U0152464

李崇峰 著

CHONGFENG LI

佛教考古

从印度到中国

BUDDHIST ARCHAEOLOGY

FROM INDIA TO CHINA

修订本

I

上海古籍出版社

Shanghai Chinese Classics Publishing House

李崇峰 1960年生，男，德里大学哲学博士，现任北京大学教授，教学科研领域为印度、中亚和中国的佛教考古与佛教艺术研究。

印度阿旃陀第19窟外景

印度根赫里第3窟前廊右端壁立佛

犍陀罗塔赫特巴希遗址全景

克孜尔谷西区石窟（47窟附近）外景

克孜尔第17窟主室前壁

云冈第13窟主像

采自《云冈石窟》二，图版111

龙门石窟大卢舍那像龛

龙门擂鼓台石窟窟前遗址发掘场景

目　　录

前言…………………………………………………………………………………… 1

一、印度寺塔：天竺宗源

塔与塔庙窟…………………………………………………………………………… 3
西印度塔庙窟的分期与年代……………………………………………………… 21
阿旃陀石窟参观记………………………………………………………………… 75

二、龟兹石窟：西域传法

克孜尔中心柱窟主室正壁画塑题材及有关问题………………………………… 107
克孜尔石窟的本生故事…………………………………………………………… 131
克孜尔中心柱窟的涅槃再现……………………………………………………… 142
克孜尔中心柱窟的弥勒图像……………………………………………………… 185
克孜尔部分中心柱窟与《长阿含经》等佛典 …………………………………… 199
龟兹与犍陀罗的造像组合、题材及布局 ………………………………………… 241

三、北方佛寺：中土弘通

从犍陀罗到平城：以地面佛寺布局为中心……………………………………… 267
鸠摩罗什与中土早期石窟寺：以禅经为例……………………………………… 313
关于鼓山石窟中的高欢柩穴……………………………………………………… 357
僧璨、定禅师与水浴寺石窟 ……………………………………………………… 365
敦煌莫高窟北朝晚期洞窟的分期与研究………………………………………… 377
龙门石窟唐代窟龛分期试论：以大型窟龛为例………………………………… 441
地婆诃罗、香山寺与“石像七龛” ……………………………………………… 529

石窟寺中国化的初步考察…… 559
陕西周至大秦寺塔记…… 610

四、川滇窟龛：汉化余韵

安岳圆觉洞调查记…… 625
剑川石窟：1999 年考古调查简报 …… 639

五、史料遗迹：透视交流

汉文史料所见罽宾与中国…… 657
西行求法与罽宾道…… 707
犍陀罗、秣菟罗与中土早期佛像 …… 737
中国出土的阿育王像…… 783
金刚力士钩稽…… 799
菩提像初探…… 809

征引文献…… 835
插图目录…… 901
后记…… 935
修订本后记…… 937

Contents

Preface 1

Part One. Hinduka: The Origin of Buddhist Art

Stūpa and *Chētiyaghara* 3

A Chronology of the *Chētiyagharas* of Western India 21

Ajaṇṭā Caves: A Preliminary Survey 75

Part Two. Kucīna: The Intermediate Phase between the Buddhist Art of Hinduka and China Proper

The Main Image on the Façade of the *Stūpa*-pillar in the *Chētiyagharas* of Kizil, Kucha 107

The *Jātakas* in the Cave Temple Complex of Kizil, Kucha 131

The Representation of Buddha's *Parinirvāṇa* in the *Chētiyagharas* of Kizil, Kucha ... 142

The Image of Maitreya in the *Chētiyagharas* of Kizil, Kucha 185

The *Dīrghāgama* Text and the *Chētiyagharas* of Kizil, Kucha 199

Gandhāra and Kucha: The Case of an Iconological Relationship 254

Part Three. North China: The Sinicizing Process of Buddhist Art

From Gandhāra to Pingcheng: The Layout of a Free-standing Buddhist Monastery 289

Kumārajīva and Early Cave-temples of China: The Case of *Dhyāna-sūtras* 313

The Tomb Cave of Gao Huan in the Cave Temple Complex at Gushan, Handan ······ 357
Sengcan, the Meditation Master Ding and the Shuiyusi Caves, Handan ······ 365
A Chronology of the Rock-cut Caves of the Northern Zhou Dynasty at Mogao, Dunhuang ······ 377
A Chronology of the Rock-cut Caves of the Tang Dynasty at Longmen, Luoyang ······ 441
Divākara, Xiangshan Monastery and the "Seven Caves" at Longmen, Luoyang ··· 529
The Sinicizing Process of the Cave-temples: The Evolution of the *Lēṇa, Maṭapa* and *Chētiyaghara* ······ 585
The Daqinsi *Stūpa* at Zhouzhi, Xi'an ······ 610

Part Four. Sichuan and Yunnan: Epilogue of the Sinicizing Process of Buddhist Art

Some Questions about the Yuanjue Caves of Anyue, Sichuan ······ 625
The Jianchuan Caves: The 1999 Archaeological Survey ······ 639

Part Five. Historical Data and Remains: A Perspective on the Sino-Indian Buddhist Cultural Exchange

Jibin and China as seen from Chinese Documents ······ 657
The Geography of Transmission: The "Jibin" Route and the Propagation of Buddhism in China ······ 721
Gandhāra, Mathurā and Buddha Images of Medieval China ······ 758
The Aśoka-type Buddha Images found in China ······ 783
An Investigation of *Dvārapāla* Images ······ 799
Regarding the *Bodhi* Image ······ 809

Selected Bibliography ······ 835
List of Illustrations ······ 901
Postscript ······ 935
Revision Postscript ······ 937

前　　言

据文献记载，宗教在中世纪各个国家和民族的生活中曾一度占据重要地位。研究中世纪的佛教活动，从历史方面来说，就是对文献加以研究；从考古学的角度来讲，其遗迹和遗物是主要的研究对象。通过佛教遗迹与遗物的表象特征，结合文献分析遗迹与遗物性质，进而探求其所蕴含的诸多历史信息，最后将这些历史信息经过分析、比较和研究，揭示出某种信息的演进规律和历史内涵，从而达到部分重建或恢复历史面貌的目的，增进东西方的相互了解。

自 19 世纪中叶以来，各国学者已从不同角度对印度和中国的佛寺遗址和石窟寺进行了多层面的研究。他们既注意到了寺院的平面布局及像设、石窟寺的建筑形制及题材内容，又论述了这些佛教遗迹产生的历史背景及社会意义。既有专题论述，也有综合研究。不过，目前各国学者的研究仍大多局限于某处或某地区的佛教遗迹。随着佛教研究的深入，我们发现：佛教文化遗产从南向北，自西往东（即印度—中亚—中国）的演变过程较为复杂，甚至出现了某些明显的反馈现象。

我们认为：研究佛教文化遗产的来龙去脉，犹如勘测一条河流；要想了解其全貌，不仅要看中游和下游，而且必须考察一下上游。这样，才能对其有一总体印象。迄今通论中印佛教文化遗产的著作不多，从纵横两方面对印度、巴基斯坦和中国的佛教遗迹进行系统研究的更是鲜有发现。本专题论文集就是在这方面的初步尝试。

笔者曾在国内外受到过严格的佛教考古学训练，因而本书采用考古学方法作为主要的分析和研究手段；而在论及佛教遗迹与遗物的象征主义及其内涵时，则采用社会—历史学方法论来阐述。

佛教考古学，是运用考古学方法研究佛教有关遗迹和遗物的人文科学。中国的“佛教考古”学科，是宿师季庚先生首倡的，它的英文对应词应为 Buddhist archaeology。1884 年，英国学者比尔 (Samuel Beal) 在撰写《大唐西域记》英译本绪言时，因推重英国考古学家伯吉斯 (James Burgess) 的工作而使用了这一术语[1]。

佛教考古的对象主要分作两类，即遗迹和遗物。遗迹包括佛寺遗迹和石窟寺遗存，前者通常指地面上建造的寺塔，其中佛塔早期是地面佛寺的中心，晚期仍然是地面佛寺的重要组成部分；那些依山靠崖开凿的石窟寺，则是地面佛寺的"石化"形式，这点在印度和中国都反映得十分清楚。遗物涵盖的内容广泛，主要有造像、经典及佛教用具。本书所要讨论的内容，主要是遗迹，兼及遗物。

《佛教考古：从印度到中国》共收集文章 31 篇，实际上应为 26 篇，因为其中 5 篇为英汉双语稿，都是英语撰述在先，汉语重写在后；另有 6 篇为英文稿。全部文章分作五组：

第一组共三篇，探讨古代天竺，即佛教艺术发源地的寺塔遗迹及石窟寺。其中，1.《塔与塔庙窟》，根据窟内俗语 (Prākṛta/Prakrit) 题铭，结合巴利语 (Pāli)、梵语 (Saṁskṛta/Sanskrit) 和汉译佛典，阐释了塔的起源、塔的种类、塔与塔庙窟之关系等。2.《西印度塔庙窟的分期与年代》，系在实地调查印度佛教遗迹的基础上，用考古学方法对西印度现存塔庙窟进行类型分析，进而归纳出各期洞窟的主要特点及年代，最后勾勒出其发展、演变的轨迹。3.《阿旃陀石窟参观记》，是在前后三次现场调查记录的基础上，对这处世界文化遗产所做的综合介绍。

第二组共六篇，都是关于古代龟兹，即今新疆库车、拜城地区佛教石窟寺的讨论文章。这一地区的佛教遗迹，堪称古代天竺与中国内地佛教艺术的"媒介体 (intermedia)"。其中，1.《克孜尔中心柱窟主室正壁画塑题材及有关问题》，比较全面地整理了"帝释窟"所涉史料和前人研究成果，并列举了印度和中亚地区出土的大量实物材料，之后论述了《长阿含经》与龟兹中心柱窟的关系，提出龟兹早期曾奉小乘佛教"法藏部"。2. 克孜尔中心柱窟主室券顶两侧的壁画内容主要是本生和因缘。本生故事画所据原典，多与汉译《贤愚经》吻合，但有些故事似仅见于巴利语 *Jātaka*（《本生经》）。The *Jātakas* in the Cave Temple Complex of Kizil, Kucha（《克孜尔石窟的本生故事》)，举例说明了汉译佛经之外其他语本佛典对研究龟兹石窟本生故事的重要性。3. The Representation of Buddha's *Parinirvāṇa* in the *Chētiyagharas* of Kizil, Kucha（《克孜尔中心柱窟的涅槃再现》)，依据新近出土的犍陀罗语 (Gāndhārī) 及梵语写本，对照早期汉译及巴利语相关佛典，经与犍陀罗出土的涅槃图像进行比较后撰写而成。克孜尔中心柱窟的涅槃画塑，在构图及细部处理上与犍陀罗的涅槃浮

[1] 伯吉斯 (James Burgess) 当时在印度主要从事佛教遗迹的调查与研究，是印度佛教考古的创始人之一。参见：*Si-Yu-Ki: Buddhist Records of the Western World; Chinese Accounts of India,* translated from the Chinese of Hiuen-Tsiang by Samuel Beal, London: Trubners, 1884: 10.

雕极为相似,应主要根据与汉译《长阿含经·游行经》相当的佛典创作而成。4. The Image of Maitreya in the *Chētiyagharas* of Kizil, Kucha (《克孜尔中心柱窟的弥勒图像》),解读了克孜尔石窟中的弥勒及其与犍陀罗同类造像的关系。5.《克孜尔部分中心柱窟与〈长阿含经〉等佛典》,通过分析和比较有关佛典,结合犍陀罗出土的系列浮雕,认为克孜尔部分中心柱窟的画塑,吸收了犍陀罗佛教艺术中的有益成分,是主要依据与汉译《长阿含经》等相当的佛典创作的。之后,借鉴近年发现的犍陀罗语及梵语写本佛经,推断法藏部曾在玄奘游历龟兹之前的几个世纪中盛行于该地。6.《龟兹与犍陀罗的造像组合、题材及布局》/Gandhāra and Kucha: The Case of an Iconological Relationship一文认为:克孜尔中心柱窟的造像组合或题材布局,即“帝释窟”与“佛涅槃”画面搭配、“佛涅槃”与“弥勒示现”场景对应,大致是汲取犍陀罗原型设计的;其创作理念,除图像志外,主要源自与汉译《长阿含经》相当的其他语本佛典。这种密切关联的图像志或圣像设计,不但与佛典所记次第相同,而且与信徒在中心柱窟内的礼拜程序一致。

第三组共九篇,主要研讨中原北方地区现存的地面佛寺遗址和石窟寺。这一地区是佛教艺术中国化或汉化的中心区。其中,1.《从犍陀罗到平城:以地面佛寺布局为中心》/From Gandhāra to Pingcheng: The Layout of a Free-standing Buddhist Monastery,根据近年在云冈石窟的考古发掘,结合汉译佛典和犍陀罗地区的地面佛寺遗迹,推测云冈西部冈上出土的遗址,为《金碑》所记武州山“上方一位石室数间”,乃武州山石窟寺“天竺僧陁翻经之地”。当初设计时,“犹依天竺旧状而重构之”,把塔院与僧院合二为一,浮图居中建造,僧房周匝设置。这应是天竺僧伽蓝(saṃghārāma)中国化的最初尝试。2. Kumārajīva and the Early Cave-temples of China: The Case of *Dhyāna-sūtras* (《鸠摩罗什与中土早期石窟寺:以禅经为例》),通过整理鸠摩罗什前后的汉译佛典及相关史料,参阅前人研究,探讨了“旧译”禅经与中土早期石窟寺之关系。3.《资治通鉴》记载高欢死后“潜凿成安鼓山石窟佛寺之旁为穴,纳其柩而塞之”。2001年,笔者登临北响堂山石窟(鼓山石窟)北洞塔柱南壁顶部一深穴并做了测绘,《关于鼓山石窟中的高欢柩穴》就是对这一传说所做的初步解读。4. 水浴寺西窟供养人“僧璨”,早年疑为中土禅宗三祖僧璨。僧璨与另一位供养人“定禅师”,同为禅宗二祖惠可弟子,且为同学密友。《僧璨、定禅师与水浴寺石窟》一文据此推测西窟前壁门道两侧浮雕的僧璨和定禅师,分别为中土禅宗第三祖僧璨和北齐后期统领佛事的最高僧官——昭玄大统神定。5.《敦煌莫高窟北朝晚期洞窟的分期与研究》,以前人研究成果为起点,以纪年洞窟为标尺,首先用考古学方法对莫高窟北朝晚期15座洞窟做了初步分期,之后探讨了北朝晚期洞窟演变所反映出的若干历史问题，最后根据敦煌藏经洞出土的纪年写卷的存佚，认为北周武帝灭佛影响了莫高窟的开窟造像活动。6.《龙门石窟唐代窟龛分期试论》，是为撰写《龙门石窟擂鼓台区考古报告》所做的准备工作之一。本文运用考古学方法对龙门现存唐代大型窟龛做了类型分析，总结了各期窟龛的特点，并推测了各期的年代。在此基础上，探讨了大卢舍那像龛与法藏的关系、武则天"好大喜功"与龙门大型窟龛的营造、武则天退位与龙门部分窟龛工程的中辍、中宗复辟迄玄宗前期龙门窟龛营造骤减等问题，最后阐述了大型窟龛与小型窟龛之关系。7.《地婆诃罗、香山寺与"石像七龛"》，原为《龙门石窟唐代窟龛分期试论》的一个附录，在唐代窟龛分期的基础上，首先对武氏家庙高僧地婆诃罗的译经及个人喜好做了初步梳理，之后探讨皇家大寺——香山寺的设置，最后推测龙门东山现存七座大窟，即擂鼓台三洞、高平郡王洞、看经寺、二莲花洞，应为文献记载的香山寺"石像七龛"。8. 印度的佛教石窟，依据洞窟形制和使用性质，大体可以分作栖止禅定生活用窟和礼忏供养等佛事用窟两类。《石窟寺中国化的初步考察》/The Sinicizing Process of the Cave-temples: The Evolution of the *Lēṇa, Maṭapa* and *Chētiyaghara,* 在分析印度石窟类型的基础上，论述了僧坊窟及方形窟的中国化，之后阐述了塔庙窟之嬗变。9.《陕西周至大秦寺塔记》，是作者实地调查大秦寺遗址后所提交的一份报告。

第四组共两篇，都是探讨西南地区佛教遗迹的。其中，1.《安岳圆觉洞调查记》系作者 2002 年秋冬之际考察四川安岳县圆觉洞窟群后所思考的几个问题的札记。2.《剑川石窟：1999 年考古调查简报》，是我们当时调查云南剑川石窟的初步小结，大体分作两部分。前面部分讲述了剑川石窟的研究史和那次调查的新发现；后面部分重点讨论了剑川石窟的分期和若干造像题材的渊源与流变。

第五组共六篇，通过史料、遗迹与遗物研讨印、巴、中三国的古代文化交流。1. Jibin and China as seen from Chinese Documents (《汉文史料所见罽宾与中国》)，系统整理了佛陀耶舍等十三位罽宾僧人的译经，阐释了罽宾佛教及其部派、中国早期佛教部执或律典的南北差异，以及现存汉译佛典和出土遗物所反映出的两地文化交往。2.《西行求法与罽宾道》/The Geography of Transmission: The "Jibin" Route and the Propagation of Buddhism in China，主要讨论了汉魏两晋南北朝时期中土高僧西行求法及游履路线。3. 犍陀罗艺术与秣菟罗艺术既是两种不同的艺术流派 (school)，又代表了两种截然不同的艺术模式 (style)。《犍陀罗、秣菟罗与中土早期佛像》/Gandhāra, Mathurā and the Buddha Images of Medieval China，对犍陀罗和秣菟罗出土及传世的佛像分别做了分期，之后以炳灵寺第 169 窟、云冈昙曜五窟以及成都和青州出土的造像为例，探讨了中土早期佛像与犍陀罗和秣菟罗佛教艺术的关系。4. The Aśoka-type Buddha Images found in China (《中国出土的阿育王像》)，以成都过去半个世纪出土的阿育王像为中心，研讨了当时阿育王像的流行、益州佛教与建康佛教的关系以及南朝与印度本土的文化交流。5.《金刚力士钩稽》，原为《龙门石窟唐代窟龛分期试论》的一个附录。金刚力士，通常对称雕造于石窟寺前庭正壁门道两侧，应源于印度佛教寺塔及石窟寺前的执杖药叉，即门神。云冈石窟门道两侧雕造的金刚力士，可能是平城工匠在印度寺塔门前“执杖药叉”及金刚力士“守护诸佛及佛住处”等理念的汉化或再创造，后来中原北方佛教窟龛与造像碑的雕造深受其影响，故当时碑铭有“金刚力士，在户之旁”之语。6.《菩提像初探》，原为《龙门石窟唐代窟龛分期试论》的另一附录。菩提像“珠瓔宝冠，奇珍交饰”，偏袒右肩，结跏趺坐，左手内敛置于腹前，右手垂作触地印。王玄策三次奉使印度，有两次游历摩诃菩提寺，瞻仰菩提像，因感“此乃旷代所未见，史籍所未详”，故请工匠宋法智图写圣颜带回京都，“道俗竞摸”，武则天前后尤为朝野所重。

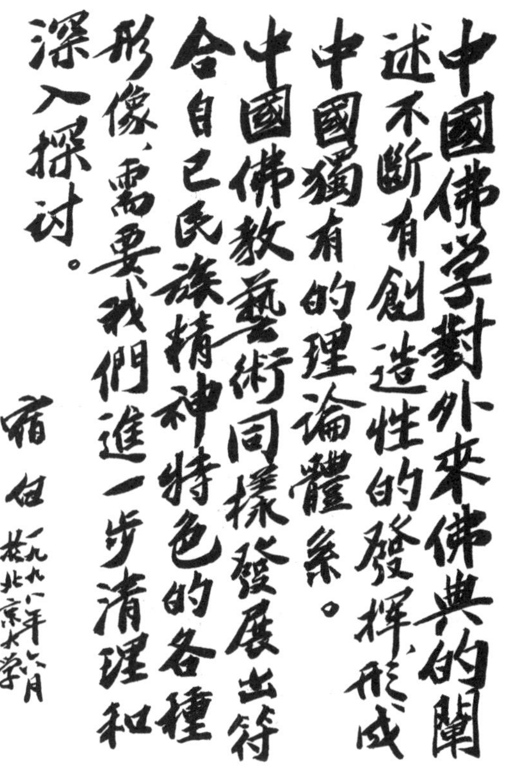

宿师季庚先生多次教诲：“中国佛学对外来佛典的阐述不断有创造性的发挥，形成中国独有的理论体系。中国佛教艺术同样发展出符合自己民族精神特色的各种形象，需要我们进一步清理和深入探讨。”

过去三十多年间，笔者曾在中国、印度和巴基斯坦实地调查了许多佛教遗迹，并收集到大量第一手资料。本专题论文集，就是对地面佛寺与石窟寺在印度的发生与发展和它在中国的流布与演化所做的初步探索。对印度学者来说，本书使其探求目光从桑吉大塔和阿旃陀石窟延伸到龟兹石窟和龙门龛像，从而可以了解古代天竺佛教文化及艺术的普遍意义；而对中国学者来讲，本书为起源于印度的某些重要的中国文化现象，提供了颇具启迪意义的图文材料。

李崇峰

2013年7月8日

一、印度寺塔：

天竺宗源

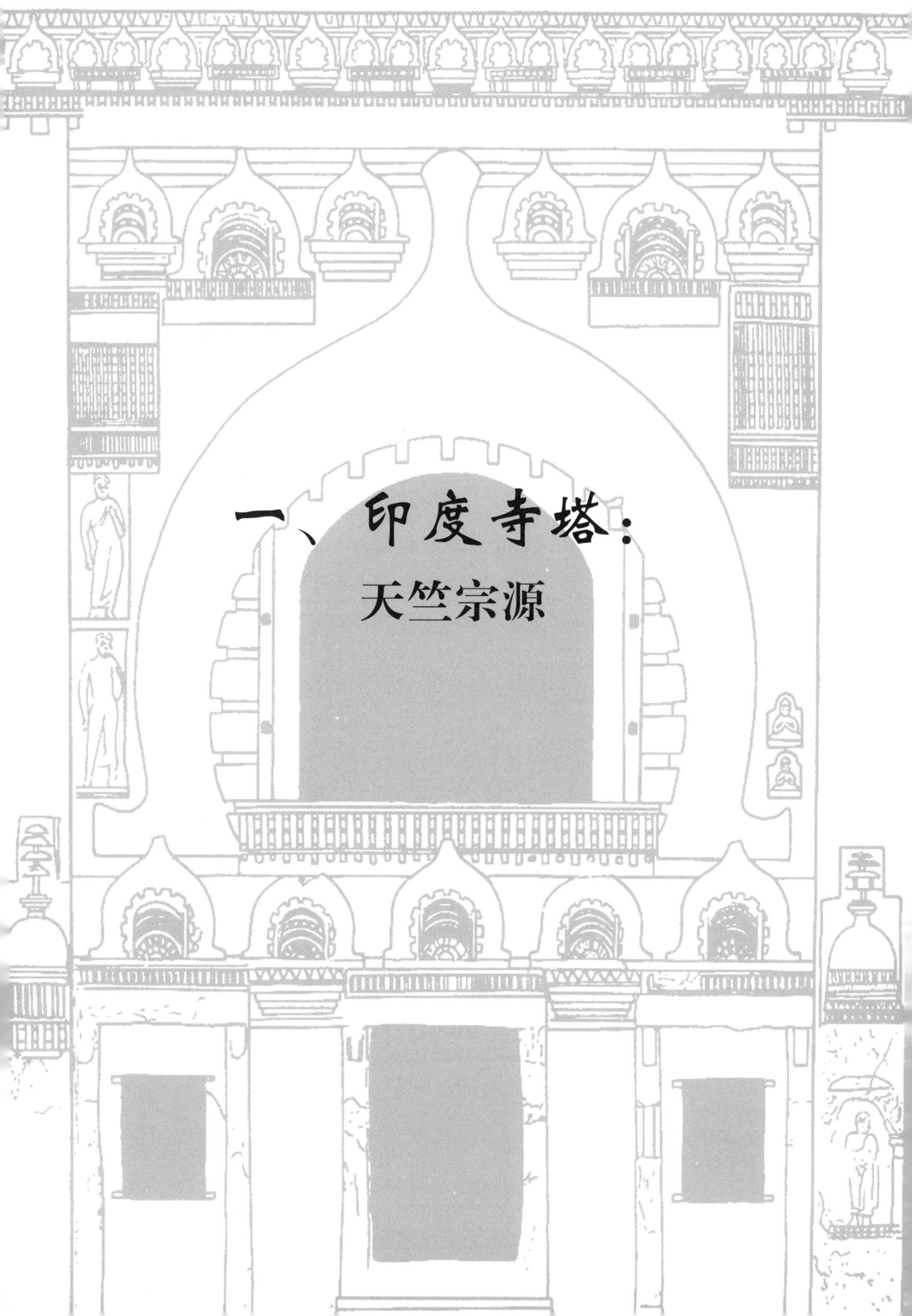

塔与塔庙窟

根据洞窟形制并参照窟内原始俗语(Prākṛta/Prākṛit/Prakrit)题铭,印度佛教石窟主要有两种类型：一种为 lēṇa[1],译作僧坊窟(图 1)；另一种是 chētiyaghara[2],译为塔庙窟或支提窟。塔庙窟的主体是其内部的thupa/thuba[3]或chētiya[4],即窣睹波(stūpa)(图 2)。窣睹波这种建筑,无疑是从古代陵墓得到的启示。在理论上,它是藏纳圣者遗骨的,来此进香朝拜的人,最后绕其一周作结束[5]。

一、Stūpa 与 Caitya

梵语 stūpa[6],俗语为 thūpa 或 thuba[7],巴利语作 thūpa[8],汉语音译作"窣

---

[1] H. Lüders, "A List of Brāhmī Inscriptions from the Earliest Times to about A.D. 400 with the Exception of those of Aśōka", in: *Epigraphia Indica,* Volume X (1909-10), Appendix, Calcutta: Superintendent Government Printing, 1912: Nos. 998, 1000, 1001, 1006-1007, 1012, 1014, 1016, 1020-1021, 1024, 1039-1041, 1048, 1051, 1060, 1062-1063, 1065-1066, 1073, 1107, 1123-1126, 1131-1133, 1138, 1140, 1144, 1152, 1175, etc.

[2] 1) H. Lüders, *opere citato*: Nos. 1050, 1058, 1072, 1141, 1153, 1178, 1179, 1183, etc.; 2) Jas. Burgess, *Report on the Buddhist Cave Temples and Their Inscriptions; supplementary to the volume on "The Cave Temples of India", Archaeological Survey of Western India,* Vol. IV, 1883: 86, No. 13; 87, No. 20; 114, No. 3; 99, No. 4; 93, No. 4; 94, No. 9; 94, No. 11; 94, No. 12.

[3] 珀贾(Bhājā)第 20 窟内共有 14 座圆雕石塔,其中第 8 号塔覆钵上的俗语题刻作 thupa,第 7 号塔身上的题刻也作 thupa,贝德萨(Beḍsā)第 3 窟(塔庙窟)后壁上的俗语铭文亦刻作 thupa。不过,根赫里(Kāṇhēri)第 4 窟(塔庙窟)石塔方龛上的俗语题刻则为 thuba。参见：1) H. Lüders, *opere citato*: Nos. 1080, 1081, 1110, 993; 2) Jas. Burgess, *opere citato*: 82-83, 89.

[4] 据 Étienne Lamotte 研究,印度塔庙中雕造的 stūpa 当时有的也称作 caitya。参见 Étienne Lamotte, *Histoire du Bouddhisme Indien: des Origines à l'ére Šaka,* Bibliothèque du Muséon 43, Louvain: Institut Orientaliste de Louvain, 1958: 342.

[5] 雷奈·格鲁塞著《印度的文明》,常任侠、袁音译,北京：商务印书馆,1965 年,第 39 页。

[6] Monier Monier-Williams, *A Sanskrit-English Dictionary,* London: Oxford University Press, 1899: 1260.

[7] 参见荻原雲來《漢訳対照梵和大辭典》,東京：鈴木学術財団/講談社,1974 年,第 563b 页。

[8] T. W. Rhys Davids and William Stede, *Pali-English Dictionary,* London: Pali Text Society, 1925: 309.

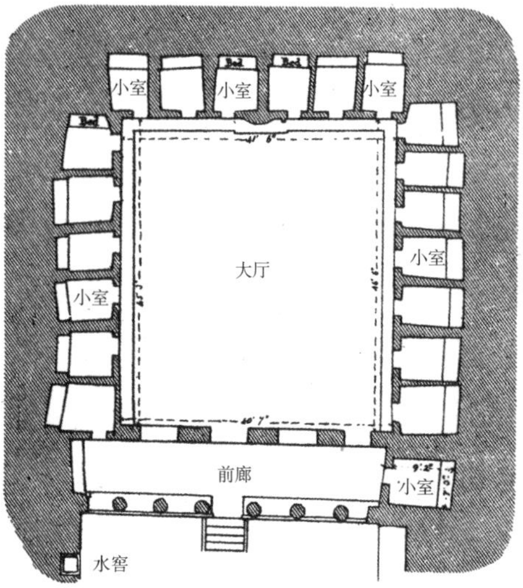

图 1　印度纳西克 (Nāsik) 第 3 窟平面图

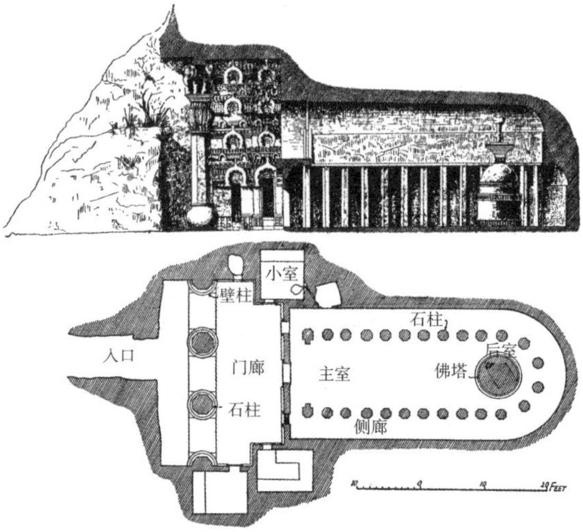

图 2　印度根赫里 (Kāṇhēri) 第 3 窟平面及纵向垂直剖面图

睹波，或窣堵波、薮斗波、数斗波、苏偷婆、素睹波、私鍮簸，或兜婆、偷婆、鍮婆、塔婆”等，意译为“塔、庙、塔庙、佛塔、坟、冢、方坟、圆冢、高显处、大聚、聚相、功德聚”等[1]。“复以塔之外表，辄有图绘雕刻，故亦称浮图，或称佛图。”[2]

Stūpa 这个词，最早出现在《梨俱吠陀》(*Ṛgveda*)[3]中，意为“柱”或“树干”[4]，二词皆富于稳定之义；而在《鹧鸪氏本集》(*Taittirīya Saṁhitā*)[5]中，则被译作“发髻”[6]，暗指至高或最高地位。据法云《翻译名义集》卷七，塔“义为灵庙。刘熙《释

[1] 参见：1) 荻原雲來，上引书，第 563b、1512a 页；2) 塚本善隆《望月佛教大辭典》，東京：世界聖典刊行協會，1978 年，第 3832-3839 页。

不过，Robert E. Buswell 认为“偷婆、兜婆、塔婆”应译自 Middle Indic（中世印度语）*thūpa*. 参见 Robert E. Buswell, Jr., “Prakritic Phonological Elements in Chinese Buddhist Transcriptions: Data from Xuanying's *Yiqiejing Yinyi*”, in: *Collection of Essays 1993: Buddhism Across Boundaries-Chinese Buddhism and Western Religions* by Erik Zürcher, Lore Sander and others, ed. John R. McRae and Jan Nattier, Taipei: Foguang Cultural Enterprise Co., Ltd, 1999: 187-217, esp. 201-203.

[2] 黄宝瑜《中国佛教建筑》，载章嘉等著《中国佛教史论集》III，台北：中华文化出版事业委员会，1956 年，第 881 页。

[3] Friedrich Max Müller, ed, *Ṛgveda-saṃhitā,* VII. 2. 1, I. 24. 7.

[4] G. T. K. Griffith, *The Hymns of the Ṛgveda,* translated with a popular commentary, 4th ed, Varanari: Chowkhamba Sanskrit Series Office, 1963, II: 3, I: 31.

[5] Ernst Windisch ed., *Taittirīya Saṃhitā,* III: 3. 6. 5.

[6] A. Macdonell and A. B. Keith, *Vedic Index of Names and Subjects,* London, rep., New Delhi: Motilal Banersidass, 1984: 483.

名》云：'庙，貌也，先祖形貌所在也。'"[1]由此我们知道：塔是一种纪念物，作为纪念先哲的一种可视形式，塔成为最高地位和等级稳定的象征[2]。由于塔具有上述含义，因而受到了古代帝王的极大推崇。他们乞望死后仍能享受尘世的最高权力，维持现有地位并保持国家稳定。

佛教创始后，这种建筑形式也被移植到佛国中来。据东晋佛陀跋陀罗与法显共译《摩诃僧祇律》卷三十三："过去世时，迦叶佛般泥洹后，吉利王为佛起塔，四面作龛，上作狮子、象种种彩画，前作栏楯，安置花处。龛内悬缯幡盖……塔四面造种种园林。"[3]而在佛陀什与竺道生共译《弥沙塞部和醯五分律》卷二十六："佛言：所有四种人应起塔，如来、圣弟子、辟支佛、转轮圣王。"[4]从上述律典中，我们不难看出：在佛陀时代，为佛教先哲和圣人起塔已成为一种时尚。据巴利语《大般涅槃经》(*Mahāparinibbāna Sutta*)，佛行将入灭之时，阿难曾问及如来遗体作何处理。佛嘱阿难道：大王过世后，尸体在香積上火化，其子民便在四个路口为其起塔。"既然人们如此处理王者遗体，那么，他们亦应如此料理如来后事，于四冲道上各为如来造一塔，无论谁到那里，只要献花或香料或香粉或拜谒或于现场全身静默，都将获益无穷。"[5]黎明前瞬间，佛涅槃即将来临，他再次嘱咐阿难他入灭后应火化。"帝王驾崩，敛骨灰于坛中，上建塔。佛陀也应如是。"[6]这里，正是佛陀自己用塔作为他新教说和教主身份的象征性纪念物，"地位的稳定和合法变成达磨的永恒和神圣"[7]。据《魏书·释老志》，"佛既谢世，香木焚尸，灵骨分碎，大小如粒，击之不坏，焚亦不焦，或有光明神验。胡言谓之'舍利'。弟子收奉，置之宝瓶，竭香花，致敬慕，建宫宇，谓为'塔'。塔亦胡言，犹宗庙也，故世称塔庙。"[8]

总之，塔既是佛教统治的视觉标志，也是佛法尊崇和永恒的象征。而且，它还可

---

[1] 1)《大正新脩大藏經》(100卷，高楠順次朗、渡邊海旭都監，東京：大正一切經刊行會，1924-1934年，下文简作《大正藏》)，第54卷，第1168a页；2)刘熙《释名》，毕沅疏证，王先谦补，北京：中华书局，2008年，第181页。

[2] Lokesh Chandra, "Introduction", in: G. Tucci, *Stupa: Art, Architectonics and Symbolism*, tr. by U. M. Vesci, New Delhi: Aditya Prakashan, 1988: XIV.

[3]《大正藏》第22卷，第498a页。

[4]《大正藏》第22卷，第173a页。

[5] *Mahāparinibhāna Sutta*, 5. 26, tr. by T. W. Rhys Davids and Hermann Oldenberg, in: *SBE* (*The Sacred Books of the East*), XI: 93.

[6] A. K. Warder, *Indian Buddhism*, 2nd rev. ed., Delhi: Motilal Banarsidass Publishers Pvt. Ltd., 1980: 78.

[7] Lokesh Chandra, *opere citato*: xxv.

[8]《魏书》，点校本，北京：中华书局，1974年，第3028页。

以被看作佛主的化身。

除窣睹波之外，另一个与之含义接近的梵语词汇是 caitya，亦作 chaitya，俗语作 chetiya[1]，巴利语为 cetiya[2]，汉语音译作支提、枝提、支帝、制底、制多、制帝、脂帝、质底、制底耶、脂帝浮图、脂帝浮都、支提浮图等，意译为塔、庙、寺、塔庙、灵庙、方坟、高坟、积聚、聚相、归宗、无上塔、请福处、生净信、可供养处、灭恶生善处等[3]。Caitya 这个词，本身亦可追溯到吠陀时期。它源于吠陀火祭坛 citi，是围绕火祭坛或吠陀 citi 建立的一种建筑[4]。支提在佛教产生之前就有悠久的传统。"佛在世时，大多数支提奉献给了药叉或诸天，在萨兰达陀支提 (Sārandada-cetiya)，佛向离车毗人 (Licchavis) 做过有关保证他们幸福和繁荣七要素 (satta aparihāṇīya-dhammā) 的著名说教，劝告他们把支提作为七种达磨之一来朝拜。这样，前佛教的传统支提便转化为佛教的圣所，并作为新教说的中心而获新生。"[5]

根据 19 世纪俄国学者 Von Joh. Minayeff 发现的一卷巴利语佛教残卷，参照传统习惯并从功能上划分，印度早期佛教共有四种支提：1. paribhotta-cetiya 或作 paribhoga-cetiya（藏纳佛陀用具）；2. dhātu-cetiya 或 sārīrika-cetiya（藏纳佛舍利或圣者尸骨）；3. dhammā-cetiye 或 uddesika-cetiya（藏缘起法颂或供奉造像）[6]；4. vratānuṣṭhita-cetiye（特专意善行、修业、奉献、净戒之用）[7]。而据汉译佛典，尚有四大制底（支提），即佛诞生处、得道处、初转法轮处和涅槃处，以及八大制底之说[8]。

因此，支提是一种多功能的佛教纪念物。佛世时，它是奉献给药叉和天人的。后

---

[1] H. Lüders, *opere citato*: Nos. 987, 1216.

[2] T. W. Rhys Davids and William Stede, *opere citato*: 272.

[3] 参见：1) 荻原雲来，上引书，第 479-480 页；2) 塚本善隆，上引书，第 1875 页。不过，Robert E. Buswell 认为"脂帝浮都、支提浮图"应译自 Gāndhārī（犍陀罗语）*caityabhūta*。参见 Robert E. Buswell, Jr., *opere citato*: 203-213.

[4] A. K. Coomaraswamy, *History of Indian and Indonesian Art,* 1ST Indian ed., New Delhi: Munshiram Manoharlal, 1972: 47.

[5] Lokesh Chandra, *opere citato*: xv.

[6] 这件巴利语残卷开头作"tividhaṃ hi buddhacetiyaṃ paribhottacetiyaṃ dhātucetiyaṃ dhammacetiyan'ti." Von Joh. Minayeff, "Buddhistische Fragmente", in: *Bulletin de l'Académie Impériale des Sciences de Saint-Pétersbourg,* 1871: 70-85, esp. 78-83. 此文系笔者 1998 年客座台南艺术学院时，承蒙同任该校客座教授的俄罗斯爱米塔什博物馆陆柏 (Lubo-Lesnichenko) 博士帮助复印。陆柏教授前几年已驾鹤西去，谨祈陆柏博士冥福。

[7] 这种 cetiya 系作者 1991 至 1995 年在印度德里大学佛教研究系攻读博士学位时，承蒙该系教师 Priya Sen Singh 博士相告，谨此致谢。

[8] 义净译《根本说一切有部毗奈耶杂事》及《根本说一切有部百一羯磨》，参见《大正藏》第 24 卷，第 408、496 页。

来，通过藏纳佛的用具、佛或先哲的舍利或遗骨、经典或造像，以及仅仅对佛一生中重要事件之纪念，重新变得神圣起来。

至于窣睹波与支提的区别，它是随着时代的发展而富于变化的。据《摩诃僧祇律》卷二十九："尔时商人欢喜，前白佛言：愿赐爪发还，起支提。佛即剪爪剃发，与之起塔。"[1]而同书卷三十三，则明确阐明："有舍利者名塔，无舍利者名枝提，如佛生处、得道处、转法轮处、般泥洹处、菩萨像、辟支佛窟、佛脚迹。此诸枝提，得安佛华盖供养具。"[2]这说明5世纪初[3]，窣睹波与支提二词于佛典上的主要区别为：窣睹波有舍利，支提则藏纳造像或其他圣物，或者仅仅是佛教重要事件之标志。不过，二词混淆情况当时亦有存在。据现存最早的大藏经音义，即唐初玄应所编《众经音义》卷六《妙法莲华经音义》："宝塔……诸经论中或作薮斗波，或作塔婆，或云兜婆，或言偷婆，或言苏偷婆，或言脂帝浮都，亦言支提浮图，皆讹略也。正言窣睹波，此译云庙，或云方坟，此义翻也。或云大聚，或云聚相，谓累石等高以为相也。案塔字，诸书所无。唯葛洪《字苑》云：'塔，佛堂也。'"[4]这条音义告诉我们：窣睹波是聚相的方坟，这种方坟既是佛庙，也是佛堂。塔作为佛庙或佛堂，至迟应是东晋以来中国人的看法[5]。而同书卷五《施灯功德经音义》则说："支提，又名脂帝浮图，此云聚相。谓累石等高以为相。或言方坟，或言庙，皆随义释也。"[6]这表明：窣睹波与支提意义相同。玄应为唐初高僧，曾参与玄奘的译场。他博学字书，撰写《众经音义》之前，曾对佛经的音义做过比较研究。因此，玄应对翻译过来的名词和唐初汉僧自己使用的名词的解释，应有一定的权威性，或者说它代表了那个时代的标准[7]。到了7世纪下半叶，义净游历印度之后撰写《南海寄归内法传》时，窣睹波与支提二词之间在涵义上已没有什么区别了。"上言制底畔睇者，或云制底畔弹那。大师世尊既涅槃后，人天并集，以火焚之。众聚香柴，遂成大積，即名此处以为质底，是积聚义。据从生理，遂有制底之名。又释，一想世尊众德俱聚于此，二乃积砖土而成之，详传字义如

[1]《大正藏》第22卷，第461b-c页。

[2]《大正藏》第22卷，第498b页。

[3] 此经系东晋义熙十二年(416年)十一月法显与佛陀跋陀罗共同译出。参见费长房《历代三宝记》，见《大正藏》第49卷，第71a页。

[4] 玄应《众经音义》，见《大日本校訂縮刻大藏經》，東京：弘教書院，1881-1885年，函"为七"，第23页。

[5] 这一观点，是笔者1985年至1987年在北京大学考古系攻读硕士学位时，宿师季庚先生在讲授《汉文佛籍版本与目录》时提出的。

[6] 玄应，上引书，第21页。

[7] 上引季庚师《汉文佛籍版本与目录》观点。

是。或名窣睹波，义亦同此。旧总云塔，别道支提，斯皆讹矣。或可俱是，众共了名，不论其义……畔睇者，敬礼也。凡欲出外礼拜尊像，有人问云：'何所之适？' 答曰：'我向某处制底畔睇。'"[1]后来，支提又引申为一般的寺庙或朝圣地，如成书于807年的慧琳《一切经音义》写到："制多，古译或云制底，或云支提，皆梵语声转耳，其实一也。此译为庙，即寺宇、伽蓝、塔庙等是也。窣堵波……亦梵语，塔也。古云苏偷婆，古译不正也，即碎身舍利砖塔也。古译或曰浮图也。"[2]"塔，梵云窣堵波，此云高显。制多，此云灵庙，律云塔婆，无舍利云支提。今塔，即窣堵，讹云塔。古书无塔字。葛洪《字苑》及《切韵》[3]：'塔即佛堂；佛塔，庙也'。"[4]而到南宋初年法云撰《翻译名义集》时，则作如下解释："窣堵波……此翻方坟，亦翻圆冢，亦翻高显，义翻灵庙……又梵名塔婆，《发轸》[5]曰：《说文》元无此字，徐铉[6]新加，云：西国浮图也。言浮图者，此翻聚相。" "支提，或名难提、脂帝、制底、制多，此翻可供养处，或翻灭恶生善处。"[7]

根据上述文献，我们不难看出：尽管支提与窣睹波意义大体相同，但支提本身更偏重 "可供养处" 和 "庙" 的含义。"它是一个适于任何神圣之物、意义广泛的名称。"[8]二者皆为佛事而非殡葬之建筑，通称塔。

由于窣睹波具有至高、稳定之性质，支提又在窣睹波含义的基础上，更加强调 "积聚"、"供养" 和 "灭恶生善"，因而对其崇拜由来已久。作为皇家之塔，它以早期形式和功能表现了群体社会和经济生活的稳定，它是王中之王的纪念物。佛陀时代，它是供养佛陀、尊礼佛教之象征；佛灭之后，窣睹波和支提不仅成为达磨的标志和佛的化身，而且也是佛国世界拓展的视觉界标。礼塔——窣睹波和支提就是礼佛的思想，牢固地树立在佛教信徒的脑海之中。建造佛塔，就是为了满足上述要求。

现在，多数学者认为 "佛塔是欧亚图兰人 (Turāniāns) 坟冢的直接派生物，包括埃特鲁里亚人 (Etrurians)、吕底亚人 (Lydians) 和北方草原上的斯基泰人 (Skythians)"[9]。佛塔的形制与建造，可以上溯到佛陀时代。据说释迦牟尼成道之

[1] 义净《南海寄归内法传》，王邦维校注，北京：中华书局，1995年，第145-146页。

[2]《大正藏》第54卷，第321a-b页。

[3]《切韵》为隋代陆法言所作。

[4]《大正藏》第54卷，第483b页。

[5] 发轸曾作《寺记》，似不见著录。参见：宿白《〈大金西京武州山重修大石窟寺碑〉校注》，载宿白《中国石窟寺研究》(第52-75页)，北京：文物出版社，1996年，第64页注一五。

[6] 徐铉 (916-991年)，五代、宋初诗人和书法家。

[7]《大正藏》第54卷，第1168a页。

[8] M. N. Deshpande, "The (Ajanta) Caves: Their Historical Perspective", in: *Ajanta Murals,* ed. A. Ghosh, New Delhi: Archaeological Survey of India, 1967: 16.

[9] James Fergusson et al, *History of Indian and Eastern Architecture,* rev. ed, London: Murray, 1910, I: 65.

后，首先对当时北印度商人提谓和波利说人天之教，并授予发爪使之造塔。此事佛典中多有记载，但以玄奘所述《大唐西域记》为详：“（缚喝国）大城西北五十余里，至提谓城。城北四十余里有波利城。城中各有一窣堵波，高余三丈。昔者如来初证佛果，起菩提树，方诣鹿园。时二长者遇被威光，随其行路之资，遂献麨蜜，世尊为说人天之福，最初得闻五戒十善也。既闻法诲，请所供养，如来遂授其发爪焉。二长者将还本国，请礼敬之仪式。如来以僧伽胝方叠布下，次郁多罗僧，次僧却崎。又覆钵、竖锡杖，如是次第为窣堵波。二人承命，各还其城，拟仪圣旨，式修崇建，斯则释迦法中最初窣堵波也。”[1]这段文字清楚地告诉我们：释迦以僧衣、饭钵和锡杖教示人们如何建造窣睹波。这种窣睹波，应是覆钵塔的原型。后世佛教信徒在印度建造的大多数窣睹波，都因循这一基本形制。

汉译佛典中关于当时造塔及塔形的描述不乏其例。据《摩诃僧衹律》卷三十三，“作塔法者，下基四方，周匝栏楯，圆起二重，方牙四出，上施槃盖，长表轮相”。[2]《根本说一切有部毗奈耶杂事》卷十八云：“我今欲于显敞之处，以尊者骨起窣睹波，得使众人随情供养。佛言：长者随意当作。长者便念：云何而作？佛言：应可用砖两重作基，次安塔身，上安覆钵，随意高下；上置平头，高一、二尺，方二、三尺，准量大小，中竖轮杆，次着相轮。其相轮重数，或一、二、三、四乃至十三，次安宝瓶……佛告长者：若为如来造窣睹波者，应可如前具足而作。若为独觉，勿安宝瓶；若阿罗汉，相轮四重，不还至三，一来应二，预流应一；凡夫善人，但可平头，无有轮盖。如世尊说，如是应作。”[3]又，《根本说一切有部毗奈耶药事》卷三补充道：“尔时世尊，以神变力持佛发、爪与邬波斯迦。彼得发爪，便立窣睹波。时彼逝多林天神，便以百枝伞，插窣睹波中。白言：世尊，我常供养此塔。作是言已，便依塔住。时诸人等号为宅神塔，或呼为薄拘罗树中心柱。”[4]

尽管佛陀时代所造之塔没有实物保存下来，但从上述文献我们可以推测其基本形状为：塔基方形两重，次安圆柱形塔身，上置半球形覆钵，再上为平头，中竖轮杆，次着相轮。塔周围绕以栏楯，四面开门。这种特有之形式，无疑是从古代圆锥型墓冢演化出来的；其原型在德干高原和南印度皆有发现[5]。传说释迦牟尼涅槃后所建原

---

[1] 玄奘《大唐西域记》，季羡林等校注，北京：中华书局，1985年，第122页。

[2]《大正藏》第22卷，第498a页。

[3]《大正藏》第24卷，第291c页。

[4]《大正藏》第24卷，第14c-15a页。又，“薄拘罗树中心柱”，梵语为Bakula-medhī。其中，bakula又作vakula，为一种树木，传说当被喷撒美女口中的花蜜时，它会争相开花。Medhī特指塔身，medhī有时亦作methi或methī，意为柱子或中心柱。中国人俗称支提窟/塔庙窟为中心柱窟，其意与此不谋而合。

[5] A. H. Longhurst, *The Story of the Stūpa*, rep., New Delhi: Asian Educational Services, 1979: 12.

始十塔，“八座藏纳舍利，一座藏坛，一座纳灰烬”[1]。这些原始佛塔，应是上部半圆、下基方形之土冢，与佛陀教示之塔相同。汉译佛典有译窣睹波为“方坟”者，可能就是因为早期塔基为方形之故。

大约在佛涅槃后两百余年，由于孔雀帝国阿育王(Aśoka)的弘扬，佛教得到了空前发展。阿育王传播佛教的方法之一，就是在各地广建佛塔。由于他的倡导，窣睹波具有了特殊的地位，被视为佛教的象征和佛主崇拜的对象。根据阿育王在位第十四年(约前255年)的一方刻铭，他曾在尼泊尔的尼伽里萨伽(Nigâli Sâgar)扩建了拘那含牟尼佛(Buddha Koṇāgamana)的寺塔[2]。传说他曾打开多数原始佛塔，从中取出舍利。尔后，“有王阿育，以神力分佛舍利，役诸鬼神，造八万四千塔，布于世界，皆同日而就”[3]。通过建造窣睹波，阿育王既可以达到供奉佛陀与传播佛法之目的，又可以使佛教变成全体臣民可以感性接受的东西。当时，阿育王可能意识到有必要向佛教徒提供一种可视的有形物，以集中他们的思想和祈祷；而佛塔是最合适的。不管他当初抱有何种目的，那些存放佛舍利的窣睹波，影响是深远而持久的。佛舍利固然受到崇拜，可是到后来，不论窣睹波中是否藏纳舍利，它本身也被视为佛的象征物，因而也就成了值得崇拜的东西。“人等百千金，持用行布施；不如一善心，恭敬礼佛塔。”[4]由于对塔的崇拜到了如此程度，以至于仅仅是造塔，不论大小，不管用何种材料，也成了一种做功德的方式。建塔者及供养人，可以因此在进入极乐世界的道路上又迈进了一步[5]。至于阿育王时期所造佛塔之形制，由于所有原始窣睹波[6]现皆成废墟或为后世覆盖，我们不得不假定它们均奉循佛陀教示之塔式。

随着佛教的发展，塔的形式也有了变化。据考古调查，桑吉(Sāñcī)1号塔(俗称桑吉大塔)之内核，系阿育王时建造，为低矮的半球形砖筑覆钵塔，其直径几乎为现存大塔的一半(图3)[7]，应依据佛陀教示的原型构造而成。后来，这种塔的塔身逐渐

---

[1] *Mahāparinibhāna Sutta*, 6. 51-62, tr. by T. W. Rhys Davids and Hermann Oldenberg, in: *SBE*, XI: 131-135.

[2] Jules Bloch, *Les inscriptions d'Aśoka* (Collection Émile Senart 8), Paris: Institut de Civilisation Indienne, 1950: 158.

[3]《魏书》，点校本，北京：中华书局，1974年，第3028页。

[4] 佛陀跋陀罗、法显译《摩诃僧祇律》卷三十三，参见《大正藏》第22卷，第497c页。

[5] John Marshall, *Buddhist Art of Gandhara: The Story of the Early School; Its Birth, Growth and Decline*, London: Cambridge University Press, 1960: 3-4.

[6] 尼泊尔蓝比尼(Lumbinī)城东大约50公里处的蓝莫塔(梵语作Rāmagrāma，巴利语为Rāmagāma)遗址，是释迦牟尼涅槃后所建原始八塔之一，传说是唯一没有被阿育王打开的原始佛塔。

[7] John Marshall, “The Monuments of Sanchi: Their Exploration and Conservation”, in: *Archaeological Survey of India; Annual Report 1913-14*: 1-39.

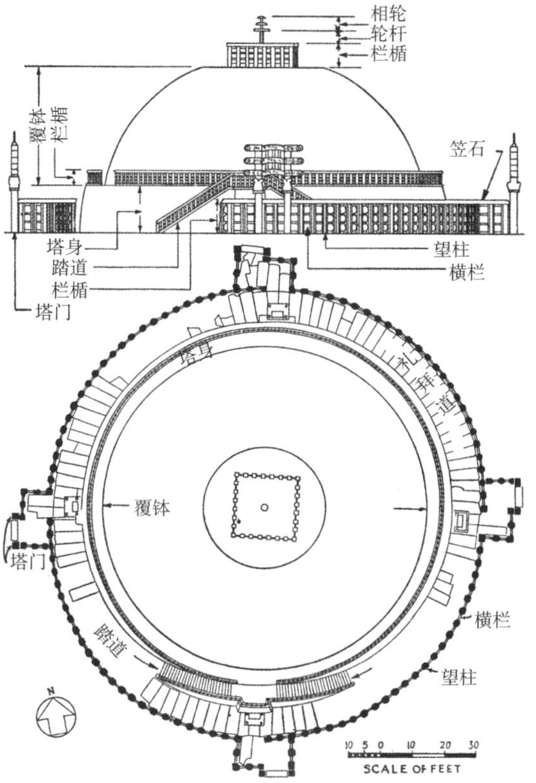

图 3　印度桑吉大塔立面及平面图

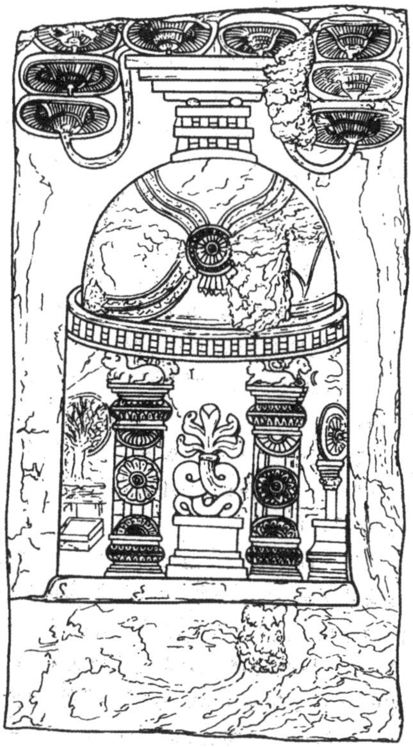

图 4　印度阿默拉沃蒂大塔塔基饰板浮雕佛塔

增高,成为圆柱形,如阿默拉沃蒂 (Amarāvatī) 大塔塔身饰板浮雕所示 (图 4)。这种圆柱形塔身继续演变,就形成了佛陀伽耶 (Bodh-Gayā) 大菩提寺 (Mahābodhi Vihāra) 那种高层建筑。

众所周知,中国的佛教文化,与古代犍陀罗 (Gandhāra) 有着极为密切的关系。佛教传入犍陀罗,最早也不过公元前 3 世纪中叶。当时新皈依佛教的阿育王,曾向其所有属地系统地派遣了佛教使团[1]。遣往罽宾和犍陀罗的使团由中际 (Madhyāntika) 率领。他们在那里不但传布了佛教,而且开辟了文化[2]。到了公元 2 世纪时,贵霜帝国国王迦腻色迦 (Kaniṣka) 皈依佛教。他的帝国以犍陀罗为中心,首都在库巴 (Kubha) 河谷的弗楼沙 (Puruṣapura) 或布色羯逻伐底 (Puṣkalāvatī),陪都在秣菟罗 (Mathurā)。迦腻色迦在支持佛教和容忍一切宗教方面与阿育王争胜。在佛教艺术上,他开创了高塔型窣睹波[3],大大不同于以前的半球覆钵形

[1] É. Lamotte, *opere citato*: 320-329.
[2] A. K. Warder, *opere citato*: 265.
[3] A. K. Warder, *opere citato*: 345.

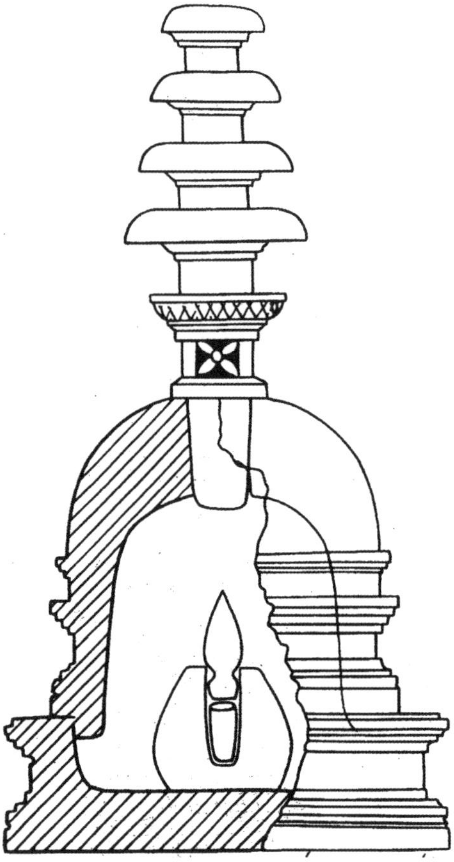

图 5 犍陀罗曼吉亚拉 (Mankīyala) 大塔出土的塔形舍利盒

(图 5)[1]。最著名者，为当时北印度佛教中心白沙瓦的“雀离浮图”，即今 Shā-jī-ki-Ḍhērī 遗址。除了高塔型窣睹波外，犍陀罗佛塔的另一显著特征，是其逐渐精巧和日渐繁复。“这种繁复，表现在塔基、塔身和半球形覆钵表面的全部雕刻和装饰上。尤其值得注意的是，它们都特别强调上部建筑。”[2]

中国的佛塔，主要为高层楼阁型木塔和砖塔。此外，尚有少量的单檐灰身塔（墓塔）、金刚宝座式塔和喇嘛塔等。这种高层楼阁型大塔，与印度覆钵塔乃至犍陀罗高塔究竟有什么关系，长期以来一直有争议。有的学者认为中国的高层大塔系模仿犍陀罗雀离浮图而造；有的认为中国的高层楼阁型大塔系受印度佛陀伽耶大菩提寺塔的影响；也有的学者认为印度的覆钵塔传入犍陀罗时，塔身已经升高，逐渐形成了北魏嵩岳寺塔（图 6）之形式；还有的学者认为中国的楼阁型大塔，塔顶上的相轮和露盘为印度所传入，而塔身则为中国固有之形式。实际上，这个问题颇为复杂。中国佛塔之形成，当具各种因素。

---

[1] 印度秣菟罗城出土的一根建筑横梁，正面雕刻佛的象征物，背面中央刻画帝释窟，雕造时代应为公元一世纪前后。象征物中有菩提屋（中央）、狮驮法论（右侧）和一座三层浮图（左侧），分别表示悉达多太子菩提树下成道、佛于鹿野苑初转法轮和拘夷那竭涅槃。其中，三层浮图应是迄今所知印度发现最早的多层佛塔。巴特那市库姆拉哈尔 (Kumrāhār) 遗址出土的“佛陀伽耶饰板 (Bodhgayā plaque)”，表现的是直角尖塔 (śikhara)，且有佉卢字母题刻，应为公元一、二世纪之物，也是高层建筑。此外，秣菟罗博物馆还藏有一件贵霜时期的高层建筑浮雕，时间应在公元二世纪。这种高层佛塔或高层建筑，与中国传统的楼阁型佛塔之关系，值得我们深入探讨。参见：1) R.C. Sharma, *Buddhist Art: Mathurā School,* New Delhi: Wiley Eastern Limited & New Age International Limited, 1995, Plates 61-64; 2) A. K. Coomaraswamy, *History of Indian and Indonesian Art,* New York: E. Weyhe / London: E. Goldston, 1927: 80-81, Pls. XVII, 62; XIX, 69.

[2] B. Rowland, *The Art and Architecture of India: Buddhist/Hindu/Jain,* rev. ed., New York: Penguin Books, 1977: 141.

首先,中国古代文明中最重要的一个观念,就是“把世界分成不同的层次,其中主要的便是‘天’和‘地’。不同层次之间的关系不是严密隔绝、彼此不相往来的。中国古代许多仪式、宗教思想和行为的很重要的任务,就是在这种世界的不同层次之间进行沟通。进行沟通的人物,就是中国古代的巫、觋。从另一个角度看,中国古代文明是所谓萨满式(Shamanistic)的文明”[1]。古代巫觋沟通天地之间所用的工具之一,就是地柱(axis mundi),或称中心柱(central axis)[2]。这种柱子从地下通到天上。通天地的巫觋通过爬这根柱子,可以从一个世界到另一个世界中去[3]。从某种意义上说,这就是中国古代的宇宙观。其次,中国古代的“台谢”建筑形成很早。这种台谢建筑,自赋予神仙方士之说后,便产生了高台建筑,如汉武帝(前140至前87年)时所修建的柏梁台、通天台、神明台等[4]。这种高台,系多层的木构高楼,高达数十丈[5],是汉武帝“置祠具其下,招来神仙之属”[6],“上通于天也”[7]。此外,山东、河北、河南、陕西、甘肃等地出土的许多汉代明器楼院和望楼,平面多作正方形,高达四五层,每层用斗拱承托腰檐,其上置平座,将楼阁划分数层(图7)。这从另一方面反映出汉代高层建筑颇为流行,甚为

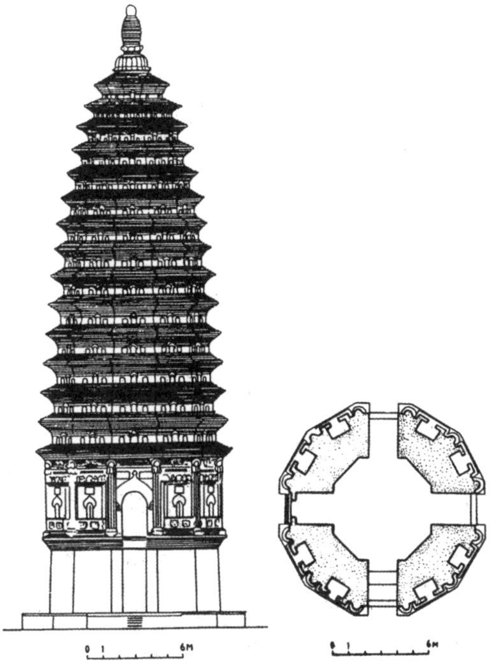

图6 河南登封嵩岳寺塔平面及立面图

[1] 张光直《考古学专题六讲》,北京:文物出版社,1986年,第4页。

[2] 这一术语原为美国芝加哥大学宗教史系教授、美籍罗马尼亚人埃里亚德(Mircea Eliade)所假定,亦作Cosmic mundi, Axis, Axis of World。

[3] Mircea Eliade, *Shamanism: Archaic Techniques of Ecstasy,* tr. from the French by W. R. Trask, London: Arkana, 1989:259-266. 又,古代通天地的工具除地柱外,尚有神山(The Cosmic Mountain)和天地树(The World Tree)等。参见Mircea Eliade上引书第266-274页。需要指出的是,中国古代巫觋沟通天地时所用的工具,与世界上其他地区萨满式文化所使用的工具大致相同。

[4] 司马迁《史记》,点校本,北京:中华书局,1959年,第459、479、482页。

[5] 据唐司马贞《史记索隐》卷四证引《三辅故事》,柏梁“台高二十丈,用香柏为殿,香闻十里”。同书卷四引《汉书旧议》,通天“台高三十丈,去长安二百里,望见长安城也”。同书卷四征引《汉宫阙疏》云“(神明)台高五十丈,上有九宫,常置九天道士百人也”。司马贞《史记索隐》,汲古阁本。

[6] 司马迁,上引书,第479页。

[7] 班固《汉书》卷六,颜师古注,点校本,北京:中华书局,1962年,第193页。

a

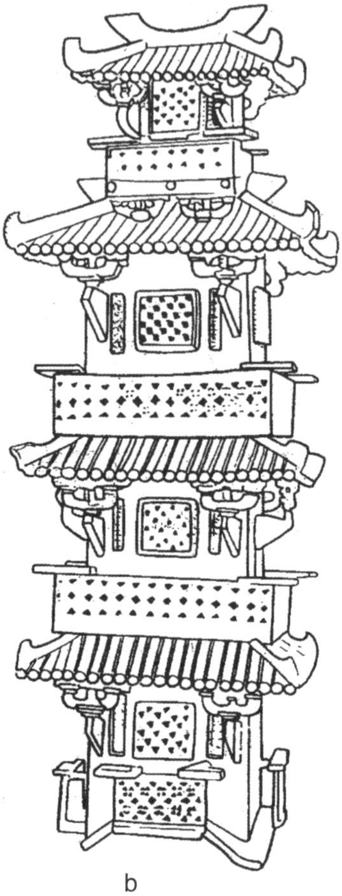

b

图 7a　张掖郭家沙滩东汉墓出土的陶楼院
b　山东高唐汉墓出土的陶望楼

发达[1]。佛教传入中土后,印度的佛教思想与中国古代的宇宙观及固有的神仙思想相结合,应是高层楼阁型佛塔出现的最恰当理由。从构造上讲,印度早期佛塔所包括的主要部分有塔基、塔身(medhī)、覆钵(aṇḍa)、方龛(harmikā)、平头(chūḍamaṇi)、轮杆(yaṣṭi)和轮盖(chattra)。这些构件与中国古代的神山、地柱观念及方士所用的望楼[2]相结合,随之置于古代帝王祀神之"神台型"木构高楼之顶,以示对佛和佛法之崇敬,应是最合理之办法。因为佛教在汉代,本视为道术之一种,"其流行之教

[1] 陈明达先生认为"汉代建筑中,高层建筑已是常见的形式"。陈明达《关于汉代建筑的几个重要发现》,见《文物参考资料》,1954 年第 9 期,第 92 页。

[2] 抗日战争时期,梁思成先生在四川南溪县李庄撰写《中国建筑史》时,认为:"二层或三层之望楼,殆即望候神人之'台'。其平面均正方形,各层有檐有平坐。魏晋以后木塔,乃由此式多层建筑蜕变而成,殆无疑义。"梁思成《梁思成文集》三,北京:中国建筑工业出版社,1985 年,第 36 页。

理行为,与当时中国的黄老方技相通”[1]。“育王创遗身之塔,架迥浮空;魏主起通天之台,仁祠切汉。”[2]就是到了北魏,这种佛道混杂现象依然存在。高允《鹿苑赋》中“凿仙窟以居禅,辟重阶以通术”[3]的重阶通术,就“有通天台之意”[4]。

因此,正如已故著名建筑史学家梁思成、林徽音、刘敦桢所强调的那样:“塔虽是佛教象征意义最重的建筑物,传到中土,却中国化了,变成这中印合璧的规模,而在全个结构及外观上中国成分,实又占得多。如果《后汉书·陶谦传》所记载的,不是虚伪,此种木塔,在东汉末期,恐怕已经布下种子了?”[5]此后,由于佛教盛行中土,佛塔之构建日益增多,形制亦多样。但不管怎样,中国佛塔创建伊始就以楼阁型木塔为主,且一直兴盛不衰。及至唐代,由此衍化出的楼阁型砖塔及砖石结构的密檐塔,渐有喧宾夺主之势[6]。至于单檐塔和金刚宝座式塔,尽管它们各自出现得也较早,但数量不多,构不成主流;而与印度原始覆钵塔形制最为接近的喇嘛塔,直到宋和西夏时才开始出现[7],蒙元时大盛,可以代表后期佛塔的一个发展阶段。

二、Caityagṛha 与 Chētiyaghara

在佛教术语中通称的支提殿或塔庙,实际上就是一座祈祷堂,梵语称 caityagṛha[8],巴利语作 cetiyagharā。这种建筑内的主体是窣睹波,通称“支提”。从梵语、巴利语我们不难发现:caityagṛha (cetiyagharā) 是由两个截然不同的名词组合在一起,即 caitya (cetiya) 和 gṛha (gharā)。caitya (cetiya) 的含义我们在上文中已做了讨论,此不赘;而梵语 gṛha 意为房、屋、殿、堂、庙等[9],巴利语 gharā 之意与此相同[10]。顾名思义,caityagṛha 或 cetiyagharā 就是支提殿,即塔庙。

---

[1] 汤用彤《汉魏两晋南北朝佛教史》,北京:中华书局,1983 年,第 83 页。

[2] 道世《法苑珠林》卷三十六,周叔迦、苏晋仁校注,北京:中华书局,2003 年,第 1137 页。

[3] 道宣《广弘明集》卷二十九,《大正藏》第 52 卷,第 339b 页。

[4] 汤用彤,上引书,第 558 页。

[5] 梁思成、林徽音、刘敦桢《云冈石窟中所表现的北魏建筑》,见《中国营造学社汇刊》,第 4 卷第 3/4 期合刊本 (1934 年),第 193-194 页。

[6] 刘敦桢《中国之塔》,刊《公共工程专刊》第一集 (1945 年),参见《刘敦桢文集》四,北京:中国建筑工业出版社,1992 年,第 4 页。

[7] 参见:1) 黄宝瑜《中国佛教建筑》,载章嘉等著《中国佛教史论集》III,台北:中华文化出版事业委员会,1956 年,第 890 页;2) 刘敦桢,上引书,第 10 页。

[8] 这一术语有时简作 caitya,亦作 chaitya,或 chaitya-gṛiha, chaitya building 或 chaitya hall。

[9] 参见:1) Monier Monier-Williams, *opere citato*: 361; 2) 荻原雲來,上引书,第 432 页。

[10] T. W. Rhys Davids and William Stede, *opere citato*: 272.

关于塔庙的起源，许多学者都曾做过有益的探索。印度考古学家米特拉 (Debala Mitra) 女士认为：塔庙的产生，显然是为了向佛教徒提供一便利的场所。在那里，他们可以不受天气的干扰而进行佛教朝拜活动，否则的话，在同一地方同时建造一座露天塔和一座塔庙就无法解释了。因此，功利主义和宗教仪式的迫切需要，是这种特殊建筑形式产生的基础[1]。笔者的看法与此基本相同，而且最近检出的汉文佛典，更证实了这一点。

据义净译《根本说一切有部毗奈耶杂事》卷十四："缘在室罗伐城时，诸苾刍于夏雨时旋绕制底，有泥污足。佛言：'应可布砖，上以碎砖和泥打之。复安礓石、灰泥。'塔大难遍。佛言：'应齐一寻。'此亦难办。佛言：'安版。'复更难求。佛言：'步步安砖。'苾刍寺门及寺内地多有泥陷。佛言：'如上所做，准事应为。'"[2]《四分律》卷五十二记述："彼塔露地，华香、灯油、幡盖、妓乐、供养具，雨渍风飘、日曝尘土坌及乌鸟不净污。佛言：'听作种种屋覆，一切作屋所须应与……'时无外墙障，牛马入无限。佛言：'听作墙，若须门，听作。'"又同卷有"彼安如来塔，置不好房中；已在上好房宿。佛言：'不应尔，应安如来塔，置上好房中，已在不好房宿。'"[3]上引律典说明：比丘在雨季旋绕佛塔时，为防止污足可布砖；为防止"雨渍、风飘、日曝、尘坌"等，应在塔及供养具上方覆盖棚顶，甚或把塔置于上好房中。此外，《弥沙塞部和醯五分律》卷二十六的一段话，对我们研讨塔的种类、形制及其附属设施等，具有重要价值。"佛言：'所有四种人应起塔，如来、圣弟子、辟支佛、转轮圣王。'诸比丘欲作露塔、屋塔、无壁塔，欲于内作龛像，于外作栏楯，欲作承露盘，欲于塔前作铜、铁、石、木柱，上作象、狮子种种兽形，欲于塔左右种树。佛皆听之。"[4]由此我们获知：1. 如来、圣弟子、辟支佛和转轮圣王应造塔供养。2. 佛在世时，允许比丘建造三种佛塔：一为露塔，一为屋塔，一为无壁塔。其中的露塔，就像桑吉大塔那种露天所建之样式；无壁塔，是在塔上方以木或竹搭一顶棚，用以遮挡雨水和较强的阳光，唯棚下无墙壁，就像帕鲁德 (Bhārhut) 大塔栏楯上的浮雕塔庙 (图 8) 所示；而屋塔，大概就是《四分律》中把塔"屋覆"、"置上好房中"的那种，为 stūpa-gṛha 或 thūpa-gharā。汉译时所据原文，可能就是 grihya-chaitya 或 caityagṛha，只是我们现在无法找到原本对勘罢了。不过值得注意的是，汉译律藏明确阐明屋塔是佛

[1] Debala Mitra, *Buddhist Monuments,* Calcutta: Sahitya Samsad, 1971: 41.

[2]《大正藏》第 24 卷，第 270c 页。

[3]《大正藏》第 22 卷，第 956c-957c 页。

[4]《大正藏》第 22 卷，第 173a 页。

陀允许建造的三种佛塔之一，在功能上它与露塔和无壁塔相同。这种屋塔，可能在佛陀时代就已经产生了。3. 佛允许比丘在塔上开龛造像，这后来在许多地区的佛塔上，如犍陀罗和阿默拉沃蒂大塔都实施了。当然，这种作法也许在佛陀时代就已经产生，或许当时为彩画或木雕，无法保存至今。但不管怎么说，后世各地盛行开龛造像之制，大多是凭借佛说（经），遵循律典进行的。4. 佛亦许可比丘于塔顶作承露盘，塔周围作栏楯，桑吉大塔覆钵上巽伽(Śuṅga) 时期修建的相轮及塔周围的栏楯，皆属此制。5. 比丘获许于塔前做铜、铁、石和木柱，柱顶雕像或狮子等动物形象；同时可以在塔左右种树。有关佛陀时代的铜、铁、石、木柱，现不得而知；不过桑吉大塔南门附近现存的阿育王石柱，可证实这点。此外，萨尔那特 (Sārnāth) 与吠舍厘 (Vaiśālī) 的阿育王石柱及其柱头上的石狮子，也立于佛塔附近[1]。至于植树之制，桑吉和帕鲁德大塔栏楯上的浮雕佛塔左右就有树。

图 8　印度帕鲁德大塔栏楯上浮雕的无壁塔

现存最早的屋塔（塔庙）遗址，是在印度拉贾斯坦邦首府斋普尔东北 75 公里处拜拉特 (Bairāṭ)[2] 铭文山 (Bījak-kī-pahārī) 发掘出土的，时代为阿育王时期。拜拉特遗址底层平面圆形的塔殿直径为 8.29 米，内壁由 27 根八角木柱做骨架，柱间砌砖，呈楔形结构[3]；柱间大砖似为后来补砌，八角木柱原应独立环绕主体朝拜物——塔，柱间敞开[4]。在中央环形列柱（内壁）与外墙之间，是宽约 2.13 米的环形礼拜道，环形列柱[5] 与外壁皆于东侧开门道。后来，在这座圆形塔殿周围，又补建了一座平面长

[1] Krishna Deva, “Northern Buddhist Monuments”, in: *Archaeological Remains, Monuments & Museums,* Part I, New Delhi: Archaeological Survey of India, 1964: 89, 92.

[2] 现在多数学者认为 “Bairāṭ” 是玄奘《大唐西域记》卷四所记述的 “波里夜呾罗国 (Pāriyātra)”。参见：玄奘，上引书，第 376-377 页。

[3] D. R. Sahni, *Archaeological Remains and Excavations at Bairat,* Jaipur: Department of Archaeology & Historical Research, Jaipur State, 1937: 28-32, Pl. VII a & b.

[4] S. Piggot, “The Earliest Buddhist Shrines”, in: *Antiquity,* 1943, XVII (65): 2-6.

[5] 这种列柱，在功能上也许相当于露塔周围的栏楯。

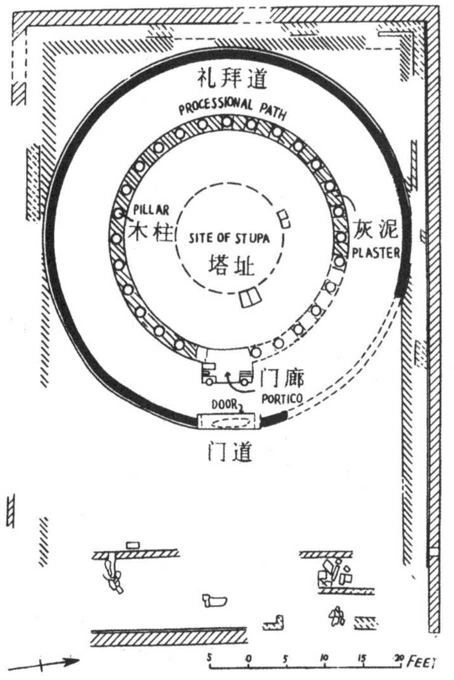

图 9　印度拜拉特圆形塔庙遗址平面图

方形建筑，其东半部为集会厅 (图 9)。此外，中央圆形主室之顶虽已不存，但原来似为瓦作，并冠以陶质尖饰；而礼拜道上之顶棚，则架于环形外墙与中央主室八角木柱顶部额枋之上[1]。

随着佛教石窟寺在西高止 (Ghats) 山麓的出现，当时人们也许感到了雕造 grihya-chaitya 之必要[2]。为了满足那些永久居留在石窟寺院的僧俗以及其他信徒的需要，尤其在天气不适宜举行宗教仪式之时，这种木结构的圆形塔庙也就自然而然地石化了。据《十诵律》卷四十八："佛听我作窟者善。佛言：'听作。'又言：佛听我窟中作塔者善。佛言：'听窟中起塔。'佛听我施窟门者善，是事白佛。佛言：'听作。'佛听我覆窟中塔者善。佛言：'听覆。'……佛听我施柱作塔者善。佛言：'听作。'佛听我以彩色、赫土、白灰庄严塔柱者善。佛言：'听庄严柱。'佛听我画柱塔上者善。佛言：'除男女合像，余者听作。'"[3]这表明：开凿石窟、窟中造塔、施柱作塔和庄严塔柱，皆符合佛说与律典。作为永久性的佛教建筑，既然初期的僧坊窟 (lēṇa) 是模仿地面木构僧坊 (vihāra) 而建，那么塔庙窟 (chētiyaghara)[4]也应是当时砖木结构塔庙或粗陋泥笆墙围遮的屋塔的石化形式。这点已为均讷尔 (Junnar) 地区杜尔贾莱纳 (Tūljālēṇa) 第 3 窟充分证实。杜尔贾莱纳第 3 窟 (图 10)，系忠实地模仿了拜拉特式木构塔庙。其平面圆形，中央为石雕窣睹波，周围绕以 12 根八角素面石柱，柱间无物[5]。中央窣睹波上面窟顶为穹隆形，

[1] D. R. Sahni, *opere citato*: 28-32, Pl. VII a & b.

[2] M. C. Joshi, "Buddhist Rock-cut Architecture: A Survey", in: *Proceedings of the International Seminar on Cave Art of India and China,* Theme I: Historical Perspective, New Delhi: Indira Gandhi National Centre for the Arts, November 25, 1991: 1-28, esp. 7-8.

[3]《大正藏》第 23 卷，第 351c-352a 页。后在同卷第 354c-355a 页有类似的记载。

[4] 印度石窟内的俗语铭文 chētiyaghara，由 chētiya 与 ghara 两词合成。其中，chētiya 意为支提 / 塔，ghara 意为窟，chētiyaghara 即支提窟或塔庙窟。参见 H. Lüders, *opere citato*: Nos. 1050, 1058, 1092, 1140, 1141, 1153, 1178, 1179, 1183, etc. 在中国，这种石窟建筑通称中心柱窟，也作支提窟、制底窟、塔洞、塔庙窟、中心塔柱窟等，忠实地表达了原词的含义。

[5] 这也证实了我们上述的推断，即拜拉特塔庙内八角木柱之间原无砖构。

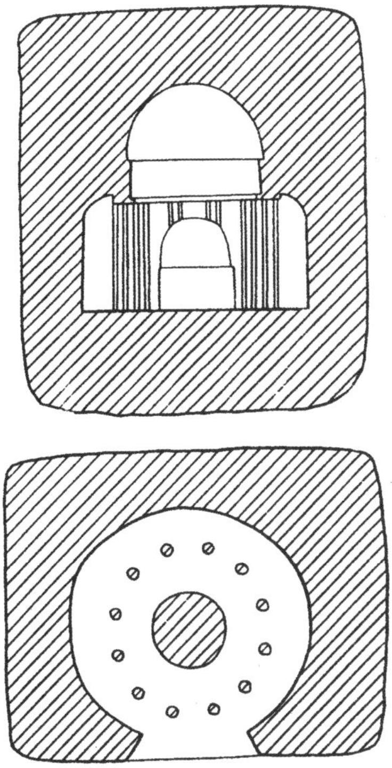

图 10　印度杜尔贾莱纳第 3 窟平面及横向垂直剖面图

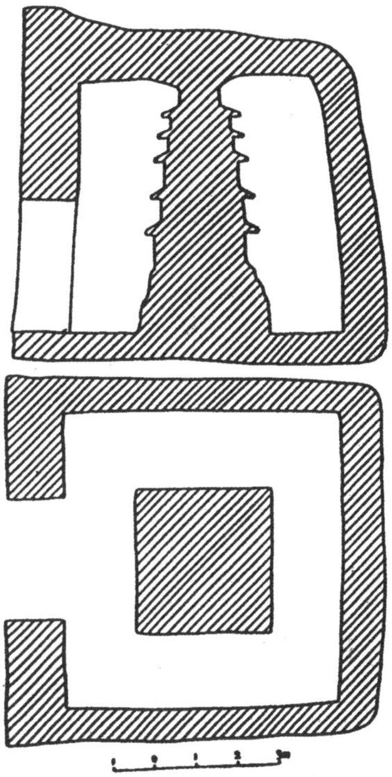

图 11　云冈石窟第 39 窟平面及纵向垂直剖面图

犹如一巨大半球扣在一座圆筒拱廊之上；而列柱与窟壁之间的环形礼拜道，即侧廊之顶则为扇形，且较主室之顶略低。此外，半球形穹隆顶之表面，原来曾安置纵横交错的木构梁椽，以示对木结构塔庙屋顶的模仿[1]。

随着佛教的迅速发展，僧团的日益扩大，这种平面圆形的塔庙窟已不能满足越来越多的信徒在窟内礼拜和集合的需求，尤其是对一处大型的石窟寺院组织来说更是如此。这种宗教上的发展，要求将那种平面圆形的小型屋塔扩大为带有集合厅的巨大塔庙。这样，倒 U 字形平面屋塔——最流行的塔庙窟便出现了，而且不久就成为塔庙窟的正规形式。后来雕凿的塔庙窟，皆在此基础上演化。至于塔庙窟内的主体——窣睹波之形式，则随着露塔的发展而变化，与之同步演进，中印两国情况皆如此（图 11）。

不论木构还是石雕，早期塔庙似乎都“体现了那种赋予窣睹波外貌上同样玄奥

[1] 著名的贡土巴利 (Guntupalli) 塔庙窟，平面亦作圆形，唯佛塔周围无石柱，穹隆顶表面雕出纵横交错之石椽，整体结构与杜尔贾莱纳第 3 窟颇为接近。过去，有学者把它看作印度现存最早的塔庙窟。经与拜拉特木构塔庙进行比较，我们认为：在缺少可靠材料的前提下，很难把它雕凿的年代定得很早。参见：Debala Mitra, *opere citato*: 44.

的象征主义。就像欧洲中世纪的大教堂那样，其十字形平面和广博的繁复装饰，曾是神体的象征外貌和微观世界内宇宙的重建。故而，塔庙应被视作宇宙屋的物化形式。宇宙屋就是万有，其入口就是世界之门”[1]。当佛教徒右绕佛塔时，这种塔庙内部苏醒过来，充满生气。绕塔礼拜乃独出心裁的举措，它为人们从尘世到佛国铺设了一条方便之路。实际上，佛教徒所采纳的旋绕仪式，是一具有悠久传统并享有盛誉的印度宗教仪式。《百道梵书》(*Śatapatha-brāhmaṇa*) 规定：信徒面向祭坛，“从右向左旋绕三圈，并在坛上铺满吉祥草。当从右向左铺满三层草时，他留下了足够铺放草束的数量。而后，他再从左向右旋绕祭坛三圈。之所以从左向右再转三圈，是因为当他最初从这里紧随三代祖先远行之后，又从他们那里回到了现世”[2]。在这个微观世界里，任何人都可以对那未知世界做一次旅行并安然返回。对一位佛教徒来说，到一处著名的塔庙做一次朝拜，大概意味着他到另一个世界做了一次旅行。假定从左侧廊进入，他自然会沿着顺时针方向右旋绕佛塔。“最初，通过记数走过的柱子，他尚能计算所进入未知世界的深度。不过当他一步又一步谨慎地前移时，光线变得愈来愈暗，从每个柱子上反射回来的光亮，也在黑暗中渐渐消逝，未知世界只有靠他默默揣度了。突然从柱间，他辨识出半圆形亮点——窣睹波之覆钵。覆钵在来自明窗的光线中反光、发亮。这是计算极为精确的效果。窟内列柱大体相同，他在柱间与塔的视角，则随着他每迈一步而增大。当他最终靠近佛塔时，他的最大视角和他与塔的距离相结合，使朝拜焦点太强以致不能凝视。”[3]这种由朦胧和分柱法设定的神秘，似乎把各种事物都溶解了，致使信徒以及各种各样的朝拜者感到他们自身已置于一个虚构的魔幻世界之中，肉体正飘向天堂，精神正在升华。

［本文初刊于（北京）经济科学出版社 1997 年出版的《中国博士后社科前沿问题论集》第 216-238 页，后收入北京大学出版社 1998 年出版的《北京大学百年国学文粹：考古卷》第 691-701 页。此次重刊前做了些许修改，并增补了最后一段。另外，斯里兰卡学者罗兰德·席尔瓦 (Roland Silva) 2004 年出版了 *Thūpa, Thūpaghara and Thūpa-pāsāda*，对斯里兰卡的“塔与塔庙”做了全面分析，可参看。］

---

[1] D. Mitra, *opere citato*: 44.

[2] Julius Eggeling tr., *Śatapatha-brāhmaṇa*, in: *SBE*. XII: 425.

[3] N. I. Wu, *Chinese and Indian Architecture: The City of Man, the Mountain of God and the Realm of the Immortals*, New York: George Braziller Inc., 1963: 16.

西印度塔庙窟的分期与年代

一、引　　言

据我们调查，印度的佛教石窟，大体可区分为僧众栖止、禅修生活用窟和供养、礼忏佛事用窟两类。作为宗教场所，后者应占主导地位，前者只是为后者服务的；前者以僧坊窟（lēṇa）为主，后者以塔庙窟（chētiyaghara，亦作支提窟）为代表。一座塔庙窟与若干僧坊窟组成一个寺，许多寺连在一起，由此构成规模宏大的石窟寺院。作为供养、礼忏的主体，印度塔庙窟是随着佛教的发展而变化的。如早期塔庙窟内的石塔无像无龛；而到晚期，由于大乘佛教的兴起，龛像都进入了窟内，石塔也变得复杂起来。因而相对僧坊窟来说，塔庙窟本身的发展更具有时代气息。

实际上，印度的佛教石窟主要集中在西印度，更确切地说，集中在今马哈拉施特拉邦境内。那里的洞窟数量多、类型齐备、时代延续较长。从某种意义上讲，该邦可以看作是世界石窟建筑的摇篮。

在西印度阿旃陀（Ajaṇṭā）、奥兰伽巴德（Aurangābād）、贝德萨（Bēdsā）、珀贾（Bhājā）、埃洛拉（Ellorā）、均讷尔（Junnar）、根赫里（Kāṇhēri）、格拉德（Karādh）、伽尔拉（Kārlā）、贡德恩（Kondāṇē）、贡迪维蒂（Kondivitē）、古达（Kudā）、默哈德（Mahād）、纳西克（Nāsik）、比德尔科拉（Pitalkhōrā）等地的石窟群中都可以看到塔庙窟这种形制，有的一处石窟群，塔庙窟多达四五座。如比德尔科拉现存石窟 13 座，其中塔庙窟 5 座（第 3、10、11、12、13 窟），占总数的 38%；阿旃陀现存洞窟 30 座，其中塔庙窟也为 5 座［第 9、10、19、26、29（第 29 窟未按计划完工）窟］，约占总数的 17%。因此可以说，塔庙窟是印度佛教石窟寺中一种很有代表性的重要窟形。此外，我们也注意到，塔庙窟在西印度延续时间较长，分布地域也较广。

前人在对西印度佛教石窟寺的调查和研究中，涉及许多塔庙窟，注意到了这种洞窟的平面、立面及整个形制。有些学者也对其中的若干组成部分，如塔的结构、题材布局等进行过考证和研究。但在对塔庙窟进行系统探讨方面，目前仍存在学术上的空白。随着佛教石窟寺研究的深入，对某一类型石窟进行专门研究，显得尤为重要。本文就是笔者在这方面的一点尝试和探索。

在印度德里大学攻读博士学位期间，笔者利用那里的天时地利之便，对印度大多数石窟群及地面佛寺遗址进行了现场调查，取得了大量的文字和图像资料。同时，对印度许多图书馆收藏的有关材料，特别是印度考古调查局 (Archaeological Survey of India) 公开刊布和内部印行的考古报告做了深入的研究。印度的塔庙窟，除少数有纪年铭刻之外，大多数洞窟无题记。即便有题记，由于人为或自然的损伤，有些题记已漫漶不清或残缺不全，语义不明。又，限于目前条件，依靠碑铭字体来断定石窟的年代，尚有一定困难。这些都给研究工作，尤其是从纵、横两方面进行比较研究，带来诸多不便。要想深入，必须解决分期和年代问题。

笔者曾受过严格的佛教考古学训练，因而本文拟采用考古类型学作为主要的分析手段。从窟龛形制和题材布局等方面入手，对西印度塔庙窟进行分类排比，从中找出洞窟各组成部分之关系及其前后发展的演变规律，进而设定一编年框架。作为一礼拜场所，塔庙窟本身是由诸多部分，如外观、石塔、窟顶、列柱、造像以及装饰图案等组成的一个复杂的文化集合体。通过运用考古学之分类法，对其各部分进行全面梳理、分析、排比，最后可以得出一可靠的塔庙窟发展演化链。这种考古学方法论中所采用的原则，就是根据其形式，将各组成部分分作若干类型、亚类型和式，找出每一部分的自身发展序列，然后将形式相同的进行归类，尔后插入每一相应的组队之中。如果它们属于同一有限的区域和同一文化圈，可以认为同类型的各部分属于同一时代。也就是说，在同一地理文化环境中的诸文化，总是相同和一样的。类型学上相似体的同步性原则，可以应用到这里。根据事物从简单型向复杂型发展的演化原则，或更确切地说，通过识别引起类型变异的因素，诸如技术之发展、社会文化需求和审美情趣之变化等，在一定程度上可以找出这些年代类型的相对年代位置。因此，运用考古学方法研究古代石窟寺，愈来愈受到各国学者的欢迎。

在考古学分析的基础上，我们可以把不同遗址中的塔庙窟归入某一相应的组队之中进行分期，而后总结出每一组乃至每一处石窟群的特点，并根据题铭及其他可对比材料推定其年代，最后探讨有关问题。

总之，本文是在占有大量第一手资料的前提下，在前人研究的基础上，从考古学角度对西印度塔庙窟试做初步的分期研究。

二、西印度塔庙窟的类型分析

根据目前刊布的资料和笔者的现场调查,西印度马哈拉施特拉邦境内现存塔庙窟55座[1]。每座塔庙窟主要由以下六部分构成,即平面、外立面、明窗、窟顶、列柱和石塔,并具有分期意义[2]。

以上述六部分的类型分析为起点,通过建筑形式和题材布局的演化,我们便有了编排这一地区塔庙窟年代框架的良好基础。根据这个框架,可以对西印度塔庙窟进行初步的分期和编年研究。

(一)平面

根据洞窟平面形制的不同,西印度塔庙窟可分作下列三型。

A型:平面圆形,正中置塔。下分三式。

Ai式:穹隆顶或平顶圆形小窟,窟内仅有一塔,无集聚空间(图1)。5座,贝德萨(Bēdsā)[3]第1、3窟,珀贾(Bhājā)[4]第26窟,根赫里(Kāṇhēri)[5]第4、36窟[6]。

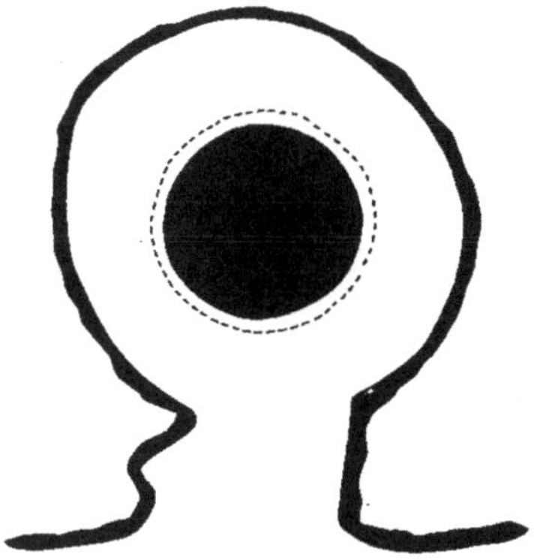

图1 珀贾第26窟平面图

Aii式:穹隆顶圆形窟,列柱环绕中央石塔,列柱与窟壁之间为环形礼拜道

[1] 珀贾第20窟内现存石塔20座,塔身直径1.6-2.5米不等,高度1.8-3米,塔形富于变化,时代早晚相距较大,故暂时不纳入本文分期和排年之列。

[2] 以塔庙窟的明窗为例,小乘时期开凿的珀贾第12窟,因为前壁系用木材建造,故明窗也为木构;而大乘时期开凿的阿旃陀第19窟,则为仿木石雕。因此,木构明窗及前壁,绝对早于石质明窗和前壁。又,小乘时期开凿的塔庙窟,窟内石塔通常较简朴,仅雕出塔身和覆钵,方龛以上部分多分体制作,如珀贾第12窟;而大乘时期塔庙窟内的佛塔,既雕出方龛、平头乃至相轮,还在塔基和塔身正面开龛造像。因此可以推断:珀贾第12窟无疑要早于阿旃陀第19窟。参见本文四之(一)、(二)节。

[3] 关于印度石窟所在地的汉字译名,凡中国地名委员会编辑的《外国地名译名手册》(北京:商务印书馆1983年版)和萧德荣主编的《世界地名翻译手册》(北京:知识出版社1988年版)中已有的,本文一律照用。其余均按中国地名委员会制定的《外国地名汉字译写通则》译出。又,为便于读者,同名译异者附后,如贝德萨(Bēdsā),一译巴特萨等。

[4] 珀贾(Bhājā),一译巴迦、巴贾、巴雅、巴阇等。

[5] 根赫里(Kāṇhēri),一译坎黑里。

[6] 根赫里第36窟平面不太规则,暂入此式。

(图2)。1座，均讷尔(Junnar)地区杜尔贾莱纳(Tūljālēṇa)第3窟。

Aiii式：前部为平顶长方形大厅，后部为圆形平面穹隆顶塔殿(图3)。1座，贡迪维蒂(Kondivitē)[1]第9窟。

B型：平面倒U字形，前部空间较大，作集聚之用；后部中央造石塔。下分五式。

Bia式：倒U字形平面纵券顶塔庙窟。窟平面通常由两排列柱纵向分作三部分，即一个主室和两个侧廊。两列柱在后端呈半圆形相接。石塔位于主室末端，其与侧壁和后壁间距相等。主室前端敞开[2](图4)。4座，阿旃陀(Ajaṇṭā)[3]第10窟、珀贾第12窟、贡德恩(Kondāṇē)[4]第1窟和比德尔科拉(Pitalkhōrā)[5]第3窟。

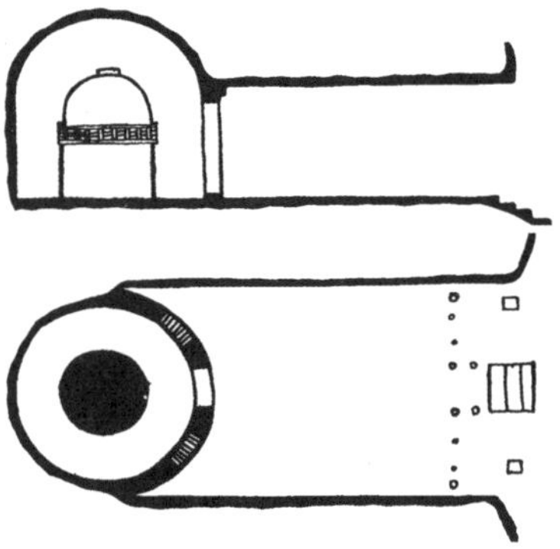

图3　贡迪维蒂第9窟平面及纵向垂直剖面图

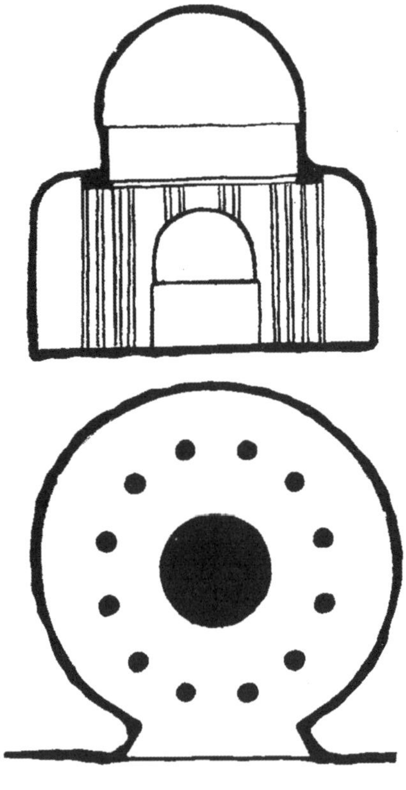

图2　杜尔贾莱纳第3窟平面及横向垂直剖面图

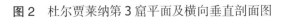

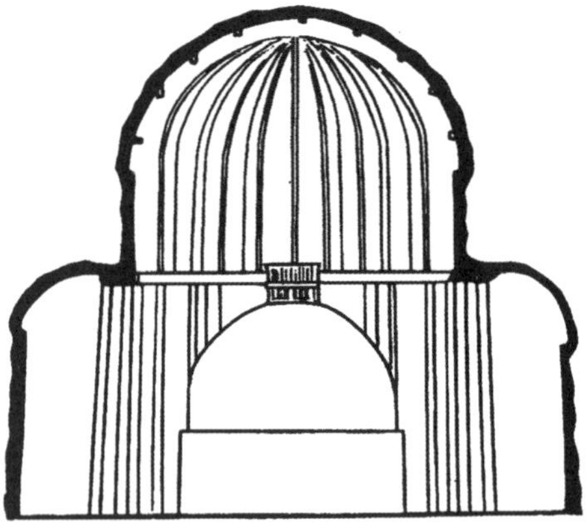

图4　珀贾第12窟横向垂直剖面图

[1] 贡迪维蒂(Kondivitē)，一译昆底福提。

[2] 这种塔庙窟的前端，原曾安置木构门屏，因为现存主室两侧壁前端及顶部，尚残留若干用来固定门屏的卯眼和地栿槽。

[3] 阿旃陀(Ajaṇṭā)，一译阿姜塔。

[4] 贡德恩(Kondāṇē)，一译昆达诺。

[5] 比德尔科拉(Pitalkhōrā)，一译皮塔尔阔拉、皮塔尔科拉等。

Bib 式：与 Bia 式相似，唯窟前端雕造石质屏墙，墙中央下部开门道（图 5）。5 座，阿旃陀第 9 窟[1]、奥兰伽巴德 (Aurrangābād) 第 4 窟[2]、均讷尔地区门莫迪 (J-Manmodi) 第 40 窟[3]、纳西克 (Nāsik)[4]第 18 窟和比德尔科拉第 13 窟。

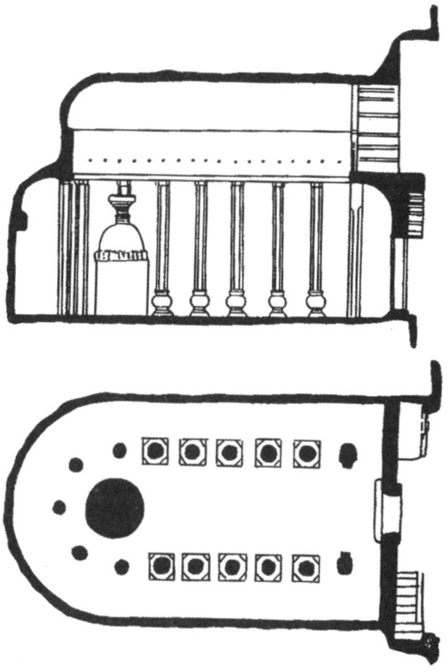

图 5　纳西克第 18 窟平面及纵向垂直剖面图

Biia 式：内无列柱，塔置于后端。窟前壁外有天井式前室（图 6）。5 座，均讷尔地区伽内什·伯哈 (Ganesh Parhar) 第 34 窟、格拉德 (Karādh) 第 5 窟、讷德苏尔 (Nāḍsūr) 第 8 窟和比德尔科拉第 10、12 窟。

Biib 式：列柱把窟内分作中央主室、两侧廊和横向长方形前廊四部分，塔置于主室后端，窟前有天井式敞口前室（图 7）。5 座，贝德萨第 7 窟、伽内什·伯哈第 6 窟、根赫里第 3 窟、伽尔拉 (Kārlā)[5]第 8 窟和门莫迪第 26 窟[6]。

Biii 式：与 Biib 式接近。由于列柱顶端的托架柱头连接额枋及深楣 (triforium-frieze)，这种倒 U 字形大厅平面看起来像一柱殿 (colonnade-sanctum)。前壁外的横廊或封闭天井式前室两侧凿有小室（图 8）。3 座，阿旃陀第 19、26 窟，埃洛拉 (Ellorā)[7]第 10 窟。

---

［1］阿旃陀第 9 窟平面虽为长方形，但整个平面布局与阿旃陀第 10 窟等相同，故暂入此式。

［2］奥兰伽巴德 (Aurrangābād，一译奥兰加巴德）第 4 窟前半部已塌毁。其现存遗迹与阿旃陀第 9 窟相似，故暂入此式。

［3］此窟未按计划完工。从现存遗迹断判：这座塔庙窟原计划凿成倒 U 字形平面，且右壁前端已凿出若干列柱，故暂入此式。

［4］纳西克 (Nāsik)，一译纳希克、纳锡克、讷希克等。

［5］伽尔拉 (Kārlā，亦作 Kārlē，Kārlī)，一译卡尔拉、卡莱、卡尔利、迦尔梨等。

［6］门莫迪第 26 窟未按计划完工。

［7］埃洛拉 (Ellorā，亦作 Ēlūra)，一译艾罗拉、爱罗拉、埃罗拉、爱洛尔。

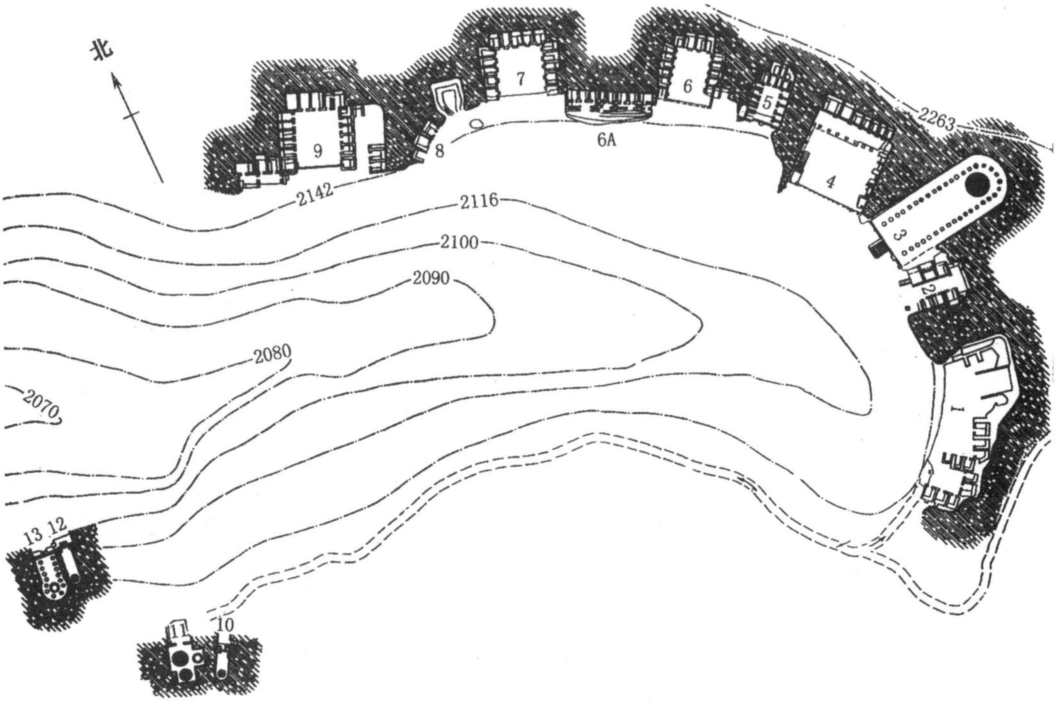

图 6　比德尔科拉石窟连续平面图

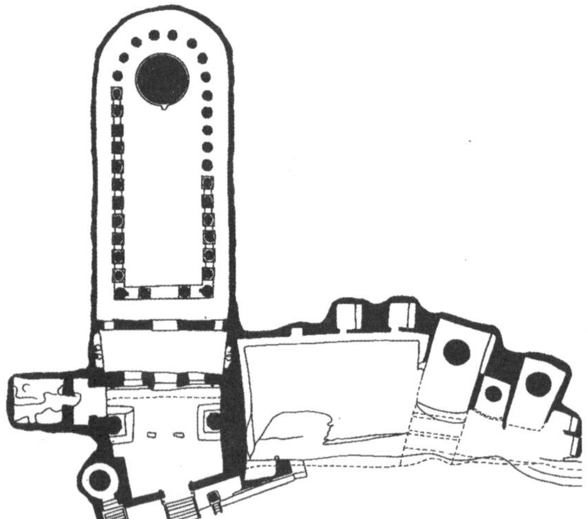

图 7　根赫里第 2、3 窟连续平面图

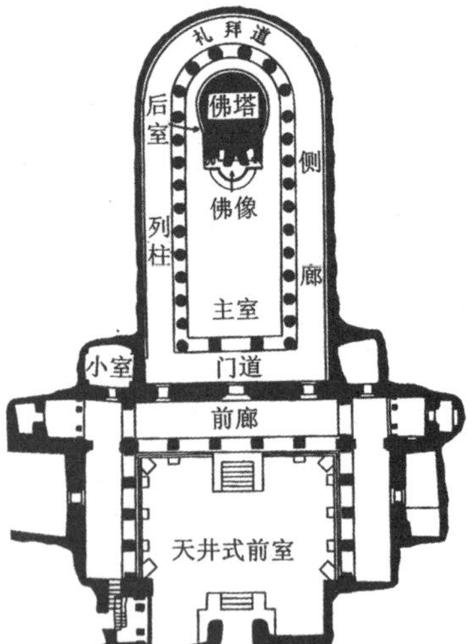

图 8　埃洛拉第 10 窟平面图

C 型：平面长方形平顶窟室，塔造里端。下分四式。

Ci 式：单一的长方形窟室，里端置塔，大多有前室（图 9）。16 座，伽内什·伯哈第 14 窟，根赫里第 2c、2d、2e 窟，格拉德第 11 窟，古达

(Kudā) 第 21 窟，默哈德 (Mahād) 第 15[1]、21 窟，门莫迪第 2[2]、25 窟，伯瓦拉 (Pawala) 第 2 窟，比德尔科拉第 11 窟，均讷尔地区锡万内里 (Sivaneri) 第 2、43、56[3]、66 窟。

Ciia 式：平顶长方形塔殿，塔置后部中央，有前廊和前室。前廊两侧各开一、二个小室（图 10）。2 座，古达第 9、15 窟。

Ciib 式：平顶长方形塔庙窟由下述部分（自内而外）构成：塔殿、塔殿前廊、方形大厅、前廊及前室（图 11）。4 座，格拉德第 6、16 窟，古达第 1、6 窟。

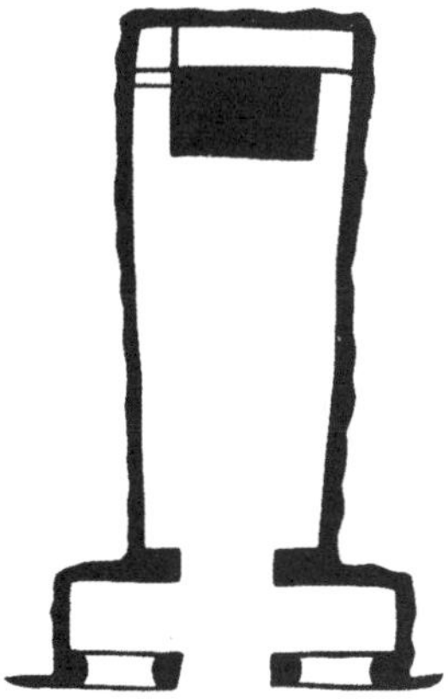

图 9　门莫迪第 2 窟平面图

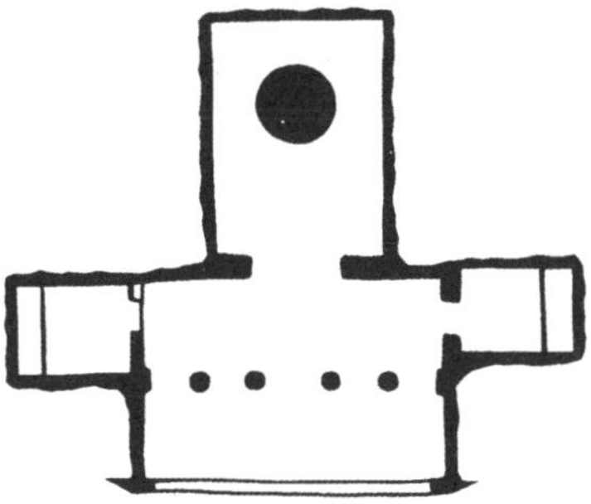

图 10　古达第 15 窟平面图

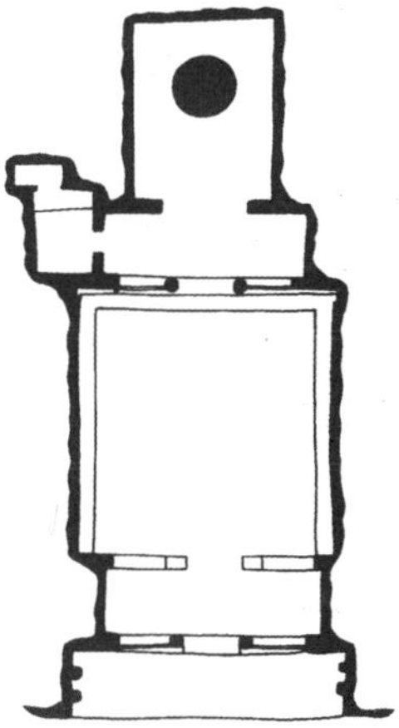

图 11　古达第 6 窟平面图

Ciic 式：塔庙僧坊混成式（图 12）。后为塔殿，前为方形大厅或横长廊，大厅或长廊周围开小室（僧坊）。3 座，格拉德第 48 窟、默哈德第 8 窟、谢拉尔瓦迪 (Shelārwādi) 第 8 窟。

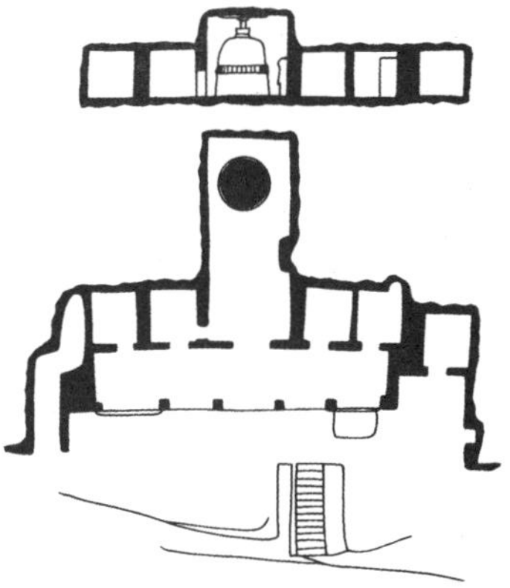

图 12　格拉德第 48 窟平面及横向垂直剖面图

（二）外立面

西印度塔庙窟的外立面可以分作下列三式。

I 式：无前壁[4]，巨大的尖楣圆拱形入口两侧浮

[1] 这是一座长方形小室，后壁凿出高浮雕石塔，暂入此式。

[2] 门莫迪第 2 窟内的石塔未完工。

[3] 此窟现毁坏严重，且已改作印度教 Sivābāi 女神庙。

[4] 贝得萨第 1 窟，珀贾第 26 窟，根赫里第 4、36 窟，默哈德第 15、21 窟等皆有宽大的长方形门道，应属此类。暂列入。

雕出支提盲窗[1]、栏楯等图案(图 13)。7 座,阿旃陀第 10 窟、珀贾第 12 窟、根赫里第 2e 窟[2]、贡德恩第 1 窟、贡迪维蒂第 9 窟、比德尔科拉第 3 窟[3]、杜尔贾莱纳第 3 窟。

II 式：前壁分为上、下两部分,上部为宽大的明窗,下部开 1-3 个门道。门道上方及明窗两侧浮雕出支提盲窗和栏楯等装饰图案(图 14)。6 座,阿旃陀第 9 窟,伽内什 · 伯哈第 34 窟,门莫迪第 40 窟,纳西克第 18 窟,比德尔科拉第 12、13 窟。

图 13　珀贾第 12 窟外立面

图 14　阿旃陀第 9 窟外立面

III 式：与 II 式相似,唯窟前有前廊或前室(图 15)。28 座,阿旃陀第 19、26 窟,贝德萨第 7 窟,埃洛拉第 10 窟,伽内什 · 伯哈第 6、14 窟,根赫里第 3 窟,格拉德第 5、6、11、16、48 窟,伽尔拉第 8 窟,古达第 1、6、9、15、21 窟,默哈德第 8 窟,门莫迪第 2、26 窟,伯瓦拉第 2 窟,比德尔科拉第 10、11 窟、锡万内里第 2、43、66 窟,谢拉尔瓦迪第 8 窟。

---

[1] Caitya arch 或 chaitya arch,可译作支提拱,意为支提窗、明窗或太阳窗等,因雕刻于塔庙窟门道上方而得名。这种支提窗早期主要用作采光,后来也用这种造型作装饰,如支提盲窗等。

[2] 根赫里第 2e 窟的左右侧壁已残,从窟前端的地面遗迹看,原安置木质门屏。

[3] 比德尔科拉第 3 窟的支提拱,现仅存左拱脚。参见 M. N. Deshpande, " The Rock-cut Caves of Pitalkhōrā in the Deccan", in: *Ancient India*, 15 (1959): Pl. XLV Ⅲ B.

（三）明窗

图 15　格拉德第 5 窟外立面图

作为塔庙窟外立面的一个重要组成部分，明窗在设计和雕刻处理上随时代的发展而多有变化，可分作六式。

I 式：巨大的拱形明窗似由两列倾斜石柱承托，以消减纵券顶之推力。支提拱的底部，即拱翼跨度最宽，看上去像一半圆形（图 16b）。4 座，阿旃陀第 10 窟、珀贾第 12 窟、贡德恩第 1 窟、比德尔科拉第 3 窟。

II 式：拱形明窗内侧各雕一壁柱，拱腹雕出截面为长方形之凸起椽头。拱翼由一拉杆（横梁）[1]连接，拱脚外凸。拱形明窗下的栏额表面，通常雕出栏楯图案。拱翼弯曲幅度较大，整个拱形明窗看似一马蹄形（图 16c）。8 座，阿旃陀第 9 窟、贝德萨第 7 窟、伽内什·伯哈第 34 窟、根赫里第 3 窟[2]、伽尔拉第 8 窟、门莫迪第 40 窟、纳西克第 18 窟、比德尔科拉第 12 窟。

III 式：整体造型与 II 式相似，唯拱内盲窗上开一方窗（图 15）。2 座，格拉德第 5 窟、比德尔科拉第 10 窟。

IV 式：与 II 式接近，唯拱翼内曲较大，拱翼末端外翻如脚爪（图 16d）。2 座，门莫迪第 2[3]、26 窟。

V 式：与 IV 式相似，拱顶有涡卷形装饰，拱翼末端外翻如火焰状（图 16e）。3 座，阿旃陀第 19、26、29 窟[4]。

VI 式：拱形设计与 V 式接近。整体造型为三叶拱，圆形明窗开在最上部（图 16f）。1 座，埃洛拉第 10 窟。

---

[1] 这种拉杆最早用于木构建筑之中，以使双翼达到完美的弯曲程度。在石窟中雕出这种构件，从另一方面证实塔庙窟系高度仿造地面木结构塔庙而建。

[2] 根赫里第 3 窟拱形明窗表面无任何雕饰。

[3] 门莫迪第 2 窟明窗为盲窗。

[4] 阿旃陀第 29 窟未按计划完工，但拱形明窗属于此式。

图 16　明窗演变示意图

a. 洛马斯 · 里希石窟门道上部；b. 珀贾第 12 窟明窗；c. 伽尔拉第 8 窟明窗；d. 门莫迪第 26 窟明窗；e. 阿旃陀第 19 窟明窗；f. 埃洛拉第 10 窟明窗

（四）窟顶

西印度塔庙窟的窟顶样式,可分下列二型。

A 型：拱顶[1],下分五式。

Ai 式：塔上方窟顶为穹隆形（参见图 3)。2 座,贝德萨第 3 窟、贡迪维蒂第 9 窟。

Aiia 式：石塔上方窟顶为穹隆状,形如一半球扣在一圆筒之上；侧廊之扇形顶,自窟壁起拱且与列柱顶部额枋相接（参见图 2)。1 座,杜尔贾莱纳第 3 窟。

Aiib 式：塔上方为半穹隆形,主室为纵向筒拱,侧廊之顶为扇形（参见图

[1] 拱顶包括穹隆顶和筒拱,二者最适合于初期木构建筑之需要。

13)。10 座,阿旃陀第 10 窟,贝德萨第 7 窟,珀贾第 12 窟,伽内什・伯哈第 6 窟,贡德恩第 1 窟,门莫迪第 26、40 窟[1],纳西克第 18 窟,比德尔科拉第 3、13 窟[2]。

Aiic 式:塔上方为半穹隆形,主室为筒拱,侧廊为平顶(图 17)。7 座,阿旃陀第 9、19、26 窟,奥兰伽巴德第 4 窟,埃洛拉第 10 窟,根赫里第 3 窟,伽尔拉第 8 窟。

Aiii 式:简洁之筒拱(图 18)。5 座,伽内什・伯哈第 34 窟,格拉德第 5 窟,讷德苏尔第 8 窟,比德尔科拉第 10、12 窟。

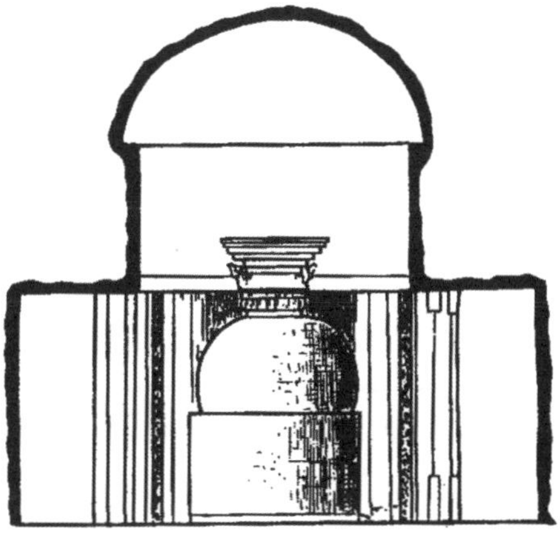

图 17　阿旃陀第 9 窟横向垂直剖面图

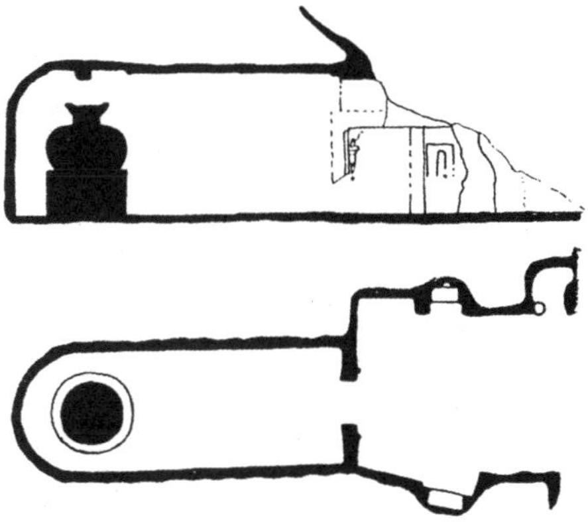

图 18　格拉德第 5 窟平面及纵向垂直剖面图

B 型:平顶,下分四式。

Bi 式:简洁之平顶(图 19)。10 座,贝德萨第 1 窟,珀贾第 26 窟,根赫里第 2c、2d、2e、4、36 窟,默哈德第 15、21 窟,门莫迪第 25 窟。

Bii 式:前室窟顶较主室为高(图 20)。2 座,门莫迪第 2 窟、比德尔科拉第 11 窟。

Biii 式:前室窟顶较主室为低(图 21)。6 座,伽内什・伯哈第 14 窟,默哈德第 8 窟,锡万内里第 2、43、56、66 窟。

Biv 式:主室与前室窟顶等高(图 22)。11 座,格拉德第 6、11、16、48 窟,古达第 1、6、9、15、21 窟,伯瓦拉第 2 窟,谢拉尔瓦迪第 8 窟。

---

[1] 门莫迪第 26、40 窟未按计划完工。其侧廊和列柱虽然尚未雕出,但已有雕刻列柱之趋向。现存顶部几乎为葱形拱(ogee),系在侧壁之上 5 厘米深的壁架上起架。

[2] 比德尔科拉第 13 窟侧廊之顶看上去如弧状(弓形)。参见:M. N. Deshpande, *opere citato*: 79.

图 19　根赫里第 2e 窟横向垂直剖面图

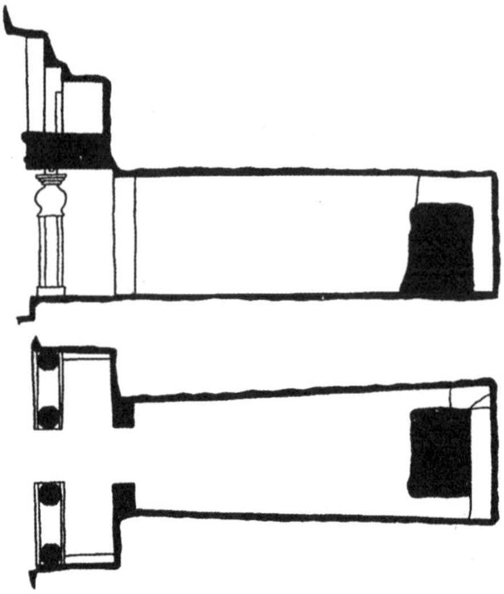

图 20　门莫迪第 2 窟平面及纵向垂直剖面图

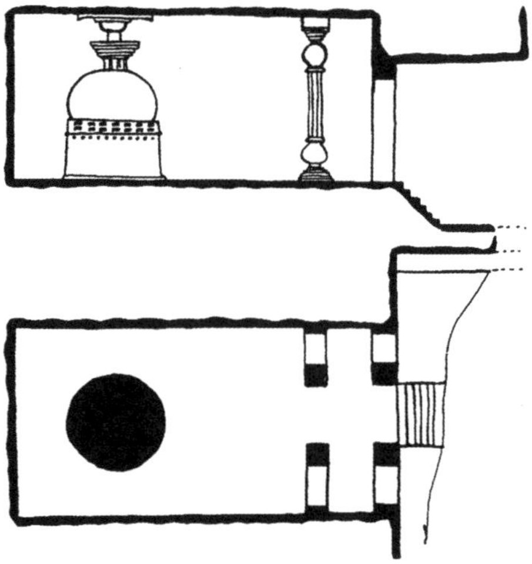

图 21　锡万内里第 43 窟平面及纵向垂直剖面图

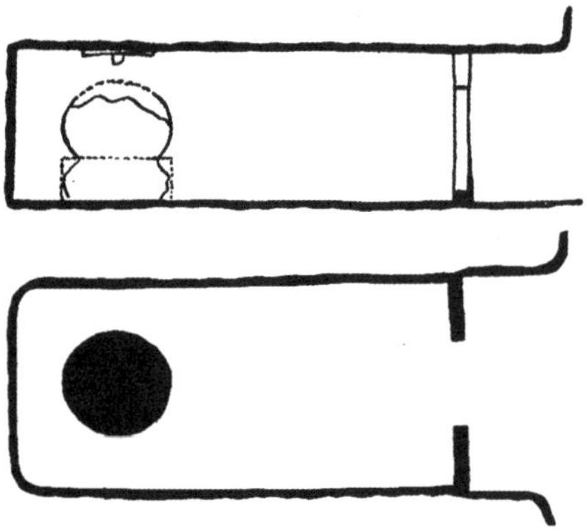

图 22　伯瓦拉第 2 窟平面及纵向垂直剖面图

(五) 石柱

西印度塔庙窟中的石柱，几乎成为一种牢固的排年标识。正如纳伽拉翥 (S. Nagaraju) 所指出的那样：同类柱子在不同纪念物中使用，经常表明它们在年代上接近，尤其在排比那些由不同类型的柱子构成的建筑时更是如此[1]。依据外形，西印度塔庙窟中的石柱，可以分作二型。

[1] S. Nagaraju, *Buddhist Architecture of Western India (C. 250 BC-C. AD 300)*, Delhi: Agam Kala Prakashan, 1981: 77.

A 型：石柱既无柱头，也无柱础。下分三式。

Ai 式：柱身八角形，向上有收分，且顶部略内倾（图 23a）。6 座，阿旃陀第 10 窟，珀贾第 12 窟，贡德恩第 1 窟，比德尔科拉第 3、13 窟，杜尔贾莱纳第 3 窟。

Aii 式：与 Ai 式相似，唯柱身向上收分及内倾幅度消减甚或不见。8 座，阿旃陀第 9 窟、奥兰伽巴德第 4 窟、贝德萨第 7 窟、伽内什·伯哈第 6 窟、根赫里第 3 窟、伽尔拉第 8 窟、门莫迪第 40 窟[1]、纳西克第 18 窟。

Aiii 式：八角、六角或四角石柱，大多有一面凸起[2]（图 23b）。5 座，阿旃陀第 9 窟、贝德萨第 7 窟、根赫里第 3 窟、伽尔拉第 8 窟、纳西克第 18 窟。

B 型：石柱有柱础或柱头，或二者兼具。下分八式。

Bi 式：八角柱、壶形础，下有方形金字塔状叠涩式柱顶石，即础座（图 23c）。1 座，纳西克第 18 窟。

Bii 式：方形叠涩式柱顶石、壶形础、八角或六角形柱身、“钟形”柱头上置倒金字塔形柱顶盘座面，再上为动物雕像（图 23d、e）。2 座，贝德萨第 7 窟、伽尔拉第 8 窟。

Biii 式：与 Bii 式类似，唯钟形柱头表面无脊棱，“钟”看上去像一只口沿外卷之球形壶。个别柱子为低方础，取代了 Bii 式壶形础（图 23f）。3 座，伽内什·伯哈第 6 窟、根赫里第 3 窟、格拉德第 5 窟。

Biv 式：与 Biii 式接近，唯柱顶盘座面上无动物雕像。个别柱子无壶形础（图 23g）。9 座，伽内什·伯哈第 14 窟，格拉德第 6 窟，古达第 9 窟，默哈德第 8 窟，门莫迪第 2、26 窟，锡万内里第 2、43、66 窟。

Bv 式：八角或四角柱，方形础（图 23h）。5 座，格拉德第 16、48 窟，古达第 1、6、15 窟。

Bvi 式：石柱分柱础、柱身、柱头三部分。柱身雕刻有凹槽、条形饰、圆带花以及精巧的网眼图案；柱身顶部是带有舟形托架枕之罗曼式柱头（图 23i）。托架上雕饰的图案繁复，如佛、大象、飞天以及四臂矮神等。2 座，阿旃陀第 19、26 窟。

---

[1] 虽然该窟未按计划完工，但右侧的柱子轮廓表明，它们原来要雕成简洁的八角柱。

[2] 这种柱子多置于列柱最前端，且对称出现。

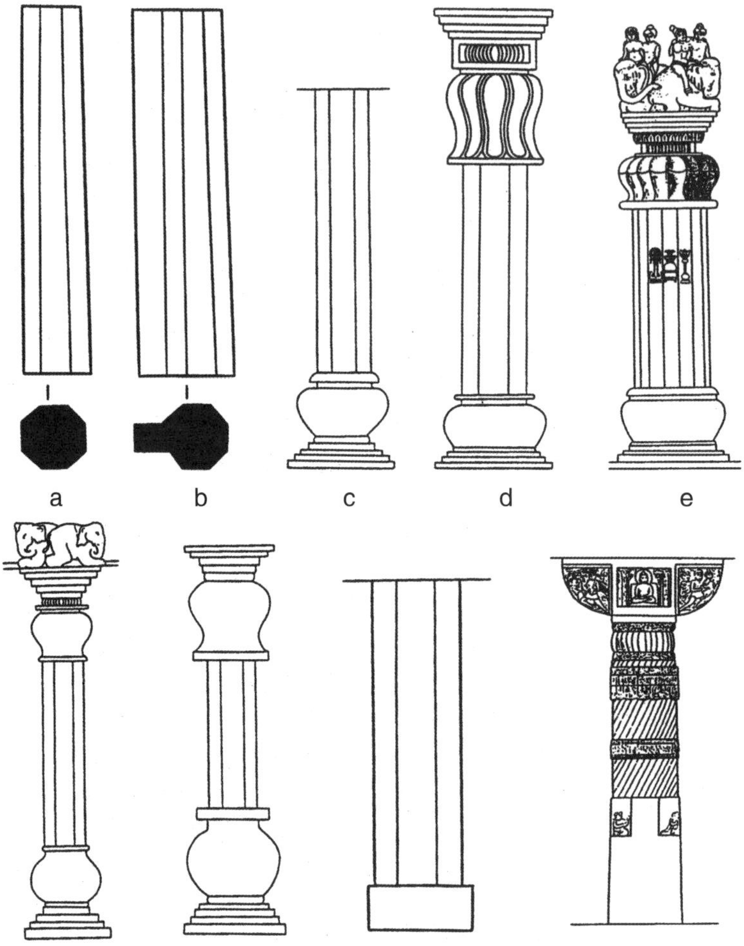

图 23　石柱类型示意图

a. 珀贾第 12 窟石柱；b. 阿旃陀第 9 窟石柱；c. 纳西克第 18 窟石柱；d. 贝德萨第 7 窟石柱；e. 伽尔拉第 8 窟石柱；f. 伽内什 · 伯哈第 6 窟石柱；g. 门莫迪第 26 窟石柱；h. 格拉德第 16 窟石柱；i. 阿旃陀第 19 窟石柱

Bvii 式：无柱础、八角柱身、素面舟形柱头。有的柱身上雕出沙漏 (hourglass) 图案。2 座，阿旃陀第 26 窟、埃洛拉第 10 窟。

Bviii 式：无础方柱，长方形托架式柱头。方柱上半部自下而上依次雕 8 面、16 面条形饰，带花及“花瓶与垂叶”图案。托架柱头表面常常刻出几何形装饰线条 (图 24)。1 座，埃洛拉第 10 窟。

（六） 塔

作为供养、礼忏的主体，一座完整的佛塔通常由塔基、塔身 (medhī)、覆钵 (aṇḍa)、方龛 (harmikā)、平头 (chūḍamaṇi)、轮杆 (yaṣṭi) 和轮盖 (chattra) 等部分构

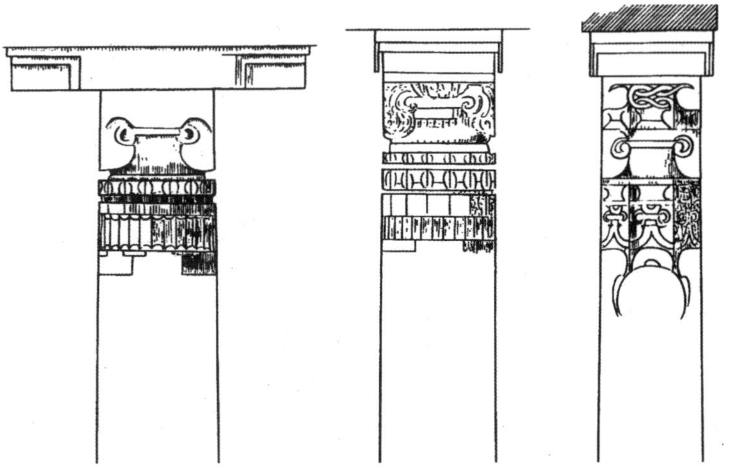

图 24　埃洛拉第 10 窟前室石柱

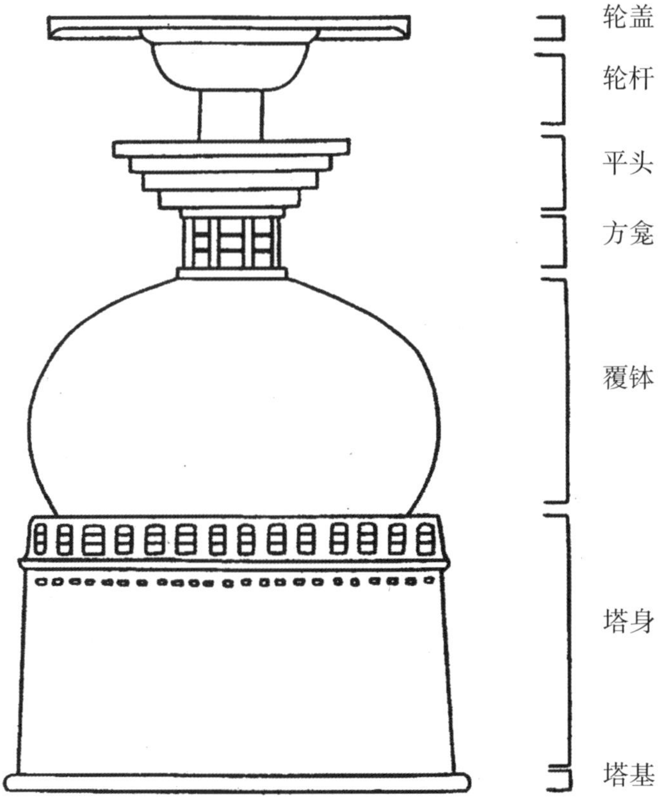

图 25　西印度塔庙窟内佛塔结构示意图

成，如图 25 所示。依据其结构，西印度塔庙窟中的石塔，可以分作下列四型。

A 型：仅塔身和覆钵系独石雕成，塔身与地面相连。其余部分，即方龛、平头、轮杆和轮盖等，原用石头或木料单独制做，这可从覆钵顶部的卯眼判明。下分二式。

Ai 式：塔素面、无任何雕饰（图 26a）。6 座，珀贾第 26 窟，根赫里第 2d、2e 窟，门莫迪第 40 窟，讷德苏尔第 8 窟，杜尔贾莱纳第 3 窟。

Aii 式：与 Ai 式相同，唯塔身上沿雕饰一匝栏楯图案（图 26b）。4 座，贝德萨第 1、3 窟，贡迪维蒂第 9 窟，比德尔科拉第 12 窟[1]。

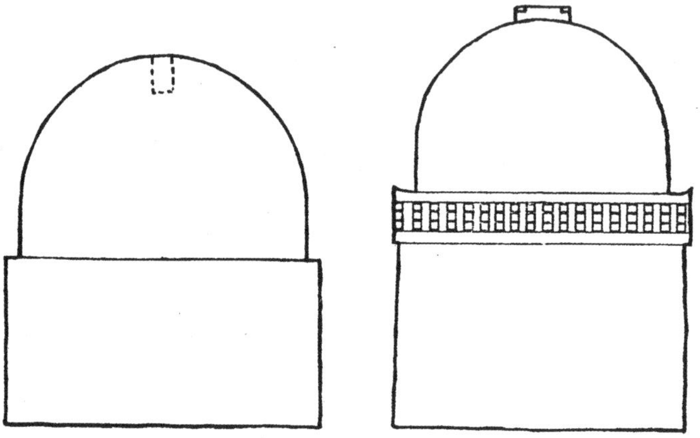

图 26　佛塔

a. 杜尔贾莱纳第 3 窟内佛塔；b. 贡迪维蒂第 9 窟内佛塔

B 型：塔基、塔身、覆钵、方龛乃至平头系独石雕作，塔身与窟地面相连。平头作叠涩式倒金字塔形。根据叠涩情况可分作二式。

Bi 式：无倒金字塔形叠涩式平头或平头由三至四层子涩构成，有的塔身边沿雕饰几何形图案（图 27a、b）。4 座，阿旃陀第 10 窟、奥兰伽巴德第 4 窟、珀贾第 12 窟、贡德恩第 1 窟。

Bii 式：倒金字塔形叠涩式平头由五层或更多子涩构成。有的塔身雕出二三匝栏楯图案，有的甚至在栏楯图案下加雕一列方孔或球形突出物（图 27c、d）。10 座，阿旃陀第 9 窟，贝德萨第 7 窟，伽内什·伯哈第 6、34[2]窟，根赫里第 3 窟，伽尔拉第 8 窟，纳西克第 18 窟，比德尔科拉第 10、11[3]窟，锡万内里第 66 窟[4]。

---

［1］据德什班德 (M. N. Deshpande) 先生撰写的考古简报，在进行考古清理时，第 12 窟内的塔“已毁坏了，覆钵上的长方形卯眼用来连接方龛的榫头。方龛原置覆钵之上，但覆钵崩裂后滑了下来，现存窟内”。参见：M. N. Deshpande, *opere citato*: 29.

［2］伽内什·伯哈第 34 窟中堆满了草捆，高度与塔顶相等。据纳伽拉蕭调查，该“塔顶可见一较平的方形物，中央有卯眼。这可能就是倒金字塔形叠涩式平头之表面”。参见：S. Nagaraju, *opere citato*: 302。故暂时把它归入此式。

［3］这是指比德尔科拉第 11 窟前室内石塔，其方龛已毁坏。

［4］由于根赫里第 3 窟、比德尔科拉第 10 窟和锡万内里第 66 窟内塔的方龛以上部分残毁或不见，笔者为了慎重，暂时将它们归入此式。

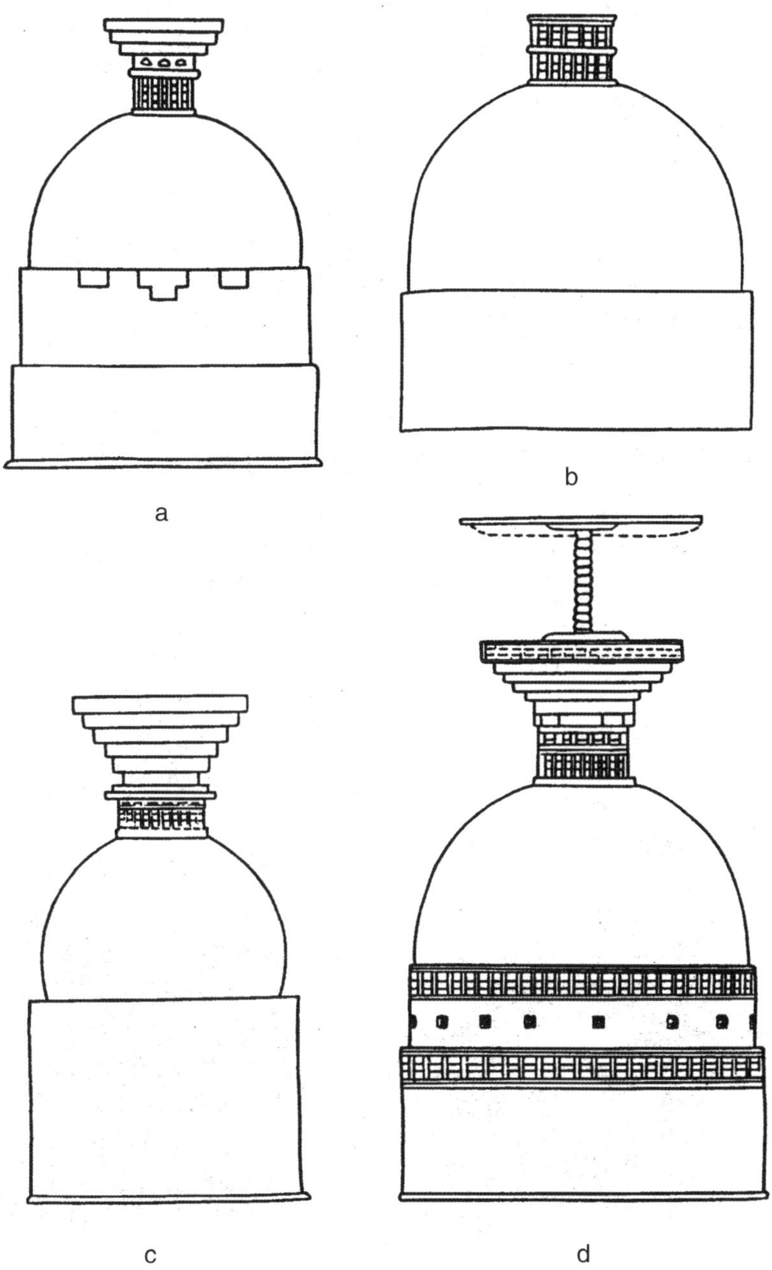

图 27　佛塔

a. 阿旃陀第 10 窟内佛塔；b. 珀贾第 12 窟内佛塔；c. 阿旃陀第 9 窟内佛塔；d. 伽尔拉第 8 窟内佛塔

C 型：塔基、塔身、覆钵、方龛、平头乃至轮盖以独石雕成，上下分别与窟顶和地面相连。下分二式。

Ci 式：塔基平面圆形，塔身向上渐收，边沿雕饰栏楯图案。覆钵雕成扁球形，像一个 2/3 或 4/5 球体置于塔身之上。方龛四面雕饰栏楯图案。倒金字塔形叠涩式平头由五层或更多子涩构成，再上是轮杆和轮盖。圆形轮盖雕于窟顶表面（图 28a）。16 座，伽内什·伯哈第 14 窟，根赫里第 2c、4、36 窟，格拉德第 5、6、11、16、48 窟，古达第 6 窟，默哈德第 8 窟[1]，门莫迪第 25 窟，伯瓦拉第 2 窟，比德尔科拉第 11 窟[2]，锡万内里第 43、56[3]窟。

Cii 式：与 Ci 式相似，唯轮杆和轮盖不见，倒金字塔形叠涩式平头与窟顶直接相连（图 28b）。7 座，古达第 1、9、15、21[4]窟，默哈德第 15、21 窟，谢拉尔瓦迪第 8 窟。

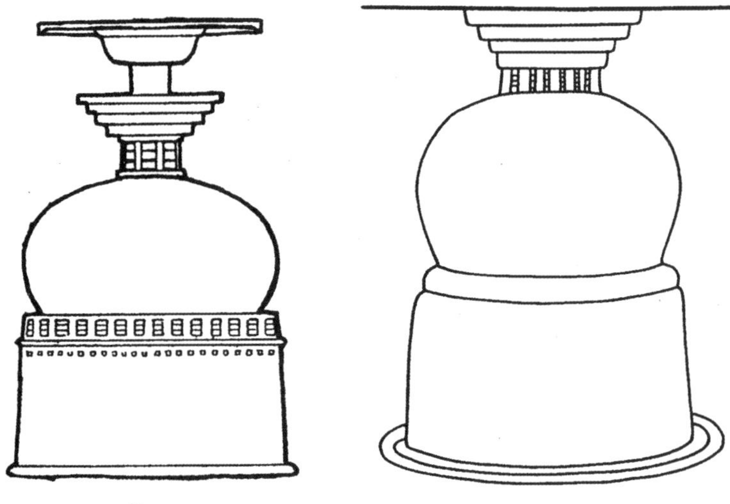

图 28　佛塔

a. 锡万内里第 43 窟内佛塔；b. 古达第 15 窟内佛塔

D 型：塔基、塔身、覆钵、方龛、平头等以独石雕成，塔正面雕出龛像。据主像姿势及塔形，下分二式。

Di 式：混合式石塔。低基座，细高塔身。塔身正面由两根壁柱承托一弓

[1] 默哈德第 8 窟内石塔已毁，唯窟顶上的轮盖尚存。

[2] 这里指比德尔科拉第 11 窟后室及东室的石塔。

[3] 尽管锡万内里第 56 窟内石塔已毁，但雕在窟顶的轮盖尚存。故入此式。

[4] 古达第 21 窟未按计划完工，但其后部粗犷的方形岩体表明，它原计划雕成类似第 15 窟那样的塔形。

架（圆栱）结构，内有高浮雕佛立像。覆钵像一个球体的 4/5 置于塔身之上。方龛正面雕一坐佛。倒金字塔形叠涩式平头由四层多边多角形子涩构成。平头之上为三重相轮，每重四面皆雕一小像。相轮顶上雕饰另一小塔，其小方龛几乎抵至窟顶（图 29a）。1 座，阿旃陀第 19 窟。

Dii 式：塔体近于圆柱形，正面[1]雕出龛像，龛内佛像为倚坐式。塔体周围雕饰宽、窄相间的方格，每格内雕姿势不同的坐像或立像。覆钵呈扁鼓状。平头或为倒金字塔式方形，或为多边多角形（图 29b）。2 座，阿旃陀第 26 窟、埃洛拉第 10 窟。

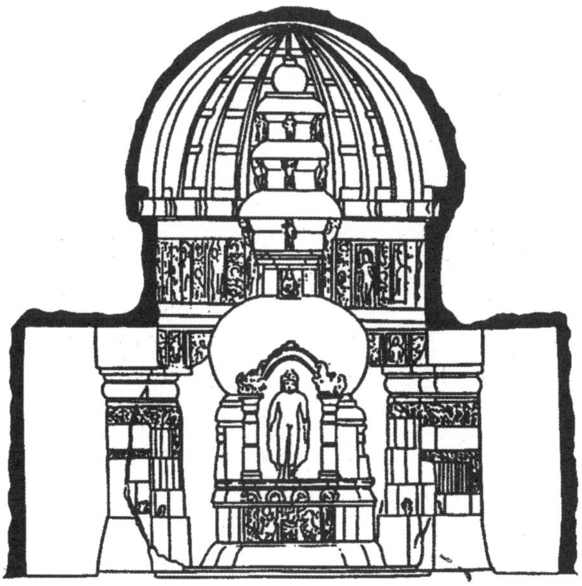
a

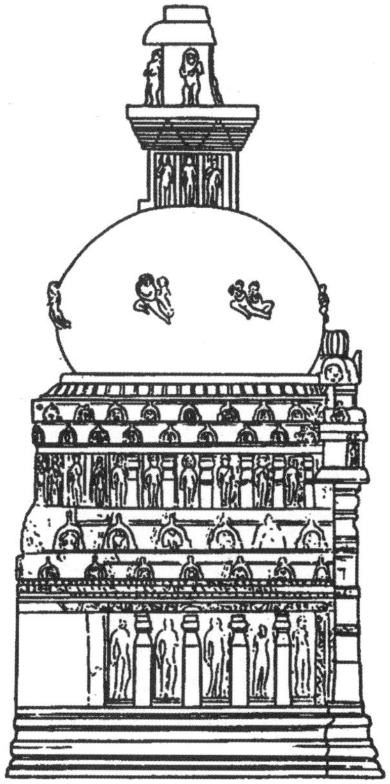
b

图 29　佛塔

a. 阿旃陀第 19 窟内佛塔；b. 阿旃陀第 26 窟内佛塔

[1] 埃洛拉第 10 窟有一巨大岩体作塔的主立面。

三、西印度塔庙窟的分组与分期

(一) 塔庙窟的分组

由于自然和人为的破坏,西印度境内55座塔庙窟的现存状况不完全一样。上述六个组成部分,有时在一座塔庙窟中仅存二三项,难以反映洞窟全貌。据我们统计,其中有39座四项保存相对完好的塔庙窟[1]。

为了客观排比西印度塔庙窟的演化序列,我们拟选取这39座洞窟作为我们分析和比较的对象。在此基础上,推断出一编年框架。另外16座保存相对不完整的塔庙窟,参照已推定的编年框架,可以较容易地被归入相应的演化序列之中。为了便于归纳它们的异同和演化关系,现将这39座塔庙窟的每个组成部分列表说明(表一)。

从表一中我们发现：顺序号第1至6号塔庙窟的大多数组成部分之类型是相同的,尽管个别部分显示出细微的差异。因此,这些塔庙窟可以看作是一组,暂定为A组。而第7至12号塔庙窟每一组成分之类型也基本相同,可以看成另一组,暂定B组。第13至19号塔庙窟每一部分基本上无差异,可以看作第三组,即C组。第20至27号窟的所有组成部分,除个别孤例外,是完全相同的,毫无疑问构成另一组,暂定D组。第28至36号塔庙窟的绝大部分在类型上是相同或接近的,暂定为E组。阿旃陀第19、26窟和埃洛拉第10窟,即序号中的第37至39窟,在类型上基本接近,可以构成最后一组,即F组。这样,表一所示西印度境内的39座塔庙窟,根据各组成部分的类型,可以分作A、B、C、D、E、F六组。

A组包括6座塔庙窟。洞窟平面有Aii、Aiii式或Bia式,以后者为主。外立面和明窗皆为I式。窟顶为Ai、Aiia和Aiib式,以后者为主。石柱皆为Ai式。石塔有Ai、Aii式和Bi式之分。

B组也包括6座洞窟。平面有Bib式或Biia式,以前者为主。外立面和明窗皆为II式。窟顶属于Aiib、Aiic或Aiii式,以Aiib式稍多。石柱富于变化,有Ai、Aii、Aiii式和Bi式之分,且以Aii式为多。石塔类型分作Ai、Aii式和Bii式,以后者为主。

C组包括7座塔庙窟。平面作Biia和Biib式,以后者为主。外立面为III式。明窗分II、III、IV式,以II式为主。窟顶分作Aiib、Aiic和Aiii式,以Aiib式略多。石

[1] 大多数无柱式长方形平面塔庙窟原来不雕明窗。

表一　西印度塔庙窟分期表

序号	石窟名称	窟平面	外立面	明窗	窟顶	石柱	塔	组别	段别	期别
1	杜尔贾莱纳第 3 窟	Aii	I		Aiia	Ai	Ai	A	1	一
2	贡迪维蒂第 9 窟	Aiii	I		Ai		Aii			
3	珀贾第 12 窟	Bia	I	I	Aiib	Ai	Bi			
4	阿旃陀第 10 窟	Bia	I	I	Aiib	Ai	Bi			
5	比德尔科拉第 3 窟	Bia	I	I	Aiib	Ai	×			
6	贡德恩第 1 窟	Bia	I	I	Aiib	Ai	Bi			
7	比德尔科拉第 13 窟	Bib	II		Aiib	Ai	×	B	2	二
8	门莫迪第 40 窟	Bib	II	II	Aiib	Aii	Ai			
9	阿旃陀第 9 窟	Bib	II	II	Aiic	Aii/Aiii	Bii			
10	纳西克第 18 窟	Bib	II	II	Aiib	Aii/Aiii/Bi	Bii			
11	比德尔科拉第 12 窟	Biia	II	II	Aiii		Aii			
12	伽内什・伯哈第 34 窟	Biia	II	II	Aiii		Bii			
13	贝德萨第 7 窟	Biib	III	II	Aiib	Aii/Aiii/Bii	Bii	C	3	
14	伽尔拉第 8 窟	Biib	III	II	Aiic	Aii/Aiii/Bii	Bii			
15	根赫里第 3 窟	Biib	III	II	Aiic	Aii/Aiii/Biii	Bii			
16	伽内什・伯哈第 6 窟	Biib	III		Aiib	Aii/Biii	Bii			
17	比德尔科拉第 10 窟	Biia	III	III	Aiii		Bii			
18	格拉德第 5 窟	Biia	III	III	Aiii	Biii	Ci			
19	门莫迪第 26 窟	Biib	III	IV	Aiib	Biv	×			
20	门莫迪第 2 窟	Ci	III	IV	Bii	Biv	×	D	4	三
21	锡万内里第 66 窟	Ci	III		Biii	Biv	Bii			
22	比德尔科拉第 11 窟	Ci	III		Bii		Bii/Ci			
23	锡万内里第 43 窟	Ci	III		Biii	Biv	Ci			
24	伽内什・伯哈第 14 窟	Ci	III		Biii	Biv	Ci			
25	锡万内里第 2 窟	Ci	III		Biii	Biv	×			
26	格拉德第 11 窟	Ci	III		Biv		Ci			
27	伯瓦拉第 2 窟	Ci	III		Biv		Ci			
28	古达第 9 窟	Ciia	III		Biv	Biv	Cii	E	5	
29	古达第 15 窟	Ciia	III		Biv	Bv	Cii			
30	格拉德第 6 窟	Ciib	III		Biv	Biv	Ci			
31	格拉德第 16 窟	Ciib	III		Biv	Bv	Ci			
32	古达第 6 窟	Ciib	III		Biv	Bv	Ci			
33	古达第 1 窟	Ciib	III		Biv	Bv	Cii			
34	默哈德第 8 窟	Ciic	III		Biii	Biv	Ci			
35	格拉德第 48 窟	Ciic	III		Biv	Bv	Ci			
36	谢拉尔瓦迪第 8 窟	Ciic	III		Biv		Cii			
37	阿旃陀第 19 窟	Biii	III	V	Aiic	Bvi	Di	F	6	四
38	阿旃陀第 26 窟	Biii	III	V	Aiic	Bvi/Bvii	Dii			
39	埃洛拉第 10 窟	Biii	III	VI	Aiic	Bvii/Bviii	Dii			
	阿旃陀第 29 窟			V				F	6	四
	奥兰伽巴德第 4 窟	Bib			Aiic	Aii	Bi	B	2	二
	贝德萨第 1 窟	Ai			Bi		Aii	B	2	二
	贝德萨第 3 窟	Ai			Ai		Aii	B	2	二
	珀贾第 26 窟	Ai			Bi		Ai	A	1	一
	根赫里第 2c 窟	Ci			Bi		Ci	D	4	三
	根赫里第 2d 窟	Ci			Bi		Ai	D	4	三
	根赫里第 2e 窟	Ci	I		Bi		Ai	A	1	一
	根赫里第 4 窟	Ai			Bi		Ci	D	4	三
	根赫里第 36 窟	Ai			Bi		Ci	D	4	三
	古达第 21 窟	Ci	III		Biv		Cii	E	5	三
	默哈德第 15 窟	Ci			Bi		Cii	E	5	三
	默哈德第 21 窟	Ci			Bi		Cii	E	5	三
	门莫迪第 25 窟	Ci			Bi		Ci	D	4	三
	讷德苏尔第 8 窟	Biia			Aiii		Ai	B	2	二
	锡万内里第 56 窟	Ci			Biii		Ci	D	4	三

序列号第 1-39 窟各部分类型中的 × 表示该部分已毁

柱类型多样，有 Aii、Aiii 式，Bii、Biii 和 Biv 式等五种，以 Aii 式为主。除格拉德第 5 窟内石塔为 Ci 式之外，其余石塔皆采用 Bii 式。

D 组包括 8 座塔庙窟。所有洞窟皆采纳 Ci 式平面。外立面也作 III 式。除门莫迪第 2 窟明窗为 IV 式外，其余塔庙窟皆无明窗。窟顶分作 Bii、Biii 和 Biv 式，以 Biii 式为主。石柱类型皆为 Biv 式。除锡万内里第 66 窟和比德尔科拉第 11 窟前室（Bii 式）外，其余窟内石塔皆为 Ci 式。

E 组包括 9 座塔庙窟。平面有 Ciia、Ciib 和 Ciic 三式，以前者少见。外立面为 III 式。所有洞窟皆无明窗。窟顶除默哈德第 8 窟（Biii 式）外，其余皆为 Biv 式。石柱分作 Biv 和 Bv 二式，以后者为主。石塔或作 Ci 式，或为 Cii 式。

阿旃陀第 19、26 窟和埃洛拉第 10 窟是最后一组，即 F 组。这组洞窟的平面（Biii 式）、外立面（III 式）和窟顶（Aiic 式）的类型相同。明窗有 V、VI 两式，以前者为主。石柱分为 Bvi、Bvii 和 Bviii 三式。塔或作 Di 式，或为 Dii 式。

其余 16 座保存相对不完整的塔庙窟（见表一），经与上述塔庙窟各组成部分的类型进行对比，可以分别归入上述各组之中。

其中，珀贾第 26 窟的平面（Ai 式）和塔（Ai 式），与杜尔贾莱纳第 3 窟的相似。根赫里第 2e[1]窟的外立面（I 式）和石塔（Ai 式）类型，也与杜尔贾莱纳第 3 窟的相应部分接近。因此，这两座洞窟可以归入 A 组塔庙窟之中。

奥兰伽巴德第 4 窟残存的平面（Bib）、窟顶（Aiic 式）、石柱（Aii 式）和石塔（Bi 式）类型，大多与阿旃陀第 9 窟的相应部分接近。讷德苏尔第 8 窟的平面（Biia 式）、窟顶（Aiii 式）和石塔（Ai 式），与比德尔科拉第 12 窟的相应部分没有差异。因此，这两座塔庙窟可以归入 B 组之中。尽管贝德萨第 3 窟的平面（Ai 式）、窟顶（Ai 式）和石塔（Aii 式）表明它属于早期之作，但在没有找出绝对可靠的证据之前，为了谨慎起见，我们暂时把它归入 B 组之中。与贝德萨第 3 窟毗邻的第 1 窟，由于未按计划完工，也暂时归入这一组。

根赫里第 2c、2d 窟和门莫迪第 25 窟，以及锡万内里第 56 窟的平面（Ci 式）、

---

[1] 根赫里第 2e 窟左壁后来被拓展扩大，其窟顶与根赫里第 2f 窟顶在同一水平高度上；而 2f 窟显然在修建时打破了 2e 窟，也就是说 2f 窟的开凿年代要晚于第 2e 窟。另外，第 2e 窟后壁补雕了若干大乘造像。因此，第 2e 窟顶及后壁的原始状况不得而知。现在有人认为 2f 窟是西印度最早的僧坊窟之一（参见 M. C. Joshi, "Buddhist Rock-cut Architecture: A Survey", in: *Proceedings of the International Seminar on Cave Art of India and China,* Theme I: Historical Perspective, New Delhi: Indira Gandhi National Centre for the Arts, November 25, 1991: 1-28, esp. 9）。倘若这一观点成立，那么根赫里第 2e 窟应定为最早的塔庙窟之一。

窟顶（Bi、Biii 式）和石塔（Ai 或 Ci 式）的类型，与格拉德第 11 窟和伯瓦拉第 2 窟相应部分的类型大都接近。根赫里第 4、36 窟内的石塔（Ci 式），与根赫里第 2c 窟的石塔毫无二致，尽管前二者的平面皆作 Ai 式。因此，这 6 座塔庙窟可以归入 D 组。

虽然默哈德第 15、21 窟的平面（Ci 式）及窟顶（Bi 式）显示年代较早，但其塔型（Cii 式）与古达第 9 窟的相似。此外，古达第 21 窟[1]的平面（Ci 式）、外立面（III 式）和窟顶（Biv 式）之类型，与古达第 9、15 窟的相应部分接近。因此，上述三窟可归入 E 组之中。

鉴于阿旃陀第 29 窟未按计划完工，可以把它暂时归入 F 组[2]。

（二）塔庙窟的演化序列

既然我们依据各组成部分把西印度的塔庙窟分作上述六组，那么就有必要进一步探讨这六组塔庙窟的演化顺序。从表一所示保存相对完整的 39 座洞窟的分组情况，我们认为西印度塔庙窟有如下演化过程。

1. 平面

A 组：圆形平面大殿内列柱环绕中央石塔（Aii 式）→圆形平面塔殿 + 长方形平面大厅（Aiii 式）→敞口式倒 U 字形平面（Bia 式）；

B 组：封闭式（带前壁）倒 U 字形平面（Bib 式）→无列柱式倒 U 字形平面主室 + 敞开式天井形前室（Biia 式）；

C 组：倒 U 字形平面主室 + 前室（Biib 式）↔无列柱式倒 U 字形平面主室 + 敞开式天井形前室（Biia 式）→倒 U 字形平面主室 + 前室（Biib 式）；

D 组：简洁的长方形平面主室 + 前室（Ci 式）；

E 组：长方形平面主室 + 前廊 + 敞开式天井形前室（Ciia 式）→塔殿 + 塔殿前廊 + 大厅 + 前室（Ciib 式）→塔庙僧坊混成式（Ciic 式）；

F 组：主要由 Biib 式演化而来，倒 U 字形平面柱殿式主室 + 前室（Biii 式）。

[1] 古达第 21 窟内未完工的石塔，原打算雕成 Cii 式。

[2] 正如 M. N. 德什班德先生所指出的那样，“其未完工之外立面和窟内拱顶表明它系晚期开凿”。参见 M. N. Deshpande, “The (Ajanta) Caves: Their Historical Perspective”, in: *Ajanta Murals*, ed. A. Ghosh, New Delhi: Archaeological Survey of India, 1967: 20.

2. 外立面

A 组：敞口式塔庙窟 (I 式)；
↓
B 组：封闭式塔庙窟 (II 式)；
↓
C 组：带前廊或天井形前室塔庙窟 (III 式)；
↓
D 组：同 C 组；
↓
E 组：同 C 组；
↓
F 组：同 C 组。

3. 明窗

A 组：拱翼底部张开幅度最大，明窗形如半圆 (I 式)；
↓
B 组：拱翼内曲，末端以连杆相接，明窗作马蹄形 (II 式)；
↓
C 组：马蹄形明窗 (II 式) →半圆形盲拱内开方形明窗 (III 式) →拱翼内曲较大，末端外翻如脚爪，明窗近圆形 (IV 式)；
↓
D 组：拱翼内曲较大，末端外翻如脚爪，明窗近圆形 (IV 式)；
↓
E 组：无；
↓
F 组：拱翼末端外翻如火焰状，拱顶有涡卷形饰，明窗近椭圆 (V 式) →三叶拱，顶部开圆形明窗 (VI 式)。

4. 窟顶

A 组：塔上方为穹隆顶 (Ai 式) →塔上方为穹隆顶，侧廊顶部作扇形 (Aiia 式) →塔上方为半穹隆顶，主室顶为纵向筒拱，侧廊顶作扇形 (Aiib 式)；
↓

B 组：塔上方为半穹隆顶，主室顶为筒拱，侧廊顶作扇形（Aiib 式）→塔上方为半穹隆顶，主室顶为筒拱，侧廊作平顶（Aiic 式）→塔上方为半穹隆顶，主室顶为筒拱（Aiii 式）；

↓ ↘

C 组：基本同 B 组；

↓

D 组：主室平顶较前室平顶略低（Bii 式）→主室平顶较前室平顶略高（Biii 式）→主室平顶与前室平顶等高（Biv 式）；

↓

E 组：主室平顶与前室平顶等高（Biv 式）↔主室平顶较前室平顶略高（Biii 式）→主室平顶与前室平顶等高（Biv 式）；

↓

F 组：塔上方为半穹隆顶，主室顶为筒拱，侧廊为平顶（Aiic 式）。

5. 石柱

A 组：八角柱身既无柱头也无柱础，柱身向上有收分且于顶部内倾（Ai 式）；

↓

B 组：顶部内倾之八角柱，既无柱头也无柱础（Ai 式）→直立八角柱，无柱头、无柱础（Aii 式）→八角、六角柱或方柱，既无柱头也无柱础，但有一面凸起（Aiii 式）→八角柱身、壶形柱础（Bi 式）；

↓

C 组：直立八角柱身，既无柱头也无柱础（Aii 式）→八角形、六角形或方柱，既无柱头也无柱础，但有一面凸起（Aiii 式）→八角柱身、壶形柱础、钟形柱头，柱头上有动物雕像（Bii 式）→八角柱身、壶形或方形柱础，壶形柱头上有动物雕像（Biii 式）→八角柱身、壶形柱头、壶形柱础（Biv 式）；

↓

D 组：八角柱身、壶形柱头、壶形柱础（Biv 式）；

↓

E 组：八角柱身、壶形柱头、壶形柱础（Biv 式）→八角或方形柱身、方形柱础（Bv 式）；

↓

F 组：柱身雕饰繁复、16 边形低柱础、罗曼式柱头，舟形托架（Bvi 式）→八角柱、素面舟形柱头（Bvii 式）→高方柱、花冠式柱头、长方形托架（Bviii 式）。

6. 塔

A 组：塔身、覆钵为独石雕成（Ai 式）→塔身、覆钵系独石雕作，塔身上沿雕刻栏楯图案（Aii 式）→塔基、塔身、覆钵、方龛、3-4 层倒叠涩式平头系独石雕作（Bi 式）；

↓

B 组：塔身、覆钵系独石雕成（Ai 式）→塔身、覆钵为独石雕作，塔身上沿镌饰栏楯图案（Aii 式）→塔基、塔身、覆钵、方龛及五层以上倒叠涩式平头系独石雕作（Bii 式）；

↓

C 组：塔基、塔身、覆钵、方龛及五层以上倒叠涩式平头为独石雕成 (Bii 式) →塔基、塔身、覆钵、方龛、五层以上倒叠涩式平头、轮杆、轮盖系独石雕作；轮盖与窟顶相连 (Ci 式)；

↓

D 组：同 C 组。

↓

E 组：塔基、塔身、覆钵、方龛、倒叠涩式平头系独石雕作，且与窟顶直接相连 (Cii 式) ↔塔基、塔身、覆钵、方龛、倒叠涩式平头、轮杆、轮盖为独石雕成，且与窟顶相连 (Ci 式) →塔基、塔身、覆钵、方龛、倒叠涩式平头系独石雕成，且与窟顶相连 (Cii 式)；

↓

F 组：塔基、塔身、覆钵、方龛、倒叠涩式平头、相轮为独石所作，塔身及覆体底部正面雕龛像 (Di 式) →塔身、覆钵、方龛、倒叠涩式平头系独石雕成，塔身正面雕出龛像 (Dii 式)。

(三) 塔庙窟的分期

上述演化序列表明：西印度塔庙窟应该是从 A 组向 F 组演进的。实际上，这也符合事物从简单形式向复杂形式发展之原则。这里我们还想提出两点，以进一步证实我们的推论。

1. 众所周知，佛教石窟寺系模仿地面木构寺院建造而成。因此，早期塔庙窟实际上是岩石与木构的结合。A 组塔庙窟的敞开外立面，原来曾安装有木质门窗。只是由于自然和人为的破坏以及“风飘雨渍”之侵蚀，它早已不复存在。而木构门窗后来，即在 B 组中，为石质门窗所取代。此外，有些塔庙窟的主室甚至侧廊顶部表面原覆置木质肋拱 (弯梁) 和椽子，彼此交接呈网格状，如 A 组的珀贾第 12 窟、阿旃陀第 10 窟、比德尔科拉第 3 窟和贡德恩第 1 窟，B 组的比德尔科拉第 12、13 窟，阿旃陀第 9 窟，纳西克第 18 窟，C 组的贝德萨第 7 窟、伽尔拉第 8 窟和根赫里第 3 窟等。其余各组，即在 D-F 组塔庙窟中，是见不到这种木质梁、椽的，其弯梁与椽子皆系石雕而成。因此，D-F 组塔庙窟，较 A-C 组洞窟无疑要晚。

2. 在小乘佛教盛行期间，佛教艺术奉循不雕造偶像的原则。因此，在这一时期开凿的塔庙或僧坊窟中，看不到佛的任何形象。大乘佛教流行之后，佛教信徒开始朝拜佛像，结果出现了造像及像龛。F 组塔庙窟内佛塔前的龛像，无疑是大乘佛教的作品；而此前五组塔庙窟中绝无任何佛的造像。这意味着 F 组石窟，较其他五组塔庙窟要晚。

因此，上述例证从另一不同角度充分证实了西印度塔庙窟是从 A 组向 F 组演进的，而不应反其道而行之。这样，上述六组洞窟代表了西印度塔庙窟从早到晚六个不同的演化阶段。换言之，上述六组洞窟也就是六个不同阶段开凿的洞窟，即六组也就是六段，但有些尚可进一步合并。

B、C 组洞窟平面皆为 Biia 式，支提窗亦多作 II 式，窟顶、列柱和石塔也多有共存关系，可以合并为一期。

D、E 组洞窟的外立面相同，窟顶和石柱的演化有一段平行期，塔的形制也接近，它们可以合并为一期。

其余各组单独为一期。

这样，我们可以把西印度境内的塔庙窟分作如下四期六段。

第一期，包括 A 组的所有塔庙窟和另外两座不完整洞窟，即杜尔贾莱纳第 3 窟、贡迪维蒂第 9 窟、珀贾第 12 窟、阿旃陀第 10 窟、比德尔科拉第 3 窟、贡德恩第 1 窟、珀贾第 26 窟、根赫里第 2e 窟。

第二期分前、后两段。前段洞窟包括 B 组所有塔庙窟和四座保存不完整的洞窟，即比德尔科拉第 13 窟，门莫迪第 40 窟，阿旃陀第 9 窟，纳西克第 18 窟，比德尔科拉第 12 窟，伽内什 · 伯哈第 34 窟，奥兰伽巴德第 4 窟，讷德苏尔第 8 窟，贝德萨第 3、1 窟；后段包括 C 组所有洞窟，即贝德萨第 7 窟、伽尔拉第 8 窟、根赫里第 3 窟、伽内什 · 伯哈第 6 窟、比德尔科拉第 10 窟、格拉德第 5 窟、门莫迪第 26 窟。

第三期也分前、后两段。前段石窟包括 D 组所有塔庙窟和六座保存不完整的洞窟，即门莫迪第 2 窟，锡万内里第 66 窟，比德尔科拉第 11 窟，锡万内里第 43 窟，伽内什 · 伯哈第 14 窟，锡万内里第 2 窟，格拉德第 11 窟，伯瓦拉第 2 窟，根赫里第 2c、2d、4、36 窟，门莫迪第 25 窟，锡万内里第 56 窟；后段石窟包括 E 组全部塔庙窟及三座保存不完整的洞窟，即古达第 9、15 窟，格拉德第 6、16 窟，古达第 6、1 窟，默哈德第 8 窟，格拉德第 48 窟，谢拉尔瓦迪第 8 窟，默哈德第 15、21 窟和古达第 21 窟。

第四期，包括 F 组全部塔庙窟和一座未完工洞窟，即阿旃陀第 19、26 窟，埃洛拉第 10 窟和阿旃陀第 29 窟。

四、西印度塔庙窟各期的主要特征

西印度塔庙窟各期的主要特点可以归纳如下：

（一）第一期

作为一种新兴的建筑形式，本期塔庙窟在形制上变化多样。从平面上看，主要有五种类型：①平顶圆形平面窟，塔置中央（Ai 式）；②穹隆顶列柱式圆形平面窟，塔置中央（Aii 式）；③方圆混成式窟，前为平顶长方形平面大厅，后为圆形平面穹隆顶塔殿（Aiii 式）；④纵券顶列柱式倒 U 字形平面窟，塔置半圆形后室中央（Bia 式）；⑤平顶方形平面窟，塔置后部中央（Ci 式）。其中，以倒 U 字形平面列柱窟为主。除平顶圆形平面窟窟口（门道）较小外，其余塔庙窟的窟口均高大敞开。据地栿槽和门道两侧的卯眼判断，第一期塔庙窟原无石质前壁，而以高大的木结构门屏替代。倒 U 字形平面塔庙窟的拱形大明窗与门道相连。拱形明窗内侧（拱腹）皆有椽头装饰。拱两翼垂直向下，拱脚外张，拱顶呈尖状。尽管拱翼表面及拱内木构件已毁，但从外立面的浮雕图案推断，拱内木构原为太阳拱（I 式）。这是第一期塔庙窟所特有的形式。窟外立面大多无装饰，有的于拱形明窗两侧浮雕栏楯及太阳拱图案[1]。倒 U 字形平面塔庙窟的主室为纵券顶，侧廊顶部作扇形，半圆形后室之顶呈半穹隆状。主室及后室之顶表面原覆木质弯梁和椽子；侧廊的扇形顶表面，有的亦覆置木构梁、椽[2]，有的以岩石仿木雕出（Aiib 式）。穹隆顶列柱式圆形平面窟和倒 U 字形平面纵券顶列柱窟内的石柱，皆作素面八角形，上细下粗，顶端略内倾。这种类型的石柱（Ai 式）后来极少见。

作为佛陀允许建造的三种佛塔之一，塔庙窟的主体当然是雕在窟内的石塔，下与地面相连。第一期石塔共有三种形式：①第一种塔，塔身和覆钵为整块岩石雕成且极为简朴，而方龛、平头及轮盖则分体制作，或为石雕或为木构，这点可以从覆钵顶部的卯眼判定（Ai 式）；②第二种塔与 Ai 式相似，只是在塔身上沿雕出栏楯图案（Aii 式）；③第三种石塔，塔基单层较矮，塔身升高为二层，并与半球形覆钵、方龛及三层倒叠涩式平头雕在一起，轮杆及轮盖分体雕制（Bi 式）。在上述三类石塔中，第一种和第二种是本期流行的形式[3]。值得注意的是，塔庙窟内塔的形式，与露天所造基本一致。这进一步证实了笔者的推论，即塔庙窟的产生，是源于人们向佛教信徒提供一处方便场所之理念。在这里，他们可以进行宗教礼拜活动，不受外界及天气的影响。

除了上述主要特征之外，这一期的塔庙窟也有许多不见于第二期的独特之处：

[1] 圆形平面或平顶长方形平面塔庙窟无支提明窗。

[2] 由于长期以来自然腐朽和人为破坏，早期塔庙窟内的木质弯梁及横椽有些已毁，但其原来位置尚可辨识，如阿旃陀第 10 窟和比德尔科拉第 3 窟等。

[3] 比德尔科拉第 3 窟内佛塔系半雕半砌而成。这种状况系雕造佛塔时岩石崩裂所致。另外，清理此窟时，在塔内发现了几只水晶舍利盒，它们被安置于塔身后面特意凿出的长方形小洞之内，外用石板封堵。参见：M. N. Deshpande, *opere citato* (The Rock-cut Caves...): 72-73, 88-90.

有的窟壁内倾（阿旃陀第 10 窟）；有的绘有壁画，内容为本生和佛传故事等（阿旃陀第 10 窟）[1]；有的于外立面雕饰男女人像（贡德恩第 1 窟）；有的塔内藏纳舍利盒（比德尔科拉第 3 窟）。尤为重要的是，本期塔庙窟大都忠实地模仿地面木构原型，有些部分，如拱门、弯梁等甚至直接以木料做出。

（二）第二期

第二期可分作前后两段。前段洞窟平面，除贝德萨第 1、3 窟沿袭第一期的 Ai 式外，其余洞窟皆采用两种新形式：①纵券顶倒 U 字形或长方形平面列柱式塔庙窟（Bib 式）；②纵券顶倒 U 字形平面塔庙窟，内无列柱（Biia 式）。除 Ai 式平面窟外，其余平面洞窟皆雕出前壁，代替了第一期的木构门屏。窟外立面平行分作上下二层：下层中央开门道，有的于门道两侧各加开一采光窗；上层中央即门道上方曲拱顶部凿出拱形大明窗[2]。拱形明窗内侧雕出两根壁柱及横梁，拱腹雕出截面为长方形之凸起椽头；拱内壁柱及拱腹上有若干槽孔，表明拱形大明窗之内原镶装木构太阳拱，故习称此类明窗为太阳窗。拱形明窗的下部，即两翼末端向内弯曲，拱脚外翻如同人脚（II 式），个别的拱脚弯曲形如大脚趾（如阿旃陀第 9 窟）。拱形明窗两侧壁面大多浮雕出太阳拱、法轮及栏楯图案，有的还雕出人物形象。不过，简朴的平顶圆形平面窟，仅开一方形入口，外立面素面无饰。

这一段的窟顶形制，亦丰富多样。除沿袭第一期的 Ai、Aiib 式和 Bi 式之外，又出现了两种新类型：一种主室为纵券顶，侧廊为平顶（Aiic 式）；另一种为简朴的纵券（Aiii 式）。除阿旃陀第 9 窟主室券顶表面原覆置木构弯梁和椽子之外，其余纵券顶表面皆为仿木构雕出的石梁和石椽。这两种新出现的窟顶在后段仍然流行。

平面倒 U 字形或长方形列柱式塔庙窟内的石柱，除个别为 Ai 式外，又出现了三种新样式：①素面八角柱，既无柱头也无柱础；有的顶端略细、微内倾（Aii 式）；②石柱为八角形或方形，中段刻棱且有一小块长方形凸起物（Aiii 式），这种石柱通常位于列柱的前端，且对称雕造；③八角柱身下有壶形柱础及四层叠涩式础座（Bi 式）。后三种柱子在后段仍然使用。

---

［1］阿旃陀第 10 窟右壁现存睒子本生和六牙象本生壁画，构图皆作横卷式；左壁壁画也为巨幅横卷式，但残破严重。前人曾把左壁的两个画面定为“皇室过城门”和“礼拜佛塔”；不过据德国学者施林洛甫（D. Schlingloff）的研究，这幅壁画表现的是佛传中的几个重要情节：有护明菩萨上升兜率天听法、树下诞生、自行七步、树下思维、降魔成道、初转法轮、八王分舍利等。笔者暂从此说。参见 D. Schlingloff, *Studies in the Ajaṇṭā Paintings: Identifications and Interpretations,* Delhi: Ajanta Publication, 1988: 1-13.

［2］门莫迪第 40 窟拱形窗为盲窗。

前段塔庙窟内的石塔共有四种类型。其中三种沿袭第一期旧制，分别为 Ai、Aii 式和 Bi 式。另一种是新出现的：其塔基、塔身、覆钵及方龛与第一期的 Bi 式相似，唯平头之倒叠涩为五层或更多；平头顶板上可见若干卯眼，原为固定轮盖和幡杆之用 (Bii 式)。最后这种塔不仅是前段，而且也是后段的主流。

除了上述共有特征之外，第二期前段塔庙窟也有若干独特之处：①就如我们在阿旃陀第 9 窟和奥兰伽巴德第 4 窟[1]所注意到的那样，将长方形平面引入到塔庙窟的设计中，是一种新的尝试。②这一阶段中，装饰性的栏楯、太阳拱、托架、梯级城齿、塔以及动物和那伽 (蛇) 等图案组合在一起，似乎当时印度所知晓的全部装饰成分，都在这里采纳了[2]。③纳西克第 18 窟外立面门道上方所雕一列椽头引人注目，每一椽头相间雕出一人物头像。这在西印度塔庙窟中是一孤例，其含义尚待探讨。④伽内什 · 伯哈第 34 窟的窟前部分，看上去像一长方形凹室 (alcove)，这可能是后段出现的塔庙窟前室之雏形，应是保护雕刻的一项创举。⑤伽内什 · 伯哈第 34 窟支提窗外侧雕有藤蔓花纹，这大概是藤蔓花纹图案在石窟中的最早使用。此外，在栏楯图案中插雕树木，看来是德干艺术中装饰主题的孤例[3]。⑥某些支提窗，如门莫迪第 40 窟和纳西克第 18 窟，有若干浅浮雕，如佛教象征物、藤蔓图案和动物等。⑦比德尔科拉第 12 窟佛塔方龛上的男女双人 (mithunā) 雕像是独一无二的，西印度塔庙窟的这一部位再未发现这种造像[4]。

第二期后段洞窟，除比德尔科拉第 10 窟和格拉德第 5 窟的平面沿袭前段旧制 (Biia 式) 外，其余洞窟平面皆为 Biib 式。这是本段新出现的一种类型，由纵券顶倒 U 字形平面主室和一平顶前室或柱式门廊构成；有的甚至在主室与前室之间增开一横廊，如伽尔拉第 8 窟和根赫里第 3 窟。

由于洞窟出现了前室，这一段塔庙窟的外立面变得复杂了 (III 式)。前室与主室之间的屏墙，即前室后壁，也同前段一样水平分作上、下两层：下层开门道一或三个，若为三个，则中央大的通向主室，两边小的通向侧廊，如伽尔拉第 8 窟和根赫里第 3 窟；上层部分，除伽内什 · 伯哈第 6 窟[5]外，其余皆凿出拱形明窗。前室前端或由列柱构作，如贝德萨第 7 窟和门莫迪第 26 窟；或由柱上的隔墙遮挡，如伽尔拉第

[1] 尽管奥兰伽巴德第 4 窟的前部已经崩毁，但残存的后半部表明它的平面呈长方形。

[2] S. Nagaraju, *opere citato*: 279.

[3] S. Nagaraju, *opere citato*: 171, pl. 75, 77.

[4] M. N. Deshpande, *opere citato* (The Rock-cut Caves...): 79.

[5] 伽内什 · 伯哈第 6 窟前室后壁上部，可见三个磨光了的几何形，中间那个呈半圆形，其上面的两个为长方形。如果我们对其相对位置作进一步观察，就会发现：这一位置，原来计划雕凿支提窗。三处磨光位置的布局，与门莫迪第 40 窟的外立面相似；不过半圆形及其延伸的栏楯图案，又与门莫迪第 2 窟支提盲窗的处理接近。

8窟和根赫里第3窟。本段塔庙窟的前室后壁及左右侧壁，有的素面，无任何装饰图案；有的浮雕出高水平的装饰图案，如太阳拱、栏楯，甚至男女双人像[1]。这种设计，让人感到它好像是一座中央开大支提明窗的四五层建筑，如贝德萨第7窟和伽尔拉第8窟。此外，伽尔拉第8窟和根赫里第3窟[2]的前室左右侧壁前端，原来各有一巨大的附墙柱，柱头上有动物形象。

第二期后段的拱形明窗有三种类型。一种为II式，沿袭前段旧制，此不赘述[3]。另外两种是新出现的：一种是III式，为半圆形拱，拱腹雕出方形椽头，拱面中央凿出一长方形明窗[4]。另一种是IV式，在II式基础上演化而来，拱翼两端向内弯曲形如一个半圆，拱脚外凸且向上微翻卷；拱内两侧各雕出一壁柱，拱顶尖略变宽，凸缘，唯拱腹未雕出椽头。

后段塔庙窟的所有前室皆作简洁的平顶。主室窟顶均袭前段旧制，有三种形式，分别为Aiib、Aiic和Aiii式[5]。

塔庙窟内的石柱，除了沿袭前段Aii和Aiii式外，又出现了三种新形式。第一种为Bii式，由四至五层叠涩础座、壶形柱础、八角形柱身、钟形柱头、四至五层倒叠涩式柱顶盘座面（冠板）及上面的动物和骑手雕像构成。第二种为Biii式，除了钟形柱头改作壶状之外，余与Bii式相同。第三种为Biv式，除了柱顶托盘座面上无动物及骑手像外，余与Biii式相同。最后这种柱式在下期流行。

第二期后段塔庙窟内的石塔，大多为Bii式。单层矮塔基、圆柱形塔身、半球状覆钵、方形宝匣（方龛）、五层以上倒叠涩式平头系独石雕作；轮杆及轮盖单独制作，或为木构或为石雕。圆柱形塔身上沿常雕出栏楯图案。此外，本段新出现的Ci式塔，在下期极为盛行。

---

[1] 根赫里第3窟前室后壁所雕男女双人像及佛像，应为晚期补雕之作，特别是横廊右端的立佛，高达6.85米，堪称该处石窟群的造像杰作。

[2] 根赫里第3窟右侧的巨大石柱现已毁坏，但残柱桩尚存。

[3] 根赫里第3窟前室后壁上部开一半圆形明窗，光线通过明窗可照射到里面的石塔上。虽然在明窗表面及拱腹下未发现任何装饰，但在明窗顶部及拱腹内却发现了若干卯眼和槽孔，这表明原来有些木构装饰曾安在卯眼和槽孔之内。又，尽管这个明窗的半圆形状与II式明窗类似，但其素面拱腹却与III式接近。因此，它的造型介于II式与III式明窗之间。

[4] 这种半圆拱长方形窗，在西印度塔庙窟中是断前绝后的；但方形明窗，在中国早期塔庙窟中则又是普遍存在的。二者或许有某种联系。

[5] 贝德萨第7窟主室和侧廊顶部覆有木质弯梁和椽子，伽尔拉第8窟和根赫里第3窟主室之顶也有木构梁、椽承托，伽内什·伯哈第6窟主室及侧廊顶部雕出仿木石梁和石椽，门莫迪第26窟由于未按计划完工，其窟顶几乎作葱形拱。

（三）第三期

在印度石窟寺营造史上，自从倒U字形平面纵券顶列柱式塔庙窟产生以来，建筑设计中从创建伊始就存在的传统与实用二者之间的矛盾，到此终于结束了。建造上的实用和经济冲破了传统的束缚。“艺术家们这种心理上的变化，似乎诱导他们甚至在外立面上也避免使用传统的但不实用的装饰性题材。”[1]从第三期开始，塔庙窟逐渐变得更加实用，无关紧要的部分及装饰尽可能地被排除在设计之外。总之，整体布局的极度简朴和实用，是第三期前段塔庙窟的最显著特征。

除根赫里第4、36窟为小型平顶圆形平面窟外，其余所有塔庙窟皆为平顶长方形平面，有前室；佛塔雕于主室后部，窟内列柱消失（Ci式）[2]。前室外端雕出两立柱和两壁柱[3]。除门莫迪第2窟和锡万内里第43窟[4]外，其余塔庙窟的外立面没有任何装饰。在第三期前段14座塔庙窟中，只有门莫迪第2窟前室后壁上方雕出支提拱。石窟的雕造者，可能原来打算在此开一支提窗，但由于第2窟是平顶塔庙窟，主室顶部低矮，无法按传统营造法式开凿，故只镌刻成一个盲窗。其整体造型，与门莫迪第26窟的支提窗相似，外表无任何装饰，突出的拱尖亦未雕出。

第三期前段洞窟最显著的建筑特征，是主室的平顶结构和窟内列柱的消失。二者表明，这种塔庙窟在设计上已完全不同于纵券顶列柱式塔庙窟。尽管前段的所有塔庙窟，无论平面是圆形还是平面为长方形，皆作相似的平顶结构，但尚可区分为四种类型：①简洁的平顶（Bi式）；②主室窟顶低于前室之顶（Bii式）；③主室窟顶高于前室之顶（Biii式）；④主室窟顶与前室之顶等高（Biv式）。其中，本段塔庙窟以Bi和Biii式窟顶为主。在前段的14座塔庙窟中，仅有五座雕出柱子和壁柱，且均在前廊。石柱皆为Biv式，由四至五层叠涩式础座、壶形柱础、八角形柱身、壶形柱头、四层倒叠涩式柱顶盘座面构成。柱顶盘座面之上无动物雕像。

---

[1] S. Nagaraju, *opere citato*: 175.

[2] 比德尔科拉第11窟由三座平顶小室构成，每室皆有一塔。据现存遗迹推断：三个小室不是同时开凿的。

[3] 锡万内里第43窟设计独特，其主室有一外横廊或门厅，横廊由两根立柱和两个壁柱与主室隔断而成。这种设计，给人感觉是一个主室加一廊道，就像我们在纵券顶列柱式塔庙窟中所见到的那样。这应该是从纵券顶塔庙窟向平顶塔庙窟过渡的一种应变措施。

[4] 门莫迪第2窟外立面雕有支提盲窗和栏楯图案，锡万内里第43窟外立面仅有栏楯图案。

前段塔庙窟内的石塔，除少数为 Bii 式外[1]，大多数为 Ci 式。这种塔的塔基较薄，塔身向上略内收，上沿雕出栏楯图案。覆钵呈大半球形，底部内收。方龛四面雕出栏楯图案。方龛之上为四至五层叠涩式平头，再上为粗轮杆及轮盖。值得注意的是，塔的所有组成部分，即塔基、塔身、覆钵、方龛、平头、轮杆、轮盖皆为独石雕作，且上下分别与窟顶和地面相连，如轮盖就是雕在窟顶表面的。这种塔，最终舍弃了唯一的木质附件——轮盖，标志着建筑设计上的进步。这种 Ci 式石塔和后段的 Cii 式石塔，尤其是 Cii 式塔，对中国塔庙窟内塔的设计影响颇大；后者主要承袭了这种建制，即塔与窟顶相连，同时舍弃不必要的构件。

上述特征表明：第三期前段塔庙窟与第二期相比，在风格上和建筑上皆有较大的进步，无关紧要的部分及附件皆被舍去，致使塔庙窟变得愈加简朴和实用。促使石窟建造者选择这种简洁而先进设计的主要原因，可能是当时日益增长的功利主义实用思潮。此外，人力与财力的匮乏恐为另一缘由。

第三期后段塔庙窟，平面布局多样化。除了沿袭前段简洁的Ci式方形平面窟外，新出现了三种类型：①第一种为平顶长方形平面塔庙窟，塔置主室后部中央，前室两侧壁各开 1-2 个小禅室 (Ciia 式)；②第二种为 Ciib 式，由平顶长方形平面塔殿 + 塔殿前廊 + 中央大厅 + 横廊 + 前室构成；③第三种为塔庙僧坊混成式 (Ciic 式)，后为塔殿，前面大厅周围凿出小禅室[2]。这种塔庙窟兼具僧坊性质，后来大乘时期开凿的僧坊窟就是在此基础上演进的。

除默哈德第 15、21 窟窟口敞开外，其余塔庙窟皆有一前廊或前室，前廊或前室的前端各由两立柱和两壁柱承托[3]。后段塔庙窟均不开明窗，窟内采光都是通过门道射入的。虽然塔庙窟皆作平顶，沿用前段旧制，但 Biv 式窟顶则是本段流行的形式，即前室之顶与大厅或主室等高。

同前段一样，后段塔庙窟主室内列柱消失。现存柱子分作两种：一种为 Biv 式，沿袭前段旧制，此不赘述。另一种是新出现的，为 Bv 式。这种石柱的柱础作方形，柱

[1] 这一段塔庙窟中属于 Bii 式石塔的只有两座。一座在锡万内里第 66 窟，另一座在比德尔科拉第 11 窟前室。前者窟内的石塔仅存塔身、覆钵及其顶上的单层冠板。后者石塔尽管已经残破，但覆钵上的方龛仍在。两塔皆未把轮盖雕于窟顶表面。此外，门莫迪第 2 窟、锡万内里第 2 窟和根赫里第 2d 窟内的残塔也属于此式。在门莫迪第 2 窟主室内，靠后壁处有一块高约 2.4 米的岩石。这块石头原来好像是雕造佛塔的，但没有完工。锡万内里第 2 窟和根赫里第 2d 窟的佛塔仅存塔身，窟顶无轮盖遗迹。

[2] 除谢拉尔瓦迪第 8 窟外，在塔庙窟大厅四周开凿的所有小禅室 (僧房) 后部皆有一矮床，这暗示僧人原来曾居住在里面。此外，中央大厅内墙底下也凿出一圈低矮的石凳。

[3] 谢拉尔瓦迪第 8 窟的前壁早已崩毁。在距原壁向内几英尺处又砌造了一堵厚墙，形成一新的前墙。从现存遗迹推测，第 8 窟前部原来有立柱和壁柱承托大厅。

身为八角形或方形，无柱头。窟两侧的壁柱大多也作方形，有的表面刻水漏图案。本段凿作的柱子或壁柱大多用来承托前廊或前室，个别的用以分隔中央大厅和前室，如古达第 1、6 窟。

后段塔庙窟内的石塔，可分作两种类型：一种为Ci式，沿袭前段旧制[1]；另一种为 Cii 式，是本段新出现的。这种塔有三层薄基座，圆柱形塔身上沿雕出素面边饰或栏楯图案；再上为覆钵和方龛，由四至五层倒叠涩构作的平头与窟顶直接相连[2]。

此外，第三期后段塔庙窟也有若干雕像，如古达第 6 窟的大象、动物及骑手、单身及男女双人像和格拉德第 48 窟的人物形象。纳西克第 18 窟和根赫里第 3 窟的类似造像，也是这段补雕的。

总之，虽然这段塔庙窟继续奉循前段形式，但也取得了不少进展并做了许多革新。

(四) 第四期

第四期塔庙窟，主室平面为倒 U 字形，后部中央雕佛塔，列柱再次重新出现；主室窟顶作纵券，侧廊为平顶。本期塔庙窟的总体布局与第二期后段接近，只是较其更加繁复。窟前部分各具特色，如阿旃陀第 19 窟有一凸起柱式门廊和一封闭式前室，前室两侧壁各开两个小室。阿旃陀第 26 窟与一宽敞的前廊相连，前廊前端由四根立柱承托，但立柱已残、廊顶坍塌；前室两端各开一小室，小室前各有两立柱和两壁柱。埃洛拉第 10 窟窟前有一巨大的敞开式天井，除前面外，天井其余三面绕以柱廊，廊外侧凿出小室。这一期塔庙窟的所有窟前部分与上段塔庙窟，尤其是与古达第 15 窟和谢拉尔瓦迪第 8 窟的同一部分相似。

本期塔庙窟的外立面（即前室后壁），亦平行分作上、下两部分。上层的主体是设计华丽的拱形明窗，下层是柱式门廊，门廊顶部是阳台（露台）[3]。整个外立面及前室侧壁雕出丰富精美的造像及装饰图案，如佛、菩萨、药叉、飞天像以及太阳拱和栏楯等图案。拱形大明窗分作两种：一为 V 式，拱翼两端向内弯曲，拱脚上卷如火焰，拱顶尖雕出涡卷纹饰，拱腹雕出椽头，拱面有边饰；另一种为 VI 式，系由 V 式演化而来，拱呈三叶形，中央偏上开圆窗，拱顶亦雕出涡卷形纹饰，拱脚上翻呈火焰状，三叶

[1] 除了该窟地面粗糙的圆形痕迹和窟顶表面雕出的轮盖之外，默哈德第 8 窟内的石塔现已不存。尽管该塔的整体形状不得而知，但残存的遗迹，尤其是窟顶表面雕出的轮盖，表明它属于 Ci 式。另外，格拉德第 6、16、48 窟内的塔顶，只有一方石（方龛）承托轮杆及雕于窟顶上的轮盖，方龛上无倒叠涩式平头。

[2] 谢拉尔瓦迪第 8 窟内的石塔早被铲除，塔殿现为一座小型的 Saiva 祭坛。不过，雕在窟顶上的 Cii 式平头残迹尚可辨识。又，默哈德第 15 窟内的佛塔，是刻在后壁上的高浮雕。

[3] 虽然阿旃陀第 26 窟前室已部分残毁，但阳台遗迹尚存。

拱内雕出曲拱和椽头。

尽管本期塔庙窟的主室纵券顶和侧廊平顶奉循第二期旧制，但为仿木石作，无任何木构。窟内列柱及前廊石柱的样式也都是新出现的，有三种：①第一种为 Bvi 式，方形高柱础、圆柱形柱身、罗曼式柱头，柱身表面雕有凹槽、条形饰、圆带花纹以及精巧的网眼饰；罗曼式柱头上的舟形托架表面雕饰繁复，有佛、胁侍、飞天等形象。②第二种为 Bvii 式，圆形薄柱础、八角形素面柱身、舟形托架式柱头。③第三种为 Bviii 式，高方础，上为多边形与圆柱形相间之柱身、长方形托架式柱头，柱头上刻少量几何纹。此外，列柱之上的环形深楣于每柱间分隔，由此构成一系列小方框，每一框内皆雕佛及胁侍像。

与上述三期石塔相比，第四期塔庙窟内的大塔结构极为复杂，可分作两种形式。第一种为 Di 式，低塔基、高塔身、近球形覆钵、高方龛，叠涩式平头上承三重相轮，相轮顶上的宝瓶与窟顶几乎相连；塔身前面所开大龛设计精巧，龛内为高浮雕佛立像。第二种为 Dii 式，塔身为圆柱形，但附一宽大的主立面 (frontispiece)，主立面前雕刻倚坐佛像及胁侍；塔身其余部分垂直分作若干方框，每一框内皆雕佛像，姿态各异。覆钵呈扁球形。方龛有两种形制：一为通常所见之方形，其上为倒叠涩式平头和相轮，如阿旃陀第 26 窟。另一种是新出现的，平面呈亚字形，如埃洛拉第 10 窟。值得注意的是，这座暗示入灭大师且受到信徒及香客朝拜之塔，现已成为塔龛。这样，便略微改变了其原有属性。

除了建筑和雕刻细部的富丽之外，塔庙窟完全以岩石雕作，则是第四期另一特点。不仅主室及侧廊顶部的弯梁、椽子和塔的轮盖为仿木雕出，而且外立面的所有装饰部分均为石作。从这个角度来看，它们发扬了第三期塔庙窟的传统，表明了它们与上期塔庙窟的关系。

第四期塔庙窟最显著的特征，是佛教造像遍布窟内外。它们既雕在外立面，也镌于窟内四壁；既在塔身开龛造像，也于柱头上刻画如来及胁侍。根据题材和内容，这些造像可大体分作四类：①单体佛像，既有坐像，也有立像，手印多样，在外立面和窟内大量雕造。②一佛二菩萨，这种一铺三身像在塔庙窟中最早出现在阿旃陀第 19 窟，稍后在阿旃陀第 26 窟和埃洛拉第 10 窟的外立面和窟内多有发现。这种造像甚至也雕在了埃洛拉第 10 窟佛塔的主立面上。③佛传场景，如阿旃陀第 19 窟外立面的燃灯佛及佛与妻儿相会、阿旃陀第 26 窟主室右壁的降魔与涅槃浮雕。④其他从属造像，如飞天、那伽以至观世音救八难等也大量出现。这些佛教造像，不仅是本期塔庙窟最显著的特征，也是信徒的朝拜对象。“中央佛像的安详及所具有的魔力，控制着礼拜殿内温和的宗教气氛。在千变万化的现象中和灾难深重的世界里，他似乎象征着永恒。”[1]这是与上述三期塔庙窟最根本和最主要的不同之处[2]。

简言之,第四期塔庙窟在形制上基本保留了早期,尤其是第二期后段洞窟的特点,只是木构部分完全为石雕替代,洞窟结构更加复杂。通过建筑与雕刻的融合,从整体上表现了审美的统一。从这个意义上说,它们可以看作是早期塔庙窟的复兴。本期塔庙窟最显著的特征,是大乘多佛思想的流行。除了刻在外立面和窟内的小型佛教造像之外,大乘观念主要通过雕在塔身正面的佛像来表现的。此外,第四期塔庙窟兼有塔殿和佛殿二重属性,而尤以后者为重。

五、西印度塔庙窟的年代

事实上,由于迄今为止在西印度塔庙窟中没有发现任何有关洞窟兴建的明确记录,因此要确定每一期塔庙窟的年代绝非易事。自 19 世纪初以来,各国学者对此问题做了许多有益的探索,但同时也存在着无尽的争议。笔者拟在前人研究的基础上,以洞窟题铭、历史背景及 ^{14}C 测年资料为依据,并与其他相关纪年实物对比,试对上述四期六段塔庙窟的年代做一初步推断。

(一)第一期

就相对年代而言,第一期塔庙窟无疑较其他三期洞窟要早。但第一期塔庙窟到底始凿于何时,目前尚无定论。实际上,根据其他年代比较清楚的材料,并参照古铭文学(palaeography),第一期塔庙窟的年代,还是可以确定的。换言之,通过考证石刻题铭的字体演化规律,并与其他纪年材料对比,我们可以大体推定第一期洞窟的年代。

1. 杜尔贾莱纳第 3 窟的结构,与帕鲁德大塔西门阿阇世望柱上浮雕所表现的内容类似,后者刻画了一座圆形平面无壁塔外貌(图 30),因而,“它们在年代上可能相距不远”[3]。贡迪维蒂第 9 窟的平面及整体结构,与巴拉巴尔山上苏达玛窟(图 31)极为接近。除了前者窟体与崖体正交之外,二者前部皆为长方形大厅,后部为圆形平面小室。由于苏达玛窟体的中轴线与岩体表面平行,入口必然开在一侧,这是较早的技术。又,贡迪维蒂第 9 窟和杜尔贾莱纳第 3 窟的设计极为独特,除此之外在西印度

[1] M. N. Deshpande, *opere citato* [The (Ajanta) Caves...]: 30.

[2] 此外,上述三期塔庙窟外立面和窟内所雕刻的佛教造像,如阿旃陀第 9 窟外立面上的佛像,也是第四期补雕的。

[3] James Fergusson & Jas. Burgess, *The Cave Temples of India,* London: W. H. Allen & Co., 1880: 253.

图 30　帕鲁德大塔栏循上浮雕无壁塔

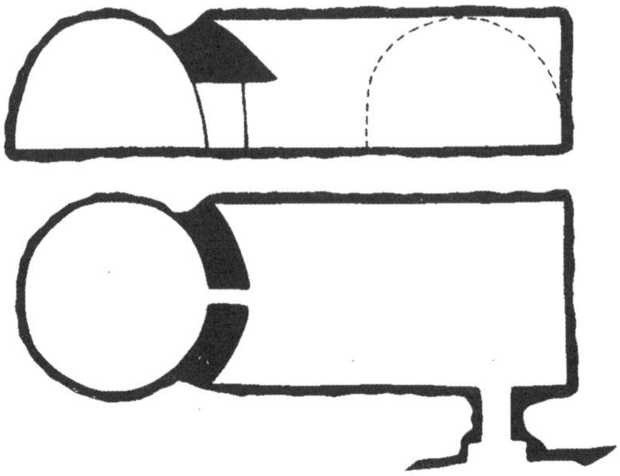

图 31　苏达玛石窟平面及纵向垂直剖面图

尚未发现与之相似的塔庙窟，这应是创始期全方位探索洞窟形制的结果。珀贾第 12 窟的拱形大明窗，应从巴拉巴尔山洛马斯·里希石窟等外立面（图 16a）演化而来。前者的拱形明窗表面现存三排钉孔，说明原有某些木质饰面覆盖其上，就像帕鲁德大塔陀兰纳（toraṇa，塔门）及栏楯浮雕所显示的那样[1]。

2. 由简朴的塔基、塔身、覆钵、方龛和三层倒叠涩式平头构成的佛塔，如阿旃陀第 10 窟[2]，是帕鲁德大塔塔门或栏楯雕刻中浮雕塔的共同特征。有些帕鲁德大塔塔门或栏楯上的浮雕塔清晰地显示方龛是木构的，这与第一期塔庙窟的 Ai 式塔相同[3]。此外，贡德恩第 1 窟的支提明窗，也可在帕鲁德大塔塔门或栏楯浮雕中的类似物上见到[4]。

3. 贡德恩第 1 窟明窗起拱点（springing）两侧的舞者像（图 32），与珀贾第 12 窟外立面上的浮雕极为相似；其身体的块面结构、姿态及装饰等，也与帕鲁德大塔西门阿阇世望柱上层的浮雕人物近似[5]。至于比德尔科拉第 3 窟的执杖药叉（图 33），其身体各部分的平板、块面处理，接近于帕鲁德大塔塔门或栏楯浮雕的风格，与头部

---

[1] James Fergusson & Jas. Burgess, *opere citato*: 225-226.

[2] 由于第一期其他塔庙窟内塔的平头以上部分与覆钵和塔身不是用同一独石雕作的，故平头的倒叠涩层数不得而知。不过，塔身和覆钵部分极为简朴。

[3] B. Barua, *Bharhut*, Book III: *Aspects of Life and Art*, rep., Patna: Indological Book Corporation, 1979: Pl. LII, LIII.

[4] B. Barua, *opere citato*: Pl. XLIX, XCI.

[5] A. Cunningham, *The Stūpa of Bhārhut; A Buddhist monument ornamented with numerous sculptures illustrated of Buddhist legend and history in the third century BC*, 2nd ed., Varanasi: Indological Book House, 1962: Pl. XVI.

图 32 贡德恩第 1 窟外立面双身像

图 33 比德尔科拉第 3 窟外立面药叉

丰圆的造型形成鲜明的对照,尤其是双眼的外轮廓线,使人立即想起帕鲁德大塔塔门或栏楯造像中眼部的类似处理手法[1]。

4. 既然当时佛像尚未出现,那么阿旃陀第 10 窟最早的壁画,同帕鲁德甚至桑吉大塔塔门或栏楯上的浮雕一样,表现的是传统的小乘题材,如本生故事和佛传场景,与古老的叙事风格相应[2]。作为早期绘画的一个突出例证,阿旃陀第10窟佛传"画面本身,富于想象力。在构图和表现手法上,与帕鲁德和桑吉大塔同时代的浮雕作品相近"[3]。画面中有些人物的造型(图34),与帕鲁德大塔塔门波斯匿(Prasenajit)望柱上浮雕人物的姿态完全相同[4]。

5. 至于西印度第一期塔庙窟现存的铭刻与题记,在珀贾第 12 窟有三处:一处镌在外立面上,两处刻在窟内木质弯梁上[5]。阿旃陀第10窟发现四条:第一条刻在

[1] V. Dehejia, *Early Buddhist Rock Temples: A Chronological Study,* London: Thames and Hudson, 1972: 119. See B. Barua, *opere citato*: Pl. IV-VIII.

[2] D. Mitra, *Ajanta,* 10th ed., New Delhi: Archaeological Survey of India, 1992: 43.

[3] I. Aall, "The (Ajanta) Murals: Their Art", in: *Ajanta Murals,* ed. A. Ghose, New Delhi: Achaeological Survey of India, 1967: 41.

[4] D. Schlingloff, *opere citato*: 7.

[5] M. N. Deshpande, "Important Epigraphical Records from the Chaitya Cave, Bhaja", in: *Lalita Kala,* 1959 (6): 31.

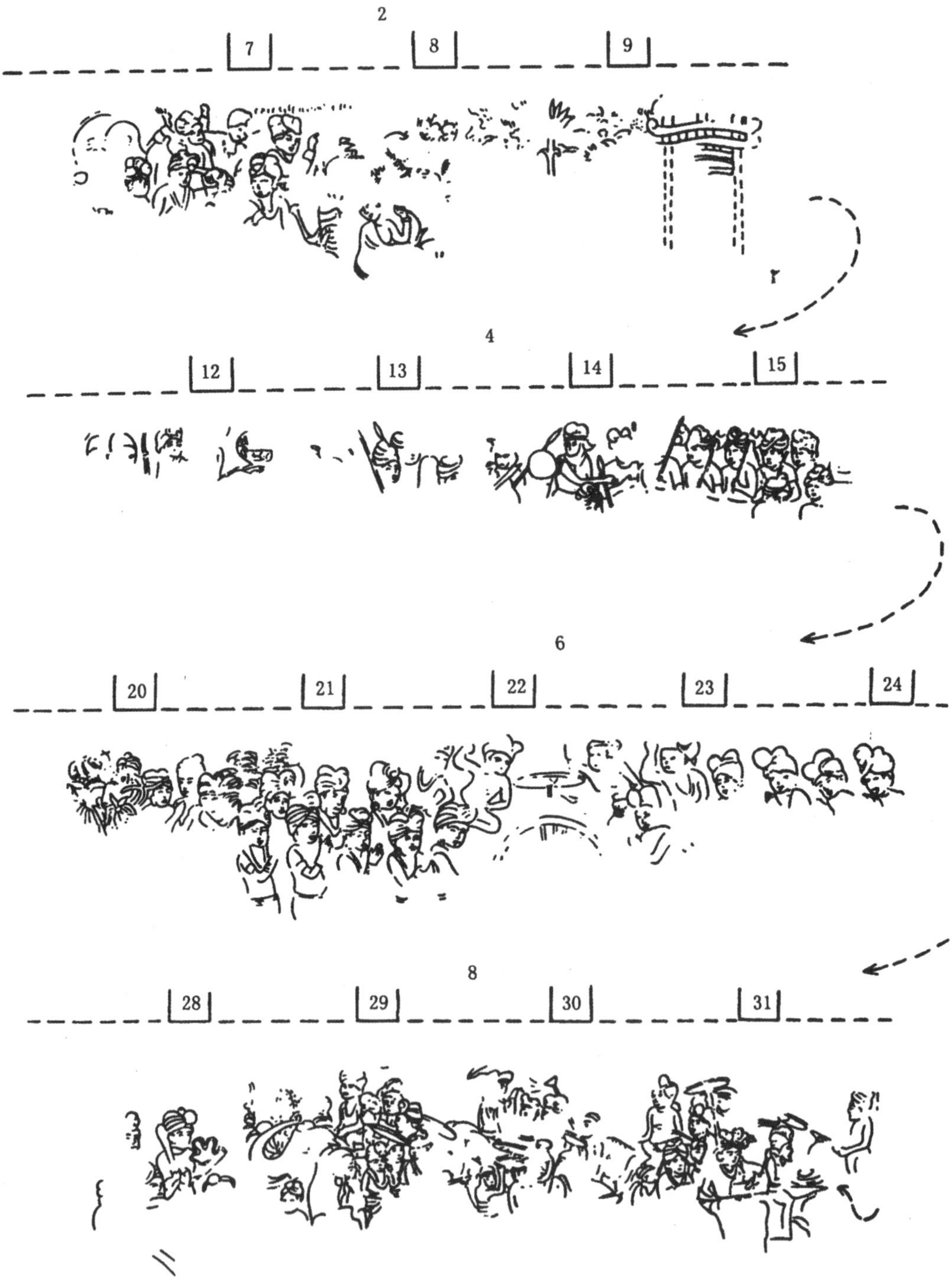

图 34　阿旃陀第 10 窟左侧壁佛传故事画

拱形大明窗左侧的外立面上,叙及外立面是由瓦西什特 (Vāsishṭha) 的儿子克特哈迪 (Katahādi) 捐助[1];第二条位于主室左侧廊第一至第三根弯梁下面的泥层底下,是根哈诃 (Kaṇhaka) 出资开凿此壁的记录[2];第三条题写于左侧廊第三根椽子上,记述它是达摩德拉 (Dhamadera) 施与苦行者的[3];第四条题写在左侧壁第三根石柱对面的壁画上,残毁严重[4]。比德尔科拉第3窟现存题铭两则,分别刻在主室右侧从外向里数第十和十一根石柱上:一根柱子是香料商弥陀提婆 (Mitradeva) 所做的功德,另一根则是僧伽诃 (Saṃghaka) 儿子捐献的,两家都是波提弹那 (Patiṭhāna) 人[5]。贡德恩第1窟外立面上的题铭,刻在残破的雕像头旁,记述它是根哈 (Kaṇha) 弟子巴拉诃 (Balaka) 雕造的[6]。

所有这些铭文的字体,属于石窟题铭的第一系。现在多数学者把第一系石窟铭文定在公元前2世纪的后半,即公元前150年至公元前100年[7]。

从上述比较及分析中我们发现:西印度第一期塔庙窟,较孔雀王朝开凿的洛马斯·里希和苏达玛石窟之设计,显示出建造技术上的进步。它们在许多方面与帕鲁德大塔塔门或栏楯雕刻的相关部分类似,故而二者的雕造年代应该接近。帕鲁德大塔塔门及栏楯上的浮雕,现被多数学者定为公元前2世纪中叶,至迟不会晚于公元前2世纪末[8]。根据上述分析并证以铭文字体,我们把第一期塔庙窟的年代定在公元前2世纪中、末叶这一阶段,即公元前150年至公元前100年左右。

(二)第二期

1. 前段洞窟题铭

第二期前段塔庙窟,也没有关于洞窟开凿年代的绝对记录及可资对比分析的显

[1] Jas. Burgess, *Report on the Buddhist Cave Temples and Their Inscriptions; ASWI*, IV, 1883: 45, 116.

[2] A. Ghosh, "Two early Brāhmī records from Ajaṇṭā", in: *Epigraphia Indica*, 37 (1968): 241-243.

[3] *ibidem.*

[4] Jas. Burgess and B. Indraji, *Inscriptions from the Cave Temples of Western India; ASWI*, X, Bombay: Government Central Press, 1881: 84.

[5] M. N. Deshpande, *opere citato* (The Rock-cut Caves...): 72.

[6] James Burgese, *opere citato*: 83.

[7] 1) M. N. Deshpande, *opere citato* (Important Epigraphical Records...): 31; 2) M. N. Deshpande, *opere citato* (The Rock-cut Caves...): 70; 3) Jas. Burgess, *opere citato*: 116.

[8] 1) B. Barua, *Bārhut*, Book I: *Stone as a Story-teller*, rep., Patna: Indological Book Corporation, 1979: 29-37; 2) John Marshall, *The Buddhist Art of Gandhāra: The Story of the early School, its birth, growth and decline*, London: Cambridge University Press, 1960: 7; 3) V. Dehejia, *opere citato*: 35.

著材料。在这种情况下，窟中刻写的题铭，值得我们特别注意。

(1) 在门莫迪第 40 窟支提盲窗的莲花雕刻中有一短铭，记述这是臾那世界 (Yavana) 钱德拉 (Chandra) 所做的功德[1]。

(2) 纳西克第 18 窟可辨识的题记有三条：第一条刻在门道上部的拱顶下，记述门道或整个外立面是纳西克人的功德[2]；第二条竖直刻在窟内的两根立柱上，记述塔庙窟是由多人出资开凿的[3]；第三条题记刻在门道左侧药叉像上方的圆边上，记述该药叉像是那达西里亚 (Nādasiriyā) 雕造的[4]。

(3) 讷德苏尔第 8 窟右壁现存一短铭，记述这是弥陀罗 (Mitra) 所做的功德[5]。

(4) 贝德萨第 3 窟石塔背面的题铭，记述该塔是阿萨拉弥陀 (Asalāmita) 雕造的，他是住在马拉古达 (Mārakuda) 的托钵僧戈布提 (Gobhūti) 的弟子[6]。

关于这些铭文的字体形态，大多数学者认为它们接续前段刻写。不过涉及到具体时代，意见存在着分歧。

据纳伽拉翥研究，纳西克第 18 窟外立面上的题铭属于第 IIB 系古字体，即公元前 150 年至公元前 125 年；而纳西克第 18 窟列柱上的铭文和门莫迪第 40 窟外立面上的题记则属于第 III 系古字体，即公元前 125 年至公元前 60 年；贝德萨第 3 窟石塔上的题铭属于第 IVA 系古字体，即公元前 60 年至公元元年；纳西克第 18 窟药叉像上方的题记则属于 VA 系古字体，即公元 100 年至 140 年[7]。这样，所有上述题铭是在公元前 150 年到公元 140 年之间雕刻的。鉴于纳西克第 18 窟门道左侧的药叉像，系后代补雕之作[8]，因此，第二期前段塔庙窟的主体铭文，应刻于公元前 150 年到公元元年之间。

戴赫佳 (V. Dehejia) 对这些铭文字体的研究，则与纳伽拉翥略有不同。她认为纳西克第 18 窟外立面和讷德苏尔第 8 窟右壁上的铭文属于第 IB 系古字体，即公元前 70 至公元前 60 年；纳西克第 18 窟列柱上的铭文属于第 ID 系，即公元前 40 年至公元前 25 年。至于门莫迪第 40 窟外立面上的题刻，则属于第 II 系古字体，即

---

[1] Jas. Burgess, *opere citato*: 95.

[2] H. Lüders, "A List of Brāhmī Inscriptions from the Earliest Times to about A.D. 400 with the Exception of those of Aśōka", in: *Epigraphia Indica,* Vol. X (1909-10), Appendix, Calcutta: Superintendent Government Printing, 1912: No. 1142.

[3] H. Lüders, *opere citato*: No. 1141.

[4] H. Lüders, *opere citato*: No. 1143.

[5] H. Cousens, "An Account of the Caves at Nadsur and Karsambla", in: *ASWI,* 1891, XII: 7.

[6] Jas. Burgess, *opere citato*: 89.

[7] S. Nagaraju, *opere citato*: 63, 108, 153, 273.

[8] *ibidem.*

公元50年至70年。这样,所有题铭应镌刻于公元前70年至公元70年之间[1]。不过,门莫迪第40窟外立面上的雕刻属晚期补作,大约完成于公元60年；这座塔庙窟的主体,大约在公元前50年左右已完工[2]。这样,第二期前段塔庙窟主体上的所有题铭应刻于公元前70年至公元前25年之间。

由于缺少其他对比资料,根据上述学者的观点[3],我们不得不暂时把铭文刻写的年代,看作是第二期前段塔庙窟开凿的年代。既然第二期前段洞窟的开凿接续第一期,那么雕造的年代就应在其后。也就是说,第二期前段塔庙窟是在公元前100年至公元元年之间完成的。至于其下限的具体年代,容后述。

2. 后段洞窟题铭

(1) 贝德萨第7窟前室右端小室门楣上所刻题记[4],据有些学者研究,字体年代较早,可定为公元前40年以前[5]。

(2) 伽尔拉第8窟可辨识的铭刻多达31条,大多记述了各组成部分的雕作,如马哈拉提·阿哥尼弥陀那伽(Mahārathi Agnimitranaka)施舍狮子柱,香料商辛哈德塔(Simhadata)捐资雕造窟门,以及彭亚姆塔·因德提婆(Bhamyamta Imdadēva)长者出资制作上下栏楯和大象等[6]。不过,刻在入口右侧带形装饰表面、与大明窗起拱点在同一水平线上的那方是最重要的一处。文云：这是"咯喇吉迦(Karajika)村民施与住在瓦卢拉迦(Valūraka)石窟中僧侣的功德,以赞助迪尼迦(Dinika)之子、克哈拉塔(Khaharāta)王的女婿乌萨珀德塔(Usabhadāta)统领区域内的四方僧伽。克哈拉塔王即是Khatapa (Kshatrapa) Nahapāna,曾向伯那萨(Baṇāsā)河畔及帕珀萨(Pabhāsa)地区的婆罗门捐施功德"[7]。铭文中的这位纳哈帕纳(Nahapāna),曾是沙多婆汉那王朝(Sātavāhanas/玄奘译作"娑多婆诃")的一位统治者,在位46年

[1] V. Dehejia, *opere citato*: 47-65, Tables 9, 11.

[2] V. Dehejia, *opere citato*: Table 11.

[3] 这一阶段塔庙窟内新出现的Bii式石塔,是本段和下段流行的式样。其四至五层倒叠涩式平头,与桑吉大塔塔门及栏楯上雕刻的所有典型佛塔上的平头,是极为接近的。

[4] Jas. Burgess, *opere citato*: 89.

[5] 戴赫佳推断这座塔庙窟雕造于公元前50-前40年,参见：V. Dehejia, *opere citato*: Table ll；纳伽拉翥则把它定为公元前1世纪之作,参见：S. Nagaraju, *opere citato*: 110.

[6] 1) É. Senart, "The Inscriptions of the Caves at Kārlē", in: *Epigraphia Indica,* VII (1903): 47 ff, No. 1-19; 2) M. S. Vats, "Unpublished Votive Inscriptions in the Chaitya Cave at Kārlē", in: *Epigraphia Indica,* XVIII (1925-1926): 325 ff, no. 1-12.

[7] É. Senart, *opere citato*: No. 13.

(即78至126年)[1],后被瞿昙弥普特拉·萨塔迦尼(Gautamīputra Sātakarṇi)击败。这条“铭刻清楚地说明：在纳哈帕纳向婆罗门捐施之时,该窟业已存在了”[2]。而且,它也显示出伽尔拉第8窟始凿时的题刻,“与纳哈帕纳铭文在字体上相距甚远”[3]。因此,我们认为这座塔庙窟至迟在公元124年已经被使用。

(3) 根赫里第3窟现已发现题记两则：一条刻在前室入口右侧壁上,记述商人建造了一座塔庙[4]；另一条镌于入口左侧壁上,提到了各种功德[5]。两则铭文在刻写特征上属于第VA系古字体,即公元100年至130年[6]。

(4) 门莫迪第26窟现存题记多达8条[7],记述了各种用来植树的土地,与洞窟本身的雕造无关。铭文中最早的属于第VB系古字体,即公元130年至180年[8]。这说明,第26窟那时已经完成了。

3. 后段雕刻与建筑

在贝德萨第7窟石柱的柱顶盘座面上,雕刻许多呈蹲跪状的马、牛和大象,且上有骑手,整体造型十分优美(图35a)。伽尔拉第8窟石柱的柱顶盘座面上,也有这种造像(图35b、c)[9]。“这些造像,与桑吉大塔塔门上雕刻的那些动物及骑手(图35d)是相似的。”[10]

伽尔拉第8窟前室正壁、明窗起拱点内以及石柱的柱头上,雕有许多男女双人像(图36、37)。这种形象,最早见于比德尔科拉第12窟佛塔的方龛上,第二期后段开始流行,下期极盛。其高贵而充满活力的亲切表情,丰润的形体以及头饰、项圈和臀部周围的珠饰等,与桑吉大塔塔门上的男女双人像(图38)非常相似。二者之间的相似性,令人感到它们是由同一设计师和雕刻家完成的。

第二期后段大多数塔庙窟内的石塔属于Bii式。这种塔在前段开始出现,本段流

---

[1] 多数学者赞同这个年代。不过,戴赫佳认为“纳哈帕纳在公元71年已经在位了”,公元68年应是纳哈帕纳开始统治的最晚年头。参见：V. Dehejia, *opere citato*: 25-26.

[2] S. Nagaraju, *opere citato*: 226.

[3] *ibidem*.

[4] H. Lüders, *opere citato*: No. 987.

[5] H. Lüders, *opere citato*: No. 988.

[6] S. Nagaraju, *opere citato*: 63.

[7] H. Lüders, *opere citato*: Nos. 1158, 1159, 1162-1167.

[8] S. Nagaraju, *opere citato*: 147.

[9] 在伽尔拉第8窟侧廊列柱上,亦出现了斯芬克斯(Sphinx)像。

[10] V. Dehejia, *opere citato*: 127.

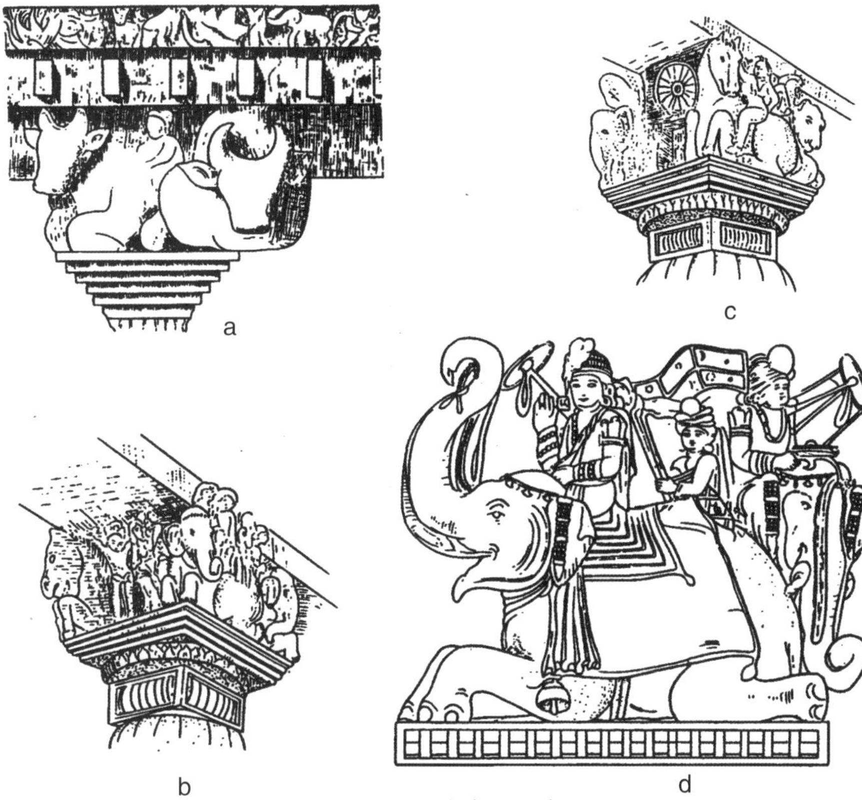

图 35　柱头类型示意图

a. 贝德萨第 7 窟柱头；b. 伽尔拉第 8 窟柱头；c. 伽尔拉第 8 窟柱头；d. 桑吉大塔南门柱头

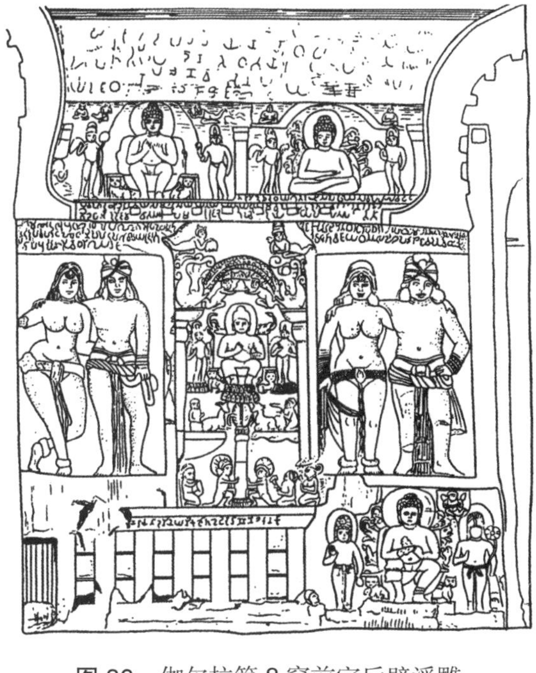

图 36　伽尔拉第 8 窟前室后壁浮雕

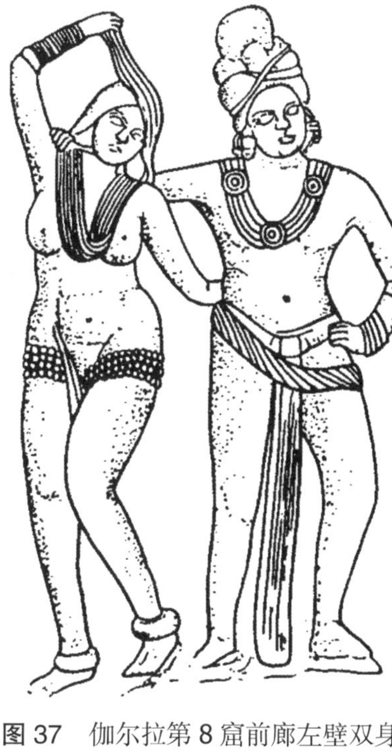

图 37　伽尔拉第 8 窟前廊左壁双身像

图 38　桑吉大塔西门右柱内侧田园浮雕

行；其四至五层倒叠涩式平头，与“桑吉塔门浮雕中所有塔的典型形式”[1]极为相似。至于桑吉大塔塔门的雕造年代，多数学者把它定在公元前 50 年至公元前 25 年[2]。

4. ^{14}C 年代测定

1964 年，巴克 (H. Barker) 与麦基 (J. Mackey) 首次公布伽尔拉第 8 窟内一木楔的放射性 ^{14}C 年代为公元前 290 ± 150 年[3]。两年后，又测定出同窟内木质弯梁的年代为公元前 230 ± 95 年和公元前 125 ± 100 年[4]。不过，考虑到建筑样式、铭文的古字体形态以及当时的历史背景等，多数学者无法认同这些年代判断[5]。因此，^{14}C 测定结果长期以来被忽略了。后来，纳伽拉翥对这个问题又做了新的探索，宣称上述

---

[1] James Fergusson, *Tree and Serpent Worship,* 2nd ed., London: Indian Office, 1873: 121.

[2] 1) Percy Brown, *Indian Architecture: Buddhist and Hindu Periods,* 3rd rev & enl. Ed., Bombay: Taraporevala Sons & Co., 1959: 18; 2) John Marshall, "The Monuments of Sanchi: Their Exploration and Conservation", in: *Archaeological Survey of India; Annual Report 1913-14*: 7.

[3] H. Barker and J. Mackey, "British Museum Natural Radiocarbon Measurements III", in: *British Museum Quarterly,* XXVII (1963-1964): 55.

[4] D. P. Agrawal and S. Kusumgar, "Tata Institute Radiocarbon Date List IV", in: *Radiocarbon,* 1966 (8): 448.

[5] V. Dehejia, *opere citato*: 189-190.

"放射性 ^{14}C 年代的通常跨度是公元前 325 年至公元前 40 年"[1]。任何有关伽尔拉第 8 窟是在公元前 4 世纪或前 3 世纪雕造的推断,毫无疑问是不正确的。其建筑样式、雕刻风格以及铭文字体,暗示出伽尔拉第 8 窟可能晚至公元前 1 世纪的前半叶。考虑到所有编年证据,即历史背景、^{14}C 年代测定、建筑风格和铭文字体,纳伽拉翥推测:伽尔拉第 8 窟,"至多在公元前 40 年或前 30 年已经完成"[2]。笔者同意他的观点。

根据上述比较和分析,我们认为,既然伽尔拉第 8 窟可能完成于公元前 40 年至公元前 30 年左右,那么这一段其他塔庙窟的年代,由建筑和雕刻样式判定,与之不应相距太远。考虑到从倒 U 字平面塔庙窟向长方形平面塔庙窟演变的过程,我们可以推定,这段塔庙窟大概始凿于公元前 1 世纪的后半,绝大多数约完成于公元 1 世纪的前半叶,即公元前 50 年至公元 50 年。根赫里第 3 窟前室及门莫迪第 26 窟的某些部分,可能延至下期才完工。

第二期前段塔庙窟的年代,根据归谬法,可以定在公元前 100 年至公元前 50 年之间。这样,第二期塔庙窟可定在公元前 100 年至公元 50 年左右。

(三)第三期

第三期塔庙窟,接续第二期洞窟开凿。尽管两期石窟在风格上存在若干共同特征,诸如支提明窗和塔的样式,但第二期塔庙窟与第三期石窟在结构和设计上有较大差异。前者为纵券顶倒 U 字形平面,后者为平顶长方形平面。因此我们认为,应有一段从纵券顶倒 U 字形平面塔庙窟向简朴的平顶长方形平面塔庙窟转变和过渡的时期。也就是说,在石窟寺营造史上应有一短暂的间隙或缺环。至于为何在设计上出现这样一种转变,我们尚未发现任何有关此问题的可靠材料,故仅有前述推论。关于第三期塔庙窟的年代,我们拟从铭文字体、雕刻样式和历史背景等方面进行探讨。

1. 前段洞窟铭文

第三期前段塔庙窟的若干题刻,对于断定这段洞窟的年代颇具参考价值。

(1) 锡万内里第 43 窟前室,现存题记一条,铭文刻作三行,云:"这座塔庙窟,献给整个世界的繁荣和幸福。"[3]从铭文采用的字体,伯吉斯 (Jas. Burgess) 推断:"它

[1] S. Nagaraju, *opere citato*: 49.

[2] S. Nagaraju, *opere citato*: 227.

[3] Jas. Burgess, *opere citato*: 93.

可能镌刻于公历纪元前后，或更早一点。”[1]不过，戴赫佳认为它刻于公元130年左右[2]。

(2) 锡万内里第66窟门道上方，也保存一方题铭，文云：“塔庙窟，系乌伽诃(Ugāha)之子伊西伯利塔(Isipālīta)及全家捐施。”[3]戴赫佳认为这则铭文属于第IV系古字体，即公元120年至130年[4]；而纳伽拉翥推断“这条题记的字母，属于VC系古字体，即公元150年至180年”[5]。

(3) 伽内什·伯哈第14窟前室后壁的题记刻作两行，可释读为：“塔庙窟，阿难陀施舍……”[6]关于这条题刻，伯吉斯推断“可能至迟镌于公元前100年”[7]；但纳伽拉翥认为“这条题刻属于第VB系古字体，即公元130年至150年”[8]。

(4) 根赫里第4窟内石塔方龛上有一题刻，文云：“珀亚塔·达摩伯拉(Bhayata Dhammapāla)长者之塔……”[9]纳伽拉翥认为“这条铭文的字母可定为第VA系古字体，即公元100年至130年”[10]。

根据建筑样式并参考上述铭文字体，第三期前段塔庙窟可定为公元50年至150年之作；而联想到从纵券顶倒U字平面塔庙窟向平顶长方形洞窟的过渡，第三期前段塔庙窟应该雕造于2世纪的前半叶，即公元100年至150年之间。

2. 后段雕刻样式

古达第6窟中央大厅后壁底部保存的动物与牧人浮雕(图39)，值得我们注意。其主题、布局以及人与动物的姿态，与阿默拉沃蒂大塔栏楯上的浮雕相似[11]；后者的年代，一般定为公元150年至200年[12]。在第6窟同壁动物与牧人浮雕的上方，就是众所周知的男女双人像。其中左侧的那幅，雕一男一女两个等身像和另一矮小的

---

[1] James Fergusson & Jas. Burgess, *opere citato*: 252.

[2] V. Dehejia, *opere citato*: 68, Table 11.

[3] Jas. Burgess, *opere citato*: 94.

[4] V. Dehejia, *opere citato*: 68.

[5] S. Nagaraju, *opere citato*: 189.

[6] Jas. Burgess, *opere citato*: 94.

[7] James Fergusson & Jas. Burgess, *opere citato*: 257.

[8] S. Nagaraju, *opere citato*: 167.

[9] H. Lüders, *opere citato*: No. 993.

[10] S. Nagaraju, *opere citato*: 198.

[11] James Fergusson, *opere citato*: Pl. LXXXIII, LVII.

[12] K. R. Srinivasan, “Southern Buddhist Monuments”, in: *Archaeological Remains, Monuments & Museums*, Part I, New Delhi: Archaeological Survey of India, 1964: 105.

图 39　古达第 6 窟浮雕动物与牧人

侍从(图 40)。画面中,男性缠裹厚重的头巾,戴大耳环及长管状手镯,袒上身,环腰缠一织物。女性着类似的头饰,唯式样略有不同,额前有圆形饰。除头饰及环腰带状物之外,她几乎裸体。女性的左侧,跪一矮小的侍从,她正握持女主人左脚,似乎在调整其厚重的圆形脚镯。右侧的浮雕与之颇为相似。

图 40　古达第 6 窟浮雕双身像

"这些雕像与伽尔拉塔庙窟(第 8 窟)前壁上的那些,有着惊人的相似性"[1](见前引图 37),尤其是两者中的男性,甚至在细部,如身体轮廓、服装及饰物上都非常相像,以至于人们最初把它们定为同一年代。然而进一步观察,则显露出它们之间的差异。古达第 6 窟的形象、姿态及表情更加大方,潇洒自如,并且胸前无项饰。与伽尔拉雕像相比,它们的年代似乎要晚[2]。

3. 后段洞窟铭文

在第三期后段雕造的 12 座塔庙窟中,有 6 座洞窟刻有题铭。而这些题铭,对确定洞窟的年代是极为重要的。

(1) 古达第 9 窟前室右侧壁,现存题记一则,文作:"珀伊拉 (Bhayila) 施舍塔庙窟……"[3]

---

[1] James Fergusson & Jas. Burgess, *opere citato*: 207-208.

[2] V. Dehejia, *opere citato*: 130.

[3] Jas. Burgess, *opere citato*: 86.

(2) 古达第 15 窟前室左侧壁题记云：拉默德塔 (Rāmadata) 施舍塔庙窟及一小室……[1]

(3) 古达第 1 窟前室后壁的一则题刻,记述这座洞窟是会赐福的[2]。

(4) 古达第 6 窟前室左侧壁的题铭,提到该窟是由锡瓦马 (Sivama) 施舍的[3]。

(5) 在默哈德第 8 窟右壁前端窟檐下,现存一则铭刻:"僧坊窟、塔庙窟、八个小室、僧坊窟两侧的两个水池以及通往僧坊窟的小径,是由格纳博阿 · 弗赫努巴利塔 (Kāṇabhōa Vheṇupālita) 王子施资雕造的。"[4]

(6) 谢拉尔瓦迪第 8 窟,现存题刻两则：一则刻在右侧一小室的前面,记载该石室由锡亚古塔尼迦(Siagutaṇikā)施资雕建[5]。另一则镌于中央大厅后壁,记述该塔庙窟由布阏 (Buddhā) 和森迦 (Sanghā) 捐资修造[6]。

关于上述铭文的年代,学者们存有争议。从字形判断,伯吉斯推测古达第 1 窟题记"属于公元前 2 世纪之作"[7]。不过,戴赫佳推断古达第 9 窟和默哈德第 8 窟的题铭应定为第 III 系古字体,即 110 年；而古达第 1、6、15 窟以及谢拉尔瓦迪第 8 窟的铭记,则属于第 IV 系古字体,即 140 年左右[8]。纳伽拉翥认为,除了古达第 9 窟题记可定作第 V 系古字体 (即 100-180 年) 外,古达第 1、6 窟,默哈德第 8 窟和谢拉尔瓦迪第 8 窟的题铭都属于第 VII 系,即 230 年之后；而古达第 15 窟的题记,应定在古达第 9 窟与古达第 1 窟的年代之间[9]。

上述所有题刻的年代,从铭文字体学角度,可定在公元前 2 世纪到公元 3 世纪之间。

4. 历史背景

众所周知,佛教的发展与传布,与统治阶级的支持及宗教容忍政策是密切相关的。倘若没有阿育王的大力弘扬,佛教也许不会成为世界性宗教；假如迦腻色迦不

[1] Jas. Burgess, *opere citato*: 87.

[2] Jas. Burgess, *opere citato*: 84.

[3] Jas. Burgess, *opere citato*: 85. 又,古达第 6 窟铭文中的 Sivabhuti 录事,与古达第 1 窟铭文中的 Sivabhuti 录事应为同一人。倘若此推断不误的话,说明二窟的时代相距不会太远 。这也从另一方面证明我们类型排比的可靠性和科学性。

[4] H. Lüders, *opere citato*: No. 1072.

[5] Jas. Burgess, *opere citato*: 92.

[6] C. C. Das Gupta, "Shelārwādi Cave Inscription" , in: *Epigraphia Indica,* XXVIII (1950): 77.

[7] James Fergusson & Jas. Burgess, *opere citato*: 206.

[8] V. Dehejia, *opere citato*: 67-68, Table 11.

[9] S. Nagaraju, *opere citato*: 295.

皈依佛法,藏纳舍利的高层佛塔可能也不会出现。恰恰是"沙多婆汉那王朝,开始将土地捐赠给婆罗门和佛教僧侣,并免其税收"[1],才使佛教又有了长足的发展。当时皇室成员及地方民众大多佞佛,结果在这段时间里雕造了一大批佛教石窟,如默哈德第8窟就是由格纳博阿·弗赫努巴利塔王子施舍建造的。此外,"从经济观点来看,这一时期印度与西方世界之间的贸易繁荣起来。印度国内商道贯穿各地,有的商道甚至通到了中亚和西亚"[2]。佛教石窟寺,通常都沿着商路开凿,尤其是穿越西高止山山脉的商道附近多有石窟寺。"显然,这些石窟寺也是人们旅程中的重要驿站,充当商队的休息地、供给所和钱庄。"[3]

随着沙多婆汉那王朝在2世纪末的衰落以及3世纪上半叶的消亡[4],佛教及佛教活动,如在露天营造佛塔和在山崖开凿石窟寺,一定受到了影响。这是宗教历史发展的必然规律。

总之,根据雕刻样式、铭文形态,并证以历史背景,第三期后段塔庙窟的上限接续第三期前段,下限不晚于3世纪上半叶。换言之,这组塔庙窟应雕造于公元150年至250年之间,其大多数应完工于2世纪的后半叶,即公元150年至200年左右。

(四)第四期

据研究,大乘佛教起源于公元1世纪的南印度[5]。然而依据《八千颂般若波罗密多经》(*Aśṭasāhasrikāprajñapārimitā*),南印度的佛教徒在佛灭后似乎已知晓大乘了;大乘佛教先向西传布,后向北发展[6]。在西印度马哈拉施特拉地区,大乘佛教的出现可能较晚;不过大约在4、5世纪时,它在那里已呈现发展状态[7]。

大乘佛教的主要标志是菩萨教旨(学说),这是早期佛教思想发展的必然结果。随着时间的推移,大乘佛教最终"创造出由高尚而慈善的菩萨组成的众神。佛陀自身日益被看作是伟大神灵在尘世的化身,他从宗教师长上升为救世的上帝。对佛偶像的朝拜,加上精心制订的佛教仪式、祷辞和符咒等,很快取代了先前对他的朴素信

---

[1] D. N. Jha, *Ancient India: An Introductory Outline,* New Delhi: People's Publishing House, 1977: 79.

[2] D. N. Jha, *opere citato*: 80.

[3] D. N. Jha, *opere citato*: 86.

[4] 1) R. C. Majumdar et al, *An Advanced History of India,* 4th ed., Madras: MaCmillan Company of India Limited, 1978: 110; 2) D. N. Jha, *opere citato*: 77; 3) S. Nagaraju, *opere citato: 25.*

[5] A. K. Warder, *Indian Buddhism,* 2nd rev ed., Delhi: Motilal Banarsidass, 1980: 352.

[6] R. Mitra, ed., *Aśṭasāhasrikāprajñapārimitā*, Rev. ed., Calcutta: 1960: 225.

[7] M. C. Joshi, *opere citato*: 16-23.

仰"[1]。佛的偶像变得越来越普遍，越来越重要。

在石雕艺术中，大乘观念主要是通过人形化了的佛像来表现；世尊被改造成为人格化的神，其信徒在危难之中可以向他祈求救援[2]。因此，洞窟平面的演进、精雕细镌的外立面和窟内外佛像与菩萨像的出现，都暗示着这期塔庙窟较上述三期塔庙窟的时代要晚。至于第四期塔庙窟的具体年代，我们将根据相关题记和建筑样式来推定。

阿旃陀第 17 窟现存的一则铭文，记述了在从属于赫里申那 (Harishēṇa) 的一位族长的赞助下，一座珍宝般 (gem-like) 的独石方形窟 (第 17 窟)，连带一佛龛及毗邻的蓄水池和西侧的佛殿(gandha-kuṭi)被雕造完成[3]。关于铭文内容，大多数学者认为：毗邻蓄水池就是与第17窟相连的那座洞窟；而佛殿就是第19窟[4]。铭文中的赫里申那，曾是瓦加塔格 (Vākāṭakas) 王朝最后一位君王，在位时间为公元 475 年至 500 年左右[5]。因此，阿旃陀第 19 窟可以定在赫里申那统治时期，即公元 475 年至 500 年左右。

阿旃陀第 26 窟外立面上的刻铭，记述该窟是由阿折罗 (Sthavira Achala) 建立的[6]。这位阿折罗，应该是玄奘公元637年左右游历摩诃剌侘国，即今马哈拉施特拉邦[7]时所记述的阿折罗[8]。《大唐西域记》不仅记载了阿折罗伽蓝及石窟状况，而且详细描述了"伽蓝大精舍，高百余尺；中有石佛像，高七十余尺，上有石盖七重，虚悬无缀，盖间相去各三尺余。闻诸先志曰：斯乃罗汉愿力之所持也。或曰神通之力，或曰药术之功。考厥实录，未详其致。精舍四周雕镂石壁，作如来在昔修菩萨行诸因地事。证圣果之祯祥，入寂灭之灵应，巨细无遗，备尽镌镂"[9]。

根据阿旃陀现存洞窟，第 26 窟比较符合玄奘法师的记述。窟内主塔前面雕"石佛像"，只是"石盖"上部已残毁；窟右壁雕出降魔图，以"证圣果之祯祥"；并刻涅槃

[1] D. N. Jha, *opere citato*: 88.

[2] *ibidem.*

[3] V. V. Mirashi, ed., *Inscriptions of the Vākāṭakas: Corpus Inscriptionum Indicarum,* V, Ootacamund: Government Epigraphist for India, 1963: 124-129.

[4] 1) V. V. Mirashi, *opere citato*: lxxiii; 2) M. N. Deshpande, *opere citato* [The (Ajanta) Caves: Their Historical...]: 16.

[5] V. V. Mirashi, *opere citato*: vi-viii.

[6] Jas. Burgess, *opere citato*: 133-136.

[7] 杨廷福《玄奘论集》，济南：齐鲁书社，1986 年，第 117 页。

[8] 玄奘《大唐西域记》，季羡林等校注，北京：中华书局，1985 年，第 895 页。

[9] 玄奘，上引书，第 897 页。

巨像与之相接，表“入寂灭之灵应”。如果这种推断不误的话，那么意味着玄奘公元637年前后游访阿旃陀时，“因年代久远，只有第26窟为众人所知”[1]。换句话说，阿旃陀第26窟在玄奘游历时早已存在了。

从风格与样式判断，阿旃陀第26窟明窗的形制、外立面的雕刻、窟顶甚至石柱的类型等，与阿旃陀第19窟的相关部分相似。两者的前室左右侧壁，皆凿出供僧众居住的小禅室。这些特征，暗示出它们在年代上接近。不过，阿旃陀第26窟出现的若干新因素，诸如素面托架式柱头及塔前主佛的倚坐姿势，表明它的时代稍晚。

考虑到洞窟铭文、历史文献及建筑式样，阿旃陀第26窟的开凿年代，应定为6世纪[2]。

至于埃洛拉第10窟的开凿年代，目前很难确定。根据天井平面、三叶拱明窗、佛塔侧面结构以及前室石柱的长条形托架式柱头，我们应把它的年代定得很晚。不过，该窟的素面舟形托架式柱头、窟顶形制、塔身侧壁浮雕及塔前立像的姿态等，则与阿旃陀第26窟的相关部分接近。

考虑到婆罗门教（新婆罗门教 / 印度教）7世纪中叶在埃洛拉的复兴及佛教在此地的逐渐衰落，我们推断埃洛拉第10窟可能在6世纪末已经开凿，但雕造工作一直延续到7世纪上半叶的前期，即该窟的雕造年代大约为公元575年至625年左右[3]。

根据以上论证，我们可以把第四期塔庙窟的年代定为公元475年至625年左右。另外，早期上座部系统石窟，如贡迪维蒂第9窟、阿旃陀第9窟、伽尔拉第8窟、根赫里第2e和4窟及古达第6窟的人格化佛像，也属于这一时期补刻。

综上所述，西印度塔庙窟的年代可以暂时推定如下：

第一期塔庙窟：公元前150年至公元前100年左右。

第二期塔庙窟：公元前100年至公元50年左右；其中前段为公元前100年至公元前50年左右，后段为公元前50年至公元50年左右。

第三期塔庙窟：公元50年至250年左右；其中前段为公元50年至150年左右，后段为公元150年至250年左右。

第四期塔庙窟：公元475年至625年左右。

---

[1] M. C. Joshi, *opere citato*: 22-23.

[2] 1) M. C. Joshi, *ibidem;* 2) Percy Brown, *opere citato*: 57; 3) M. N. Deshpande, *opere citato* (The Caves: Their Historical...): 21.

[3] K. V. Soundara Rajan, “Keynote Address (at the National Seminar on Ellorā Caves)”, in: *Ellorā Caves: Sculptures and Architecture,* ed. R. Parimoo et al, New Delhi: Books & Books, 1988: 37.

六、结　　语

作为石窟寺的一个重要组成部分，塔庙窟的开凿可能比僧坊窟要晚一些。不过，作为佛陀允许建造的三种佛塔之一，地面上的木构塔庙 / 屋塔可能早在佛陀时代就已经出现了。限于笔者的学识及获取的有限材料，拜拉特铭文山上的木构塔庙应是现存最早的。

大约在孔雀帝国崩溃之后，即公元前 200 年左右，作为内陆贸易扩展和佛教从北天竺向西南沙多婆汉那王国传布之结果，石窟寺沿着西高止山脉出现了。也许在"德干高原山丘中漫游之时，佛教僧侣已意识到了这些幽静的地点，有益于健康的寺院生活。因此，随着俗人的慷慨捐赠并通过僧侣百折不挠的努力，出现了许多石窟寺"[1]。作为地面佛寺不可分割的一部分，在僧坊窟出现之后，土木结构的塔庙也被"石化"(petrified) 了。与拜拉德木构塔庙最接近的一个例证，就是均讷尔地区杜尔贾莱纳第 3 窟。

随着僧伽的扩大和大众追随者的增多，这种圆形平面塔庙窟已难以适应朝圣者在窟内集聚并举行宗教仪式的需要。这导致西印度石窟的设计者，于公元前 2 世纪中叶创造出了倒 U 字形平面塔庙窟，以满足住持及栖息僧侣和游方者的需求。这种倒 U 字形平面塔庙窟，曾广为传布，并连续使用了很长的时间。实际上，后来开凿的塔庙窟都是由此发展和演化而来的，沿着倒 U 字形平面——长方形平面——倒 U 字形平面轨迹运作。不过朝拜的主体，即窟内塔的形制，与露天塔无异，并自始至终保持不变。

在本文研讨的 18 处石窟寺中，塔庙窟最早的开凿活动是在公元前 2 世纪后半叶于七个地点展开的。这七个地点包括杜尔贾莱纳、贡迪维蒂、珀贾、阿旃陀、比德尔科拉、贡德恩和根赫里，即本文第一期塔庙窟。稍后不久，雕造活动开始出现在纳西克、门莫迪、伽内什 · 伯哈、奥兰伽巴德、讷德苏尔和贝德萨等地区，时间为公元前 1 世纪的前半叶，即第二期前段。到了公元前 1 世纪的后半叶，伽尔拉开始营建；此外，格拉德出现塔庙窟，是公元 1 世纪前 50 年内的事情，即第二期后段。到了第三期前段，即公元 1 世纪后半到 2 世纪前半叶，第一、二期繁盛的大多数石窟群，如阿旃陀、贝德萨、珀贾、伽尔拉、贡德恩、贡迪维蒂、纳西克等，雕造活动都停止了。塔庙窟的营造活动，那时集中在门莫迪、锡万内里、伽内什 · 伯哈和根赫里，洞窟结构发生了较大变

[1] D. K. Barua, *Vihāras in Ancient India,* Calcutta: Indian Publications, 1969: 19.

化，石窟建筑更加简朴和实用，这可以说是塔庙窟雕造史上的一次革命。接下来营造的塔庙窟，分布在伯瓦拉、古达、格拉德、默哈德和谢拉尔瓦迪，时间是公元 2 世纪后半到 3 世纪初。

从上述编年，我们不难发现：西印度塔庙窟营造的端绪，几乎与定都普拉蒂什塔纳 (Pratishṭhāna，今 Paithan)[1]的沙多婆汉那王朝（娑多婆诃）的崛起相吻合；而佛教洞窟雕造活动的起落，也与沙多婆汉那王朝的盛衰密切相关。沙多婆汉那王朝的统治者，虽然自身为婆罗门教徒，但允诺佛教在其领土上传布、弘扬和发展。在沙多婆汉那统治者的容忍和支持下，伴随着公众的大力捐赠，佛教石窟寺迅速发展，保存至今的塔庙窟多达 51 座。而且，在许多塔庙窟中发现的题铭，提到了各种组成部分的捐赠，诸如外立面、门道、栏楯、石柱、塔、水池、小室等等，这表明大多数石窟寺是通过合作方式协力开凿的。当时"窟内住持僧人及石窟建造活动的主要财源，是社会各阶层，尤其是以村邑形式为主的捐献和布施，同时也靠无尽藏 (akṣayāvini) 的利息。这种无尽藏是由布施者和商贾或钱庄老板联合管理的一种永久性存款。钱庄的倒闭、王室布施的丧失、公共场所的变化、商路的改道以及其他社会—经济原因等，都可能导致一处石窟寺的关闭或者营造活动的延缓甚至停止"[2]。

由于沙多婆汉那王朝的衰亡，西印度的石窟寺雕造活动大约在公元 3 世纪后半到 5 世纪前半叶出现了一段空白。不过，当大乘佛教于 4 世纪左右到来之后，西印度，特别是阿旃陀、奥兰伽巴德、埃洛拉以及纳西克的石窟寺营造活动又接踵兴盛起来。结果，在瓦加塔格王朝统治者的支持和赞助下，一大批洞窟在 5 世纪后半到 7 世纪前半叶完成了，个别洞窟的"装饰和细部，可能延续到 8、9 世纪，那时执政的是拉什特拉库塔 (Rāshtṛakūṭas)"[3]。像沙多婆汉那王朝一样，瓦加塔格王朝的统治者自身信仰婆罗门教，但他们对佛教也采取兼容并包的政策[4]。这一时期雕造的塔庙窟保留了早期塔庙，尤其是第二期塔庙窟的基本特征，全部构件皆仿木石作。塔庙窟中的大乘概念，除了外立面及窟内侧壁上众多的小型造像外，主要是通过主塔前人格化佛像来表现的，建造佛殿在当时被看作是获得解脱与超度的一种手段[5]。不过值得

---

[1] M. N. Deshpande, *opere citato*［The (Ajanta) Caves: Their Historical...］: 15.

[2] M. C. Joshi, *opere citato*: 25-27.

[3] K. R. Srinivasan, "Rock-cut Monuments", in: *Archaeological Remains, Monuments & Museums,* Part I, New Delhi: Archaeological Survey of India, 1964: 124-125.

[4] V. V. Mirashi, ed., *opere citato*: XL-XLIII.

[5] G. Yazdani, *Ajanta*: *The Colour and Monochrome Reproductions of the Ajanta Frescoes based on Photography,* IV, London: Oxford University Press, 1955: 116-118.

注意的是，这一时期开凿的塔庙窟，仅有三座（阿旃陀第29窟未完成）保存到现在，与数量众多的僧坊窟形成鲜明对比。究其原因，除了印度教（新婆罗门教）于7世纪兴起、佛教逐渐衰微之外，大乘佛教认为保持独立式祈祷殿已非必要恐为另一缘由。这一时期雕造的僧坊窟，本身设施齐备，雕造辉煌，配齐了主要和从属龛像。僧坊窟“后端雕造佛殿，是礼拜佛像的主要场所”[1]。因此，这种僧坊窟具有双重属性，它既是朝拜之地，又是修行之所[2]。实际上，这种洞窟的形成，受到了第三期后段“塔庙僧坊混成式”窟的极大影响。

总之，印度的塔庙窟，自从公元前2世纪中叶创始以来，一直沿着自己特有的轨迹演化，先后经历了四个显著阶段，即创始期（第一期）、繁盛期（第二期）、功利期（第三期）和复兴期（第四期）。最初，它们的中心位于普拉蒂什塔纳的西部和北部，后来在功利主义时期的后段曾一度移至南部，而到复兴期再度迁到它的北部。但不管怎样迁移，它们均在古代天竺通往普拉蒂什塔纳的商路沿线及附近。普拉蒂什塔纳既是当时沙多婆汉那王朝的首都，同时又是纪元前后几世纪一处巨大的商贸中心[3]。此外，这些塔庙窟的营造，自始至终大多限定在西印度境内[4]。

［本文原刊（北京）文物出版社2002年出版的《宿白先生八秩华诞纪念文集》第681-738页，后修订为《中印佛教石窟寺比较研究：以塔庙窟为中心》第三章。这次重刊前，调整了注释体例，并改正了若干错误。］

---

［1］K. V. Soundara Rajan, *opere citato*: 34.

［2］O. C. Kail, *Buddhist Cave Temples of India,* Bombay: D. B. Taraporevala Sons & Co. Pvd Ltd, 1975: 122.

［3］M. N. Deshpande, *opere citato* (The Rock-cut Caves...): 67-69.

［4］南印度的贡土巴利 (Guntupalli) 有一塔庙窟，但时代有争论。除此之外，印度其他地区不闻有塔庙窟。

阿旃陀石窟参观记

阿旃陀石窟，位于印度马哈拉施特拉邦奥兰伽巴德市东北 106 公里处。石窟开凿于新月形溪谷岩壁上，海拔 534 米，俯临瓦哥拉河 (Waghora)，从东向西绵延 550 米，编号洞窟 30 个 (图 1-3)。

图 1 阿旃陀石窟远景

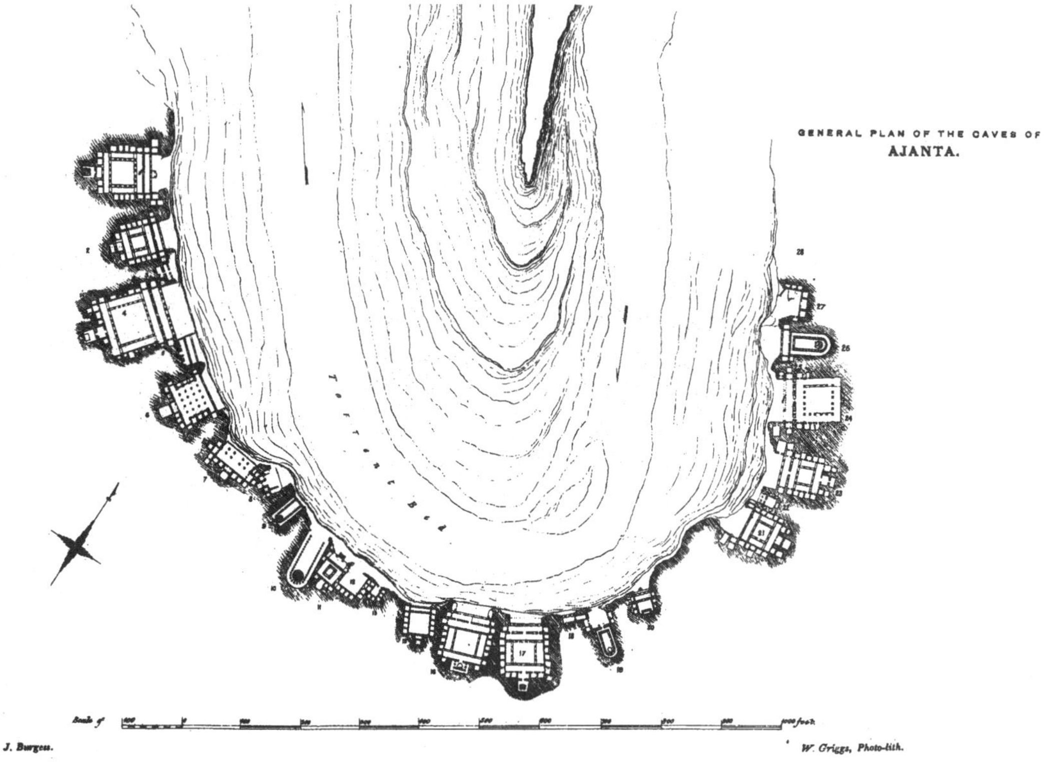

图2　阿旃陀石窟连续平面图

图3　阿旃陀第6至10窟外景

现存阿旃陀石窟的唯一古代文献，是中国唐代高僧玄奘的《大唐西域记》。该书卷十一“摩诃剌侘国”条记述了“阿折罗伽蓝”：

> 国东境有大山，迭岭连障，重峦绝巘，爰有伽蓝，基于幽谷，高堂邃宇，疏崖枕峰；重阁层台，背岩面壑，阿折罗唐言所行阿罗汉所建……伽蓝大精舍，高百余尺。中有石佛像，高七十余尺，上有石盖七重，虚悬无缀，盖间相去各三尺余。闻诸先志曰：斯乃罗汉愿力之所持也。或曰神通之力，或曰药术之功。考厥实录，未详其致。精舍四周雕镂石壁，作如来在昔修菩萨行诸因地事；证圣果之祯祥，入寂灭之灵应，巨细无遗，备尽镌镂。伽蓝门外南北左右，各一石象。闻之土俗曰：此象时大声吼，地为震动。昔陈那菩萨多止此伽蓝。[1]

《大唐西域记》关于阿折罗伽蓝的记载，早已被阿旃陀第 26 窟发现的碑铭（图 4）证实。玄奘所记阿折罗阿罗汉，即碑铭中的圣者阿折罗 (Sthavir-Āchalena)，阿折罗伽蓝即今阿旃陀石窟[2]。

图 4　阿旃陀第 26 窟“阿折罗”题铭

[1] 玄奘《大唐西域记》，季羡林等校注，北京：中华书局，1985 年，第 895、897 页。

[2] 1) Jas. Burgess, *Report on the Buddhist Cave Temples and Their Inscriptions; supplementary to the volume on "The Cave Temples of India "*, in: *Archaeological Survey of Western India,* Vol. IV (1883): 132-136, esp. 134-135; 2) B. Ch. Chhabra, "The Incised Inscriptions" , in: *Ajanta: The colour and monochrome reproductions of the Ajanta frescoes based on photography,* ed. G. Yazdani, London: Oxford University Press, Part IV, 1955, Appendix: 112-124, esp. 115-118.

玄奘之后，由于佛教在印度的衰落，僧侣相率离散，石窟自然荒废。以后渐为崩塌、泥石湮没，直到1819年才被英国马德拉斯军团(Madras Army)约翰·史密斯(John Smith)等几位军官在瓦哥拉山谷狩猎时偶然发现，并以附近村镇阿旃陀为其命名。1829年开始，有关阿旃陀石窟的报道陆续见于各种报刊[1]。

阿旃陀石窟，集建筑、雕刻、绘画三者为一体。关于建筑，它乃地面佛寺的"石化"形式，在印度古代建筑史上占有举足轻重的地位；至于其雕刻，亦颇具特色，虽远离都市并藏于洞窟之中，但大多数雕刻未被自然侵蚀和异教徒破坏，皆具较高的艺术水平；说到其绘画，更是驰名世界，尤为可贵。鉴于其卓越的艺术形式，印度考古学家德什班德(M. N. Deshpande)先生把这种凿岩为寺，融合建筑、雕刻、绘画为一体的视觉艺术表现形式，称为"阿旃陀主义(Ajantaism)"。这种阿旃陀主义，在佛教领域的不同地区呈现出多种新形式[2]。下面我们拟从三个方面简要作一介绍。

一、营　造

阿旃陀石窟的雕造，可以明显分作早、晚两个阶段，即通称的小乘时期和大乘时期。

其中，第9、10窟是小乘时期开凿的两座塔庙窟，在年代上以第10窟为早。该窟体量高大，雕建辉煌。窟平面呈倒U字形，39根素面八角列柱将洞窟分作长方形主室、两侧廊和半圆形后室四部分，后室中央雕造石塔(图5)。主室窟顶为纵券，表面原覆木质弯梁和横椽，彼此交接呈网格状；木质梁椽架于下粗上细顶端略内倾的八角石柱顶端深楣之上，给人以木结构之感(图6)。窟前壁原为木质门屏。第9窟与第10窟毗邻开凿，时代略晚。该窟平面作长方形，窟内列柱与第10窟相似，窟顶表

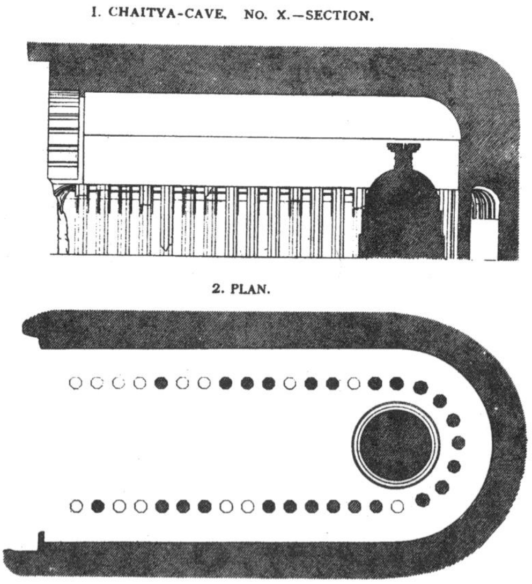

图5　阿旃陀第10窟平面及纵向垂直剖面图

[1] James Fergusson and James Burgess, *The Cave Temples of India,* London: W. H. Allen & Co., 1880: 280-346.

[2] M. N. Deshpande, "The (Ajanta) Caves: Their Historical Perspective", in: *Ajanta Murals*, ed. A. Ghosh, New Delhi: Archaeological Survey of India, 1967: 14-21, esp. 17.

图 6　阿旃陀第 10 窟内景

面亦覆置木质梁椽,唯主室前壁石雕而成。前壁分作上、下两层,下层中央开门道,上层中央雕出拱形大明窗,窗内原镶嵌木质太阳拱,俗称支提窗 (chaitya arch)。至于第 9 窟外立面及窟前两侧壁的佛教造像,则是大乘时期补雕的。

小乘时期开凿的僧坊窟,现存有第 8、12、13 和 15A 窟。其中,最后一座是 20 世纪 50 年代清理出来的,故编号 15A (图 7)。以第 12 窟为例,僧坊窟中央为方形或长方形大厅,大厅的左、右、后三面凿出供僧侣栖息之小禅室,即僧房 (图 8-10)。僧坊窟外观极为简朴,唯一的装饰是小禅室门道上方的太阳拱、栏楯及阶梯状城齿浮雕图案。这种极端简朴的建筑风格,应是寺院中僧侣苦修生活的折射。

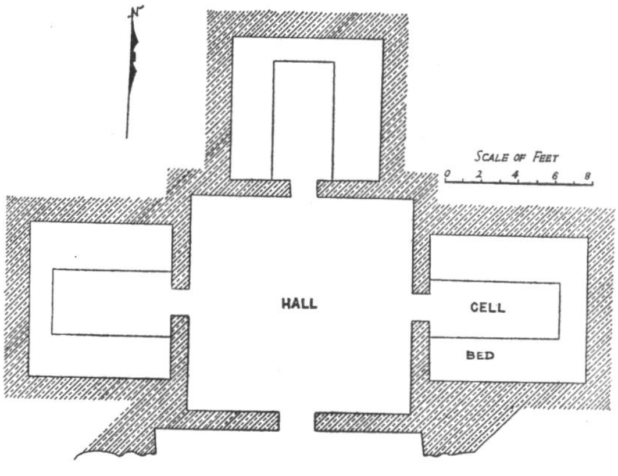

图 7　阿旃陀第 15A 窟平面图

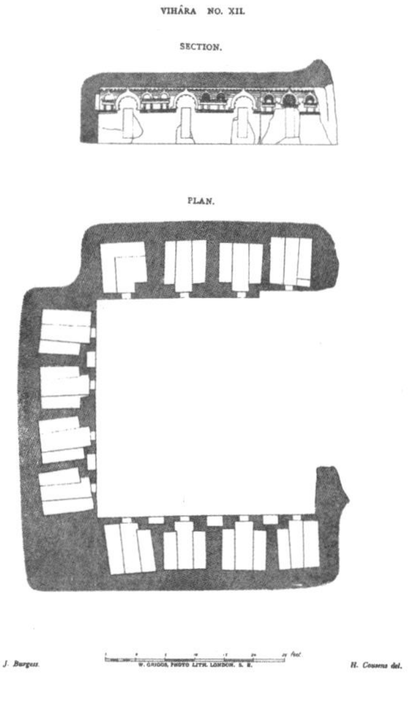

图 8　阿旃陀第 12 窟平面及纵向垂直剖面图

图 9　阿旃陀第 12 窟内景

图 10　阿旃陀第 12 窟后壁小室（僧房）内石床

至于阿旃陀小乘洞窟的开凿年代，现代学者通常把它们定在公元前 2 世纪至公元 1 世纪的沙多婆汉那 (Sātavāhanas，娑多婆诃) 统治时期。依据窟内现存的古代题铭，第 10 窟由瓦西什特 (Vāsishṭha) 之子克特哈迪 (Kaṭahādi) 捐资兴建，第 12 窟由富商格纳默德德 (Ghanāmadaḍa) 施舍雕造。[1]

阿旃陀大乘洞窟的开凿，约始于六百年之后。当时庞大的开窟活动，计划环绕整个马蹄形溪谷，以迎合信徒日益增长的需求。那时统治这一区域的瓦加塔格 (Vākāṭakas) 王朝，虽然自身信奉婆罗门教，但同前任沙多婆汉那一样，对佛教采取了兼容并包的政策。阿旃陀第 16 窟发现的一则题铭，详细记载了瓦加塔格王朝末代国王赫里申那 (Harishēṇa，约 475-500 年) 的宠臣瓦拉赫提婆 (Varāhadēva) 捐资雕建该僧坊之情景[2]；而第17窟的另一通题刻，明确记述赫里申那的一位封邑王子舍财开凿该窟及其附属设施[3]。瓦加塔格王朝曾与笈多 (Gupta) 王朝联姻结盟。笈多王朝当时正值鼎盛，文治武功，各方面均取得了卓越成就。他们以坚实的经济实力为基础，把印度的文化和艺术向前推进了一大步。在宗教上，尽管笈多诸王皈依婆罗门教 (印度教)，但对佛教并不排斥；在艺术上，既创立了笈多式雕刻，又于绘画方面极力摆脱不合时宜之规范。

属于瓦加塔格时期开凿的石窟，包括阿旃陀现存第 19、26、29 号三座塔庙窟 (第 29 窟未完工) 和第 1、2、4、6、7、11、15、16、17、20-24 号等十几座僧坊窟。由此可见，公元 5 至 6 世纪阿旃陀的开窟活动极为繁盛。当时的开窟造像，充分利用旧有崖面，选择适宜雕刻岩壁的不同区段同时进行。第 1、2、4、6、7 窟开凿于溪谷的东端；第 11、16、17 和 20 窟雕造在中段；而第 21-24 窟与第 26 窟一道稍后营建于溪谷的西端。这些洞窟大多完成于公元 5-6 世纪，个别的延续至 7 世纪。

其中，宏伟壮观的塔庙窟各具特色。第 19 窟沿袭小乘时期塔庙窟通用的平面形制，但较其繁复，并在外立面加雕门廊。门廊两侧建筑的细部雕刻及装饰图案，令人瞩目。大约公元 6 世纪初兴建的第 26 窟，把第 19 窟那种柱式门廊扩展为柱式前廊，廊顶形成一宽大的露台 (图 11、12)。需要注意的是，这两窟皆有一前庭，前庭外侧凿出小室，供僧侣禅修、起居之用。第 29 窟虽未按计划完成，但现存外观及窟内拱顶表明它的原设计亦为塔庙。

---

[1] Jas. Burgess, *opere citato*: 45, 116.

[2] V. V. Mirashi, ed., *Inscriptions of the Vākāṭakas*: *Corpus Inscriptionum Indicarum*, V, Ootacamund: Government Epigraphist for India, 1963: 103-111.

[3] V. V. Mirashi, ed., *opere citato*: 120-129.

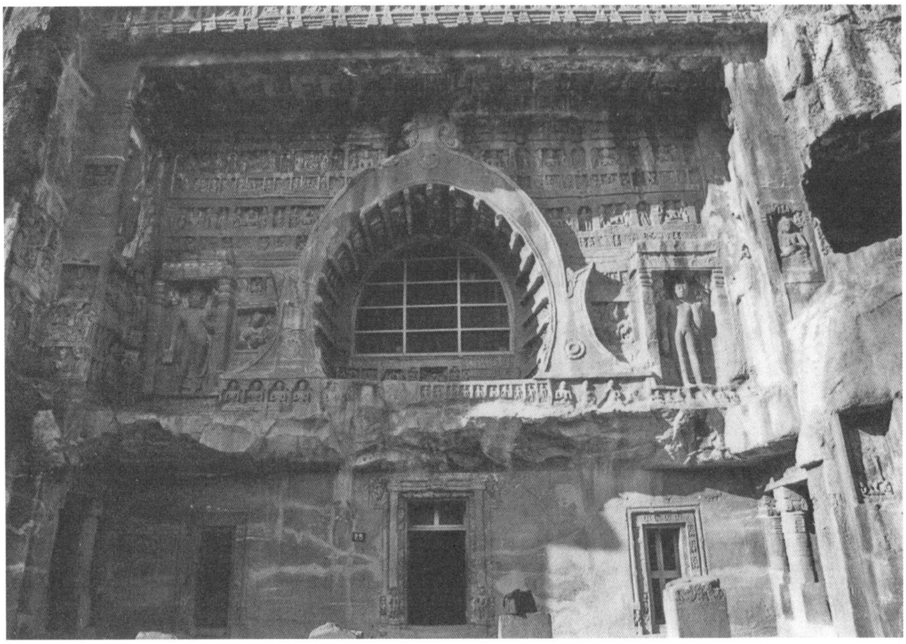

图 11　阿旃陀第 26 窟外立面

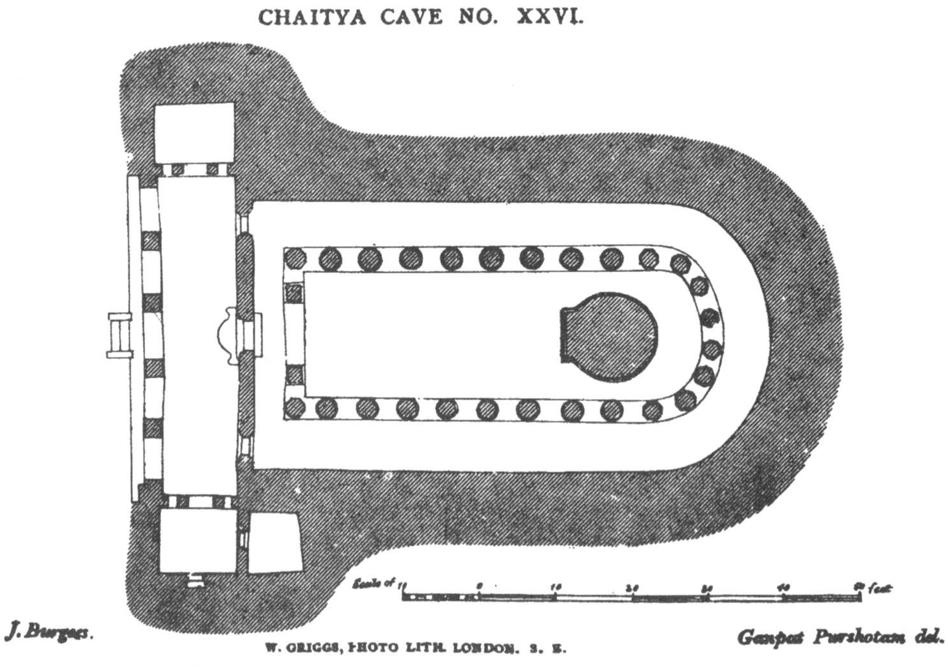

图 12　阿旃陀第 26 窟平面图

大乘时期开凿的僧坊窟,较小乘时期所造体量宽大、结构繁复。窟外崖面雕饰富丽(图 13),每窟皆在大厅后壁(正壁)中央向外凿出内殿(garbha-gṛha/garbha-griha,胎藏殿,即佛殿),这是与小乘时期僧坊窟的最大不同。此外,有些僧坊窟除了主佛殿之外,尚雕单独的佛或菩萨像龛及药叉龛。阿旃陀大乘时期开凿的僧坊窟,第 1 窟可作代表。该窟平面由前廊、中央柱式大厅、大厅周匝小室和正壁所开佛殿构成(图 14)。其中,前廊后部正中开门道,门道两侧各凿一较大的明窗(有些洞窟的明窗为门道替代),以利于中央大厅和侧壁,尤其是侧壁壁画的采光。因而我们推测:当初石窟的设计者,在决定于僧坊窟中雕造附属佛殿时,一定认为适度的采光是必不可少的。此外,阿旃陀第 1 窟尚有一柱式前廊,就像第 26 窟的前廊那样。其他僧坊窟,如第 2、16、17 窟等,亦遵循同样的设计,依据其各自的窟内题铭,可以定在 5 世纪末。而阿旃陀最大的僧坊窟——第 4 窟,根据 20 世纪 60 年代在内殿佛座上发现的题铭,与第 1、2、16 和 17 窟的年代相当或稍晚一些。至于第 6 窟的构造,则较为独特。该窟分上、下两层,下层大厅中央雕造 4 排石柱,每排 4 根,共 16 根。上层的布局,与下层大体接近,且在佛殿内雕造佛像。这种结构虽与阿旃陀其他僧坊窟不同,但埃洛拉第 11 和 12 窟的设计,可能与之相关。

图 13　阿旃陀第 1 窟外立面

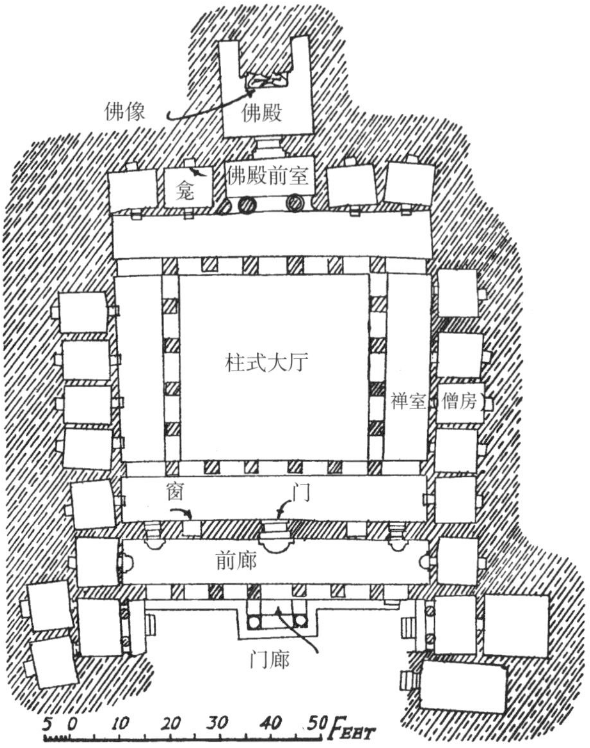

图 14　阿旃陀第 1 窟（佛殿僧坊混成式窟）平面图

二、雕　　刻

对于大多数人来说，一谈到阿旃陀石窟，往往想到的只是它的壁画，而忽略了它的雕刻。事实上，阿旃陀的雕刻可与壁画媲美，且有许多独特之处。倘若我们仔细观察，就会发现阿旃陀石窟的许多雕刻，如第 1、2、16、17 窟的雕像，表面曾贴敷一层灰泥及彩绘。其目的就是通过雕、画合璧之法，增强作品的明暗视觉效果和庄严法相。

诚如印度考古学家 M. N. 德什班德先生所强调的那样，开凿石窟本身就是一种雕刻活动。当时雕刻家的艺术创造，已远远脱离刻画凡人和动物形象。他们所雕造的不仅仅是一种非结构性建筑，而且更重要的是通过榔头对凿子的每一次撞击，让雕刻家的梦幻成真[1]。当地面佛寺完全石化之后，在佛教图像化思潮的冲击和影响之下，他们也效仿地面佛寺的建制与布局，将信徒礼拜的对象巧妙地移植进来，并雕刻

[1] M. N. Deshpande, "The (Ajanta) Caves: Their Sculpture", in: *Ajanta Murals,* ed. A. Ghose, New Delhi: Archaeological Survey of India, 1967: 22-34, esp. 22-23.

在洞窟内的主要部位。而且随着时间的推移，它们逐渐扩散至窟内外，题材和内容亦渐广泛。经过我们实地考察，阿旃陀石窟的雕刻题材和内容可以归纳为如下几类。

图 15　阿旃陀第 26 窟佛塔正面主像

1. 佛像

至少在 5 世纪时，德干地区的石窟寺院开始雕造佛像，信徒把释迦牟尼作为救世主来供养、礼忏。当时不论在塔庙窟里还是在僧坊窟中，佛像均成为必不可少的主体朝拜物[1]。以阿旃陀石窟为例，塔庙窟的主尊，是石塔正面的佛像（图 15）；而僧坊窟的佛殿，则必然成为佛像雕置之所（图 16）。佛像分为坐像和立像两类。坐佛通常结跏趺坐 (vajrāsana)，少数倚坐，手作转法轮印 (dharmacakra-pravartanamudrā)；佛的胁侍皆手持麈尾或佛两侧分立金刚手和莲花手。立佛手相多施无畏印 (abhayamudrā)，少数作与愿印 (varadamudrā)。此外，阿旃陀石窟中还雕造了长过 7 米的涅槃巨像（图 17）及降魔场景（图 18），场面颇为宏大、繁复。

图 16　阿旃陀第 17 窟佛殿正面

[1] M. N. Deshpande, *opere citato*: 23-24.

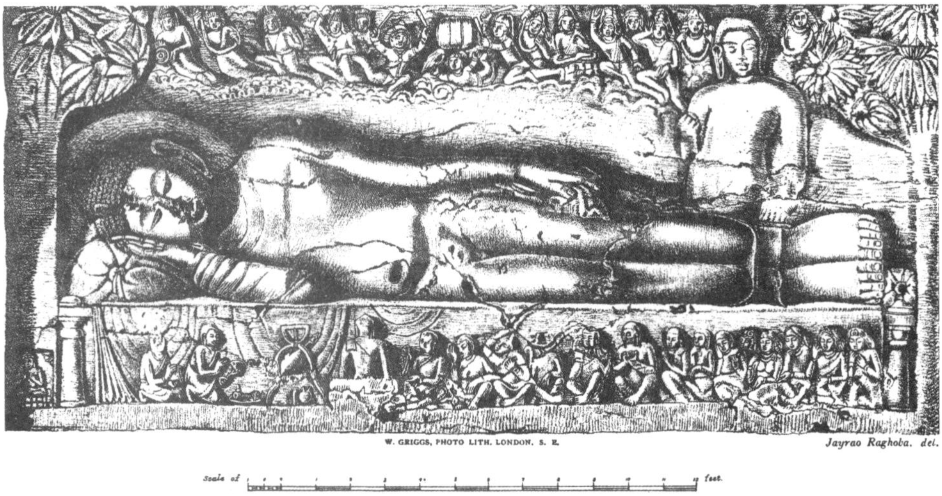

a

b

图 17a　阿旃陀第 26 窟右壁涅槃浮雕；
b　阿旃陀第 26 窟右侧列柱及右壁涅槃浮雕

a

b

图 18　阿旃陀第 26 窟右壁降魔浮雕
a. 1883 年伯吉斯测绘；b. 2001 年作者拍摄

2. 菩萨像

由于大乘多神论 (polytheism of Mahāyāna) 的影响,佛教万神殿在印度逐渐产生。集人情特质、自我牺牲和最高智慧于一身的菩萨,此时成为信徒,尤其是居士阶层青睐的主要对象,并超越以往单一的胁侍地位,开始独立出现。特别是观音像,当时对佛教徒具有无法抗拒的吸引力。观音救八难,系当时最流行的雕刻题材之一。其基本构图为：观音长发垂肩,头顶阿弥陀佛,一手持青莲,一手执念珠。其左右各有四铺情景,分别叙述人们在遇到野狮、大象、毒蛇、刺客、牢狱、火灾、海难等艰险和困苦时,如何向观音求救,后者如何保护信徒脱离苦难的慈悲之举 (图 19)。这些内容对从事海陆贸易的人们,具有特别的吸引力和感召力。

图 19　阿旃陀第 26 窟前庭左侧龛像

3. 龙王与药叉

自然神崇拜在印度有悠久的传统，印度古代文学作品，如佛本生故事，充满着大量的自然神事迹。其中，尤以水中之龙王 (nāga) 和统领四方之药叉 (yakṣas) 最为盛行，且后来都成为佛教的守护神。阿旃陀石窟中的龙王，如第 1、2、19、23 窟的龙王，头顶多雕出 5-7 只蛇形头；而依偎其旁的王后，则多作单头 (图 20)。第 16 窟还出现了神人同形之作，即龙王坐在自己蜷曲的身体之上，并在题铭中特别予以记载。此外，在舍卫城神变中，难陀和优波难陀二龙王兄弟共同为佛支撑莲座，以及第 1、2 窟中多次出现的与龙王有关的本生故事画，也从另一方面反映出该题材在当时颇为流行。

图 20　阿旃陀第 19 窟前庭右侧壁龙王及王后

至于护持佛塔四方之药叉和药叉女 (yakṣīs)，也是印度早期雕刻中常见的题材。在小乘时期的佛教石窟中，它们被雕刻在窟门两侧。到了大乘时期，雕刻家和工匠在沿用早期习俗的基础上，如在塔庙窟的拱形明窗两侧雕出药叉外，开始出现单独设龛之制。阿旃陀第 2 窟的两身药叉，头戴冠、佩项饰、挂璎珞、服饰繁复，并有胁侍相护，以示尊贵。

4. 天人

作为佛和菩萨的从属，香音神乾达婆 (gandharvas)、乐神紧那罗 (kiṃnaras) 和献花环者持明仙 (vidyādharas) 在阿旃陀石窟雕刻和壁画中多有刻画，尤以后者为多。画面中,我们常常看到乾达婆大展歌喉,人面鸟身的紧那罗全身心演奏,而持明仙正于虚空之中向佛敬献花环。乾达婆和紧那罗常常各自以男女双人像表现,即 gandharva-mithunas 和 kiṃnara-mithunas,大多女性极为温情地依偎在男性身旁。

5. 河神、财神、繁殖女神及其他

崇拜河神,在印度也是一种古老习俗。恒河 (Gaṅgā) 女神和阎牟那河 (Yamunā) 女神通常分立于摩竭 (makara) 和龟 (kūrma) 之上,雕造于宗教建筑入口的两侧。在阿旃陀石窟中,如第 16 窟,二河神分居窟门两侧,在果实累累的树下,她们分别脚踏摩竭和龟,皆为漂亮的少女形象 (图 21)。

图 21　阿旃陀第 16 窟门道上方河神

财神般遮迦 (Pāñcika) 及其配偶繁殖女神诃利帝 (Hāritī,鬼子母),据说是受犍陀罗雕刻影响才在印度本土出现的。在大乘时期开凿的洞窟中有时单独为其设龛,说明它们也是颇为流行的一种题材。阿旃陀第 2、23 等窟中刻有二神的形象。

男女 (mithuna,意为年轻伴侣) 双人像在小乘时期的洞窟中,如比德尔科拉 (Pitalkhōrā) 第 3 窟和伽尔拉 (Kārlā) 第 8 窟中,都有表现。在阿旃陀大乘石窟里,这种题材多雕刻在窟门两侧,表示幸运和吉祥。

6. 装饰图案

在阿旃陀石窟的外立面、侧壁和列柱上,我们常常发现许多雕刻精美的装饰性图案。内容既有动物和禽鸟,如丛林中的大象、争斗的水牛、莲池中的天鹅以及摩竭、海贝等;也有植物花卉,如莲花、缠枝蔓草、联珠以及其他纹样等。这些装饰,构成了一个色彩斑斓的世界,为宗教建筑添加了一种温馨气氛。

三、壁　　画

西藏高僧多罗那它在《印度佛教史》中写到:“凡是有佛教的地方,精巧的造像工艺就发达。凡是蔑戾车统治的地方,造像的工艺就衰落。凡是外道盛行的地方,就流行不精巧的造像工艺。”[1]为了倡导佛陀信念，增强教化效果，印度古代艺术家开创了宗教绘画艺术。佛教徒借此为布道工具，传教于民众。那些描绘佛传之卷轴，便于携带，为僧徒游说时所习用。西藏及尼泊尔犹存之唐卡 (tangka) 传统，应为印度初期以雕画布道之余风。与文字相比，绘画更易于为下层民众所理解。

阿旃陀与巴格 (Bagh) 石窟的壁画，可谓印度中古佛教绘画之代表；尤其前者的壁画，堪称印度石窟艺术的辉煌典范 (图 22)。遗憾的是，由于千百年来自然和人为的破坏，阿旃陀石窟中的壁画现仅有第 1、2、16、17 窟保存较为完好。以第 17 窟为例，该窟前廊右壁残存轮回图 (wheel of saṁsāra)；前廊正壁的壁画内容自右向左依次为：须大拏本生、帝释天与飞天、人间佛 (mānuṣi Buddha)、乾达婆与飞天、降服狂象等；中央方形柱式大厅四壁，自门道右侧前壁起经右壁、正壁、左壁至门道左侧前壁止，壁画题材依次为：六牙象本生、猿王本生、象本生、鹅本生、须大拏本生、须陀须摩本生、三十三天说法、佛与妻儿、舍卫城神变、舍罗步鹿本生、象王本生、鱼本生、睒子本生、水牛本生、狮子国因缘、尸毗王本生、智慧鹿本生、榕鹿本生等 (图 23、24)[2]，由此可以想见当时其他洞窟之辉煌情景。据实地考察，阿旃陀石窟现存的壁画题材可以大体分作七类。

图 22　阿旃陀第 1 窟大厅前壁

[1] 多罗那它著《印度佛教史》，张建木译，成都：四川民族出版社，1988 年，第 270 页。

[2] V. V. Mirashi, ed., *opere citato*: lxix-lxxiii.

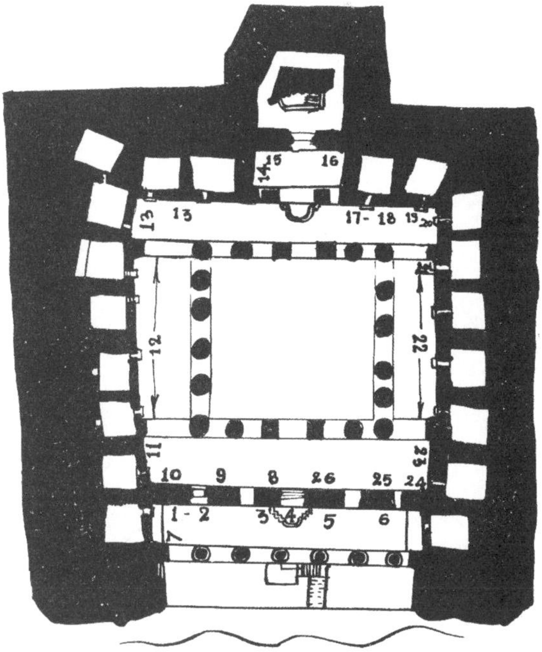

Index of Paintings in Cave XVII at Ajṇṭā
(The Numbers are as in the Plan of the Cave.)

1-2. Scenes from the Viśvantara Jātaka.
3. Fiying indra and Apsarases.
4. The Mānushi Buddha.
5. Gandharvas and Apsarases adoring the Buddha.
6. The Taming of the Furious Elephant Nālāgiri.
7. The wheel of Saṁsāra.
8. The Shaḍ-danta Jātaka.
9. The Mahākapi Jātaka.
10. The Hasti Jātaka.
11. The Haṁsa Jātaka.
12. The Viśvantara Jātaka.
13. The Sutasōma Jātaka.
14. The Buddha preaching in the Tushita Heaven.
15. The Buddha, Yaṣōdharā and Rāhula.
16. The Miracle at Śrāvasti.
17. The Śarabha Jātaka.
18. The Mātṛi-pōshaka Jātaka.
19. The Matsya Jātaka.
20. The Śyāma Jātaka.
21. The Mahisha Jātaka.
22. The Ṣimhalavadāna.
23. The Śibi Jātaka.
24. The Mṛiga Jātaka.
25. The Riksha Jātaka.
26. The Nyagrōdha-mriga Jātaka.

图 23　阿旃陀第 17 窟平面及壁画题材分布示意图

图 24　阿旃陀第 17 窟柱式大厅后壁

1. 本生与譬喻故事

本生 (jātaka)，音译阇陀伽，系记载佛陀前生所修种种善行，也就是释迦牟尼的前世故事。这是印度最古老、最完整的民间故事总集，经常受到佛教画家的青睐。在这些故事中，佛以菩萨身份出现，有时为凡人，有时变天神，有时作小鸟，有时成大象。每一故事都表现他竭尽全力发扬十善，反映出他那种自我牺牲、无私奉献、大慈大悲的高贵品格。这些逼真而又具非凡想象力的本生故事，曾给佛教信徒以强大的震撼；而画家采用写实主义手法敏锐地表达的现实生活，也必然会在香客和朝圣者的心目中留下难以忘怀的深刻印象。如，象王本生故事中所反映出的菩萨的无限慷慨，贤者本生中所透视出的菩萨的无上智慧，须大拏本生中所表现出的菩萨的无尽施舍等。据我们不完全统计，阿旃陀石窟中现存本生故事可考订者有 21 种之多。它们是：

(1) 六牙象本生 (Chaddantajātaka/Chhaddanta Jātaka/Shaḍ-danta Jātaka)，现存第 10(图 25) 和 17 窟，故事内容参见 E. B. Cowell 编辑的 *The Jātakas,* No. 514[1]。

(2) 龙王本生 (Champeyya Jātaka/Campeyyajātaka)，第 1 窟 (图 26)，参见 *The Jātakas,* No. 506[2]。

(3) 鹅本生 (Haṁsajātaka/Mahāhaṁsa Jātaka)，第 2 和 17 窟，参见 *The Jātakas,* No. 502[3]。

(4) 象本生 (Hastijātaka)，第 16 和 17 窟，参见 H. Kern 所辑 *The Jātaka-mālā*[4]。

(5) 羼提本生 (Khantijātaka/Kshānti Jātaka)，第 2 窟，参见 *The Jātaka-mālā*[5]。

(6) 鱼本生 (Macchajātaka/Machchha Jātaka/Matsya Jātaka)，第 17 窟，参见 *The*

---

[1] 1) E. B. Cowell ed., *The Jātaka or Stories of the Buddha's Former Births;* translated from the Pāli by various hands, Cambridge: Cambridge University Press, 1895-1907, 6 vols., Vol. V: 20-31; 2) G. Yazdani, *Ajanta: The colour and monochrome reproductions of the Ajanta frescoes based on photography,* London: Oxford University Press, 1930-1955, 4 parts, Part III: 32-37, Pls. XXX-XXXIV; Part IV: 30-33, Plate X, XIA, XIIa-b.

[2] 1) E. B. Cowell ed., *opere citato*, Vol. IV: 281-290; 2) G. Yazdani, *opere citato*, Part I: 38-43, Plates XXXIV-XXXVIa.

[3] 1) E. B. Cowell ed., *opere citato,* Vol. IV: 264-267; 2) G. Yazdani, *opere citato,* Part II: 12-15, Plates XV-XVI; Part IV: 40-41, Plates XVIIa-b.

[4] 1) H. Kern, ed., *The Jātaka-mālā,* Harvard Oriental Series, Cambridge: Harvard University Press, 1914: 200; 2) G. Yazdani, *opere citato,* Part III: 46-47, Plates XLVIIIb-XLIX; Part IV: 35-36, Plates XIVa-b.

[5] H. Kern, ed., *opere citato*: 181.

图 25　阿旃陀第 10 窟右壁壁画线描

a

b

图 26　阿旃陀第 1 窟柱式大厅后壁左侧龙王本生
a. 1883 年伯吉斯调查绘制；b. 2001 年作者拍摄

Jātakas, No. 75[1]。

(7) 摩诃阇迦樊或大施本生 (Mahājanakajātaka),第 1 窟,参见 *The Jātakas,* No. 539[2]。

(8) 猿王本生 (Mahākapijātaka),第 17 窟,参见 *The Jātakas,* No. 407 和 516[3]。

(9) 须陀须摩或普明王本生 (Mahāsutasomajātaka/Sutasōma Jātaka),第 16 和 17 窟,参见 *The Jātakas,* No. 537[4]。

(10) 大隧道本生 (Mahāummaggajātaka),第 1 和 16 窟,参见 *The Jātakas,* No. 546[5]。

(11) 水牛本生 (Mahisajātaka),第 17 窟,参见 *The Jātakas,* No. 278[6]。

(12) 象王本生 (Mātiposakajātaka/Mātṛiposaka Jātaka),第 17 窟,参见 *The Jātakas,* No. 455[7]。

(13) 榕鹿本生 (Nigrodhamigajātaka/Nyagrōdha-mriga Jātaka),第 17 窟,参见 *The Jātakas,* No. 12[8]。

(14) 智慧鹿或鹿本生 (Rurujātaka/Mṛiga Jātaka),第 2 和 17 窟,参见 *The Jātakas,* No. 482[9]。

(15) 龙王本生 (Saṅkhapālajātaka/Saṁkhapāla Jātaka/Śaṅkhapāla Jātaka),第 1 窟,参见 *The Jātakas,* No. 524[10]。

---

[1] 1) E. B. Cowell ed., *opere citato,* Vol. I: 183-185; 2) G. Yazdani, *opere citato,* Part IV: 78-79, Plates XLIXa-La.

[2] 1) E. B. Cowell ed., *opere citato,* Vol. VI: 19-37; 2) G. Yazdani, *opere citato,* Part I: 15-26, Plates XII-XIII.

[3] 1) E. B. Cowell ed., *opere citato,* Vol. III: 225-227; Vol. V: 37-41; 2) G. Yazdani, *opere citato,* Part IV: 33-35, 53-54, Plates XIb, XIIc-e, XIIIa-b, XXIXa.

[4] 1) E. B. Cowell ed., *opere citato,* Vol. V: 246-279; 2) G. Yazdani, *opere citato,* Part III: 44-45, Pl. XLVIb; Part IV: 54-66, Plate XXVIIc-XXXVII.

[5] 1) E. B. Cowell ed., *opere citato,* Vol. VI: 156-246; 2) G. Yazdani, *opere citato,* Part I: 26, Plate XXIIIa; Part III: 47-49, Plates L-LI.

[6] 1) E. B. Cowell ed., *opere citato,* Vol. II: 262-263; 2) G. Yazdani, *opere citato,* Part IV: 81, Plate LIa.

[7] E. B. Cowell ed., *opere citato,* Vol. IV: 58-61.

[8] 1) E. B. Cowell ed., *opere citato,* Vol. I: 36-42; 2) G. Yazdani, *opere citato,* Part IV: 103-105, Plates Lb, LXIXc, LXXa-b.

[9] 1) E. B. Cowell ed., *opere citato,* Vol. IV: 161-166; 2) G. Yazdani, *opere citato,* Part IV: 100-102, Plates LXVIIIa-c.

[10] 1) E. B. Cowell ed., *opere citato,* Vol. V: 84-91; 2) G. Yazdani, *opere citato,* Part I: 13-14, Plate XI.

(16) 睒子本生 (Sāmajātaka/Śyāma Jātaka)，第 10 和 17 窟，参见 *The Jātakas,* No. 540[1]。

(17) 舍罗步鹿本生 (Sarabhamigajātaka/Sarabhāmiga Jātaka/Śarabha Jātaka)，第 17 窟，参见 *The Jātakas,* No. 483[2]。

(18) 尸毗王本生 (Sivijātaka/Śibi Jātaka)，第 1 窟和 17 窟，参见 *The Jātakas,* No. 499[3]。

(19) 云马本生 (Valāhassajātaka)，第 17 窟，参见 *The Jātakas,* No. 196[4]。

(20) 须大拏本生 (Vessantarajātaka/Viśvantara Jātaka)，第 17 窟，参见 *The Jātakas,* No. 547[5]。

(21) 贤者本生 (Vidhurapaṇḍitajātaka)，第 2 窟，参见 *The Jātakas,* No. 545[6]。

根据上述不完全统计，我们发现：阿旃陀大乘时期洞窟壁画，即从 5 世纪末叶开始，本生故事颇为流行。本生故事画面多采用连续构图，有时几幅本生合图一壁。为了分隔画面或情节，画家时常插入建筑、草木、花卉以及其他图案。需要说明的是，这些本生故事大多舍弃了印度早期雕刻，如珀鲁德 (Bhārhut)、桑吉 (Sāñcī) 和阿默拉沃蒂 (Amarāvatī) 等传统的"上画下记"之法，但在绘制罕见题材或自由表现主题时，往往于画像之下标记主体人物名字，以利辨识。如第 2 窟的羼提本生和第 17 窟的尸毗王本生。中国古代传统绘画中亦采纳"左榜右壁"之法，看来东方文化艺术在许多方面是相通的。

譬喻 (avadāna)，音译阿波陀那。欧美学者对于 avadāna 字义的解说，是以"行为" (karma) 或"英雄行为"为中心的；日本学者大多认为 avadāna 含有"譬喻"之意。因此可以说，avadāna 特重"行为"与"譬喻"两种涵义，即以譬喻宣说法义。阿旃陀现存的譬喻故事，可以确定的仅有两种，分别为：

---

[1] 1) E. B. Cowell ed., *opere citato,* Vol. VI: 38-52; 2) G. Yazdani, *opere citato,* Part III: 29-30, Plates XXVIIIb-XXIXb; Part IV: 79-80, Plate XLIXb.

[2] 1) E. B. Cowell ed., *opere citato,* Vol. IV: 166-174; 2) G. Yazdani, *opere citato,* Part IV: 73-76, Plates XLIV-XLVI.

[3] 1) E. B. Cowell ed., *opere citato,* Vol. IV: 250-256; 2) G. Yazdani, *opere citato,* Part I: 4-7, Plate V; Part IV: 96-99, Plates LXVc-LXVII.

[4] E. B. Cowell ed., *opere citato,* Vol. II: 89-91.

[5] 1) E. B. Cowell ed., *opere citato,* Vol. VI: 246-305; 2) G. Yazdani, *opere citato,* Part IV: 43-52, Plates XIX-XXVI.

[6] 1) E. B. Cowell ed., *opere citato,* Vol. VI: 126-156; 2) G. Yazdani, *opere citato,* Part II: 36-45, Plates XXXV-XLI.

(1) 富楼那因缘 (Pūrṇa-avadāna)，现存第 2 窟，故事内容参见 E. B. Cowell 和 R. A. Neil 编辑的 *Divyāvadāna*[1]。

(2) 狮子国因缘 (Siṃhalāvadāna)，第 17 窟（图 27），参见 *Divyāvadāna*[2]。

图 27　阿旃陀第 17 窟柱式大厅左侧壁狮子国因缘

2. 佛传

佛传乃佛陀一生的事迹。阿旃陀的佛传故事画，可分作早、晚两个阶段。早期佛传似仅见于第 10 窟左壁。该壁画题材以前被称作“皇室过城门”和“礼拜佛塔”[3]。不过，德国学者施林洛甫 (D. Schlingloff) 近年把它重新考定为巨幅“佛传”[4]，唯画面中仍循奉早期以象征物表现佛陀之习俗，在风格上与珀鲁德和桑吉雕刻相似。从

[1] 1) E. B. Cowell and R. A. Neil ed., *Divyāvadāna,* Cambridge: Cambridge University Press, 1886: 24; 2) G. Yazdani, *opere citato,* Part II: 45-49, Plate XLII.

[2] 1) E. B. Cowell and R. A. Neil ed., *opere citato*: 523-528; 2) G. Yazdani, *opere citato,* Part IV: 82-95, Plates LIb-LXIVa.

[3] G. Yazdani, *opere citato,* Part III: 27-29, Plates XXIVb, XXVIIIa, XXIVc.

[4] Dieter Schlingloff, *Studies in the Ajanta Paintings: Identifications and Interpretations,* Delhi: Ajanta Publications (India), 1987: 1-13.

阿旃陀石窟早期壁画中，我们不难看出：印度当时的绘画水平已达到相当高度，绘画方法及技巧臻于完善。阿旃陀现存壁画，是那些受过高级艺术训练的画师所作，代表了印度古老而伟大的传承。画家和匠师当时丝毫不受隐蔽崖穴之障隔，对人生和现实生活皆有充分的体验。这在壁画的题材和内容上反映得一清二楚。

大乘时期的佛传壁画，与同内容的雕刻相辅相成，互有补充。由于故事情节在石雕上展开多有局限，阿旃陀的画师和工匠以画笔和五彩缤纷的颜色将那些有益教化的佛传故事尽情地图绘于窟壁之上。现存第16和17窟的壁画，可以作为此时佛传绘画的代表。以第16窟的佛传为例，该窟壁画以传统的"叙事风格"向我们展示了佛传中的许多情景，从中央柱式大厅左壁前端起经正壁至右壁前端止，画面依次为：摩耶夫人临梦、阿私陀占相、悉达多上学、太子试艺、出游四门、乳女奉糜、初转法轮、阿阇世拜佛、说法图、人间佛、难陀皈依、孙陀利临终等。此外，在前庭右壁尚保存有三十三天说法[1]。据我们调查，阿旃陀现存大乘时期佛传壁画较为重要的情节有：

(1) 降魔成道

作为佛传中一极为重要的情节，阿旃陀石窟的雕刻家和画师对佛陀降魔之相多有表现。这与印度本土当时流行的四相和八相图的刻画，应有某种必然联系。如第1窟的降魔成道（图28），画面中，佛居中结跏趺坐，瞑然静虑；围绕其左右的群魔，异形怪貌，纷来惊扰；佛前之魔女，妖媚诱惑，姿态极妍[2]。

(2) 鹿野苑初转法轮

该题材既为供养人及信徒喜爱，也倍受阿旃陀雕刻家和画师青睐。以第17窟的初转法轮为例，画面中佛居中结跏趺坐，罗汉、天人、王公贵族和大众信徒环绕左右，完全是一幅活生生的佛教法会。

(3) 忉利天说法

画面中展示了佛陀在三十三天，即忉利天为母说法和自三十三天降下两个情景，表现了天上和人间两种截然不同的境界。

(4) 舍卫城神变

这个在犍陀罗和阿默拉沃蒂颇为流行的雕刻题材，在阿旃陀石窟壁画中也得以进一步表现。佛的化身，在主尊上下有序、左右成列地被绘画出来，对信徒产生强大的震撼。

---

[1] V. V. Mirashi, ed., *opere citato*: LXVI-LXIX.

[2] 冉云华《试论敦煌与阿旃陀的〈降魔变〉》，见《敦煌石窟研究国际讨论会文集：石窟艺术》，沈阳：辽宁美术出版社，1991年，第194-206页。

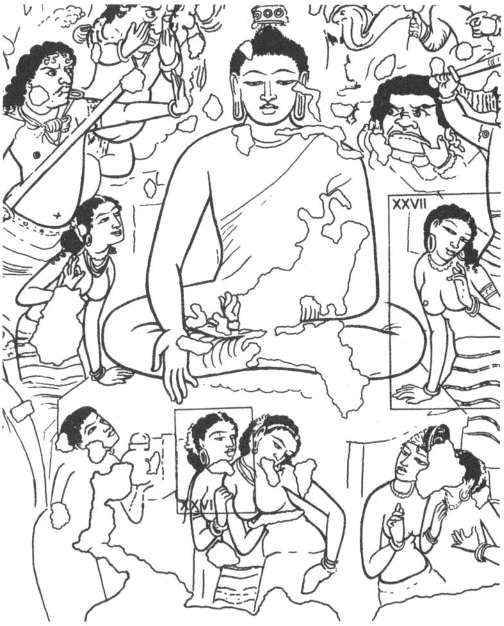

a

b

图 28　阿旃陀第 1 窟佛殿前室右壁降魔变
a. 1967 年线描图；b. 2001 年现场拍摄照片

(5) 佛与妻儿相会

第 16 窟所绘佛与耶输陀罗及罗喉罗相会，构图和技法颇为优雅，可惜原画业已破坏。

(6) 难陀出家

第 17 窟前廊所绘难陀出家场景，表现一黑肤王子正与妻子极尽燕婉之情。旁边侍女，有的捧杯侍奉，有的临窗窥看，还有的自门外张盖而来，完全是现实生活的再现。

3. 佛与菩萨像

除佛传之外，阿旃陀大乘时期开凿的洞窟中亦出现了单体佛像、七佛(图29)和千佛等。其中，第2窟佛殿前廊后壁门道右侧的千佛壁画(图30)，每排佛像头上方皆有墨书题记，应记述千佛(Buddhāsahasa)供养，年代可定在6世纪，惜字迹皆漶漫不清[1]。这种千佛题名作法，与新疆和甘肃石窟中的千佛壁画及其题名应有一定联系。同雕刻一样，这时的有些菩萨已改变原有身份，从佛的胁侍中分离出来并单独绘画，如第1窟佛殿前廊门道两侧著名的拈花菩萨和观音菩萨(图31)。

图29　阿旃陀第17窟中央门道上部雕刻及绘画

图30　阿旃陀第2窟佛殿前廊右侧壁及后壁千佛壁画

---

[1] 1) John Allan, "A Note on the Inscriptions of Cave II", in: *Ajanta: The colour and monochrome reproductions of the Ajanta frescoes based on photography,* ed. G. Yazdani, London: Oxford University Press, 1930-1955, 4 parts, Part II, Appendix: 57-65, esp. 64; 2) M. N. Deshpande, "The (Ajanta) Murals: Their Theme & Content", in: *Ajanta Murals,* ed. A. Ghose, New Delhi: Archaeological Survey of India, 1967: 35-39, esp. 39.

a

b

图 31　阿旃陀第 1 窟佛殿前廊门道两侧，即柱式大厅后壁壁画
a. 拈花菩萨；b. 观音菩萨

4. 天人

阿旃陀石窟侧壁和窟顶所绘翱翔于天国之中的天神，如紧那罗、乾达婆和持明仙等，是日益增长的大乘佛教信条——延续佛教乐土的一种反映。飞天造型及天国构图，较之石雕的同一内容，更加丰富多彩，充分展示了画家当时非凡的艺术想象与创造力。

5. 轮回图

在阿旃陀第 17 窟前廊右壁，残存一幅轮回图。残轮为两只大手扶持，当初完整时应有 8 个轮辐。这轮辐，应是印度庄严独特的哲学命题——四有轮或因果轮回的完美图示。每一轮辐间皆描绘出生活的不同方面，可辨识的有：神猴、大象、豪宅、民舍、花园、市场以及陶瓷作坊等。整个画面表现生命之体，一直处在循环不息的轮回之中（图 32）。中国新疆龟兹和四川大足石窟中绘有与之相似的题材，这或许透视出中印石窟渊源关系的一个侧面。

a

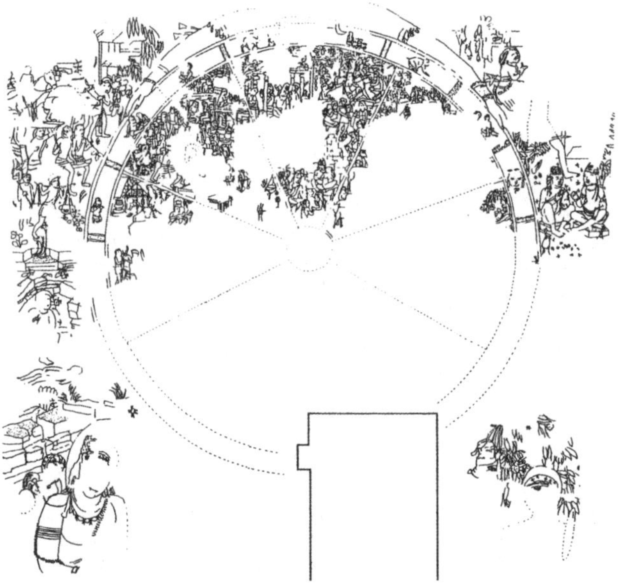

b

图 32　阿旃陀第 17 窟前廊右侧壁轮回图

6. 世俗生活

虽然阿旃陀壁画大多表现的是佛教题材，但有些画面却真实地反映出印度当时的社会状况。换言之，尽管阿旃陀壁画性质是宗教的，但画面本身却充满了人间情趣。不论是佛前世种种善行的刻画，还是现世的诞生、成长、出家、成道、游说以及涅槃和分舍利等的图绘，都或多或少地表现出宫廷之豪华、山林之美妙、田园之秀丽以及战争之残酷等，折射出印度当时物质和精神生活之面貌。

此外，第 1 窟所画波斯使节朝献图，虽已残损，但仍不失原风貌。画面中，波斯使节坐于画面中央偏左，擎杯豪饮，醉意朦胧；一女侍抚肩软语，似在劝饮；两抱瓶者轮番把斟，两持果盘者座前服侍。整个酒宴图，真实地展现了饮酒人醺然欲醉之态（图 33）。关于此图中的主角，多数学者推测为波斯国王库思老 (Khosrau Parviz, 591-628 年）所派朝献摩诃剌陀国王普拉勒辛二世 (Pulalesin II) 的使臣，但也有的学者，如法国学者傅塞 (A. Foucher)，认为表现的是财神般遮迦。不管怎么说，本图在庄严的宗教气氛中，添加了不少生活情趣。

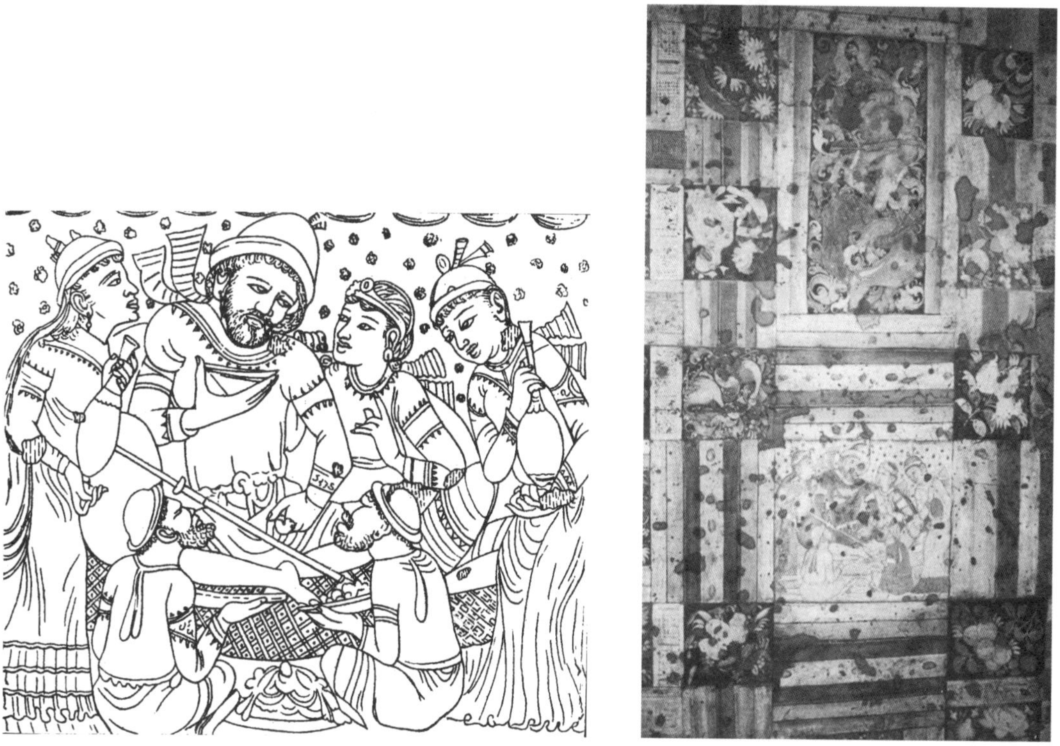

a　　　　b

图 33　阿旃陀第 1 窟柱式大厅顶部壁画
a. 1883 年伯吉斯调查绘制；b. 2001 年作者拍摄

7. 装饰图案

阿旃陀壁画中的装饰性题材，尤其是僧坊窟顶部的壁画，极为繁复，包括花草、几何图形、禽鸟以及神话等。画面中绘有嬉戏的鸟儿、角力的水牛、打斗的公鸡等图景，充分反映出当时画家对现实生活的敏锐观察。特别是第 1、2 窟前廊、天井和列柱所画人像与建筑相配合之图案，画家以写实之意匠，着丰富之色彩，堪称印度古代装饰艺术的代表（图 34）。第 2 窟药叉龛顶部所绘 23 只呈人字形飞翔的大雁，

图 34　阿旃陀第 2 窟前廊顶部装饰图案

只只栩栩如生，更是画家对大自然的真实写照。至于许多平棋图案中的斗四构图，在中国敦煌石窟中可以发现极为相似的“经营”。

1991 年 12 月 16 日第一次游历阿旃陀，深为这处世界文化遗产所震撼。后来因为学习和研究印度石窟寺，又曾几次前往这处著名的佛教艺术圣地。2000 年 12 月中旬参加新德里英迪拉·甘地国立艺术中心举办的“新疆的艺术与宗教国际学术研讨会”后，在印度考古调查局副局长 R. C. Agrawal 博士的周到安排下，笔者再次对西印度石窟群进行了系统调查与记录，前后历时一个半月。其间，于 2001 年 1 月 2-7 日在阿旃陀石窟考察，并借住阿旃陀石窟保管所内部客房，每天与该所职工一道上下班。这次整理佛教考古书稿，先把有关阿旃陀记录的一部分梳理出来，请同好指正。

二、龟兹石窟：

西域传法

克孜尔中心柱窟主室正壁画塑题材及有关问题

一、引　　言

克孜尔中心柱窟主室正壁，由于龛内主尊早已不存，龛外上部及两侧浮雕大多残毁，因而自20世纪初以来，学者一般依据现存遗迹把它定为龛内塑坐佛、龛外影塑菱形山峦的"说法图像"。不过，也有的学者进一步把它推测为"帝释窟说法"，其代表人物有德国的格林威德尔(A. Grünwedel)、美国的索伯(A. C. Soper)和中国的姚士宏。

1905年12月至1907年4月，德国柏林人种学博物馆的格林威德尔教授率领普鲁士第三次考察队对古代龟兹、焉耆和高昌的佛寺遗址进行了全面的学术调查，并于1912年在柏林出版了由格林威德尔撰写的考察报告《新疆的古代佛寺》(*Altbuddhistische Kultstätten in Chinesisch-Turkistan*)。该书第37至181页，详细记录了1906年2月26日至5月14日德国学者对克孜尔石窟的洞窟形制、壁画题材及保存状况等的详细调查。格林威德尔认为：克孜尔部分洞窟[1]主室正壁残存的许多小木桩或木桩孔，原来曾以其为芯按菱形有规律地塑出各种色彩的山峦；山峦之间塑有神像、禅定像和各种禽兽，但现皆已脱落不见，唯正壁龛外两侧有的尚存释提桓因(Indra)[2]与般遮翼(Pañcasikha)[3]形象。根据这些遗迹，格林威德尔推

---

[1] 格林威德尔所指洞窟包括Höhlengruppe mit dem Kamin A（现编第4窟）、Höhle mit dem Musikerchor（现编第38窟）、Kāśyapa-Höhle（现编第63窟）、Höllentopf-Höhle（现编第80窟）、Höhle "mit der Äffin"（现编第92窟）、Höhle "mit den ringtragenden Tauben"（现编第123窟）、Nāgarājahöhle（现编第193窟）、Ajātaśatru-Höhle（现编第219窟）、Höhle der Maler（现编第207窟）、Höhle mit der Fußwaschung（编第206窟）、Māyāhöhle der 3 Anlage（现编第224窟）等。

[2] 一译帝释、帝释天、天帝释等，亦作Śakra. 汉文"释提桓因"似译自犍陀罗语Śakra-devaṇa iṃtra/Śakra devana iṃdra。

[3] 一译天乐般遮、般遮迦、五髻乾达婆等。

测：克孜尔石窟主室正壁中央是帝释窟（Indraśailaguhâ），窟内塑佛像；周围布满峰峦，峰峦间插塑天神、禅师和禽鸟等[1]。

20世纪40年代末、50年代初，美国东方艺术史学家索伯在《亚洲艺术》(*Artibus Asiae*)上分三期连载了他撰写的《犍陀罗雕刻中之光明象征》(Aspects of Light Symbolism in Gandhāran Sculpture)。全文分"造访"碑、佛与太阳神、影窟、英雄与蛇神、窟中熟睡之英雄、黑暗中之光芒、燃灯佛授记、夜半逾城及补遗等九个子目[2]。虽然索伯赞同格林威德尔对克孜尔部分洞窟主室正壁画塑题材的考证，但却用较长篇幅探讨了犍陀罗地区这一雕刻题材的象征意义及其与西方文化艺术之关系[3]。

20世纪80年代，时任克孜尔石窟文物保管所所长的姚士宏，专门论述了克孜尔石窟部分洞窟主室正壁的塑画题材。姚士宏认为：弄清克孜尔部分洞窟主室正壁的画塑题材，"对我们认识龟兹佛教及其艺术不无意义。然而，这一值得重视的问题，迄今为止尚无定说，有必要加以专门讨论。鉴于龛外浮塑菱形山峦部分，本身就比较简单，加之多已脱落，目前仅存固定菱形山峦的木橛孔，缺乏据以探讨的资料；而龛外绘画部分，幸有不少保存下来。因此，本文着重就这部分做些考释"[4]。经过现场调查，姚士宏确定克孜尔石窟有20座洞窟涉及此题材，并选取了其中的11座洞窟做了详细的记录。最后认为上述洞窟主室正壁"是采取塑绘结合的手法，即以龛内塑像为主，以龛外壁画作补充，表现了一个完整的佛传题材——佛为帝释宣说正法"[5]。遗憾的是，限于种种客观原因，该文作者未能注意到域外的同一内容雕刻。

笔者依据留学时对印度佛教遗迹所做的系统调查和在新疆克孜尔石窟前后四次近七个月的考察记录，完全同意上述学者关于该题材的推论，同时拟对克孜尔石窟主室正壁画塑题材之源流及有关问题做进一步探讨。

---

[1] Albert Grünwedel, *Altbuddhistische Kultstätten in Chinesisch-Turkistan*: *Bericht über archäologische Arbeiten von 1906 bis 1907 bei Kuča, Qarašahr und in der oase Turfan;* Königlich Preussische Turfan-Expeditionen, Berlin: Druck und Verlag von Georg Reimer, 1912: 44, 63, 80, 99, 101, 121, 131, 145, 150, 158, 174.

[2] 九个子目依次为：The "Visit" Stele, The Buddha and Mithra, The Cave of the Shadow, Hero and Serpent God, The Hero Asleep in a Cave, The Light Shining in the Darkness, The Dīpaṃkara Buddha Motif, The Midnight Departure and Addendum.

[3] A. C. Soper, "Aspects of Light Symbolism in Gandhāran Sculpture", in: *Artibus Asiae,* 1949, XII (3): 252-283; (4): 314-330; 1950, XIII (1/2): 63-85.

[4] 姚士宏《克孜尔石窟部分洞窟主室正壁塑绘题材》，载新疆维吾尔自治区文物管理委员会、拜城县克孜尔千佛洞文物保管所、北京大学考古系编《中国石窟·克孜尔石窟》三，北京：文物出版社，1997年，第178页。

[5] 姚士宏，上引书，第179-181页。

二、帝释窟图像

帝释窟这一题材,内容大体如下:释提桓因获悉佛在摩竭陀国奄婆罗村北毗陀山因陀沙罗窟入火焰三昧,与般遮翼及其他诸天前往。释提桓因把四十二件疑难事情画在石头上向佛询问,后者给他们做了解释。关于这个传说,现存巴利语经藏《长尼迦耶》(*Dīghanikāya*)[1]中的《帝释所问经》(*Sakka-pañha suttanta*)[2],梵语[3]和汉译佛典《长阿含经·释提桓因问经》[4]、《中阿含经·释问经》[5]、《佛说帝释所问经》[6]、《杂宝藏经·帝释问事缘》[7],以及《法显传》[8]和玄奘《大唐西域记》[9]等都有详略不同的记载。

1. 印度本土

据目前掌握的资料,现存最早的帝释窟图像,是印度帕鲁特大塔周围建于公元前2世纪栏楯上的一幅浮雕(参见文后所附《印度和巴基斯坦所见帝释窟雕刻统计表》,下文简称《统计表》,第1号)。这件浮雕曾一度被人用作伯丹马拉(Batanmāra)纪念碑框缘,凿掉了圆形浮雕的两边,唯中央部分保存完好,现藏于加尔各答印度博物馆。1879年,英国人坎宁安(Alexander Cunningham)在撰写《帕鲁特大塔》时,曾注意到画面上方与之同时镌刻的婆罗米字母题铭,把它用拉丁字母转写为 Ida Sâla

---

[1]《长尼迦耶》系巴利语五部《尼迦耶(Nikāya)》之一。据研究,尼迦耶原意是集合体、类或部。上座部将巴利语经藏(Suttapiṭaka)称作"尼迦耶",意思是"佛陀言论汇编"。阿含(Āgama,或译阿笈摩)意指传承的经典或圣典,说一切有部等部派佛教用它指称经藏。阿含原是印度传统用语,耆那教和婆罗门教也用它指称自己的一些经典。在巴利语佛典中,有时也用阿含指称经藏。因此,在佛教范围内,完全可以把尼迦耶和阿含视为同义词。参见郭良鋆《佛陀和原始佛教思想》,北京:中国社会科学出版社,1997年,第7页。

[2]参见 T. W. Rhys Davids and J. Estlin Carpenter, ed., *The Dīgha Nikāya*, Vol. II, London: Oxford University Press, 1903: 263-289. 英文译本见 T. W. and C. A. F. Rhys Davids, tr., *Dialogues of the Buddha*, Vol. II, London: Oxford University Press, 1910: 299-321.

[3] 20世纪初德国格林威德尔和勒考克(A. von Le Coq)率领的新疆考察队曾携回数量庞大的梵语《阿含经》残本,其中就包括《释提桓因问经》。详见后述。

[4]《大正藏》第1卷,第62b-66a页。

[5]《大正藏》第1卷,第632c-638c页。

[6]《大正藏》第1卷,第246b-250c页。据吕澂先生研究,该经系出自《中阿含经》卷三十三《释问经》。参见吕澂《新编汉文大藏经目录》,济南:齐鲁书社,1980年,第45页。

[7]《大正藏》第4卷,第476a-478b页。

[8]法显《法显传》,章巽校注,上海:上海古籍出版社,1985年,第111页。

[9]玄奘《大唐西域记》,季羡林等校注,北京:中华书局,1985年,第769页。

guha，并译作 The Cave Hall of Indra[1]；德国教授路得施(Heinrich Lüders，一译吕德斯)转写为 Idasālaguha，迻译 The Idasāla (Indraśāla) cave[2]；印度学者伯鲁阿(Benimadhab Barua)转写作 Iṁdasāla-guhā，译为 The Indraśāla-cave[3]；上述迻录皆可汉译"帝释窟"。依据铭文并参考巴利语文献及法显和玄奘的记载，坎宁安辨识出释提桓因的琴师——般遮翼被雕刻在圆形浮雕的左侧，手持箜篌（琉璃琴）；浮雕中部的坐像，应是释提桓因及其侍从。由于佛在帕鲁特雕刻中尚未以人格化形式出现，所以他的存在是通过伞盖下的空座表示的。窟上的层叠岩壁，表现的是毗陀山；整个浮雕，刻画的是帝释窟情景[4]。坎宁安对这一雕刻题材的考释，在学术上具有重要的贡献，后来发现的大量同一内容雕刻之考证，在某种意义上应归功于他的研究成果。

至于画面中可辨识的其他细部还有：佛座表面刻出若干花卉纹饰，两花环自伞盖边缘垂下；释提桓因[5]及其他天神在佛座前结跏趺坐，双手合十；般遮翼形体大部残毁，但所持琉璃琴的前半部尚清晰可见；窟内地面岩石错落有致，唯窟壁磨光；窟上方刻出一棵大树[6]，两只猴子面对面坐在岩石之上，两头大熊正从洞穴中微微探出头来。雕刻家或工匠当时意欲表现猴子在山中尽情窜上跳下，野熊随意钻进爬出之情景（图 1）[7]，这与文献记载完全切合。

大约半个世纪之后，即公元前 100 年左右，佛陀伽耶大塔栏楯也出现了这一题材。在该地发现的一根望柱顶部的浮雕（参见《统计表》第 2 号）之中，我们看到：帝释窟显系人工雕造而成，外面加凿踏道和栏楯，窟右侧刻出一棵大树。释提桓因在浮雕中没有出现，也许他还没有到达；但般遮翼则如上件浮雕一样，呈立姿雕在窟

[1] A. Cunningham, *The Stūpa of Bhārhut: A Buddhist Monument ornamented with numerous sculptures illustrated of Buddhist legend and history in the third century B. C.*, London: W. H. Allen & Co., 1879: 138, Plates XXVIII, LV.

[2] 1) H. Lüders, "A List of Brāhmī Inscriptions from the Earliest Times to about A.D. 400 with the Exception of those of Aśōka", in: *Epigraphia Indica,* Volume X (1909-10), Appendix, Calcutta: Superintendent Government Printing, 1912: No. 805; 2) H. Lüders ed., *Bharhut Inscriptions,* revised by E. Waldschmidt and M. A. Mehendale, New Delhi: Archaeological Survey of India, 1963: 109-110, Plates XIX, XL B35.

[3] B. Barua, *Barhut,* Book II: *Jātaka-scenes,* rep., Patna: Indological Book Corporation, 1979: 55, Plate LIV.

[4] A. Cunningham, *opere citato*: 88-89. See H. Lüders ed., *opere citato*: 109-110.

[5] 库马拉斯瓦米 (A. K. Coomaraswamy) 曾怀疑圆形浮雕残失的右边，原来可能刻画天帝释，或者他坐于佛座前的朝拜者当中。当然，也不排除整个圆形浮雕并未表现天帝释，就像佛陀伽耶的浮雕所示。如果说佛座前的信徒中有天帝释的话，他应是背向观众的那身。参见 A. K. Coomaraswamy, "Early Indian Iconography: I. Indra, with special reference to 'Indra's Visit'", in: *Eastern Art,* 1928, I (1): 35.

[6] 帝释窟上方所雕大树，与佛音对"帝释窟"的诠释完全相符，参见本文 127 页注[2]。

[7] B. Barua, *opere citato*: 55-56.

右侧,头顶发髻卷曲,披发至肩,袒上身,下着裙,左手执琉璃琴,右手上举作弹拨状。佛同前件浮雕,以空座表示,唯顶部伞盖不见。这或许是该题材最简朴的表现形式[1]。

图 1 帕鲁德大塔栏楯浮雕帝释窟

桑吉大塔现存栏楯浮雕,可定在公元前100年至公元前50年左右,表现的帝释窟题材共有两幅[2]。其中,大塔北门左柱顶部内侧的浮雕(参见《统计表》第3号)可作代表。浮雕分上下两部分,帝释窟雕于上半部中央,外立面作太阳拱形,与同时期塔庙窟外立面的造型接近;而表示佛陀之空座,明显雕置于窟外。岩石与动物之刻画,与前述浮雕大体相似,唯岩石表面呈锯齿状,顶部放射出火焰光芒。传说这种光是由于释提桓因及其他诸天莅临所致[3]。至于动物形象,窟左侧裂缝处雕刻两只人面山羊,右侧为两只半狮半狗之怪兽[4]。下半部所刻十身立像分为两排,其中上排中央面向帝释窟者应为释提桓因,左边束高髻、袒上身、下着裙、持琉璃琴者无疑是般遮翼;其余人物应是释提桓因之随从。

以上所述浮雕,皆属佛陀尚以象征物表现的时期。大约又过了100年左右,即公元1世纪后半,以人格化形式表现的帝释窟,开始出现在秣菟罗雕刻之中,稍后亦见于犍陀罗,并逐渐成为秣菟罗和犍陀罗雕刻家特别喜爱的题材[5]。尤其是在前者为数不多的佛传图中,只这一题材的雕刻就有6件;不过,其构图与布局基本沿袭早

[1] A. C. Soper, *opere citato,* XII (3): 256.

[2] John Marshall and Alfred Foucher, *The Monuments of Sāñchī,* Calcutta: Archaeological Survey of India, 1940: 218, Plates 35b1, 64a3.

[3] A. K. Coomaraswamy, *opere citato*: 37.

[4] James Fergusson, *Tree and Serpent Worship*: or *Illustrations of Mythology and Art in India in the first and fourth centuries after Christ from the Sculptures of the Buddhist Topes at Sanchi and Amravati,* London: Indian Office, 1873: 124.

[5] 参见:1) 高田修《佛像の起源》,東京:岩波書店,1967 年,第 359 页;2) J. Ph. Vogel, *Catalogue of the Archaeological Museum at Mathurā,* Allahabad,1910:166.

期的传统形式。为便于了解该题材在印度本土发展的全貌，现分述如下：

秣菟罗博物馆收藏的一根陀兰那（toraṇa，塔门）横梁具有极为重要的价值（参见《统计表》第 5 号），因为它是佛教从象征物向偶像刻画过渡的真实反映（图 2a）。换言之，这件浮雕应是迄今所见秣菟罗雕刻家创作的最早的一件出现佛陀的帝释窟，时间可定在 1 世纪末 2 世纪初。横梁的正面，分别刻出佛塔、菩提殿和狮驮法轮以及其他人物；背面中央雕出帝释窟，窟内为人格化佛像。同早期雕刻一样，帝释窟右侧是束高髻、袒上身、下着裙、左手持琉璃琴的般遮翼，般遮翼之后为六身手持花环的女性天神；窟左侧是头戴高冠、袒上身、下着裙、双手合十作礼拜状的释提桓因及其天妃与坐骑——大象。值得注意的是，帝释窟上下左右皆不见动物，唯岩石雕刻富于层理，帝释窟似自然洞穴（图 2b）。

秣菟罗博物馆收藏的一件奉献塔（参见《统计表》第 7 号），原出土于秣菟罗的特拉夫·蒂拉（Dhruv Ṭīlā）遗址，时间也为 1 世纪末 2 世纪初。塔身表面所雕佛传场面颇多，有诞生、灌顶、成道、四天王奉钵、初转法轮、帝释窟、三十三天降下等[1]。其中，帝释窟的形制及其外观、释提桓因和般遮翼的位置及造型，与前述秣菟罗的帝释窟雕刻基本相同。

加尔各答印度博物馆所藏另一件帝释窟浮雕（参见《统计表》第 10 号），原出土于秣菟罗的杰马勒布尔（Jamalpur）。该浮雕的构图，与图 2 所示相似，唯窟外岩石多作数列菱形及少量不规则几何形。窟上方刻出一匹狼和一只孔雀，窟下雕镌一头龟缩于巢穴之中、正探头观望的大熊或野猪。般遮翼与释提桓因的位置，较前述浮雕中二者的经营相反，即佛陀左侧为般遮翼[2]，右侧是释提桓因及其侍从和坐骑，人物姿态同前者（图 3）。

秣菟罗出土的另一件浮雕（参见《统计表》第 8 号），原为巴黎的罗森堡（M. L. Rosenberg）收藏，系一根横梁残件。横梁上的浮雕，构图严格遵循旧式。帝释窟系人工雕造，边缘整齐光滑，但窟外岩石则多与前件浮雕相似，刻作三角形、菱形和其他几何形状。窟外上方岩石之中有金刚手和孔雀（？），窟下有野熊龟缩于巢穴之内。窟内佛陀作禅定印，佛左侧的释提桓因，头戴高冠、袒上身、下着裙，双手合十作拜谒状；右侧人物已残毁。

此外，勒克瑙（Lucknow）博物馆和秣菟罗博物馆各自收藏的一件建筑构件，表现

[1] R. C. Sharma, *Buddhist Art: Mathurā School,* New Delhi: Wiley Eastern Limited & New Age International Limited, 1995: 243, Plates 169-170. 不过，该书作者认为：这件塔身和上件横梁的年代应定在公元 1 世纪。

[2] 浮雕中的般遮翼已残损，但所持琉璃琴尚清晰可见。

a

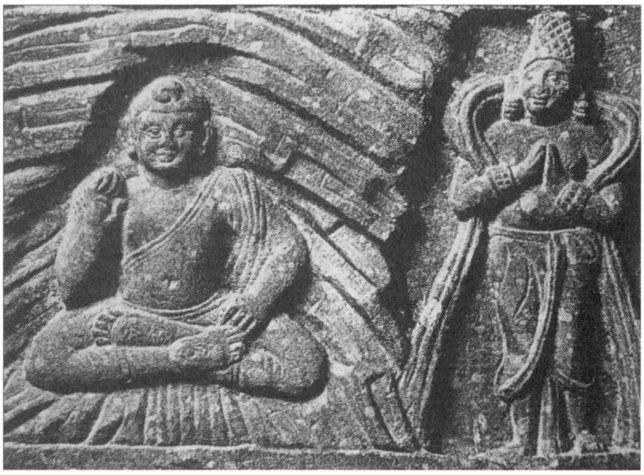

b

图2　秣菟罗博物馆藏陀兰纳(塔门)横梁浮雕佛传
a. 全景；b. 横梁背面中央帝释窟局部

的是多情节的佛传，时代应为贵霜后期。其中帝释窟这一内容，布局及构图与前两件浮雕接近。以后者为例，该横梁（参见《统计表》第9号）原出土于秣菟罗，帝释窟的造型与图3所示非常相似。佛于帝释窟居中而坐，窟外两侧菱形或三角形岩石上各雕出一熊或狮子头部，窟顶上方镌刻一只孔雀。窟左侧上部残存一头大象，应为帝释天坐骑；下部残留三身交脚坐像，其中靠近窟口者，应为帝释天。窟右侧共有五身立像，其中靠近窟口者应是般遮翼[1]。帝释窟顶部正中圆拱龛内，雕出悉达

[1] 1) J. Ph. Vogel, *opere citato*: 130, pl. vib; 2) J. Ph. Vogel, *La sculpture de Mathurā*, Paris et Bruxelles: Les Editions G. van Oest, 1930: 58-59.

图3　加尔各答印度博物馆藏帝释窟浮雕

多肉髻 (uṣṇīṣa of Siddhārtha) 或顶髻筵 (cūḍā-maha，即太子头巾)，其两侧龛内之天神均面向顶髻朝拜 (图 4)。由此看出，帝释窟题材在早期佛传雕刻中占据重要位置，其他佛传情节皆围绕中央帝释窟经营。这从另一方面反映出，当时僧俗极为青睐这一题材；这也是帝释窟浮雕出土数量如此之多的主要原因。至于勒克瑙博物馆收藏的那件帝释窟浮雕 (参见《统计表》第 6 号)，几乎是图 4 的复制品，唯窟顶的孔雀雕在了窟右侧下方，左侧的野熊换成了小鹿或山羊。般遮翼的琉璃琴尚见局部。

2. 犍陀罗

作为贵霜王朝的中心区域，犍陀罗出现佛像大约在公元 1 世纪；它是在信徒接受了创作偶像思想的基础上，受希腊罗马造型艺术影响的结果。现存帝释窟浮雕，最

图 4　秣菟罗博物馆藏建筑构件上的帝释窟浮雕

早者可以定在1世纪末2世纪初[1],2世纪后半到3世纪前半达到高峰。遗存至今的作品,据笔者不完全统计,达23件之多(参见《统计表》第12至34号)。依据构图与布局,这些浮雕大体可以分作两种类型。

A型：构图与佛陀伽耶望柱顶部的帝释窟相似,繁简不一。复杂者,佛坐于帝释窟之中,窟边缘刻出火焰纹,窟顶上方雕出鹿或羊,窟下巢穴中雕出熊、狮、野猪等。般遮翼和释提桓因及其侍从皆雕在窟右侧。般遮翼头顶作多卷发髻,袒上身,下着裙,左手持琉璃琴(图5),如《统计表》第12至15号。

图5　拉合尔博物馆藏锡克里佛塔塔身饰板上的帝释窟

B型：帝释窟位于浮雕中央,佛居窟内而坐,般遮翼和释提桓因分雕窟外两侧,可分二式。

Bi式：佛多坐于窟内正中方座上,"入火焰三昧",窟壁边缘刻出火焰。大多数佛座或窟下雕出狮子、野猪、熊及其巢穴,窟左右和其顶部尚雕出丛林及生活其中的鹿、野羊、猴子、孔雀以及其他动物和禽鸟。这些动物和禽鸟在此不仅表示故事发生场景之荒凉,而且象征众

[1] 索伯认为帝释窟题材在犍陀罗雕刻出现的时间为2世纪后半,且主要承袭印度本土传统。参见：A. C. Soper, *opere citato,* XII (3): 253-254.

生在佛陀面前皆安宁祥和。头戴高冠的释提桓因从左侧恭敬地走向佛陀，双手合十作朝拜状；般遮翼与释提桓因相对，立于佛右侧，左手持琉璃琴。复杂者，尚于窟左右及顶部雕出其他人物及向佛礼敬、散花之天神（图 6），如《统计表》第 16-28 号等。

图 6　加尔各答印度博物馆藏帝释窟浮雕

Bii 式：构图与 Bi 式接近，佛多坐于窟内地面上，手作禅定印。佛座或窟下雕出一排人像，多为般遮翼和释提桓因的随从，有时释提桓因以其坐骑替代；少数是过去七佛和弥勒菩萨。窟外四周被隔成若干长条形，其内雕出若干小像。窟顶部多刻丛林、山石及活跃其中的孔雀、鹿、羊、野猪、狮子、熊以及其他人物（图 7），如《统计表》第 29-34 号等。

从上述分类我们可以看出：犍陀罗帝释窟雕刻，尤其是完成于 2 世纪后半叶的 Bi 式帝释窟，布局和构图与秣菟罗的帝释窟浮雕有密切关系；只是犍陀罗雕刻家和工匠进一步发展了印度本土雕刻，生动地表现出故事细节，如释提桓因的坐骑和坐在岩石中守护佛主的金刚手以及背景所雕刻的岩石、树木、禽鸟和野兽等。帝释窟浮雕在印度本土不过是一幅展现山水、花鸟、动物和人类生活的典型卷轴，佛周围所泛动的微光，具有强烈的动感。犍陀罗的雕刻家和工匠，由于缺少印度人那种天赋，只能以类似的视点和方法来解决这一问题。虽然犍陀罗流行“帝释窟”，但我们通常很难解释他们为何偏重这一题材。不过，这种展现印度古老的超级神祇——释提桓因来到新宗教创始者面前的谦恭之会，对于佛教的传播具有显著的推动作用。尽管帝释窟故事没有纳入标准的巴利语和梵语佛传之中，但却出现在其他经典里，甚至以单本经形式流传。帝释所问和佛陀所答，补充了正统的教说[1]。而在 Bi 式基础上演进的 Bii 式，时代多在 3 世纪前半，应是后期帝释窟雕刻的代表。

---

[1] A. C. Soper, *opere citato*: 258.

a

b

图 7　白沙瓦博物馆藏帝释窟浮雕

a. 全景；b. 局部

3. 龟兹石窟

克孜尔中心柱窟主室正壁，从构图和布局来看，也可以大体分作两种类型：

A 型：正壁中央开一圆拱形大龛。从现存遗迹看，龛内原塑坐佛，龛外上部悬塑出一排排纵横交错、色彩多变的菱形山峦。不过，菱形山峦现已大多残毁，仅在壁面遗存原悬塑山峦所用之木桩、木桩孔及山峦的菱形痕迹；龛下部亦残存木桩、木桩孔及菱形痕迹，有的尚在下部残存一至三个较大的浅孔洞[1]；龛两侧各有一至两个较大的木桩孔，原应固定造像之用[2]（图8）。如第 4、7、13、38、43、91、114、171、196、205、207、224 窟等。

B 型：正壁中央亦开一圆拱形大龛，龛内塑坐佛，唯塑像已残毁。龛上绘出菱格山峦，有的在山峦中插画动物和禽鸟，有的画出诸天；龛两侧分别绘出释提桓因和般遮翼，后者通常画在龛左侧[3]，持琉璃琴；龛台或龛内两下角画出熊、狮子、鹿等，有的在龛台正中画坐像（图 9）。如第 58、63、80、92、99、126、159、175、178、179、186、206 窟等。

从上述秣菟罗、犍陀罗与克孜尔的帝释窟图像，我们不难看出克孜尔的帝释窟造

[1] 龛台表面残存的浅孔洞，根据秣菟罗和犍陀罗同一内容的浮雕判断，原应塑造动物，如熊、野猪等。

[2] 龛两侧壁面所存较大的木桩孔，原应安置释提桓因和般遮翼塑像。

[3] 般遮翼绘在帝释窟左侧，与图 3 布局相同，这或许暗示出两者之间的渊源关系。

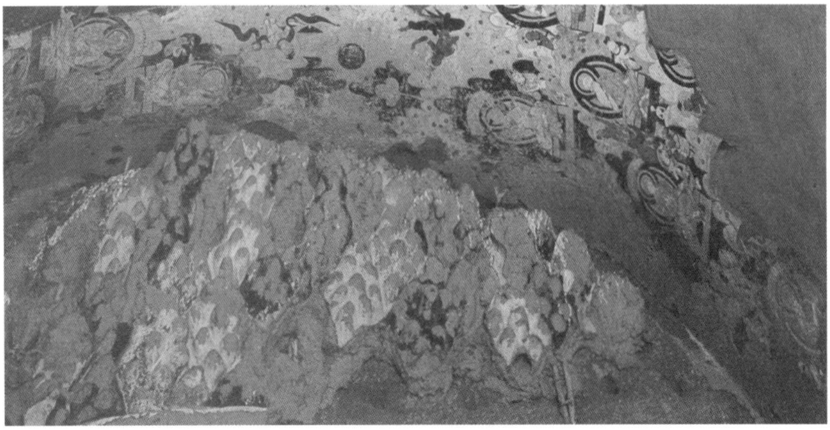

图 8　克孜尔第 196 窟主室正壁佛龛上部悬塑菱形山峦

图 9　克孜尔第 80 窟主室正壁佛龛左侧壁画

型，基本上延续了秣菟罗和犍陀罗帝释窟的构图，在布局及细部特征的经营上更接近犍陀罗的 B 型帝释窟。

经检索巴利语《尼迦耶》和汉译佛典，我们发现：龟兹地区帝释窟题材之塑绘，在吸收秣菟罗和犍陀罗同一内容雕刻的基础上，主要依据的是与汉译《长阿含经·释提桓因问经》相当的佛典。鉴于新疆发现的犍陀罗语和梵语《长阿含经》均为残卷，我们拟以汉译本作为主要的参照依据。

如是我闻，一时佛在摩竭陀国奄婆罗村北毗陀山因陀娑罗窟中。尔时释提桓因发微妙善心，欲来见佛。“今我当往至世尊所。”时诸忉利天，闻释提桓因发妙善心欲诣佛所，即寻诣帝释，白言：“善哉，帝释。发妙善心欲诣如来，我等亦乐侍从诣世尊所。”时释提桓因即告执乐神般遮翼，曰：“我今欲诣世尊所，汝可俱行。此忉利诸天亦当与我俱诣佛所。”对曰：“唯然。”时般遮翼持琉璃琴，于帝释前忉利天众中鼓琴供养。时释提桓因、忉利诸天及般遮翼于法堂上忽然不现，譬如力士屈伸臂，顷至摩竭陀国北毗陀山中。尔时世尊入火焰三昧，彼毗陀山同一火色。时国人见，自相谓言："此毗陀山同一火色，将是如来、诸天之力。"时释提桓因告般遮翼曰："如来至真甚难得睹，而能垂降此闲静处，寂默无声、禽兽为侣，此处常有诸大神天侍卫世尊。汝可于前鼓琉璃琴，娱乐世尊。吾与诸天寻于后往。"对曰："唯然。"即受教已，持琉璃琴于先诣佛……头面礼足，于一面住。白世尊言："释提桓因及忉利诸天，故遣我来问讯世尊起居轻利游步强耶？"世尊报曰："使汝帝释及忉利天，寿命延长、快乐无患。所以然者，诸天世人及阿须轮诸众生等，皆贪寿命，安乐无患。"尔时帝释复自念言："我等宜往礼觐世尊。"即与忉利诸天往诣佛所，头面礼足，却住一面。时帝释白佛言："不审我今去世尊远，近可坐？"佛告帝释曰："汝天众多，但近我坐。"时世尊所止因陀罗窟，自然广博，无所障碍。尔时帝释与忉利诸天及般遮翼，皆礼佛足，于一面坐。帝释白佛……[1]

克孜尔第99窟，位于谷内区。虽然该窟被后代严重熏黑，但在正壁龛上以菱形山峦为背景的壁画中仍可辨识出狮子、兔、禽鸟等动物以及草庐中的禅僧。尤其龛两侧的人物，保存基本完好，清晰可辨。其中，龛右侧共绘出5身人像。最上面两身立像，一为高僧，一为天人，皆双手合十；中间两身，一男一女，头戴高冠，双腿斜交坐于高方座上；座前有一躬身伏地作叩拜状的弟子像（图10a）。龛左侧壁面共画四身人像。其中，上部绘一男一女两个天人，皆头戴花蔓冠，身饰珠宝璎珞，双手合十，其中内侧那身女像，袒露上身，双乳丰腴，作扭腰曲肢之态；中间的天人，呈蹲跪状，半裸，右膝之上置一琉璃琴，左手上举持琴颈，右手作弹拨状；最下面是另一伏地叩拜的弟子（图10b）。两侧壁面所画形象，皆面向龛内主尊。主龛下部的壁画，已残蚀不清。

依据壁画内容及布局，我们认为：克孜尔第99窟中心柱正壁，应是《长阿含经·释提桓因问经》的完整变相。主龛内原塑佛像，应是居于帝释窟的世尊；龛上的壁画，表现的是宁静的高岩——毗陀山，山中寂默无声，禽兽为侣；龛右侧一男一女两身坐像，应为释提桓因（帝释）及其眷属；龛左侧持琉璃琴者，应是乐神般遮翼；其余皆为诸天大神。

克孜尔第80窟中心柱正壁画塑，似由两部分构成。正壁上半部壁画，疑为释迦降服六师外道；正壁下半部中央开一圆拱形大龛，唯龛内塑像已毁，仅存背光、身光及两只狮子（？）残迹。龛右上方，残存两像上半部及一对飞鸟。其中，前一身像，头戴宝冠，袒上身，右手置胸前，作捻珠状；后一身女性，头戴花蔓冠，着短袖衣，作世俗装，右手于胸前上扬，左手于腹前反掌向下。龛左上方，二天人并坐于高方座上，

[1] 佛陀耶舍、竺佛念译《长阿含经·释提桓因问经》，《大正藏》第1卷，第62b-63b页。

a

b

图 10　克孜尔第 99 窟主室正壁佛龛两侧壁画
a. 右侧壁画；b. 左侧壁画

双腿斜舒。其中，前一身半裸，腹前置一琉璃琴，左手上举持其颈，右手高举似作弹拨状；后一身头戴花冠，着世俗装，右臂弯曲，倚于前者左肩之上，左手持花。左右两侧人物背景，皆为菱形山峦，并缀以花树。显然，持琉璃琴者为娱乐世尊的般遮翼，与之相对而坐的应是释提桓因及其眷属。值得注意的是，正壁龛内两下角各画出一动物（狮子？），龛右上方绘出禽鸟（图 11）[1]。

上述两窟中的帝释窟，是克孜尔中心柱窟 B 型主室正壁的情况。至于那些龛上悬塑菱形山峦、龛两侧残存较大孔洞的 A 型正壁，如第 13、38、196、205 窟等，表现的应是同一题材，只是以塑代画而已。

---

[1] 第 80 窟中心柱正壁龛台下方两侧各有一鹿（？），左右甬道上方各有两个在洞中禅修的高僧。故而，整个中心柱正壁下半部画塑应为“帝释窟”。

图 11　克孜尔第 80 窟主室正壁佛龛及两侧壁画

从上述材料我们不难看出：克孜尔石窟“帝释窟”之构图与布局，即在山体结构及外观、龛形、人物配置、动物刻画等方面，与秣菟罗出土的同一内容雕刻，如图 3、4 颇为相似；同时接受了犍陀罗雕刻如图 6、7 对禽鸟的处理方法，形成了具有龟兹地方特色的新型帝释窟[1]。

值得注意的是，德国柏林亚洲艺术博物馆收藏的一件编号 III302 的木雕，是 20 世纪初德人从库车劫掠的，原应表现帝释窟场景。木雕高 115 厘米，残宽 74 厘米。其中，正中佛龛高 76. 5 厘米，宽 45 厘米。佛龛左右两侧底部各雕一小龛，周围刻出菱形山峦，惟右半部及龛内造像残失（图 12）。这件木雕说明：帝释窟这一主题在古龟兹地区的佛教艺术中极为流行，既能大量雕造石窟之内，也可单独置于寺院或家庙之中。

如前所述，“帝释窟”这一画塑题材所据原典，应是小乘教派信奉的《长阿含经》。

三、经典依据

1919 年，鲁道夫 · 霍恩勒 (A. F. Rudolf Hoernle) 简要介绍了《新疆发现的写本佛教文献》。在该文论及的七件梵语《阿含经》残卷中，属于《长阿含经》的有两件，即《众集经》(*Saṅgītisūtra*) 和《阿吒那智经》(*Āṭānāṭikasūtra*)[2]。《众集经》，相当于

[1] 印度 6 世纪开凿的根赫里第 90 窟，也雕出了帝释窟。这说明该题材自始至终一直受到印度僧俗的喜爱。参见 D. Mitra, *Buddhist Monuments,* Calcutta: Sahitya Samsad, 1971: 165.

[2] A. F. Rudolf Hoernle, *Manuscript Remains of Buddhist Literature found in Eastern Turkestan,* Oxford: Clarendon Press, 1916: 16-52.

图 12　柏林亚洲艺术博物馆收藏的帝释窟木雕

巴利语《长尼迦耶》的《等诵经》(*Saṅgītisuttanta*) 和汉译《长阿含经·众集经》,属于有部[1]所传[2]。《阿咤那智经》,仅存一纸,相当于巴利语《长尼迦耶》的《阿咤囊胝经》(*Āṭānāṭiyasuttanta*),现存汉译《长阿含经》未收入,但此经的同本异译名称则散见于汉译诸经之中,如《善见律毗婆沙》[3]、《十诵律》[4]等。经过仔细研究,渡边海旭认为它是汉译阙本《阿咤那智经》[5]残原卷,并由此推断：法藏部所传汉译《长阿含经》之外,尚有其他各部所传的《长阿含经》存在[6]。

---

[1] 通常意义上的有部,包括新、旧两派。后者指传十诵律的萨婆多部；前者为义净所传的根本说一切有部。参见高楠顺次郎《新文化原理としての佛教》,東京：大藏出版社：1946 年,第 252 页。

[2] 岡教邃《梵語の阿含經と漢譯原本の考察》,刊《哲學雜誌》482 號 (1927 年),第 354-357 页；483 號 (1927 年),第 421-425 页。1955 年,林冶公布了德国考察队在新疆收集的说一切有部《长阿含经》残卷《众集经》(*Saṇgītisūtra*)。参见 E. Waldschmidt, "Die Einleitung des Saṇgītisūtra", in: *Zeitschrift der Deutschen Morgenländischen Gesellschaft,* 105 (1955): 298-318.

[3] 名作《阿咤那咤》,参见《大正藏》第 24 卷,第 753c 页。

[4] 名作《阿咤那剑》,晋言《鬼神戒经》。参见《大正藏》第 23 卷,第 174b 页。

[5] 此经于唐龙朔三年(663 年)3 月由沙门那提译出,但智昇开元十八年(730 年)撰写《开元释教录》时已散佚。参见《大正藏》第 55 卷,第 563a-b 页。

[6] 渡邊海旭《新發見の阿含諸經の梵语》,刊《新佛教》,1909 年第 10 卷 2 期；渡邊海旭《真言秘經の起源及發達の實例》,刊《哲學研究》,第 231-232 號,1906 年。两文后均收入渡邊海旭《壺月全集》上,東京：壺月全集刊行会,1933 年,第 564-569 页、357-404 页。

专长佛典比较研究的林冶(Ernst Waldschmidt[1],一译瓦尔德施密特/瓦尔德施米特/瓦尔特施密特),在1926年完成博士论文《有部〈比丘尼戒本〉校注》[2]之后,于1932年公布了他对德人从新疆吐鲁番带回的一件梵语写卷的整理成果。据林冶研究,新疆出土的这件梵语写本,包括《幢经》(*Dhvajāgrasūtra*)、《转轮圣王修行经》(*Dharmacakra-pravartanasūtra*)、《大本缘经》(*Mahānidānasūtra*)、《释提桓因问经》(*Śakrapraśnasūtra*)、《频婆娑罗经》(*Bimbasārasūtra*)、《大会经》(*Mahāsamājasūtra*)和《十力经》(*Daśabala-sūtra*)。经与汉文和巴利语佛典对照,林冶认定这件残卷是有部《阿含经》的梵语原典[3]。20世纪40年代末,林冶致力于小乘《大般涅槃经》的研究[4]。他先把新疆发现的梵语残卷与巴利语及汉译四本做了详细的对勘[5],之后拼接了德人在硕尔楚克、图木舒克等地发掘出土的四

[1] 据陈寅恪先生记载,柏林大学路得施教授(Prof. Henrich Lüders,一作吕德斯)"学术有盛名于世"。1920年,林冶赴柏林师从路得施教授学习吠陀、古文字学及佛教梵语写本,同时也兼修汉语和藏文。1921年,陈先生"寅恪曾游普鲁士,从教授治东方古文字学"。"往岁德意志林冶君Ernst Waldschmidt校释说一切有部梵语比丘尼婆罗提木叉残本Bruchstücke des,予适游柏林,偶与之讨论。"参见:1) Lore Sander, "Ernst Waldschmidt's Contribution to the Study of the 'Turfan Finds'", in: *Turfan Revisited-The First Century of Research into the Arts and Cultures of the Silk Road,* ed. Desmond Durkin-Meisterernst et al, Berlin: Dietrich Reimer Verlag, 2004: 303-309; 2) 陈寅恪《敦煌本十诵比丘尼波罗提木叉跋》及《童受喻鬘论梵语残本跋》(原刊《清华学报》4卷2号),二文均收入陈寅恪《金明馆丛稿二编》,上海:上海古籍出版社,1980年,第207-211页、258-260页。

[2] E. Waldschmidt, *Bruchstücke des Bhikṣuṇī-Prātimokṣa der Sarvāstivādins*: *Mit einer Darstellung der Überlieferung des Bhikṣuṇī-Prātimokṣa in den verschiedenen Schulen* (Kleinere Sanskrittexte III), Leipzig: Deutschen Morgenländische Gesellschaft, 1926. 传世文献和出土残卷都证明:该戒本系当时西域佛教诸寺"常所用者也",尤为龟兹高僧佛图舍弥所重。参见僧佑《出三藏记集》,苏晋仁、萧錬子点校,北京:中华书局,1995年,第411页。

[3] E. Waldschmidt, *Bruchstücke buddhistischer Sūtras aus dem zentralasiatischen Sanskritkanon I: herausgegeben und im Zusammenhang mit ihren Parallelversionen bearbeitet* (Kleinere Sanskrittexte IV), Leipzig: Deutschen Morgenländische Gesellschaft, 1932.

1976年,在德国哥廷根举行的"佛教研讨会:II最古的佛教传承语言"上,林冶提交了《中亚佛经残本及其与汉译〈阿含经〉之关系》(Central Asian Sūtra Fragments and their Relation to the Chinese Āgamas)。该文进一步论述了这件写卷上的七个佛经,林冶认为:尽管它们长短不一,无法构成正典《阿含经》的任何一部,但的确是中亚寺院中流行的一部佛经。参见*Die Sprache der ältesten buddhistischen Überlieferung; The Language of the Earliest Buddhist Tradition* (Symp II), H. Bechert, hrsg, Göttingen: Vandenhoeck & Ruprecht, 1980: 137-162.

[4] E. Waldschmidt, "Beiträge zur Textgeschichte des Mahāparinirvāṇasūtra", in: *Nachrichten der Akademie der Wissenschaften in Göttingen,* 1939: 55-94.

[5] E. Waldschmidt, *Die Überlieferung vom Lebensende des Buddha*: *Eine vergleichende Analyse des Mahāparinirvāṇasūtra und seiner Textentsprechungen,* Teil 1 und 2 (Abhandlungen der Akademie der Wissenschaften in Göttingen III, 29, 30), Göttingen: Vandenhoeck & Ruprecht, 1944, 1948.

种写本 (S360,TM361,S362,S364)[1]及无数小梵语残片,并把它和《根本说一切有部毗奈耶杂事》的巴利原典、汉译及藏译诸本进行了详细的比较研究[2]。此外,林冶后来又整理出版了阿含类梵语原典《四众经》(*Catuṣpariṣatsūtra*)[3]和《大本经》(*Mahāvadānasūtra*)[4]。1992 年,哈特曼 (Jens-Uwe Hartmann) 向哥廷根提交了"高校教师资格论文 (Habilitationsschrift)"——《说一切有部〈长阿含经〉研究》(*Untersuchungen zum Dīrghāgama der Sarvāstivādins*)。依据《新疆出土梵语写本目录》(*Sanskrithandschriften aus den Turfanfunden*)[5]及有关资料,哈特曼对新疆出土梵语《长阿含经》之《六经》(*Ṣaṭsūtrakanipāta*),即《十上经》(*Daśottarasūtra*)、《广义法门经》(*Arthavistarasūtra* 或作 *Arthavistara-nāma-dharmaparyāya*)、《众集经》(*Saṅgītisūtra*)、《四众经》(*Catuṣpariṣatsūtra*)、《大譬喻经》(*Mahāvadānasūtra*)和《大般涅槃经》(*Mahāparinirvāṇasūtra*) 做了系统梳理,认为龟兹及焉耆地区出土的《阿含经》残本大多属于"六经"范畴,因此,"六经"可能是当时两地流行的佛典,惟汉译无全本[6]。

根据新疆发现的梵语残本并参照汉译《阿含经》,笔者认为：新疆地区出土的

[1] 林冶认为这些写本是 6、7 世纪之物,系根本说一切有部所传。

[2] E. Waldschmidt, *Das Mahāparinirvāṇasūtra*: *Text in Sanskrit und Tibetisch, verglichen mit dem Pāli nebst einer Übersetzung der chinesischen Entsprechung im Vinaya der Mūlasarvāstivādins,* Teil I-III (Abhandlungen der Deutschen Akademie der Wissenschaften zu Berlin, Klasse für Sprachen, Literatur und Kunst, 1950, 2, 3), Berlin: Akademie-Verlag, 1950-1951.

[3] E. Waldschmidt, *Das Catuṣpariṣaṭsūtra*: *Eine kanonische Lehrschrift über die Begründung der buddhistischen Gemeinde*. Teil I-III (Abhandlungen der Deutschen Akademie der Wissenschaften zu Berlin, Klasse für Sprachen, Literatur und Kunst, 1952, 2; 1956, 1; 1960, 1), Berlin: Akademie-Verlag, 1952, 1957, 1962. 此经是属于根本说一切有部《长阿含经》的一种佛传,与之相当的汉译是宋法贤的《众许摩诃帝经》和唐义净《根本说一切有部毗奈耶破僧事》。

[4] E. Waldschmidt, *Das Mahāvadānasūtra*: *Ein kanonischer Text über die sieben letzten Buddhas,* Teil 1, 2 (Abhandlungen der Deutschen Akademie der Wissenschaften zu Berlin, Klasse für Sprachen, Literatur und Kunst, 1952, 8; 1954, 3), Berlin: Akademie-Verlag, 1953, 1956. 此经相当于巴利语的 *Mahāpadānasuttanta,* 汉译《长阿含经》以外尚有包括法天译本在内的 4 种异译。

[5] Ernst Waldschmidt, Lore Sander, und Klaus Wille, ed., *Sanskrithandschriften aus den Turfanfunden,* pts. 1-8, Wiesbaden/Stuttgart: Franz Steiner Verlag, 1965-2000.

[6] 该文仅为哈特曼博士申请高校教师资格论文,即通常所说的"教授论文",未刊。曾蒙作者厚意,笔者获赠该文,谨此谢忱。有关该专题论文的内容,请参见 Jens-Uwe Hartmann, "Buddhist Sanskrit Texts from Northern Turkestan and their relation to the Chinese Tripiṭaka", in: John R. McRae, Jan Nattier, eds., *Collection of Essays 1993: Buddhism Across Boundaries—Chinese Buddhism and Western Religions,* by Erik Zürcher, Lore Sander, and others, Taipei: Foguang Cultural Enterprise Co., Ltd, 1999: 107-136.

《阿含经》,尤其是《长阿含经》残本数量如此之多,足以说明当时它在新疆地区极为流行。克孜尔中心柱窟主室正壁画塑题材,与汉译《长阿含经·释提桓因问经》内容相符;后室每窟必画或塑的涅槃图像及其与之相关的须跋先佛入灭和荼毗焚棺等,又都与汉译《长阿含经·游行经》内容吻合。因此,画塑所据佛典不言自明。此外,根据林冶对新疆出土《四众经》和《大本经》的整理研究,我们推测:克孜尔中心柱窟主室侧壁及窟顶所绘因缘佛传,即从菩提树下成道开始,历经梵天劝请、二商主供养、初转法轮、耶舍出家、迦叶和频婆娑罗王皈依等,是与《长阿含经·游行经》叙述的释迦牟尼最后游行相照应的另一种佛传形式;而这种把最初弘法和四众教团成立之事汇集在一起的就是《四众经》。换言之,主室侧壁和窟顶的因缘佛传壁画或许与《四众经》有关[1]。至于《大本经》中毗婆尸等七佛内容,在克孜尔中心柱窟中也是习见的题材[2]。因此从某种意义上说,克孜尔中心柱窟几乎是小乘佛典《长阿含经》[3]的完整再现。这种状况与新疆,或更确切地说,与龟兹地区的佛教历史是极为相符的。史载曾经统辖达慕蓝等九寺、被后世尊称为龟兹小乘佛教领袖的高僧佛图舍弥,

[1] 参见:E. Waldschmidt, *opere citato* (*Das Catuṣpariṣaṭsūtra*: *Eine kanonische Lehrschrift...*). 这件梵语写本之英译,见 Ria Kloppenborg, *The Sūtra on the Foundation of the Buddhist Order (Das Catuṣpariṣatsūtra)*: *Relating the events from the Bodhisattva's enlightenment up to the conversion of Upatiṣya (Śāriputra) and Kolita (Maudgalyāyana)*, Leiden: E. J. Brill, 1973. 又,关于因缘佛传壁画,容另文探讨。

[2] 如克孜尔第 13 窟中心柱正壁两侧甬道上方各画三身佛像,它们与龛内主尊共同构成七佛题材;而犍陀罗出土的一件帝释窟浮雕(参见《统计表》第 33 号),主尊下共雕出六佛(其中左端的已残,但从位置判断,应有一像,故也应视作七佛题材)和一弥勒。实际上,克孜尔第 13 窟前壁已毁,否则的话,门道上方应绘弥勒于兜率天说法。另外,克孜尔有些中心柱窟,如谷内区第 100 和 104 窟中心柱左右两侧壁各画二身立佛,后壁(中心柱后壁)画三身立佛。这是否也是另一种形式的七佛?此外,第 114 窟门道上方画有七佛。

[3] 新疆发现的《长阿含经》,除梵语写本外,尚有用其他当地语言书写的《长阿含经》,而汉译《长阿含经》所据原典,可能是用"西北俗语",即"犍陀罗语 (Gāndhārī)"写成的。参见:E. Waldschmidt, "Central Asian Sūtra Fragments and their Relation to the Chinese Āgamas", in: *opere citato*: 137-174, esp. 167, 137, 163-164。不过,克孜尔中心柱窟画塑所据《长阿含经》,到底是犍陀罗语写卷,还是梵语写本,抑或当地"胡语"原典,现不得而知。

至于《长阿含经》究竟属于何部所传,从来就没有一致的意见,但多数学者认为它可能出自法藏部。参见:1) E. Waldschmidt, *opere citato* (*Bruchstücke buddhistischer Sūtras...*): 229; 2). E. Waldschmidt, *opere citato* (Central Asian Sūtra...): 136-137; 3) 石川海淨《長阿含經成立の再檢討》,見《立正大學論叢》,1941 年,創刊號,第 118-143 页;4) 田光烈《长阿含经》,见《中国佛教》三,中国佛教协会编,上海:知识出版社,1989 年,第 181-184 页。

倘若此说成立,可能在玄奘游访龟兹之前,当地曾流行法藏部;克孜尔石窟大量开凿中心柱窟(塔庙窟),或许是法藏部重视供养佛塔的一种反映。

就是“阿含学者也”[1]；其势力，可能对当时龟兹地上寺院的营建和石窟寺的开凿产生相当影响[2]。

四、菱形山峦

关于克孜尔石窟中的菱形山峦构图，学者多有探讨，笔者借此略陈管见。帝释窟说法这个故事，发生在摩揭陀国奄婆罗村北毗陀山因陀娑罗窟 (Vediyake pabbate Indasāla-guhāyaṃ)[3]中。毗陀，梵语作 Vediyaka，巴利语作 Vediyake，汉文译作毗陀、毗陀提、毗提泗、毗提醯以及小孤石山和因陀罗势罗娄诃山等。关于毗陀山之涵义，现存唯一的诠释是佛音 (Buddhaghosa) 对巴利语《长尼迦耶 / 长部经》的注疏《吉祥悦意论》(*Sumaṅgalavilāsinī*):

“*Vediyake pabbate ti so kira pabbato pabbata-pāde jātena maṇi-vedikā-sadisena nīla-vana-saṇḍena samantā parikkhitto tasmā Vediya-pabbato tv'eva saṅkhaŋ gato.* ”[4]

这段巴利语原文可译作：毗陀山，实际上是一座四周完全被山脚下生长的一簇簇绿色丛林所覆盖的山丘，表面看上去形如众多的 Maṇi-vedikā。

佛音注疏中的 Maṇi-vedikā，由两个词构成，即 Maṇi 和 vedikā。其中，Maṇi 音译摩尼珠、摩尼、末尼，意译珠、意珠、宝珠、如意宝珠、明珠、珠宝、宝等[5]。Vedikā，巴利语、梵语和俗语拼法相同，唯重音有别。巴利语 vedikā 意为雪檐、飞檐、栏杆或栅栏[6]。尽管该故事的发生地位于北印度，但形容山形作雪檐或飞檐状显然是不合适的。梵语 vedikā 汉译为栏楯、轩槛、轩阶、栏杆、边框等[7]。俗语 vedikā，据德国学者路得施解释为 railing，即栏楯、栏杆、栅栏[8]。此外，比利时学者拉莫特 (É. Lamotte)

---

[1] 僧佑，上引书，第 411 页。

[2] 克孜尔石窟早期盛行的大像窟，如第 47 和 77 窟，是大立佛形象与塔庙合壁于一窟的极好实例。这种设计，应与《长阿含经》先叙释迦游行布道，后讲涅槃造塔的内容有密切关系。这也是阿含势力强烈影响石窟建造的结果。参见宿白《武威天梯山早期石窟参观记》，见《燕京学报》，新 8 期 (2000 年)，第 221-223 页。

[3] T. W. Rhys Davids and J. Estlin Carpenter ed., *opere citato*: 263.

[4] W. Stede ed., *The Sumaṅgala-vilāsinī: Buddhaghosa's Commentary on the Dīgha-Nikāya*, III, London: Oxford University Press, 1932: 1.

[5] 荻原雲來《漢訳対照梵和大辭典》，東京：鈴木学術財団 / 講談社，1974 年，第 986a 页。

[6] T. W. Rhys Davids and William Stede, *Pali-English Dictionary*, London: Pali Text Society, 1925: 648.

[7] 荻原雲來，上引书，第 1277a 页。

[8] H. Lüders, *opere citato*: No. 340.

认为：印度词汇 vedikā 的主要意思是 balustrade，即栏杆；其次是 palisade，即栅栏[1]。由此我们可以看出，vedikā 的涵义主要是指栏楯或栏杆，也就是说，毗陀山表面覆盖的绿色植被，形如众多的摩尼栏楯，即宝珠栏楯。

至于帝释窟，汉译佛典亦作因陀娑罗窟、因陀罗石室、帝释岩等，佛音对此也做了诠释，现以拉丁字母转写如下：

> Indasāla-guhāyan ti pubbe pi sā dvinnaŋ pabbatānaŋ antare guhā. Indasā-rukkho c'assa dvāre tasmā Indasāla-guhā ti saṅkhaŋ gatā. Atha naŋ kuḍḍehi parikkhipitvā dvāra-vātapānāni yojetvā suparinitthita-sudhākamma-mālākamma-latākamma-vicittaŋ leṇaŋ katvā Bhagavato adaŋsu. Purima-vohāra-vasen'eva pana Indasāla-guhā tv'eva naŋ sañjānanti. Taŋ sandhāya vuttaŋ Indasāla-guhāyan ti.[2]

这段巴利语原文大意为：帝释窟是位于两悬崖间的一座石室，窟口有一棵高大的因陀娑罗 (Inda-sāla) 树，故称之因陀娑罗 (Inda-sāla) 窟。后来，村邑给石室补建泥巴墙，安置了门窗，并以各式磨光的灰泥涡卷、藤蔓浮雕和花环进行装饰，最后奉献世尊。

佛音，一译觉音或佛陀瞿沙，是南传上座部巴利语系佛教学者。据《小史》(*Culavaṃsa*) 记载，佛音 4 世纪后半出生于佛陀伽耶附近的婆罗门家庭，知晓科学、艺术和技巧，精通吠陀学，后皈依佛教并开始研究三藏。“因其演说同佛说一样深刻，他被称作佛音 (Buddhaghosa)。”锡兰国王摩诃那摩 (Mahānāma) 在位时，佛音前往锡兰大寺 (Mahāvihāra) 研读佛典，曾让比丘“把所有的书都给我（佛音），我要作注”。锡兰人赞其学德，崇为弥勒菩萨 (Metteyya)。佛音后移住根陀迦罗寺 (Ganthākara-vihāra)，把所有三藏的僧伽罗语注疏全部翻译为原始的摩竭陀语，使上座部的所有大师都像原始佛典一样采用它们[3]。在印度佛教史上，佛音堪称最伟大的注疏家和义学大师[4]，被称作“巴利语佛典注释的权威”[5]。因此，他对巴利语《长尼迦耶》的注

---

[1] Étienne Lamotte, *History of Indian Buddhism from the Origins to the Saka era,* tr. By Sara Webb-Boin, Louvain-la-Neuve: Institut Orientaliste de l'Université Catholique de Louvain/Louvain: Peeters Press, 1988: 856.

[2] W. Stede ed., *opere citato*: 1.

[3] Wilhelm Geiger ed. & tr., *Cūḷavaṃsa being the more recent part of the Mahāvaṃsa,* 37. 224-246, translated from the German into English by C. Mabel Rickmers, London: Pali Text Society, 1929, Part I: 24-26.

[4] G. P. Malalasekera, *The Pāli Literature of Ceylon,* Colombo: M. D. Gunasena & Co., Ltd, 1928: 79-101.

[5] 季羡林《原始佛教的语言问题》，见季羡林《印度古代语言论集》，北京：中国社会科学出版社，1982 年，第 404、406 页。

疏，应该代表了 5 世纪天竺学者对该经的权威理解。换言之，佛音对毗陀山及帝释窟的解释，是当时印度人对毗陀山外貌及帝释窟的普遍认识。

克孜尔中心柱窟主室正壁表现的菱形山峦，应为当地画工和雕塑匠人在吸收印度艺匠对这一题材传统的菱形、四边形或三角形山峦刻画的基础上，采纳印度人当时对毗陀山的惯常记述塑绘而成。也就是说，克孜尔帝释窟及其所在的菱形山峦，是印度摩竭陀国奄婆罗村北毗陀山因陀娑罗窟的真实再现，这点在克孜尔第 163 窟窟顶的菱格因缘（图 13）和 172 窟窟顶的菱格本生中折射得极为显著；后两者的菱形山峦，形如众多的摩尼栏楯构造而成。

图 13　克孜尔第 163 窟主室窟顶菱格构图

［本文原刊（北京）文物出版社 2000 年出版的《汉唐之间的宗教艺术与考古》第 209-233 页，本次重刊除改正错误外，还补写了柏林亚洲艺术博物馆所藏木雕“帝释窟”一段，增加了三条注释并调整了注释体例。］

附表：印度和巴基斯坦所见帝释窟雕刻统计表

序号	出土地点	收藏地	尺寸	材料来源
1	Railing pillar, Barhut stūpa	Indian Musuem		*The Stūpa of Bharhut,* pl. xxviii; *Barhut,* Book III, pl. liv.
2	Railing pillar, Mahābodhī	*in situ*		*Mahābodhī or The great Buddhist temple under the Bodhi tree at Buddha Gayā,* pl. viii; *L'Art gréco-bouddhique du Gandhâra,* Vol. I, fig.248.
3	Northern gate, Stūpa 1, Sāñcī	*in situ*		*Tree and Serpent Worship,* pl. xxix, fig.1; *The Monuments of Sāñchī,* pl. 35b. 1.
4	Western gate, Stūpa 1, Sāñcī	*in situ*		*The Monuments of Sāñchī,* pl. 64a. 3.
5	Mathurā city	Mathurā Museum	19cm H 252cm L	*History of Indian and Indonesian Art,* fig.76; *La sculpture de Mathurā,* pl. vii; *The "Scythian" Period,* pl. xxii, fig.35; 佛像の起源, pl. 57; *Buddhist Art: Mathurā School,* pl. 61-64.
6	Jamalpur, Mathurā	Lucknow Museum		*Archaeological Survey of India: Annual Report 1909-10,* pl. xxva; *The "Scythian" Period,* pl. xxix, fig.53; *Buddhist Art: Mathurā School,* pl. 106.
7	Dhruv Ṭīlā	Mathurā Museum	20cm H 62cm R	*La sculpture de Mathurā,* pl. vib; *Buddhist Art: Mathurā School,* pl. 169.
8	Mathurā	Rosenberg 藏		*Archaeological Survey of India: Annual Report 1909-10, pl. xxviiia; Eastern Art,* Vol. I, pl. xvi, fig.7.
9	Mathurā	Mathurā Museum	46cm H	*Catalogue of the Archaeological Museum at Mathurā,* pl. iiia; *Eastern Art,* Vol. I, pl. xvii, fig.11; *La sculpture de Mathurā,* pl. lib.
10	Jamalpur	Indian Museum	61cm H	*La sculpture de Mathurā,* pl. liiib; 佛像の起源, pl. 58.
11	Cave 90, Kāṇhēri	in situ		*Buddhist Monuments,* p. 165.
12	Sikrī stūpa	Lahore Museum	33cm H	*L'Art gréco-bouddhique du Gandhâra,* Vol. I, fig.247; *"Scythian" Period,* pl. iii, fig.3; *Gandhāran Art in Pakistan,* pl. 129; ガンダーラ美術, Vol. I, fig.332.
13		Peshawar Museum		ガンダーラ美術, Vol. I, fig.336.
14		Peshawar Museum		ガンダーラ美術, Vol. I, fig.337.
15		日本私人收藏	21cm H	ガンダーラ美術, Vol. I, P3-X.

（续表）

序号	出土地点	收藏地	尺寸	材料来源
16		Lahore Museum	18cm H	*Gandhāran Art in Pakistan,* pl. 128; ガンダーラ美術, Vol. I, fig.340.
17	Giri, Taxila	Taxila Museum	54cm H	*Taxila,* Vol. iii, pl. 219, no. 113; *Gandhāran Art in Pakistan,* pl. 132; *Buddhist Art of Gandhara,* pl. 74; ガンダーラ美術, Vol. I, fig.335.
18	Takht-ī-Bāhī	Peshawar Museum	21cn H	*Gandhāran Art in Pakistan,* pl. 134.
19	Sikrī, Gandhāra	Lahore Museum	72. 5cm H	*Gandhāran Art in Pakistan,* pl. 168; ガンダーラ美術, Vol. I, fig.340.
20		日本私人收藏	46cm H	ガンダーラ美術, Vol.I, fig.331.
21	Buner, Gandhāra	British Museum	20. 4cm H	*Gandhâra,* pl. 277; ガンダーラ美術, Vol. II, fig.867; *A Catalogue of the Gandhāra Sculpture in the British Museum,* fig.219.
22	Sahrī-Bahlol?	日本私人收藏	78cm H	ガンダーラ美術, Vol. I, PIII-VI.
23	Karamar, Gandhāra	Lahore Museum	83cm H	ガンダーラ美術, Vol. I, fig.466.
24	Jamālgaṛhī, Gandhāra	British Museum	14. 2cm H	*A Catalogue of the Gandhāra Sculpture in the British Museum,* fig.220.
25		日本私人收藏	78cm H	ガンダーラ美術, Vol. I, fig.338.
26		日本私人收藏	31cm H	ガンダーラ美術, Vol. I, fig.439.
27		Indian Museum		*Gandhâra,* pl. 16.
28	Loriyān Tāṅgai	Indian Museum	114. 5cm H	*L'Art gréco-bouddhique du Gandhâra,* Vol. I, fig.246; *Buddhist Art of Gandhara,* pl. 83; ガンダーラ美術, Vol. I, fig.334.
29		British Museum	34cm H	*Gandhāran Art in Pakistan,* pl. xviii3; ガンダーラ美術, Vol. I, fig.333; *A Catalogue of the Gandhāra Sculpture in the British Museum,* fig.221.
30	Mamāne Ḍheri	Peshawar Museum	76cm H	Kharoshṭhī Inscriptions, pl.xxxiv3; The "Scythian" Period, pl.vi, fig.9; Gandhāran Art in Pakistan, pl.131; Buddhist Art of Gandhara, pl.85.
31	Jauliāñ, Taxila	Taxila Museum	82. 5cm H	*Taxila,* Vol. iii, pl. 221, no. 4; *Gandhāran Art in Pakistan,* pl. 130.
32		Lahore Museum	35. 5cm H	*Gandhāran Art in Pakistan,* pl. 133.
33		Lahore Museum	33cm H	*Gandhāran Art in Pakistan,* pl. 135.
34		A. M. Khan 藏	64cm H	ガンダーラ美術, Vol. II, fig.866.

The *Jātakas* in the Cave Temple Complex of Kizil, Kucha

The subject of wall-paintings in Kizil is mainly of Buddhist stories. Among them, the stories from the *jātakas* and *avadāna*s as well as episodes from Buddha's last life are very rich and colourful. The *jātakas* are stories of the previous births of Gautama Buddha who, as a Bodhisattva, is believed to have passed through innumerable existences, both human and animal, persistently qualifying himself for Buddhahood by the greatest acquisition of all kinds of virtues. More than five hundred *jātakas* were widely popular among Buddhist followers and people in general[1]. Presently, the Pāli version consisting of 547 stories can be found in libraries and even scholars' private book collections, but it is a pity that the Chinese version, which also contains more than five hundreds *jātakas,* did not reach the same degree of popularity and was transmitted in translation during the reign period of Emperor Wu [武帝, 482-493 AD] of the Southern Qi dynasty [萧齐][2].

---

[1] 1) Xuanzang [玄奘] tr. *Apidamo dapiposha lun* [阿毗达磨大毗婆沙论, *Abhidharmamahāvibhāṣā-śāstra*], fascicle 126, in: *Taishō shinshū daizōkyō* [大正新脩大藏經, *Taishō Revised Tripiṭaka*], 100 vols., ed. Junjirō Takakusu [高楠顺次朗] and Kaikyoku Watanabe [渡邊海旭], Tokyo: Taishō Issaikyō Kankōkai, 1924-1934 (hereafter abbreviated to *Taishō*), Vol. 27: 660a; 2) Yijing [义净], *Nanhai ji gui neifa zhuan* [南海寄归内法传, *Record of Buddhist Monastic Traditions of Southern Asia*], emended and annotated by Wang Bangwei [王邦维], Beijing: Zhonghua Book Company, 1995: 182-183; *confer Taisho,* Vol. 54: 238a.

[2] Sengyou [僧佑], *Chu sanzang ji ji* [出三藏记集, *A Collection of Records concerning the Tripiṭaka or A Collection of Records of Translations of the Tripiṭaka*], emended and annotated by Su Jinren [苏晋仁] and Xiao Lianzi [萧鍊子], Beijing: Zhonghua Book Company, 1995: 63; *confer Taishō,* Vol. 55: 13b.

The *jātakas* were depicted in painting and relief in large numbers in the Buddhist art of India, Central Asia and China, for example, the bas-reliefs on the *toraṇa* of Bhārhut, the murals of Ajaṇṭā and the murals of the Chinese cave temples. On the basis of our *in situ* investigation, the *jātakas* painted in one cave at Kizil generally amount to dozens, and sometimes even go up to more then 80, such as the *jātakas* in Cave 69. Therefore we are told that the content as well as the variety of the *jātakas* in the Kizil caves, which approximates 100, is the largest among all the cave-temples both in India and China[1]. About 70% of them have been identified so far[2].

As for the composition of the Kizil *jātakas,* they can be roughly classified into three types according to their shape: rhombic or diamond, square, and horizontal scroll.

The first type of *jātakas* was mostly painted on both sides of the barrel-vault of the main chamber of central-pillar-caves (*chētiyagharas*), as in the Caves 7, 13, 17, 69, 114, 178 and 198 (fig.1). One or two typical moments of the story were depicted. Since the *jātakas* were painted in the rhombus and had a chain of mountains as the background, this type is called "rhombic *jātakas*" for short. The rhombic composition is the most characteristic of the representation of Kizil *jātakas*.

The second type appears on the side walls of the Kizil caves, as in the murals on the lower part of the side walls of the Caves 110, 184 and 186 (fig.2)[3]. This type of painting, similar to what we have seen in the preceding example, also takes one or two typical moments for depiction. The *jātaka* paintings of this type are infrequent, and most of them belong to late periods.

---

[1] Ma Shichang [马世长], *Zhongguo fojiao shiku kaogu wenji* [中国佛教石窟考古文集, *Essays on the Buddhist Cave Temples of China*], Taipei: Chueh Feng Buddhist Art & Culture Foundation, 2001: 25, 76.

[2] 1) E. Waldschmidt, "Über die Darstellungen und den Stil der Wandgemälde aus Qyzil bei Kutscha I", in: *Die buddhistische Spätantike in Mittelasien,* ed, A. von Leq, E. Waldschmidt, VI: Neue Bildwerke II, Berlin, 1928: 9-62; 2) Ma Shichang, *opere citato*: 35-122.

[3] E. Waldschmidt mistakenly regarded the murals which were taken back to Berlin from Cave 184 as coming from Cave 206 (Fußwaschungshöhle). *confer*: E. Waldschmidt, *opere citato*: 17.

fig.1 Mural of the *jātakas* on the ceiling of Cave 17 at Kizil, Kucha

fig.2 Mural of the *jātakas* on the side wall of Cave 186 at Kizil

In the third type of composition, many scenes were depicted to display a complete and continuous story developing like in a horizontal scroll; here the contents of the episodes are closely linked in order to make the painting dovetail. For instance, the *Vessantarajātaka* in Cave 81 at Kizil, painted on the four side walls of that square cave, is formed by more than twenty sequential episodes (fig.3). In addition, this *jātaka* was also depicted on the lower parts of the side walls of the Caves 184 and 186, with the same composition[1].

Since so many varieties of *jātakas* have been discovered in the Kizil caves, we would certainly inquire about their origin. Were they influenced by the themes of the wall-paintings in the Bāmiyān caves? The answer is, of course, negative,

[1] E. Waldschmidt, *opere citato*: 38-39.

fig.3 Mural of the *Vessantarajātaka* on the side wall of Cave 81 at Kizil

because stories of this kind have not yet been discovered in Bāmiyān, except for five fragments of murals depicting the *parinirvāṇa* Buddha. Under such circumstances, scholars naturally assumed or have to admit that *jātaka* stories as well as the story of Buddha's life in the Kizil caves stemmed directly from Gandhāra[1].

In fact, sculptors of the early Indian school of art (150 BC to 50 AD) left a great number of carvings on Buddhist monuments such as the *toraṇas* and *vedikās* at the Bhārhut *stūpa,* the Sāñcī *stūpa* and the Mahābodhi *vihāra* at Bodhgayā. "The purpose of these sculptures was to glorify the Buddha. This they did by recounting episodes from the story of his life and of his previous births, or sometimes, but only rarely, from the subsequent history of the Buddhist Church. In the earliest monuments the stories of his previous births, or *Jātakas,* as they were called, greatly predominated. Later on, interest shifted to the events of his

[1] Takayasu Higuchi [樋口隆康], "From Bāmiyān to Dunhuang", in: *Dunhuang shiku yanjiu guoji taolunhui wenji: shiku kaogu bian* [敦煌石窟研究国际讨论会文集：石窟考古编, *Proceedings of 1987 International Conference on Dunhuang Cave Temples; Archaeological Section*], Shenyang: Liaoning Fine Arts Press, 1990: 121.

last earthly life, and still later to his image, which was destined to eclipse all else in Buddhist art. But that was not until the School of Gandhāra had initiated the idea and established the practice of portraying the Buddha in bodily form" [1].

Therefore, it is appropriate to say that the *jātaka* stories as well as the *avadāna* stories in the Kizil caves were influenced by those of central India at large rather than by those of Gandhāra, because the *jātakas* and the story of the life of Buddha had been the main subjects of Indian sculpture as well as painting from beginning to end. They are not only common at Bhārhut, Sāñcī and Bodhgayā but occur also in the paintings of the Ajaṇṭā caves.

Viewed from the aspect of composition, we feel that the rhombic *jātaka* might have a direct relationship with Indian art. Taking the *Mṛgajātaka* as an example, in a bas-relief on the *toraṇa* of the Bhārhut *stūpa* which dates from the 2nd century BC, the *mṛga* (deer) is depicted as crouching at the lower left, while the king who stands at the upper right is about to shoot an arrow at the *mṛga*. All the scenes of this story were arranged and enclosed within a circular medallion (fig.4). However, the same story in a relief from Gandhāra, which was carved in the third century AD, was depicted in the form of a frieze running from right to left, that is, in a horizontal composition (fig.5) [2]. In the Kizil wall-paintings, this *jātaka* was illustrated in a

fig.4 *Mṛgajātaka* in bas-relief on the *toraṇa* of the Bhārhut *stūpa*

[1] John Marshall, *Buddhist Art of Gandhara: The Story of the Early School; its birth, growth and decline,* London: Cambridge University Press, 1960: 7.

[2] Dieter Schlingloff, *Studies in the Ajanta Paintings: Identifications and Interpretations,* Delhi: Ajanta Publications (India), 1987: 403.

fig.5 *Mṛgajātaka* in bas-relief from Gandhāra

fig.6 *Mṛgajātaka* painted on the ceiling of Cave 38 at Kizil

rhombus, with the *mṛga* crouching at the lower right and the king on a horse at the upper left in the act of killing the deer with his sword (fig.6). From the above examples, therefore, we become aware that the rhombic *jātaka* of the *mṛga* in Kizil may be inherently related to an Indian model, such as that of Bhārhut. It is obvious that the former was modeled on the latter, only it transformed the circular composition into the rhombic one.

As for the *jātakas* in square and horizontal scroll format, we can find similar reliefs in Sāñcī (fig.7) and similar murals in the Ajaṇṭā caves. There are more than 21 varieties of *jātakas* that are still preserved in the Caves 1, 2, 10, 16, 17 in Ajaṇṭā (fig.8)[1], and most of them are of horizontal or square type. For instance, the *Śyāmajātaka/Sāma*

[1] They are: *Chaddantajātaka, Campeyyajātaka, Haṁsajātaka, Hastijātaka, Ksāntijātaka, Macchajātaka, Mahājanakajātaka, Mahākapijātaka, Mahāsutasōmajātaka, Mahāummaggajātaka, Mahisajātaka, Mātiposakajātaka, Nigrodhamigajātaka, Rurujātaka, Saṁkhapālajātaka, Sāmajātaka, Sarabhāmigajātaka, Sivijātaka, Valāhassajātaka, Vessantarajātaka, Vidhurapaṇḍitajātaka. confer* 1) D. Mitra. *Ajanta*, 10th ed., New Delhi: Archaeological Survey of India. 1992: 20-68; 2) Chongfeng Li [李崇峰] "*Azhantuo shiku canguan ji* [阿旃陀石窟参观记, Ajaṇṭā caves: A Preliminary Survey]".

fig.7 *Śyāmajātaka* in bas-relief on the *toraṇa* of Sāñcī

fig.8 *Haṃsajātaka* painted on the side wall of Cave 17 at Ajaṇṭā

Jātaka on the right side wall of Cave 10 is the oldest depiction of this legend in a wall painting. It consists of seven scenes in a row of pictures (fig.9), dating from around the 2nd century BC[1]. But, it is very interesting that the order of the pictures does not correspond to the narrative order of the story, which is different from that of the Kizil *jātaka* murals. Moreover, the *jātaka* stories in relief from Gandhāra have a similar composition. Thus, the origin of the *jātaka* composition in square or horizontal scroll in Kizil is self-evident.

fig.9 *Śyāmajātaka* painted on the side wall of Cave 10 at Ajaṇṭā

Besides the pictorial tradition, the original text for the depiction of the *jātakas* in Kizil is still an outstanding question. They might have been created on the basis of texts in Gāndhārī or Prākṛta or Sanskrit or even some other vernacular languages. According to incomplete statistics, nearly 70 of the *jātaka* murals in Kizil can be found in various Chinese sources, most of which are also available in the Pāli version. The source for the remaining *jātakas* in Kizil, which is estimated to form 30% of the whole *jātaka* body and which have not been interpreted yet, are most likely in the versions of Gāndhārī or Sanskrit or even some other vernacular languages. Although the Pāli version itself was not the original source for the depiction of *jātaka* in Kizil, it is presently the most referential texts, for us, to identify *jātakas* there. For instance, the *Naḷapānajātaka,* which appears in Kizil Caves 17, 63, 91, 99, 101, 114, 178, 188, 192 and 206[2], was depicted as

[1] D. Schlingloff, *opere citato*: 67.

[2] Xinjiang Qiuzi shiku yanjiusuo [新疆龟兹石窟研究所, Kucha Cave Research Institute], *Kezi'er shiku neirong zonglu* [克孜尔石窟内容总录, *A Descriptive Catalogue of the Cave Temple Complex at Kizil*], Urumchi: Xinjiang Art & Photograph Publishing House, 2000: 294.

follows: two or three monkeys standing around a pond use reeds to drink water and in the center of the pond, a head of a water-ogre appears (fig.10a/b). This *jātaka* is described in great detail in the Pāli source:

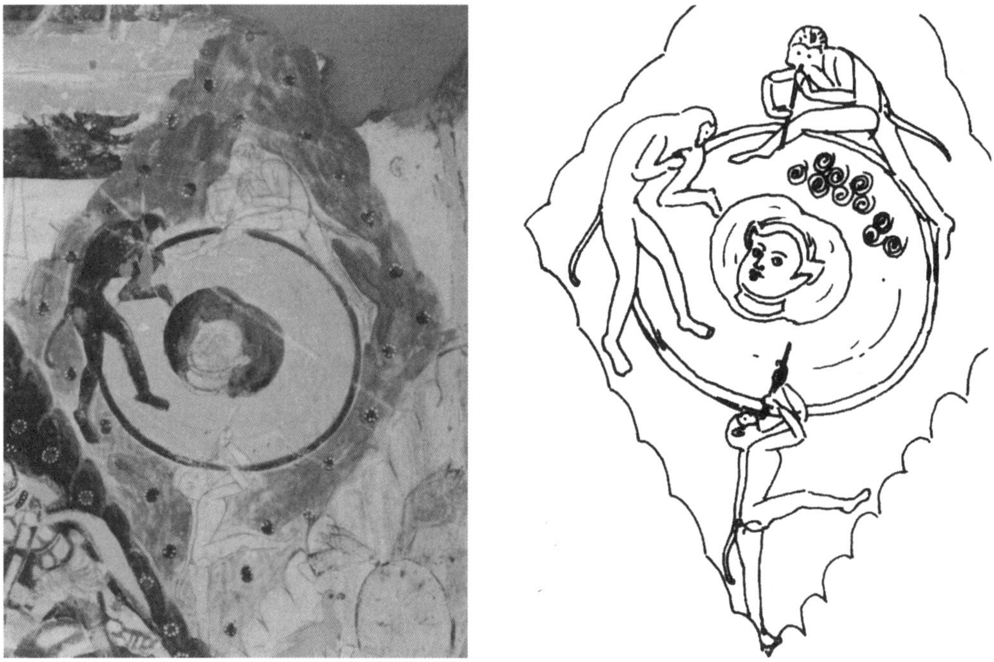

a b

fig.10a Mural of the *Naḷapānajātaka* on the ceiling of Cave 17 at Kizil
b line-drawing of *Naḷapānajātaka* on the ceiling of Cave 17 at Kizil

In past times, we are told, there was a thick forest on this spot. And in the lake here dwelt a water-ogre who used to devour everyone who went down into the water. In those days the Bodhisattva had come to life as the king of the monkeys, and was as big as the fawn of a red deer; he lived in that forest at the head of a troop of no less than eighty thousand monkeys whom he shielded from harm. Thus did he counsel his subjects:— "My friends, in this forest there are trees that are poisonous and lakes that are haunted by ogres. Mind to ask me first before you either eat any fruit which you have not eaten before, or drink of any water where you have not drink before" . "Certainly" , said they readily.

One day they came to a spot they had never visited before. As they were searching for water to drink after their day's wanderings, they came on this lake. But they did not drink; on the contrary they sat down watching for the coming of the

Bodhisattva.

When he came up, he said, "Well, my friends, why don't you drink?"

"We waited for you to come."

"Quite right, my friends," said the Bodhisattva. Then he made a circuit of the lake, and scrutinized the footprints round, with the result that he found that all the footsteps led down into the water and none came up again. "Without doubt," thought he to himself, "this is the haunt of an ogre." So he said to his followers, "You are quite right, my friends, in not drinking of this water; for the lake is haunted by an ogre."

When the water-ogre realized that they were not entering his domain, he assumed the shape of a horrible monster with a blue belly, a white face, and bright-red hands and feet; in this shape he came out from the water, and said, "Why are you seated here? Go down into the lake and drink." But the Bodhisattva said to him, "Are not you the ogre of this water?" "Yes, I am," was the answer. "Do you take as your prey all those who go down into this water?" "Yes, I do; from small birds upwards, I never let anything go which comes down into my water. I will eat the lot of you too." "But we shall not let you eat us." "Just drink the water." "Yes, we will drink the water, and yet not fall into your power." "How do you propose to drink the water, then?" "Ah, you think we shall have to go down into the water to drink; whereas we shall not enter the water at all, but the whole eighty thousand of us will take a cane each and drink therewith from your lake as easily as we could through the hollow stalk of a lotus. And so you will not be able to eat us." And he repeated the latter half of the following stanza (the first half being added by the Master when, as Buddha, he recalled the incident):—

I found the footprints all lead down, none back.

With canes we'll drink; you shall not take my life.

So saying, the Bodhisattva had a cane brought to him. Then, calling to mind the Ten Perfections displayed by him, he recited them in a solemn asseveration, and blew down the cane. Straightway the cane became hollow throughout, without a single knot being left in all its length. In this fashion he had another and another brought and blew down them. (But if this were so, he could never have finished; and accordingly the forgoing sentence must not be understood in this—literal—sense).

Next the Bodhisattva made the tour of the lake, and commanded, saying, 'Let all canes growing here become hollow throughout. ' Now, thanks to the great virtues of the saying goodness of Bodhisattvas, their commands are always fulfilled. And thenceforth every single cane that grew round that lake became hollow throughout.

After giving this command, the Bodhisattva seated himself with a cane in his hands. All the other eighty thousand monkeys too seated themselves round the lake, each with a cane in his hands. And at the same moment when the Bodhisattva sucked the water up through his cane, they all drank too in the same manner, as they sat on the bank. This was the way they drank, and not one of them could the water-ogre get; so he went off in a rage to his own habitation. The Bodhisattva, too, with his following went back into the forest. [1]

From the murals, it is evident that the ancient painters in Kucha reproduced, on the wall, scenes from the *Naḷapānajātaka* [2]. This story, which is also narrated in the *Mahāvastu* [3], seems not to be found in any extant texts in Chinese. It proves, therefore, that the contents and the subjects of the murals in the Kizil caves were borrowed from those of India and central Asia. In addition, the *Naḷapānajātaka* painted in Kizil is the only representation of this story, in visual form preserved now in the whole world, so far as I know.

(This paper was published in the *Turfan Revisited*: *The First Century of Research into the Arts and Cultures of the Silk Road,* edited by M. Yaldiz et al, Berlin: Dietrich Reimer Verlag, 2004: 163-168.)

---

[1] E. B. Cowell ed., *The Jātaka or Stories of the Buddha's Former Births,* translated from the Pāli by various hands, 6 volumes, Cambridge: Cambridge University Press, Vol. I, 1895; Vol. II, 1895; Vol. III, 1895; Vol. IV, 1895; Vol. V, 1905; Vol. VI, 1907; Vol. I: 54-56, No. 20.

[2] Ma Shichang, *opere citato*: 26-27, 50.

[3] É. Snart ed., *Mahāvastu*, III, 1897: 29-30.

The Representation of Buddha's *Parinirvāṇa* in the *Chētiyagharas* of Kizil, Kucha[1]

I. Introduction

The term *Parinirvāṇa* [涅槃] refers to the death of the Buddha, which is the final transcendence of Sākyamuni Buddha who escaped from the endless cycle of reincarnation. "Upon death only the *nirvāṇa* dharma, so to speak, exists as all other dharmas have disintegrated. This is represented in the art of Kizil [克孜尔] almost obsessively, in the form of monumental sculptures and mural paintings and in some cases as a combination of both"[2]. Scenes of the Buddha's *Parinirvāṇa* and episodes of related events were generally portrayed on the side walls of the back corridor, back part of the circumambulatory passageway, or the rear chamber of the *chētiyaghara* [塔庙窟 rock-cut *caityagṛha*, 中心柱窟 central-pillar-cave] in

[1] In this article, I use *chētiyaghara* as a convention for the characteristic cave structure of Kizil with a central *chētiya/stūpa* surrounded by an open circumambulatory passageway. The term is known from Prākṛit inscriptions from the Buddhist caves of the Western Ghats, and has been popularized since the time of colonial Indology.

[2] Rajeshwari Ghose, "The Kizil Caves: Dates, Art, and Iconography", in: *Kizil on the Silk Road: Crossroads of Commerce & Meeting of Minds*, ed. Rajeshwari Ghose, Mumbai: Marg Publications, 2008: 40-65, esp. 50.

Kizil, Kucīna［龟兹］[1]/Kucha［龟兹 / 库车］[2]. These scenes usually include: Subhadra［须 跋］who had entered *samādhi*［三 昧］meditation and passed away before the Buddha's *Parinirvāṇa*, Mahākāśyapa［大迦叶］'s worship of the Buddha's feet[3], cremation of the Buddha's body, distribution of the relics and worship of the *stūpa*. More specifically, the *Parinirvāṇa* was regularly depicted on the rear wall of the back corridor or the rear chamber, the cremation of the body on the opposite wall and the distribution of the relics on the side wall at a right angle to the cremation episode. These representations indicate that the Buddha's *Parinirvāṇa* and related events were very popular in ancient Kucha. Especially, the scene of the Buddha's *Parinirvāṇa*, which occurs almost without exception in all the *chētiyagharas*[4] dating from the end of the third century AD to the late

---

［1］*confer*：1) Li Yan［礼言］, *Fanyu zaming*［梵语杂名, *Sundry Names in Sanskrit*］, in: *Taishō*, No. 2135, Vol. 54: 1236a; 2) Unrai Ogiwara［荻原雲来］, *Bon-wa Daijiten*［漢訳対照梵和大辭典, *A Sanskrit-Chinese-Japanese Dictionary*］, Tōkyō: Kōdansha, 1974: 352b.

［2］1) Su Bai［宿白］, "*Xinjiang baicheng kezi'er shiku bufen dongku de leixing yu niandai*［新疆拜城克孜尔石窟部分洞窟的类型与年代, Types and Dating of Some Caves at Kizil in Baicheng, Xinjiang］", in: *Zhongguo shikusi yanjiu*［中国石窟寺研究, *Studies of the Cave-temples of China*］, Beijing: Cultural Relics Press, 1996：21-38, esp. 22-33; 2) Jia Yingyi［贾应逸］, "*Kezi'er yu mogaoku de niepan jingbian bijiao yanjiu*［克孜尔与莫高窟的涅槃经变比较研究, A Comparative Study of Kizil and Mogaoku *Nirvāṇa-sūtra* Paintings］", in: *Qiuzi fojiao wenhua lunji*［龟兹佛教文化论集, *Collected Essays on Kucha Buddhist Culture*］, ed. Kucha Cave Research Institute, Urumchi: Xinjiang Art & Photograph Publishing House, 1993: 229-240.

［3］The story of the Buddha's *Parinirvāṇa*, in a general way, ends up with Mahākāśyapa's worship of the feet of the Buddha. *confer:* Akira Miyaji［宫治昭］, *Nehan to Miroku no zuzōgaku: Indo kara Chūō Ajia e*［涅槃と弥勒の図像学——インドから中央アジアへ, *Iconology of Parinirvāṇa and Maitreya: from India to Central Asia*］, Tokyo: Yoshikawa Kōbunkan, 1992: 139.

［4］According to the statistics that the author collected *in situ*, the Cave Nos. 63, 100, 123 at Kizil do not have scenes of the Buddha's *Parinirvāṇa* portrayed in the rear chambers of *chētiyagharas*. It is noteworthy that in the ratio of frequency of the texts in the German Turfan Collection, as well as the fragments in the Hoernle and Pelliot Collections, the *Mahāparinirvāṇa-sūtra* is one of the four Buddhist texts copied most often, while the text represented by the largest number of manuscripts is the *Udānavarga*［优陀那品, i. e. 法集要诵经］, followed, in proper order, by *Bhikṣuprātimokṣasūtra*［比丘戒本］, Mātṛceṭa's *Buddhastotras*［摩咥里制吒《佛赞》］and the *Mahāparinirvāṇa-sūtra*［大般涅槃经］. *confer*: 1) Dieter Schlingloff, *Die Buddhastotras des Mātṛceṭa, Faksimilewiedergabe der Handschriften* (Abhandlungen der Deutschen Akademie der Wissenschaften zu Berlin 1968, Nr. 2), Berlin: Akademie-Verlag, 1968: 5; 2) Jens-Uwe Hartmann, "Buddhism along the Silk Road: On the Relationship between the Buddhist Sanskrit Texts from Northern Turkestan and those from Afghanistan", *Turfan Revisited-The First Century of Research into the Arts and Cultures of the Silk Road,* eds. Desmond Durkin-Meisterernst et al, Berlin: Dietrich Reimer Verlag, 2004: 125-128, esp. 126.

eighth century AD[1].

The *chētiyaghara* of Kizil, in general, can be divided into three parts: front chamber, main chamber and back corridor or rear chamber. Most of the front chambers collapsed long ago and only their rear section remains, although sometimes the façade of the cave has survived with remnants of the murals. On the façade of the central *stūpa*-pillar shaped like a mushroom, which corresponds to the back wall of the main chamber of the *chētiyaghara*, is represented the Indraśāla-guhā［帝释窟］, i. e., Indra's visit to the Buddha. In the lunette above the entrance, namely the upper part of the front wall of the main chamber, is the Bodhisattva Maitreya who is preaching in Tuṣita Heaven［兜率天］. The main chamber's sidewalls and ceiling are filled with mural paintings. These include scenes of the Buddha's preaching depicted on the sidewalls and representations of *jātakas*［本生］, as well as *avadāna*［因缘］stories, on the ceiling. The back corridor or the rear chamber is mainly occupied by the Buddha's *Parinirvāṇa* cycle; in other words, the side walls of the entire back corridor are covered with the narrative scenes that took place before and after the Buddha's *Parinirvāṇa*, the latter being the focal point for pilgrims while they circumambulate the mushroom-like *stūpa* (central pillar) in the *chētiyaghara* (fig.1).

The scene of the Buddha's *Parinirvāṇa* is depicted according to a convention derived from *sūtra* texts, which remains practically unchanged and has become fixed iconography. The figure of the Buddha is shown lying on his right side, with his head resting on his right arm or on the palm of his right hand, while his left arm is stretched along his side and his left foot is placed over the other. The great sorrow or lamentation of the participants was generally portrayed at the upper right of the reclining Buddha and a cycle of narratives connected with the Buddha's final events in his life was depicted around the reclining body.

---

［1］Chongfeng Li［李崇峰］, *Zhongyin fojiao shikusi bijiao yanjiu: yi tamiaoku wei zhongxin*［中印佛教石窟寺比较研究：以塔庙窟为中心, *Chētiyagharas in Indian and Chinese Buddhist Cave-temples: A Comparative Study*］, Beijing: Peking University Press, 2003: 167-176.

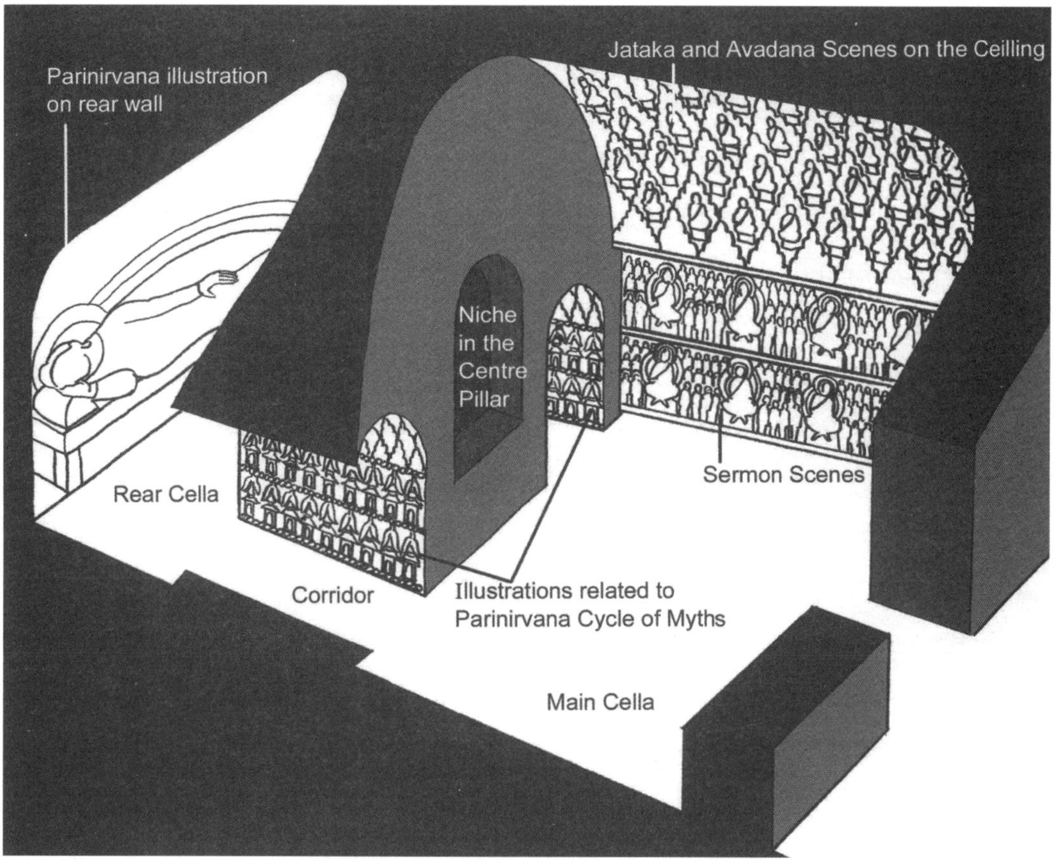

fig.1 Typical iconographic program of a *chētiyaghara* (central pillar cave) at Kizil

II. Visual *Parinirvāṇa* in Kucha

On the basis of the composition, the visual or pictorial representations related to the Buddha's *Parinirvāṇa* cycle at Kizil can be classified as follows.

Type A: The scene of the *Parinirvāṇa* is depicted on the rear wall of the back corridor of the *chētiyaghara*. The Buddha is lying on a couch between two *śāla* trees［娑罗树］, with one foot resting on the other. The Buddha's drapery folds, instead of falling straight over the couch, curve toward his feet just as they would as if he were standing. The aureole behind his body sometimes has flames issuing from it. Concerning this composition, details may differ in the caves of Kizil[1]. For instance, in Caves 7 and 171, the composition is kept to a minimum; the Buddha is shown reclining on the couch, with an old monk kneeling before his feet, who may be identified as Mahākāśyapa[2]. Mahākāśyapa's gaze is fixed on Buddha's feet as he gently strokes them. This rendering refers to the episode in which the body of the Buddha refused to burn until the disciple Mahākāśyapa paid his last homage to his teacher. In more complicated depictions, as in Caves 179 and 205, additional narratives and events are conflated and merged into a big scene of the *Parinirvāṇa* and lamentation. Thus, the monk sitting in front of the couch and viewed from behind is probably Subhadra, the last convert to Buddhism during the Buddha's lifetime; by the feet of the reclining Buddha one sees a kneeling figure, no doubt the monk Mahākāśyapa. Behind the couch are celestials, *devas*, as well as princely personages, who are perhaps the nobles of Kuśinagara［拘尸那揭罗］, the Mallā［末罗］chieftains, likewise in attitudes of grief. According to the subjects painted on the opposite walls, which are also part of the *Parinirvāṇa* cycle in the back corridor of the *chētiyaghara*, the Type A composition can be divided into three sub-types:

Type Ai: The scene of the Buddha's *Parinirvāṇa* is depicted on the rear wall of the back corridor, with *śārīra stūpas*［舍利塔］portrayed on the opposite wall, i. e., the rear wall of the mushroom-like *stūpa*, as in the Caves 7[3], 38, 107A, 171, 172 etc. (figs. 2a, 2b).

Type Aii: The scene of the *Parinirvāṇa* is depicted on the rear wall of the back corridor, with the cremation of the Buddha's body painted on the opposite wall. The Buddha's body, wrapped in multiple layers of cloth, is lying in a coffin in the

［1］Ding Mingyi［丁明夷］et al., "*Kezi'er shiku de fozhuan bihua*［克孜尔石窟的佛传壁画, Representation of the Buddha's Life-story in the Mural Paintings at Kizil Caves, Kucha］", in: *Zhongguo shiku: Kezi'er shiku*［中国石窟·克孜尔石窟, *The Cave-temples of China: Kizil Caves*］Vol. 1, Beijing: Cultural Relics Press, 1989: 185-222, esp. 197.

［2］Albert von Le Coq und Ernst Waldschmidt, *Die Buddhistische Spätantike in Mittelasien*, vi, Neue Bildwerke ii, Berlin: D. Reimer, 1928: 73, Tafel 11.

［3］A set of *śārīra stūpas* was depicted over the tableau of the cremation on the front wall of the back corridor of Cave No. 7 at Kizil.

a

b

fig.2a *Parinirvāṇa* of the Buddha, mural painting from the rear wall of the back corridor of Cave 171 at Kizil

b *Śārīra stūpas,* mural on the front wall of the back corridor of Cave 171 at Kizil, *in situ*

process of being burnt. In some cases, a monk is opening the lid of the coffin[1]

[1] A monk who is opening the lid of the coffin is something unique in the scene of the Buddha's *Parinirvāṇa* at Kizil. The monk may be identified as Mahākāśyapa because there is an inscription on the forehead of a monk in such a position in Kizil Cave No. 48 that has been recently deciphered which identifies him by name. This narrative, to my knowledge, occurs in both the Chinese version of the *Mūlasarvāstivāda-vinaya-kṣudraka-vastu* [根本说一切有部毗奈耶杂事] and the Sanskrit version of *Mahāparinirvāṇasūtra* of the Sarvāstivāda-Mūlasarvāstivāda school edited by Ernst Waldschmidt. *confer* 1) Rajeshwari Ghose, *opere citato*: 53; 2) *Taishō,* No. 1451, Vol. 24: 207-414, esp. 401b.

and in others is kneeling at the foot of the couch. The Type Aii representations are found in the Caves 4, 98, 163, 178, 179, 205 etc. (figs.3a, 3b).

Type Aiii: The scene of the *Parinirvāṇa* is depicted on the rear or front wall of the back corridor, while a tableau showing the distribution of the relics or the impending war among the eight contenders for the relics of the Buddha is

a

b

fig.3a *Parinirvāṇa* of the Buddha, mural painting on the rear wall of the back corridor of Cave 205 at Kizil, *in situ*

b Cremation of the Buddha, mural painting from the front wall of the back corridor of Cave 205 at Kizil typically portrayed on the opposite wall, as in the Caves 27[1], 58[2], 80, 114, 192 etc. (figs.4a, 4b).

Type B: The back corridor of the *chētiyaghara* was transformed into a rear chamber, a rock-cut couch was carved against the rear wall and a large-sized painted clay sculpture of the Buddha in *Parinirvāṇa* was installed on the couch

a

b

fig.4a *Parinirvāṇa* of the Buddha, mural painting on the front wall of the back corridor of Cave 58 at Kizil, *in situ*

b Distribution of the relics, mural painting on the rear wall of the back corridor of Cave 58 at Kizil, *in situ*

---

[1] The scene of the cremation of the body and that of the impending war among the eight contenders for the relics of the Buddha were depicted together on the front wall of the back corridor of Cave No. 27 at Kizil. The former is painted on the left and the latter on the right.

[2] The scene of the *Parinirvāṇa* was depicted on the front wall of the back corridor of Cave 58 at Kizil, and the tableau of the war among the eight contenders for the relics was portrayed on the opposite wall.

(fig.5a), with adoring people and flying deities depicted on the surrounding side walls and ceiling, executed either in painted clay or painted. Most of these large-sized clay sculptures of the *Parinivāṇa* Buddha have been damaged or have totally disappeared. The front wall, i. e., the rear wall of the mushroom-like *stūpa*, is decorated with either the scene of the cremation, as in the Caves 175, 224, 227, etc., or with the scene of distribution of the relics, as in the Caves 8, 34 and Cave New No. 1, etc. (fig.5b). In general, the scene of the cremation is

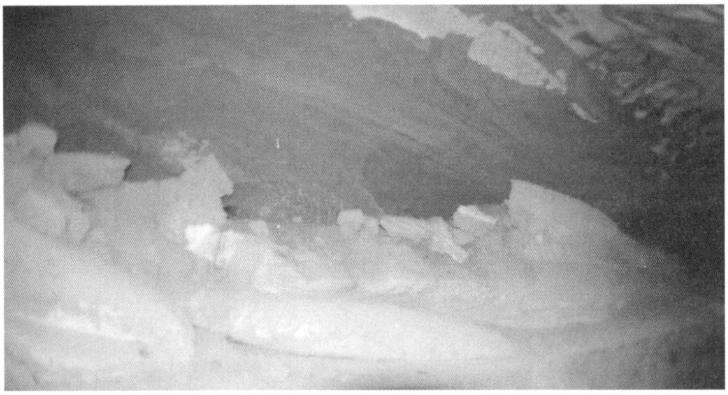

a

b

fig.5a *Parinirvāṇa* of the Buddha, painted clay sculpture on a rock-cut couch against the rear wall of the rear chamber of Cave New No.1 at Kizil, *in situ*

b Distribution of the relics, mural painting on the front wall of the rear chamber of Cave New No.1 at Kizil, *in situ* formed chiefly by two parts (fig.6a). The lower part of the wall is painted with the cremation of the Buddha, whose body, wrapped in multiple layers of cloth, is stretched out in a coffin. The lid of the coffin is decorated with a herringbone pattern, with a dragon head on the front and a dragon tail on the back. Monks, princely personages and other figures are gathered around the coffin. Sometimes a monk is placed at the head of the coffin in the act of lifting the lid and staring upon the remains of the Buddha, and another monk is kneeling at the end of the coffin, with his hands clasped in adoration. In addition, some are shown paying their last respects to the expired Buddha and others are pouring oil on the coffin. Most of these personages are filled with deep sorrow. In the upper part of the wall is painted the great lamentation showing those who were grieving over the Buddha's passing away. Some are shown inflicting harm on themselves resulting in different kinds of injuries (fig.6b)[1].

The scene of the Buddha's *Parinirvāṇa* represented by Type Ai composition was depicted on the rear wall of the back corridor of the *chētiyagharas* in the first period, about the end of the third century AD to the middle of the fourth century AD, which is similar to such reliefs of Gandhāra in design. From the second period, about the middle of the fourth century AD to the end of the fifth century AD, onwards, some of the back corridors of the *chētiyagharas* at Kizil were enlarged and made higher and wider to form a rear chamber with a rock-cut couch carved against the rear wall on which was placed a huge clay statue of the reclining Buddha. This sculpture dominated the rear chamber of the *chētiyaghara*. All the scenes of the Buddha's *Parinirvāṇa* cycle were further developed and a new composition, much different from the reliefs of Greater Gandhāra [罽宾], was created during the sixth and seventh centuries AD, such as those of Type Aii and Type Aiii, as well as Type B. This indicates that the ideal or notion of the Buddha's *Parinirvāṇa* was further enhanced by that time in Kucha[2].

---

[1] Dharmarakṣa [竺法护] tr., *Fo bonihuan jing* [佛般泥洹经, *Buddha's Parinirvāṇa Sūtra*], in: *Taishō*, No. 5, Vol. 1: 160-175, esp. 171a.

[2] Chongfeng Li, *opere citato*: 151-176.

a

b

fig.6a Cremation of the Buddha and great lamentation, mural painting from the front wall of the rear chamber of Cave 224 at Kizil

b Great lamentation, detail of upper part of fig.6a, line-drawing

III. Gandhāran Prototype

Regarding the final events in Buddha's life, that is, the *Parinirvāṇa* cycle, there are numerous records in the Buddhist canon, such as the *Mahāparinibbāna-sutta* of the Pāli *Dīghanikāya*, the *Mahāparinirvāṇasūtra* in the Sanskrit *Dīrghāgama*[1], the Gāndhārī [犍陀罗语][2] and Chinese versions of the above text as well as the Sanskrit *Mūlasarvāstivāda-vinaya-kṣudraka-vastu* and its Chinese version. Among these texts, the *Mahāparinibhāna-sutta* in the Pāli *Dīghanikāya* was believed to be the original or one of the oldest versions of such a Buddhist *sūtra*[3], and the *Youxing jing* [游行经, *The Sūtra of (the Buddha's) Travels to Preach/ Sūtra of (the Buddha) Preaching Travels*], Fascicle 2 to 4 in the Chinese *Dīrghāgama* [长阿含经, the *Chang ahanjing* or *Long Āgama Sūtra*][4], which corresponds closely to a Gāndhārī parallel, is

---

[1] The Sanskrit *Mahāparinirvāṇasūtra* in the *Dīrghāgama* edition, which belongs to the Sarvāstivāda-Mūlasarvāstivāda school, is fundamentally based on numerous fragments retrieved in Xinjiang. *confer:* 1) Ernst Waldschmidt, *Die Überlieferung vom Lebensende des Buddha: Eine vergleichende Analyse des Mahāparinirvāṇasūtra und seiner Textentsprechungen*, Teil 1 und 2 (Abhandlungen der Akademie der Wissenschaften in Göttingen, Philologisch-historische Klasse, 3. Folge, Nr. 29, 30), Göttingen: Vandenhoeck & Ruprecht, 1944, 1948; 2) Ernst Waldschmidt, *Das Mahāparinirvāṇasūtra*: *Text in Sanskrit und Tibetisch, verglichen mit dem Pāli nebst einer Übersetzung der chinesischen Entsprechung im Vinaya der Mūlasarvāstivādins*, Teil I-III (Abhandlungen der Deutschen Akademie der Wissenschaften zu Berlin, Klasse für Sprachen, Literatur und Kunst, no. 1, 1949; No. 2, 3, 1950), Berlin: Akademie-Verlag, 1950-1951.

A tremendous number of Buddhist manuscripts in Indian languages have found their way from the area of Greater Gandhāra to the Western rare book market in recent years. Of which, a manuscript containing a Sanskrit version of the *Dīrghāgama* has been confirmed, and fragments of the *Mahāparinirvāṇasūtra* are shown a little in folio 111 of this manuscript. *confer*: Jens-Uwe Hartmann, "Contents and Structure of the Dīrghāgama of the (Mūla-) Sarvāstivādins", *Annual Report of The International Research Institute for Advanced Buddhology at Soka University* 7 (2004): 119-137.

[2] A small fragment of a Gāndhārī *Mahāparinirvāṇasūtra* from Xinjiang has come to light in the Oldenberg collection of St Petersburg, which seems to belong to the Dharmaguptakas. *confer* B. A. Litvinsky, ed., *History of Civilizations of Central Asia*, Vol. 3: *The Crossroads of Civilization:* AD 250-750, Multiple History Series, Paris: UNESCO, 1996: 436.

[3] T. W. Rhys Davids, *Buddhist India*, rev. ed., Delhi: Bharatiya Kala Prakashan, 2007: 111.

[4] *Taishō*, No. 1, Vol. 1: 11-30.

relatively complete and coherent when compared to the Pāli parallel, the *Mahāparinibbāna-sutta* of the *Dīghanikāya*.

The Buddha's *Parinirvāṇa* was depicted in the visual form as early as the second century BC, but was represented only aniconically, "those on the East Gate (at Bhārhut) symbolize just an event in the life of the Buddha, namely, his great decease"[1]. The scene of the Buddha's *Parinirvāṇa* in human form, however, was a creation of the Gandhāran artists, the scene may have been modeled on Hellenistic and Roman funerary arts[2] and became one of the most favorite subjects popular in the Greater Gandhāra region[3]. More than 70 reliefs that depict the scene of the Buddha's *Parinirvāṇa* have been discovered so far in this region. They were models or prototypes for the representation of the same theme not only in India proper[4], but also in central Asia and eastern Asia[5]. The representations apparently remained popular in India[6] and central Asia during the fifth to sixth century AD, as evidenced by the huge *Parinirvāṇa* sculpture at Kuśīnagara and that in Cave 26 at Ajaṇṭā［阿折罗 / 阿旃陀］, as well as the representation in the form of monumental sculptures and mural paintings

[1] Benimadhab Barua, *Bārhut*, Book III, *Aspects of Life and Art*: Patna: Indological Book Corporation, 1979: 22, Figs. 54-55. *confer* 1) Jas. Burgess, *The Buddhist Stūpas of Amarāvatī and Jaggayapeṭa in Krishna District, Madras Presidency, surveyed in 1882*, in: *Archaeological Survey of Southern India*, VI, London: 1886, rep., New Delhi: Archaeological Survey of India, 1996: Pls. XLI, XLVI, XLVIII; 2) James Fergusson, *Tree and Serpent Worship: or Illustrations of Mythology and Art in India in the first and fourth centuries after Christ from the Sculptures of the Buddhist Topes at Sāñchī and Amrāvatī*, London: Indian Office, 1873: Pls. XCIV, XCVII, LXXV.

[2] Akira Miyaji, *opere citato*: 597.

[3] John Marshall, *The Buddhist Art of Gandhāra: The Story of the Early School; its birth, growth and decline*, London: Cambridge University Press, 1960: 55, Figs. 68, 72, 87, 127, 128, 129.

[4] R. C. Sharma, *Buddhist Art: Mathura School*, New Delhi: Wiley Eastern Limited & New Age International Limited, 1995: 245, Figs. 168, 178, 179.

[5] Akira Miyaji, *opere citato*: 113, 148-150.

[6] According to R. C. Sharma, "before the cremation the body of the Buddha was placed in a coffin after wrapping it in five hundred layers of cotton cloth. The iron case was filled with oil. The theme was very popular with the Gandhāran artists but there is only one sculpture depicting this theme in Mathura art" . R. C. Sharma, *opere citato*: 245.

at Bāmiyān［梵衍那 / 巴米杨］[1].

The *Parinirvāṇa* cycle represented in Greater Gandhāra includes not only the scene of the Buddha's *Parinirvāṇa* itself, but also episodes concerning the events before and after the moment of the *Parinirvāṇa*, such as Subhadra's passing away beforehand; the great lamentation; wrapping the Buddha's remains; placing the body in a coffin; the funeral procession; the Buddha extending his feet out of the coffin; the cremation of the Buddha's body; guarding the urn; veneration of the relics; fight for the relics; distribution of the relics; transportation of the relics; enshrinement of the relics; as well as construction of the *stūpa* and the cult of the *stūpa*[2]. This series of scenes of the Buddha's *Parinirvāṇa* cycle were commonly used as *stūpa* casings[3] and form the main "part of the Gandhāra repertoire"[4] of the early period. Among these various scenes, "the death of the Buddha was one of the earliest and most familiar subjects of Gandhāra art."[5] Of the many *Parinirvāṇa* scenes known to us, the oldest might be the one from the Guides' Mess Collection (fig.7a). "In this composition—the earliest that has survived but by no means the first of its kind"[6], the Buddha is shown lying on a couch in the centre of the panel, with a richly decorated cloth covering the mattress. The artist has made a brave effort to disclose the lines of the form of the reclining Buddha beneath the folds of the robe, and to make it appear as

---

［1］1) D. R. Patil, *Kuśīnagara*, New Delhi: Archaeological Survey of India, 1957: 20; 2) James Fergusson and James Burgess, *The Cave Temples of India*, London: W. H. Allen & Co., 1880: Plate L; 3) Samuel Beal, *Si-Yu-Ki: Buddhist Records of the Western World; Chinese Accounts of India*, London: Trubner, 1884: 114-115; 4) Takayasu Higuchi［樋口隆康］ed., バーミヤーン：アフガニスタンにおける仏教石窟寺院の美術考古学的調查 1970-1978 年 (*Bāmiyān: Art and archaeological researches on the Buddhist cave temples in Afghanistan 1970-1978*), 京都大學中央アシア學術調查報告：第 I 巻図版篇 (壁画), 第 II 巻図版篇 (石窟構造)1983；第 III 巻本文篇, 第 IV 巻英文 / 実測図篇, 1984 (4 vols., Vol. I: Plates / Murals, Vol. II: Plates / Construction of Caves, 1983; Vol. III: Text, Vol. IV: Summary / Plans, 1984), 京都：同朋舎 (Kyoto: Dōhōsha), 1983-1984 年 , Vol. I: Pls. 7, 57-2, 66, 69-1, 70-2.

［2］Kurita Isao［栗田功］, *Gandhāra bijutsu*［ガンダーラ美術 , *Gandhāran Art*］, I 佛伝 (Vol. I *The Buddha's Life Story*): Tokyo: Nigensha, 1988: 233-262.

［3］W. Zwalf, *A Catalogue of the Gandhāra Sculpture in the British Museum,* Vol. I, London: British Museum Press, 1996: 50.

［4］Rajeshwari Ghose, *opere citato*: 54.

［5］John Marshall, *opere citato*: 54.

［6］John Marshall, *opere citato*: 49.

if the dead Buddha were sleeping, relaxed and peaceful on his side. Near the head of the couch stands a bearded Vajrapāṇi [金刚手], with his hand holding the thunderbolt. At the foot of the couch, one may still see the outline of a standing figure, probably Mahākāśyapa, who rushed to the funeral pyre after he learned that the Buddha had been dead for a week. In front of the couch, three monks can be seen sitting on the ground, expressing their feelings of grievous loss in different ways. Behind the couch, four princely personages, likewise in attitudes of grief, are perhaps Mallā chieftains, nobles of Kuśīnagara. To complete the scene, two *śāla* trees were added in the background, with dryads or tree-spirits ensconced among their foliage[1].

Scenes of the same theme depicted later follow the principle of this basic composition, but decorative elements have been accentuated by increasing the number of figures, although the effect is more natural and spontaneous in the earlier works. In all of them, the essential elements were well established by tradition and are unalterable, namely, the Buddha stretched at full length on his couch, with mourners around him. A striking peculiarity of this and most of the other Gandhāran *Parinirvāṇa* reliefs is the rendering of the Buddha's drapery (*saṃghāṭī*) folds. Instead of folds falling straight over the couch, they curve toward his feet, just as they would as if he were standing. As for the group of figures around the couch, we may recognize Subhadra sitting in front of the couch[2], Vajrapāṇi by the vajra in his hand[3], the flywhisk holder Upavāna[4], Mahākāśyapa, the *devas*, as well as the *śāla* trees in the background, and frequently, but not invariably, the Mallā chieftains. In the treatment of the individual figures and their grouping, however, there was

[1] 1) A. Foucher, *L'art gréco-bouddhique du Gandhāra: Étude sur les origines de l'influence classique dans l'art Bouddhique de l' Inde et de l'Extréme-Orient* , 2 Bde, I, 1905; II1, 1918; II2, 1922; II3, 1951, Paris: Imprimerie Nationale/ E. Leroux, 1905-51, Tome I: 557, Fig. 276; 2) Harald Ingholt, *Gandhāran Art in Pakistan*, New York: Pantheon Books, 1957: 92-93; 3) John Marshall, *opere citato*: 49-50.

[2] A. Foucher, *opere citato*, Tome I (1905), 567.

[3] A. Foucher, *opere citato*, Tome I (1905), 565, Fig. 281; Tome II. 1 (1918), 48-64.

[4] A. Foucher, *opere citato*, Tome I (1905), 566.

plenty of space for the imagination and skill of the artist. Thus, there are some differences between this relief and later versions of the same scene. For instance, Mahākāśyapa was represented in three different kinds of posture in the reliefs of Greater Gandhāra. In the first posture, he is shown standing near the head or feet of the expired Buddha, sometimes with a staff in his hand; the nude figure beside him might be Nirgrantha-putra [尼乾子] who had given him the news of the Buddha's death (fig.7b). In the second posture, Mahākāśyapa is shown bowing slightly from the waist in the act of veneration at the feet of the expired Buddha after he arrived at the funeral pyre, with his right hand or two hands gently touching or stroking the Buddha's feet. In the third posture, this venerable monk is shown going down on one knee or kneeling at the foot of the couch, with his hands clasped in adoration or gently stroking the feet of the Buddha (fig.7c). The representation of the third posture of Mahākāśyapa belongs to the later period of Gandhāran art[1]. Furthermore, Ānanda [阿难], who has collapsed in front of the couch, is being helped from the ground by Aniruddha [阿那律] at the head of the couch[2]. It is difficult to know whether the other figures are meant to be celestials or Mallā chieftains (figs. 7b, 7c, 8a)[3]. Among these figures, Subhadra and Mahākāśyapa are the two most important ones in the representation of the Buddha's *Parinirvāṇa* cycle in the Greater Gandhāra.

In addition to the usual depiction of the Buddha's *Parinirvāṇa*, some other events concerning the *Parinirvāṇa* cycle were also added in Gandhāran art. For instance, the Buddha's body was cleaned by perfumed ointments and his hands and feet were enveloped in the folds of his drapery, and the mourners are depicted behind the couch all making gestures of grief. One monk by the Buddha's feet seems to be arranging and smoothing out the cloth with his left hand (fig.8b). In fig.8c, the body of the Buddha is shown covered from head to foot by the cloth, which indicates that the body was covered by new cotton

---

[1] Akira Miyaji, *opere citato*: 139-142.

[2] A. Foucher, *opere citato*: Tome I: 565-566, Figs. 277, 281, 284.

[3] 1) A. Foucher, *opere citato* Tome I: 555-573; 2) John Marshall, *opere citato*: 54-55, 97-98; 3) Akira Miyaji, *opere citato*: 113-151.

a

b

c

fig.7a *Parinirvāṇa* of the Buddha, bas-relief, Peshawar Museum, Peshawar
b *Parinirvāṇa* of the Buddha, bas-relief, British Museum
c *Parinirvāṇa* of the Buddha, bas-relief, National Museum of Afghanistan, Kabul

and then wrapped in five hundred successive layers of cotton cloth. According to the Buddhist *sūtras* [经] and *vinayas* [律], after the Buddha's body was wrapped in multiple layers of cotton and cotton cloth in preparation for the actual cremation, it was placed into a golden inner coffin filled with linseed oil,

a

b

c

fig.8a *Parinirvāṇa* of the Buddha, bas-relief, Pakistan

b The Expired Buddha covered by a drapery, bas-relief, from Swāt, Royal Ontario Museum

c The Buddha's body wrapped in multiple layers of cloth, bas-relief, Museum für Asiatische Kunst, Berlin over which was placed a double cover of iron, covered in turn by an outer coffin made of sandalwood[1]. The outer coffin in fig.9a is surrounded by monks only, seven in all, and in front of the bier, a small altar or an incense burner has been placed in the center. The coffin is scattered with a number of divine *mandāraka* flowers [文陀罗花] and one can see clearly the clamps which fastened the outer coffin[2]. In the next relief, however, the outer coffin is fastened by a leaf-like band made of cloth or silk, and monks, as well as believers, seem to be getting ready to carry the coffin (fig.9b). The outer coffin in these two reliefs seems to be made of sandalwood. In addition, in the art of Gandhāra, a miraculous event is shown as the Buddha extended his feet out of the coffin when Mahākāśyapa paid his last respects to the Buddha once he reached the place of the funeral pyre (fig.9c).

IV. Records on the *Parinirvāṇa* Cycle

The composition of all the reliefs discovered from Greater Gandhāra are closely related to the text of the *Sūtra of* [*the Buddha's*] *Travels to Preach* in the Chinese *Dīrghāgama*[3], but they somewhat differ from the corresponding text of the *Mahāparinibbāna-sutta* in the Pāli *Dīghanikāya*[4] and also from the Sanskrit version of the *Mahāparinirvāṇasūtra*. In other words, the Chinese *Dīrghāgama* follows the wording and contents of the Pāli version, but it distances itself from the Pāli *Dīghanikāya* in structure and classification, as well

[1] Buddhayaśas [佛陀耶舍] tr., *Chang ahanjing* [长阿含经, *Dīrghāgama / The Long Āgama Sūtra*], in: *Taishō*, No. 1, Vol. 1: 1-149, esp. 28b.

[2] Harald Ingholt, *opere citato*: 94-95.

[3] Buddhayaśas, *opere citato*: 25a-29a.

[4] T. W. Rhys Davids and J. Estlin Carpenter, eds., *Dīgha Nikāya, XVI, Mahā-Parinibbāna-Suttanta*, Pali Text Society, London: Oxford University Press, 1938: 149-165. *confer* 1) Maurice Walshe tr., *The Long Discourses of the Buddha*, Boston: Wisdom Publications, 1995: 262-268; 2) T. W. and C. A. F. Rhys Davids tr., *Dialogues of Buddha*, London: Oxford University Press, 1910: 164-186.

a c

b

fig.9a Coffin of the Buddha, bas-relief, Institute of Silk Road Studies
b Transporting of the Coffin, bas-relief, National Museum of Pakistan
c Cremation of the Buddha, bas-relief, Museum für Asiatische Kunst

as in some details[1].

For instance, the story of King Mahāsudarśana [大善见王] is presented

[1] 1) Ernst Waldschmidt, "Central Asian Sūtra Fragments and their Relation to the Chinese Āgamas", in: *Die Sprache der ältesten buddhistischen Überlieferung; The Language of the Earliest Buddhist Tradition* (Symposien zur Buddhismusforschung ii), Abhandlungen der Akademie der Wissenschaften in Göttingen: Philologisch-historische Klasse, Ser. 3, Vol. 117, Heinz Bechert, hrsg, Göttingen: Vandenhoeck & Ruprecht, 1980: 136-174, esp. 149; 2) Guo Liangyun [郭良鋆], *Fotuo he yuanshi fojiao sixiang* [佛陀和原始佛教思想, *Buddha and Thought of Primitive Buddhism*], Beijing: Chinese Social Science Press, 1997: 7.

as a separate *suttanta* (xvii) in the Pāli *Dīghanikāya,* which follows the *Mahā-Parinibbāna-Suttanta* (xvi) in the same *Nikāya*[1]. The Chinese version of the *Dīrghāgama* combines the *Mahāparinirvāṇasūtra* and the *Mahāsudarśanasūtra* into the *Sūtra of* [*the Buddha's*] *Travels to Preach*. In other words, the story of King Mahāsudarśana and the *Mahāparinirvāṇasūtra* were incorporated in fascicule 3 of the Chinese *Dīrghāgama.* This indicates that the ordering and structure of the *Dīrghāgama* were probably adapted in the Gāndhārī version after the Prākṛit original had been transmitted to northwestern India[2]. It seems to be confirmed by the Mahāsudarśana text, which was also included within the Gāndhārī version of the *Mahāparinirvāṇasūtra* in the Schøyen Collection[3]. Therefore, in some *chētiyagharas* of Kizil, a panel comprising two figures, a male standing on the left and a female on the right, always occurs on the right wall of the back corridor (figs. 10a, 10b), close to the head of the reclining Buddha. Some scholars identify this as the conversion of the Gandharva Shan'ai［善爱健闼婆王］[4]. However, we consider these two figures probably to refer to King Mahāsudarśana and his *strī-ratna* concubine[5], whose story was placed ahead of the event of Subhadra in the *Sūtra of* [*the Buddha's*] *Travels to Preach* of the Chinese *Dīrghāgama*. That is the reason why the two personages were given such an honored position in the scenes of the *Parinirvāṇa* cycle.

With regard to Subhadra, the Pāli *Dīghanikāya* records him as follows:

> And Subhadda said to the Venerable Ānanda: "Friend Ānanda, it is a great gain for you all, it is very profitable for you, that you have obtained the consecration of

[1] T. W. Rhys Davids and J. Estlin Carpenter eds., *opere citato*: 169-199.

[2] The Sanskrit *Dīrghāgama* of the Sarvāstivāda-Mūlasarvāstivāda school seems to adopt this structure and content division because the *Mahāsudarśanasūtra* appears in its central Asian Sanskrit version as incorporated in the *Mahāparinirvāṇasūtra*. *confer* Ernst Waldschmidt, *opere citato* (*Das Mahāparinirvāṇasūtra*: *Text in Sanskrit*...) 1951: 304-354.

[3] Mark Allon and Richard Salomon, "Kharoṣṭhī fragments of a Gāndhārī version of the *Mahāparinirvāṇasūtra*", in: *Manuscripts in the Schøyen Collection 1; Buddhist Manuscripts,* Vol. I, ed. Jens Braarvig, Oslo: Hermes Publishing, 2000: 243-284, esp. 244.

[4] 1) Ding Mingyi et al., *opere citato*: 196-197; 2) Akira Miyaji, *opere citato*: 498-500.

[5] Jia Yingyi, *opere citato*: 235.

a

b

fig.10a Mahāsudarśana and his *strī-ratna* (jade-like) concubine, mural painting on the right wall of the back corridor of Cave 7 at Kizil, *in situ*

b Mahāsudarśana and his strī-ratna concubine, line-drawing of mural painting on the right wall of the back corridor of Cave 13 at Kizil

discipleship in the Teacher's presence."

Then Subhadda received the going-forth in the Lord's presence, and the ordination. And from the moment of his ordination the Venerable Subhadda, alone, secluded, unwearying, zealous and resolute, in a short time attained to that for which young men of good family go forth from the household life into homelessness, that unexcelled culmination of the holy life, having realized it here and now by his own insight, and dwelt therein: "Birth is destroyed, the holy life has been lived, what had to be done has been done, there is nothing further here." And the Venerable Subhadda became another of the Arhants. He was the last personal disciple of the Lord[1].

---

[1] Maurice Walshe tr., *opere citato*: 269 (§5. 30). *confer* 1) Rhys Davids and J. Estlin Carpenter eds., *opere citato*: 148, 153; 2) T. W. and C. A. F. Rhys Davids tr., *opere citato*: 169.

This last sentence, "he was the last personal disciple of the Lord, " was added according to Buddhaghosa［佛音］by the reciters of the First Council[1]. The content of the first half of the *Sūtra of* [*the Buddha's*] *Travels to Preach* of the Chinese *Dīrghāgama* is more or less similar, but adds the fact that "Subhadda had passed away immediately before the *Parinirvāṇa* of the Buddha took place. "[2] Subhadra, whose story was fully represented in the reliefs (see figs. 7b, 7c, 8a, 8c) of Greater Gandhāra, is shown entering the stage of *samādhi*, and flames above his shoulders can be seen in some tableaux[3].

The process of anointing the dead body with *candana-vāri* (perfumed ointments or liquids) does not have a parallel in the *Mahāparinibbāna-sutta* of the Pāli *Dīghanikāya* nor in the Sanskrit version of the *Mahāparinirvāṇasūtra*, but it does appear in the Chinese version of the *Dīrghāgama* and the Kharoṣṭhī［佉卢字母］fragments of a Gāndhārī version of the *Mahāparinirvāṇasūtra*[4].

As for Mahākāśyapa's worship of the Buddha's feet, the *Mahāparinibbāna-sutta* of the Pāli *Dīghanikāya* narrates as follows:

> Then the Venerable Kassapa the Great went to the Mallas' shrine at Makuṭa-Bandhana to the Lord's funeral pyre and, covering one shoulder with his robe, joined his hands in salutation, circumambulated the pyre three times and, uncovering the Lord's feet, paid homage with his head to them, and the five hundred monks did likewise. And when this was done, the Lord's funeral pyre ignited of itself.[5]

The Chinese version of the *Dīrghāgama*, however, not only adds some details, but particularly accentuates the fact that the Buddha extended his feet out of the coffin so that the disciples could venerate them:

---

［1］Yang-Gyu An, trans., *The Buddha's Last Days, Buddhaghosa's Commentary on the Mahāpainibbana Sutta*, Oxford: The Pali Text Society, 2003: 175.

［2］*Taishō*, Vol. 1: 25b.

［3］Akira Miyaji, *opere citato*: 530.

［4］Mark Allon and Richard Salomon, *opere citato*: 258.

［5］Maurice Walshe tr., *opere citato*: 275 (§6. 22). *Confer*: 1) T. W. Rhys Davids and J. Estlin Carpenter eds., *opere citato*: 163; 2) T. W. and C. A. F. Rhys Davids tr., *opere citato*: 183.

After having heard of the Buddha's *Parinirvāṇa*, Mahākāśyapa ordered his follower *bhikṣus* to tidy in dress and to pay a formal visit to the *śāla* trees in Kuśinagara. They hoped to see the remains of the Buddha in person before the cremation took place. Then, Mahākāśyapa who was accompanied by his followers crossed the Nairañjanā [尼连禅河] and finally arrived at Makusa-bandhana [天冠寺 Mauli temple] where they met Ānanda in his residence. After saying greeting to each other, Mahākāśyapa asked Ānanda whether they could pay their last respects to the remains of the Buddha in person before the cremation. Ānanda was embarrassed to tell Mahākāśyapa and his followers that although the body was not cremated, it was hard to see the remains, because the body of the Buddha was first cleaned and anointed with *candana-vāri* [香汤, perfumed liquids] and then the body was wrapped in new *karpāsa* [劫贝, cotton] and *karpāsa-picu* or *paṭaka* [氎, cotton cloth or cotton shirting] one by one until it was wrapped in five hundred successive layers of the cotton cloth or cotton shirting, moreover, the body was put into a golden inner coffin filled with *gandha-taila* [麻油, linseed oil], over which a double cover made of iron was then placed, and finally it was covered by an outer coffin made of sandalwood. That's why it is hard to see the remains of the Buddha in person. Mahākāśyapa made the request three times, but Ānanda could not satisfy his demands and repeated what he had said before, believing that the remains of the Buddha were hard to see in person. When Mahākāśyapa came up to the *gandha-sugandha* (funeral pyre), the Buddha himself immediately extended his feet out of the inner and outer coffins. The color of Buddha's feet looked quite unusual. Mahākāśyapa felt surprised after he saw the Buddha's feet and asked Ānanda why the color of the Buddha's feet looked golden. Ānanda told Mahākāśyapa that an old woman had been overcome with deep grief and stroked the Buddha's feet gently, and her tears dropped on the feet. That's why the feet of the Buddha looked abnormal. After hearing this, Mahākāśyapa, with an annoyed expression, went to the *gandha-sugandha* (funeral pyre), bowing down with clasped hands and doing his last homage to the remains of the Buddha. In the meanwhile, the disciples, the *devas* and four kinds of believers also paid their respects to the remains of the Buddha. The feet of the Buddha suddenly disappeared just at this moment. Then, Mahākāśyapa thrice walked reverently around the pyre reciting *gathas* or verses ... As soon as the venerable Mahākāśyapa finished singing the praises of the Buddha, the funeral pyre on which the body of the expired Buddha was placed caught fire by itself and burst into flames.[1]

When transposed into the visual or pictorial realm, according to Sonya S. Lee, "the episode assumes a form rather different from what the text describes. The pictorialization can best be broached by two pictorial details: the feet-touching figure and the exposure of the Buddha's body." The reclining Buddha can be seen as a self-conscious reformulation of narrative time as articulated in the text. The body is rendered invariably visible at the moment of the disciple making his final homage, long after the moment of the Nirvāṇa, which is different from the scriptural version, as described in the Chinese *Dīrghāgama.* In selecting an exposed recumbent body, "the temporal sequentiality characteristic of any textual narrative is altered such that episodes registering different narrative times were all compressed into one spatial setting" (see figs. 7c, 8a), which "suggests that the configuration selected was not the result of some misunderstanding of the iconographic tradition or textual account, but rather a deliberate departure from both. "[2] The episode of this final event of Buddha's life was rarely represented, but in fig.9c the Buddha is shown remarkably extending his feet out of the double coffins, which were not uncovered by Mahākāśyapa as recorded in the Pāli *Dīghanikāya*. This depiction remains, however, quite faithful to the textual account of the Chinese *Dīrghāgama*.

Finally, in the tableau of the great lamentation, we may see mourners deeply grieving the Buddha's passing. Some are shown pulling their hair, pounding their head or striking their chest, as well as suffering other kinds of self-inflicted pain, such as wounding or disabling themselves by scratching their faces or noses or even cutting their chests (see fig.6b). Such scenes or narratives cannot be found

---

[1] *Taishō*, Vol. 1: 28c-29a. A similar statement can also be found in the Sanskrit version of the *Mahāparinirvāṇasūtra* of the Sarvāstivāda-Mūlasarvāstivāda school edited by Waldschmidt (§40. 46-49).

[2] Sonya S. Lee, *Surviving Nirvana: Death of the Buddha in Chinese Visual Culture*, Hong Kong: Hong Kong University Press, 2010: 58.

in the Pāli *Mahāparinibbāna-sutta* nor in the Sanskrit *Mahāparinirvāṇasūtra* of the Sarvāstivāda-Mūlasarvāstivāda school [说一切有部 / 根本说一切有部] edited by Ernst Waldschmidt. One may find details of such grief in the *Fo bonihuan jing* [佛般泥洹经, *The Buddha's Parinirvāṇa Sūtra*][1], a variant version parallel to the *Sūtra of [the Buddha's] Travels to Preach* text in the Chinese *Dīrghāgama,* which was translated by Dharmarakṣa [竺法护] in 269 AD[2]. Expressions of such a kind of deep grief used to be a Scythian custom that developed and merged with the local habit and culture of the people living in Chinese Central Asia[3].

With regard to the pictorial transformation or representation of the Buddha's *Parinirvāṇa* cycle in Kizil, the artists and painters, on the basis of the Gandhāran models, had copied the prototype of Gandhāran reliefs (see figs. 7a, 7b, 7c, 8a) in part only and made three or four events, such as Subhadra's passing away beforehand, the Buddha in *Parinirvāṇa*, Mahākāśyapa's worship of the Buddha's feet, as well as the cremation of the body, into one big scene (see figs. 2a, 11a), showing the great ingenuity of the local artists and craftsmen. In terms of composition, the reclining Buddha indicates the *Parinirvāṇa* of the Enlightened One, the posture of Subhadra[4], who is covered over from head to foot, expresses his passing away before the Buddha's *Parinirvāṇa* (fig.11b), and flames around the nimbus of the Buddha suggest the cremation of the body. Mahākāśyapa, in particular, appears in almost every scene related to the Buddha's

---

[1] Dharmarakṣa tr., *Fo bonihuan jing* (*Buddha's Parinirvāṇa Sūtra*), in: *Taishō,* No. 5, Vol. 1: 160-175, esp. 171a.

[2] Lü Cheng [吕澂], *Xinbian hanwen dazangjing mulu* [新编汉文大藏经目录, *A New Catalogue of the Chinese Versions of the Buddhist Tripiṭaka*], Ji'nan: Qilu Publishing House, 1980: 48.

[3] A. von Le Coq und Ernst Waldschmidt, *opere citato*: 80-81.

[4] According to CA MPS, Subhadra decides that it would not be suitable for him to witness the Teacher's *Parinirvāṇa*, and he should pass away before him. Ernst Waldschmidt, *opere citato*: 49 (§40. 48). The Pāli *Mahāparinibhāna Sutta* states that, "the venerable Subhadda became another of the Arahants. He was the last personal disciple of the Lord". Maurice Walshe, *opere citato*: 269 (§5. 30). The content of the third section of "*The Sūtra of [Buddha's] Travels to Preach*", viz. Fascicle 4 of the Chinese *Dīrghāgama*, is more or less similar, but adds the fact that "Subhadra achieved the *arhat* state and became the last disciple of Buddha. Then Subhadda had been in extinction of reincarnation and passed away immediately before the *Parinirvāṇa* of Buddha took place". *Taishō*, Vol. 1: 25b. Subhadra, whose story was fully represented in the reliefs of Greater Gandhāra, is shown, in some cases, being covered from head to foot by drapery and even flames above his shoulders can be seen in some tableaux, which seem to depict Subhadda had entered the *samādhi* state in a sitting posture.

passing away, whether in the tableau of the *Parinirvāṇa* itself or in the episode of the cremation at Kizil. Mahākāśyapa is shown kneeling at the end of the couch and bowing down with clasped hands, sometimes gently touching or stroking the feet of the expired Buddha (fig.11c). The episode of Subhadra passing away before the Buddha's *Parinirvāṇa*, and that of Mahākāśyapa worshipping the Buddha's feet, came into vogue in Kucha. The two personages became two indispensable figures in the composition of the Buddha's *Parinirvāṇa* at Kizil, especially in the earlier period[1].

If one considers the iconographic characteristics of the representations of the Buddha, Subhadra, and Mahākāśyapa, as well as their postures, one may conclude that the Kizil interpretation of the *Parinirvāṇa* scene is the heir of the iconography developed in Greater Gandhāra. The iconographic composition and its details are related to the notion of the Buddha's *Parinirvāṇa* popular in India, as well as central Asia. This could be regarded as a sign of the revival of the symbolism of the *Parinirvāṇa*. Combining the mural paintings of the *Parinirvāṇa* in Kizil with the reliefs of the same theme from Greater Gandhāra, as well as the *sūtras* and *vinayas*, we are inclined to conclude that the Kizil scene of the Buddha's *Parinirvāṇa* was mainly composed on the basis of a text[2] parallel to

[1] Akira Miyaji, *opere citato*: 142-143, 501, 534.

[2] The *Parinirvāṇa-sūtras* of the Hīnayāṇa schools are not focused as much on Buddha's preaching, but focus on descriptions of the final events of his life, his entry into *Nirvāṇa*, and the distribution of his relics. According to Hubert Durt, "the Mahāyānic *Mahāparinirvāṇasūtra* does not contain regulations on funerals." Hubert Durt, "The Long and Short Nirvāṇa Sūtras" , in: *Problems of Chronology and Eschatology,* Four Lectures on the *Essay on Buddhism* by Tominaga Nakamoto (1715-1746), Kyoto: Istituto Italiano di Cultura Scuola di Studi sull' Asia Orientale, 1994: 57-74, esp. 58. In the light of *Chu sanzang ji ji* [出三藏记集, *A Collection of Records concerning the Tripiṭaka*] by monk Sengyou [僧佑] between 494 and 497 AD and *Kaiyuan shijiao lu* [开元释教录, *Kaiyuan Era Catalogue of the Buddhist Canon*] by monk Zhisheng [智昇] in 730 AD, the two-volume *Buddha's Parinirvāṇa Sūtra* translated by Dharmarakṣa in 269 AD is a variant version parallel to the *Sūtra of* [*the Buddha's*] *Travels to Preach* in the Chinese *Dīrghāgama,* the three-volume *Dabo niepan jing* [大般涅槃经, *Mahāparinirvāṇasūtra*] translated by Faxian [法显 ?-c. 423 AD] between 416 and 418 AD is parallel to the two-volume *Buddha's Parinirvāṇa Sūtra*, and the two-volume *Bonihuan jing* [般泥洹经, *Parinirvāṇa Sūtra*] by an unknown translator of the Eastern Jin Dynasty [东晋, 317-420 AD] is also parallel to the two-volume *Buddha's Parinirvāṇa Sūtra*. *confer* Lü Cheng, *opere citato*: 48. These variant versions indicate that the *Parinirvāṇa sūtra* used to be very popular in the various local regions at that time.

a

b

c

fig.11a *Parinirvāṇa* of the Buddha, mural painting on the rear wall of the back corridor of Cave 38 at Kizil, *in situ*

b Details of the scene of the Buddha's *parinirvāṇa,* Subhadra perishing before the *parinirvāṇa* of the Buddha, mural painting on right section of the rear wall of the back corridor of Cave 38 at Kizil, *in situ*

c Details of the scene of the Buddha's *parinirvāṇa,* Mahākāśyapa's worship of the Buddha's feet, mural painting on the left section of the rear wall of the back corridor of Cave 38 at Kizil, *in situ* the *Sūtra of* [*the Buddha's*] *Travels to Preach* of the Chinese *Dīrghāgama*[1]. These two texts carry a rather abbreviated version of the Buddha's *Parinirvāṇa* cycle.

The centrality and supremacy of the *Parinirvāṇa* scene in Kizil is absolutely a unique aspect of central Asian art because "the last *Parinirvāṇa* that shows the Buddha-*dhātu* [佛性 nature of the Buddha]" is the ultimate goal sought after by the Buddhist followers of central Asia, especially of Kucha[2].

V. *Dharmaguptakas* and Kuchean *Chētiyaghara*

According to the *Mahāparinibbāna-sutta* of the Pāli *Dīghanikāya*, before the *Parinirvāṇa*, Ānanda asked the Buddha how to treat his remains after his passing:

> "What should be done, lord, with the remains of the Tathāgata?" "As men treat the remains of a king of kings, so, Ānanda, should they treat the remains of a Tathāgata. " "And how, lord, do they treat the remains of a king of kings?" "They wrap the body of a king of kings, Ānanda, in a new cloth. When that is done they wrap it in carded cotton wool. When that is done they wrap in a new cloth, and so on till they have wrapped the body in five hundred successive layers of both kinds. Then they place the body in an oil vessel of iron, and cover that close up with another oil vessel of iron. They then build a funeral pyre of all kinds of perfume, and burn the body of the king of kings. And then at the four cross roads they erect a cairn to the king of kings. This, Ānanda, is the way in which they treat the remains of a king of kings." "And as they treat the remains of a king of kings, so,

---

[1] *confer* Huo Xuchu [霍旭初] and Wang Jianlin [王建林], "*Danqing banbo qianqiu zhuangguan: Kezi'er shiku bihua yishu ji fenqi gaishu* [丹青斑驳　千秋壮观：克孜尔石窟壁画艺术及分期概述, Evidence of the Treasure House of a Great Art: A Survey of Kizil Mural Art and its Periodization]", in: *Qiuzi fojiao wenhua lunji* (*Collected Essays on Kucha Buddhist Culture*), ed. Kucha Cave Research Institute, Urumchi: Xinjiang Art & Photograph Publishing House, 1993: 201-228, esp. 211-212.

[2] Sengyou, *Chu sanzang ji ji* (*A Collection of Records concerning the Tripiṭaka* or *A Collection of Records of Translations of the Tripiṭaka*), emended and annotated by Su Jinren [苏晋仁] and Xiao Lianzi [萧錬子], Beijing: Zhonghua Book Company, 1995: 232. *confer*: *Taishō,* No. 2145, Vol. 55: 1-114, esp. 40c.

Ānanda, should they treat the remains of the Tathāgata. At the four cross roads a cairn should be erected to the Tathāgata. And whosoever shall there place garlands or perfumes or paint, or make salutation there, or become in its presence calm in heart—that shall long be to them for a profit and a joy." [1]

Later, when the Mallā chieftains of Kuśīnagara asked Ānanda how to treat the remains of the expired Buddha, the latter repeated again what he had learnt from the Buddha[2].A parallel to the above text in the *Mahāparinibbāna-sutta* of the Pāli *Dīghanikāya*, however, can be found in the Sanskrit version of the *Mahāparinirvāṇasūtra*[3]. Moreover, Ānanda's inquiry regarding the funeral practice, that is, the conversation between the Buddha and Ānanda, as well as what Ānanda told the Mallā chieftains, also occurs in the *Sūtra of* [*the Buddha's*] *Travels to Preach*, in Fascicle 3 of the Chinese *Dīrghāgama*:

Ānanda, you should treat my remains as those of the *cakravartin* [转轮圣王]. My body should be first cleaned and anointed with *candana-vāri* (perfumed liquids); afterwards, you should wrap the body from head to foot in a new *karpāsa* (cotton) and then in a *karpāsa-picu* or *paṭaka* (cotton cloth or cotton shirting) until the body is wrapped in five hundred successive layers of cotton cloth or cotton shirting. When that is done, the body should be put into a golden inner coffin filled with *gandha-taila* (linseed oil), over which a double cover made of iron is then placed, and finally it is covered again by an outer coffin made of sandalwood. After that, you build a funeral pyre of all kinds of perfume and then cremate the body covered with thick cloths and collect the relics. Later, a *stūpa* should be erected to the Buddha at the four crossroads, with a sign marked for the central pillar (of the *stūpa*) and banners hung atop the *stūpa*. And whosoever shall be there, see the *stūpa* and think of the Tathāgata as well as his dharma with respect and veneration-that shall be long to them for a profit and a joy, and they will be reborn

[1] Maurice Walshe tr., *opere citato*: 264 (§5. 11). *confer* 1) T. W. Rhys Davids and J. E. Carpenter eds., *opere citato*: 141-142; 2) T. W. and C. A. F. Rhys Davids tr., *opere citato*: 155-156.

[2] T. W. Rhys Davids and J. E. Carpenter eds., *opere citato*: 161 (Pāli); for translations, *confer*: 1) Maurice Walshe, *opere citato*: 274 (§6. 17); 2) T. W. and C. A. F. Rhys Davids, *opere citato*: 182-183.

[3] Ernst Waldschmidt, *opere citato* (*Die Überlieferung*...) Teil 2: 213-214, 294-295.

after death in a happy realm of the heaven ... And, anyone who worships the *stūpa* will obtain the immeasurable happiness.[1]

The Chinese *Dīrghāgama* has added the process of anointing the body with perfumed liquids[2] and changed the oil vessel of iron into a golden coffin. Moreover, it is noteworthy that the Chinese *Dīrghāgama* lays particular stress on the fact that anyone who worships the *stūpa* will obtain immeasurable happiness and they will be reborn after death in a happy realm of the heaven. In fascicule 4 of the Chinese *Dīrghāgama*, the Buddha's order is repeated, accentuating the fact that a *stūpa* should be erected to the Buddha at the four crossroads. Anyone who worships the *stūpa* will obtain the immeasurable happiness and they will be reborn after death in a happy realm of the heaven[3]. Such a message, however, cannot be found in the other versions of the *Mahāparinirvāṇasūtra*[4]. In short,

---

[1] *Taishō*, Vol. 1: 20a-b.

[2] The process of anointing the body with perfumed liquids in the Chinese *Dīrghāgama* neither has parallel in the Pāli *Dīghanikāya* and Sanskrit version of the *Mahāparinirvāṇasūtra*, nor in the variant versions of the *Sūtra of* [*the Buddha's*] *Travels to Preach* in the Chinese *Dīrghāgama*. *confer* 1) Ernst Waldschmidt, *opere citato* (Die Überlieferung...): 213-214; 2) *Taishō*, Vol. 1: 169a-b, 186c, 199c-200a.

[3] *Taishō*, Vol. 1: 28b.

[4] Similar sentences or paragraphs can not be found in the variant versions of the *Sūtra of* [*the Buddha's*] *Travels to Preach* of the Chinese *Dīrghāgama*, such as the two-volume *Buddha's Parinirvāṇa Sūtra* translated by Dharmarakṣa, the two-volume *Parinirvāṇa Sūtra* translated by an unknown person, and the three-volume *Mahāparinirvāṇasūtra* translated by Faxian. *confer Taishō*, Vol. 1: 169b, 173a; 186c, 189a; 199c. In a newly found Kharoṣṭhī fragment of a Gāndhārī version of the *Mahāparinirvāṇasūtra* in the Schøyen Collection, i. e., SC 2179/44a, there is a paragraph describing the death and funeral ceremonies of King Mahāsudarśana: "... they put it in a vat ... After an interval of a week, they took (it) out of the vat of oil and bathed the body with all fragrant liquids ... They wrapped the body with (five) hundred pairs of (unbeaten) cloth. Having wrapped the body with five hundred pairs of unbeaten cloth, (they filled?) an iron vat with oil ... after building a pyre of (all) fragrant [woods], they burned the body of King Mahāsudarśana. They built a *stūpa* at the crossing of four main roads. " As pointed out by Mark Allon and Richard Salomon, although the "description of the treatment of Mahāsudarśana's body is similar to that prescribed for the body of a cakravartin and the Buddha in MPS-P (DN II 141-2 and 161) and in MPS-S (§§ 36. 7, 46. 7), but the details and their ordering differ from the Pāli and Sanskrit versions. For example, in the G text the body is put in a vat for a week before it is removed, anointed, wrapped, and then placed in an iron vat again, while in the other versions, the body is put in the vat only once, after being wrapped. The process of anointing the body with perfumed liquids has no parallel in P and S, but it does appear in C-DA. " Mark Allon and Richard Salmon, *opere citato*: 247, 258-262.

emphasis on the merit of *stūpa* worship or the cult of the *stūpa* is also a distinguishing feature of the *Sūtra of* [*the Buddha's*] *Travels to Preach* of the Chinese *Dīrghāgama.*

In terms of the early Buddhist tradition, the *bhikṣus* were allowed to build three types of *stūpa* during the life-time of the Buddha, viz., *luta* [露塔, an open-air *stūpa*], *wuta* [屋塔, a housed-*stūpa*] and *wubita* [无壁塔, a wall-less roofed *stūpa*][1]. Here, the open-air *stūpa* is the usual one such as the Sāñcī *stūpa* (fig.12a), while the housed-*stūpa*, as well as the wall-less roofed *stūpa*, appears to be two kinds of *caityagṛha*. The structure of a wall-less roofed *stūpa* is rather similar to that depicted in the relief on the railing of Bhārhut (fig.12b)[2], and the housed-*stūpa*, which means a *stūpa* to be placed in a room, is probably a substitute of the *stūpa-gṛha* in Sanskrit or *thūpa-gharā* in Pāli (fig.12c). Before this text was translated into Chinese, the original word was most likely *chētiyaghara* in Prākṛit or *grihya-chaitya/caityagṛha/stūpa-gṛha* in Sanskrit, only that the original has not been found, yet. Moreover, the Chinese version of this *vinaya* text clearly indicates that a housed-*stūpa/stūpa-gṛha* or *grihya-chaitya/caityagṛha* is one of the three kinds of *stūpa* allowed by the Buddha to be built, its function and nature being identical to that of the open-air *stūpa*. In any case, such a housed-*stūpa/stūpa-gṛha* or *grihya-*

[1] Buddhajiva [佛驮什] tr., *Mishasai lü* [弥沙塞律, *Mahīśāsaka-vinaya*], in: *Taishō*, No. 1421, Vol. 22: 1-194., esp. 173a. *The Mishasai lü* (*Mahīśāsaka-vinaya*), translated into Chinese by Buddhajiva in 424 AD (Sengyou, *opere citato*: 119-120; *confer Taishō*, Vol. 55: 21a-b), was also called *Wufen lü* [五分律, *Fivefold Vinaya* or *Mahīśāsaka Fivefold Vinaya*] in the Tang Dynasty. Zhisheng, *Kaiyuan shijiao lu* (*The Kaiyuan Era Catalogue of the Buddhist Canon* or *A Catalogue of the Buddhist Sacred Books of the Kaiyuan Period* or *A Catalogue of the Buddhist Canon compiled in the Kaiyuan Period*), in: *Taishō*, No. 2154, Vol. 55: 477-723, esp. 523c. According to some documents, the Mahīśāsaka school is an offshoot of the Sarvāstivāda school from which the Dharmagupataka school eventually branched off. Charles Willemen, "Sarvāstivāda Developments in Northwestern India and in China", in: *The Indian International Journal of Buddhist Studies* (New Series in continuation of the *Indian Journal of Buddhist Studies*), Vol. X, Varanasi: B. J. K. Institute of Buddhist and Asian Studies, No. 2 (2001): 163-169, esp. 164.

[2] James Fergusson, *History of Indian and Eastern Architecture*, rev. ed., Vol. 1, London: Murray, 1910: Fig.81.

a

b

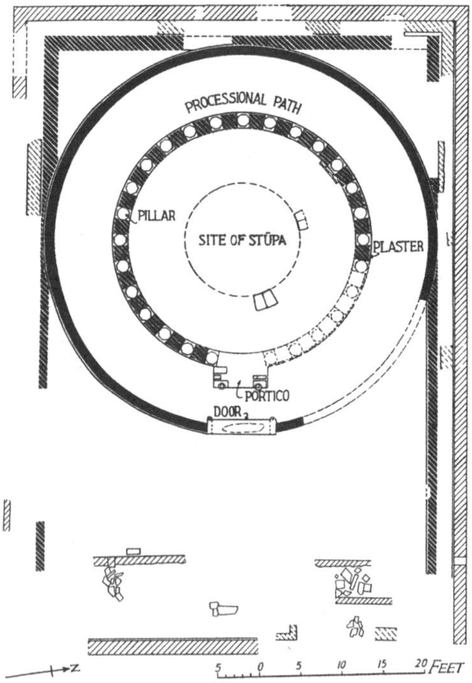

c

fig.12a *Stūpa* 1 at Sāñcī

b Circular wall-less roofed *caityagṛha,* drawing of a bas-relief from Bhārhut

c Circular *caityagṛha* at Bairāṭ, plan

chaitya/caityagṛha came into existence as early as during the Buddha's lifetime[1]. In this regard, the *chētiyaghara* (figs. 13a-b), a term that is attested in the Prākṛit inscriptions engraved on the rock-cut caves of western India and is an equivalent of Sanskrit *caityagṛha*[2], can be regarded as one of the three kinds of *stūpa* allowed to be built by the Buddha.

There are about 60 *chētiyagharas* (fig.13c) being extant at Kizil, making up one third of the total cave temples *in situ*, which are strong evidence that *stūpa* worship was popular in Kucha. Moreover, the *śārīra stūpas* depicted on the front wall, and even on the side walls of the back corridor of the *chētiyaghara*, indicate that Kizil attached great importance to *stūpa* worship. The *chētiyagharas* built both in Xinjiang and northern China (fig.13d), however, derived from the Indian prototype and may be also regarded as housed-*stūpa/stūpa-gṛha* (figs. 14a-c).

In light of the *Yibu zonglun lun*［异部宗轮论, *Samayabhedoparacanacakra, The Doctrines of the Different Schools*］by Vasumitra［世友］, translated into Chinese by Xuanzang［玄奘, ca. 602-664 AD］in 662 AD[3], the Dharmaguptakas［法藏部］emphasized the merit acquired through *stūpa* worship. Whoever took the cult of the *stūpa* seriously would obtain great profit and good retribution[4]. According to the *Sifen sengjieben*［四分僧戒本, *Fourfold Bhikṣuprātimokṣasūtra*］[5], translated into Chinese by Buddhayaśas between 410-413 AD, more than 24 items of *śīla* concerning the *stūpa* were set down in the rules of monastic discipline for the *bhikṣus* of the Dharmaguptaka school[6]; these particular rules cannot be found

［1］Chongfeng Li, *opere citato*: 54.

［2］H. Lüders, "A List of Brāhmī Inscriptions from the Earliest Times to about A.D. 400 with the Exception of those of Aśōka", Appendix to *Epigraphia Indica* X, Calcutta: Superintendent Government Printing, 1912: Nos. 1050, 1058, 1140, 1141, 1153, 1178, 1179, 1183, etc.

［3］Zhisheng, *opere citato*: 557b.

［4］*Xuanzang* tr., *Yibu zonglun lun* (*Samayabhedoparacanacakra*, *The Doctrines of the Different Schools*), in: *Taishō*, No. 2031, Vol. 49: 15-17, esp. 17a.

［5］*Sifen sengjieben* (*Fourfold Bhikṣuprātimokṣasūtra*) used to be called *Tanwude jieben*［昙无德戒本, *Bhikṣuprātimokṣasūtra of the Dharmaguptaka school*］, both of them refer to the *Dharamaguptaka-bhikṣu-prātimokṣa-sūtra*. 1) Sengyou, *opere citato*: 51-52; *confer Taishō*, Vol. 55: 11b; 2) Zhisheng, *opere citato*: 516b.

［6］Buddhayaśas tr., *Sifen sengjieben* (*Fourfold Bhikṣuprātimokṣa-sūtra*), in: *Taishō*, No. 1430, Vol. 22: 1023-1030, esp. 1029b.

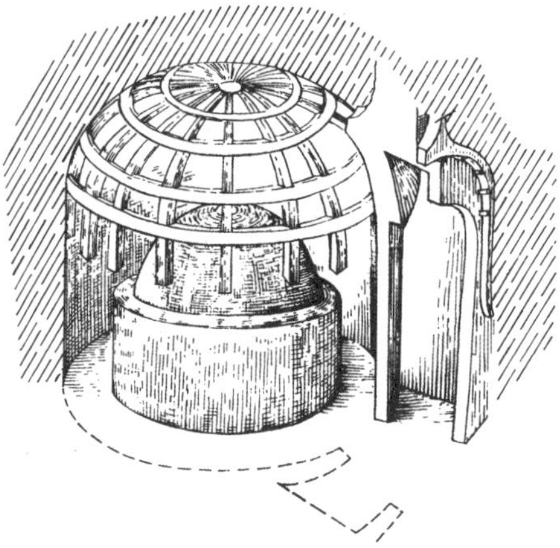

a

b

c

d

fig.13a A rock-cut circular *caityagṛha* (*chētiyaghara*) at Guntupalli, section

b Interior of Cave 8 (*chētiyaghara*) at Kārlā

c Interior of Cave 38 (*chētiyaghara*) at Kizil

d Interior of Cave 2 (*chētiyaghara*) at Yungang

a

b

c

fig.14 *Stūpa* inside the *chētiyagharas in situ:*
a. Cave 12 at Bhājā; b. Cave 224 at Kizil; c. Cave 39 at Yungang

in any other extant versions of the *prātimokṣas* or *vinayas*. It indicates that the *stūpa* played a very important role in the life of the Dharmaguptakas; in other words, the Dharmaguptakas particularly stressed the *stūpa* cult[1].

The Sanskrit version of the *Mahāparinirvāṇasūtra* of the Sarvāstivāda-Mūlasarvāstivāda school, which has often been recognized as the probable literary source of the Kizil *Parinirvāṇa* figures[2], was edited by Ernst Waldschmidt on the basis of numerous fragments dating to the sixth and seventh centuries AD in the German Turfan Collection[3]. Since then, several new fragments of this *sūtra* have been brought to our attention. For example, a fragment of the *Mahāparinirvāṇasūtra* of the Dharmaguptakas, which was written in the Northern Turkistan Brāhmī (type A) from the seventh or eighth century AD and discovered in Murtuq［木头沟］, is different from that of the German Turfan Collection[4]. A "small fragment of palm leaf bearing a text in the Kharoṣṭhī script in Gāndhārī, evidently an excerpt from the Hīnayāna version of the *Mahāparinirvāṇasūtra*," according to M. I. Vorob' eva-Desjatovskaja, has come to light in the S. F. Oldenburg Collection in the Institute of Oriental Studies of the Russian Academy of Science in St. Petersburg[5]; this fragment was probably discovered in Kucha[6].

The Dharmaguptakas, a proto-Mahāyāna sect, were prominent in north-western India and neighboring regions of the Iranian world in the early centuries of the Christian era and played a central role in the early transmission of Buddhism beyond

---

［1］Lü Cheng, "*Lun lüxue yu shibabu fenpai zhi guanxi*［论律学与十八部分派之关系，On the Relationship between Studies of Discipline and Schism of Eighteen Hīnayāna Schools］", in: *Lü Cheng foxue lunzhu xuanji*［吕澂佛学论著选集，*Collected Works of Lü Cheng on Buddhism*］, Ji'nan: Qilu Publishing House, Vol. I, 1991: 131-143, esp. 142.

［2］Akira Miyaji, *opere citato*: 486-502.

［3］1) Ernst Waldschmidt, *opere citato* (*Das Mahāparinirvāṇasūtra*...*);* 2) E. Waldschmidt, *opere citato* (Central Asian Sūtra Fragments...): 136-174, esp. 142.

［4］1) Ernst Waldschmidt, "Drei Fragmente buddhistischer Sūtras aus den Turfanhandschriften", in: *Nachrichten der Akademie der Wissenschaften,* Phil. -hist. Kl., Göttingen, 1968, 3-26, esp. 3-16; 2) Waldschmidt, *opere citato* (Central Asian Sūtra Fragments...)：167-169.

［5］B. A. Litvinsky ed., *opere citato*: 435.

［6］Chongfeng Li, "*Kezi'er bufen zhongxinzhuku yu Chang'ahanjing deng fodian*［克孜尔部分中心柱窟与《长阿含经》等佛典，The *Dīrghāgama* Text and the *Chētiyagharas* of Kizil, Kucha］", *Xu Pingfang xiansheng ji'nian wenji*［徐苹芳先生纪念文集，*Papers in Commemoration of Professor Xu Pingfang*］, Shanghai: Shanghai Chinese Classics Publishing House, 2012: 419-465, esp. 436.

the Indian homeland[1]. "The language used by the Dharmaguptas sect for its texts in the period in question, both in India and in central Asia, was Gāndhārī. "[2] According to Waldschmidt:

... widespread agreement has been reached meanwhile in attributing the *Dīrghāgama* (*Chang a'hanjing*) to the school of the Dharmaguptakas, ... [which has] been recognized as obviously not translated from the Sanskrit but from some Middle Indic or mixed dialect of Prakrit with Sanskrit elements. In the case of the *Dīrghāgama* it is probably the "North-western Prakrit" for which the name "Gāndhārī" has come into use[3].

Many scholars have concluded that the Chinese *Dīrghāgama*, which was translated by Buddhayaśas in 413 AD with the help of the monk Zhu Fonian [竺佛念, Buddhasmṛti?] who took down what Buddhayaśas dictated[4], is a Dharmaguptaka text[5]. Buddhayaśas, who came from Jibin [罽宾, Greater

---

[1] Franz Bernhard demonstrated in 1970 that "an early mission of the sect of the *Dharmaguptakas* using the Gāndhārī dialect preceded the propaganda of the Buddhist schools of the *Sarvāstivādins* and *Mūlasarvāstivādins* and the followers of the Mahāyanā using Sanskrit as known to us from the mass of central Asian manuscripts" . Franz Bernhard, "Gāndhārī and the Buddhist Mission in Central Asia" , in: *Aňjali, Papers on Indology and Buddhism: A Felicitation Volume Presented to Oliver Hector de Alwis Wijesekara on His Sixtieth Birthday*, ed. J. Tilakasiri, Peradeniya: University of Ceylon, 1970: 55-62, esp. 61.

[2] Richard Salomon, *Ancient Buddhist Scrolls from Gandhāra: The British Library Kharoṣṭhī Fragments,* Seattle: University of Washington Press, 1999: 173.

[3] E. Waldschmidt, *opere citato* (Central Asian Sūtra Fragments...): 136-174, esp. 136-37.

[4] Sengyou, *opere citato*: 336-337; *confer Taishō*, 55: 63c.

[5] 1) Waldschmidt, *Bruchstücke buddhistischer Sūtras aus dem zentralasiatischen Sanskritkanon I: herausgegeben und im Zusammenhang mit ihren Parallelversionen bearbeitet* (Königlich Preußische Turfan-Expeditionen, Kleinere Sanskrit-Texte IV), Leipzig: Deutschen Morgenländischen Gesellschaft, 1932: 229-234; 2) H. W. Bailey, "Gāndhārī" , in: *Bulletin of the School of Oriental and African Studies*, XI (1946): 764-797, esp. 765; 3) Étienne Lamotte, *Histoire du Bouddhisme Indien: des origines à l'ère Šaka*, Bibliothèque du Muséon 43, Louvain: Institut Orientaliste de Louvain, 1958: 629-630; 4) Lü Cheng, "Āgama" , in: *Encyclopedia of Buddhism*, ed. G. P. Malalasekera, Colombo: The Government of Ceylon, 1961-1965, Vol. I: 241-244; 5) John Brough, *The Gāndhārī Dharmapada*, London Oriental Series 7, London: Oxford University Press, 1962: 48-54, esp. 50; 6) André Bareau, "L'origine du Dīrgha-āgama traduit en Chinois par Buddhayaśas" , in: *Essays Offered to G. H. Luce by His Colleagues and Friends in Honour of His Seventy-fifth Birthday*, Vol. 1, *Papers on Asian History, Religion, Languages, Literature, Music, Folklore and Anthropology*, *Artibus Asiae* Supplementum 23. 1, eds. Ba Shin, Jean Boisselier and A. B. Griswold, Ascona: Artibus Asiae, 1966: 49-58; 7) E. Waldschmidt, *opere citato* (Central Asian Sūtra Fragments...): 136-174, esp. 136-137; 8) Richard Salomon, *opere citato*: 173.

Gandhāra][1], was a monk of the Dharmaguptaka school[2]. The original version of the Chinese *Dīrghāgama*, which was written in some kind of archaic Prākṛit and not in Sanskrit[3], might be the earliest dated version of the *Dīrghāgama* besides the Pāli *Dīghanikāya*. The Pāli *Dīghanikāya*, which may have been collected and was probably finalized sometime before King Aśoka [阿育王]'s reign, is one of the five fundamental *Nikāyas* of early Indian Buddhism[4].

Within the past two decades, new Buddhist manuscripts or scrolls containing texts in Kharoṣṭhī script have been unearthed in Afghanistan, such as the Kharoṣṭhī fragments in the British Library, the Kharoṣṭhī manuscripts in the Schøyen Collection, as well as those in other private collections[5]. Although the Gāndhārī version of the *Mahāparinirvāṇasūtra* in the Schøyen Collection "does not correspond in all respects to any other single version of the *sūtra*, it does have some notable similarities to the Chinese *Dīrghāgama* version; these similarities could eventually prove to have some special textual and historical

---

[1] Fei Zhangfang [费长房], *Lidai sanbo ji* [历代三宝记, *Record of the Triratna through the Ages* or *Record concerning the Triratna under Successive Dynasties*], in: *Taishō,* No. 2034, Vol. 49: 22-127, esp. 79c.

With respect to Jibin, there have been many opinions about its location and territory. According to Charles Willemen, Jibin "was northwestern India, of which Kaśmīra was an important part, but not the only part. Jibin, by the way, is not necessarily a phonetic rendering, but it may indicate the region of foreigners, guests [bin, 宾], who use ji [罽], a kind of cloth, very appreciated by the Han. Udyāna, the Gilgit area, may have been the original area, but it gradually developed to encompass the whole northwestern area, certainly in the 4th century. " Charles Willemen, *opere citato*: 163-169, esp. 167. *confer* 1) Edouard Chavannes, *Documents sur les Tou-kiue* (*Turcs*) *Occidentaux: Recueillis et commentés*, St-Pétersbourg: Académie Impériale des Sciences de St-Pétersbourg, 1903: 130-132; 2) Chongfeng Li, "The Geography of Transmission: The 'Jibin' Route and the Propagation of Buddhism in China" , in: *Kizil on the Silk Road: Crossroads of Commerce & Meeting of Minds,* ed. Rajeshwari Ghose, Mumbai: Marg Publications, 2008: 24-31, esp. 25.

[2] 1) *Sifenlü xu* [四分律序, Preface to *Caturvarga-vinaya* or *The Fourfold Rules of Discipline*] by unknown author, *Taishō*, Vol. 22: 567a; 2) Chongfeng Li, *opere citato* (*Kezi'er bufen zhongxinzhuku*...): 419-465, esp. 436-437.

[3] 1) John Brough, *opere citato*: 50-54; 2) Richard Salomon, *opere citato*: 170; 3) Ernst Waldschmidt, *opere citato* (Central Asian Sūtra Fragments...): 136-174, esp. 163.

[4] T. W. Rhys Davids, *Buddhist India*, rev. ed., Delhi: Bharatiya Kala Prakashan, 2007: 110-112.

[5] 1) Richard Salomon, *opere citato*: 59-66; 2) Mark Allon and Richard Salomon, *opere citato*: 243-284.

significance" [1]. Moreover, some texts written on birch bark scrolls in the British Library Kharoṣṭhī Manuscripts are closely related to the texts of related *sūtras* in the Chinese *Dīrghāgama*. For instance, "the number and sequence of the topics in the newly discovered Gāndhārī version of the *Saṅgīti-sūtra* agree almost perfectly with the corresponding *sūtra* in the Chinese *Dīrghāgama* but differ widely from both the Sanskrit and Pāli versions of the same text". "This must mean that they represent the texts of one and the same school, especially since the ordering of topics in this important list, like the ordering of rules in the *prātimokṣa*, is the type of feature that is most likely to be distinctive in different sectarian traditions." [2]

Therefore, it has been tentatively concluded that some, if not all of the British Library Kharoṣṭhī manuscripts, represent the textual tradition of the Dharmaguptakas. "In light of the apparent similarities between the MPS-G and the corresponding text of the Dharmaguptaka *Dīrghāgama,* we might consider the possibility that the Schøyen Kharoṣṭhī fragments too, or at least the MPS fragments therein, also belonged to that school. " [3] Furthermore, "the linguistic argument, combined with the textual evidence, makes the theory of a Dharmaguptaka origin for the Chinese *Dīrghāgama* very strong. " [4]

In terms of the *Prātimokṣasūtra*, although Ca. -No. 656, a fragment probably discovered in Kizil and now preserved in the German Turfan Collection, "is a very small piece of the *prātimokṣa* of the Dharmaguptaka school written in 'early Turkistan characters' of about the fifth or sixth century AD" [5], it does suggest that the Dharmaguptakas were still active in Kucha at that time.

On the basis of the new discoveries and after due consideration of the *sūtras*

---

[1] Mark Allon and Richard Salomon, *opere citato*: 243-244.

[2] Richard Salomon, *opere citato*: 173.

[3] Mark Allon and Richard Salomon, *opere citato*: 273.

[4] Richard Salomon, *opere citato*: 174.

[5] 1) Ernst Waldschmidt, *Sanskrithandschriften aus den Turfanfunden,* T. 1, unter Mitarbeit von Walter Clawiter und Lore Holzmann hrsg. und mit einer Einleitung versehen von Ernst Waldschmidt, Wiesbaden: Franz Steiner Verlag, 1965: 297-298, No. 656; 2) E. Waldschmidt, *opere citato* (Central Asian Sūtra Fragments...): 136-174, esp. 164-167.

and *vinayas* on the Buddha's *Parinirvāṇa* cycle, we assume that a Prākṛit version, probably Gāndhārī, which is closely related to the Chinese *Dīrghāgama* and was transmitted by the Dharmaguptakas[1], could well have been the literary source of the Kuchean representation of the Buddha's *Parinirvāṇa* as well as its related events. The *Mahāparinibbāna-sutta* of the Pāli *Dīghanikāya* does not include many of the events portrayed in the Kizil murals[2] and, in any case, the Pāli texts, as we know them today, were redacted and written down in Sri Lanka-they are not known to have been transmitted in North India, let alone Central Asia[3]. The Chinese *Dīrghāgama* version, "though independent, is not seldom more closely in agreement with the Pāli text. "[4]

Some details of the *Parinirvāṇa* and related events, such as Subhadra's passing away before the Buddha, the Buddha in *Parinirvāṇa*, cremation of the Buddha's body, distribution of the relics as well as the Ajātasatru-Varṣākāra［阿阇世王灵梦沐浴］episode and the first Buddhist council, can also be found in *Genben shuoyiqieyoubu pi'naiye zashi*［根本说一切有部毗奈耶杂事, *Mūlasarvāstivāda-vinaya-kṣudraka-vastu* or *Monastic Rules of the Mūlasarvāstivāda School*

---

［1］Chongfeng Li, *opere citato* (*Kezi'er bufen zhongxinzhuku...*): 419-465, esp. 448-454.

［2］Rajeshwari Ghose, "Introduction: Kizil on the Silk Road" , in: *Kizil on the Silk Road: Crossroads of Commerce & Meeting of Minds.* ed. Rajeshwari Ghose, Mumbai: Marg Publications, 2008: 8-23, esp. 21-22, note 8.

［3］T. W. Rhys Davids believes that the Pāli version is the original or oldest version of such a Buddhist *sūtra*, but he wrote long before the Sanskrit (Turfan) version became available, before numerous comparative studies, and before the recent Schøyen and other finds. I was told by Dr. Peter Skilling in an email dated 8 December, 2010 as follows: "The status of the Pāli texts as 'the oldest' is now challenged, and few accept that the Pāli texts are 'original' vis-à-vis other version like Gāndhārī or even early Chinese translations. " Further, "not many scholars today think that the MPS would have had a Pāli 'original' . Pāli is seen as another translation from an earlier Prākṛit, which was progressively standardized in Sri Lanka until it turned into a literary language. Something similar may have happened with the Gāndhārī versions—they are translations, or transpositions, from an earlier Prākṛit (better, earlier Prākṛits) into Northwestern Prākṛit. Like the Pāli, they are early versions of texts that were transmitted orally in the early centuries of Buddhism. There is no evidence that the Pāli versions were ever transmitted in NW India, Gandhāra" . Here, I want to express my sincere thanks to Dr. Peter Skilling.

［4］Ernst Waldschmidt, *opere citato* (Central Asian Sūtra Fragments...): 136-174, esp. 139.

on Various Matters][1], which was compiled by the Mūlasarvāstivādins and translated into Chinese by Yijing (635-713 AD) in 710[2]. This text only became popular in India during the time of Yijing's visit[3]. It means that some episodes of the Buddha's *Parinirvāṇa* cycle painted in the rock-cut caves at Kizil in the later period, such as Mahākāśyapa opening the lid of the coffin[4], probably belong to the Sarvāstivāda or Mūlasarvāstivāda school. This would confirm that the Dharamaguptakas preceded the Sarvāstivādins in Kucha[5]; and, should this

---

[1] Yijing tr., *Genben shuoyiqieyoubu pi'naiye zashi* (*Mūlasarvāstivāda-vinaya-kṣudraka-vastu, Monastic Rules of the Mūlasarvāstivāda School on Various Matters*), in: *Taishō,* No. 1451, Vol. 24: 207-414, esp. 392b-408c.

[2] Zhisheng, *opere citato*: 477-723, esp. 568a.

[3] 1) Lü Cheng, *Yindu foxue yuanliu luejiang* [印度佛学源流略讲, *A Survey of Indian Buddhism*], Shanghai: Shanghai People's Publishing House, 1979: 50-51; 2) Charles Willemen, et al., *Sarvāstivāda Buddhist Scholasticism*, Leiden: Brill, 1998: 125.

[4] In the episode of Mahākāśyapa worshiping the feet of Buddha, as observed by John Strong, "he is described in our sources as doing this in a variety of ways. In the Pāli tradition, he merely uncovers Buddha's feet and venerates them before proceeding with the cremation. In the Sanskrit, he actually opens the coffin and unwraps the whole of Buddha's body in order to venerate it. He then rewraps and re-encoffins it before lighting the pyre. In several Chinese accounts, he asks Ānanda for permission to view the body, but Ānanda refuses, apparently because it would be too difficult to take the coffin down from the pyre, open it, and unwrap the thousand shrouds. " John S. Strong, "Buddha's Funeral", in: *The Buddhist Dead: Practices, Discourses, Representations*, eds. Bryan J. Cuevas and Jacqueline I. Stone, Honolulu: University of Hawaii Press, 2007: 32-59, esp. 43. Such differences in the Buddhist sources might be probably the result of different Hīnayāna schools laying emphasis on their own interest.

[5] As summarized by Ann Heirman, several schools gained importance in northwestern India during and after King Aśoka's reign, mainly the Dharmaguptakas and Sarvāstivādins and later, mainly the Mūlasarvāstivādins. The Dharmaguptakas originally used Northwest Prākṛit, i. e., Gāndhārī, then gradually turned to Buddhist Sanskrit at a later stage and eventually used normal Sanskrit. The transition from the Gāndhārī to the Sanskrit tradition must have occurred mainly in the fifth or sixth century. On the basis of Bu-ston's record, the monks who used Sanskrit often belonged to the Sarvāstivāda school. However, the date of the translation of the first *vinaya* texts is also used as an argument to prove that the Dharmaguptakas were among the earliest monks in China; although in the fifth century AD, the *Sarvāstivādavinaya* was widely spread and studied in China. 1) Ann Heirman, "Can we trace the early Dharmaguptakas?", in: *T'oung Pao* [通报], Vol. LXXXVIII (2002), Fasc. 4-5: 396-429, esp. 399-409; 2) Franz Bernhard, *opere citato*: 55-62, esp. 61; 3) Bu-ston rin-chen grub [布顿], *Bde-bar-gšegs-pahi bstan-pahi gsal-byed, Chos-kyi hbyuń-gnas gsuń-rab-rin-po-chehi mdsod ces-bya-ba* [佛教史大宝藏论, *History of Buddhism*], trans. Guo, Heqing [郭和卿], Beijing: Minzu Publishing House, 1986: 116; 4) Chongfeng Li, *opere citato* (*Kezi'er bufen zhongxinzhuku*...): 419-465, esp. 456-462.

inference be correct, would indicate that the Dharmaguptaka school was very popular in Kucha in the early period, presumably before Xuanzang's visit to that area in 629 AD[1].

(The paper was published in the *Buddhist Narrative in Asia and Beyond,* Vol. I, eds. Peter Skilling and Justin McDaniel, Bangkok: Institute of Thai Studies, Chulalongkorn University, 2012: 59-81.)

[1] Chongfeng Li, *opere citato*: 462-464.

The Image of Maitreya in the *Chētiyagharas* of Kizil, Kucha

The *chētiyaghara* (*stūpa*-cave/central pillar cave) in the cave temple complex at Kizil, which comprises a main chamber (nave), a *stūpa* and a rear chamber (cella), was chiefly used by the Buddhist followers or devotees for worship and monastic activity. Most of the *chētiyagharas* seem to have a unified iconographic scheme in design, such as the *Indraśālaguhā* scene (Indra's visit to the Buddha) on the façade of the *stūpa*, a series of scenes of the Buddha's sermons on the lateral walls, *jātaka* and *avadāna* tales on the barrel vaulted ceiling of the main chamber, the Buddha in *Parinirvāṇa* and related events on the sidewalls of the rear chamber, and the Bodhisattva Maitreya preaching in Tuṣita Heaven in the lunette above the entrance (fig.1).

Such a pictorial scheme clearly represents the former life of Śākyamuni, his preaching and *Parinirvāṇa* in the present *kalpa*, and also includes Maitreya, Śākyamuni's spiritual heir. These scenes, especially Indra's visit to the Buddha, the Buddha's preaching, as well as his *Parinirvāṇa,* are possibly derived from the Buddhist scriptures or *sūtras* corresponding to the Chinese *Dīrghāgama*[1].

---

[1] 1) Chongfeng Li [李崇峰], "*Kezi'er zhongxinzhuku zhushi zhengbi huasu ticai ji youguan wenti* [克孜尔中心柱窟主室正壁画塑题材及有关问题, The Main Image on the Façade of the *Stūpa*-pillar in the *Chētiyagharas* of Kizil, Kucha]", in: *Between Han and Tang: Religious Art and Archaeology in a Transformative Period,* ed. Wu Hung, Beijing: Cultural Relics Press, 2000: 209-233; 2) Chongfeng Li, "*Kezi'er bufen zhongxinzhuku yu Chang'ahanjing deng fodian* [克孜尔部分中心柱窟与《长阿含经》等佛典, The *Dīrghāgama* Text and the *Chētiyagharas* of Kizil, Kucha]", in: *Xu Pingfang xiansheng ji'nian wenji* [徐苹芳先生纪念文集, *Papers in Commemoration of Professor Xu Pingfang*], Shanghai: Shanghai Chinese Classics Publishing House, 2012: 419-465; 3) Chongfeng Li, "The Representation of Buddha's *Parinirvāṇa* in the *Chētiyagharas* of Kizil, Kucha", in: *Buddhist Narrative in Asia and Beyond*, Vol. I, eds. Peter Skilling and Justin McDaniel, Bangkok: Institute of Thai Studies, Chulalongkorn University, 2012: 59-81.

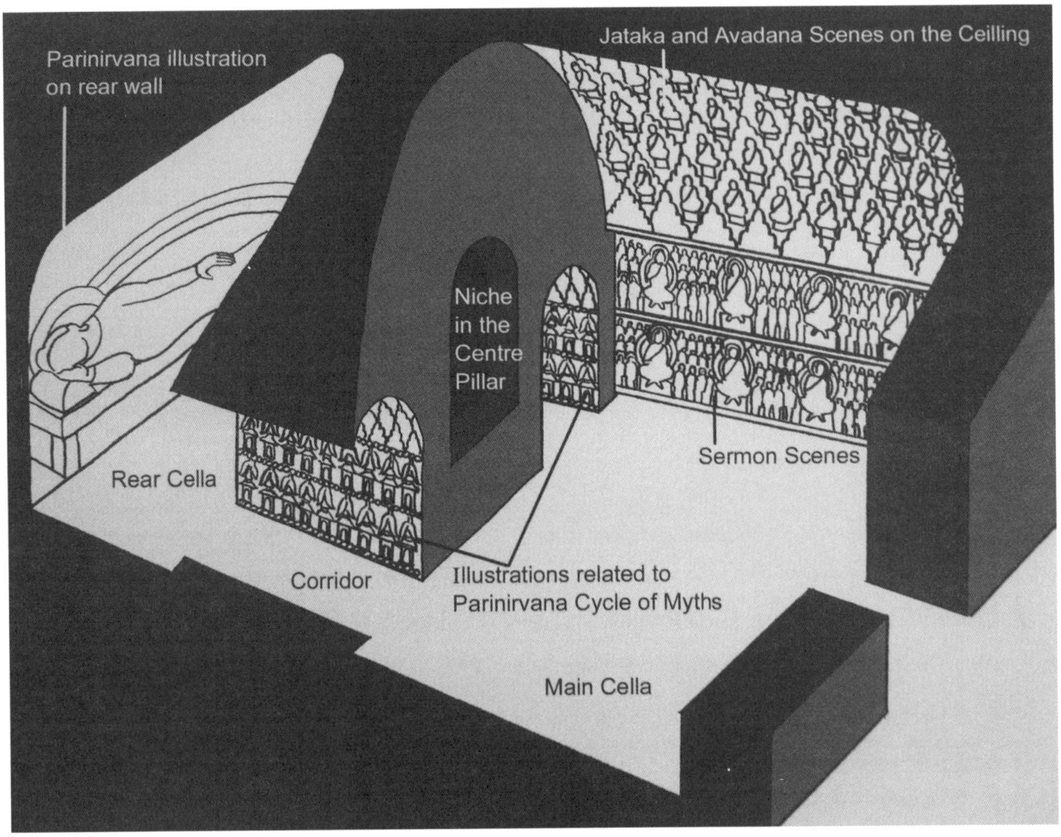

fig.1 Typical iconographic program of a *chētiyaghara* (central pillar cave) at Kizil

The painting of the Bodhisattva Maitreya and his attendants in the lunette is immediately recognizable by the worshipers, who return to the main chamber after having circumambulated the mushroom-shaped *stūpa* and paid respect to the image of the Buddha's *Parinirvāṇa* in the back corridor or the rear chamber[1]. The lunette composition is dominated by Maitreya, who is shown frontally seated in a low, squatting position with legs crisscrossed at the ankles, manifesting himself, preaching his doctrine or giving a benediction (fig.2).

[1] Albert Grünwedel inferred that the mittelpfeiler (central pillar) along with a corridor around it and main image-niche carved in its façade were built for the pilgrims to carry on the Buddhist service or ritual, to be precise, to practice the rite of *pradakṣiṇā* (circumambulation of the *stūpa*) and to pay religious respects to the image of the Buddha. Albert Grünwedel, *Altbuddhistische Kultstätten in Chinesisch-Turkistan, Bericht über archäologische Arbeiten von 1906 bis 1907 bei Kuča, Qaraśahr und in der oase Turfan,* Königlich Preussische Turfan-Expeditionen, Berlin: Druck und Verlag von Georg Reimer, 1912: 9.

fig.2 Maitreya's manifestation and preaching in the lunette above the entrance in Cave 17 at Kizil in situ

In 1906, Albert Grünwedel and his team members carried out a reconnaissance of the Buddhist sites and remains in Kucha, making a survey, taking notes and copying the murals. During this trip, the German scholars identified nearly every bodhisattva sitting in the center of the lunette above the entrance of Kuchean *chētiyagharas* as Maitreya, for example, the painting in Cave 23 at Kumtura. The only reason or grounds for his identification was that Maitreya sits in a European posture and holds his characteristic water flask (*kamaṇdalu*) in the left hand[1], with additional deities surrounding him. In

---

[1] Alexander C. Soper summarized three distinguishing attributes or features of Maitreya's appearance as follows: First, his long, curly hair is tied in a knot on the top of his head without any turban or crown; second, his left hand holds a water bottle; and third one is his special seated posture. "The knees are widely separated, as in the traditional Buddha post, but the lower legs, instead of being tightly folded against each other, are allowed to hang down on diagonal lines, crossing at the ankles" . Alexander C. Soper, *Literary Evidence for Early Buddhist Art in China,* Ascona: Artibus Asiae Publishers, 1959: 216-217.

almost all representations of this iconography in Kucha, the posture of Maitreya and the attending deities are rather similar in appearance[1]. One hundred years later, Marianne Yaldiz presented a paper entitled "Maitreya in Literature and in the Art of Xinjiang", which focuses on a relationship between the literary and the visual[2]. Because "there is a total absence of any inscription which could have given us a clue as to their identity", she concludes that "identifying the visual representations of the Bodhisattva and future Buddha Maitreya in the art of Chinese Central Asia on the basis of the literary evidence is quite difficult"[3].

Within the past two decades, I have devoted myself to the study of the *chētiyagharas* in both India and China and have found some texts or *sūtras* in Chinese which are of particular importance for us to understand the unified iconographic scheme designed for this special kind of rock-cut cave.

At the end of the *Zhuanlunshengwang xiuxing jing* [转轮圣王修行经, *Sūtra on the Wheel-turning Sage-king's Practice* or *Cakkavattisīhanādasutta*], fascicle 6 of the Chinese *Dīrghāgama* [长阿含经, the *Chang ahanjing* or *Long Āgama Sūtra*][4], we read that a Buddha will come into the world in the future whose name is Maitreya Tathāgata. Maitreya will attain an awakening to the true nature of life as well as all things and possess all the ten titles of a Buddha, in the same way as the present Tathāgata achieved. Maitreya will manifest himself among all *devas,* Buddhist followers, *Brāhman*, Māra, demons, divine beings, all the *śramaṇas*, *Brāhmaṇa*, *devatā* and *manuṣya*, who form his retinue as proclaimer of the truth, in a manner similar to what the present Tathāgata has done prior. Maitreya will

---

[1] In Kucha, according to Albert Grünwedel, Maitreya is possibly depicted in a number of *chētiyagharas*, such as the Caves 23, 46 at Kumtura, Cave Nos. 7, 17, 38, 80, 205, 219, 224 at Kizil and Cave no. 1 at Kiris (Simsim). Albert Grünwedel, *opere citato*: 22, 34, 49, 59, 63, 95, 163, 143, 174, 191.

[2] Akira Miyaji has cited numerous texts and *sūtras* on Maitreya in his study of the iconology of *Parinirvāṇa* and Maitreya from India to Central Asia. Akira Miyaji [宫治昭], *Nehan to Miroku no zuzōgaku: Indo kara Chūō Ajia e* [涅槃と弥勒の図像学——インドガら中央アジアへ, *Iconology of Parinirvāṇa and Maitreya: from India to Central Asia*], Tokyo: Yoshikawa Kōbunkan, 1992: 396-401.

[3] Marianne Yaldiz, "Maitreya in Literature and in the Art of Xinjiang", in: *Kizil on the Silk Road: Crossroads of Commerce & Meeting of Minds*, ed. Rajeshwari Ghose, Mumbai: Marg Publications, 2008: 66-83, esp. 82.

[4] *Taishō,* No. 1, Vol. 1: 39-42.

deliver his preaching just like the present Buddha has done[1]. According to this *sūtra*, the legend of Maitreya and Śākyamuni are quite similar. Maitreya will attain enlightenment, preach and convert his followers as Śākyamuni has done.

One may find details, moreover, from some *sūtras* on the relationship between the Buddha's *Parinirvāṇa* and Maitreya's manifestation, as in the *Fo bonihuan jing* [佛般泥洹经, *Buddha's Parinirvāṇa Sūtra*][2] translated by Dharmarakṣa [竺法护] in 269 AD, which is a variant version of and parallel to the *Youxing jing* [游行经, *The Sūtra of (the Buddha's) Travels to Preach* or *Sūtra of (the Buddha) Preaching Travels*], fascicle 2 to 4 in the Chinese *Dīrghāgama*[3] or *Bonihuan jing* [般泥洹经, *Parinirvāṇa Sūtra*][4] by an unknown translator of the Eastern Jin Dynasty (317-420 AD), which is parallel to the *Buddha's Parinirvāṇa Sūtra*[5]. They both clearly record and narrate a belief in Maitreya after Śākyamuni Buddha's *Parinirvāṇa.*

According to fascicle 2 of the *Buddha's Parinirvāṇa Sūtra,* after the Buddha was cremated, Mahākāśyapa, Aniruddha and other *arhats* believed that more than 300, 000 followers of the Buddha as well as subjects of the Kuśīnagara King will be finally reborn at the court of Maitreya in Tuṣita Heaven. Once Maitreya becomes a future Buddha, he would, first of all, deliver his preaching. As a result, 9.6 billion *bhikṣus* will become *arhats*. Maitreya would teach all followers and worshippers that those who used to build *stūpas* during Śākyamuni's lifetime will be rewarded with *ṛddhi-prabhūta* (magic power) or privilege, while those, who hung banners, offered incense, lighted lamps as well as just followed *prātimokṣa*, will all be *upāsakas* and *upasikās*[6].

---

[1] *Taishō,* No. 1, Vol. 1: 39-42, esp. 41c.

[2] *Taishō,* No. 5, Vol. 1: 160-175.

[3] *Taishō,* No. 1, Vol. 1: 11-30.

[4] *Taishō,* No. 6, Vol. 1: 176-191.

[5] Lü Cheng (吕澂), *Xinbian hanwen dazangjing mulu* [新编汉文大藏经目录, *A New Catalogue of the Chinese Versions of the Buddhist Tripiṭāka*], Ji'nan: Qilu Publishing House, 1980: 48.

[6] *Taishō,* No. 5, Vol. 1: 160-175, esp. 174c. *confer: Bonihuan jing* [*Parinirvāṇa Sūtra*], in: *Taishō,* No. 6, Vol. 1: 176-191, esp. 190c.

In fascicle 2 of the *Parinirvāṇa Sūtra*, however, we read that in the First Buddhist Council held 90 days after the Buddha's *Parinirvāṇa*, Mahākāśyapa, Aniruddha and the *bhikṣus* were first told by Ānanda that Buddha had predicted Maitreya would succeed him as a future Buddha. Those who begin to follow the *dharma* should learn from him and will attain their enlightenment[1].

On the basis of these *sūtras*, it becomes evident that a belief in a future Buddha already existed during the lifetime of the historic Buddha[2].

In terms of the visual representation, most of the Greater Gandhāran reliefs depicting Maitreya's preaching were set in an architectural space which uses various types of arches to recreate his inner court in Tuṣita (figs.3, 4); some, like a relief kept in the Archaeological Museum at Taxila (fig.5), even arranged Maitreya's preaching in conjunction with Buddha's *Parinirvāṇa*. "This linkage of the images of Śākyamuni and Maitreya is a characteristic of Buddhist sculpture in the Kushanshahr." The reason is that, according to John M. Rosenfield, firstly, Maitreya would explain to the hundreds of millions of followers and worshippers gathered to hear him how they gained this privilege. Secondly, in the past they had rendered homage to Śākyamuni with parasols, banners, incense as well as garlands, and they had given to the *stūpas* saffron mixed with water; to the *saṃgha*, clothes, food, drink, and medicine, and also kept the various fasts. For these deeds, they are rewarded by Maitreya's instruction which leads to salvation. Thirdly, "this basic relationship in the visual arts is confirmed by a uniform series of passages in texts of this period in which Śākyamuni is described as predicting the future career of Maitreya"[3]. The Chinese sources, however, do help us to infer that the Buddha's *Parinirvāṇa* and Maitreya's preaching in the *chētiyagharas* of Kizil were basically modeled on the sculpture of the same iconographic scheme from Greater Gandhāra. The similarity is particularly evident in the structure and composition, even in the posture of Maitreya and his surrounding deities.

[1] *Taishō,* No. 6, Vol. 1: 176-191, esp. 191a. *confer Fo bonihuan jing* (*Buddha's Parinirvāṇa Sūtra*), in: *Taishō,* No. 5, Vol. 1: 160-175, esp. 175b.

[2] Marianne Yaldiz, *opere citato*: 68.

[3] John M. Rosenfield, *The Dynastic Arts of the Kushans*, Berkeley: University of California Press, 1967: 232-234.

fig.3 Maitreya's manifestation and preaching in Tuṣita, from Chārsadda, Gandhāra, Museum für Asiatische Kunst, SMPK, Berlin

fig.4 Maitreya's manifestation and preaching in Tuṣita, from Shotorak, Afghanistan, Musée Guimet, Paris

fig.5 Buddha's *parinirvāṇa* along with Maitreya's manifestation and preaching, Archaeological Museum at Taxila, Taxila

As a Buddhist center in Xinjiang, Kucha, which lies midway between the center of Greater Gandhāra and China proper (figs.6, 7), should have shared its great neighbor's enthusiasm for the 'historic' Buddha and Buddha-to-be. As a result, balancing the Buddha-to-be vis-à-vis the 'historic' Buddha is a visual innovation in the Kizil composition. The main image in the niche carved in the façade of the mushroom-shaped *stūpa* should be Śākyamuni, while in the lunette above the entrance, opposite to the main image, is shown Maitreya. This pictorial alignment also proves that Maitreya is the spiritual heir of Śākyamuni[1]. From the perspective of Buddhist ritual, moreover, the Buddha's *Parinirvāṇa* depicted or sculpted on the back-wall of the back corridor or the rear chamber clearly forms a set with Maitreya in Tuṣita portrayed in the lunette above the entrance of the main chamber. This joint iconographic program-*Parinirvāṇa* Buddha and Buddha-to-be Maitreya—reflects the wish of monks and worshippers, who, based their faith on the relics as well as the Dharma after the Buddha's *Parinirvāṇa*, will be reborn in Tuṣita Heaven in the presence of Maitreya after their deaths[2]. This linked program not only is identical with the order of the *sūtra* narrative, but is also consistent with the rituals that Buddhist followers carry on in the *chētiyagharas*[3]. The "*Indraśālaguhā* in conjunction with Buddha's *Parinirvāṇa*" (fig.8) and the "Buddha's *Parinirvāṇa* in combination with Maitreya in Tuṣita" (fig.5) were basically designed after the models or prototypes of Greater Gandhāra and principally represented on the basis of the variant *sūtras* corresponding to the Chinese *Dīrghāgama*. They become, therefore, a standard iconography strikingly developed from the Buddhist art of Gandhāra. In addition, in the early Chinese transcriptions the name of Maitreya is expressed with two characters 弥

[1] *Zhuanlunshengwang xiuxing jing* (*Sūtra on the Wheel-turning Sage-king's Practice* or *Cakkavattisīhanādasutta*), Fascicle 6 of the Chinese *Dīrghāgama*, in: *Taishō,* No. 1, Vol. 1: 39-42, esp. 41c-42a.

[2] Akira Miyaji, *opere citato*: 512-517.

[3] The lunette above the entrance of the *chētiyaghara* of Kizil is connected with the barrel vault of the main chamber. Maitreya who sits in the lunette seems to suggest his staying in Tuṣita Heaven, because the middle of the barrel vault is depicted with celestial beings such as sun-god and moon-god in the sky. If so, Maitreya depicted in the lunette of the *chētiyaghara* in Kucha is absolutely the Buddha-to-be in the heaven.

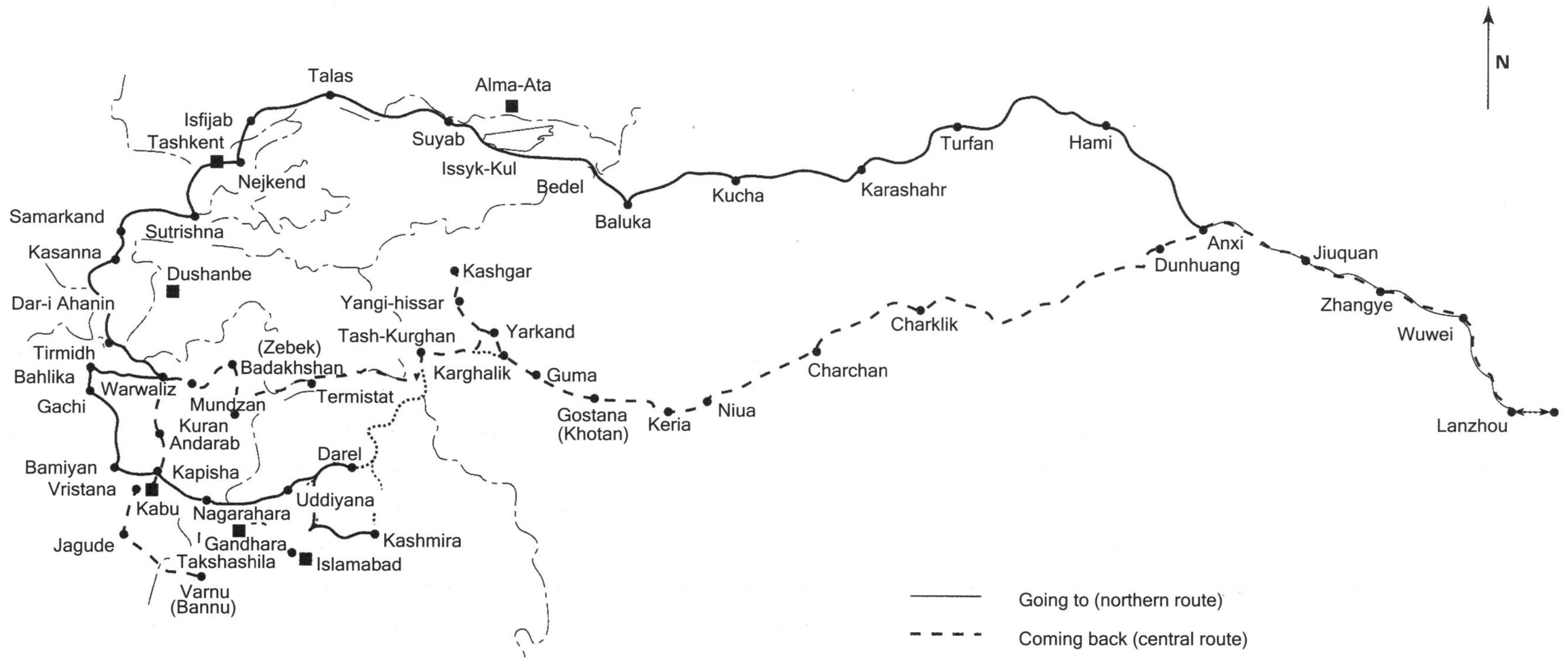

fig.6 A sketch map of Xuanzang's pilgrimage to India

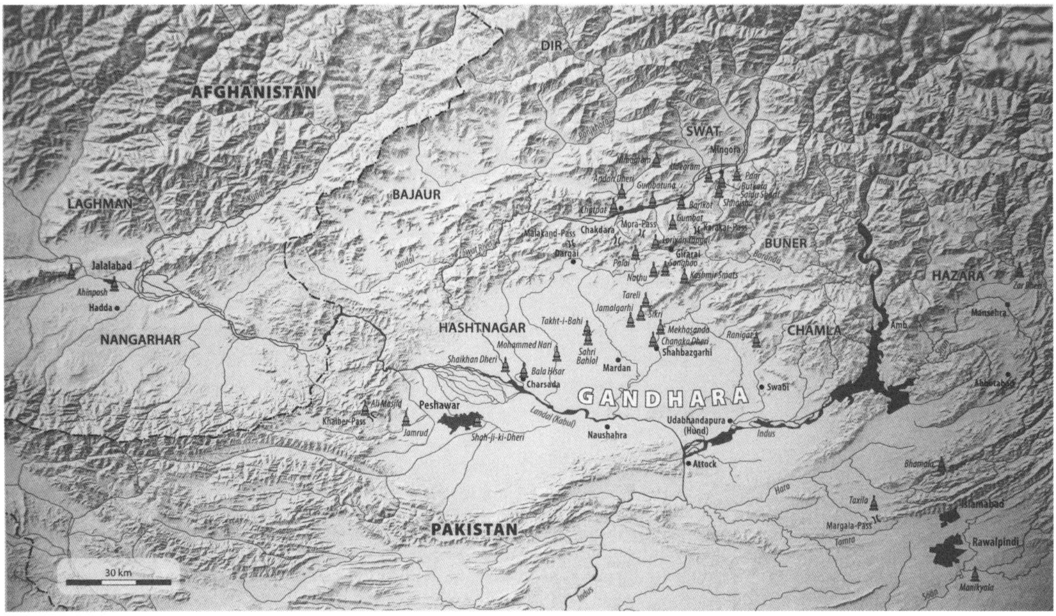

fig.7 A sketch map of Greater Gandhāra

fig.8 *Indraśālaguhā* in conjunction with Buddha's *parinirvāṇa*, from Chatpat, Archaeological Museum at Dir, Chakdara

勒 for which a middle Chinese pronunciation *mjię-lək* can be reconstructed. In the Gāndhārī dialect forms such as '*metraya/metreya: metraga*' are to be found together or even with the loss of the suffix consonant: '*metrae/metre*', from which an East-Tocharian '*metrak*' and a Chinese '*mjię-lək*' can be derived[1].

The cult of Maitreya as the Buddhist Messiah was established in northern

[1] Franz Bernhard, "Gāndhārī and the Buddhist Mission in Central Asia", in: *Añjali, Papers on Indology and Buddhism: A Felicitation Volume Presented to Oliver Hector de Alwis Wijesekara on His Sixtieth Birthday*, ed. J. Tilakasiri, Peradeniya: University of Ceylon, 1970: 55-62, esp. 58.

India as early as the Kushan period. According to the Buddhist texts as well as archaeological discoveries, Maitreya worship spread widely in northwest India[1], the Tarim basin and northwest China, but the center of his cult was definitely in Gandhāra proper. From the accounts of early Chinese travelers and pilgrims, we know, that one of the important pilgrimage cults of this region centered on a colossal Maitreya statue, which was carved out of sandalwood and erected in the little mountain principality of Darel, up-river from Gandhāra[2]. Most of the Chinese pilgrims to Greater Gandhāra or even to India proper around 400 AD did pay special attention to this image[3]. Among them, Baoyun［宝云］[4], Faxian［法显］[5] and Fasheng［法

---

［1］John M. Rosenfield, *opere citato*: 229-230, Figure 32; 2) R. C. Sharma, *Buddhist Art: Mathurā School*, New Delhi: Wiley Eastern Limited & New Age International Limited, 1995: 181, fig.94.

［2］Alexander C. Soper, *opere citato*: 216-218.

［3］Alexander C. Soper convincingly suggests that this image must have been made about the beginning of the third century AD. Alexander C. Soper, *opere citato*: 270.

［4］On the basis of *Hagiography of Bao yun* in the *Mingseng Zhuan*［名僧传, *Biographies of Famous Monks*］by Baochang［宝唱］, preserved in the Japanese *Meisōden-shō*［名僧传抄, *A Transcript of the Biographies of Famous Monks*］by Shū-shō［宗性］, "in a small kingdom named Tuoli, Baoyun saw the image of Maitreya as a Buddha, being 80 feet tall and covered with gold foil. He started to repent and confessed his sins［启忏］at the feet of Maitreya image, with the utmost devotion for 50 days. Then, he saw a supernatural light shining forth at night, which is as bright as the rising sun. Those who witnessed this filled the roads". 1) Shū-shō, *Meisōden-shō*, fascicle 26, in: *Dainihon Zoku Zōkyō*［大日本續藏經, *Continued Tripiṭaka of Japan*］, Vol. 7, No. 1: 13; 2) Alexander C. Soper, *opere citato*: 268.

［5］According to Faxian's record, in a small country called Tuoli (Darēl) "there was formerly an *arhat* who, using his divine power, carried a clever artisan up to Tuṣita Heaven to observe the height, complexion, and features of Bodhisattva Maitreya, so that when he came down he might carve an image of Maitreya in wood. Altogether he made three journeys for observation and afterwards executed an image eighty feet in height, the folded legs of which measured eight feet across. On fast-days it always shines with a brilliant light ... On the basis of an old tradition *śramanas* from India began to bring the *sūtras* and *vinayas* across this river (Indus) from the date of setting up the image of Maitreya Bodhisattva. It was said that the Great Doctrine began to spread abroad from the setting up of the image, and that but for our ghostly Master, Maitreya, who is to succeed Śākyamuni, who could have caused the Precious Trinity to be preached afar and foreigners to become acquainted with the Faith? Thus we know that the revelation of these mysteries was clearly not the work of human beings, and that the dream of the Emperor Mingdi of the Han dynasty was not without foundation". H. A. Giles, *The Travels of Fa-hsien* (399-414 AD), *or Record of the Buddhistic Kingdoms,* by Faxian, rep. Delhi: Indological Book House, 1972: 9-10.

盛][1] were said to have won the first fruit of salvation and drew a close tie with Maitreya for future salvation. The setting up of the Imperial Temple of Maitreya at Turfan by Juqu Anzhou [沮渠安周] in 445 AD[2], however, might be influenced by the Maitreya image at Darel, because Fasheng who saw the image personally *in situ* used to stay in Turfan for some time[3]. Although Maitreya depicted in the lunette of Kizil *chētiyaghara* is a component part of the whole iconographic scheme based on the *sūtras* corresponding to the Chinese *Dīrghāgama*, the Darel Maitreya image may have contributed to the formation of Kuchean iconography or at least put the design scheme forward. By the time that Xuanzang visited this area, the image, -which is golden colored and very dazzling in appearance, -still possessed a secret spiritual power of miracle[4].

In the light of the literary records, *The Sūtra on Wheel-turning Sage-king's Practice* and variant versions parallel to *The Sūtra of* (*the Buddha's*) *Travels to Preach* in the Chinese *Dīrghāgama*, an exact correspondence to a parallel *Gāndhārī* version that has been ascribed to the

---

[1] In the light of the *Hagiography of Fasheng* in the *Biographies of Famous Monks*, "in the northeast of Udyāna, Fasheng and his followers saw the Maitreya image made of sandalwood, which is 80 feet high and constantly emits light. Many worshippers from afar become attendants to the image, confessing their faults and praying that they may overcome all obstacles. Those who win thereby the first fruit of salvation number several tens yearly. Fasheng joined with monks and laymen coming from various lands, totaling 500, to worship and to pray that when they discarded their bodies they would infallibly see Maitreya. These prayers might be acceptable, his incense smoke swirled up to the right, and in an instant all the [threads of] smoke joined in a shape like a canopy, which revolved three circuits to the right before it gradually dissipated" . 1) Shū-shō, *ibidem*; 2) Alexander C. Soper, *opere citato*: 268-269.

[2] 1) Albert Grünwedel, *Bericht über archäologische Arbeiten in Idikutschari und Umgebung im Winter* 1902-1903, München: G. Franz'scher Verlag, 1906: 27-28, Fig. 20; 2) Rong Xinjiang, "Juqu Anzhou's Inscription and the Daliang Kingdom in Turfan" , in: *Turfan Revisited—The First Century of Research into the Arts and Cultures of the Silk Road*, ed. Desmond Durkin-Meisterernst et al, Berlin: Dietrich Reimer Verlag, 2004: 268-275.

[3] 1) Shū-shō, *ibidem*; 2) Alexander C. Soper, *opere citato*: 268.

[4] Samuel Beal, *Si-Yu-Ki—Buddhist Records of the Western World; Chinese Accounts of India*, translated from the Chinese of Hiuen Tsiang, London: Trubner, 1884: 177.

Dharmaguptakas[1], appear to be the original of Maitreya's story[2]. On the basis of some new discoveries, a lost *Prākṛit* or vernacular version which is closely related to the Chinese *Dīrghāgama* could well have been the literary source of Maitreya's manifestation and preaching, which make up a unified composition with the other visual motifs in the *chētiyagharas* of Kizil[3]. They seem to be entirely derived from the *sūtras* corresponding to the Chinese translation of the *Dīrghāgama*.

If such an inference is correct, it means that the *Dharmaguptakas* were very popular in Kucha before Xuanzang's visit to the area[4], because in Central Asia, as Franz Bernhard demonstrated, "an early mission of the sect of the

---

[1] 1) Ernst Waldschmidt, *Bruchstücke buddhistischer Sūtras aus dem zentralasiatischen Sanskritkanon I: herausgegeben und im Zusammenhang mit ihren Parallelversionen bearbeitet* (Königlich Preußischo Turfan-Expeditionen), Kleinere Sanskrit-Texte iv, Leipzig: Deutschen Morgenländischen Gesellschaft, 1932: 229-234; 2) H. W. Bailey, "Gāndhārī", in: *Bulletin of the School of Oriental And African Studies*, XI (1946): 764-797, esp. 765; 3) André Bareau, *Les sectes bouddhiques du Petit Véhicule,* Paris: Publications de l'École française d'Extrême-Orient 38, 1955: 191; 4) Étienne Lamotte, *Histoire du Bouddhisme Indien: des origines à l'ère Saka,* Bibliothèque du Muséon 43, Louvain: Institut Orientaliste de Louvain, 1958: 629-30; 5) John Brough, *The Gāndhārī Dharmapada*, London Oriental Series 7, London: Oxford University Press, 1962: 48-54, esp. 50; 6) André Bareau, "L' origine du Dīrgha-āgama traduit en Chinois par Buddhayaśas", in: *Essays Offered to G. H. Luce by His Colleagues and Friends in Honour of His Seventy-fifth Birthday*, eds. Ba Shin, Jean Boisselier and A. B. Griswold, Vol. 1, *Papers on Asian History, Religion, Languages, Literature, Music, Folklore and Anthropology*, *Artibus Asiae* Supplementum 23. 1, Ascona: Artibus Asiae, 1966: 49-58; 7) Ernst Waldschmidt, "Central Asian Sūtra Fragments and their Relation to the Chinese Āgamas", in: *Die Sprache der ältesten buddhistischen Überlieferung; The Language of the early Buddhist Tradition* (Symposien zur Buddhismusforschung ii), Abhandlungen der Akademie der Wissenschaften in Göttingen: Philologisch-historische Klasse, Ser. 3, Vol. 117, Heinz Bechert, hrsg, Göttingen: Vandenhoeck & Ruprecht, 1980: 136-174, esp. 136-137; 8) Richard Salomon, *Ancient Buddhist Scrolls from Gandhāra: The British Library Kharoṣṭhī Fragments,* Seattle: University of Washington Press, 1999:173.

[2] Maitreya seems to be paid attention to by the Dharmaguptakas, because a Bodhisattva image found at Girdharpur, Mathurā, has an inscription that records in the year 29 of the Mahārāja Huvishka this image was installed in the *vihāra* for the acceptance of the Dharmaguptikas. John M. Rosenfield, *opere citato*: 229-230, Figure 32.

[3] Chongfeng Li, *opere citato* (*Kezi'er bufen zhongxinzhuku*...): 419-465, esp. 420-431.

John M. Rosenfield indicted that most figures in Indo-Scythian dress "are devotees of Maitreya or of Sākyamuni in conjunction with Maitreya". John M. Rosenfield, *opere citato*: 227.

[4] Chongfeng Li, *opere citato*: 462-464.

Dharmaguptakas using the Gāndhārī dialect preceded the propaganda of the Buddhist schools of the *Sarvāstivādins* and *Mūlasarvāstivādins* and the followers of the *Mahāyanā* using Sanskrit as known to us from the mass of central Asian manuscripts"[1]. The *Dharmaguptakas* had a primordial role in the evangelization of Central Asia and China and were strong supporters of the cult of the Bodhisattvas[2].

(The paper was presented to the first International Workshop on Gandhāran Studies held on December 1-3, 2010 by Quaid-i-Azam Unviersity, Islamabad, Pakistan and was published in the seventh volume of *Gandhāran Studies*: 11-22)

[1] Franz Bernhard, *opere citato*: 61.
[2] John M. Rosenfield, *opere citato*: 230.

克孜尔部分中心柱窟与《长阿含经》等佛典

一、画塑经营与佛典依据

根据洞窟形制及性质并参考印度石窟寺原型，克孜尔现存洞窟大体可以分作四种类型：中心柱窟[1]、大像窟、方形窟[2]和僧房窟[3]。其中，中心柱窟是佛教信徒供养、礼忏和进行宗教仪式的主要场所。

克孜尔中心柱窟按结构可以分作前室、主室、中心塔柱和后室四部分，唯前室多残毁。其中，主室正壁，即中心塔柱前壁画塑题材（图1、2）近半为"帝释窟"[4]，雕

---

[1] 中心柱窟，即塔庙窟或塔洞，相当于印度石窟寺中俗语(Prākṛita/ Prākṛit)题铭的chētiyaghara，梵语(Sanskrit)应作caityagṛha 或chaityagriha，意译塔庙窟，音译支提窟，英译为chaitya building或central-pillar-cave；包括大像窟，英译为colossal-Buddha-image-cave。参见H. Lüders, "A List of Brāhmī Inscriptions from the Earliest Times to about A.D. 400 with the Exception of those of Aśōka", in: *Epigraphia Indica*, Volume X (1909-10), Appendix, Calcutta: Superintendent Government Printing, 1912: No. 1050, 1058, 1140, 1141, 1153, 1178, 1179, 1183, etc.

[2] 方形窟，相当于印度石窟寺中俗语题铭的maṭapa或maḍapa，梵语应作mandapa，英译为hall或square-cave。参见：H. Lüders, *opere citato*: Nos. 1106, 1174, etc.

[3] 僧房窟，即单室僧坊，相当于印度石窟寺中俗语题铭的lēṇa，梵语应作vihāra，意译僧坊窟，音译毗诃罗窟，英译为cave或dwelling cave。参见：H. Lüders, *opere citato*: Nos. 998-1002, 1005-1007, etc.

[4] 1) Albert Grünwedel, *Altbuddhistische Kultstätten in Chinesisch-Turkistan: Bericht über archäologische Arbeiten von 1906 bis 1907 bei Kuča, Qarašahr und in der oase Turfan;* Königlich Preussische Turfan-Expeditionen, Berlin: Druck und Verlag von Georg Reimer, 1912: 44, 63, 80, 99, 101, 121, 131, 145, 150, 158, 174; 2) Alexander C. Soper, "Aspects of Light Symbolism in Gandhāran Sculpture", in: *Artibus Asiae,* 1949, XII (3): 252-283; (4): 314-330; 1950, XIII (1/2): 63-85; 3) 姚士宏《克孜尔石窟部分洞窟主室正壁塑绘题材》，见新疆维吾尔自治区文物管理委员会、拜城县克孜尔千佛洞文物保管所、北京大学考古系编《中国石窟·克孜尔石窟》三，北京：文物出版社，1997年，第178-186页；4) 宫治昭著《涅槃と彌勒の図像学——インドから中央アジアへ——》，東京：吉川弘文館，1992年，第440-442页；5) 李崇峰《克孜尔中心柱窟主室正壁画塑题材及有关问题》，见巫鸿主编《汉唐之间的宗教艺术与考古》，北京：文物出版社，2000年，第209-233页。

图 1　克孜尔第 38 窟中心柱正壁“帝释窟”雕塑遗迹

图 2　克孜尔第 80 窟中心柱正壁“帝释窟”壁画

塑或绘制年代约从公元 3 世纪末到 8 世纪下半叶[1]。帝释窟这一题材，内容大体如下：在摩竭陀国奄婆罗村北毗陀山，佛于因陀沙罗窟中入火焰三昧，释提桓因获悉后与乐神般遮翼及其他诸天前往，并把四十二件疑难事情画在石头上向佛询问，后者为他们做了解释。关于这个传说，现存巴利语经藏《长尼迦耶》(*Dīghanikāya*) 中的《帝释所问经》(*Sakka-pañha suttanta*)，汉译《长阿含经 · 释提桓因问经》、《中阿含经 · 释问经》、《佛说帝释所问经》、《杂宝藏经 · 帝释问事缘》以及《法显传》和玄奘《大唐西域记》等都有详略不同的记载[2]。经检索上述佛典并与秣菟罗 (图 3) 和犍陀罗 (图 4) 出土的佛教造像进行对比，我们发现：克孜尔中心柱窟中帝释窟之塑绘，即山体结构及外观[3]、龛形、人物配置、动物刻画等方面，在吸收秣菟罗和犍陀罗同一内容雕刻的基础上，主要依据与汉译《长阿含经 · 释提桓因问经》相当的佛典创作[4]，是当时龟兹石窟极为流行的造像题材。

克孜尔中心柱窟主室侧壁壁画，左侧壁与右侧壁布局对称，通常分作上下二栏或三栏，每栏三铺或四铺，内容主要是因缘佛传，俗称“说法图”。克孜尔现存中心柱窟中，有 34 座洞窟主室侧壁壁画表现了这种题材 (图 5)，由此可见它是中心柱窟主室

[1] 李崇峰《中印佛教石窟寺比较研究：以塔庙窟为中心》，北京：北京大学出版社，2003 年，第 167-176 页。

[2] 李崇峰《克孜尔中心柱窟主室正壁画塑题材及有关问题》，上引书，第 210 页。

[3] 克孜尔中心柱窟主室正壁的整体结构，与犍陀罗出土的“帝释窟”浮雕外观，尤其如图 4 所示，极为相似，这或许不是巧合。若然，克孜尔中心柱窟主室正壁采用中亚佛教艺术这一流行题材乃情理中事。

[4] 李崇峰《克孜尔中心柱窟主室正壁画塑题材及有关问题》，上引书，第 217-218 页。

图 3　秣菟罗“帝释窟”浮雕，出土地不详，现藏印度秣菟罗博物馆

图 4　犍陀罗“帝释窟”浮雕，出土于 Loriyān Tangai，现藏加尔各答印度博物馆

图 5　克孜尔第 17 窟侧壁“因缘佛传”壁画

侧壁比较固定的壁画内容。不过，由于壁画多被磨蚀，加之某些现存画面仅为原壁画局部，因此对侧壁因缘佛传壁画的内容考证比较困难。尽管如此，现已考订出的因缘佛传画面有[1]：梵志燃灯（第 163 窟）、燃灯佛授记(63、69、114 窟）、树下诞生(99*、175*、205 窟）、七步宣言(99*、175* 窟）、龙浴太子（九龙灌顶，99* 窟）、阿私陀占相

[1] 据我们调查，克孜尔中心柱窟的因缘佛传大多绘在主室左右侧壁，少数绘在主室正壁或前壁乃至甬道侧壁或券顶。为此，凡因缘佛传未绘于主室侧壁者，在下述窟号后加 * 作标记。

(175* 窟)、参诣天祠(224 窟)、树下观耕(38、227 窟)、出游四门(99*、175* 窟)、太子惊梦(99* 窟)、乳女奉糜(114 窟)、吉祥施草(80、163、171 窟)、降魔成道(98*、163、171、175*、198、205 窟)、诸天朝贺(224 窟)、梵天劝请(98 窟)、初转法轮(38、43*、69、98、192、193、198*、205、207、224 窟)、降伏火龙(63*、205* 窟)、观察世间(80*、227* 窟)、龙王守护(205、207、224 窟)、尼拘陀树神(207 窟)、频毗娑罗王皈依(207 窟)、耶舍出家(163、224 窟)、富楼那出家(38、224 窟)、降伏迦叶(迦叶皈依，4、8、98、114、171、175*、192*、193、196*、205*、207、224 窟)、舞狮女化作比丘尼(舞狮女皈依，101、163、171、193、206 窟)、佛度恶牛(192* 窟)、提婆达多伤佛(175* 窟)、布施竹园(77、207 窟)、教化五百苦行仙(175* 窟)、六师论道(降伏六师外道，80*、97*、192、207 窟)、舍卫城神变(123 窟)、度旷野药叉(163 窟)、惟楼勒王率兵诛释种(80、193 窟)、须摩提女请佛(178*、198*、205*、224* 窟)、罗怙罗命名(8、17、163、192、206、207、224 窟)、为净饭王说法(227 窟)、毗舍佉出家(17、77、99、163、219、224 窟)和婆提唎迦继位(38、171、207 窟)等[1]，绘制年代约从公元 3 世纪末到 8 世纪下半叶[2]。

自佛像在公元 1 世纪中叶出现之后，用象征手法表现佛陀形象的方式就自然结束了，传统的佛传故事也随之发扬光大。于是，在印度本土和犍陀罗地区创作了许多重要的佛传雕刻和绘画。以犍陀罗为例，遗存至今的佛传内容雕刻有：燃灯佛授记、梦象入胎、树下诞生、七步宣言、龙浴太子、阿私陀占相、太子上学、角力、树下观耕、宫中娱乐、逾城出家、吉祥施草、降魔成道、四天王奉钵、初转法轮、布施竹园、布施芒果园、舍卫城神变、降伏黑蛇、降伏火龙、难陀皈依、涅槃入灭及荼毗焚棺等[3]，主要为 1 世纪中叶到 3 世纪中叶之作，少数可延续到 4、5 世纪[4]。从题材内容及构图考量，犍陀罗出土的佛传浮雕与克孜尔石窟的佛传壁画有密切关系。以“吉祥施草”为例，

[1] 克孜尔中心柱窟中的因缘佛传内容，主要依据《克孜尔石窟的佛传壁画》和《克孜尔石窟内容总录》统计。参见：1) 丁明夷、马世长、雄西《克孜尔石窟的佛传壁画》，见新疆维吾尔自治区文物管理委员会、拜城县克孜尔千佛洞文物保管所、北京大学考古系编《中国石窟 · 克孜尔石窟》一，北京：文物出版社，1989 年，第 186-207 页；2) 新疆龟兹石窟研究所编《克孜尔石窟内容总录》，乌鲁木齐：新疆美术摄影出版社，2000 年，第 299-300 页附录三。

[2] 李崇峰，上引书，第 167-176 页。

[3] John H. Marshall, *Buddhist Art of Gandhara: The Story of the Early School; its birth, growth and decline*, London: Cambridge University Press, 1960: Figs. 53-141.

[4] Chongfeng Li, “Gandhāra, Mathurā and Buddhist Sculptures of Mediaeval China”, in: *Glory of the Kushans: Recent Discoveries and Interpretations*, ed. Vidula Jayaswal, New Delhi: Aryan Books International, 2012: 378-391, esp. 379-380.

依据目前刊布的资料,这一题材的浮雕在犍陀罗地区迄今出土过15件[1],足以说明它在当地非常流行。现以拉合尔博物馆收藏的出土于锡克里(Sikri)佛塔上的浮雕为例,简述犍陀罗地区这一题材的构图情况。画面中,佛于中央偏右而立,其右侧为佛座;刈草人双手奉施一捆净草,佛陀以右手示意放在座上(图6);佛周围雕出若干天人[2]。克孜尔现存中心柱窟壁画中也有这一题材,如第80、163、171窟等[3]。其中第171窟的吉祥施草,构图亦作方形;佛左侧上方画一方座,右下方跪一人,双手捧草,向佛作供奉状(图7)。克孜尔石窟以东,不闻有此题材的雕刻或绘画。因此,不论从题材上,还是从构图上,克孜尔石窟中的"吉祥施草"壁画与犍陀罗出土的"吉祥施草"浮雕,有密切关系[4]。

图6　犍陀罗佛塔塔基"吉祥施草"浮雕,出土于Sikri,现藏巴基斯坦拉合尔博物馆

[1] 宫治昭等《佛傳美術の傳播と變容——シルクロードに沿つて》,見《シルクロード學研究》,1997年,第3辑,第169页。除犍陀罗本土外,在阿富汗的Shotorak,也曾出土一件这种题材的浮雕,参见Jacques Meunié, *Shotorak, Mémoires de la Délégation Archéologique française en Afghanistan*, X, Paris: Les Éditions d'Art et d'Historie, 1942: 133.

[2] John Marshall, *opere citato*: 57-58, fig.76.

[3] 丁明夷、马世长、雄西《克孜尔石窟的佛传壁画》,上引书,第189页。

[4] 尽管"吉祥施草"在早期汉译佛典,如《修行本起经》、《普曜经》、《过去现在因果经》和《佛本行集经》等都有记述,但以《佛本行集经》描述最详,且与犍陀罗出土的浮雕和克孜尔中心柱窟主室侧壁的同类故事画面相近。

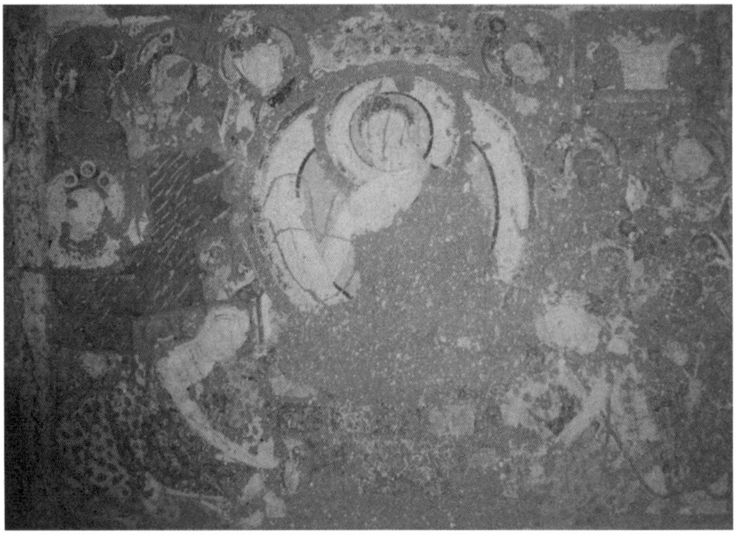

图 7　克孜尔第 171 窟右壁“吉祥施草”壁画

经检索佛典，克孜尔中心柱窟的因缘佛传壁画和犍陀罗出土的佛传浮雕内容，大多见于汉译《佛本行集经》、《长阿含经》以及《普曜经》、《方广大庄严经》和《根本说一切有部毗奈耶破僧事》等[1]，有些内容，似仅见于《佛本行集经》，如“富楼那出家”、“婆提唎迦继位”[2]等。因此，克孜尔中心柱窟主室侧壁的因缘佛传壁画，受犍陀罗佛传雕刻或绘画之影响[3]，似主要依据与汉译《佛本行集经》和《长阿含经》相当的佛典绘制。

克孜尔中心柱窟主室券顶两侧壁画的内容主要是本生和因缘，二者皆画在以山峦为背景的菱形格内，分别简称“菱格本生”或“菱格因缘”[4]。

菱格本生，画面中不出现佛像，仅画出该故事最具特征的一个情节(图 8)。有的一窟之内画出本生故事几十种，多者一窟竟达八十余种。据马世长先生研究，“克孜尔石窟菱格本生故事的内容，大约近九十余种。本生故事种类之多，内容之丰富，在国内外石窟中都是极少见的”[5]。菱格因缘，画面正中绘出佛像，故事情节及内容则

---

[1] 丁明夷、马世长、雄西《克孜尔石窟的佛传壁画》，上引书，第 186-197、202-207、218-219 页。

[2] 阇那崛多《佛本行集经》，参见《大正藏》，No. 190，第 3 卷，第 824a-825a、921a-923a 页。

[3] 李崇峰，上引书，第 197-200 页。

[4] 李崇峰，上引书，第 196-197 页。

[5] 马世长《克孜尔中心柱窟主室券顶与后室的壁画》，见《中国石窟·克孜尔石窟》二，北京：文物出版社，1996 年，第 198 页。德国学者林冶 20 世纪 30 年代根据格林威德尔 (A. Grünwedel) 及他自己的研究，曾统计出约 80 个不同的本生故事及譬喻故事。参见 Ernst Waldschmidt, “Über die Darstellungen und den Stil der Wandgemälde aus Qyzil bei Kutscha I”, in: A. von Leq, E. Waldschmidt (ed.), *Die buddhistische Spätantike in Mittelasien*, VI: Neue Bildwerke II, Berlin, 1928: 9-62.

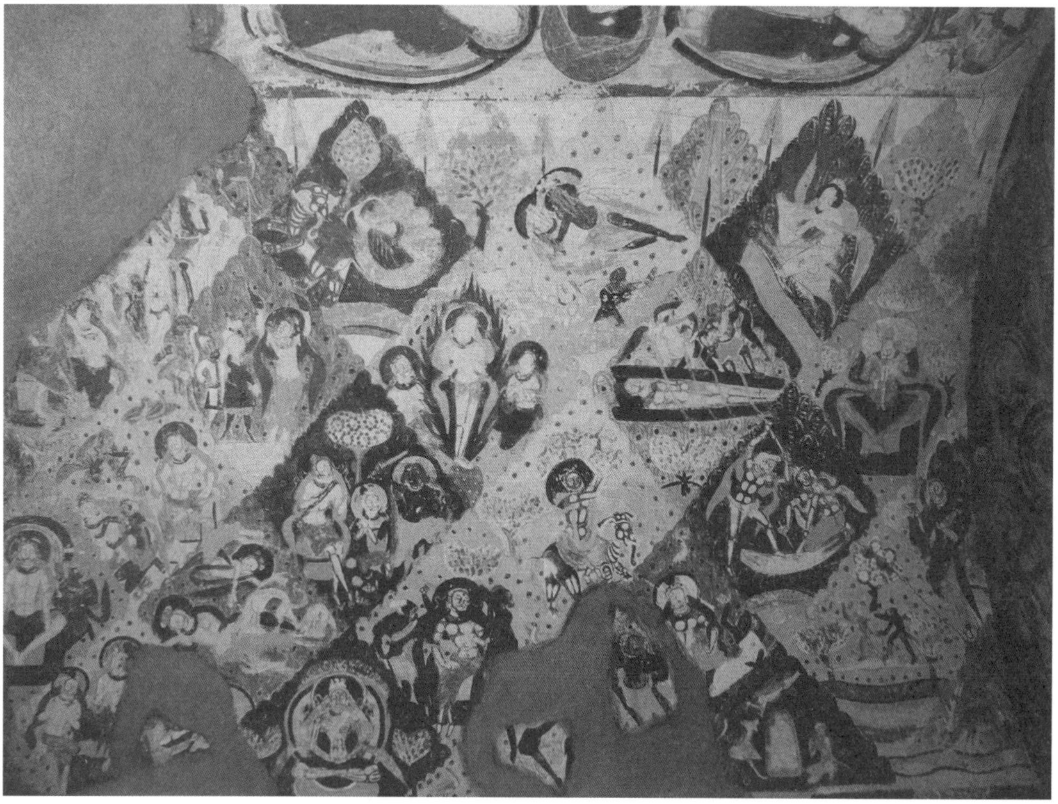

图 8　克孜尔第 17 窟券顶“本生故事”壁画

安排在佛像的两侧或下方(图 9)。克孜尔中心柱窟的菱格因缘故事,仅第 80 窟券顶所画就有八十种左右。因而估计,克孜尔石窟“因缘故事的总数大约不少于九十种。无疑,克孜尔石窟因缘故事画数量之多,内容之丰富,也不亚于本生故事画。两者同是克孜尔石窟中心柱窟券顶壁画的主要题材”[1]。

至于克孜尔中心柱窟菱格本生所据经典,多与汉译《贤愚经》[2]吻合,少数见于汉译《六度集经》、《杂宝藏经》、《经律异相》以及巴利语《本生经》(*The Jātaka*)

[1] 马世长《克孜尔中心柱窟主室券顶与后室的壁画》,上引书,第 208 页。

[2] 据僧佑《出三藏记集》卷九《贤愚经记》,《贤愚经》也作《贤愚因缘经》,十三卷,是叙述因缘故事的典籍。它是昙学(一作慧觉)、威德等八人在于阗参加般遮于瑟会时,分别所做的会中长老讲诵经律的汉译记录;445 年抵高昌后,昙学等八僧汇集各自记录,即“始集次经”,其原典似为于阗语。参见:1) 僧佑《出三藏记集》,苏晋仁、萧錬子点校,北京:中华书局,1995 年,第 351 页;2)Victor Mair, “The Khotanese Antecedents of *the Sūtra of the Wise and Foolish* (*Xianyujing*)”, in: *Collection of Essays 1993: Buddhism Across Boundaries—Chinese Buddhism and Western Religions* by Erik Zürcher, Lore Sander and others, eds. John R. McRae, Jan Nattier, Taipei: Foguang Cultural Enterprise Co., Ltd, 1999: 361-420.

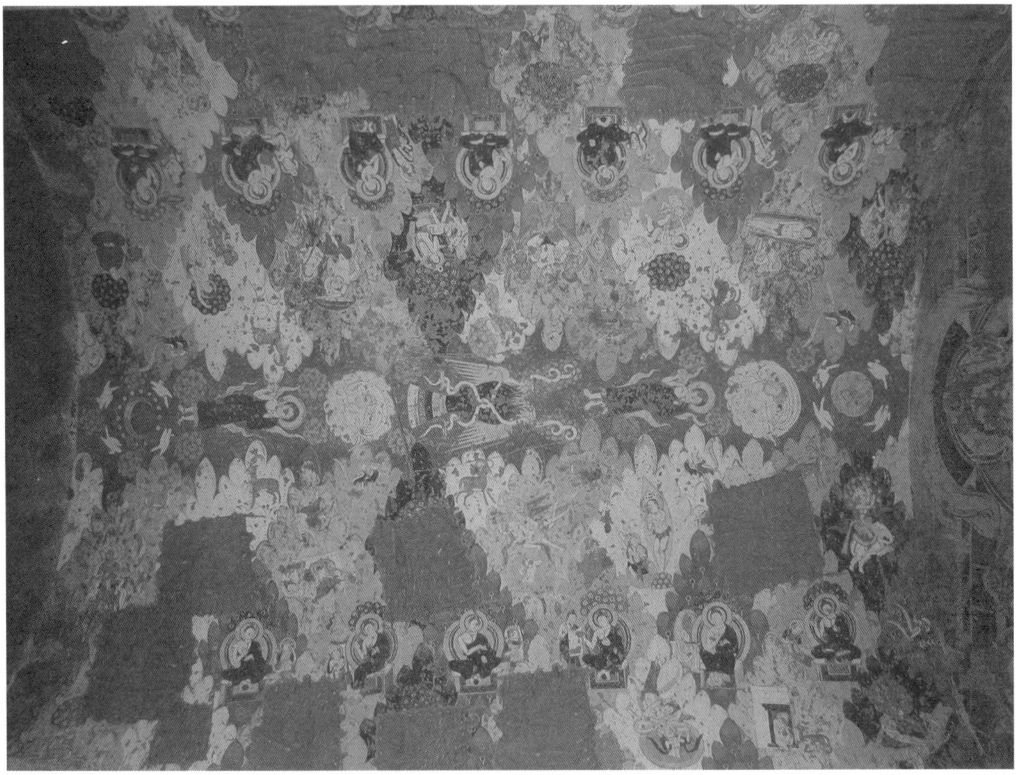

图 9　克孜尔第 38 窟券顶“因缘故事”壁画

等佛典中[1]。实际上，新疆中古时期曾流行一部《十业譬喻鬘》(*Daśa-karmapatha-avadānamālā*)。该经中的譬喻故事，与汉译《贤愚经》相同或相近[2]。美国学者梅维恒 (Victor Mair) 认为：这部《十业譬喻鬘》原典为龟兹语，后从龟兹语本 (Tokharian B) 译成焉耆语 (Tokharian A)，再由焉耆语本译为回鹘文；至于粟特文《十业譬喻鬘》，可能是从龟兹语本译出的。现有充分证据显示，《贤愚经》中的譬喻及其他类型故事[3]，在

[1] 1) 马世长《克孜尔中心柱窟主室券顶与后室的壁画》，上引书，第 178-198 页；2) Chongfeng Li, “The Representation of Jātakas in Kizil Caves, Kucha” , in: *Turfan Revisited—The First Century of Research into the Arts and Cultures of the Silk Road*, ed. Desmond Durkin-Meisterernst et al, Berlin: Dietrich Reimer Verlag, 2004: 163-168.

[2] 1) Sylvain Lévi, “Le sūtra du sage et du fou dans la littérature de l’Asie Centrale” , in: *Journal Asiatique,* Sér. 12, 6, Vol. 207 / 2 (October-December, 1925): 304-332, esp. 312-317; 2) Victor Mair, “The Khotanese Antecedents of the *Sūtra of the Wise and Foolish* (*Xianyujing*)” , in: *opere citato*: 361-420, esp. 402.

[3] 陈寅恪先生认为：“《贤愚经》者，本当时昙学等八僧听讲之笔记也。今检其内容，乃一杂集印度故事之书。以此推之，可知当日中央亚细亚说经，例引故事以阐经义。此风盖导源于天竺。”陈寅恪《西游记玄奘弟子故事之演变》，见陈寅恪《金明馆丛稿》二编，上海：上海古籍出版社，1980 年，第 192 页。

高僧法成9世纪编译藏文本之时,新疆尚存于阗语、龟兹语、焉耆语以及粟特文、回鹘文,尤其是印度语本。至于觉贤等八人在于阗听诵的原典应为印度语,《贤愚经》可能是以西北俗语的于阗化型(Khotanized form of Northwest Prākrit)诵出的[1],因为6世纪以前新疆地区的佛典似乎仅用印度语言传诵[2]。若然,龟兹地区最早流行的本生故事原典,或为西北俗语。菱格因缘所据经典,多见于汉译《撰集百缘经》、《杂宝藏经》、《贤愚经》和《佛本行集经》等佛典中[3]。这种譬喻故事及上述因缘佛传,似乎都属于本行范畴,在佛典分类上,“本生、本事、譬喻、因缘各籍,原为律藏之支分”[4]。

克孜尔中心柱窟后室及中心塔柱后壁壁画的主要题材,是涅槃图像及其相关内容,如须跋先佛入灭、涅槃、荼毗焚棺、八王分舍利以及舍利塔供养或塔中坐佛等,尤其涅槃图像可以说每窟必有[5],绘制年代大约从公元3世纪末到8世纪下半叶左右[6]。涅槃图像的构图与画面繁简不一,一般在卧佛上方画出诸天、菩萨、弟子多身(图10)。最简单者,画面中仅出现卧佛和其双足下方所跪一老比丘,余无其他内容,如第7窟;复杂者,在佛床周围加入须跋先佛入灭,摩耶夫人自忉利天降下观佛涅槃等,如第179窟。克孜尔中心柱窟的涅槃图像,第一期[7]皆画在后甬道后壁。从第二期[8]开始,后甬道被拓宽加高成后室,且于后室后壁下部向前凿出涅槃台,上塑涅槃像。这表明佛教涅槃思想进一步加强了。实际上,佛的涅槃故事,早在公元前2世纪就已在印度本土创作,只是以象征物表现

[1] Victor Mair, “The Khotanese Antecedents of the *Sūtra of the Wise and Foolish* (*Xianyujing*)”, in: *opere citato*: 361-420, esp. 402-420.

[2] 1) Jan Willem de Jong, *Buddha's Word in China, The Twenty-eighth George Ernest Morrison Lecture in Ethnology,* Canberra: The Australian National University, 1968:11; 2) Jan Nattier, “Church Language and Vernacular Language in Central Asian Buddhism”, in: *Numen* (International Review for the History of Religion), Vol. 37 (1990), No. 2: 195-219.

[3] 马世长《克孜尔中心柱窟主室券顶与后室的壁画》,上引书,第198-211页。

[4] 吕澂《新编汉文大藏经目录》,济南:齐鲁书社,1980年,第13页。

[5] 克孜尔中心柱窟后甬道或后室未见或未塑绘涅槃图像的较少,据统计只有第63、100、101、123窟等。其中,第63窟的画塑已毁,第101窟、第123窟壁画残失,原画内容不明。参见:新疆龟兹石窟研究所编,上引书,第74、130、153页。

[6] 李崇峰,上引书,第167-176页。

[7] 克孜尔第一期中心柱窟开凿的时间,大约从3世纪末到4世纪中叶左右。参见:李崇峰,上引书,第151-152、167、176页。

[8] 克孜尔第二期中心柱窟开凿的时间,大约从4世纪中叶到5世纪末左右。参见:李崇峰,上引书,第153-156、168-169、176页。

图 10　克孜尔第 38 窟后室 "涅槃" 壁画

而已[1]。秣菟罗和犍陀罗的艺术家及工匠，在分别引入偶像观念并创作出佛像之后，"涅槃变" 乃成为两地佛教艺术的流行题材之一（图 11）[2]，并且很快向各地传播，一直为佛教徒所重[3]。克孜尔石窟中的涅槃图像，应与印度、中亚流行的涅槃思想有

[1] 1) Benimadhab Barua, *Barhut*, 3 vols., Book I: *Stone as a story teller*, Book II: *Jātaka-scenes*, Book III: *Aspects of life and art*, rep., Patna: Indological Book Corporation, 1979, esp. Book III: 22, Figs. 54-55; 2) Jas. Burgess, *The Buddhist Stūpas of Amarāvatī and Jaggayapeṭa in Krishna District, Madras Presidency, surveyed in 1882*, in: *Archaeological Survey of Southern India*, VI, London: 1886, rep., New Delhi: Archaeological Survey of India, 1996: Pls. XLI, XLVI, XLVIII, XLIV; 3) James Fergusson, *Tree and Serpent Worship*: or *Illustrations of Mythology and Art in India in the first and fourth centuries after Christ from the Sculptures of the Buddhist Topes at Sāñchī and Amrāvatī*, London: Indian Office, 1873: 171, Pls. XCIV, XCVII, LXXV.

[2] 1) R. C. Sharma, *Buddhist Art: Mathurā School*, New Delhi: Wiley Eastern Limited & New Age International Limited, 1995: 245, Figs. 168, 178, 179; 2) John Marshall, *opere citato*: 55, Figs. 68, 72, 87, 127, 128, 129.

[3] 1) V. S. Agrawala, *Sārnāth*, New Delhi: Archaeological Survey of India, 1980: 20, Pl. IX; 2) D. R. Patil, *Kuśīnagara*, New Delhi: Archaeological Survey of India, 1957: 20; 3) James Fergusson and James Burgess, *The Cave Temples of India*, London: W. H. Allen & Co., 1880: Pl. L; 4) 樋口隆康《バーミヤーン：アフガニスタンにおける仏教石窟寺院の美術考古学的調查 1970-1978 年》，京都大學中央アシア學術調查報告：第 I 卷図版篇（壁画），第 II 卷図版篇（石窟構造）1983；第 III 卷本文篇，第 IV 卷英文 / 実测図篇，1984，京都：同朋舍，1983-1984 年，4 卷；第 I 卷図版篇（壁畫），图版第 7、57-2、66、69-1、70-2。

图 11 犍陀罗"涅槃"浮雕,出土地不详,现藏伦敦不列颠博物院

着极为密切的关系[1]。

通过对上述涅槃图像进行比较,我们发现：克孜尔中心柱窟的涅槃画塑,不论在构图上,还是在细部处理上,都与犍陀罗地区出土的涅槃浮雕极为相似。在仔细观察画面的基础上,通过分析犍陀罗语、巴利语、梵语和汉译有关涅槃之佛典[2],我们认为克孜尔中心柱窟后室及中心塔柱后壁的涅槃图像,主要根据与汉译《长阿含经 · 游行经》[3]相当的佛典创作而成[4]。

至于主室前壁门道上方半圆形壁面所画弥勒及"慈子"(图 12、13),乃信徒绕塔礼拜、观瞻涅槃及荼毗后返回主室所目睹[5],或许依据与汉译《长阿含经 · 转轮圣王

[1] 参见：李崇峰,上引书,第 200-202 页。

[2] 丁明夷、马世长、雄西《克孜尔石窟的佛传壁画》,上引书,第 216 页。

[3] 据僧佑《出三藏记集》和智昇《开元释教录》,西晋竺法护泰始五年(269 年)翻译的《佛般泥洹经》,后作帛法祖译,勘出《长阿含经》第二至四卷初分《游行经》；东晋法显译《大般涅槃经》,勘同《佛般泥洹经》；失译《般泥洹经》,先作刘宋求那跋陀罗译,后附东晋录,勘同《佛般泥洹经》。参见：吕澂,上引书,第 48 页。有关涅槃经典的一再传译,反映出这一时期它们在当地颇为流行。

[4] Chongfeng Li, "Representation of the Buddha's Parinirvāṇa in the Cetiyagharas of Kizil, Kucha", in: *Buddhist Narrative in Asia and Beyond,* Vol. I, eds. Peter Skilling and Justin McDaniel, Bangkok: Institute of Thai Studies, Chulalongkorn University, 2012: 59-81. 参见霍旭初、王建林《丹青斑驳—千秋壮观：克孜尔石窟壁画艺术及分期概述》,见新疆龟兹石窟研究所编《龟兹佛教文化论集》,乌鲁木齐：新疆美术摄影出版社,1993 年,第 211-212 页。

[5] 宫治昭,上引书,第 512-520 页。

图 12　克孜尔第 224 窟前壁门道上方“弥勒菩萨兜率天说法”壁画，现藏德国柏林亚洲艺术博物馆

图 13　克孜尔第 17 窟前壁门道上方“弥勒菩萨兜率天说法”壁画

修行经》相当的佛典及有关文献[1]并模仿犍陀罗弥勒菩萨图像（图 14-16）经营而

[1]《长阿含经》卷六《转轮圣王修行经》记“有佛出世，名为弥勒如来，至真等正觉，十号具足，如今如来十号具足。彼于诸天、释、梵、魔、若魔、天、诸沙门、婆罗门、诸天、世人中，自身作证，亦如我今于诸天、释、梵、魔、若魔、天、沙门、婆罗门、诸天、世人中，自身作证。彼当说法，初言亦善，中、下亦善，义味具足，净修梵行，如我今日说法。上中下言，皆悉真正义味具足，梵行清净。彼众弟子有无数千万，如我今日弟子数百。彼时，人民称其弟子号曰慈子，如我弟子号曰释子”。参见《大正藏》第 1 卷，第 41c 页。此外，《长阿含经·游行经》异译本《佛般泥洹经》与《般泥洹经》之末，有关于释迦入灭后弥勒信仰的记载，如“弥勒当下作佛”、“弥勒世尊当为天说经法”等。《大正藏》第 1 卷，第 191a、175c 页。

图 14　犍陀罗“佛说法图与弥勒菩萨兜率天示现”浮雕，约 1865-1880 年拍摄

图 15　犍陀罗“佛说法图与弥勒菩萨兜率天示现”浮雕细部，原藏巴基斯坦拉合尔博物馆，现藏印度昌迪加尔博物馆

图 16　犍陀罗“弥勒菩萨兜率天示现”浮雕，出土于 Chārsada，原藏巴基斯坦拉合尔博物馆，现藏德国柏林亚洲艺术博物馆

成[1],因为早期西行求法之高僧,如宝云[2]、法显[3]、法盛[4]等多记乌苌弥勒[5]结缘；甚至到了玄奘游历之时,该菩萨像尚“灵鉴潜通”[6]。

二、汉译经律与法藏部“五藏”

克孜尔中心柱窟主室正壁（中心塔柱前壁）画塑题材,与汉译《长阿含经·释提桓因问经》内容相符；每窟后室后壁和中心塔柱后壁与侧壁必画或塑的涅槃图像及其与之相关的须跋先佛入灭和荼毗焚棺等,又都与汉译《长阿含经·游行经》内容吻合。因此,画塑所据佛典不言自明[7]。新疆发现的《长阿含经》除梵语写本外,尚有佉卢字母犍陀罗语[8]写本。不过,克孜尔中心柱窟画塑所据的《长阿含经》,到底是犍陀罗语写本,还是梵语本,抑或当地龟兹语所传,现不得而知。

通常所说的《阿含经》,包括《长阿含经》、《中阿含经》、《杂阿含经》和《增一阿含经》等四部。据吕澂先生研究,“小乘各部所传四《阿含》,每每以编次异序为区别”,如说一切有部四阿含的编排次第与别部有异,将《相应》视为根本经典,置于首位。关于汉译《阿含经》,“《瑜伽》事教乃在《杂含》,所举契经存有部说……《杂含》

---

[1] 犍陀罗出土的弥勒菩萨兜率天说法,整体构图多作半圆形,疑为克孜尔中心柱窟前壁门道上方半圆形壁面“弥勒菩萨兜率天说法”经营之源。Chongfeng Li, “The Image of Maitreya in the Chētiyagharas of Kizil, Kucha”, in: *Gandhāran Studies,* Vol. VII: 11-22.

[2] 宝唱《名僧传》第二十六《宝云传》,见宗性《名僧传抄》,载《大日本續藏經》,第壹輯第貳編乙第七套第壹册,第十三叶。

[3] 法显《法显传》,章巽校注,上海：上海古籍出版社,1985年,第26页。

[4] 宝唱《名僧传》第二十六《法盛传》,上引书,第十三叶。

[5] 北凉承平三年(445年)沮渠安周于高昌兴造皇家大寺“弥勒祠”,疑受其影响所建,因为前述法盛昔年“寓于高昌”。参见：1) Albert Grünwedel, *Bericht über archäologische Arbeiten in Idikutschari und Umgebung im Winter 1902-1903*, München: G. Franz'scher Verlag, 1906: 27-28, Fig. 20; 2) Rong Xinjiang, “Juqu Anzhou's Inscription and the Daliang Kingdom in Turfan”, in: *Turfan Revisited—The First Century of Research into the Arts and Cultures of the Silk Road*, ed. Desmond Durkin-Meisterernst et al, Berlin: Dietrich Reimer Verlag, 2004: 268-275.

[6] 玄奘《大唐西域记》,季羡林等校注,北京：中华书局,1985年,第295-296页。

[7] 参见本书所收《克孜尔中心柱窟主室正壁画塑题材及有关问题》。

[8] 据俄国学者M. I. 沃罗比耶娃—捷夏托夫斯卡娅介绍,在俄国圣彼得堡俄罗斯科学院东方研究所的S. F. 鄂登堡藏品中,有一件用佉卢字母犍陀罗语书写在棕榈叶上的佛经残片,显然是小乘《大般涅槃经》。参见B. A. 李特文斯基主编《中亚文明史》第三卷,马小鹤译,北京：中国对外翻译出版公司,2003年,第372页。这件重要残片的出土地点不清,不过依据有关材料,鄂登堡1909年第一次在新疆考察时,主要踏查了库车、焉耆和吐鲁番地区；1914年第二次考察的重点是敦煌等地。因此,我们怀疑这件残片或许采自库车。

旧译部别未详，今由《本母》厘正次第，勘为同本”[1]。因此，宋元嘉二十年(443年)中印度三藏法师求那跋陀罗所出《杂阿含经》就等同于《相应阿含经》，为有部经典。此外，汉译《中阿含经》也属于一切有部所传[2]，汉译《增一阿含经》或为大众部传本，汉译《别译杂阿含经》则出于化地部或法藏部所传[3]。“《长阿含经》的译者先诵出《四分律》，属于法藏部；既而又诵出本经，虽其中各经次序和《四分律》所说不同，但经文中表现了对于供养佛塔的重视以及阿罗汉身无漏的思想，都合乎法藏部的主张，故无妨看做和法藏部相近的部派传本。”[4]

汉译《长阿含经》属于法藏部所传，现已得到学界的广泛认同[5]。译者佛陀耶舍(Buddhayaśas)来自罽宾(西北印度)，在翻译《长阿含经》之前曾译出《四分律》[6]。据窥基《妙法莲华经玄赞》卷一，“四分律是法藏部义”[7]。汉译本《四分律序》记载：“壬辰之年(392年)，有晋国沙门支法领，感边土之乖圣，慨正化之未夷，乃亡身以俎险，庶弘道于无闻。西越流沙，远期天竺，路经于阗，会遇昙无德部、体大乘三藏沙门佛陀耶舍，才体博闻，明炼经、律，三藏、方等，皆讽诵通利。”[8]故而，佛陀耶舍为昙无

---

[1] 吕澂《杂阿含经刊定记》，原刊《内学》第一辑(1924年)，后收入《吕澂佛学论著选集》一，济南：齐鲁书社，1991年，第15、29页。

[2] 赤沼智善《佛教經典史論》，名古屋：三寶書院，1939年，第41-46页。

[3] 1) 吕澂《阿含经》，见中国佛教协会编《中国佛教》三，上海：知识出版社，1989年，第160页；2) 水野弘元《別譯雜阿含について》，刊《印度學佛教學研究》18 (2) 號，第41-51页；3) 静谷正雄《漢譯〈增一阿含經〉の所屬部派》，刊《印度學佛教學研究》22 (1) 號，第54-59页。

[4] 吕澂《阿含经》，上引书，第158页。参见：赤沼智善，上引书，第29-35页。

[5] 参见：1) A. Bareau, *Les sectes bouddhiques du Petit Véhicule,* Paris: Publications de l'École française d'Extrême-Orient 38, 1955: 191; 2) É. Lamotte, *Histoire du Bouddhisme Indien: des origines à l'ére Šaka,* Bibliothèque du Muséon 43, Louvain: Institut Orientaliste de Louvain, 1958: 629-30; 3) Ernst Waldschmidt, "Central Asian Sūtra Fragments and their Relation to the Chinese Āgamas", in: *Die Sprache der ältesten buddhistischen Überlieferung; The Language of the Earliest Buddhist Tradition* (Symposien zur Buddhismusforschung ii), Abhandlungen der Akademie der Wissenschaften in Göttingen: Philologisch-historische Klasse, Ser. 3, Vol. 117, Heinz. Bechert, hrsg, Göttingen: Vandenhoeck & Ruprecht, 1980: 136-174, esp. 136-137; 4) 吕澂《阿含经》，上引书，第158页。

[6] 据费长房《历代三宝记》卷八《译经・符秦、姚秦录》，佛陀耶舍译“《长阿含经》二十二卷，弘始十五年(413年)出，竺佛念笔受……弘始十二年(410年)译《四分律》”。参见《大正藏》第49卷，第79c-80b页。又，据僧佑《释迦谱》卷一，“遮迦越，齐言飞行皇帝，即转轮王也。《长阿含》及《昙无德律》序转轮世数甚明，已显于前”；《大智论》云：“昔日种王，名师子颊，有四子，长名净饭。《长阿含》与《昙无德律》并同”。参见《大正藏》第50卷，第3c-4b页。这或许暗示《长阿含经》与《四分律》(即《昙无德律》)属同一部派所传。

[7] 窥基《妙法莲华经玄赞》，《大正藏》第34卷，第657a页。

[8] 佛陀耶舍 / 竺佛念译《四分律》，《大正藏》第22卷，第567a页。

德部（法藏部）三藏法师[1]。

据《摩诃僧祇律》卷四十所附东晋义熙十四年（418年）法显《〈摩诃僧祇律〉私记》，“佛泥洹后，大迦叶集律藏为大师宗，具持八万法藏……尊者优波崛多……而亦能具持八万法藏，于是遂有五部名生。初昙摩崛多别为一部（法藏部），次弥沙塞别为一部（化地部），次迦叶维复为一部（饮光部），次萨婆多（说一切有部）……于是五部并立，纷然竞起，各以自义为是”[2]。梁僧佑《出三藏记集》卷十二《萨婆多部记目录序》更强调：“中代异执，五部各分；既分五部，则随师得传习。”[3]因此，既为法藏部高僧，应“诵持”法藏部经律，这是部派佛教徒必须遵循的教规。故而，依据多年实地考察和研究印度律藏之经历，义净在《南海寄归内法传》序言中特别指出：“出家之侣，各依部执，无宜取他轻事，替己重条，用自开文，见嫌余制。若尔，则部别之义不著，许遮之理莫分。岂得以其一身，遍行于四？裂裳金杖之喻，乃表证灭不殊。行法之徒，须依自部。”[4]

此外，从佛典编排分析，汉译《长阿含经》偏重佛陀，因此以第一分集录有关佛陀经典，而把佛弟子、阿罗汉修行之道置于第三分；汉译《长阿含经》与巴利语《长尼迦耶》之三分，前者依佛、法、僧之次第，后者按僧、佛、法之顺序，因而两者在编排上有较大差异[5]。又，从佛典内容考虑，汉译《长阿含经·游行经》强调供养佛塔，这点不见于巴利语《大般涅槃经》，而与法藏部偏重佛塔相一致[6]。崇奉佛塔，乃法藏部特有主张之一；法藏部在“四分戒本学处”加入塔事数十则，为他派部执律藏所不见[7]。关于十二分教之顺序，《长阿含经》与《四分律》近似；至于释迦族谱，《长阿含经》与《四分律》之记载[8]几乎完全相同，但与其他佛典则有较大差异。另

---

[1] 据慧皎记载，“（律藏）……昙无德部佛陀耶舍所翻，即四分律也”。慧皎《高僧传》，汤用彤校注，北京：中华书局，1992年，第443页。

[2] 佛陀跋陀罗 / 法显译《摩诃僧祇律》，《大正藏》第22卷，第548a-b页。

[3] 僧佑，上引书，第466页。

[4] 义净《南海寄归内法传》，王邦维校注，北京：中华书局，1995年，第19页。

[5] 1) 赤沼智善，上引书，第29-35页；2) 水野弘元《國譯一切經：四阿含解題の補遺・長含》，東京：大東出版社，1968年，第499-515页。

[6] 1) 干潟龍祥《漢巴對照長阿含研究概括》，見《佛教學雜誌》，1919年，第3卷6號，第11页；2) 吕澂《阿含经》，上引书，第160页。

[7] 1) 佛陀耶舍译《四分僧戒本》及《四分比丘尼戒本》，《大正藏》第22卷，第1029b、1039c-1040a页；2) 吕澂《诸家戒本通论》及附录《论律学与十八部分派之关系》，载《吕澂佛学论著选集》一，济南：齐鲁书社，1991年，第89-143页。

[8] 1) 佛陀耶舍译《长阿含经》卷二十二《世记经》，《大正藏》第1卷，第148c-149a页；2) 佛陀耶舍译《四分律》卷三十一《受戒揵度》，《大正藏》第22卷，第779a-b页。

外,汉译《长阿含经》卷二“菴婆婆梨女施果园”[1]与《四分律》卷五十“瓶沙王施竹园”[2]描述的施园仪式及措辞相似,但与其他部派如上座部和化地部的类似记载有别;这反映出在佛与僧伽施奉的相对值上,各派冲突的学说态度[3]。因此,汉译《长阿含经》应属于法藏部所传[4];而“四分本是上座末宗,西域流行较盛”[5]。

汉译《佛本行集经》是一部完整的佛传。它把五部不同佛传汇集一起,以法藏部《释迦牟尼佛本行》(*Śākyamuni-Buddhacarita*)为名,称作《集经》[6]。据隋费长房记载:《佛本行集经》,为“北天竺揵达国(即犍陀罗)三藏法师阇那崛多(Jńānagupta,隋言至德)译,又云佛德,周明帝世武成年初(559 年)共同学耶舍崛多,随厥师主摩伽陀国三藏禅师阇那耶舍赍经入国。师徒、同学悉习方言二十余年,崛多最善。周世在京及往蜀地,随处并皆宣译新经,或接先阙,文义咸允”[7]。唐智昇编著《开元释教录》时进一步补充道:“阇那崛多,隋云志德,北贤豆揵陀啰国人也,隋云香行国,居富留沙富逻城,隋云丈夫宫也,刹帝利种,姓金步……崛多道性纯厚,神志刚正;爱德无厌,求法不懈;博闻三藏,远究真宗;遍学五明,兼闲世论。经行得道场之趣,总持通神咒之

[1]《大正藏》第 1 卷,第 13b-14c 页。

[2]《大正藏》第 22 卷,第 936b-c 页。

[3] André Bareau, “L' origine du Dīrgha-āgama traduit en Chinois par Buddhayaśas”, in: *Essays Offered to G. H. Luce by His Colleagues and Friends in Honour of His Seventy-fifth Birthday,* Vol. 1, *Papers on Asian History, Religion, Languages, Literature, Music, Folklore and Anthropology, Artibus Asiae* Supplementum 23. 1, eds. Ba Shin, Jean Boisselier and A. B. Griswold, Ascona: Artibus Asiae, 1966: 49-58, esp. 49.

[4] 1) 干潟龍祥,《漢巴對照長阿含研究概括》,上引书,第 11 页;2) E. Waldschmidt, *Bruchstücke buddhistischer Sūtras aus dem zentralasiatischen Sanskritkanon I: herausgegeben und im Zusammenhang mit ihren Parallelversionen bearbeitet* (Königlich Preußische Turfan-Expeditionen, Kleinere Sanskrit-texte IV), Leipzig: Deutschen Morgenländische Gesellschaft, 1932: 229-234; 3) 赤沼智善,上引书,第 29-35 页; 4) H. W. Bailey, “Gāndhārī”, in: *Bulletin of the School of Oriental And African Studies*, XI (1946): 764-797, esp. 765; 5) John Brough, *The Gāndhārī Dharmapada, London Oriental Series 7. London: Oxford University Press, 1962: 48-54, esp. 50;* 6) André Bareau, *opere citato*: 49-58; 7) 水野弘元,上引书,第 499-515 页; 8) Richard Salomon, *Ancient Buddhist Scrolls from Gandhāra: The British Library Kharoṣṭhī Fragments,* Seattle: University of Washington Press, 1999:173.

[5] 吕澂《诸家戒本通论》,上引书,第 128 页。

[6] 印度部派佛教时期各派律中的佛传,都从佛的家世、出家以至成道后六年回家为止,此后的活动均无记载,《佛本行集经》也是如此。参见吕澂《印度佛学源流略讲》,上海:上海人民出版社,1979 年,第 13 页。

[7] 费长房《历代三宝记》卷十二《译经·大隋录》,《大正藏》第 49 卷,第 104a 页。

理……自开皇五年讫仁寿之末，出《护国》等经，总三十九部、合一百九十二卷"[1]。其中，"《佛本行集经》六十卷，开皇七年（587年）七月起手，十二年二月讫功，沙门僧昙、学士费长房、刘凭等笔受，沙门彦琮制序"[2]。该经在隋费长房《历代三宝记》及后世佛经目录中皆有记载[3]，属小乘经[4]。据《佛本行集经》卷六十《阿难因缘品》，此经"摩诃僧祇（大众部）师名为《大事》，萨婆多（说一切有部）师名此经为《大庄严》，迦叶维（饮光部）师名为《佛生因缘》，昙无德（法藏部）师名为《释迦牟尼佛本行》，尼沙塞（化地部）师名为《毗尼藏根本》"[5]。因此，出生于法藏部重镇富留沙富逻城（今白沙瓦）的阇那崛多，应为昙无德部（法藏部）高僧，所译佛典应为法藏部当时所传[6]。

法藏部[7]乃印度小乘佛教部派之一[8]，一作昙摩毱多、昙摩崛多、昙无德部、法护部、法镜部、法密部、法正部等[9]。据《出三藏记集》卷三《新集律来汉地四部记录》，"中夏闻法，亦先经而后律。律藏稍广，始自晋末……昙无德者，梁言法镜，一音昙摩毱多。如来涅槃后，有诸弟子颠倒解义，覆隐法藏。以覆法故，名昙摩毱多"[10]。通常认为法藏部从化地部分裂而来[11]，起源于印度西海岸阿跋兰多（Aparānta，即

---

[1] 智昇《开元释教录》卷七《总括群经录》上，《大正藏》第55卷，第549a-550b页。不过，费长房《历代三宝记》卷十二《译经·大隋录》作"三十一部，合一百六十五卷"，《大正藏》第49卷，第104a页。道宣《大唐内典录》卷五《隋代传译佛经录》作"三十七部，合一百七十六卷"，《大正藏》第55卷，第276b页。

[2] 费长房《历代三宝记》卷十二《译经·大隋录》，《大正藏》第49卷，第103b页。

[3] 如［隋］费长房《历代三宝记》卷十四《小乘录入藏目》、［隋］法经等《众经目录》卷二《贤圣集传》、［唐］道宣《大唐内典录》卷八《贤圣集传》、［武周］明佺《大周刊定众经目录》卷十三《大乘重译经》和［唐］智昇《开元释教录》卷十三《小乘经单译》等。参见《大正藏》第49卷，第115c页；第55卷，第161b、312a、461c、616b页。

[4] 据《开元释教录》卷十三《小乘经单译》，"此《佛本行经》，《大周录》中编为'大乘重译'，云与七卷《本行经》同本异译者，误也。彼是偈赞，与此悬殊。诸录或在'大乘经'中，或编'集传'之内，恐将乖僻。今移编此"。《大正藏》第55卷，第616b页。

[5]《大正藏》第3卷，第932a页。

[6] 1) Hajime Nakamura［中村元］, *Indian Buddhism: A Survey with Bibliographical Notes*, Delhi: Motilal Banarsidass Publishers, 1987: 132; 2) Akira Hirakawa［平川彰］, *A History of Indian Buddhism: From Śākyamuni to Early Mahāyāna,* tr. Paul Groner, Asian Studies at Hawaii 36, Honolulu: University of Hawaii Press, 1990: 263.

[7] 法藏部一词，梵语拉丁字母转写为 Dharmagupta 或 Dharmaguptaka，巴利语作 Dhammaguttika，犍陀罗语为 Dhamaüteaṇa 或 Dharma'ute'a。

[8] 1) É. Lamotte, *opere citato*: 571-606; 2) 吕澂《诸家戒本通论》附录《论律学与十八部分派之关系》，上引书，第131-143页。

[9] 元照《四分律行事钞资持记》上，载《大正藏》第40卷，第176b页。

[10] 僧佑，上引书，第116-117页。

[11] 据智昇《开元释教录》卷十三《有译有本录》中《声闻三藏录·调伏藏》，"法密部……佛圆寂后三百年中，从化地部之所出也"。《大正藏》第55卷，第618c页。

Kōnkan 和 Malakar 地区)。后来,他们循着贸易路线到达乌苌(Uḍḍiyāna)和安息(Parthia)。在他们向西发展远至安息并树立根基之后,又沿着丝路主线向东发展,越过中亚直抵中国,并于公元2、3世纪在那里有效地奠定了佛教基础[1]。在中亚及汉地早期佛教中,法藏部是最具影响的主要部派[2];即使后来,法藏部毗奈耶始终是汉地佛教戒律的基础[3]。当法藏部从化地部分裂之时,北方和西方的一切有部仍然维持它在舍卫城以及孔雀城(秣菟罗)的原有地盘,后来才逐渐集中到迦湿迷罗和犍陀罗,即罽宾[4]。结果,这一地区成为新的说一切有部的中心;再后来,新疆和汉地出现说一切有部[5]。因此可以说,最早立足于中亚乃至新疆的佛教徒可能属于法藏部[6]。

实际上,关于佛灭后佛教部派分裂次第以及各派异执较完整的记载,现存汉译佛典,仅见于玄奘译《异部宗轮论》。虽然该论可能出自有部大家世友之手,主要内容完全依照有部宗旨叙述,但它确是研究部派佛教的主要文献。

据《异部宗轮论》卷一:"法藏部本宗同义,谓佛虽在僧中所摄,然别施佛,果大非僧;于窣堵波,兴供养业,获广大果。佛与二乘解脱虽一,而圣道异。无诸外道能得

---

[1] 1) Étienne Lamotte, *opere citato*: 549; 2) 渥德尔《印度佛教史》,王世安译,北京:商务印书馆,1987年,第271页。

[2] 1) Franz Bernhard, "Gāndhārī and the Buddhist Mission in Central Asia", in: *Aňjali, Papers on Indology and Buddhism: A Felicitation Volume Presented to Oliver Hector de Alwis Wijesekara on His Sixtieth Birthday*, ed. J. Tilakasiri, Peradeniya: University of Ceylon, 1970: 55-62, esp. 59, 61; 2) Étienne Lamotte, *opere citato*: 549.

[3] 据道宣《四分律删繁补阙行事钞》卷一,"今昙无德部,人法有序,轨用多方。提诱唯存生善,立教意居显约;上则通明教兴,今据当宗以辨。夫教不孤起必因人,人既不同教亦非一。故摄诱弘济,轨用实多;贵在得其本诠,诚难核其条绪。所以约开制验,旨在为人;显持犯谅,意存无过"。《大正藏》第40卷,第1c-2a页。后来,义净在《南海寄归内法传》序中强调:"东夏大纲,多行法护;关中诸处,僧祇旧兼;江南岭表,有部先盛。"义净《南海寄归内法传》,王邦维校注,北京:中华书局,1995年,第19页。参见Ann Heirman, "Can we trace the early Dharmaguptakas?" in: *T'oung Pao* (通报), Vol. LXXXVIII (2002). Fasc. 4-5: 396-429.

[4] 据失译(今附秦录)《萨婆多毗尼毗婆沙》卷五《第十五结新作尼师檀因缘》,"以罽宾佛教炽盛……有二种僧,一萨婆多、二昙无德"。由此看出说一切有部与法藏部曾共存于罽宾。参见:1)《大正藏》第23卷,第534c页;2) 吕澂,上引书,第61页。

[5] 渥德尔,上引书,第268-271页。

[6] 据德国学者桑德尔(Lore Sander)博士研究,法藏部不仅存在于塔里木盆地南沿,甚至也许在说一切有部于迦腻色迦一世开始成功地传播佛法之前,在北沿的龟兹绿洲也曾存在过。该派遗迹显示他们在盆地北沿一直"杂行"到7世纪,而在吐鲁番绿洲甚至更晚些。参见Lore Sander, "Early Prakrit and Sanskrit Manuscripts from Xinjiang (second to fifth/sixth centuries C. E.): Paleography, Literary Evidence and Their Relation to Buddhist Schools", in: *Collection of Essays 1993: Buddhism Across Boundaries—Chinese Buddhism and Western Religions* by Erik Zürcher, Lore Sander and others, eds. John R. McRae, Jan Nattier, Taipei: Foguang Cultural Enterprise Co., Ltd, 1999: 61-106, esp. 67-68, 75.

五通，阿罗汉身皆是无漏。余义多同大众部执。”[1]对此，唐代高僧窥基注疏得更为具体：“法密部谓佛虽在僧，摄等者以别施佛，其心无简别，但为施世尊，极上极胜，一心平等，恭敬无差，故得福多。若佛在僧，亦兼施者，即心宽慢，又复大慢，又起简别。佛为无上，僧为有上，故普施僧，果少别福。于窣堵波，兴供养业，获广大果；于窣堵波供养得大果者，以佛舍利安在其中，见此处时如见于佛，其心既重，故得大果。以佛亦许供养舍利，如佛无异，故果极大，法等亦然。不为无摄受，便无大果。佛自开许，摄受施故。佛与二乘，解脱虽一而圣道异。”[2]

“法藏部由佛与二乘同一解脱而不同圣道的根本主张演绎出佛在僧数，所以它对僧团资具所有权的观点不同，解释亦异……又由它的根本主张演绎出施佛果大而盛行塔的供养，所以在《四分律》众学法里有关于佛塔的举法二十六条[3]，皆他家戒本之所无，乃至和它同一血脉的南传戒律里也没有。”[4]换言之，法藏部特别重视对佛陀的布施供养，超过僧团，同时强调供养佛塔的重要性。供养佛塔原因很多，《长阿含经》卷三《游行经》第二之二表述：“于四衢道起立塔庙，表刹悬缯，使诸行人皆见佛塔，思慕如来法王道化，生获福利，死得上天”；后在卷四《游行经》第二之三中再次重复同一言语[5]。由此可见，当初造塔是为了思慕如来，不忘佛陀教诲，多所饶益；“以佛舍利安在其中，见此处时如见于佛，其心既重，故得大果”。因此，《羯磨》、《昙无德律部杂羯磨》及《四分律》“异本同文”告诉信徒：“汝当善受教法，应当劝化作福治塔。”[6]唐代高僧道世更明言“安塔有其三意：一表人胜，二令他信，三为报恩”[7]。

除强调供养佛塔外，法藏部还特立“五藏”。据隋吉藏《三论玄义》卷一，“法护部……自撰为五藏，三藏如常，四咒藏、五菩萨藏。有信其所说者，故别成一部也”[8]。唐神清《北山录》卷九特别指出：“昙无德部，此云法镜部，即化地部分出也，俗艺咒术，为

---

[1]《大正藏》第 49 卷，第 17a 页。

[2] 窥基《异部宗轮论疏述记》卷一，参见《卍新纂大日本續藏經》第 53 卷，第 589a 页。

[3] 应为 24 条。参见《四分僧戒本》，《大正藏》第 22 卷，第 1029b-c 页。

[4] 吕澂《律学重光的先决问题》，刊《法音》，3 期 (1998 年)，第 8-11 页。此文乃吕澂先生 1953 年 10 月 28 日稿。

[5]《大正藏》第 1 卷，第 20b、28b 页。

[6] 1) 昙谛译《羯磨》卷一，《大正藏》第 22 卷，第 1054a 页；2) 康僧铠译《昙无德律部杂羯磨》卷一，《大正藏》第 22 卷，第 1043a 页；3) 佛陀耶舍共竺佛念译《四分律》卷三十五，《大正藏》第 22 卷，第 816a 页。据吕澂研究，《羯磨》、《昙无德律部杂羯磨》皆从昙无德律 (《四分律》) 抄出。吕澂《新编汉文大藏经目录》，济南：齐鲁书社，1980 年，第 62 页。

[7] 道世《法苑珠林》卷三十七《敬塔篇 · 兴造部》，周叔迦、苏晋仁校注，北京：中华书局，2003 年，第 1188 页。

[8]《大正藏》第 45 卷，第 9c 页。

防己害,兼以闲邪开学不犯也。其宗立五藏：一律、二经、三论、四咒、五菩萨藏也。”[1]

法藏部在传统三藏基础上,增加了咒藏[2]和菩萨藏,且特重后两藏,开后来大乘密教之端绪。他们似乎设计出许多方法包括咒术普及佛法,以适应新的皈依者,因为当地人比较喜欢佛法的神秘方面,而非它的哲理,这在印度—斯基泰统领的乌苌及其他地区非常明显[3]。据法显记载,“乌苌国是正北天竺……佛法甚盛,名众僧止住处为僧伽蓝,凡有五百僧伽蓝,皆小乘学……宿呵多国,其国佛法亦盛……(犍陀卫国),人多小乘学……(竺刹尸罗)国王臣民竞兴供养……(弗楼沙国)有七百余僧……(那竭国醯罗城)中有佛顶骨精舍……诸国王亦恒遣使供养”[4]。实际上,乌苌国、宿呵多国、犍陀卫国、竺刹尸罗国、弗楼沙国以及那竭国,皆在西北印度[5]范畴,或可通称罽宾[6],西方学者现称“大犍陀罗 (Greater Gandhāra,图 17)”或“犍陀罗文化圈(Gandhāran Cultural Area)”[7]。这一地区早期盛行小乘,尤重法藏部律

[1]《大正藏》第 52 卷,第 461c 页。

[2] 西方学者把咒藏还原作 Dhāraṇī,意为 formules magiques(魔术)或 mnemonical formulas(记忆术)。参见：1) É. Lamotte, *opere citato*: 152, 549; 2) Charles Willemen, “Sarvāstivāda Developments in Northwestern India and in China”, in: *The Indian International Journal of Buddhist Studies*, (New Series in continuation of the *Indian Journal of Buddhist Studies*, Vol. X, Varanasi: B. J. K. Institute of Buddhist and Asian Studies) No. 2 (2001): 163-169, esp. 164-165.

[3] 1) É. Lamotte, *opere citato*: 549; 2) John Rosenfield, *The Dynastic Arts of the Kushans*, Berkeley: University of California Press, 1967: 230; 3) 渥德尔,上引书,第 268 页。

[4] 法显《法显传》,章巽校注,上海：上海古籍出版社,1985 年,第 33-46 页。

[5] 现代学界一般认为：西北印度 (North-West India) 即迦湿迷罗—犍陀罗 (Kāśmīra-Gandhāra),西北俗语 (North-Western Prākṛit) 即犍陀罗语 (Gāndhārī)。参见：É Lamotte, *opere citato*: 628.

[6] 据慧琳《一切经音义》卷二十二引慧苑《新译大方广佛花严经音义》卷中,“迦叶(什)弥罗国,旧名罽宾国……其国即在北印度境乾陀罗国次北邻也……乾陀罗国,此云持地国……其国在中印度北、北印度南二界中间也”。又,慧林《一切经音义》卷四十一：“罽宾……梵语西国名也,或名罽湿弥罗,或名个湿蜜,皆古译讹略也,正梵音云：羯湿弭罗,北印度境也”。参见：1)《大正藏》第 54 卷,第 447c、574c 页；2) 李崇峰《西行求法与罽宾道》,刊《燕京学报》,新二十一期 (2006 年),第 175-187 页；3) Fumio Enomoto[榎本文雄], “A Note on Kashmir as Referred to in Chinese Literature: Ji-bin”, in: *A Study of the Nīlamata: Aspects of Hinduism in Ancient Kashmir,* ed. Yasuke Ikari, Kyoto: Kyoto University, 1994: 357-365, esp. 361.

[7] 严格说来,犍陀罗乃白沙瓦谷地之古称,相当于今巴基斯坦西北边境省,西至阿富汗边界的 Kohi Hindūrāj 山脉,东至印度河 (Indus River)。 不过“犍陀罗”这一术语,除指犍陀罗本土外,通常还包括其周边地区,尤其包括北部斯瓦特及其临近河谷地区、东部呾叉始罗地区和阿富汗的东部地区。“大犍陀罗 (Greater Gandhāra)”一词最早由法国学者富斯曼 (Gérard Fussman) 提出,后来美国学者邵瑞祺 (Richard Salomon) 对此做了更深入的论证。这一地区的文化特色,是通用犍陀罗语并采纳犍陀罗艺术的独特造型样式。因此,近年有学者将之称作 Gandhāran cultural area, i. e. non-Kāśmīra Jibin 罽宾,包括古代大夏领域。参见：1) Richard Salomon, *opere citato*: 3; 2) Charles Willemen, *Outlining the Way to Reflect*/思维略要法 (T. XV 617), Mumbai: Somaiya Publications Pvt Ltd, 2012: 16.

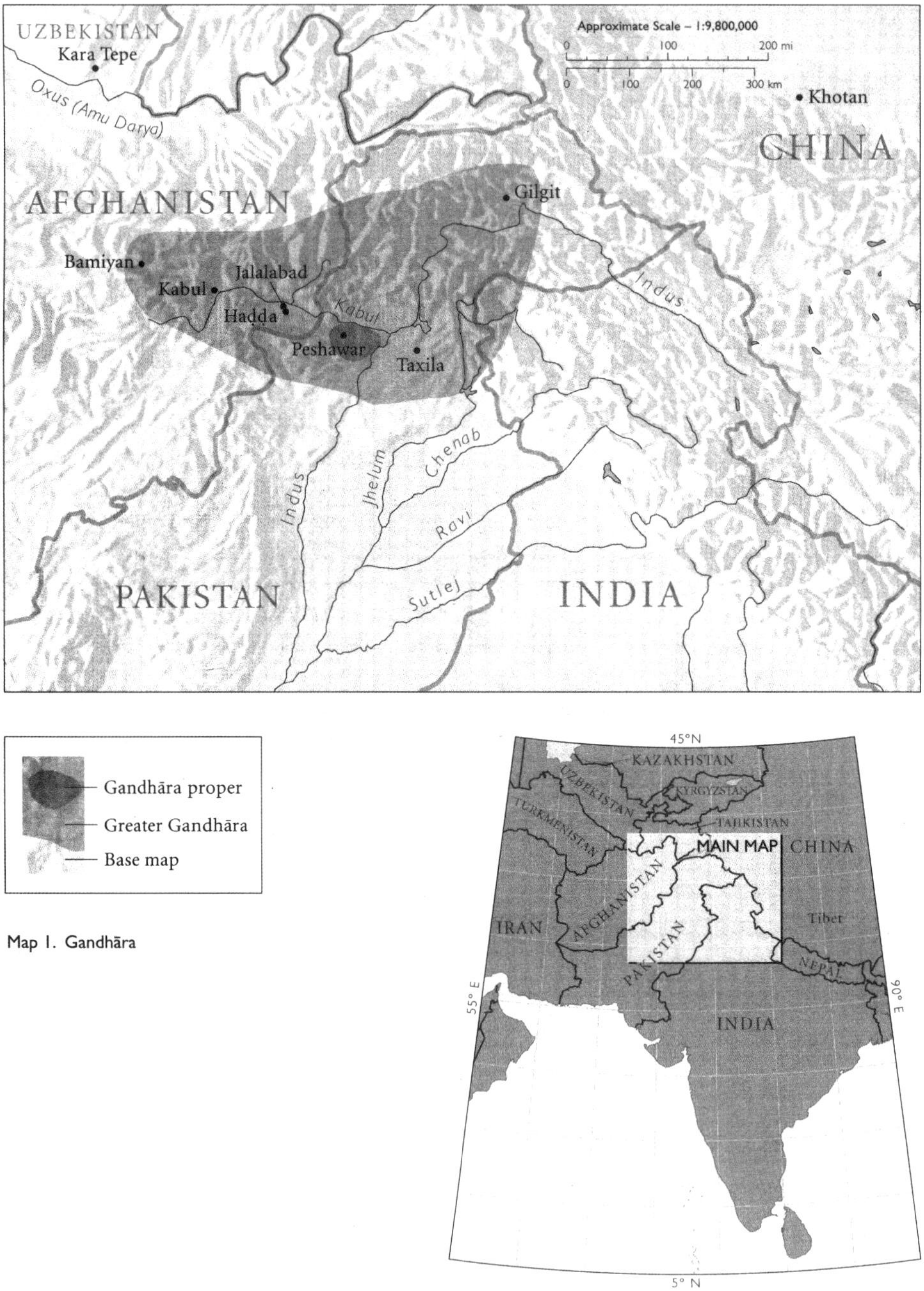

图 17　大犍陀罗区示意图

仪。到了玄奘游历乌仗那国时,还特别提到“乌仗那国(包括法显所言乌苌和宿呵多国)周五千余里,山谷相属,川泽连原……人性怯懦,俗情谲诡;好学而不功,禁咒为艺业”[1]。故而,禁咒(mantra/vidyā)既是这一地区传统之艺业[2],也是法藏部高僧传播佛法之手段,因为后者“俗艺咒术”。

据前引智昇《开元释教录》卷七《总括群经录》上,《佛本行集经》译者阇那崛多“博闻三藏,远究真宗;遍学五明,兼闲世论。经行得道场之趣,总持通神咒之理”[3]。曾参与阇那崛多译经、充当笔受的费长房强调:当时“善恭敬、善巧咒等经,崛多出”[4]。据智昇统计,阇那崛多翻译神咒及陀罗尼佛典达十二种之多[5]。这既符合法藏部之主张,也从另一方面证实他是法藏部高僧。

对于法藏部所增“咒藏”与“菩萨藏”,唐代高僧窥基曾做过简疏。据《异部宗轮论疏述记》卷一,“法藏者,部主名,亦名法密。密之与藏,义意大同。法藏、法密,二义皆得。此师含容正法,如藏之密,故言法密。从人以立部主名,此部师说,总有五藏:一经、二律、三阿毗达磨、四咒即明诸咒等、五菩萨即明菩萨本行事等”[6]。此外,

---

[1] 玄奘,上引书,第 270 页。

[2] 据杨衒之《洛阳伽蓝记》卷五引《惠生行记》、《道荣传》及《宋云家记》,位于龟兹、乌苌国之间的汉盘陀(塔什库尔干)国王,曾“向乌场国学婆罗门咒,四年之中,尽得其术”。同书卷四“法云寺”条记载该寺乃“西域乌场国胡沙门僧摩罗所立……摩罗聪慧利根,学穷释氏……京师沙门好胡法者,皆就摩罗受持之。戒行真苦,难可揄扬。秘咒神验,阎浮所无。咒枯树能生枝叶,咒人变为驴马,见之莫不忻怖”。此外,《高僧传》卷三《求那跋摩传》记载罽宾三藏法师求那跋摩颇善咒术,刘宋时曾于建业祇洹寺译出《四分羯磨》;《历代三宝记》卷九《译经·西秦、北凉、元魏、高齐、陈氏录》记载北魏“译经首”菩提流支,乃北天竺国三藏法师,“兼工杂术”并言“斯是术法,外国共行”。由此可见当时咒术流行于北印度、罽宾等地。参见:1)杨衒之《洛阳伽蓝记》,周祖谟校释,北京:中华书局,1963 年,第 192-193 页;2)慧皎《高僧传》,汤用彤校注,北京:中华书局,1992 年,第 105-114 页;3)费长房《历代三宝记》,《大正藏》第 49 卷,第 82c、86b 页。

[3]《大正藏》第 55 卷,第 550b 页。

[4] 费长房《历代三宝记》卷三《帝年》下《魏、晋、宋、齐、梁、周、大隋》,《大正藏》第 49 卷,第 48a 页。

[5] 据《开元释教录》卷七《总括群经录》上,阇那崛多译出的相关佛典包括:《虚空孕菩萨经》(与《虚空藏经》及《虚空藏神咒经》等同)、《金光明经银主陀罗尼品嘱累品》、《大方等大云请雨经》、《八佛名号经》(与《八吉祥神咒》、《八阳神咒经》等同本)、《不空羂索咒经》(亦云《不空羂索观世音心咒经》,初出;与唐译《不空羂索神咒心经》等同本)、《十二佛名神咒经》(题云《十二佛名神咒校量功德除障灭罪经》,初出;与唐译《称赞如来功德神咒经》同本)、《金刚场陀罗尼经》(与《金刚上味陀罗尼经》同本)、《如来方便善巧咒经》(与《虚空藏菩萨问佛经》同本)、《东方最胜灯王如来经》(题云《东方最胜灯王如来遣二菩萨送咒奉释迦如来助护持世间经》,与《持句神咒经》等同本)、《大法炬陀罗尼经》、《大威德陀罗尼经》、《五千五百佛名经》等。《大正藏》第 55 卷,第 548b-549a 页。参见吕澂《新编汉文大藏经目录》,第 99-122 页。

[6]《卍新纂续藏经》第 53 卷,第 577a-b 页。

窥基在《大乘法苑义林章》卷二特别指出："法藏部中说有五藏，即于此四（即四藏，一经、二律、三对法、四明咒）加菩萨藏，明诸菩萨本所行事"[1]。因此，除"诸咒"外，"菩萨本行事"或"诸菩萨本所行事"也为法藏部所特别推重[2]。

"本行"指释迦成佛以前尚在菩萨位（因位）时之行迹，乃成佛之因的根本行法。慧远《维摩义记》卷一："本行者，约果显因。菩萨所修，能为佛因，故名本行"[3]。据玄奘译《阿毗达磨顺正理论》卷四十四，"言本事者，谓说自昔展转传来，不显说人谈所说事；言本生者，谓说菩萨本所行；行或依过去事起诸言论，即由过去事言论究竟，是名本事，如《曼驮多(māndhātṛ)经》；若依现在事起诸言论，要由过去事言论究竟，是名本生，如《逻刹私(rākṣasa)经》"[4]。从历史角度看，"菩萨"这一名称既是当初悉达多·乔达摩成道前专用之称呼；也是原始佛教到部派佛教时期佛弟子对释迦牟尼佛之称号。"菩萨当为尚未成佛的佛，佛当为已经成佛的菩萨。"[5]至于题名"本行"[6]字样的汉译佛典，则有本生类如《菩萨本行经》[7]，佛传类如《佛所行赞》[8]、《佛本行集经》、《佛本行经》[9]等。

法藏部重视"菩萨本行事"或"诸菩萨本所行事"，或许与大犍陀罗区多"本行"传说有关。据法显402年夏游历该地所做记载：乌苌国是正北天竺也，传言佛至北天竺，即到此国，有佛足迹、晒衣石、度恶龙处。宿呵多国，有割肉贸鸽处，国人由是得

---

[1]《大正藏》第45卷，第271b页。

[2]吕澂先生认为：法藏部"发展了本生说，编成为一类'菩萨藏'，这是很特殊的。其他部派只把本生放在杂藏内，或分散于各经籍中，并不独立为一藏。大乘扩大菩萨在成佛以前的修行方法，把与之相关的种种行事分为六类而都可以得到解脱，这一思想，就与法藏部的重视本生有关"。吕澂《印度佛学源流略讲》，上海：上海人民出版社，1979年，第84页。

[3]《大正藏》第38卷，第427a页。

[4]《大正藏》第29卷，第595a页。另据玄奘译《大乘阿毗达磨集论》卷六，"何等譬喻？谓诸经中有比况说；何等本事？谓宣说圣弟子等前世相应事；何等本生？谓宣说菩萨本行藏相应事"。《大正藏》第31卷，第686b页。

[5]汤用彤《佛与菩萨》，见《汤用彤学术论文集》，北京：中华书局，1983年，第316-318页。参见水野弘元《佛教的真髓》第十一章《从部派佛教到大乘佛教》，香光书乡编译组译，嘉义市：香光书乡，2002年。

[6]现存佛教遗迹中题名"菩萨行"字样的最显著实例，是印度阿旃陀石窟第26窟。该窟系塔庙窟，于后部中央造塔，塔前雕一坐佛；倒U字形平面窟侧壁雕出降魔、说法以及涅槃等内容。对此，唐代高僧玄奘有较详细的记述："精舍四周雕镂石壁，作如来在昔修菩萨行诸因地事。证圣果之祯祥，入寂灭之灵应，巨细无遗，备尽镌镂。"玄奘，上引书，第897页。

[7]失译人名，今附东晋录，参见《大正藏》第3卷，第108-124页。

[8]昙无谶译《佛所行赞》，亦云《佛本行经》，参见《大正藏》第4卷，第1-54页。

[9]宝云译《佛本行经》，一名《佛本行赞传》，参见《大正藏》第4卷，第54-115页。

知,于此处起塔。犍陀卫国,是阿育王子法益所治处,佛为菩萨时于此国以眼施人,亦起大塔。竺刹尸罗,汉言截头也,佛为菩萨时,于此处以头施人和投身饿虎,此二处亦起大塔。弗楼沙国存罽腻伽大塔,众宝挍饰,凡所经见塔庙,壮丽、威严都无此比。那竭国界醯罗城中有佛顶骨精舍,那竭国城是菩萨供养定光佛处,城中亦有佛齿塔。城东北谷口有佛锡杖,亦起精舍供养;入谷口西行有佛僧伽梨精舍供养。那竭城南石室博山,佛留影此中,观之如佛真形。影西四百步许,佛在时剃发、剪爪,与弟子共造塔,以为将来塔法[1]。大犍陀罗地区流行本生、佛传故事[2]并盛行造塔,完全符合法藏部主张[3]。这一地区传说如此众多的"菩萨本行事"或"诸菩萨本所行事",疑为法藏部五部之一"菩萨藏"之源。

三、遗迹、遗物与龟兹早期"部执"

汉译《长阿含经》所据原典语言,可能是"西北俗语 (North Western Prākṛit)"[4],即"犍陀罗语 (Gāndhārī)"。"犍陀罗语"一词,乃英国学者白雷 (H. W. Bailey 一译贝利) 根据伯罗 (T. Burrow) 早年工作[5]最先拟定[6],指在犍陀罗地区发现的佛教碑铭和出土的大量写本所使用的语言,属于俗语 (Prākṛta/Prākṛit) 之一,或可称中世印度—雅利安语 (Middle Indo-Aryan),是从梵语或更确切地说古印度—雅利安方言 (Old Indo-Aryan dialect group) 演进的本地话[7]。大约在公元 2、3 世纪,犍陀罗语及其载体佉卢字母越过"犍陀罗"范围,蔓延到今天阿富汗北部、乌兹别克斯坦和塔吉克

---

[1] 法显,上引书,第 26-51 页。6 世纪上半叶宋云和惠生,7 世纪上半叶玄奘游历西北印度时,对这一地区传说的本行故事及其遗迹,分别做过较为详细的记录。参见:1) 杨衒之,上引书,第 198-225 页;2) 玄奘,上引书,第 220-312 页。

[2] 在西北印度占支配地位的小乘佛教五部派,尤其法藏部,偏重戒律和佛传。参见 É. Lamotte, *opere citato*: 605-606.

[3] 吕澂先生认为:法藏部"因佛本生遗迹均在人间,宜营塔婆香花供养……以为供塔得果"。吕澂《诸家戒本通论》附录《论律学与十八部分派之关系》,上引书,第 141 页。

[4] 1) Ernst Waldschmidt, *opere citato* (*Bruchstücke buddhistischer Sūtras...*): 229-234; 2) É. Lamotte, *opere citato*: 628-630; 3) Ernst Waldschmidt, *opere citato* (Central Asian Sūtra Fragments...): 136-174, esp. 137, 163-164, 167.

[5] 1) T. Burrow, *The Language of the Kharoṣṭhi Documents from Chinese Turkestan*, Cambridge: Cambridge University Press, 1937; 2) T. Burrow, *A Translation of the Kharoṣṭhi Documents from Chinese Turkestan,* James G. Forlong Fund 20, London: Royal Asiatic Society, 1940.

[6] H. W. Bailey, *opere citato*: 764-797.

[7] Richard Salomon, *opere citato*:3.

南部地区以及新疆塔里木盆地周边绿洲城镇[1]，它是印度文明，尤其是佛教传播新疆并最终抵达中国内地的主要媒介及最重要的语言[2]，如 20 世纪初在新疆发现的公元 3 世纪的《法句经》(*Dharmapada*)[3]及官方文书就是用佉卢字母犍陀罗语书写的。在这点上，它绝对早于梵语，且作为印度口语肯定在中亚使用了相当长的时间[4]，即使当梵语和婆罗米 (Brāhmī 一译婆罗迷) 字在佛教写本中已取代犍陀罗语和佉卢字母之后仍继续使用[5]。初期汉译佛典所据原文，有些可能用西北俗语，即犍陀罗语书写，而非后来印度佛教义学家 (Buddhist scholiasts) 所使用的古典梵语[6]；最初外来的高僧也包括法藏部僧人[7]。现有足够证据显示：汉译《长阿含经》，是从

---

[1] 1) 季羡林《中世印度雅利安语二题》，载《季羡林学术论著自选集》，北京：北京师范学院出版社，1991 年，第 343-361 页；2) Richard Salomon, *opere citato*: 4.

[2] 古代罽宾道，即今喀喇昆仑公路沿线，保存了用佉卢字母、婆罗米字母、粟特文、大夏文、藏文及汉文刻写的数量庞大的古代石刻题铭。其中，300 多通佉卢字母 (Kharoṣṭhī) 铭文代表或象征着佛教时代初期，标志着新兴宗教已载入史册；尽管这批佉卢字母题刻多系简单刻画，未涉及佛教部派，但至少说明这一地区当时流行佉卢字母。此外，大约 80% 的晚期铭文以婆罗米字母 (Brāhmī) 刻画，这是公元 3 至 8 世纪的印度第二种字母。参见：1) 豪普特曼《巴基斯坦北部印度河上游古代文物研究：兼论丝绸之路南线岩画走廊的威胁与保护》，边钰鼎译，载李崇峰主编《犍陀罗与中国》，北京：文物出版社，2019 年，第 421-474 页；2) Ann Heirman, “Can we trace the early Dharmaguptakas?” in: *T'oung Pao* (通报), Vol. Lxxxviii (2002). Fasc. 4-5: 396-429, esp. 400.

[3] John Brough, *The Gāndhārī Dharmapada*, London Oriental Series 7, London: Oxford University Press, 1962.

于阗出土的佉卢字母犍陀罗语《法句经》残本，书写于桦树皮上，可能是法藏部高僧从犍陀罗带来的。关于这部《法句经》或《犍陀罗语法句经》写本的部派归属问题讨论颇多，目前学者一致认为这件写本是法藏部佛典。参见：1) Gérard Fussman, “Gāndhārī écrite, Gāndhārī parlée” , in: *Dialectes dans les littératures indo-aryennes*, ed. Colette Caillat, Publications de l'Institut de Civilisation Indienne, série in-8°, fasc. 55, Paris: Collège de France, 1989: 433-501; 2) Lore Sander, *opere citato*: 61-106, esp. 104.

[4] 据研究，在公元前最后几个世纪中，佛教文学使用的语言为中世—印度俗语 (Middle-Indian Prākṛit)—摩揭陀语 (Māgadhī)、西北俗语 (North-Western Prākṛit)—犍陀罗语 (Gāndhārī) 和巴利语 (Pāli)；而在公元纪年最初的 3 个世纪之内，这些俗语受到了混合梵语 (mixed Sanskrit) 的强烈挑战。从笈多王朝开始 (4 世纪)，佛教梵语 (Buddhist Sanskrit) 取代了各种俗语和混合梵语。其中，这最后阶段的演化是从公元 2 世纪逐渐发展的。参见：Étienne Lamotte, *opere citato*: 645.

[5] 1) John Brough, *opere citato*: 49; 2) Franz Bernhard, *opere citato*: 55-62.

[6] Robert E. Buswell, Jr., “Prakritic Phonological Elements in Chinese Buddhist Transcriptions: Data from Xuanying's *Yiqiejing Yinyi*” , in: *Collection of Essays 1993: Buddhism Across Boundaries—Chinese Buddhism and Western Religions* by Erik Zürcher, Lore Sander and others, ed. John R. McRae, Jan Nattier, Taipei: Foguang Cultural Enterprise Co., Ltd, 1999: 187-217, esp. 189.

[7] Ann Heirman, *opere citato*: 396-429, esp. 401.

犍陀罗语原典而非其他俗语或梵语原典迻译的[1]。

1994年9月，伦敦英国图书馆东方与印度部(Oriental and India Office Collections)入藏了29件桦树皮写本。这批写本以佉卢字母犍陀罗语书写，原藏于阿富汗东部地区出土的一只陶罐中[2]。美国华盛顿大学邵瑞祺(Richard Salomon)教授应邀主持了这批写本的整理，并于1999年公布了初步报告[3]。翌年，邵瑞祺小组以《犍陀罗佛教文献》(*Gandhāran Buddhist Texts*)丛书形式陆续刊布了他们的研究成果[4]。

---

[1] 1) John Brough, *opere citato*: 50-54, esp. 54; 2) John Brough, "Comments on Third-Century Shan-shan and the History of Buddhism", in: *Bulletin of the School of Oriental and African Studies*, XXVIII (1965): 582-612, esp. 608; 3) Ernst Waldschmidt, *opere citato* (Central Asian Sūtra Fragments...): 136-174, esp. 163; 4) Daniel Boucher, "Gāndhārī and the Early Chinese Buddhist Translations Reconsidered: the Case of the *Saddharmapuṇḍarīkasūtra*", in: *Journal of American Oriental Society*, 118 (1998), No. 4: 471-506, esp. 471-75. 不过，日本学者辛嶋静志认为：《长阿含经》原语呈现出多样性特征，它是犍陀罗语之外的中世印度语、地域方言、梵语要素的十分复杂的混合体，也许从广义上可以把这种语言称为犍陀罗语，但它与西北印度碑铭上的犍陀罗语相距甚远。辛嶋静志《〈長阿含經〉の原語の研究——音写語分析を中心として》，東京：平河出版社，1994年，第51-52页。

[2] 这批写本送至伦敦英国图书馆时，一共29件，因此随机编为29个号，编号与写本本身内容没有任何关系。与这批写本一起运抵伦敦的，还有5个陶罐及26块陶片。据捐赠者陈述，这批写本最有可能出自现编D号陶罐中，地点应在古代那揭罗曷国(Nagarāhāra)的醯罗城，即今Haḍḍa。参见：Richard Salomon, *opere citato*: 20-21.

[3] Richard Salomon, *Ancient Buddhist Scrolls from Gandhāra: The British Library Kharoṣṭhī Fragments,* Seattle: University of Washington Press, 1999, xx+273pp. 参见王邦维书评，刊《敦煌吐鲁番研究》第五卷，北京：北京大学出版社，2001年，第343-353页。

[4] 迄今正式出版的《犍陀罗佛教文献》丛书有：1) Richard Salomon, *A Gāndhārī Version of the Rhinoceros Sūtra: British Library Kharoṣṭhī Fragment 5B*; Gandhāran Buddhist Texts Volume 1, Seattle and London: University of Washington Press, 2000; 同时参见陈明书评，刊《敦煌吐鲁番研究》第七卷，北京：中华书局，2004年，第451-456页；2) Mark Allon, *Three Gāndhārī Ekottarikāgama-Type Sūtras: British Library Kharoṣṭhī Fragments 12 and 14*; Gandhāran Buddhist Texts Volume 2, Seattle and London: University of Washington Press, 2001. 参见：萨尔吉书评，刊《中国学术》第十五辑，北京：商务印书馆，2003年，第315-320页；3) Tomothy Lenz, *A New Version of the Gāndhārī Dharmapada and A Collection of Previous-Birth Stories: British Library Kharoṣṭhī Fragments 16+25*; Gandhāran Buddhist Texts Volume 3, Seattle and London: University of Washington Press, 2003; 同时参见陈明书评，刊《敦煌吐鲁番研究》第八卷，北京：中华书局，2005年，第362-365页；4) Andrew Glass, *Four Gāndhārī Saṃyuktāgama Sūtras: Senior Kharoṣṭhī Fragment 5*; Gandhāran Buddhist Texts Volume 4, Seattle and London: University of Washington Press, 2007; 5) Richard Salomon, *Two Gāndhārī Manuscripts of the Songs of Lake Anavatapta* (*Anavatapta-gāthā*): *British Library Kharoṣṭhī Fragment 1 and Senior Scroll 14*; Gandhāran Buddhist Texts Volume 5, Seattle and London: University of Washington Press, 2008; 6) Timothy Lenz, *Gandhāran Avadānas: British Library Kharoṣṭhī Fragments 1-3 and 21 and Supplementary Fragments A-C*, Gandhāran Buddhist Texts Volume 6, Seattle and London: University of Washington Press, 2010.

据邵瑞祺辨认和研究，这批佉卢字母犍陀罗语写本主要包括：经及经疏 (sūtra texts and commentaries)、论及论疏 (scholastic treatises and commentaries)、偈颂 (verse texts)、譬喻及相关文献 (avadāna and related texts) 以及其他类型的杂文 (other genres and miscellaneous texts) 等，现摘要如下[1]：

这次出土的犍陀罗语"经藏"，数量相对较少，但残存最长且保存相对最好的写本之一，是犍陀罗语《众集经》(*Saṅgīti-sūtra*) 及其经疏。其子目及数序，与汉译《长阿含经》的相应部分几乎完全相同，但却与同经的梵语和巴利语本大相径庭。换言之，"犍陀罗语《众集经》和汉译《长阿含经》相应部分的编排极为相似，实际上近乎相同，这意味着它们代表的是同一部派的同一经文"[2]。此外，还残存有少量《增一阿含经》类写本[3]等。

犍陀罗语"论及论疏"类写本数量相对较多，但内容不甚清楚，有些可能是"偈颂"之注疏。注疏中的大部分"偈颂"可在巴利语经藏[4]《小部》中找到，惟排列次第与之差异较大。

犍陀罗语"偈颂"类残存三种，一为《阿耨达偈》或《无热恼池偈》(*Anavatapta-gāthā*)，在北传佛教中流布较广[5]；二是《犀角经》或《犀牛角经》(*Rhinoceros Horn Sūtra*)[6]，与巴利语本大体一致；三为《法句经》(*Dharmapada*)[7]，与于阗本

[1] 参见：Richard Salomon, *opere citato* (*Ancient Buddhist Scrolls from Gandhāra*...): 22-42.

[2] Richard Salomon, *opere citato*: 173.

[3] 三篇犍陀罗语《增一阿含经》类佛经，已经作为《犍陀罗佛教文献》丛书第 2 卷整理出版。不过，迄今尚未在梵语、巴利语本或汉、藏译本中发现与犍陀罗语本相对应之经典，部执亦不明了。参见 Mark Allon, *Three Gāndhārī Ekottarikāgama-Type Sūtras: British Library Kharoṣṭhī Fragments 12 and 14,* Gandhāran Buddhist Texts Volume 2, Seattle and London: University of Washington Press, 2001: 39-40.

[4] 有的学者认为：依据锡兰佛教传说，现存巴利语《大藏经》是阿育王胞弟（一说阿育王之子）摩哂陀 (Mahinda, 梵语作 Mahendra) 带到锡兰的，故而巴利语也就是摩揭陀语 (Māgadhā nirutti 或 Māgadhikā bhāsā)，即佛所说的话，因而"巴利语《大藏经》也就是佛教的唯一正统的经典"。参见：1) 季羡林《原始佛教的语言问题》，载《季羡林佛教学术论文集》，台北：东初出版社，1995 年，第 59 页；2) 郭良鋆《佛陀和原始佛教思想》，北京：中国社会科学出版社，1997 年，第 2-5 页。

[5] 鸠摩罗什在沙勒时曾听参军王子须利耶苏摩为其说《阿耨达经》，说明该经至少在 4 世纪时流行于疏勒地区。至于须利耶苏摩讲诵时所用语言是否为犍陀罗语，则不得而知。参见：慧皎，上引书，第 47 页。

[6] 犍陀罗语本《犀角经》，已经作为《犍陀罗佛教文献》丛书第 1 卷整理出版。该经不见汉译本，其经文结构与巴利语本基本一致，但与梵语本差异较大。参见 Richard Salomon, *A Gāndhārī Version of the Rhinoceros Sūtra: British Library Kharoṣṭhī Fragment 5B; Gandhāran Buddhist Texts I,* Seattle and London: University of Washington Press, 2000: 38-52.

[7] 这次新出土的犍陀罗语本《法句经》及《本事集》，已经作为《犍陀罗佛教文献》丛书第 3 卷整理出版。参见 Tomothy Lenz, *A New Version of the Gāndhārī Dharmapada and a Collection of Previous-Birth Stories: British Library Kharoṣṭhī Fragments 16+25;* Gandhāran Buddhist Texts Volume 3, Seattle and London: University of Washington Press, 2003.

《法句经》略有差异,乃佉卢字母犍陀罗语又一传本。

英国图书馆这次入藏的最具代表性的写本,是内容丰富的故事题材,且大多明确标记“譬喻 (avadāna)”字样。“譬喻”残本多附顺序编号的简诵,表明譬喻文字只是一概述或提纲,意味着它们要由讲诵者自己去补充。在这点上,它们与土库曼斯坦捷尔梅兹出土的、经过类似删节的拜兰 · 阿里写本 (Bairam Ali manuscript) 上的譬喻和本生相似。新出土的譬喻写本似乎可以分作两类:一类是与释迦牟尼同时代的那些为人熟知的传说人物;另一类似乎以印度—斯基泰人统治犍陀罗时期为背景,如 Jhādamitra 譬喻、Sārthadāsa 譬喻和 Ājīvika 譬喻等,后者在迄今刊布的佛典中绝无仅有。

值得注意的是,16+25 号残本包含一组特别有趣的系列故事[1],在形式上与譬喻文学接近,由同一经生书写,但多题作前世 (*provayoge*)[2],而非譬喻。与譬喻故事不同,有些前世故事确实描写了传统佛教人物的前生,如憍陈如 (Añadakoḍiña)、阿难 (Anada) 和菩萨 (bodhisatva/boṣisatva)。正是这些“前世”写本,而非题作“譬喻”的那些,更像大家熟知的典型的佛教梵语系譬喻 (avadānas) 及巴利语系譬喻 (apadānas)。此外,这些汇编的“前世”故事,有较譬喻故事更好的类似物与之对照。其中,第一个故事为菩萨前世 (Boṣisatva-provayoge),汉译《贤愚经》卷十《勒那阇耶品》[3]和《六度集经》卷六《杀身济贾人经》[4]的内容与之相似;克孜尔石窟第13窟及第 114 窟券顶壁画也绘出了该故事的主要情节 (图 18、19)[5]。第二个前世故事为著名的普护 (Viśvantara) 本生,即须大拏本生,汉译《六度集经》卷二《须大拏经》[6]及义净译《根本说一切有部毗奈耶破僧事》卷十六[7]的内容与之相似,后者似更详细些;惟汉译诸本之人名、地名与犍陀罗语本不同。关于这个故事,犍陀罗、新疆和内地都曾有视觉艺术表现。其中,犍陀罗出土的一件浮雕,刻画的是菩萨正把钱袋施舍给婆罗门 (图 20)。克孜尔石窟同一内容的壁画,现存达八幅之多[8],除个别

---

[1] 这组故事现存十一个,但只有前六个保存较好,可作分析对象;后五个极为破碎,无法恢复原貌。参见:Tomothy Lenz, *opere citato*: 79-110,209-252.

[2] 梵语作 pūrvayogaḥ,汉译为:本事、本生、往古、往古学、本生事、往昔事、昔因缘、本事因缘、本所修行等。参见荻原雲來《漢訳対照梵和大辭典》,東京:鈴木學術財団,1974 年,第 807 页。

[3]《大正藏》第 4 卷,第 421c-422b 页。

[4]《大正藏》第 3 卷,第 36a 页。

[5] 马世长《克孜尔中心柱窟主室券顶与后室的壁画》,上引书,第 190-191 页。

[6]《大正藏》第 3 卷,第 7c-11a 页。

[7]《大正藏》第 24 卷,第 181a-184b 页。

[8] 新疆龟兹石窟研究所编,上引书,第 291 页。

图 18　克孜尔第 114 窟券顶
“勒那阇耶本生”壁画

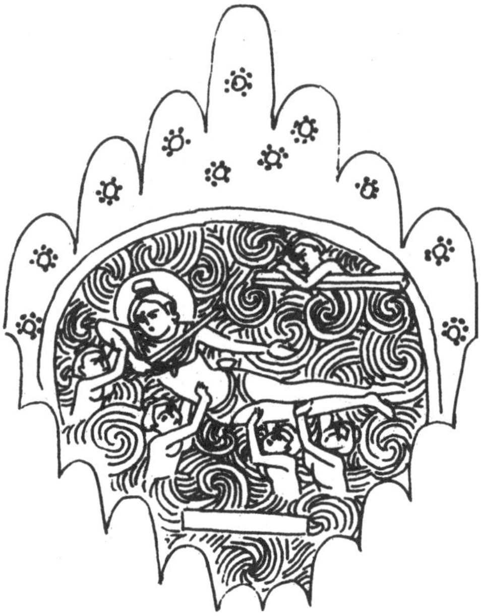

图 19　克孜尔第 114 窟券顶壁画
“勒那阇耶本生”线描

图 20　犍陀罗“*Viśvantara Jātaka*（普护本生）”浮雕，出土于 Jamālgaṛhī，现藏伦敦不列颠博物院

采用横卷式构图（图 21）外，大多使用菱形经营（图 22），主要表现菩萨“施子为奴”的情景。因此，克孜尔石窟的“前世”故事画，或许从另一方面说明当时龟兹地区可能有与汉译《贤愚经》或《六度集经》相当的犍陀罗语本存在。第三个故事描写憍陈如过去是一位陶工 (kulala)，巴利语《大事》(Mahāvastu) 也有一题作本生的前世故事，讲述憍陈如为一制陶工人 (kumbhakāra-, bhārgava-)。虽然《大事》中的故事情节与新发现的犍陀罗语写本略微相似，且在文风及语句上亦具可比性，但汉译《佛本

图 21　克孜尔第 184 窟主室侧壁“须大拏本生”壁画,现藏德国柏林亚洲艺术博物馆

行集经》卷三十四《转妙法轮品》中的“瓦师”,即长老大憍陈如比丘故事[1],却与之非常相似。第四个故事叙及阿难前生,描述颇为简略;不过在《佛本行集经》卷六十《阿难因缘品》[2]中则有类似的记载。这种超级相似性,既可说明犍陀罗地区曾流行与汉译《佛本行集经》相当的佛典,也暗示汉译《佛本行集经》之原本可能为犍陀罗语。

图 22　克孜尔第 38 窟券顶“须大拏本生”壁画,现藏德国柏林亚洲艺术博物馆

总之,伦敦英国图书馆新收藏的这批佉卢字母犍陀罗语写本,看来是公元 1 世纪初当地一座法藏部寺院的收藏或为法藏部僧众所藏,因为藏匿写本的陶罐上有明确的犍陀罗语题记[3]。虽然这批写本可

[1]《大正藏》第 3 卷,第 813c-814b 页。

[2]《大正藏》第 3 卷,第 930a-931b 页。

[3] 书写于陶罐上的佉卢字母犍陀罗语题记,可用拉丁字母转写为:“saghami caüdiśami dhamaüteaṇa[p]arig[r]ahami”,英译作“[Given] to the universal community, in the possession of the Dharmaguptakas”,意为“奉献一切众生,法藏部受持”。参见:Richard Salomon, *opere citato* (*Ancient Buddhist Scrolls*...): 214-217, pls. 28-29.

能是当年佛教徒弃之不用、却有意保存下来的[1]，但它们的确是迄今发现的年代最早的佛教文献，为我们提供了一次前所未有的零距离考察机遇，毫无疑问它们是当地流行的法藏部佛典[2]。

另外，施佛爱延（Schøyen，绥思）收藏的百余件佉卢字母写本，传说出土于阿富汗东部，是近年有关古写本佛典的另一重要发现。其中，佉卢字母犍陀罗语本《大般涅槃经》(Kharoṣṭhī fragments of a Gāndhārī version of the *Mahāparinirvāṇasūtra*) 颇具学术价值。该经书写于棕榈叶上，残存6片，包含"大善见王"故事。犍陀罗语本《大般涅槃经》虽然在各方面与诸本《大般涅槃经》不甚一致，但与汉译本却有某些特别的相同之处。如"大善见王"故事，与汉译《长阿含经》的编排次第相同，并未像巴利语《长尼伽耶》那样单列。有关大善见王尸体处理的描述，犍陀罗语本《大般涅槃经》虽然与巴利语和梵语《大般涅槃经》中转轮王和佛陀尸体处理的记载相似，但细节却与巴利语和梵语本有别。如犍陀罗语本《大般涅槃经》记载尸体用香油涂抹的步骤及流程，不见于巴利语和梵语本，但与汉译《长阿含经》的描述相同[3]。这既说明汉译《长阿含经》与犍陀罗语本《大般涅槃经》之关系，也显示出佉卢字母犍陀罗语佛典流行之范围。因此，有学者推测：西北印度的佛教法藏部，当时"已经有一部具备一定规模的犍陀罗语的大藏经(canon)"[4]。

我们认为：确定佛教部派流行某地最直接且最可靠的证据，除上述出土写本外，应来自当地铭刻。大犍陀罗地区早年发现的佉卢字母题刻，有两件涉及法藏部。一件是印度考古调查局1920-1921年冬季在杰马勒堡（Jamālgaṛhī，杰马尔格里）发掘出土的，称之为"杰马勒堡第359年铭文(Jamālgaṛhī Inscription on the Year 359)"，现藏巴基斯坦白沙瓦博物馆，馆藏号为铭文第

---

[1] Richard Salomon, *opere citato*: 81-84.

[2] 2009年8月初，笔者应邀参加了在新德里印度国际中心(Indian International Centre)举办的"阿育王与现代印度(Ashoka and the Making of Modern India)"国际学术讨论会。会后各国学者联合考察桑吉大塔时，笔者曾向负责该项目整理工作的邵瑞祺教授询问了这批写本情况，并就法藏部有关问题与之进行了交流。参见：Richard Salomon, *opere citato*: xv, 10, 15-56, 21, 23, 35-38, 36, 171-173.

[3] 1) Mark Allon and Richard Salomon, "Kharoṣṭhī fragments of a Gāndhārī version of the *Mahāparinirvāṇasūtra*", in: *Manuscripts in the Schøyen Collection 1; Buddhist Manuscripts,* Vol. I, ed. Jens Braarvig, Oslo: Hermes Publishing, 2000: 243-284, esp. 244, 247, 258-262; 2) Chongfeng Li, *opere citato* (Representation of the Buddha's Parinirvāṇa...): 59-81.

[4] 王邦维，"*Ancient Buddhist Scrolls from Gandhāra: The British Library Kharoṣṭhī Fragments* 书评"，刊《敦煌吐鲁番研究》第五卷，北京：北京大学出版社，2001年，第343-353页。

23号[1]。这件石刻出土近二十年后,路得施(H. Lüders)才正确解读它是供养法藏部(dhamaütea[na*]parigrahe)的题刻[2]。另一件是所谓的昆都士瓶(Qunduz vase),具体发现地点不清,传说出自阿富汗北部某地,即古代大夏领域。铜瓶上的铭文采用通常的措辞,记录供养法藏部法师(acariyanaṃ dhaṃmagutakana parigrahe)[3]。这两件佉卢字母[4]铭刻表明,法藏部在今巴基斯坦西北部及阿富汗北部地区具有突出地位。此外,在贵霜王朝的陪都秣菟罗也发现了两件铭文,皆镌刻在造像座上。一件是秣菟罗博物馆收藏的菩萨像(M. M. No. 10. 121),结跏趺坐,现残存下半身。像座上的铭文采用婆罗米字母混合梵语(Brāhmī/ hybrid Sanskrit)刻写,记述这尊"菩萨"像供奉在一商人家庙中,供养法藏部法师(acāryana dharmagutakāna pratigrahē)[5]。另一件造像出土于秣菟罗的吉尔特尔布尔(Girdharpur),也残存下半身,结跏趺坐,左手持净瓶,可能是弥勒。像座上的题铭亦用婆罗米字母混合梵语镌刻,记述该像系胡维色迦大王(Mahārāja Huvishka)第二十九年雨季安置于僧院,供养法藏部(vihare dharmaguptikanaṃ parigrahe)[6]。因此,我们认为法藏部流行于印度—斯基泰及贵霜诸王统领的区域之内:西至古代大夏领地,东至印度本土秣菟罗,中心是帝国的核心犍陀罗[7]。东北印度以及德干高原和南印度未发现法藏部铭

[1] Sten Konow, *Kharoshṭhī Inscriptions with the Exception of those of Aśoka*; Corpus Inscriptionum Indicarum II, Part 1, London: Oxford University Press, 1929: 110-113, No. XLV; Plate XXII1. 题刻中的 the first Aśvayuj 359, van Wijk 博士曾换算为公元 275 年 8 月 24 日。参见: Sten Konow,上引书,第 111 页。

[2] Heinrich Lüders, "Zu und aus den Kharoṣṭhī-Urkunden", in: *Acta Orientalia* 18 (1940): 15-49, esp. 17-20.

[3] Gérard Fussman, "Documents épigraphiques kouchans", in: *Bulletin de l'École française d'Extrême-Orient,* 61 (1974): 1-76, esp. 58-61.

[4] 佉卢字母使用的时间,一般认为是从公元前 3 世纪中叶到公元 4、5 世纪。参见: Sten Konow, *opere citato*: xiii.

[5] 1) J. Ph. Vogel, "The Mathurā School of Sculpture", in: *Archaeological Survey of India: Annual Report 1909-10*: 63-79, esp. 65, Plate XXIVc; 2) Heinrich Lüders, *Mathurā Inscriptions: Unpublished Papers Edited by Klaus L. Janert*, Abhandlungen der Akademie der Wissenschaften in Göttingen, Philologisch-historische Klasse, 3. 47, Göttingen: Vandenhoeck & Ruprecht, 1961: 187, No. 150; 3) R. C. Sharma, *opere citato*: 170, fig.79.

[6] John M. Rosenfield, *opere citato*: 229-230, Figure 32.

[7] Charles Willemen, "Kumārajīva's 'Explanatory Discourse' about Abhidharmic Literature", in: *Kokusai Bukkyōgaku Daigaku-in Daigaku Kenkyū Kiyō*[国際仏教大学院大学研究紀要第 12 号(平成 20 年)/*Journal of the International College for Postgraduate Buddhist Studies*], Vol. XII (2008): 37-83 (156-110), esp. 38-39 (155-154), 69 (124); 2) Charles Willemen, *opere citato* (*Outlining the Way to Reflect...*): 16.

刻，新发现的佉卢字母犍陀罗写本及早年出土或流传的法藏部题刻证实他们集中于大犍陀罗。纪元初几世纪，他们在西北印度及与古伊朗临近地区地位突出，所操语言为犍陀罗语[1]。其他部派，如说一切有部和大众部，由于受限于他们在犍陀罗地区的佛事，可能也有犍陀罗语佛典[2]，以便与采纳当地语言传法之传统相一致。尽管如此，现有证据明确显示，我们所具有的大多数犍陀罗语写本，或许全部，都属于法藏部。换言之，“尽管法藏部也许不是纪元初几个世纪内使用犍陀罗语的唯一佛教部派，但我们确知这种语言是他们（法藏部）的特征”[3]。

法藏部在印度佛教史中以往处于一种模糊状态。“这次新发现的佉卢字母犍陀罗语写本，强化了过去有些学者提出但直到现在才为考古材料所证实的理论，即犍陀罗盛行法藏部。”[4]

据慧皎《高僧传》卷十一《僧佑传》附《论》：“（阿育王）后易心归信，追悔前失，远会应真，更集三藏。于是互执见闻，各引师说。依据不同，遂成五部。而所制轻重，时或不同；开遮废立，不无小异。皆由如来往昔，善应物机；或随人随根，随时随国；或此处应开，余方则制；或此人应制，余者则开。五师虽同取佛律，而各据一边，故篇聚或时轻重，罪目不无优降。依之修学，并能得道。故如来在世，有梦迭因缘，已悬记经律应为五部。《大集经》云：‘我灭度后，遗法分为五部：颠倒解义，隐覆法藏，名

[1] 参见：1) Lore Sander, *opere citato*: 61-106, esp. 67-68; 2) Richard Salomon, *opere citato*: 168-170.

[2] John Brough, *opere citato* (*The Gāndhārī Dharmapada...*): 42.

Oskar Von Hinüber（封兴伯）曾举几例说明《中阿含经》原本以佉卢字母犍陀罗语书写。参见：1) Oskar von Hinüber, “Upali's Verses in the Majjhimanikaya and the Madhyamagama”, in: *Indological and Buddhist Studies, Volume in Honour of Professor J. W. de Jong on his Sixtieth Birthday*, eds. L. A. Hercus et al., Canberra 1982: 243-251; 2) Oskar von Hinüber, “Sanskrit und Gāndhārī in Zentralasien”, in: *Sprachen des Buddhismus in Zentralasien: Vorträge des Hamburger Symposions vom 2. Juli bis 5. Juli 1981*, eds. Klaus Röhrborn und Wolfgang Veeker, Veröffentlichungen der Societas Uralo-Altaica, Band 16, Wiesbaden: Otto Harrassowitz, 1983: 27-34.

不过，邵瑞祺认为：迄今尚未发现用犍陀罗语书写的说一切有部佛典。参见：Richard Salomon, *opere citato* (*Ancient Buddhist Scrolls...*): 171.

[3] 在整理这批佉卢字母犍陀罗语写本的初步报告中，邵瑞祺用一节篇幅专门论述法藏部及有关问题，包括法藏部与汉译《长阿含经》之关系。Richard Salomon, *opere citato*: 166-177. 参见：1) F. Bernhard, *opere citato*: 55-62, esp. 59-61; 2) Oskar von Hinüber, “Expansion to the North: Afghanistan and Central Asia”, in: *The World of Buddhism, Buddhist Monks and Nuns in Society and Culture*, eds. H. Bechert and R. Gombrich, London: Thames and Hudson, 1993: 99-107, esp. 103-104.

不过，魏查理认为：把犍陀罗语的使用局限于法藏部一派不一定合适。参见：Charles Willemen, *opere citato* (Kumārajīva's “Explanatory Discourse” ...): 37-83 (156-110), esp. 38 (155).

[4] Richard Salomon, *opere citato*: 175.

昙无毱多(法藏部),即昙无德也;读诵外书,受有三世,善能问难,说一切姓皆得受戒,名萨婆若帝婆(说一切有部),即萨婆多也;说无有我,转诸烦恼,名迦叶毗(饮光部);说有我不说空,名婆蹉富罗(犊子部);以广博遍览五部,名摩诃僧祇(大众部)。善男子,如是五部,虽各别异,而皆不妨诸佛法界及大涅槃。'"[1]

这里,慧皎在叙述部派佛教时,摘引《大集经》,把法藏部置于五部之首,或许暗示当时该部的重要地位[2]。

法显402年游历乌苌国时,当地"佛法甚盛……皆小乘学……宿呵多国,其国佛法亦盛"[3]。依据玄奘、慧立等记载,我们怀疑今天的巴基斯坦西北部地区当时存在小乘佛教五个部派,法藏部或居统领地位[4]。他们在接下来的两个世纪里为大乘佛教取代。630年玄奘游历这一地区时,记述了当时情景:"(乌仗那国)夹苏婆伐窣堵河,旧有一千四百伽蓝,多已荒芜;昔僧徒一万八千,今渐减少。并学大乘,寂定为业;善诵其文,未究深义;戒行清洁,特闲禁咒。律仪传训,有五部焉:一法密部、二化地部、三饮光部、四说一切有部、五大众部。"[5]既然当地"特闲禁咒"、法藏部律仪仍居首位,或许说明该部在乌苌仍具相当影响,尽管当地"并学大乘"。到了671年前后义净记述该地佛教时,这种情景没有改变:"有部所分三部之别,一法护、二化地、三迦摄卑(饮光部),此并不行五天,唯乌长那国及龟兹、于阗杂有行者。"[6]值得注意的是,义净在这里仍把法藏部放在首位,又特别指出他们在7世纪时仍杂行于乌苌、龟兹和于阗,尽显该部之余波。因此,我们推测法藏部盛行犍陀罗时,乌苌、龟兹[7]

---

[1] 慧皎,上引书,第442页。

[2] 法显418年所作《〈摩诃僧祇律〉私记》,也把法藏部列为五部派首位,应该不是巧合。参见《大正藏》第22卷,第548a-b页。

[3] 法显,上引书,第33页。

[4] 1) Thomas Watters, *On Yuan Chwang's Travels in India AD 629-645*, London: Royal Asiatic Society, 2 vols., Vol. I, 1904; Vol. II, 1905, esp. I: 226; 2) 慧立、彦悰《大慈恩寺三藏法师传》,孙毓棠、谢方点校,北京:中华书局,2004年,第40页。

[5] 玄奘,上引书,第270页。

[6] 义净《南海寄归内法传》,王邦维校注,北京:中华书局,1995年,第28页。

[7] 林梅村认为:至少在公元2世纪末佉卢字母已开始在龟兹流行,克孜尔出土的龟兹佉卢字母(Kuci Kharoṣṭhī)或作直体佉卢字母(Formal Kharoṣṭhī)写本应为5世纪之作。此外,英人斯坦因(Mark Aurel Stein)、法人伯希和(Paul Pelloit)、德人勒柯克(Albert von Le Coq)以及日人大谷光瑞在新疆库车、尼雅、吐鲁番等地发现的直体佉卢字母写本,可定在公元3至6世纪。1) Lin Meicun, "Kharoṣṭhī Bibliophy: The Collections from China (1897-1993)", in: *Central Asiatic Journal*, 40 (2): 188-221, esp. 197-198; 2) Lin Meicun, "A Formal Kharoṣṭhī Inscription from Subashi",载敦煌研究院编《段文杰敦煌研究五十年纪念文集》,北京:世界图书出版公司,1996年,第328-347页。又,德国学者桑德尔认为:直体佉卢字母通常用作书写经典。Lore Sander, *opere citato*: 61-106, esp. 72.

和于阗[1]或为其重镇。稍后，“他们因说一切有部 / 根本说一切有部的到来而黯然失色”[2]。

德国学者伯恩哈德 (Franz Bernhard) 认为：佛教在向中亚和汉地传播过程中，犍陀罗语起到了非常重要的桥梁作用；佛教在中亚传播的第一次浪潮，就是由法藏部发起的，该部以犍陀罗语为其媒介。在这一地区，换言之，法藏部早于说一切有部 / 根本说一切有部以及后来为大批中亚写本所证实使用梵语传法的大乘佛教[3]。此外，许多早期汉译佛典术语之原文就是犍陀罗语[4]。现存最早的犍陀罗语佛典之汉译，可能是康僧铠于曹魏嘉平四年(252年)在洛阳白马寺翻译的《昙无德律部杂羯磨》[5]。稍后，高贵乡公正元元年 (254 年) 昙谛于洛阳译出《昙无德羯磨》一卷[6]，姚兴弘始 (399-415 年) 中佛陀耶舍于长安再出《昙无德戒本》一卷[7]，宋元嘉八年 (431 年) 求那跋摩于扬州祇洹寺三译《四分羯磨》[8]。由此可见，这部规范法藏部僧众行为举止仪式之

---

[1] 除《法句经》外，于阗策勒县出土有佉卢字母佛经残本、于阗之北邻尼雅出土过法藏部《戒本》，这说明于阗最初流行小乘佛教法藏部，于阗佛教最早的经堂用语是犍陀罗语。参见林梅村《法藏部在中国》，载林梅村《汉唐西域与中国文明》，北京：文物出版社，1998 年，第 343-364 页。此外，法藏部亦重“咒藏”。斯坦因曾在新疆于阗北部尼雅遗址发现一件木椟，上有佛教神秘咒术符号；经邵瑞祺研究，这套神秘符号实际起源于犍陀罗语。Richard Salomon, “New Evidence for a Gāndhārī Origin of the Arapacana Syllabary”, in: *Journal of the American Oriental Society,* 110 (1990): 255-273.

[2] Étienne Lamotte, *opere citato*: 595.

[3] 1) Franz Bernhard, *opere citato*: 55-62, esp. 59, 61; 2) Étienne Lamotte, *opere citato*: 549.

[4] 1) H. W. Bailey, *opere citato*: 764-797; 2) John Brough, *opere citato* (*The Gāndhārī Dharmapada*...): 50-54; 3) Franz Bernhard, *opere citato*: 55-62; 4) Hiän-lin Dschi (季羡林), “On the Oldest Chinese Transliteration of the Name of Buddha (浮屠与佛)”，见季羡林《印度古代语言论集》，北京：中国社会科学出版社，1982 年，第 343-346 页；5) 季羡林《再谈“浮屠”与“佛”》，见《季羡林佛教学术论文集》，台北：东初出版社，1995 年，第 37-54 页；6) Robert E. Buswell, Jr., *opere citato*: 187-217, esp. 203-213.

[5] 据智昇《开元释教录》卷一《总括群经录》上，“《四分杂羯磨》一卷，题云：《昙无德律部杂羯磨》，以结戒场为首新附……沙门康僧铠，印度人也，广学群经，义畅幽旨，以嘉平四年壬申，于洛阳白马寺译”。《大正藏》第 55 卷，第 486c-487a 页。不过，吕澂认为：“《昙无德杂羯磨》一卷，从《昙无德律》抄出，旧误康僧铠译。” 吕澂《新编汉文大藏经目录》，济南：齐鲁书社，1980 年，第 62 页。

[6] 据费长房《历代三宝记》卷五《译经 · 魏、吴录》，“《昙无德羯磨》一卷，初出，见竺道祖《魏录》。右一卷昙无德者，魏云法藏，藏师地梨茶由，是阿踰阇第九世弟子，藏承其后，即四分律主也，自斯异部兴焉，此当佛后二百年中。后安息国沙门昙谛，以高贵乡公正元一年届乎洛阳，妙善律学，于白马寺众请译出”。《大正藏》第 49 卷，第 56c 页。不过，吕澂认为：“《昙无德羯磨》一卷，从《昙无德律》抄出，旧误曹魏昙谛译”。吕澂，上引书，第 62 页。

[7] 僧佑，上引书，第 51-52 页。

[8] 据法经《众经目录》卷五《小乘毗尼藏录 · 众律异译》，“《昙无德羯磨》一卷，魏正元年安息沙门昙谛于洛阳译；《四分羯磨》一卷，宋元嘉年求那跋摩于扬州祇桓 (洹) 寺译。右二律同本异译”。《大正藏》第 55 卷，第 140b 页。

律典[1],3世纪中叶以降盛行汉地。汉译“昙无德”,显然音译了法藏部原本之名,表明《昙无德羯磨》及《昙无德戒本》应译自犍陀罗语原典[2],因为“昙无德”乃犍陀罗语 dharma'ute'a之对音[3]。此外,汉译《四分律》[4]和《长阿含经》原本为犍陀罗语,佛陀耶舍与竺佛念于410年至413年迻译;汉译《佛本行集经》源自法藏部,犍陀罗高僧阇那崛多587年译出。这既说明犍陀罗语使用的时间下限[5],又显示出当时中亚和汉地流行法藏部;龟兹位于犍陀罗与汉地之间,当地流行法藏部乃情理中事。

塔里木盆地周边地区迄今发现的数以千计的梵语及各种当地语言写本残片,大多属于7世纪或更晚[6],极少数可能早到2、3世纪[7];现存最早的梵语纸质写本不会早于5世纪[8]。这或许说明梵语写本乃续接“西北俗语”,即犍陀罗语佛典

---

[1] 德国学者贝歇特 (Heinz Bechert) 推测:原始佛教不同部派的发展或分化源于寺院律仪之纷争,而非学说问题或救度方式。Heinz Bechert, “Notes on the Formation of Buddhist Sects and Origin of Mahāyāna”, in: *German Scholars on India*, I, ed. Cultural Department of Embassy of the Federal Republic of Germany, New Delhi/ Varanasi: Chowkhamba Sanskrit Series Office, 1973: 6-18. 吕澂明言:“佛灭后十八部之分裂,皆由戒之开遮不同”。吕澂《大般涅槃经正法分讲要》,载《吕澂佛学论著选集》二,济南:齐鲁书社,1991年,第1172页。不过,汤用彤认为:“戒律之不同,虽亦为分部之原因,而教理之异执,则于分部更为重要。”汤用彤《印度哲学史略》,北京:中华书局,1988年,第57页。

[2] Franz Bernhard, *opere citato*: 55-62, esp. 60.

[3] 德国学者路得施最早把杰马勒堡 (Jamālgaṛhī) 出土的石刻佉卢字母犍陀罗语 dharma'ute'a 断定为梵语的法藏部 (dharmaguptaka);英国学者白雷认为:汉译佛典中“昙无德”一词,即“法藏部”之音译,系来自犍陀罗语 dharma'ute'a。1) Heinrich Lüders, “Zu und aus den Kharoṣṭhī-Urkunden”, in: *opere citato*: 15-49, esp. 17; 2) H. W. Bailey, *opere citato*: 790.

[4] 安·海尔曼 (Ann Heirman) 认为:5世纪初佛陀耶舍、竺佛念共译《四分律》,其原本与犍陀罗语传统有关不是不可能。Ann Heirman, *opere citato*: 402.

[5] Franz Bernhard, *opere citato*: 60.

[6] 法国学者皮诺 (Georges-Jean Pinault) 认为:“大多数吐火罗语写本是佛教经典的翻译或改编,这些经典属说一切有部 (Sarvāstivāda),这是一个小乘的部派。说一切有部在其经典中加入了梵语,这些经典原来用的是西北俗语……最古的吐火罗语写本可以追溯到公元五世纪,但其大部分应置于公元七世纪初。”皮诺特《论吐火罗语中佛教术语翻译》,徐文堪译,见新疆龟兹石窟研究所编《鸠摩罗什和中国民族文化:纪念鸠摩罗什诞辰1650周年国际学术讨论会文集》,乌鲁木齐:新疆美术摄影出版社,2001年,第171-172页。

[7] Richard Salomon, *opere citato*: 8.

德国学者桑德尔博士曾对新疆出土的早期俗语和梵语写本 (2-6世纪) 进行了系统整理,推测:早期写本出自塔里木盆地北沿一线,系用各种婆罗米字母书写,时间可定在2-6世纪,但与7世纪以后的写本相比,资料则显得匮乏。塔里木盆地北沿出土的写本局限于库车和焉耆等西北绿洲,且大多出自克孜尔红穹顶洞 (现编66、67窟),年代远在迦腻色迦一世。Lore Sander, *opere citato*: 75-76. 笔者以为:这批材料似定得过早,因为同窟中出土的“寺院化缘簿 (Anzahl von Formularen für Schenkungen)”等残本应为7世纪之物。李崇峰,上引书,第171-172页。

[8] Lore Sander, *opere citato*: 83.

而来[1]，因为“现存各部，如说一切有部是使用的梵语，南方上座部是使用的巴利语”[2]。西藏高僧布顿1322年撰写《佛教史大宝藏论》时，记述部派佛教四大系统所用语言各不相同：有部一系，使用梵语；大众一系，使用俗语；正量一系，使用讹误语；上座一系，使用平常语[3]。这一说法，我们认为是可信的[4]。玄奘游历西域时，曾记载：“阿耆尼国……伽蓝十余所，僧徒二千余人，习学小乘教说一切有部。经教律仪，既遵印度，诸习学者，即其文而玩之……屈支国，旧曰龟兹……伽蓝百余所，僧徒五千余人，习学小乘教说一切有部。经教律仪，取则印度，其习读者，即本文矣……跋禄迦国，旧谓姑墨……文字法则同屈支国……伽蓝数十所，僧徒千余人，习学小乘教说一切有部。”[5]这种情况，与新疆出土的梵语及当地语言写本是吻合的，因为塔里木盆地北沿发现的大多数梵语写本属于说一切有部，说明它是当时佛教的主流部派[6]。据季羡林先生研究，“最早的汉译佛典的原本不是梵语或巴利语，其中可能有

---

[1] 在塔里木盆地南沿发现的公元1至4世纪的佉卢字母写本中，提到了饮光部、法藏部及大众部等部派。由于残存佛典的语言及措辞不同，佉卢字母系统佛典通常被归为法藏部。

桑德尔认为：塔里木盆地北沿出土的梵语残本，说明西部绿洲从贵霜时期以迄7世纪左右为说一切有部统领；至于北沿发现的法藏部残本，表明这一部派在当地延续了若干世纪。法藏部僧伽在塔里木盆地南、北沿一直存在到说一切有部传至该地并居统领地位之前。法藏部高僧，大概把他们用佉卢字母书写的佛典从故乡犍陀罗带到了新疆；遗憾的是，迄今我们仅知他们的《法句经》。应该说桑德尔博士关于法藏部与说一切有部之关系的论点是对的，只是把说一切有部流行北沿的时间上限过于提前了，因为如博士所言，新疆出土的早期梵语写本皆未注明日期，其断年只能通过这一地区婆罗米字母的演进来推定。笔者以为：从库车发现的佉卢字母犍陀罗语和婆罗米字母吐火罗语双语题记来看，或许法藏部与说一切有部的交替时间在6、7世纪。至于佉卢字母写本残存较少，除不易保存及损坏等因素外，或许与桑德尔博士所言早期传教仅靠高僧口诵佛典有关。参见：Lore Sander, *opere citato*: 66-67, 105, 106, 81-84.

[2] 吕澂《印度佛学源流略讲》，上海：上海人民出版社，1979年，第40页。

[3] 布顿在叙述原始佛教四大部派各自所用语言之后，又补充道：有人说大众部用平常语，正量部用俗语，上座部用讹误语。参见布顿大师《佛教史大宝藏论》，郭和卿译，北京：民族出版社，1986年，第116页。

蒲文成重译布顿书时，把上座系使用的“平常语”译作“鬼语”。此“鬼语”或为“印度西北方土语”。参见：1) 布顿・仁钦珠《布顿佛教史》，蒲文成译，兰州：甘肃民族出版社，2007年，第81页；2) 李志夫《中印佛学比较研究》，北京：中国社会科学出版社，2001年，第106页注②。

[4] 吕澂，上引书，第40页。

[5] 玄奘，上引书，第48-66页。

[6] 1) Lore Sander, *opere citato*: 85-86; 2) Lore Sander, "Ernst Waldschmidt's Contribution to the Study of the 'Turfan Finds'", in: *Turfan Revisited-The First Century of Research into the Arts and Cultures of the Silk Road*, ed., Desmond Durkin-Meisterernst et al, Berlin: Dietrich Reimer Verlag, 2004: 303-309, esp. 304-305; 3) Jens-Uwe Hartmann, "Buddhist Sanskrit Texts from Northern Turkestan and their relation to the Chinese *Tripiṭaka*", in: *Collection of Essays 1993: Buddhism Across Boundaries—Chinese Buddhism and Western Religions* by Erik Zürcher, Lore Sander and others, eds. John R. McRae, Jan Nattier, Taipei: Foguang Cultural Enterprise Co., Ltd, 1999: 107-136, esp. 117-119.

少数的犍陀罗文,而主要是中亚古代语言(包括新疆)”[1]。辛嶋静志认为:西北印度及中亚等地,在梵语之前使用的中期印度语中有犍陀罗语。汉魏两晋南北朝时期,到中土传法、译经的高僧有许多来自犍陀罗地区。因此在这一时期的汉译佛典中,有许多经律的原典语言就是犍陀罗语,或是由犍陀罗语多少梵语化的语言[2]。近年,更有学者提出:鸠摩罗什之前的汉译佛典,即“古译”主要根据犍陀罗语,或为口诵而出,或为赍本迻译[3]。印度佛典梵语化约始于公元4世纪,佛典从犍陀罗语过渡到梵语传统一定发生在5世纪[4];到了6世纪,可能基本上完成了这一变革[5]。梵语写本在新疆出现较晚,或许意味着说一切有部流行新疆地区的时间也较晚,因为该部主要用梵语传法。

因此,我们推测法藏部在玄奘游历龟兹之前的几个世纪曾盛行于该地[6]。甚至在较晚阶段,当说一切有部 / 根本说一切有部开始在这一地区占据主导地位时,尚有少量梵语写本可以归为法藏部。这些梵语写本中较可靠者,一件是《波罗提木叉》(*Prātimokṣa*,戒本)残卷(Cat. No. 656),大概出土于克孜尔,用5或6世纪的早期

---

[1] 季羡林《梅呾利耶与弥勒》,见《季羡林佛教学术论文集》,台北:东初出版社,1995年,第290页。

[2] 辛嶋静志《漢譯佛典的語言研究》及附篇,刊:《俗語言研究》第4期(1997年),第29-49頁。

[3] Charles Willemen, *opere citato* (Kumārajīva's “Explanatory Discourse” ...): 37-83 (156-110), esp. 38 (155).

[4] 1) Oskar von Hinüber, *opere citato* (Sanskrit und Gāndhārī...): 27-34; 2) Oskar von Hinüber, “Origin and Varieties of Buddhist Sanskrit”, in: *Dialectes dans les littératures indo-aryennes*, ed. Colette Caillat, Publications de l'Institut de Civilisation Indienne, śerie in 8, fasc. 55, Paris: Collège de France, 1989: 341-67, esp. 354.

[5] Edwin G. Pulleyblank, “Stages in the Transcription of Indian Words in Chinese from Han to Tang”, in: *Sprachen des Buddhismus in Zentralasien: Vorträge des Hamburger Symposions vom 2. Juli bis 5. Juli 1981*, eds. Klaus Röhrborn und Wolfgang Veenker, Veröffentlichungen der Societas Uralo-Altaica, Band 16, Wiesbaden: Otto Harrassowitz, 1983: 73-102, esp. 87-88. 不过,尼雅和龟兹地区出土的实物表明迟至7世纪,犍陀罗语尚在丝路南、北道使用。参见:Oskar von Hinüber, “Expansion to the North: Afghanistan and Central Asia”, in: *The World of Buddhism, Buddhist Monks and Nuns in Society and Culture*, eds. H. Bechert and R. Gombrich, London: Thames and Hudson, 1993: 99-107, esp. 103.

[6] 德国慕尼黑大学荣休教授施林洛甫(D. Schlingloff)博士2004年曾自费印制(privatdruck)了《TIII MQR:一座中亚藏经阁的发现及其命运》(TIII MQR Eine ostturkistanische Klosterbibliothek und ihr Schicksal)小册子,后分送相关领域专家学者,笔者蒙博士错爱也收到了一份。后来,复旦大学刘震博士迻译全文并刊布在《西域历史语言研究集刊》第五辑第33-42页。施林洛甫认为:克孜尔红穹顶窟(Rotkuppelhöhle)发现的古代写本数量不得而知,既有珍贵的古代贝叶和桦树皮写本,也有纸质写本,既有说一切有部的经典(die kanonischen Schriften der Sarvastivadin-Schule),还有法藏部和根本说一切有部的零星经文(vereinzelt kanonische Schriften der Dharmagupta-und Mulasarvastivadin-Schulen),以及极少量的大乘经典。施林洛甫推断:红穹顶窟当时发现的藏书中只有极小的一部分运到了柏林,大量写本的下落不明。若然,红穹顶窟出土的法藏部经文从另一方面说明克孜尔石窟寺曾一度信奉法藏部。

突厥字母(early Turkistan characters)书写，唯散缀俗语因素[1]；由于它与汉译《四分律》在术语及内容次第上非常相似，林冶认为它应出自法藏部之手[2]。另一件是用7或8世纪北突厥A婆罗米字母(Northern Turkistan Brāhmī A)书写的单叶《大般涅槃经》(*Mahāparinirvāṇa-sūtra*)梵语残本(Cat. No. 1024)，出土于木头沟(Murtuq)[3]。《大般涅槃经》写本之语言，较前述《波罗提木叉》进一步梵语化；内容及次第，与说一切有部/根本说一切有部的相应部分差距较大。相反，它与汉译《长阿含经·游行经》颇为一致，语言学特点亦明显，确信为法藏部所传[4]。这两件残本表明：即使在当地失去统领地位之后，法藏部仍在今新疆地区杂行。他们紧随佛典梵语化潮流，接纳婆罗米字母为佛典文字体系[5]，并在说一切有部影响下改用基于犍陀罗语的混合梵语乃至梵语雅语传教[6]。至于玄奘所记"小乘教说一

[1] 伯恩哈德认为该本乃基于俗语(犍陀罗语)原本，只是已经梵语化了。这是否说明当地早期佛典系用西北俗语传写，后来改用梵语呢？另外，伯恩哈德提到在克孜尔发现三方犍陀罗语题记，在苏巴什遗址发现一方，惜未标明出处。参见：Franz Bernhard, *opere citato*: 55-62, esp. 56, 59.

[2] 1) Ernst Waldschmidt, *Sanskrithandschriften aus den Turfanfunden*. Teil 1, Verzeichnis der orientalischen Handschriften in Deutschland, unter Mitarbeit von Walter Clawiter und Lore Holzman hrsg. und mit einer Einleitung versehen von Ernst Waldschmidt, Wiesbaden: Franz Steiner Verlag, 1965: 297-298, no. 656; 2) Ernst Waldschmidt, *opere citato* (Central Asian Sūtra Fragments...): 136-174, esp. 164-167.

[3] Ernst Waldschmidt, "Drei Fragmente buddhistischer Sūtras aus den Turfanhandschriften", in: *Nachrichten der Akademie der Wissenschaften in Göttingen,* Nr. 1, Philologisch-historische Klasse, Jg. 1968, Göttingen: Vandenhoeck & Ruprecht, 1968: 3-26, esp. 3-16.

[4] 1) Ernst Waldschmidt, *opere citato* (Central Asian Sūtra Fragments...): 136-174, esp. 167-169; 2) Jens-Uwe Hartmann, "Buddhism along the Silk Road: On the Relationship between the Buddhist Sanskrit Texts from Northern Turkestan and those from Afghanistan", *Turfan Revisited-The First Century of Research into the Arts and Cultures of the Silk Road,* eds. Desmond Durkin-Meisterernst, et al, Berlin: Dietrich Reimer Verlag, 2004: 125-128, esp. 127.

不过，也有学者认为：检讨其细节，乃未必与《长阿含经》一致，尤以此本所说十二分教之配列，与《长阿含经》或《四分律》之法藏部传承不同，而与《杂阿含经》一致。参见榎本文雄《阿含經典の成立》，見《東洋學術研究》第23卷1期，第93-108页。

[5] Lore Sander, *opere citato* (Early Prakrit and Sanskrit...): 61-106, esp. 75.

[6] 参见：1) Ernst Waldschmidt, *opere citato* (Central Asian Sūtra Fragments...): 136-174, esp. 168-169; 2) Jin-il Chung [郑镇一] und K. Wille, "Einige Bhikṣuvinayavibhaṅga-Fragmente der Dharmaguptakas in der Sammlung Pelliot", in: *Untersuchungen zur buddhistischen Literatur zweite Folge: Gustav Roth zum 80 Geburtstag gewidmet,* eds. Heinz Bechert, Sven Bretfeld und Petra Kieffer-Pülz, Sanskrit-Wörterbuch der buddhistischen Texte aus den Turfan-Funden, Beiheft 8, Göttingen: Vandenhoeck & Ruprecht, 1997: 49-94, esp. 52-53.

不过，伯恩哈德博士根据克孜尔和吐峪沟出土的残本，认为在婆罗米字母—梵语雅语取代佉卢字母—犍陀罗语很久以后，官方仍保留使用犍陀罗语之习惯。佉卢字母—俗语(即犍陀罗语)写本传统在塔里木盆地北沿一直沿用到7世纪。此外，伯恩哈德也提到了龟兹7世纪的双语简牍及题记，如库车苏巴什遗址就有佉卢字母—俗语与婆罗米字母—吐火罗语双语共存。这种双语简牍或题记，俗语部分通常在前，且较书于其后的婆罗米字母—吐火罗语详细，无疑是官方或正式文本；而婆罗米字母—吐火罗语部分乃非正式译文，(转下页注)

切有部”[1],只能反映他游历时当地佛教部派流行的情况,不宜混作龟兹等地早期部执。而且,克孜尔石窟大量开凿塔庙窟(中心柱窟)[2]且早期塔庙窟内中心塔柱左、右、后三面满绘舍利塔或塔中坐佛(图23)都反映出法藏部曾流行该地[3],因为只有该部偏重造塔及供养佛塔之功德[4]。又,克孜尔中心柱窟主室券顶中脊两侧绘制本生和因缘故事,主室两侧壁对称画出佛在不同时间、不同地点向信众说法场景,整体内容重视“菩萨本行事”。基于前述研究,“法藏部发展了本生说,编成为一类‘菩萨藏’,这是很特殊的”。因此,克孜尔中心柱窟主室侧壁与窟顶壁画的题材内容,疑与法藏部特有的二藏之一“菩萨藏”有关,即“明诸菩萨本所行事”。这从另一方面表明龟兹地区曾流行法藏部。至于龟兹地区6世纪以降中心柱窟(塔庙窟)数量剧减,疑为上述历史背景之反映。

此外,克孜尔早期盛行的大像窟,如第47和77窟,是大立佛形象与塔庙合璧于一窟的极好实例。这种设计,应与《长阿含经》先叙释迦游行布道、后讲涅槃造塔有密切关系[5]。这或许是法藏部势力强烈影响石窟建造之结果。

1999年11月,美国芝加哥大学召开“汉唐之间的宗教考古与艺术”学术研讨会。笔者在会上宣读的论文是《克孜尔中心柱窟主室正壁画塑题材及有关问

以方便不谙俗语之人。另外,法国学者皮诺博士也曾出示了佉卢字母—俗语与婆罗米字母—吐火罗语并排刻画之例证(7世纪)。参见:1) Franz Bernhard, *opere citato*: 55-62, esp. 56-57; 2) Georges-Jean Pinault, “Épigraphie koutchéenne”, in: *Mission Paul Pelliot Documents conservés au Musée Guimet et à la Bibliothèque Nationale*; *Documents Archéologiques VIII, Sites divers de la région de Koutcha,* ed. Chao Huashan, S. Gaulier, M. Maillard et G. Pinault, Paris: Center de Recherche sur l'Asie Centrale et la Haute Asie, Collège de France, 1987: 59-196, *esp*. 138, 157. 这种双语题记,疑为从佉卢字母—犍陀罗语向婆罗米字母—吐火罗语过渡之形式。

[1] 有学者认为:“犍陀罗语在佛教及其文学传入中国新疆和内地中曾起到了积极作用,当地用佉卢字母书写犍陀罗语之习惯一直延续到6世纪,那时婆罗米字母开始在大乘佛教的中心——于阗流行,好像取代了佉卢字母。”参见 B. N. Puri, *Buddhism in Central Asia*, Delhi: Motilal Banarsidass Publishers, 1987: 184-190。又,林梅村推测:玄奘7世纪游历龟兹时,当地只使用婆罗米字母,不再使用佉卢字母。Meicun Lin, *opere citato* (Kharoṣṭhī Biblioraphy...): 188-221, esp. 196.

[2] 克孜尔中心柱窟塔柱左、右、后三面通常绘制荼毗焚棺、八王分舍利、阿阇世王闻佛涅槃后闷绝复苏等内容,均与佛涅槃及荼毗焚棺后的舍利有关。因而,这种洞窟显然具有塔庙(caityagṛha)性质。另外,克孜尔中心柱窟早期塔柱的左、右、后三面多画小型舍利塔或塔中坐佛,显示其具舍利塔之意殆无疑义。在这一点上,它与印度塔庙窟内佛塔性质相同。参见:李崇峰,上引书,第176-180页。

[3] 克孜尔第211窟西壁残存直体佉卢字母题刻,但内容不明。参见:1) Albert Grünwedel, *opere citato* (*Altbuddhistische Kultstätten...*): 147; 2) Lore Sander, *opere citato*: 61-106, esp. 73.

[4] 巴基斯坦西北部,尤其斯瓦特(Swāt)地区佛教遗迹的显著特征,是佛寺遗址中央高耸的大塔及其周围的奉献塔(图24)。这应是法藏部势力影响之结果,因为法藏部曾经是这一地区极具势力的小乘部派。

[5] 宿白《武威天梯山早期石窟参观记》,见《燕京学报》,新八期(2000年),第221-223页。

图 23　克孜尔第 38 窟后甬道侧壁舍利塔壁画

图 24　巴基斯坦斯瓦特地区（乌苌国）布特卡拉 I 号遗址

题》，提出“可能在玄奘游访龟兹之前，当地曾流行法藏部；克孜尔石窟大量开凿支提窟，或许是法藏部重视供养佛塔的一种反映”。2003 年 9 月，日本龙谷大学举办“仏の来た道：シルクロードの文物と現代科学”（佛陀之道：丝绸之路的文物与现代科学）国际学术讨论会，笔者应邀讲述了“*Dīrghāgama and Kucha Chētiyagharas*（《长阿含经》与龟兹中心柱窟）”，对克孜尔部分中心柱窟与《长阿含经》等佛典之关系及其部派问题做了探讨。不过由于种种原因，该会议论文集迄今尚未出版。随着近年新发现的犍陀罗语与梵语佛典写本的刊布，笔者对这一问题做了进一步梳理。不当之处，祈望同好指正。

（本文原刊于上海古籍出版社 2012 年出版的《徐苹芳先生纪念文集》第 419-465 页，此次重刊增补两条注释。）

龟兹与犍陀罗的造像组合、题材及布局

新疆克孜尔石窟是古代龟兹境内规模最大的石窟群，现存洞窟250余个，类型齐备，延续时间较久，可以作为龟兹石窟的代表。依据洞窟形制，克孜尔石窟主要分作四种类型，即中心柱窟（塔庙窟）、大像窟、僧房窟和方形窟[1]。其中，中心柱窟（包括大像窟）应是早期信徒进行供养、礼忏仪式或从事佛事活动的主要场所[2]。克孜尔的中心柱窟，由前室、主室、塔（塔柱）和后室四部分构成。鉴于窟内经营位置相对固定，克孜尔中心柱窟的塑画，似有统一的圣像设计(iconological scheme)，即造像组合与题材布局。这种圣像设计或造像组合与题材布局，在古代西域流传范围较广、延续时间较长。

以克孜尔第38窟为例，中心塔柱正面凿作蘑菇状，合壁塑画“帝释窟”场景（图1a）[3]。主室两侧壁分栏分段，绘制佛在不同时间、不同地点的说法图（图1b）。窟顶中

---

［1］宿白《新疆拜城克孜尔石窟部分洞窟类型与年代》，载宿白《中国石窟寺研究》，北京：文物出版社，1996年，第21-38页。

［2］佛教讲究最上供养(Anuttara-pūjā)，传说共有七种最上供养。据施护译《佛说法集名数经》(*Dharma-saṃgraha*)卷上：“云何七种最上供养？所谓礼拜(vandanā)、供养(pūjānā)、忏悔(pāpa-deśanā)、随喜(anumodanā)、劝请(adhyeshaṇā)、发愿(bodhi-cittôtpāda)、回向(pariṇamanā)。”施护为北天竺乌填曩（乌仗那）人，宋太宗太平兴国五年(980年)与北印度迦湿弥罗国之天息灾同抵汴京。这种最上供养，应流行于北天竺，疑为早期佛教徒所特重，尤其是当时“志欲躬睹灵迹、广寻经要”的西行求法高僧。据宗性《名僧传抄》摘录宝唱《名僧传》，宝云“于隆安元年(397年)，乃辞入西域，誓欲眼都（睹）神迹，躬行忏悔。遂游于阗及天竺诸国，与智严、法显，发轸是同，游造各异。于陀历国，见金薄弥勒成佛像，整高八丈，(宝)云于像下革（毕）城启忏五十日”。寓于高昌的法盛，“年造十九，遇沙门智严从外国还，述诸神迹，因有志焉。辞二亲，率师友与二十九人远诣天竺，经历诸国，寻觅遗灵及诸应瑞，礼拜、供养，以申三业。□忧长国（乌仗那）东北，见牛头旃檀弥勒像……常放光明，四众伎乐四时笑乐，远人皆卒从像悔过，愿无不尅，得初道果，岁有十数。(法)盛与诸方道俗五百人，愿求舍身，必见弥勒”。因此，克孜尔中心柱窟及大像窟疑为当时信徒实施集会礼忏活动，即最上供养的主要场所。参见：1)《大正藏》第17卷，第660b页；2)Monier Monier-Williams, *A Sanskrit-English Dictionary*, London：Oxford University Press, 1899: 919, 641, 618, 37, 22, 23, 396, 594；3)宝唱《名僧传》，见宗性《名僧传抄》，载《大日本續藏經》，前田慧雲原編、中野達慧增訂，京都：藏經書院，1905-1912年，第壹輯第貳編乙第七套第壹冊，第十三叶。

［3］关于“帝释窟”画塑之具体内容，参见李崇峰《克孜尔中心柱窟主室正壁画塑题材及有关问题》，见《汉唐之间的宗教艺术与考古》，北京：文物出版社，2000年，第209-233页。

脊绘天空，内有日神、月神、立佛、金翅鸟及那伽；中脊两侧对称画出以菱形山峦为背景的本生或因缘故事（图 1c）。塔柱周围甬道，尤其是后甬道或后室侧壁，表现涅槃图像及相关内容（图 1d）。门道上方的半圆形壁面，即主室前壁上部，绘制弥勒菩萨于兜率天示现、说法（图 1e）。其中，门道上方的未来佛弥勒与帝释窟中的现在佛释

a

b

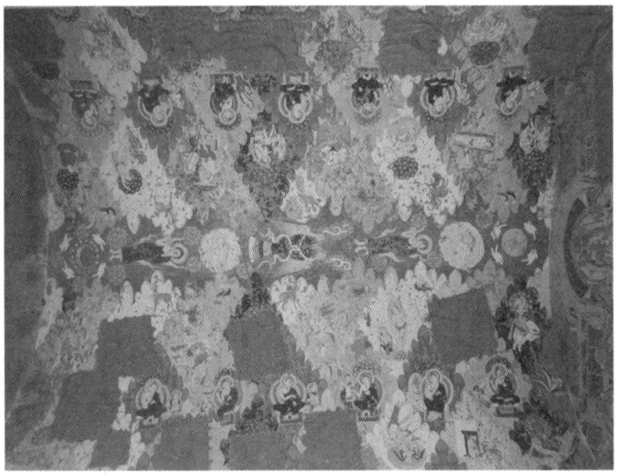

c

d

e

图 1　克孜尔第 38 窟题材布局
a. 中心柱正壁；b. 主室侧壁；
c. 主室窟顶；d. 后甬道后壁；
e. 主室门道上方半圆形壁面

迦相应经营[1]。

这种圣像设计,即造像组合与题材布局(图2),尤其是帝释窟[2]、涅槃场景[3]及弥勒示现[4],可能依据与汉译《长阿含经》相当的佛典绘制[5]。这一佛典,似与犍陀罗佛教雕刻的造像组合 (iconological composition) 密切相关。

犍陀罗出土的佛教雕刻,原来大多用作塔身饰板或佛塔装饰,少数置于寺院的佛龛之内[6]。犍陀罗地区的佛塔早已废弃,镶嵌在塔身上的原始浮雕散落后为后代地层或碎石掩埋。由于早年缺乏科学系统的考古发掘,故而,现存世界各地博物馆或私人收藏的大多数犍陀罗雕刻,皆为佛塔原始浮雕带 (relief strip) 脱落之个体,缺乏佛塔营造时整个塔身浮雕或原始造像组合之信息[7]。由于相关造像比邻内容残损、题材布局前后画面缺失,致使佛塔雕饰中的题材布局或造像的完整组合情况一直困惑学界。

不过,近半个世纪考古发掘或采集的若干佛教雕刻,对于我们认识原始佛塔的圣像设计或造像组合与题材布局颇具价值。其中,收藏在巴基斯坦迪尔 (Dir) 考古博物

[1] 李崇峰《克孜尔部分中心柱窟与〈长阿含经〉等佛典》,见《徐苹芳先生纪念文集》,上海:上海古籍出版社,2012 年,第 419-465 页。

[2] 李崇峰《克孜尔中心柱窟主室正壁画塑题材及有关问题》,上引书,第 209-233 页。

[3] Chongfeng Li, "Representation of the Buddha's Parinirvāṇa in the Cetiyagharas of Kizil, Kucha", in: *Buddhist Narrative in Asia and Beyond,* Vol. I, eds. Peter Skilling and Justin McDaniel, Bangkok: Institute of Thai Studies, Chulalongkorn University, 2012: 59-81.

[4] Chongfeng Li, "The Image of Maitreya in the Chētiyagharas of Kizil, Kucha", in: *Gandhāran Studies,* Vol. VII: 11-22.

[5] 李崇峰《克孜尔部分中心柱窟与〈长阿含经〉等佛典》,上引书,第 419-465 页。

[6] W. Zwalf, *A Catalogue of the Gandhāra Sculpture in the British Museum,* Vol. I, London: British Museum Press, 1996: 50.

[7] 现藏巴基斯坦拉合尔博物馆犍陀罗展室中央的佛塔,保存了犍陀罗地区唯一完整的塔身雕饰(图 3)。该塔系 1889 年由时任马尔丹 (Mardan) 地区助理专员 (Assistant Commissioner) 的迪恩 (Lt. Col. H. A. Deane) 在锡克里 (Sikri) 遗址发掘出土,并于同年整体搬迁至拉合尔博物馆。除礼拜道及覆钵为后来复建、方龛及轮盖取自同一地区别塔之外,其余部分皆为原作,年代可定在公元 2 世纪。塔身装饰由 13 块浮雕石板组合而成,内容为佛传,法国学者傅塞 (A. Foucher) 依次考订为:燃灯佛授记、未来佛居兜率天、树下思维、龙王夫妇赞美、刈草人铺座、四天王奉钵、梵天劝请、佛与信徒、忉利天说法、奉施芒果园、帝释窟、阿吒薄俱皈依、猕猴奉蜜等场景,唯不见涅槃图像。需要说明的是,塔身浮雕饰板的现排列顺序似有误,疑为佛塔搬迁后复原所致。不管怎样,借助这批浮雕,我们可以窥见昔日犍陀罗佛塔完整雕饰之一斑。参见:1) Alfred Foucher, *L'Art gréco-bouddhique du Gandhâra: étude sur les origines de l'influence classique dans l'art bouddhique de l'Inde et de l'Extréme-Orient*, 2 Bde, Tome I, 1905; Tome II, 1, 1918; Tome II, 2, 1922; Tome II, 3, 1951, Paris: Imprimerie Nationale/ E. Leroux, 1905-1951, I: 275, Fig. 139; 286, Fig. 145; 342, Fig. 175; 384, Fig. 194; 391, Fig. 197; 417, Fig. 210; 421, Fig. 212; 481, Fig. 242; 485, Fig. 243; 491, Fig. 245; 495, Fig. 247; 509, Fig. 252; 513, Fig. 254; 2) Humera Alam, *Gandhara Sculptures in Lahore Museum*, Lahore: Lahore Museum, 1998: 80-85.

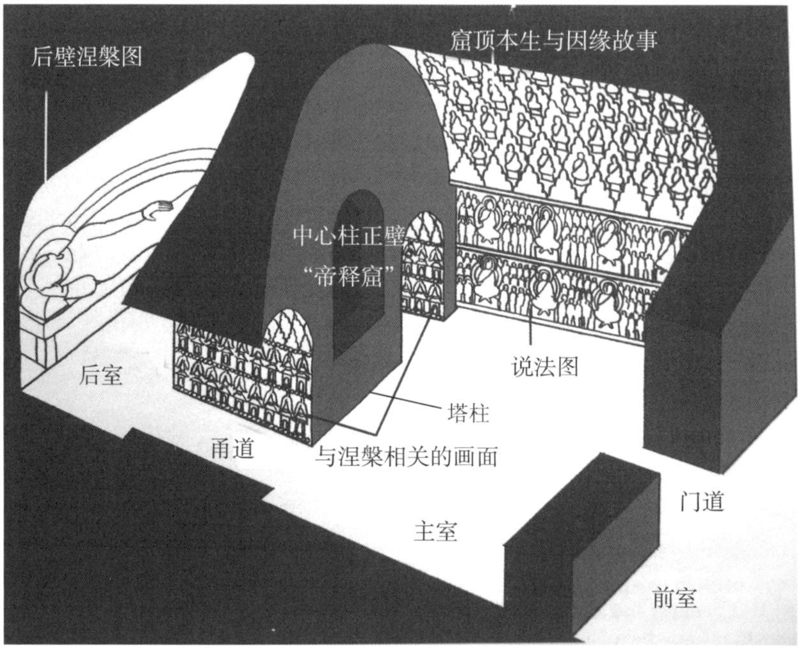

图 2　克孜尔中心柱窟题材布局示意图

图 3　锡克里佛塔，拉合尔博物馆犍陀罗艺术展厅

馆和塔克西拉考古博物馆的两件浮雕尤为重要。

迪尔考古博物馆收藏的编号 No. 85 浮雕（图 4），是在杰格德拉（Chakdara）地区杰德伯特（Chatpat）遗址发掘出土的[1]。它是一件长方形饰板，现存两个画面，中间以科林斯式壁柱相隔。

图 4　“帝释窟”与“佛涅槃”浮雕，杰德伯特遗址出土，迪尔考古博物馆

浮雕左半部，刻画释提桓因与五髻乐师拜谒佛陀，即帝释窟场景。这是犍陀罗佛教艺术中最为流行的题材之一。犍陀罗地区出土的帝释窟浮雕，现存最早者可定为 1 世纪末、2 世纪初，3 世纪时达到鼎盛[2]。依据画面结构与经营位置，犍陀罗地区出土的帝释窟浮雕，可以大体分作两种构图类型：第一种：佛陀所居帝释窟，位于画面右侧，窟口刻饰火焰；窟上方可见鸟兽及其他动物；窟下雕出鹿、羊或野猪等。释提桓因、五髻乐师（般遮翼）及其他人物皆雕在帝释窟右侧。其中，般遮翼躬立窟侧，卷发若髻，上身袒裸，下着禅裙（dhoti），手持箜篌（图 5）。第二种：帝释窟位于画面中央，佛居中禅定，释提桓因移至窟左，般遮翼仍在窟右，换言之，释提桓因与般遮翼被对称雕于帝释窟两侧。在这种构图中，除释提桓因和般遮翼外，艺术家尚在窟外分栏分段雕出众多小神祇、鸟兽及林木等（图 6）。在上述两种浮雕构图中，帝释窟中之佛陀，不论刻画正面还是侧面，均结跏趺坐、作禅定印[3]。至于杰德伯特出土的那件

[1] Abdur Rahman, “Excavation at Chatpat”, in: *Ancient Pakistan* (Bulletin of the Department of Archaeology, University of Peshawar), Vol. IV (1968-69), Plate 44.

[2] 1) 李崇峰《克孜尔中心柱窟主室正壁画塑题材及有关问题》，上引书，第 213 页；2) Chongfeng Li, “Gandhāra, Mathurā and Buddhist Sculptures of Mediaeval China”, in: *Glory of the Kushans: Recent Discoveries and Interpretations*, ed. Vidula Jayaswal, New Delhi: Aryan Books International, 2012: 378-391, esp. 379-380.

[3] 参见：1) Alfred Foucher, *opere citato*, Tome I: 492-497; 2) 李崇峰《克孜尔中心柱窟主室正壁画塑题材及有关问题》，上引书，第 213-215、230 页。

图5　帝释窟浮雕，锡克里佛塔，拉合尔博物馆

图6　帝释窟浮雕，马曼内 · 得里 (Mamāne-Dheṛī) 遗址出土，白沙瓦博物馆

浮雕,构图应属第一种。窟内雕刻趋于写实,佛大衣通肩披覆；般遮翼、释提桓因及另外二人均雕于帝释窟的右前方,窟之上下未见动物。这是犍陀罗地区同类题材雕刻中的一种简化形式。

浮雕右半部,表现佛涅槃场景。涅槃图像,“是犍陀罗佛教艺术中雕刻较早且为人熟悉的题材之一”[1],迄今所见以盖兹·梅斯 (Guides' Mess) 原藏那件 (图 7) 为最古。尽管“这件浮雕是现存年代最早的,但绝非全部浮雕中的第一幅”[2]。画面中,佛居中而卧,榻布图案繁复；艺术家竭力刻画圆寂佛陀,再现其入灭之相。榻头站一力士,手持金刚杵；榻尾尚存立像残迹,疑为大迦叶。依据佛典,迦叶获悉佛涅槃一周后,速奔天冠寺,跪拜抚佛足。榻侧前三僧席地而坐,表情沮丧；榻后所雕四人,满脸泪痕,疑为末罗贵族。此外,背景中还刻出娑罗双树及树精等[3]。

图 7　佛涅槃浮雕,现藏于白沙瓦博物馆

[1] John Marshall, *Buddhist Art of Gandhāra: The Story of the Early School; its birth, growth and decline.* London: Cambridge University Press, 1960: 54.

[2] John Marshall, *opere citato*: 49.

[3] 1) A. Foucher, *opere citato,* Tome I: 557, Fig. 276; 2) Harald Ingholt, *Gandhāran Art in Pakistan; with 577 illustrations photographed by Islay Lyons and 77 pictures from other sources, introduction and descriptive catalogue by Harald Ingholt*, New York: Pantheon Books, 1957: 92-93; 3) John Marshall, *opere citato*: 49-50.

尽管后来同一题材的雕刻，基本因循这一构图，唯附属人物及装饰成分增多。在所有涅槃浮雕中，基本因素及经营位置相对固定且始终不变：佛于榻上展身侧卧，周围环绕举哀弟子。不过，雕刻家在处理个体形象及组合时，充分发挥了自己的聪明才智并施展个性手法。因此，不同作品之间常常存在若干差异[1]。在杰德伯特出土的那件浮雕中，须跋坐于榻侧，金刚手立于榻头，大迦叶跪拜于榻尾，诸天、末罗贵族及娑罗双树等，在榻后的背景中清晰可见。

现陈列于塔克西拉考古博物馆、编号 No. WTG 6 展品，系一长方形浮雕饰板，原为瓦赫 (Wah) 收藏[2]。该浮雕也由两幅画面构成，中以科林斯式壁柱相隔 (图 8)。

图 8　“佛涅槃” 与 “弥勒示现”，现藏于塔克西拉考古博物馆

浮雕左半部，表现一菩萨结跏趺坐于悬布座上，身具头光，发式独特；面部残蚀，五官不清；身着上衣 (uttarīya)，右肩袒裸；佩平项圈，戴长项链。菩萨右臂屈举，现小臂残失，疑施无畏印；左手置于腿上，以食指和中指夹持净瓶，唯净瓶已残失。座上覆布，两端垂穗；座前置踏座。菩萨头上方的华盖，以印度—科林斯式细柱支撑，柱础系一正面狮子。菩萨两侧各有一人，似王子，皆面向菩萨，着上衣，佩项圈，戴项链，善跏趺坐 (倚坐)，双脚置踏上。二倚像后各一立像，皆双手合十，戴耳饰，佩项圈，身着上衣和下衣 (paridhāna)。 上方的露台，现天人半身。这幅画面，通常被定为弥勒菩萨于兜率天示现、说法[3]。此外，在塔克西拉法王塔遗址的发掘中，出土了

[1] Chongfeng Li, 1) “Representation of the Buddha’s Parinirvāṇa in the Cetiyagharas of Kizil, Kucha” , in: *opere citato*: 59-81; 2) A. Foucher, *opere citato*, Tome I: 555-573.

[2] Muhammad Ashraf Khan et al, *A Catalogue of the Gandhāra Stone Sculptures in the Taxila Museum*, Islamabad: Department of Archaeology and Museums, Government of Pakistan, 2005, Vol. I: 105-107, Vol. II: 34, Plate 45.

[3] 1) 宫治昭《涅槃と彌勒菩薩》，見東武美術館等編集《ブッダ展——大いなる旅路》/*Buddha: The Spread of Buddhist Art in Asia,* 東京：NHK (Japan Broadcasting Corporation) and NHK プロモーション，1998: 125; 2) Muhammad Ashraf Khan et al, *opere citato*, Vol. I: 106-107.

一件内容极为类似的浮雕（图 9a）[1]，其主像多被学者定为弥勒[2]。至于迪尔考古博物馆收藏的另一件浮雕（图 9b），可能表现的是同一内容[3]。

a　　　　b

图 9a　兜率天弥勒，法王塔遗址出土，塔克西拉考古博物馆
　　b　兜率天弥勒，迪尔考古博物馆

浮雕右半部，刻画涅槃场景，较杰德伯特遗址出土的涅槃浮雕之构图略微复杂。佛侧卧于画面中央，肉髻较大，发根系带明显，右手下为高枕；大衣覆盖整个躯体，包裹左手及双足。榻尾两人作交谈状，疑为阿难与须跋。依据佛典，佛涅槃之前，阿难曾婉拒须跋拜谒佛陀。榻侧前雕刻两人，一位作跪坐状，似为悲伤过度之阿难；另一人头及身体完全被大衣包裹，禅定而坐，应为先佛入灭之须跋。榻头两人，一位裸体，一位大衣通肩披覆，疑为裸体外道与大迦叶，前者似正向后者通报佛涅槃情况[4]。

上述两件浮雕清楚地显示："帝释窟与佛涅槃"和"佛涅槃与弥勒示现"，是两种

[1] John Marshall, *Taxila: An illustrated account of archaeological excavations carried out at Taxila under the orders of the government of India between the years 1913 and 1934*, London: Cambridge University Press, 1951, Vol. II: 712-713, Vol. III: Plate 217, No. 93.

[2] 1) John Marshall, *opere citato* (*The Buddhist Art of Gandhāra*...): 79; 2) Francine Tissot, *Gandhâra*, 2e éditon revue et corrigée; Dessins d'Anne-Marie Loth et de l'auteur, Paris: Librairie d'Amérique et d'Orient/Jean Maisonneuve, 2002: 101, Fig.239; 3) Kurt Behrendt, "Reuse of Images in Ancient Gandhara", in: *Gandhāran Studies*, ed. M. Nasim Khan, Vol. 2: 17-38, esp. 23, k.

不过，Harald Ingholt 认为这幅画面表现的是"诸神规劝悉达多太子弃离世俗生活"。Harald Ingholt, *opere citato*: 58, plate 37.

[3] Seoul Arts Center ed., *The Exhibition of Gandhara Art of Pakistan*, Seoul: Joong-Ang Ilbo, 1999: 156.

[4] 1) 宫治昭《涅槃と彌勒菩薩》，上引书，第 125 页；2) Muhammad Ashraf Khan et al, *opere citato*: 105-106.

固定的造像组合形式，二者皆为犍陀罗佛教艺术中常规的圣像设计。

作为古代西域的佛教中心，位于犍陀罗与中国内地之间的龟兹（图 10），理应分享犍陀罗佛教信徒对"历史"佛与未来佛崇拜之热情。结果，如何平衡现在佛释迦牟尼与未来佛弥勒，成为龟兹艺术家在石窟造像组合与题材布局方面的一大创造。

首先，从佛法传播角度来讲，龟兹中心柱窟塔柱正壁龛内之佛陀，欲就释提桓因提出的42个问题进行解答[1]，而与之对应的门道上方弥勒，将于兜率天示现[2]。这种题材布局设计，表明弥勒乃释迦牟尼之神圣继承者[3]。其次，从佛教礼忏仪式考量，中心柱窟后甬道或后室后壁塑画的涅槃图像，与塔柱正壁的帝释窟说法和主室门道上方的弥勒示现，构成一固定的造像组合。一旦信徒或朝圣者踏入这座神圣的洞窟，首先映入眼中的是帝释窟场景（图 11a），似乎佛陀正在回答信徒或朝圣者提出的问题[4]。之后，主室侧壁表现佛在不同地点、不同时间的说法图像及窟顶描绘的本生和因缘故事也会映入信徒的眼帘。至此，信徒或朝圣者渴望实施当时最重要的宗教仪式——绕塔礼拜。就在他们右绕佛塔、瞻仰涅槃（图 11b）并回到主室之后，立即看见了门道上方的弥勒（图 11c），后者乃信徒的终极愿望之所在，因为他们祈求当世得到弥勒决疑、死后托生兜率天堂[5]。这种密切关联的题材布局或圣像设计，不但与佛典所记顺序相同，而且与信徒在中心柱窟内实施的礼忏程序，即"最上供养"活动一致。克孜尔中心柱窟的造像组合或题材布局，即"帝释窟"与"佛涅槃"画面搭配、"佛涅槃"与"弥勒示现"场景对应，基本上依据犍陀罗原型设计；其创作理念，除图像志 (iconography) 外，主要源自与汉译《长阿含经》相当的其他语本佛典[6]。稍后，这种图像志或圣像设计成为古代西域地区中心柱窟的标准造像组合与题材布

---

[1] 李崇峰《克孜尔中心柱窟主室正壁画塑题材及有关问题》，上引书，第 210 页。

[2] 克孜尔中心柱窟主室门道上方的半圆形壁面，与主室窟顶相连。绘在半圆形壁面上的弥勒菩萨，似乎也暗示他居于兜率天，因为与之相连的主室窟顶中脊壁画表现的是天空，如日神和月神等。

[3]《长阿含经·转轮圣王修行经》，《大正藏》第 1 卷，第 41c-42a 页。

[4] 德国柏林亚洲艺术博物馆收藏的一件编号 III302 的木雕，是 20 世纪初德人从库车劫掠的，原应表现帝释窟场景。木雕高 115 厘米，残宽 74 厘米。其中，正中佛龛高 76. 5 厘米，宽 45 厘米。佛龛左右两侧底部各雕一小龛，周围刻出菱形山峦，惟右半部及龛内造像残失（图 12)。这件木雕说明：帝释窟说法这一主题在古龟兹地区的佛教艺术中极为流行，既能大量雕造石窟之内，也可单独置于寺院或家庙之中。

[5] 宫治昭《涅槃と彌勒の図像學——インドがら中央アジアへ》，東京：吉川弘文館，1992 年，第 512-517 页。

[6] 李崇峰《克孜尔部分中心柱窟与〈长阿含经〉等佛典》，上引书，第 419-465 页。

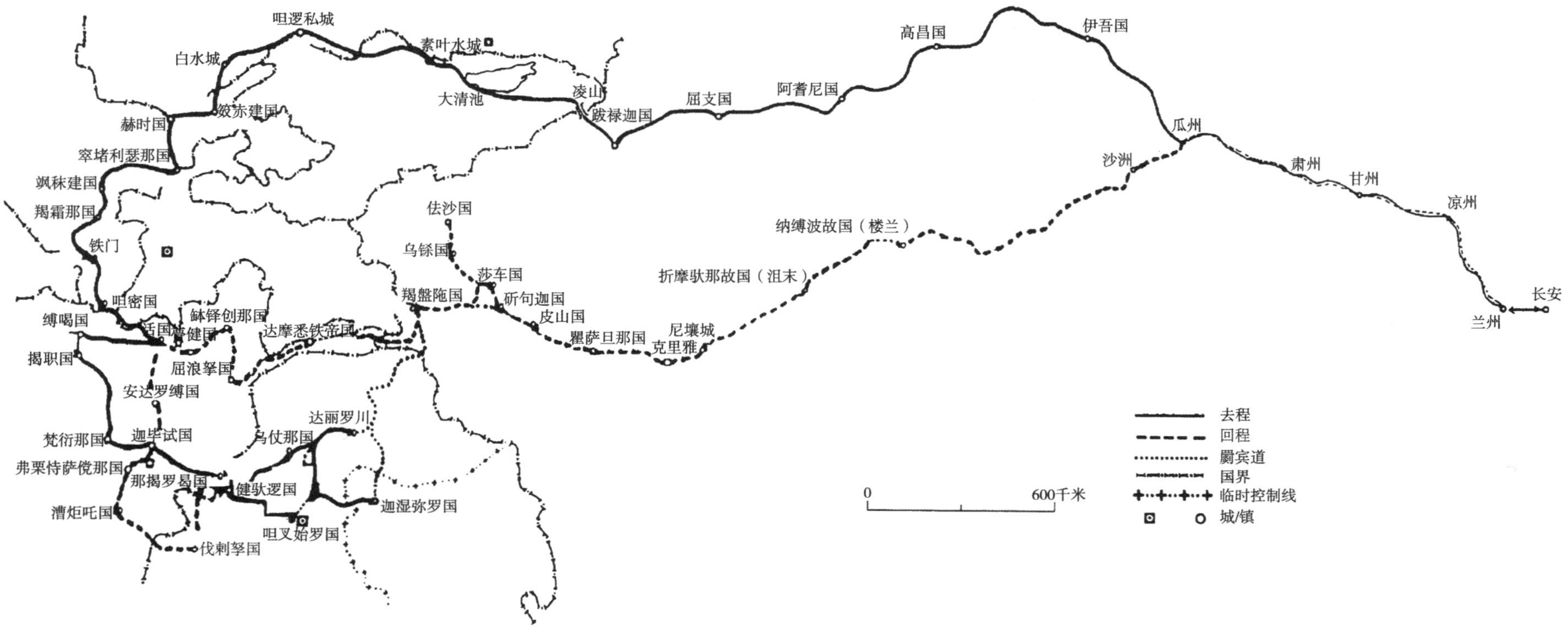

图 10　玄奘西行求法路线示意图（前半）

a

b

c

图 11　克孜尔第 38 窟圣像组合，即“帝释窟”与“佛涅槃”和“未来佛弥勒”

图 12　柏林亚洲艺术博物馆藏帝释窟木雕

局。又,龟兹佛像样式,受到了犍陀罗佛教艺术的直接影响,似在犍陀罗原型的基础上演化而来[1]。

(本文原刊文物出版社2012年出版的《中国考古学会第十四次年会论文集2011》第456-465页,此次重刊增补一个注释。)

---

[1] 德国学者格林威德尔认为:德国考古队在库木吐拉石窟附近一寺址中发现的大立像残迹,在风格上与优填王佛像的类型或样式(Typus der Buddhastatue des Königs Udayana/Typus des Udayanabuddha)有关;而优填王像类型或样式的大立佛,曾被龟兹艺术家和工匠模制于森姆塞姆第44窟的中心柱正壁。参见:Albert Grünwedel, *Altbuddhistische Kultstätten in Chinesisch-Turkistan: Bericht über archäologische Arbeiten von* 1906 *bis* 1907 *bei Kuča, Qarašahr und in der oase Turfan;* Königlich Preussische Turfan-Expeditionen, Berlin: Druck und Verlag von Georg Reimer, 1912: 6-8, 182, 186, 201.

Gandhāra and Kucha: The Case of an Iconological Relationship

The cave-temple complex at Kizil consists of four distinctive architectural designs, i. e., *chētiyaghara* (*stūpa*-cave or central pillar cave), colossal Buddha-image cave, *lēṇa* (dwelling cave) and *maṭapa* (square cave). Among them, the *chētiyaghara*, which was chiefly used by the Buddhist devotees for worship and monastic activity[1], is comprised of a front chamber, a main chamber (nave), a *stūpa* and a rear chamber. The *chētiyagharas* seem to have a unified iconological scheme in design, as portrayed in the Caves 17, 38 and 224 of Kizil, a design that

[1] The Buddhists pay great attention to the seven kinds of *Annuttara-pūjā* or highest worship. According to *Foshuo faji mingshu jing* [佛说法集名数经,*Dharma-saṃgraha*] translated into Chinese after 980 AD by Dānapāla, a Buddhist master from Udyāna, the seven kinds of *Annuttara-pūjā* comprise *libai* [礼拜 *vandanā*, worship/praise], *gongyang* [供养 *pūjānā*, respect/adoration], *chanhui* [忏悔 *pāpa-deśanā*, confession, instruction of the wicked], *suixi* [随喜 *anumodanā*, pleasing/causing pleasure], *quanqing* [劝请 *adhyeshaṇā*, to stand upon], *fayuan* [发愿 *bodhi-cittôtpāda*, thought of wisdom/to pray], *huixiang* [回向 *pariṇamanā*, change/transformation]" . These seven kinds of the highest worship were regarded as very important or taken seriously by pious adherents of Buddhism, especially for those who went on a pilgrimage to the Buddhist center and paid their respects to the Buddhist image personally.

According to the *Hagiography of Baoyun* in the *Mingseng Zhuan* [名僧传, *Biographies of Famous Monks*] by Baochang [宝唱], preserved partly in the Japanese *Meisōden-shō* [名僧传抄, *A Transcript of the Biographies of Famous Monks*] by Shū-shō [宗性], a Chinese pilgrim Baoyun went to the Western Regions in 397 AD. He took the vows to see sacred traces as well as the Buddhist remains with his own eyes and to confess before the Buddha [忏悔] personally. "In a small kingdom named Tuoli, Baoyun saw the image of Maitreya as a Buddha, being 80 feet tall and covered with gold foil. At its feet he started to repent and confessed his sins [启忏] with the utmost devotion for 50 days" . On the basis of the *Hagiography of Fasheng* in the said *Biographies* of (To be continued on the next page) spread far and wide in Xinjiang and survived for quite a long time.

In Cave 38, for instance, the *stūpa* was shaped like a mushroom, with scene of *Indraśālaguhā* (Indra's visit to the Buddha) shown in its façade (fig.1a). A series of scenes of Buddha delivering his sermon were portrayed on the lateral walls of the main chamber (fig.1b). A line of celestial beings such as the sun-god, moon-god, wind-god, standing Buddha, a *garuda* bird and even a *nāga* serpent were painted in the middle of the barrel vaulted ceiling of the main chamber, while murals depicting *jātaka* and *avadāna* stories, i. e. narratives of the Bodhisattva's sacrifices, were shown on both sides of the barrel vault (fig.1c). The Buddha in *Parinirvāṇa* and related events were depicted or sculpted on the sidewalls of the *pradakṣiṇā patha* (circumambulatory path), specifically in the rear chamber (fig.1d). In the lunette above the entrance, the upper part of the front wall or entrance wall of the main chamber, was portrayed the Bodhisattva Maitreya's manifestation and preaching in Tuṣita Heaven (fig.1e). Maitreya faces Śākyamuni Buddha in the *Indraśālaguhā*, the main image on the façade of the

---

Famous Monks, moreover, another Chinese pilgrim Fasheng and his followers travelled vastly and visited several kingdoms. They looked for the sacred remains as well as Buddhist traces of mystical reaction or response, and attended some Buddhist service, worshipping and making offerings to the Buddha in adoration. In the northeast of Udyāna, they saw the Maitreya image made of sandalwood, which is 80 feet high and constantly emits light. Many worshippers from afar become attendants to the image, confessing their faults and praying that they may overcome all obstacles. Those who win thereby the first fruit of salvation number several tens yearly. Fasheng joined with monks and laymen coming from various lands, totaling five hundred, to pray that when they discarded their bodies they would infallibly see Maitreya.

Therefore, we are inclined to infer that the *chētiyaghara* at Kizil used to be a Buddhist church, where the Buddhist followers and pilgrims could attend the religious rituals and carry on the highest worship—the *Annuttara-pūjā*.

See 1) Dānapāla [施护], tr., *Foshuo faji mingshu jing* [*Dharma-saṃgraha*], in: *Taishō,* No.764, Vol.17: 660-662, esp. 660b; 2)Monier Monier-Williams, *A Sanskrit-English Dictionary*, London: Oxford University Press, 1899: 919, 641, 618, 37, 22-23, 396, 594; 3)Baochang, *Mingseng Zhuan* (*Biographies of Famous Monks*)/*Meisōden-shō* (*A Transcript of Biographies of Famous Monks*) by Shū-shō, Fascicle 26, in: *Dainihon Zoku Zōkyō* [大日本續藏經, *Continued Tripiṭaka of Japan*], Vol. 7, No. 1: 1-17, esp. 13; 4) Alexander C. Soper, *Literary Evidence for Early Buddhist Art in China*, Artibus Asiae Supplementum XIX, Ascona: Artibus Asiae Publishers, 1959: 268-269.

stūpa [1].

Such an iconological scheme (fig.2), especially Indra's visit to the Buddha [2], the Buddha in *Parinirvāṇa* [3] and Maitreya preaching in Tuṣita [4], were likely derivative from Buddhist scriptures or *sūtras* corresponding to *Shitihuanyin wen jing* (*Sūtra on the Questions of Śakra Devānām Indra*) [5] and *Youxing jing* (*The Sūtra of* (*the Buddha's*) *Travels to Preach/The Sūtra of* (*the Buddha*) *Preaching Travels* [6] in the Chinese *Dīrghāgama* [7]. These texts seem to be related to the iconological composition or pictorial arrangement of the stone sculptures of Gandhāra.

The Buddhist sculptures discovered in Gandhāra, carved either in low relief (bas-relief) or in high relief (deep relief), were used mostly as *medhī* (drum) panels or *stūpa* casings [8]. Since most of the *stūpas* in Gandhāra have been laid in ruin a long time ago, the reliefs attached to the drum of a *stūpa* naturally fell off or were scattered and covered by later layers or debris. Because of the unsystematic excavations undertaken early on, most of the Buddhist sculptures unearthed from Gandhāra and kept in museums and private collections are incomplete tableaus extrapolated from relief strips and lack the original

[1] Chongfeng Li, "*Kezi'er bufen zhongxinzhuku yu Chang'ahanjing deng fodian* [克孜尔部分中心柱窟与《长阿含经》等佛典, The *Dīrghāgama* Text and the *Chētiyagharas* of Kizil, Kucha]", in: *Xu Pingfang xiansheng ji'nian wenji* [徐苹芳先生纪念文集, *Papers in Commemoration of Professor Xu Pingfang*], Shanghai: Shanghai Chinese Classics Publishing House, 2012: 419-465.

[2] Chongfeng Li [李崇峰], *Kezi'er zhongxinzhuku zhushi zhengbi huasu ticai ji youguan wenti* [克孜尔中心柱窟主室正壁画塑题材及有关问题, The Main Image on the Façade of the *Stūpa*-pillar in the *Chētiyagharas* of Kizil, Kucha], in: *Between Han and Tang: Religious Art and Archaeology in a Transformative Period*, ed. Wu Hung, Beijing: Cultural Relics Press, 2000: 209-233.

[3] Chongfeng Li, "Representation of the Buddha's Parinirvāṇa in the Cetiyagharas of Kizil, Kucha", in: *Buddhist Narrative in Asia and Beyond,* Vol. I, eds. Peter Skilling and Justin McDaniel, Bangkok: Institute of Thai Studies, Chulalongkorn University, 2012：58-81.

[4] Chongfeng Li, "The Image of Maitreya in the Chētiyagharas of Kizil, Kucha", in: *Gandhāran Studies,* Vol. 7: 11-22.

[5] *Taishō*, No. 1, Vol. 1: 1-149, esp. 62-66.

[6] *Taishō*, No. 1, Vol. 1: 1-149, esp. 11-30.

[7] Chongfeng Li, *opere citato* (*Kezi'er bufen zhongxinzhuku...*): 419-431.

[8] W. Zwalf, *A Catalogue of the Gandhāra Sculpture in the British Museum,* Vol. I, London: British Museum Press, 1996: 50.

surroundings of when the *stūpa* was built[1] On account of this lack of context regarding subject matter and motifs, nobody knows for certain the nature of the overall iconological scheme or the comprehensive body of sculptures used in the *stūpa decor*. Within the past 50 years, however, a few panels with Buddhist narratives have been fortunately discovered or collected, which are very important in enabling us to understand the basic arrangement of Buddhist subjects and motifs as well as their composition in the *stūpa decor*. Among them, a relief kept in the Archaeological Museum at Dir and one in the Archaeological Museum at Taxila are the most important and valuable.

Image No. 85 (fig.4) kept in the Archaeological Museum at Dir was discovered during an excavation at Chatpat[2], Chakdara; it is a long panel consisting of two scenes, divided by a Corinthian pilaster.

The left scene in the panel depicts Indra and his harpist visiting the Buddha

---

[1] As far as I know, the only *stūpa* found with all its panels intact *in situ* in Gandhāra was the one kept in the Gandhāra Gallery at the Lahore Museum, which was excavated from the site of Sikri near Jamālgaṛhi, Mardan, by H. A. Deane, the then Assistant Commissioner of Mardan, in 1889 and then brought to the Lahore Museum in the same year. "The base of the circumambulation path and the dome are the hypothetical reconstruction. The *harmikā* and *chattras* are original but belongs to another *stūpa* from the same precincts, while remaining entire structure is original" (Fig.3). The *medhī* (drum) of the *stūpa*, however, gives an excellent idea of the way in which the sculptural propaganda was carried out, which shows thirteen different episodes carved on the rectangular panels. Starting from the serial wise numbers given to the panels, each illustrates one of the significant events in the life of the Buddha as follows:

Dīpaṃkara *Jātaka*, Buddha-to-be in the Tuṣita Heaven, The first meditation of Siddhāratha, Hymn of the Nāga Kālika and his wife, Grass cutter offers grass for the seat of enlightenment, Offering of the four bowls, The gods entreat the Buddha to preach, The Buddha among the monks, The Buddha preaches to the gods in the Trāyastriṃśa Heaven, The courtesan Āmrapālī presents the Buddha with a mango grove, Indra's visit to the Buddha in the Indraśālaguhā, Conversion of the Yakṣa Āṭavika and Offering of the monkey.

See 1) Alfred Foucher, *L'Art gréco-bouddhique du Gandhâra: étude sur les origines de l'influence classique dans l'art bouddhique de l'Inde et de L'Extréme-Orient*, 2 Bde (Tome I, 1905; Tome II, 1, 1918; Tome II, 2, 1922; Tome II, 3, 1951), Paris: Imprimerie Nationale/ E. Leroux, 1905-51. I: 275, Fig. 139; 286, Fig. 145; 342, Fig. 175; 384, Fig. 194; 391, Fig. 197; 417, Fig. 210; 421, Fig. 212; 481, Fig. 242; 485, Fig. 243; 491, Fig. 245; 495, Fig. 247; 509, Fig. 252; 513, Fig. 254; 2) Humera Alam, *Gandhara Sculptures in Lahore Museum*, Lahore: Lahore Museum, 1998: 80-85.

[2] Abdur Rahman, "Excavation at Chatpat" , in: *Ancient Pakistan* (Bulletin of the Department of Archaeology, University of Peshawar), Vol. IV (1968-69), Plate 44.

in the cave (Indraśālaguhā), a most popular subject and motif in the Buddhist art of Gandhāra. The earliest surviving Gandhāran depiction of Indra's visit to the Buddha can be dated to the late first or early second century AD, while the tradition reached its height in the third century[1]. On the basis of structure and composition, the Gandhāran reliefs depicting the scene of the Indraśālaguhā may be divided into two types. In the first type, *guhā* (the cave) the Buddha sits occupies the right-hand section of the composition, while around the rim of the cave opening is carved with a flame pattern. Above the cave are carved deer or goats or similar animals, while burrows beneath the cave contain bears, lions and so on. The pañcaśikhin harpist, Indra and other protagonists are all carved to the right of the cave. The harpist standing by the cave is depicted with buns of curly hair, holding a *konghou* stringed instrument (harp) in his hands; a skirt or *dhoti* covers his lower body, but the upper body is left bare (fig.5). In the second type, the cave is carved at the centre of the composition, the harpist is still placed at the right of the cave while Indra has moved over to the left; in other words, Indra and his harpist are arranged symmetrically on both sides of the cave. In this very type, the carvers added to the original two visitors minor deities, animals and trees which are arranged in horizontal registers or bands around the cave's exterior (fig.6). Moreover, the Buddha within the cave is shown sidewise or frontally, but in both types of composition is depicted in meditation[2]. The relief discovered in Chatpat, however, belongs to the first type. The interior depiction of the cave is more realistic: the Buddha is represented with both shoulders covered and seated on a pedestal inside the cave. The harpist, Indra and two figures are all depicted to the right of the cave; no animals are visible above and below the cave. In short, this is a primitive representation of such a subject in Gandhāra.

---

[1] 1) Chongfeng Li, *opere citato* (*Kezi'er zhongxinzhuku...*): 213; 2)Chongfeng Li, "Gandhāra, Mathurā and Buddhist Sculptures of Mediaeval China", in: *Glory of the Kushans: Recent Discoveries and Interpretations*, ed. Vidula Jayaswal, New Delhi: Aryan Books International, 2012: 378-391, esp. 379-380.

[2] 1) Alfred Foucher, *opere citato*, I: 492-497; 2) Chongfeng Li, *opere citato* (*Kezi'er zhongxinzhuku...*): 213-215, 230.

The right scene in the panel depicts the Buddha in *Parinirvāṇa.* The representation of the Buddha in *Parinirvāṇa* "was one of the earliest and most familiar subjects of Gandhāra art" [1]. Among the many *Parinirvāṇa* scenes known to us, the oldest might be the one from the Guides' Mess Collection (fig.7). "In this composition—the earliest that has survived but by no means the first of its kind" [2], the Buddha is shown lying on a couch in the centre, with a richly decorated cloth covering the mattress. The artist has made a brave effort to disclose the lines of the form of the reclining Buddha beneath the folds of the monk's robe and to make it appear as if the dead Buddha were sleeping relaxed and peaceful on his side. Near the head of the couch stands a bearded Vajrapāṇi, with his hand holding the thunderbolt. At the foot of the couch, one may still see the outline of a standing figure, probably Mahākāśyapa, who rushed to the funeral pyre after he learned that the Buddha had been dead for a week. In front of the couch, three monks can be seen sitting on the ground, expressing their feelings of grievous loss in different ways. Behind the couch, four princely personages, likewise in attitudes of sorrow, are perhaps the Malla chieftains, nobles of Kuśīnagara. To complete the scene, two *śāla* trees were added to the background, with dryads or tree-spirits ensconced among their foliage [3].

Scenes of the same subject depicted later follow the principle of this basic composition, but decorative elements and additional figures have been added, although the effect is more natural and spontaneous in the earlier works. In all these interpretations, the basic elements were firmly established by tradition and unalterable, namely, the Buddha lays stretched at full length on his couch, with the mourners around him. In the treatment of the individual figures and their grouping, however, there was plenty of space for the imagination and skill of the

---

[1] John Marshall, *Buddhist Art of Gandhāra: The Story of the Early School; its birth, growth and decline*, London: Cambridge University Press, 1960: 54.

[2] John Marshall, *opere citato*: 49.

[3] 1) A. Foucher, *opere citato*, Tome I: 557, Fig.276; 2) Harald Ingholt, *Gandhāran Art in Pakistan*; *With* 577 *illustrations photographed by Islay Lyons and 77 pictures from other sources, Introduction and Descriptive Catalogue by Harald Ingholt*, New York: Pantheon Books, 1957: 92-93; 3) John Marshall, *opere citato*: 49-50.

artist. Thus, there are some differences between this relief and later versions of the same scene[1]. In the relief excavated in Chatpat, we may recognize Subhadra sitting in front of the couch, a *vajrapāṇi* standing at the head of the couch; Mahākāśyapa is shown going down on one knee at the foot of the couch, with his hands gently stroking the feet of the Buddha; the *devas* and the Malla chieftains as well as the *śāla* trees are also visible in the background.

Sculpture No. W. T. G. 6, a long panel kept in the Archaeological Museum at Taxila, used to belong to the Wah collection[2]. It also consists of two scenes, divided by a Corinthian pilaster (fig.8).

The left scene of the panel shows a Bodhisattva along with princely figures and worshippers. The Bodhisattva, who has the attributes of Maitreya, the future Buddha, is seated cross-legged on a draped throne. The haloed Bodhisattva is shown in an unusual coiffure, with locks of long curly hairs descending over his shoulders. The face of the Bodhisattva is defaced and his features are not discernible. His right hand is raised up originally in the *abhaya-mudrā,* but now is broken from the forearm; his left hand is placed on his lap and holds a water flask between the index finger and central finger, which has been severely damaged. The Bodhisattva is shown in princely attire: dressed in *uttarīya* leaving his right shoulder bare and covering the lower body; he also wears a flat neckband and a long supple necklace. The throne is covered with a cloth with tassels on the pleated ends and hanging down between the lion figures; in front of the throne there is a footstool. The baldachin over the throne is supported by tapering columns of the Indo-Corinthian type, with their bases showing a lion *affronté* or frontal. On either side of the Bodhisattva a princely figure is seated on a high couch in European fashion, his feet placed on a footrest and facing towards the Bodhisattva. Both princely figures wear the *uttarīya*, adorned with neckband and long necklace made of a flexible chain studded with gems at intervals. Behind

[1] Chongfeng Li, *opere citato* (Representation of the Buddha's *Parinirvāṇa*...)：59-81.

[2] Muhammad Ashraf Khan et al, *A Catalogue of the Gandhāra Stone Sculptures in the Taxila Museum*, Islamabad: Department of Archaeology and Museums, Government of Pakistan, 2005, Vol. I: 105-107, Vol. II: 34, Plate 45.

each is a standing figure in *añjali-mudra*, dressed in *uttarīya* and *paridhāna* and adorned with ear pendants and neckband. Above are two balconies each with busts of figures. This scene is generally acknowledged to be Maitreya in Tuṣita[1]. In addition, a relief that has a similar scene (fig.9a) was excavated from Dharmarājikā, Taxila[2], whose main figure has been identified as Maitreya by most scholars[3], and another relief kept in the Archaeological Museum at Dir (fig.9b) seems to depict such a narrative as well[4].

The right scene of the panel depicts the Buddha in *Parinirvāṇa*. This composition is more complicated than that of the relief excavated at Chatpat, Chakdara. In the centre of the composition the Buddha is lying on the couch as usual, with the drapery covering his whole body including his left hand and two feet. A large *uṣṇīṣa* fastened with a band at its base is quite obvious, under his right hand is a high pillow. At the foot of the couch, two figures are depicted talking to each other; they may be Ānanda and Subhadra. According to the *sūtra*, Ānanda politely declined Subhadra who hoped to view the Buddha personally. In front of the couch, a figure with his right leg bent below the body and the left leg stretched out to the side might be Ānanda who is almost falling to the ground on account of his deep grief over the Buddha's *Parinirvāṇa*; a meditating figure beside him, with his head wrapped and the whole body covered, might be

---

[1] Akira Miyaji, "Death of Buddha (*Nirvāṇa*) and Maitreya Bodhisattva", in: ブッダ展——大いなる旅路 / *Buddha: The Spread of Buddhist Art in Asia,* ed. Tobu Museum of Art et al, Tokyo: NHK (Japan Broadcasting Corporation) and NHK Promotions, 1998: 125; 2) Muhammad Ashraf Khan et al, *opere citato,* Vol. I: 106-107.

[2] John Marshall, *Taxila: An illustrated account of archaeological excavations carried out at Taxila under the orders of the government of India between the years* 1913 *and* 1934, London: Cambridge University Press, 1951, Vol. II: 712-713, Vol. III: Plate 217, No. 93.

[3] 1) John Marshall, *opere citato (The Buddhist Art of Gandhāra...)*: 79; 2) Tissot, Francine, *Gandhâra*, 2e éditon revue et corrigée; Dessins d'Anne-Marie Loth et de l'auteur, Paris: Librairie d'Amérique et d'Orient/Jean Maisonneuve, 2002: 101, Fig. 239; 3) Kurt Behrendt, "Reuse of Images in Ancient Gandhara", in: *Gandhāran Studies*, ed. M. Nasim Khan, Vol. 2: 17-38, esp. 23, k.

Harald Ingholt holds that this scene represents "the Gods exhort Siddhārtha to renounce the world". Harald Ingholt, *opere citato*: 58, Plate 37.

[4] Seoul Arts Center ed., *The Exhibition of Gandhara Art of Pakistan,* Seoul: Joong-Ang Ilbo, 1999: 156.

Subhadra, the last disciple whom the Buddha converted. At the head of the couch are a nude figure and a figure with drapery covering his shoulders, they may be identified as an *ajīvaka* and Mahākāśyapa separately, the former appears to tell the news of the Buddha's *Parinirvāṇa* to the latter[1].

These two reliefs clearly show that both the composition of Indra's visit to the Buddha in conjunction with the Buddha's *Parinirvāṇa* and that of the Buddha's *Parinirvāṇa* in combination with Maitreya's manifestation and preaching in Tuṣita Heaven are definitely component parts of a fixed iconological scheme in the Buddhist art of Gandhāra.

As a Buddhist center of Chinese Central Asia, Kucha which lies midway between Gandhāra and China proper (fig.10) should have shared its great neighbor's enthusiasm for the 'historic' Buddha and Buddha-to-be. As a result, balancing the Buddha-to-be vis-à-vis the 'historic' Buddha is a visual innovation in the iconography of the Kucha caves. The main image in the niche carved in the façade of the mushroom-shaped *stūpa* in the *chētiyaghara* is Śākyamuni who would answer Indra's questions related to 42 matters[2], while in the lunette above the entrance, opposite to the main image, is shown Maitreya's manifestation and preaching in Tuṣita[3]. This pictorial program and arrangement indicate that the latter is the spiritual heir of Śākyamuni Buddha[4]. From the perspective of Buddhist ritual, moreover, the Buddha's *Parinirvāṇa* depicted or sculpted on the rear wall of the back corridor or the rear chamber clearly forms a set or a fixed iconological scheme with the Buddha in the *Indraśālaguhā* on the façade of the *stūpa* and Maitreya's manifestation and preaching in Tuṣita Heaven

---

[1] 1) Akira Miyaji, *ibidem*; 2) Muhammad Ashraf Khan et al, *opere citato*: 105-106.

[2] Chongfeng Li, *opere citato* (*Kezi'er zhongxinzhuku...*): 210.

[3] The lunette above the entrance of the *chētiyaghara* is connected with the barrel vaulted ceiling of the main chamber. Maitreya who sits in the lunette seems to suggest his being in Tuṣita Heaven, because the middle of the barrel vault is depicted with celestial beings such as the sun-god and moon-god in the sky. In this case, Maitreya depicted in the lunette of the Kucha *chētiyaghara* is absolutely the Buddha-to-be in the heaven.

[4] *Zhuanlunshengwang xiuxing jing* [转轮圣王修行经, *Sūtra on the Wheel-turning Sage-king's Practice* or *Cakkavattisīhanādasutta*], fascicle 6 of the Chinese *Dīrghāgama*, in: *Taishō,* No. 1, Vol. 1: 39-42, esp. 41c-42a.

portrayed in the lunette above the entrance. Once a believer or a pilgrim enters a *chētiyaghara*, the scene of the Indraśālaguhā greets him right away, as if the Buddha is ready to answer the viewer's questions[1]; then, the scenes of the Buddha's preaching on the lateral walls along with the narrative stories such as *jātaka* and *avadāna* on the ceiling will also catch his attention. At this time, the believer or the pilgrim is very eager to circumambulate the mushroom-shaped *stūpa* and to worship the Buddha's *Parinirvāṇa.* As soon as he has completed the circumambulation and the worship and returned to the main chamber, he will immediately behold Maitreya in the lunette who will help him in strengthening his belief. Therefore, this joint iconological arrangement, namely, the Indraśālaguhā and the Buddha's *Parinirvāṇa* along with Maitreya's manifestation and preaching in Tuṣita (fig.11), reflects the wish of monks, pilgrims and worshippers; they based their faith on the relics and the dharma after the Buddha's *Parinirvāṇa*, upon their demise they will be reborn in Tuṣita Heaven in the presence of Maitreya[2]. This linked program and scheme not only is identical to the sequence of the *sūtra* narrative, but is also consistent with the rituals and the highest worship that Buddhist followers should carry on in the *chētiyagharas*. Both "the *Indraśālaguhā* in conjunction with "the *Parinirvāṇa*" and the "Buddha's *Parinirvāṇa* in combination with Maitreya's manifestation in Tuṣita" were basically designed after the prototypes of Gandhāra and principally derived from variant vernacular *sūtras* corresponding to the Chinese *Dīrghāgama*[3]. As a result, they became a standard iconological scheme in the *chētiyagharas* of Chinese Central Asia, which spread in wide areas and continued to be used for a long time. Furthermore, the style of the Buddhist images in Kucha must be regarded as

[1] The scene of the *Indraśālaguhā* was very popular in ancient Kucha, not only was it carved on the façade of the *stūpa* in the *chētiyaghara*, but also built in the free standing monastery and temple or even in the Buddha-cell of believer's privately owned house, such as a wooden niche showing scene of *Indraśālaguhā* kept in the Asian Art Museum in Berlin (Fig. 12).

[2] Akira Miyaji [宫治昭], *Nehan to Miroku no zuzōgaku: Indo kara Chūō Ajia e* [涅槃と弥勒の図像学——インドガら中央アジアへ, *Iconology of Parinirvāṇa and Maitreya: from India to Central Asia*], Tokyo: Yoshikawa Kōbunkan, 1992: 512-517.

[3] Chongfeng Li, *opere citato* (*Kezi'er bufen zhongxinzhuku...*): 419-431.

having been directly related to that of Gandhāran sculpture and having evolved, no doubt, from Gandharan prototypes[1]

(This paper was presented to the International Seminar on *Historical, Cultural and Economic Linkages between India and Xinjiang Region of China*: *New Challenges and Opportunities* held at ICSSR, New Delhi on 3-4 May 2011, by Himalayan Research and Cultural Foundation.)

---

[1] Albert Grünwedel believed that the fragmented colossal Buddha statue excavated by his team at a ruined temple site near Kumtura was stylistically related to the "Typus der Buddhastatue des Königs Udayana" or "Typus des Udayanabuddha". And, a colossal Buddha image of the "Typus der Buddhastatue des Königs Udayana" or "Typus des Udayanabuddha" was copied and set up in the façade of the *stūpa*-pillar in cave 44 at Kiriś (Simsim). See Albert Grünwedel, *opere citato*: 6-8, 182, 186, 201.

三、北方佛寺：

中土弘通

从犍陀罗到平城：以地面佛寺布局为中心

云冈石窟位于北魏都城平城（今山西大同）之西30里的武州山南麓，窟龛鳞次栉比，东西绵延约2里，现存编号洞窟45座；石窟由北魏皇室创立，史称武州山石窟寺[1]，“雕饰奇伟，冠于一世”，成为当时北魏领域内开凿石窟所参考的典型[2]。

一、武州山上寺址

1938-1940年，日人水野清一主持了云冈第8-10窟和第16-20窟的窟前遗址的发掘，参与者有小野胜年和日比野丈夫。由于当时怀疑石窟所在冈上曾建地上寺院，小野胜年与日比野丈夫1940年秋在云冈冈上，即西部台上和东部台上做了考古勘探。其中，西部台上的勘探，始于1940年10月30日，同年11月14日结束，所挖探沟大体呈H形。当时日本人没能探出一清楚的建筑平面，不过可以肯定的是，北魏时期石窟所在冈上曾建地上寺院，即遗存至今的“西部台上寺址”和“东部台上寺址”。这次发掘出土的若干建筑材料颇为重要，如莲花瓦当、“传祚无穷”瓦当以及涂饰绿釉的板瓦和指纹板瓦等[3]。

2010年，为了配合云冈石窟的防渗水工程，山西省考古研究所会同云冈石窟研究院及大同市考古研究所联合发掘了云冈石窟所在西部冈上遗址（位于第39窟西

[1] 陈垣《记大同武州山石窟寺》，载《陈垣学术论文集》第一集，北京：中华书局，1980年，第398-409页。

[2] 宿白《平城实力的集聚和“云冈模式”的形成与发展》，载宿白《中国石窟寺研究》，北京：文物出版社，1996年，第114-144页。

[3] 水野清一《雲岡發掘記 1&2》，載水野清一、長廣敏雄《雲岡石窟：西曆五世紀における中國北部佛教窟院の考古學的調查報告》；東方文化研究所調查，昭和十三年至昭和二十年，京都：京都大學人文科學研究所，第七卷，本文（1952年）第57-68、123-129頁，第29-56圖；第十五卷，本文（1955年）第91-99、185-190頁，第50-53、56-107圖。

南上方），主持人为张庆捷，发掘面积达 3600 平方米。发掘者认为：这是一处佛寺遗址，地层堆积可分现代、明清、辽金和北魏等 4 层。其中北魏文化层中残存一组较完整的寺院遗迹，包括中央佛塔及其北、东、西侧的僧房（图 1、2）。

佛塔位于长方形庭院中央，周围环绕回廊，回廊后为僧房。佛塔仅存塔基，平面方形，边长约 14 米，残高 0.35-0.7 米，南面正中有一斜坡踏道，宽 2.1 米，长 5 米，据此可通塔基顶部。塔基顶部或塔基内未发现舍利函或地宫（图 3）。

长方形庭院的北、东、西侧原来各有一排廊房。北侧廊房遗迹东西长 61.5 米，由 15 间僧房组成，其中 13 间建于北魏，余 2 间为辽金时期在北魏原址上重建。北魏僧房有的设计复杂，似套间，最大者面阔 7.4 米，进深 3.4 米。房墙为夯筑，厚 0.65-0.85 米不等。有些房内残存土炕、灶坑及烟道等。僧房前残存石质柱础 11 个，表明房前接建廊道，即前廊后室结构（图 4）。西侧廊房遗迹，南北残长 13.5 米，东西宽 5.9 米，现存房址 2 座，房前残存柱础 1 个，表明其布局与北侧廊房相同。东侧廊房遗迹，南北残长 18 米，东西宽 4.4 米，现存房址 3 座。中央佛塔及北、东、西侧僧房及廊道的上部建筑早已塌毁，原貌不清。另外，遗址南部破坏严重，没有发现门址或廊房遗迹。

这次发掘出土的遗物，主要为北魏建筑材料，数量庞大，重要者有莲花瓦当、“传

图 1　云冈石窟西部冈上遗址

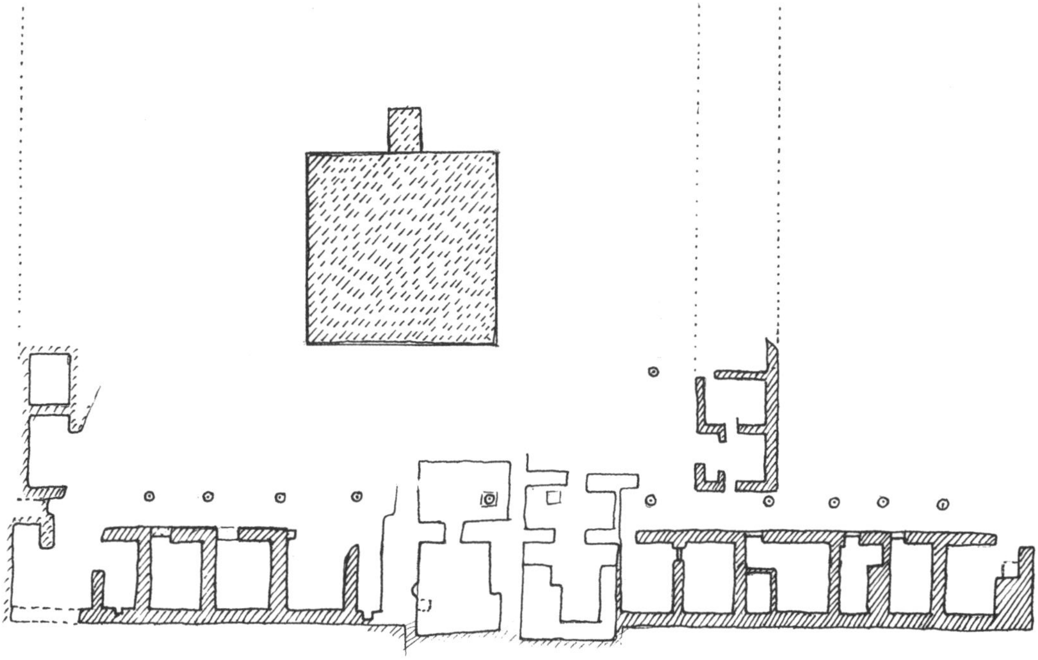

图 2 云冈石窟西部冈上遗址平面示意图

图 3 云冈石窟西部冈上遗址中央塔基

图 4 云冈石窟西部冈上遗址北侧廊房

祚无穷”瓦当以及涂饰绿釉[1]之板瓦等。此外，在遗址中还发现了若干残石佛像和供养人像残件，以及一片戳有“西窟”字样的陶器[2]。

[1] 琉璃瓦乃当时珍稀之物。据《太平御览》卷一百九十三引《郡国志》：“朔州太平城，后魏［景］穆帝治也。太极殿琉璃台瓦及鸱尾，悉以琉璃为之。”这说明北魏宫殿已经使用了琉璃瓦，过去大同方山和云冈冈上曾有发现。这次在云冈石窟西部上方寺址中再次出土琉璃瓦，表明武州山石窟寺当时地位颇高。参见《太平御览》，影印宋本，北京：中华书局，1960 年，第 932 页。

[2] 本文关于云冈石窟西部冈上寺址的描述，主要依据张庆捷的简报。参见国家文物局主编《2010 中国重要考古发现》，北京：文物出版社，2011 年，第 127-130 页。

依金皇统七年（1147年）曹衍撰《大金西京武州山重修大石窟寺碑》，“西京大石窟寺（武州山石窟寺）者，后魏之所建也，凡有十名，一通示/通乐、二灵岩、三鲸崇、四镇国、五护国、六天宫、七崇教/崇福、八童子、九华严、十兜率……明元始兴通乐，文成继起灵岩，护国、天宫则创自孝文，崇福则成于钳尔，其余诸寺次第可知。复有上方一位石室数间，按《高僧传》云：孝文时天竺僧陁[1]番（翻）经之地也”[2]。因此，云冈石窟西部冈上发掘出土的遗址，疑为金碑所记武州山“上方一位石室数间”，乃武州山石窟寺之“天竺僧陁翻经之地”[3]。

二、犍陀罗佛寺布局

中国佛寺制度传自印度，以供奉舍利的浮图/塔为中心建置。云冈石窟冈上寺址的布局，证实文献记载塔最为时人关注。魏晋南北朝时期，塔通常含有寺院之意；故葛洪《字苑》云：“塔，佛堂也。”[4]汉文史料中多有建塔即建寺的记录[5]。

> （汉）哀帝元寿元年（前2年），博士弟子秦景宪受大月氏王使伊存口授浮屠经。中土闻之，未之信了也。后孝明帝夜梦金人，项有日光，飞行殿庭，乃访群臣，傅毅始以佛对。帝遣郎中蔡愔、博士弟子秦景等使于天竺，写浮屠遗范。愔仍与沙门摄摩腾、竺法兰东还洛阳……愔之还也，以白马负经而至，汉因立白马寺于洛城雍门西……自洛中构白马寺，盛饰佛图，画迹甚妙，为四方式。凡宫塔制度，犹依天竺旧状而重构之，从一级至三、五、七、九[6]。

---

[1] 关于僧陁，宋赵汝愚编《名臣奏议》卷八十《儒学门·释老》引元祐五年（1090年）十二月岑象求《上哲宗论佛老》云：“盖四方谓寺，为伽蓝；伽蓝者，华言所谓静住也，谓其徒为僧陁；僧陁者，华言所谓乞士也。称其居为静住，目其人为乞士，则佛所以责其徒者何如哉？今不能精进戒律，笃修行业，而乃多求厚藏，享美馔、衣鲜衣，猎吾民之财，以奉其身，而严饰其居处，是大违戾其师之说也。”《四库全书》文渊阁本。

[2] 宿白《〈大金西京武州山重修大石窟寺碑〉校注——新发现的大同云冈石窟寺历史材料的初步整理》，载宿白《中国石窟寺研究》，北京：文物出版社，1996年，第52-75页。

[3] 参见：宿白，上引书，第65页［注一九］。2011年在云冈石窟东部冈上的考古发掘，大约位于第5、6窟上方，出土一座塔基遗址，但周匝似不见僧房遗迹。参见《云冈窟顶再次发现佛寺遗址》，刊2011年12月6日《中国佛教新闻网》。

[4] 玄应《一切经音义》卷六《妙法莲华经音义》，见《一切经音义三种校本合刊》，徐时仪校注，上海：上海古籍出版社，2008年，第129页。

[5] 宿白《东汉魏晋南北朝佛寺布局初探》，载宿白《魏晋南北朝唐宋考古文稿辑丛》，北京：文物出版社，2011年，第230-247页。

[6]《魏书·释老志》，点校本，北京：中华书局，1974年，第3025-3026、3029页。

天竺乃我国古代对今南亚次大陆之旧称[1]。法人沙畹认为，“印度佛教圣地有二：一在辛头河流域，一在恒河流域。中夏巡礼之僧俗多先历辛头，后赴恒河；盖中印通道中，直达中印度之尼泊尔(Népal)一道，在唐代以前似尚不知有之。常循之路，盖为葱岭(Pamirs)，南达克什米尔(Çachemire)与乌苌之路。有不少巡礼之人，如宋云、惠生之徒者，且不远赴中印度，而以弗楼沙国或呾叉尸罗(Taksaçila)为终点也。乾陀罗在佛教传播中夏中任务重大之理，盖不难知之矣”[2]。

克什米尔及乌苌等地，乃中国史书所记之罽宾[3]。关于罽宾的地域范围，学术界争议颇大[4]。虽然罽宾通常指今克什米尔地区，但至少从4世纪到6世纪初，它应包

---

[1] 有关天竺之称，参见：P. C. Bagchi “Ancient Chinese Names of India”, in: *India and China: Interactions through Buddhism and Diplomacy; A Collection of Essays by Professor Prabodh Chandra Bagchi,* compiled by Bangwei Wang and Tansen Sen, Delhi: Anthem Press India, 2011: 3-11; 2) 钱文忠《印度的古代汉语译名及其来源》，载《十世纪前的丝绸之路和东西文化交流：沙漠路线考察乌鲁木齐国际讨论会(1990年8月19-21日)》，北京：新世界出版社，1996年，第601-611页。

[2] 沙畹《宋云行纪笺注》，冯承钧译，见冯承钧《西域南海史地考证译丛六编》，后收入冯承钧《西域南海史地考证译丛》第二卷，北京：商务印书馆，1995年，第7页。

[3] 关于罽宾，班固《汉书·西域传》云：“罽宾……民巧，雕文、刻镂，治宫室，织罽、刺文绣，好治食。”李延寿《北史·西域传》延续汉以降记载，谓“其人工巧，雕文、刻镂、织罽”。玄奘《大唐西域记》记录“迦湿弥罗国，旧曰罽宾，讹也”；道宣《续高僧传》明言：“迦湿弥罗国，即此俗常传罽宾是也，莫委罽宾由何而生？”。日人辛嶋静志认为：“罽宾”可能被用作俗语Kaśpīr的音译，Kaśpīr对应的梵语形式即Kaśmīra。不过，比利时魏查理推测：罽宾不一定是语音学逐译，它可能指外国人居住区域。罽宾之“罽”，应源自瀱，“宾”为外国人或客人；“罽宾”是指使用“瀱”的外国人。参见：1)《汉书》卷九十六《西域传》，点校本，北京：中华书局，1962年，第3884页；2)《北史》卷九十七《西域传》，点校本，北京：中华书局，1974年，第3229页；3) 玄奘《大唐西域记》，季羡林等校注，北京：中华书局，1985年，第320页；4) Samuel Beal, *Si-Yu-Ki—Buddhist Records of the Western World; Chinese Accounts of India,* translated from the Chinese of Hiuen Tsiang, London: Trubner, 1884: 188, Note 86; 5) Thomas Watters, *On Yuan Chwang's Travels in India,* London: Royal Asiatic Society, 1904-1905, Vol. I (1904): 259; 6) 道宣《续高僧传·玄奘传》，见《大正藏》第50卷，第449a页；7) P. C. Bagchi, “Ki-pin and Kashmir”, in: *India and China: Interactions through Buddhism and Diplomacy; A Collection of Essays by Professor Prabodh Chandra Bagchi,* compiled by Bangwei Wang and Tansen Sen, Delhi: Anthem Press India, 2011: 145-154; 8) 辛嶋静志《汉译佛典的语言研究》，载朱庆之主编《佛教汉语研究》，北京：商务印书馆，2009年，第33-74页；9) Charles Willemen, “Sarvāstivāda Developments in Northwestern India and in China”, in: *The Indian International Journal of Buddhist Studies,* (New Series in continuation of the *Indian Journal of Buddhist Studies,* Vol. X, Varanasi: B. J. K. Institute of Buddhist and Asian Studies) No. 2 (2001): 163-169, esp. 167.

[4] 参见：1) 列维、沙畹《罽宾考》，冯承钧译，见冯承钧《西域南海史地考证译丛七编》，后收入冯承钧《西域南海史地考证译丛》第二卷，北京：商务印书馆，1995年，第58-61页；2) 足立喜六《法顯傳：中亞、印度、南海紀行の研究》第二《法顯の蔥嶺通過の研究》第二節《罽賓考》，東京：法藏館，1940年，第275-283页；3) 白鳥庫吉《罽賓國考》，见白鳥庫吉《西域史研究》上，東京：岩波書店，1944年，第377-462页；4)W. W. Tarn, *The Greeks in Bactria and India,* Cambridge: Cambridge University Press, 1951: 469-473.

含古代的乌苌、呾叉始罗、犍陀罗和迦毕试[1]。罽宾历史上应“指西北印度，迦湿弥罗是其重要组成部分，但不是唯一部分”[2]。汉文史料中记载的罽宾，基本相当于今天学界所称之大犍陀罗(Greater Gandhāra)[3]或犍陀罗文化圈(Gandhāran cultural area)[4]。

据欧阳询《艺文类聚》卷七十六《内典部》征引支僧载《外国事》：“罽宾国在舍卫之西，国王民人悉奉佛；道人及沙门，到冬，未中前饮少酒，过中不复饭。”[5]魏晋南北朝时期，“罽宾多出圣达”[6]，当时中国与罽宾的往还非常频繁[7]。文献记载抵中土译经传法的罽宾高僧，如佛驮跋陀 / 觉贤、佛大什 / 觉寿、佛陀耶舍 / 觉明、昙摩密多 / 法秀、昙摩难提 / 法喜、昙摩蜱 / 法爱、昙摩耶舍 / 法明、求那跋摩 / 功德铠、弗若多罗 / 功德华、僧伽跋澄 / 众现、僧伽提婆 / 众天、僧伽罗叉及卑摩罗叉 / 无垢眼等，在《出三藏记集》中有明确记载；至于当时赴罽宾求法或游历的中土大德，则有法勇、智猛、智严等；著名高僧鸠摩罗什，更是几进罽宾[8]。由此可见两地佛教关系之密切。

罽宾，即大犍陀罗地区保存有丰富的佛教遗迹。迄今在罽宾发现的佛寺遗址中，没有任何寺址比塔赫特巴希(Takht-i-Bāhī)更为学界所知晓，也没有其他遗址像塔赫特巴希那样引发盗宝者的肆行挖掘或受到考古学家的高度重视。一直到前几年，巴

---

[1] 1) 李崇峰《西行求法与罽宾道》，刊《燕京学报》新21期(2006年)，第175-188页；2) Chongfeng Li, “Jibin and China as seen from Chinese Documents”, in: *Archaeology of Buddhism in Asia,* ed. B. Mani, New Delhi: Archaeological Survey of India (in press). 余太山认为：“汉代罽宾国应以乾陀罗、呾叉始罗为中心，其势力范围一度包括喀布尔河上游地区和斯瓦特河(Swāt)流域。”见余太山《塞种史研究》，北京：商务印书馆，2012年，第217页。

[2] Charles Willemen, *ibidem.*

[3] Richard Salomon, *Ancient Buddhist Scrolls from Gandhāra: The British Library Kharoṣṭhī Fragments,* Seattle: University of Washington Press, 1999: 3.

[4] 1) Charles Willemen, “Kumārajīva’s ‘Explanatory Discourse’ about Abhidharmic Literature”, in: *Kokusai Bukkyōgaku Daigaku-in Daigaku Kenkyū Kiyō*[国際仏教大学院大学研究紀要第12号(平成20年),*Journal of the International College for Postgraduate Buddhist Studies*], Vol. XII (2008): 37-83 (156-110), esp. 39 (154), 69 (124); 2) Charles Willemen, *Outlining the Way to Reflect*[思维略要法](T. XV 617), Mumbai: Somaiya Publications Pvt Ltd, 2012: 16.

[5] 欧阳询《艺文类聚》，汪绍楹校，上海：上海古籍出版社，1965年，第1294页。

[6] 僧佑《出三藏记集》，苏晋仁，萧錬子点校，北京：中华书局，1995年，第545页。

[7] 据2005年10月26日《中国文物报》，2005年9月，西安市北郊南康村村民在基建工程中，发现了一座北周墓葬。墓主李诞，婆罗门种，北魏正光年间(520-525年)自罽宾归到中土，保定四年(564年)薨于万年里，春秋五十九，死后被授邯州刺史，葬中乡里。它既是迄今国内发现的第一座婆罗门后裔之墓，也是中土有明确记载的第一座罽宾人之冢。这进一步说明，当时罽宾和中国除佛教外在其他方面也有密切往来。

[8] 1) 李崇峰《西行求法与罽宾道》，上引书，第175-188页；2) Chongfeng Li, *ibidem*.

基斯坦考古工作者仍在塔赫特巴希遗址周边区域进行系统的发掘工作。

塔赫特巴希遗址，位于巴基斯坦西北边境省马尔丹市北大约 13 公里处，即古代犍陀罗的中心。建筑遗迹保存在当地一座凸起山脉的北坡顶上，沿山顶东西绵延 1.5 公里（图 5a、5b、5c），最重要者是山脊北部的寺院遗迹，较山顶本身略低，且伸展到整个遗址的东部边界。19 世纪中叶以降，欧洲学者一直特别关注这处遗迹。1871 年，威尔彻 (F. H. Wilcher) 主持了该遗址中宗教遗迹部分的发掘；1875 年，坎宁安 (A. Cunningham) 发表了他调查塔赫特巴希遗址的详细报告[1]；1907-1908 年，斯普纳 (D. B. Spooner) 对这处遗址进行了系统的考古发掘[2]；1910-1911 年，哈格里夫斯 (H. Hargreaves) 再次对该遗址做了进一步清理[3]。坎宁安等三人分别发表的考古报告，皆附有相当完善的塔赫特巴希遗址平面测绘图（图 6a、6b、6c）。

根据上述报告并参考汉译佛典[4]，塔赫特巴希遗址中的佛寺遗迹主要包括浮图 / 塔 (stūpa)、僧坊 / 僧院 (vihāra)[5]、中庭 (central court)、布萨处 / 说戒堂 (uposathāgāra) 或讲堂 (prāsāda) 以及其他附属设施如院、仓、库、廊等。因其建于陡峭山坡之上，寺院围墙颇高，有些围墙外侧高达 18.29-24.38 米，但内侧不会高于 6.1 米。佛寺主入口似开在遗址南面。由入口到中庭西端，右转向东即可进入中庭之内。从平面图及图版中可以看出，中庭内奉献塔 (votive stūpa) 密布，三面环建较大佛龛 (chapel)；一条南北向砖铺道，穿过小塔及龛像联通塔院 (stūpa court) 与僧院 (vihāra court)。塔院与僧院之地面皆高出中庭，其中后者，即僧院通过一低矮踏道 (5 踏) 与中庭相连，前者与中庭间之踏道较高，共 15 踏。

经过 15 级高踏（第一踏道），向南进入塔院。院中央有一方形台基，基前尚存若干踏子，显然是主塔塔基，只是由于长期被人肆行盗掘，主塔早已残毁（图 7a）。塔院为长方形，进深 17.22 米，面阔 13.87 米。塔基方形，边长 6.25 米，现存三层，向上内倾、

---

[1] A. Cunningham, *Archaeological Survey of India: Report for the Year 1872-73* (1875)/ Volume V: 23-36, Pl. VI-X.

[2] D. B. Spooner, "Excavations at Takht-i-Bāhī", in: *Archaeological Survey of India: Annual Report 1907-08* (1911): 132-48, Pls. XL-L。

[3] H. Hargreaves, "Excavations at Takht-i-Bāhī", in: *Archaeological Survey of India: Annual Report 1910-11* (1914): 33-39, P. XVII-XXII.

[4] 本文关于僧伽蓝 / 佛寺各组成部分之名称，主要依据唐初道宣《四分律删繁补阙行事钞》拟定，因该书就四分广律加以删繁、补阙，叙述四分律之要义，兼采律学诸家之说，详述律行之故实、制规。参见《大正藏》第 40 卷，第 1-156 页。

[5] 据善无畏讲解、一行笔录之《大毗卢遮那成佛经疏》卷三《入漫荼罗具缘真言品》："僧坊，梵音毗诃罗，译为住处，即是长福住处也。白衣为长福故，为诸比丘造房，令持戒禅慧者，得庇御风寒暑湿种种不饶益事，安心行道。"《大正藏》第 39 卷，第 615c-616a 页。

a

b

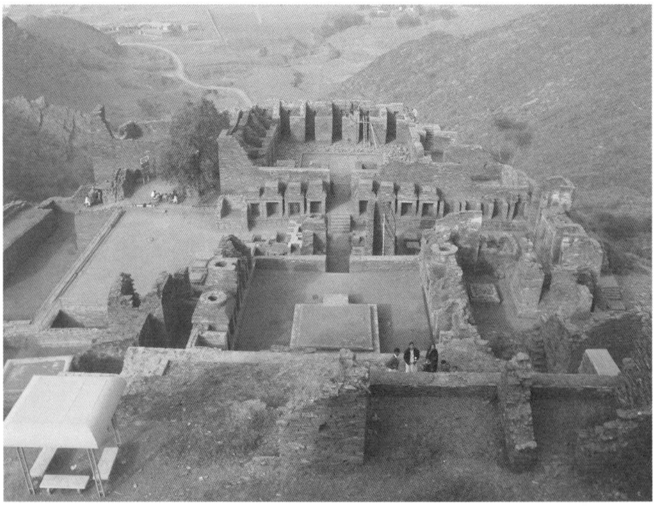

c

图 5a　塔赫特巴希佛寺遗址
　b　塔赫特巴希佛寺遗址中庭
　c　塔赫特巴希佛寺遗址

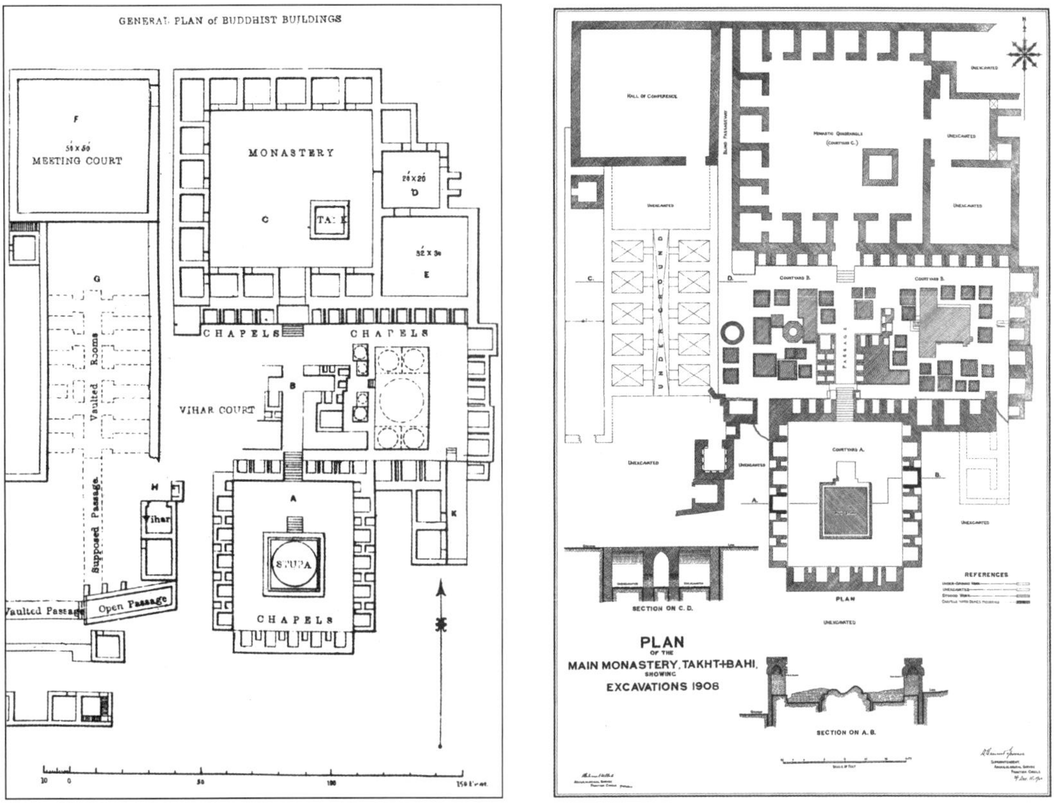

a　　b

图 6a　塔赫特巴希佛寺遗址平面图 (1873 年测绘)
　　b　塔赫特巴希佛寺遗址平面图 (1908 年测绘)

有收分，顶部 4.72 米见方，地面以上部分残高 2.6 米。塔基顶部原有右绕佛塔之礼拜道，北面中央置踏，正对塔院入口。塔院三面置佛龛，原来每面五座，每座佛龛外缘边长 2.44 米，皆向内敞开。依据现存遗迹，这些佛龛当初建造时，彼此间隔 0.86 米，均敞口。当塔院后来布满造像时，于每龛间补砌一横墙，形成类似佛龛的小神龛，故在东、南、西三面封闭了塔院。除了中庭西侧的低洼屋室外，整个塔赫特巴希遗址保存的上层建筑仅在塔院得以发现。即便在这里，也仅有两座半佛龛保存了原始屋顶。佛龛之顶以托臂 (corbels) 相承，呈穹顶，唯上部截平；穹顶之上另置环 / 系梁 (collar)，上托另一小穹顶，外观呈斜顶形，平面半圆状；外立面敞口形如三叶，上为蘑菇形小尖顶 (图 7b)。

中庭位于塔院与僧院之间，较两者地面低凹，东西长 35.36 米，南北宽 15.24 米。中庭的北、东、南三面建置佛龛，共 29 座。佛龛较窄，高 7.62-9.14 米。佛龛皆为独立式建筑，均面向中庭敞口；顶已塌毁，但原作穹顶无疑，类似于塔院中的那些。中庭内密布小型奉献塔，故有人称为“众塔之院”。从废墟中发现的诸多遗物推断，所有

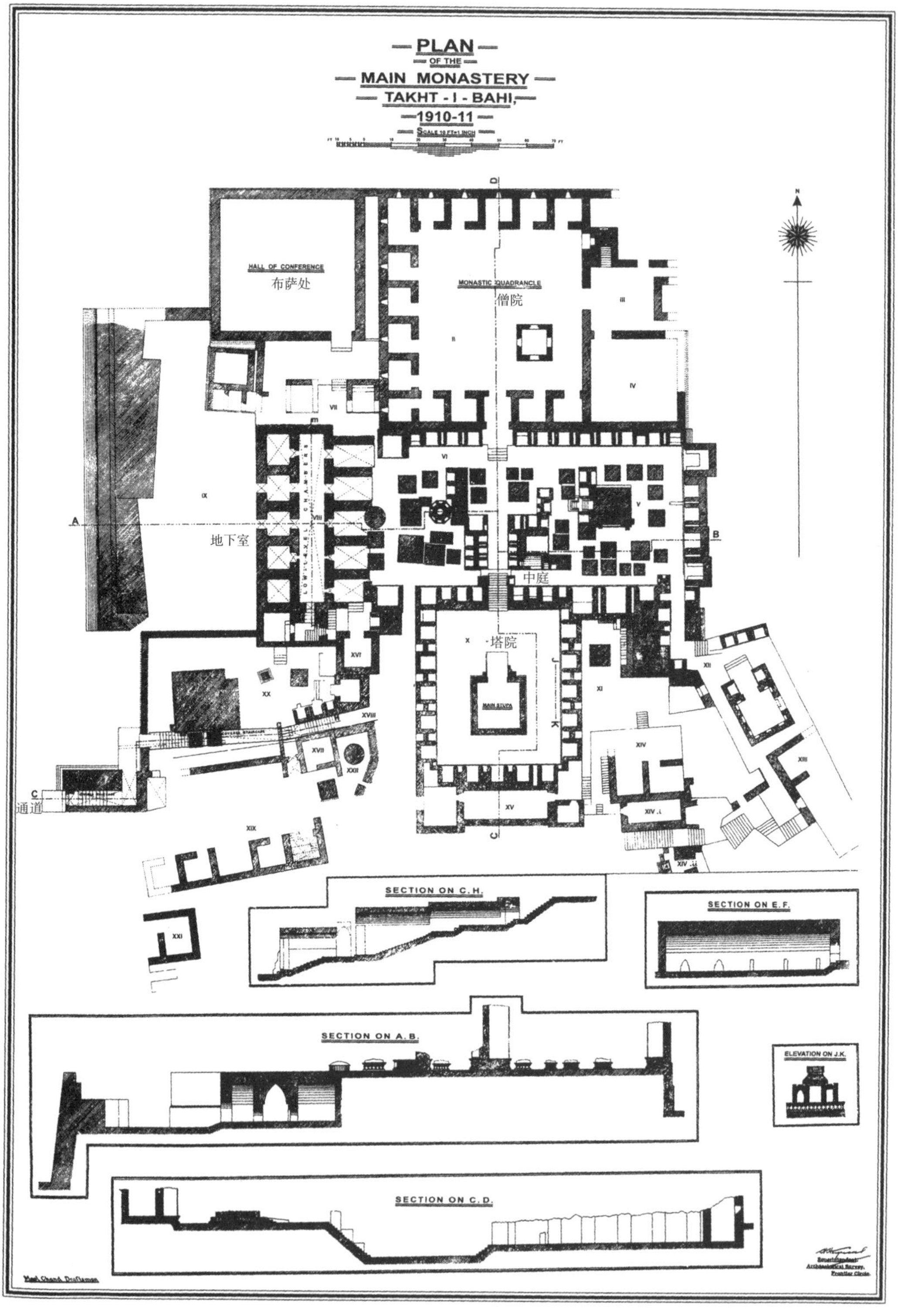

图 6c　塔赫特巴希佛寺遗址平面图 (1911 年测绘)

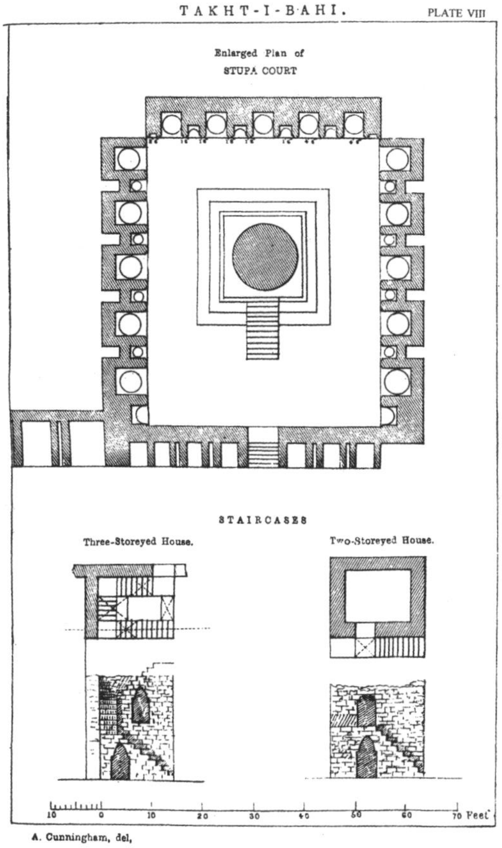

a

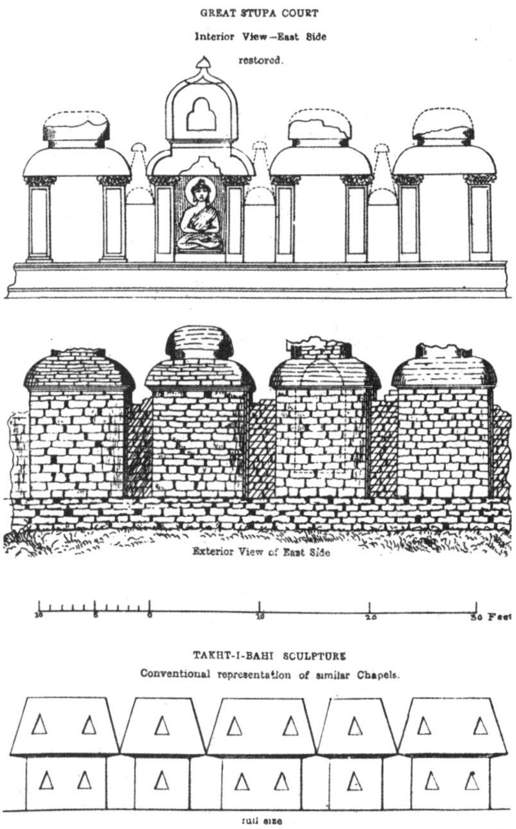

b

图 7a　塔赫特巴希佛寺遗址塔院平面图
　　b　塔赫特巴希佛寺遗址塔院周匝佛龛立面图

佛龛，或其中的绝大多数，原塑灰泥佛像。虽然其确切用途尚不明了，但中庭出土了极为丰富的石雕和泥塑。除了不成样子的残件和损毁严重无法辨识者外，仅 1907-1908 年在中庭发掘出土的石雕就多达 472 件，后来成为白沙瓦博物馆第 679 至 1151 号藏品，这还不包括当时出土的泥塑。塔赫特巴希遗址发现的大多数雕塑均出自中庭，雕塑通常表现佛陀，有时也用大幅构图浮雕佛传，具有不同的艺术价值（图 8）。

第二踏道与第一踏道对应，位于中庭北壁，通往僧坊 / 僧院。僧院地面略低于塔院，此前学者大多称其为隐修院或寺（monastic quadrangle 或 monastery）[1]。这座

[1] 据义净《大唐西域求法高僧传》卷上："毗诃罗是住处义，此云寺者不是正翻"。义净《大唐西域求法高僧传》，王邦维校注，北京：中华书局，1988 年，第 115 页。坎宁安当年撰写考古调查报告时，有时喜欢用僧坊 / 毗诃罗 (vihāra) 而不是英语的寺 (monastery) 来描述这种佛教建筑。参见：A. Cunningham, *Archaeological Survey of India*: *Report of a Tour in the Punjab in 1878-79* (1883), Volume IX: 12.

图 8　白沙瓦博物馆展示的塔赫特巴希佛寺遗址出土的佛教造像

僧院系一紧凑型单元，在整个佛寺中系体量最大的建筑。僧院方形，边长 18.9 米，共有 15 座僧房 (gābha) 置于南、西、北三面，每房进深 3.05 米，惟西北角一房较其他略宽，但进深相同。僧院东南部存一水池，其水源来自僧房顶上的排水。僧院东墙中央，有门通向一 6.1 米见方的房间——厨房。厨房北墙辟二门，一门通向另一小房，另一通往楼上；东墙两端各辟一门，皆通往室外，室外有二凸起扶壁，似为厕；南墙西侧有单门通往另一面阔 9.75 米、进深 9.14 米的大房——食堂。诸房舍屋顶皆不存，原为叠压式穹顶，但早已塌毁。

在遗址北部、紧靠僧院西侧，是一座较大的露天方院，边长 15.24 米，围墙高达 9.14 米，仅南壁东侧开一门道。关于这座方院，威尔彻推测它应为荼毗之所，坎宁安认为是僧伽集聚之处[1]，斯普纳根据傅塞 (M. Foucher) 之说推想它原作会堂[2]，笔者疑为汉译佛典之“布萨处”/“说戒堂”。布萨处的北墙和西墙自山坡起垒，迄今尚高耸。虽然这座方形建筑的内壁有灯龛若干，但墙上既无窗洞，地面也未发现任何椅座或其他小型建筑遗迹。它应是当初设计佛寺时专门辟出的僧团集合修道场所——布萨处[3]。单一门道与高墙，保证了隐避与静谧，除此之外很难想象它充当别用。

布萨处南侧，是 10 间所谓的“地下室”。实际上，这些房舍应称“低洼”屋室恰当，因为它们处于地面之下纯属偶然，不是真正的地下室。这些房舍的年代，较中庭为晚，因其倚中庭西墙而建，绝非砌合而成；顶为突拱结构，屋高 4.27 米，上覆厚泥，与中庭地面齐平 (图 9a)。坎宁安推测：这些房舍应为整个佛寺之库藏。

在“低洼”房舍之南，有另一方院及其下面通往山谷的梯道。其中，方院南墙下部的基坛上残存六身泥塑大立佛足迹，院中出土泥塑大佛头若干，故俗称“大像院”。(图 9b)

塔赫特巴希遗址中的佛寺遗迹[4]，堪称犍陀罗僧伽蓝或佛寺的典范。其中，塔院和僧院是最重要的组成部分。

位于乌苌国中心区的赛度・谢里夫 I 号 (Saidu Sharīf I) 佛教遗址，核心是“塔台 (Stūpa Terrace)”和“寺台 (Monastery Terrace)”[5]，分别表示塔院和僧院，是系统规划设计、毗邻建造而成的。其中，僧院位于塔院东侧，地面较后者略高，且呈现出与塔院确凿的同步地层及相继地面，两者以梯道相通 (图 10a)[6]。据主持该遗址发掘工作的多米尼克・法谦纳 (Domenico Faccenna，法琴纳) 研究，赛度・谢

[1] A. Cunningham, *Archaeological Survey of India*: *Report for the Year 1872-73* (1875): 23-36, esp. 32, Plate VII.

[2] D. B. Spooner, “Excavations at Takht-i-Bāhī” , in: *opere citato*: 134, Plate L.

[3] 据道宣《四分律删繁补阙行事钞》卷上《说戒正仪篇》，“中国布萨，说戒堂；至时便赴，此无别所，多在讲、食两堂。理须准承，通皆席地。中国有用绳床，类多以草布地，所以有尼师坛者，皆为舒于草上。此间古者有床，大夫已上，时复施安降斯，已下亦皆席地。东晋之后，床事始盛。今寺所设，率多床座，亦得双用，然于本事行时多有不便。”《大正藏》第 40 卷，第 35b 页。

[4] 1) A. Cunningham, *Archaeological Survey of India*: *Report for the Year 1872-73* (1875)/ Volume V: 23-36, esp. 26-33; 2) D. B. Spooner, “Excavations at Takht-i-Bāhī” , in: *opere citato*: 132-48; 3) H. Hargreaves, “Excavations at Takht-i-Bāhī” , in: *opere citato*: 33-39.

[5] Pierfrancesco Callieri, *Saidu Sharif I* (*Swat, Pakistan*) 1, *The Buddhist Sacred Area; The Monastery,* Rome: IsMEO, 1989: 3-141, esp. 4; Figs. 2-3.

[6] Domenico Faccenna, *Saidu Sharif I* (*Swat, Pakistan*) 2, *The Buddhist Sacred Area; The Stūpa Terrace,* Text, Rome: IsMEO, 1995: 143-163, esp. 145, Figs. 22-23.

a

b

图 9a　塔赫特巴希佛寺遗址布萨处及“地下房舍”顶部
　　b　塔赫特巴希佛寺遗址“大像院”

里夫 I 号遗址的宗教建筑，可能始建于公元 1 世纪，4 世纪时趋于衰微，5 世纪时废止[1]（图 10b、C）。

上述佛寺布局，不仅流行于犍陀罗和乌苌国，而且在呾叉始罗也备受欢迎，如焦莲（Jauliāñ）佛寺遗址。换言之，这种佛寺的设计，公元 2 世纪以降在罽宾地区一直盛行。据马歇尔（John Marshall）发掘报告，焦莲寺址（图 11）"包括一座中等规模之寺及其旁侧的二座塔院。二塔院的地平不同，南侧较高，北侧略低。此外，北侧塔院西边尚有一较小的方院与之衔接。主塔置于南侧高院，四周密布小塔；院四面所置佛龛，照例皆面向主塔。北侧低院及另一方院配置同样的小塔及佛龛。至于那座中等规模之寺，与莫赫拉·莫拉杜（Mohṛā Morādu）寺址的布局相同，方院周匝建置僧房；另外还有会堂、厨房及其他附属设施"[2]。实际上，马歇尔所称的"中等规模之寺"就是僧院，至于二塔院，系一座大型塔院的两个组成部分。高大浮图位于塔院南部中央，浮图周围和踏道两侧及前部密布奉献小塔、龛像等；塔院周匝建置高大佛龛。其僧院，与塔赫特巴希及赛度·谢里夫 I 号遗址的僧院相似，为两层建筑，水池、阴沟、灯龛、佛龛、经行石路及楼梯具备，布萨处 / 说戒堂、食堂、厨、仓、厕等设施完善。

这种僧伽蓝，与当时中土西行求法高僧所记罽宾佛寺的布局基本吻合。据《洛阳伽蓝记》卷五征引《惠生行记》、《宋云家记》及《道荣传》，乌苌"城北有陀罗寺，佛事最多，浮图高大，僧房逼侧，周匝金像六十躯"[3]。此外，道宣《四分律删繁补阙行事钞》卷下《主客相待篇》曰："客僧受房已，问主人已，应先礼佛塔。"[4]这说明：佛塔应为僧伽蓝之中心，僧房乃佛寺之必置；至于佛龛中的造像，更为信徒提供了良好的供养、礼忏之处。"若比丘独阿兰若处十五日，布萨时，应洒扫塔、寺、布萨处及中庭，

---

[1] 1) Francesco Noci et al, *Saidu Sharif I* (*Swat, Pakistan*) 3, *The Graveyard,* Rome: IsIAO, 1997: 107-111, esp. 111; 2) Domenico Faccenna, *opere citato*: 143-163, esp. 157-159.

[2] 1) John Marshall, *Excavations at Taxila: The Stūpas and Monastery at Jauliāñ; Memoir No. 7 of the Archaeological Survey of India,* Calcutta: Archaeological Survey of India, 1921: 3-19, esp. 3; 2) John Marshall, *Taxila*: *An illustrated account of archaeological excavations carried out at Taxila under the orders of the Government of India between the years 1913 and 1934,* London: Cambridge University Press, 1951, Volume I: 368-387.

[3] 杨衒之《洛阳伽蓝记》，周祖谟校释，北京：中华书局，1963 年，第 203 页。

意大利学者朱塞佩·图齐（Giuseppe Tucci）和多米尼克·法谦纳皆把斯瓦特的布特卡拉 I 号遗址（Butkara I）考定为陀罗寺。参见：1) Giuseppe Tucci, "Preliminary Report on an Archaeological Survey in Swāt", in: *East and West,* IX/4 (1958): 279-348, esp. 280, 288; 2) Domenico Faccenna, *Butkara I* (*Swāt, Pakistan*) *1956-1962,* Part 1, Text, Rome: IsMEO, 1980: 171-172.

[4]《大正藏》第 40 卷，第 142a 页。

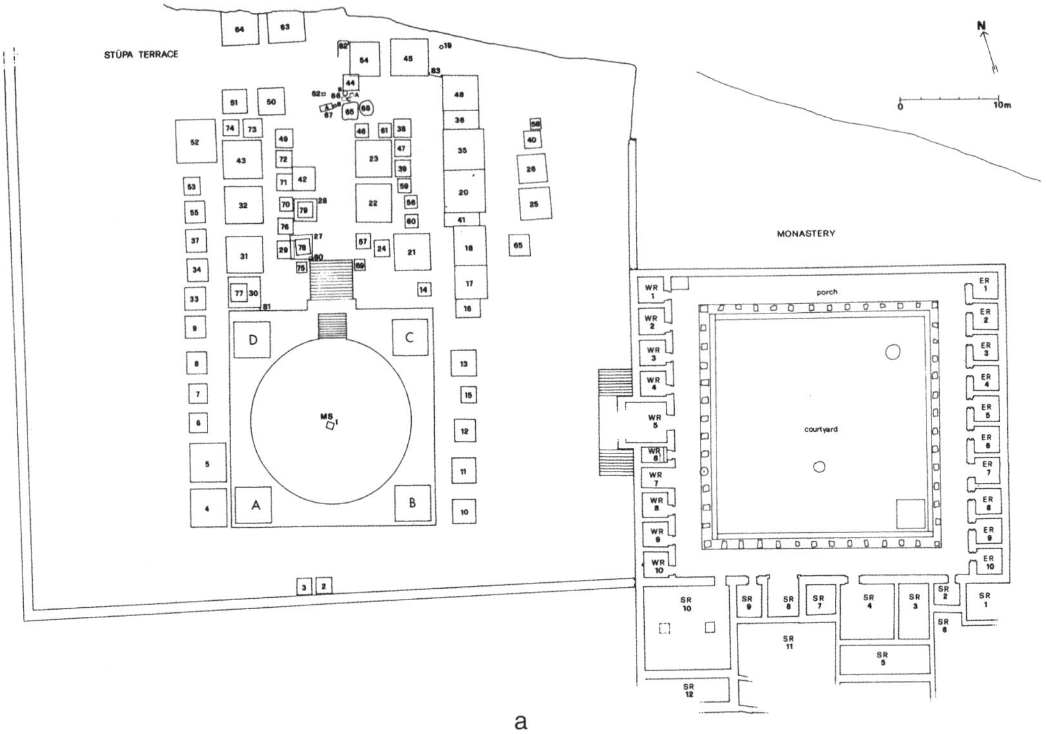

a

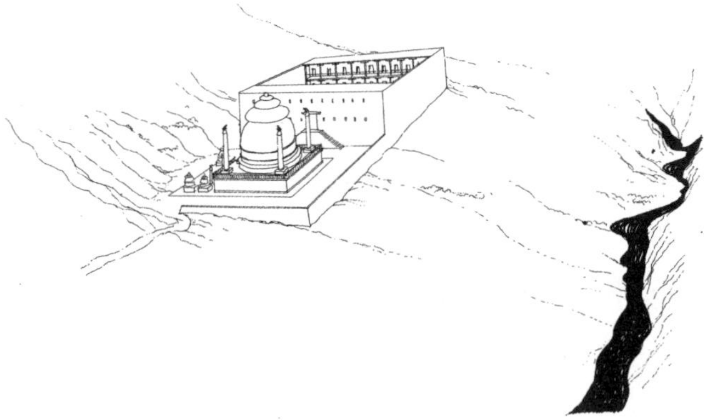

b

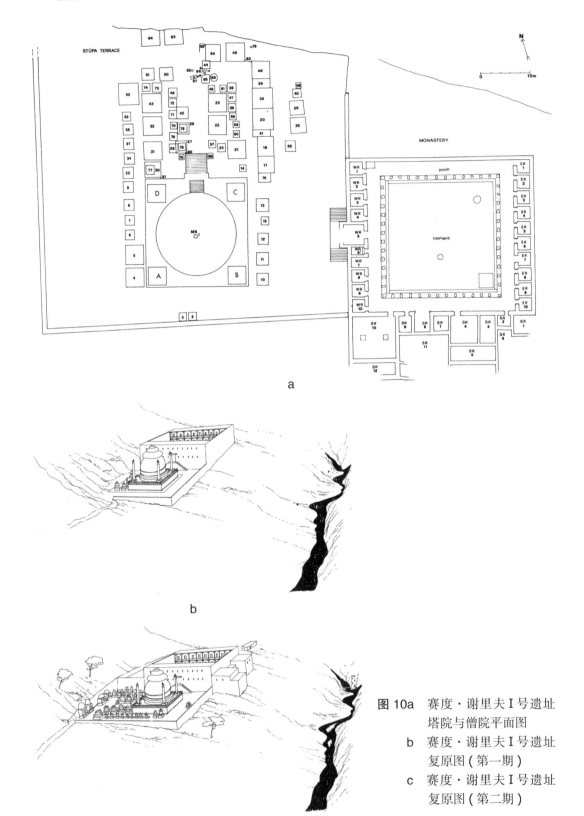

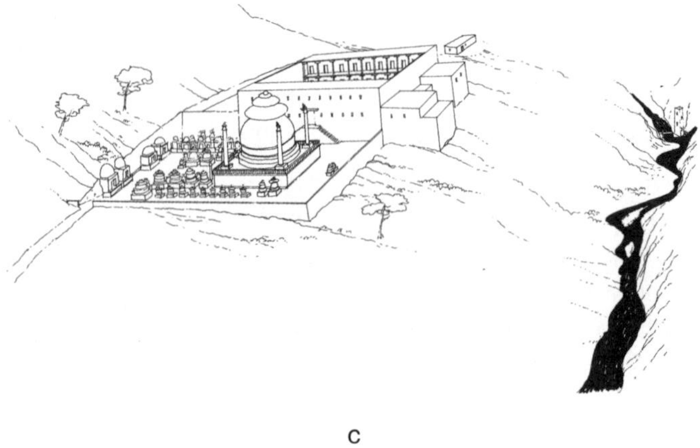

c

图 10a　赛度 · 谢里夫 I 号遗址塔院与僧院平面图
　　b　赛度 · 谢里夫 I 号遗址复原图（第一期）
　　c　赛度 · 谢里夫 I 号遗址复原图（第二期）

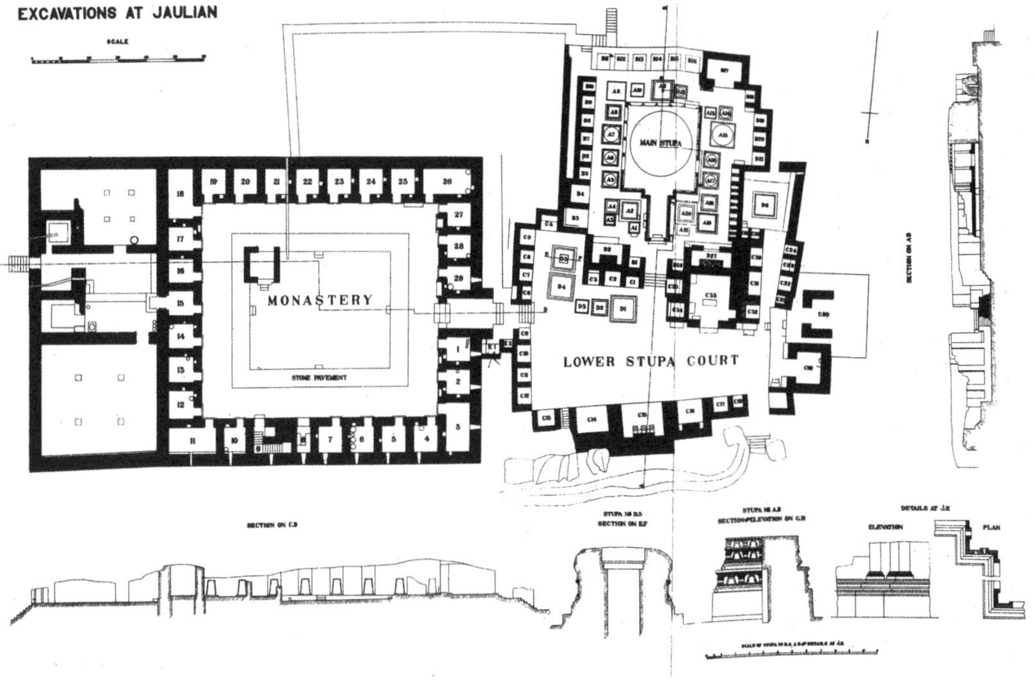

图 11　焦莲佛寺遗址平面图

次第敷座。”[1]因此，塔院、僧院、中庭及布萨处系一座大型僧伽蓝的基本组合。

依道世《法苑珠林》卷六十二《祭祠篇·献佛部》，“初立寺时，佛院、僧院各须位别。如似大寺，别造佛塔”[2]。法立与法炬共译《佛说诸德福田经》云：“佛告天帝：复有七法广施，名曰福田，行者得福，即生梵天。何谓为七？一者，兴立佛图、僧房、堂阁；二者……”[3]这里，把兴立佛图、僧房及堂阁置于福田七法之首，可见佛主对其极为重视。失译《菩萨本行经》卷中曰：“正使布施百辟支佛……所得功德，不如起塔、僧房精舍。”[4]另据吉迦夜与昙曜共译《杂宝藏经》卷五：“尔时王舍城，频婆娑罗王为佛造作浮图、僧房。有一长者……便于如来经行之处，造一讲堂，堂开四门。后时命终，生于天上……佛言：‘本在人中，造佛讲堂，由是善因，命终生天。’”[5]“尔时耆阇崛山南天竺有一长者，见频婆娑罗王为佛作好浮图、僧坊，亦请如来，为造浮图、僧房住处。其后命终生于天上……佛言：‘……由此善业，得生天上。’”[6]至于律藏，如佛陀

[1] 弗若多罗译《十诵律》卷五十六《比丘诵》，《大正藏》第 23 卷，第 411a 页。
[2] 道世《法苑珠林》，周叔迦、苏晋仁校注，北京：中华书局，2003 年，第 1831 页。
[3]《大正藏》第 16 卷，第 777b 页。
[4]《大正藏》第 3 卷，第 114c 页。
[5]《大正藏》第 4 卷，第 475c 页。
[6]《大正藏》第 4 卷，第 475c 页。

跋陀罗共法显译《摩诃僧祇律》和道宣《四分律删繁补阙行事钞》等皆推崇塔院与僧院。除了修行、礼忏之外，僧众每日"晨起……应当扫塔院、僧坊院"[1]。"晨起，扫塔院、僧院。"[2]"至布萨日，应扫塔及僧院。"[3]"若塔院、僧院内见不净者，应除去。"[4]"若作说戒，常法半月恒遵。每至说晨，令知事者点知僧众，谁在谁无？健病几人？几可扶来？几可与欲？如是知已，令拂拭塔庙、洒扫寺院。"[5]"若布萨日，扫塔、僧院。"[6]因而，"礼塔即礼佛"之传统思想和佛说兴造浮图与僧坊之善果，辅以严格之戒律，使天竺僧伽蓝中的塔院、僧院及讲堂等，在佛教信徒心目中占据着崇高地位。

除上述佛寺布局外，大犍陀罗地区发现的另外两处佛寺遗址亦值得注意。其中，一处是呾叉始罗的金迪亚尔(Jaṇḍiāl)B丘，另一处是呾叉始罗的毕钵罗(Pippala)废墟。

金迪亚尔B丘，亦称巴伯尔·汗纳(Babar-Khäna)塔寺，在坎宁安《呾叉始罗废墟图》中标为第40号遗迹，是一处塔寺遗址。浮图置于方院中央，旁侧出土若干房舍(图12a、12b)[7]。据马歇尔发掘报告，中央浮图始建于塞种·帕提亚(Śaka-Parthian)时期，3或4世纪时在原址上进行了重建。这处遗址最重要的特点，"是塔院北面和西面地基的特殊布局。浮图在塞种·帕提亚始建时，尚未出现庭院周匝对称设置成排小室(僧房)之法，后者乃晚期佛寺布局之特征。实际上，我们也不能肯定现存房舍那时曾被僧众居住过。Q、R、S那组可能用以起居，但东北角的大型建筑

[1]《摩诃僧祇律》卷二十五《明杂诵跋渠法》，《大正藏》第22卷，第429b页。

[2]《摩诃僧祇律》卷二十五《明杂诵跋渠法》，《大正藏》第22卷，第433a页。

[3]《摩诃僧祇律》卷二十七《明杂诵跋渠法》，《大正藏》第22卷，第450b页。

[4]《摩诃僧祇律》卷三十四《明威仪法》，《大正藏》第22卷，第504c页。

[5]《四分律删繁补阙行事钞》卷上《僧网大纲篇》，《大正藏》第40卷，第23c页。

[6]《四分律删繁补阙行事钞》卷上《说戒正仪篇》，《大正藏》第40卷，第35a页。

[7] 1863年，坎宁安对这处遗址进行了第一次发掘。虽然他似乎仅发掘了晚期建筑遗迹，但发表的文字记录及测绘图(图12a)显示的塔院周匝建筑引起了学界的关注。"中央浮图直径约45英尺(13.72米)，周围环绕回廊，进深8英尺(2.44米)，从而形成了一座90英尺(27.43米)见方的庭院，其后为僧房。僧房每间进深$9\frac{1}{2}$英尺(2.9米)、面阔$14\frac{1}{2}$英尺(4.42米)。" 1) A. Cunningham, *Archaeological Survey of India: Four Reports made during the years 1862-63-64-65* (1872)/Volume I: 111-135, esp. 120-121, 132, Pl. LVII; 2) A. Cunningham, *Archaeological Survey of India: Report for the Year 1872-73* (1875)/Volume V: 74-75, Pl. XX.

不过，马歇尔认为坎宁安发表的文字记录及测绘图，富于想象力且会引人误入歧途。马歇尔在他自己的发掘报告(图12b)中写道：早期建筑遗迹"不足33英尺(10.06米)见方，南面有一踏道，中央是11×14英尺(3.35×4.27米)的地宫"。从僧院入口到塔基踏道，是一狭窄的石砌小道。"当这座早期浮图及其与之相连的建筑坍塌后，在其废墟上又建造了另一佛塔及另一组建筑。晚期佛塔的塔基呈圆形，直径35英尺(10.67米)。"参见：John Marshall, *Taxila: An illustrated account of archaeological excavations carried out at Taxila under the orders of the Government of India between the years 1913 and 1934*, London: Cambridge University Press, 1951, Volume I: 355-356; Volume III: Pls. 1, 91, 92a.

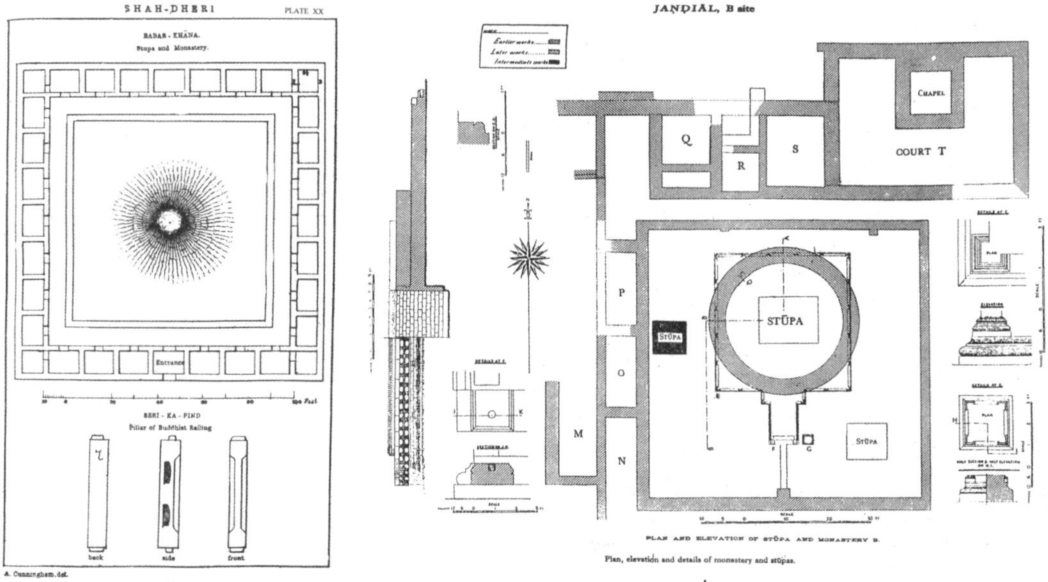

a　　　　　　　　　　b

图 12a　巴伯尔·汗纳塔寺（金迪亚尔 B 丘）遗址平面图
b　金迪亚尔 B 丘遗址平面图

T 显然是一露天方院，从其北墙中部朝院内伸出的小室，可能为佛堂。塔院西侧，乍看似乎有一组狭长房舍（N、O、P），实际上只是凸起的平台地基”[1]。

毕钵罗废墟亦分属两个时期。东侧部分为僧院，始建于帕提亚晚期或贵霜初，周匝建置僧房，中央方形塔基北向（图 13），西侧部分为后代在原址上重建[2]。

鉴于佛塔和僧坊系天竺早期辟地新建僧伽蓝 / 佛寺必不可缺的组成部分，这种僧伽蓝当时也称“塔寺”[3]。《杂宝藏经》卷五《长者夫妇造作浮图生天缘》曰：“舍卫国有一长者，作浮图、僧坊。长者得病，命终生三十三天。妇追忆夫，愁忧苦恼，以追忆故，修治浮图及与僧坊，如夫在时。夫在天上，自观察言：‘我以何缘生此天上？’知

[1] John Marshall, *opere citato*, Volume I: 356.

[2] 据马歇尔发掘报告，这座早期寺院“在 4、5 世纪之前已成废墟，因为那时在它西侧部分的上面又建起了另一寺院，其地基完全覆盖了西侧的古老廊房。与此同时，早期寺院的其余部分被改造成一座塔院，除了方院中央的浮图和周匝僧房的后墙，其余建筑一律被拆除、铲平，僧房的后墙因此变成了新院的围墙”。参见：John Marshall, *opere citato*, Volume I: 365-367, esp. 365; Volume III: Pls. 98a, 99a-b, 100a.

[3] 据慧琳《一切经音义》卷二十三引惠苑《新译大方广佛花严经音义》卷下，“盗塔寺物：塔，具云窣堵波（stūpa），谓置佛舍利处也。寺名依梵本中呼为鞞诃罗（vihāra），此云游，谓众生共游止之所也。《三苍》曰：寺，馆舍也。馆舍与游义称相近耳。又，《风俗通》曰：寺，司也。匡之有法度者也。今诸侯所止皆曰寺也。《释名》曰：寺，嗣也。治事者相继嗣于内也。今若以义立名，则佛弟子助佛杨化，住持正法同后三说。若直据梵本敌对而翻，则如初释也”。《大正藏》第 54 卷，第 453c 页。

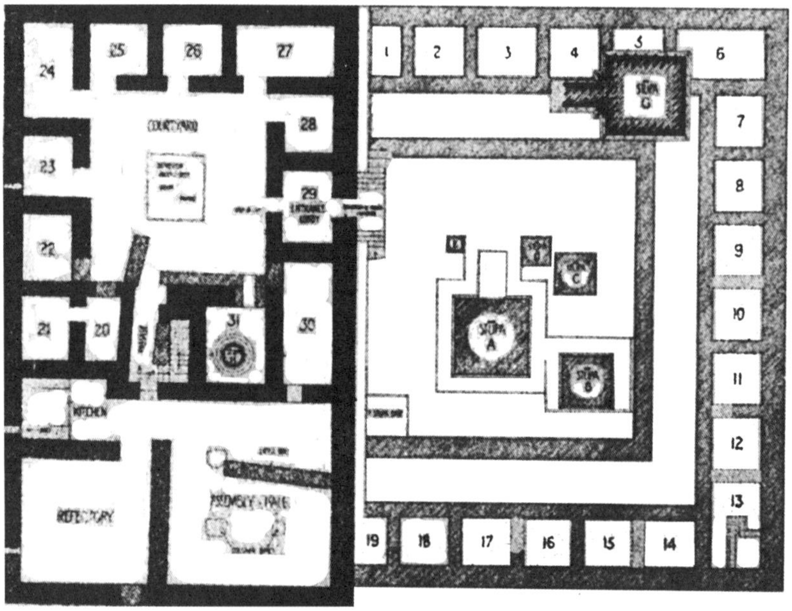

图 13　毕钵罗遗址平面图

以造作塔寺功德，是故得来。自见定是天身，心生欢喜，常念塔寺，以天眼观所作塔寺今谁料理？即见其妇，昼夜忆夫，忧愁苦恼，以其夫故，修治塔寺……供养佛僧，作众功德，发愿生天。其后命终，即生彼天宫。夫妇相将，共至佛边。佛为说法，得须陀洹。诸比丘等惊怪所以，便问：'何业缘故得生此天？'佛言：'昔在人中，作浮图、僧坊，供养佛僧。由是功德，今得生天。'"[1]据此，浮图与僧坊合称"塔寺"。另据《洛阳伽蓝记》卷五征引《惠生行记》、《宋云家记》及《道荣传》，"西行五日，至如来舍头施人处，亦有塔寺，二十余僧……至如来挑眼施人处，亦有塔寺……至如来为尸毗王救鸽之处，亦起塔寺"[2]。

三、平城佛寺渊源

《魏书·释老志》曰："和平初，师贤卒。昙曜代之，更名沙门统……昙曜白帝，于京城西武州塞，凿山石壁，开窟五所，镌建佛像各一。高者七十尺，次六十尺，雕饰奇伟，冠于一世。"[3]另据费长房《历代三宝记》卷九《译经·西秦北凉元魏高齐陈氏》记载："《入大乘论》二卷，坚意菩萨造；（元魏北台）《净度三昧经》一卷，第二出，与宝云

[1]《大正藏》第 4 卷，第 473b-c 页。
[2] 杨衒之，上引书，第 212-213、220-221 页。
[3]《魏书·释老志》，点校本，北京：中华书局，1974 年，第 3037 页。

译二卷者同，广略异耳，见《道祖录》;《付法藏传》四卷，见《菩提流支录》。右三部合七卷。宋文帝元嘉二十三年丙戌(446年)，是北魏太平真君七年，太武皇帝信纳崔皓邪佞谄谀，崇重寇谦，号为天师；残害释种，毁破浮图。至庚寅年(450年)，太武遭病，方始感悟；兼有白足禅师来相启发，生愧悔心，即诛崔皓。到壬辰岁(452年)，太武帝崩，子(孙)文成立，即起浮图，毁经七年还兴三宝。至和平三年(462年)，诏玄统沙门释昙曜，慨前凌废，欣今载兴，故于北台石窟寺内集诸僧众，译斯传经，流通后贤，庶使法藏住持无绝。"[1]后来，道世《法苑珠林》卷七十九《十恶篇·感应缘》[2]、道宣《续高僧传·昙曜传》[3]及《大唐内典录》卷四《后魏元氏翻传佛经录》[4]、靖迈《古今译经图纪》卷三"昙曜"条[5]、智昇《开元释教录》卷六《总括群经录》[6]和圆照《贞元新定释教目录》卷九《总集群经录》[7]均沿用费长房《历代三宝记》的记载。由此看出，《付法藏传》之翻译，系北魏和平三年"昭玄沙门昙曜欣三宝再兴，遂于北台石窟寺，躬译《净度三昧经》一卷、《付法藏传》四卷，流通像法也"[8]，因为此前太武帝听信崔皓之言，下诏诛沙门，废法祀，毁经像，破佛塔。毁佛诏书中并言佛法"皆是前世汉人无赖子弟刘元真、吕伯强之徒，接乞胡之诞言，用老庄之虚假，附而益之，皆非真实"[9]。另据《历代三宝记》卷九引道慧《宋齐录》，昙曜初译《付法藏传》十年后，"西域沙门吉迦夜，魏言何事，延兴二年(472年)为沙门统释昙曜于北台重译，刘孝标笔受"[10]。昙曜初译和吉迦夜重译《付法藏传》，皆在昭示佛教之由来，庶使法藏住持无绝[11]。故而，"昙曜不独为石窟寺开山的创始者，亦为石窟寺译经的创始者"[12]。

---

[1]《大正藏》第49卷，第85a-b页。

[2] 道世，上引书，第2317-2318页。

[3]《大正藏》第50卷，第427c-428a页。

[4]《大正藏》第55卷，第268b页。

[5]《大正藏》第55卷，第360a页。

[6]《大正藏》第55卷，第539c-540a页。

[7]《大正藏》第55卷，第838a页。

[8]《历代三宝记》卷三《帝年下·魏晋宋齐梁周大隋》，《大正藏》第49卷，第43a页。

[9]《魏书·释老志》，点校本，北京：中华书局，1974年，第3034页。

[10]《大正藏》第49卷，第85b页。

现存《付法藏传》的最早记录，是[梁]僧佑《出三藏记集》："《杂宝藏经》十三卷(阙)、《付法藏因缘经》六卷(阙)、《方便心论》二卷(阙)。右三部，凡二十一卷。宋明帝时，西域三藏吉迦夜于北国，以伪延兴二年，共僧正释昙曜译出，刘孝标笔受。此三经并未至京都。"僧佑，上引书，第62-63页。僧佑所记六卷本《付法藏因缘经》，应为吉迦夜重译本。陈垣先生认为："吉迦夜当时系以昙曜所译者为底本，而从新改译，又在目上加'因缘'二字也。自吉迦夜译本行，而昙曜译本遂废。"陈垣《云冈石窟寺之译经与刘孝标》，载《陈垣学术论文集》第一集(第443-448页)，北京：中华书局，1980年，第444页。

[11] 汤用彤《汉魏两晋南北朝佛教史》，北京：中华书局，1983年，第357-360页。

[12] 陈垣《云冈石窟寺之译经与刘孝标》，上引书，第443页。

依据上述文献，和平三年昙曜于北台石窟寺内召集僧众译经，似表明北台“石窟寺和平三年前已工毕”[1]。换言之，规划中的北台石窟寺[2]，倘若在和平三年尚未全部完工，其中的若干场所如“天竺僧陁番经之地”等应已投入使用；“云冈石窟寺新建，梵汉经典，正好贮藏”[3]。故而，昙曜五窟（第16-20窟）上方译经处之营造，疑与昙曜主持开窟同步。倘若此推断不误，云冈石窟西部冈上之遗址，即武州山石窟寺“上方一位石室数间”之译经处应完工于北魏和平三年之前。当初设计“天竺僧陁番经之地”时，遵循“犹依天竺旧状而重构之”原则，在罽宾佛寺制度的基础上[4]，把塔院与僧院合二为一，甚或直接采纳类似毕钵罗早期塔寺之布局[5]，浮图居中建造，僧房周匝设置[6]。这应是中原北方迄今发现的最早的佛寺遗址。稍后兴建的洛阳永宁寺，在这种布局的基础上进一步发展，堪称中国境内第一座完全汉化了的佛寺[7]。

[1] 汤用彤，上引书，第359页。

[2] 北台石窟寺，即武州山石窟寺，亦称北石窟寺，因为伊阙石窟寺（龙门石窟）时称南石窟寺。参见：陈垣《记大同武州山石窟寺》，上引书，第398-409页。

[3] 陈垣《云冈石窟寺之译经与刘孝标》，上引书，第447页。

[4] 为昙曜重译《付法藏传》的西域三藏吉迦夜，可能来自大犍陀罗。其与昙曜共译的《杂宝藏经》，故事内容多发生在犍陀罗。云冈石窟西部冈上遗址与大犍陀罗佛寺遗址布局之相似，或许不是偶然。参见：Charles Willemen, “A Chinese Kṣudrakapiṭaka (T. IV. 203),” in: *Asiatische Studien Études Asiatiques* XLVI. 1 (1992): 507-515.

[5] 这种布局设计，似不符合晚期教规。据法藏《梵网经菩萨戒本疏》，盗戒轻重罪：于僧房院地内造佛堂、塔，及于塔院地中取井水等，俱重。《大正藏》第40卷，第615a页。

[6] 印度佛教石窟寺，有些在石窟附近或周边营造地面建筑，即采用地面建筑与岩石开窟相结合的形式。根据印度考古调查局2000-2001年在阿旃陀石窟区的考古发掘，阿旃陀第4-17窟所在对面山腰，即石窟群下方瓦哥拉河(Waghora)南岸的山地上发掘出土了砖砌的建筑遗址。遗址中央为方形塔基，塔基左、右、后三面环置小室，整体布局作塔庙—僧坊混成式(stūpa-cum-vihāra)，即塔寺结构；中央方塔为僧众供养、礼忏之处，周匝小室系僧众栖止、禅修之所。根据遗址出土的陶器和一枚拜占庭狄奥多西斯(Theodosius, 402-450年）金币，发掘者推测这处地面建筑营造于4、5世纪。又，6世纪初麴氏高昌时营造的交河故城，城中大道北端的“大庙”，现编E-27号，长88米，宽59米，平面布局也是塔院、僧院合一，即塔寺布局，只是年代略晚于武州山石窟寺的冈上遗址。云冈石窟西部冈上发掘出土的寺址，与阿旃陀石窟群对岸揭露出土的寺址和犍陀罗苹钵罗寺址在平面布局上非常相似，或许不是偶然。参见：*Indian Archaeology 2000-01—A Review* (New Delhi: Archaeological Survey of India, 2006) 93-97, Plate 73.

[7] 杨衒之《洛阳伽蓝记》卷一记载永宁寺颇详，现节录如下：“永宁寺……中有九层浮图一所，架木为之，举高九十丈。上有金刹，复高十丈；合去地一千尺……浮图北有佛殿一所，形如太极殿……作工奇巧，冠于当世。僧房楼观，一千余间……寺院墙……若今宫墙也。四面各开一门。南门楼三重……形制似今端门。”参见：杨衒之，上引书，第17-24页。这处“冠于当世”的永宁寺遗址，在20世纪后半由中国社会科学院考古研究所组织专人进行了发掘，出土遗迹与文献记载基本相符。永宁寺平面布局以方形木浮图为中心，山门、木塔、佛殿自南向北排列，形成中轴线，其他附属建筑如僧房、楼观等于两侧对称建置。参见：中国社会科学院考古研究所著《北魏洛阳永宁寺：1979-1994年考古发掘报告》，北京：中国大百科全书出版社，1996年，第6-8页，图四。

From Gandhāra to Pingcheng: The Layout of a Free-standing Buddhist Monastery

The cave-temple complex at Yungang is located about 15 km to the west of Pingcheng (present-day Datong), capital of the Northern Wei dynasty (386-534 AD). The caves were carved out of the cliff of the Wuzhou Hill, along the northern bank of the Wuzhou River; the caves stand side by side covering a distance of about 1 km from east to west and comprise twenty very large, twenty-five medium, and numerous small caves and countless niches. The carving of the cave-temples was initially commissioned by the ruling family of the Northern Wei; the caves were designated as the Cave-temple Complex at Wuzhou Hill[1], showing the splendid workmanship of the dynasty and becoming a model for the rock-cut temples in the whole territory controlled by the Northern Wei[2].

---

[1] Chen Yuan [陈垣], "*Ji Datong wuzhoushan shikusi* [记大同武州山石窟寺, Notes on the Cave-temple Complex at Wuzhou Hill, Datong]", in: *Chen Yuan xueshu lunwenji* [陈垣学术论文集, *A Collection of Essays by Professor Chen Yuan*], Vol. I, Beijing: Zhonghua Book Company, 1980: 398-409.

For the Chinese literature or documents, in addition, I will first write down its name in pinyin system, followed by the Chinese characters and its English translation in bracket. Whenever the literature or document is again cited or quoted, I just use the pinyin system first and then put the English translation in bracket.

[2] Su Bai [宿白], "*Pingcheng shili de jiju he yungang moshi de xingcheng yu fazhan* [平城实力的集聚和云冈模式的形成与发展, Gathering of Manpower and Material Resources in Pingcheng and the Creation as well as Development of the 'Yungang Style']", in: *Zhongguo shikusi yanjiu* [中国石窟寺研究, *Studies of the Cave-temples of China*], Beijing: Cultural Relics Press, 1996: 114-144.

1. Monastery Site atop the Wuzhou Hill

Between the years 1938 and 1940, archaeological excavations on the remains of structural antechambers attached to Cave Nos. 8-10 and 16-20 were carried out by the Japanese scholars, Seiichi Mizuno, Katsutoshi Ono and Takeo Hibino. Since then one has debated whether a free-standing temple once stood on the crest of the Wuzhou Hill where the cave-temples were carved out; some trial excavations were initiated on the eastern and western sections on top of the hill in 1940 under the direction of Mr. K. Ono and Mr. T. Hibino. The archaeological work on the western part started on October 30th and was completed on November 14th, with an open trench made approximately in an "H" shape. Unfortunately, the excavations did not reveal a clear plan of the building complex. It is certain, however, that a free-standing temple stood on the crest of the Wuzhou Hill during the Northern Wei dynasty. The recovery of some building materials, such as round eaves tiles with a lotus-flower design or with the Chinese characters *chuan zuo wu qiong* (the Imperial Throne Continuing for Ever) and flat eaves tiles with green-glaze or with a meander design on the edge, is very significant[1].

In 2010, in coordination with work of the conservation and protection atop the Yungang cave-temples, the Shanxi Provincial Institute of Archaeology together with the Yungang Institute and the Datong Municipal Institute of Archaeology, under the direction of Mr. Zhang Qingjie, carried out a joint excavation on top of the Wuzhou Hill. This location covers an area of 3,600 square meters and has revealed four main cultures lying in stratified sequence, i. e. the modern time, the Qing (1616-1911 AD) and Ming (1368-1644 AD) dynasties, the Jin (1115-1234 AD) and Liao (907-1125 AD) dynasties,

---

[1] S. Mizuno, "Report on the Yünkang Excavation I & II [雲岡發掘記 1 & 2]", in: S. Mizuno and T. Nagahiro [長廣敏雄], *Yun-kang; The Buddhist Cave-temples of the Fifth Century AD in North China; detailed report of the archaeological survey carried out by the mission of the Tōhōbunka Kenkyūsho 1938-1945* [雲岡石窟：西曆五世紀における中國北部佛教窟院の考古學的調查報告；東方文化研究所調查，昭和十三年——昭和二十年], Kyoto: Jimbunkagaku Kenkyūshō, Kyoto University [京都大學人文科學研究所], Vol. VII (1952): 57-68, 123-129, Figs. 29-56; Vol. XV (1955): 91-99, 185-190, Figs. 50-53, 56-107.

in addition to the Northern Wei. As a result, the excavation brought to light a site of a freestanding Buddhist temple from the cultural layer of the Northern Wei, with a *stūpa* in the center and a range of monks' cells along the north, south and east flanks (figs.1, 2).

The *stūpa* which stands in the middle of an oblong court was surrounded by an open cloister, forming a square, behind which were the monks' cells. To be precise, on the three sides of the *stūpa* there was a row of rooms for the officiating monks forming a cloister where the monks could walk about (*caṅkramita*) along the three sides, besides, they performed the circumambulation of the *stūpa*. The basement of the *stūpa* was a square, 14 meters from south to north and 14.3 meters from east to west, with a height ranging from 0.35 meter to 0.7 meter. To the south there is a slope, with a 2.1 meters width and 5 meters length, indicating a flight of steps leading to the basement. No *śarīra* casket or buried relics were found in the basement (fig.3).

The cells along the north flank, which is 61.5 meters long from east to west, were 15 in number. Among them, thirteen cells were originally built in the Northern Wei and two were rebuilt in the Liao or Jin dynasties, overlapping the cells of the Northern Wei. Some of the Northern Wei cells consist of a small room opening into another or inner room, the largest one of which is 7.4 meters long and 3.4 meters broad. The earthen walls of the cells were originally rammed, their thickness ranging from 0.65 meter to 0.85 meter. Some of the cells have remains of a *kang* [1], stove as well as a flue. There are 11 stone plinths in front of the cells, indicating that a cloister or veranda used to be attached to the cells (fig.4). Two cells survive along the west flank, 13.5 meters long and 5.9 meters wide; a stone plinth was unearthed in front of the cells, which indicates that they have the same layout as the cells along the north flank. Three cells are extant on the east flank, about 18 meters long and 4.4 meters wide. The super structure of the central *stūpa* and that of the cells along the three flanks perished long ago and their

[1] The *Kang* is a brick platform built across one side or at the end of a room in a house in northern China; it is warmed by a fire underneath and is used for sleeping.

original form cannot be imagined. The southern part of the site had been destroyed and no remains of the gate and flank were found.

A significant great amount of the building materials was found and collected at the site. Among them, the aforementioned round eaves tiles with lotus-flower design or with the Chinese characters *chuan zuo wu qiong* and the flat eaves tiles with green-glaze are of historical value[1]. Some broken pieces of stone images of the Buddha as well as donor figures were also unearthed, and a pottery shard inscribed with the Chinese characters *xi ku* (western cave) came also to light[2].

According to a copy of *Dajin xijing wuzhoushan chongxiu dashikusi bei* (*A Tablet of the Restoration of the Great Cave-temple Complex at the Wuzhou Hill near the Western Capital of the Jin Dynasty*), hereafter referred to as the *Jin Tablet,* by Cao Yan in 1147 AD, the Great Cave-temple Complex at the Wuzhou Hill comprised ten temples, among which, the Tongle Temple was commissioned to be built initially by Emperor Mingyuan (409-423 AD), the Lingyan Temple was successively set up by Emperor Wencheng (452-465 AD), and the Huguo Temple as well as the Tiangong Temple were originally established by Emperor Xiaowen (471-499 AD). The Chongfu Temple, moreover, was donated or set up by Qian'er Qingshi, a famous eunuch of the Northern Wei dynasty. The free-standing temple at the crest of the Wuzhou Hill, which consists of several cells, on the basis of *Gaoseng zhuan* (*Biographies of Eminent Priests*)[3], was the place where Hinduka (present-day the South Asian Subcontinent) *bhikṣus* translated the Buddhist scriptures during the

---

[1] Glazed tiles were rare architectural material for the timber structure in early medieval China. According to documentations, the glazed tiles were used at the latest in the construction of the Palace of the Great Ultimate [太极殿] by Emperor Jingmu [穆帝] of the Northern Wei dynasty. The eaves tiles with green-glaze unearthed from the ruined temple on top of the rock-cut caves at Yungang indicate that the Great Cave-temple Complex at Wuzhou Hill was given a high position at that time. *Taiping yulan* [太平御览, *The Taiping Reign-Period Imperial Encyclopedia*], facsimile edition, Beijing: Zhonghua Book Company, 1960: 932.

[2] State Administration of Cultural Heritage [国家文物局主编] ed., *Major Archaeological Discoveries in China in 2010* [2010 中国重要考古发现], Beijing: Cultural Relics Press, 2011: 127-130.

[3] *Gaoseng zhuan* [高僧传, *Biographies of Eminent Priests*] was compiled by Huijiao [慧皎, c 495-554 AD] in 519 AD. The book title can be also translated as *The Liang Dynasty Biographies of Eminent Priests,* or *Biographies of Eminent Monks,* or *Memoirs of Eminent Monks.* Huijiao, *Gaoseng zhuan* (*Biographies of Eminent Priests*), emended and annotated by Tang Yongtong [汤用彤], Beijing: Zhonghua Book Company, 1995.

reign period of Emperor Xiaowen[1]. The free-standing temple site unearthed on the hilltop in 2010 should be the temple consisting of several cells at the crest of the Wuzhou Hill recorded in the *Jin Tablet* and used to be an important component part of the Great Cave-temple Complex at Wuzhou. It was the place where the Indian *bhikṣus* from Hinduka translated the Buddhist scriptures at the Wuzhou Cave-temple Complex during the Northern Wei[2]. This ruined temple represents the earliest site of a Buddhist monastery ever found in central China to this day.

2. Layout of Gandhāran Saṃghārāma

The scheme or design of the Chinese *samghārāma* (temple and monastery) originated from Hinduka, with a *stūpa* as the centre of a monastic complex. Layout of the free-standing temple at the crest of the Wuzhou Hill, however, coincides with a historical reference that the *stūpa* was the pivot of attraction, a *stūpa* generally implied a temple or monastery in China during the period of the Wei, Jin, Southern and Northern Dynasties (221-589 AD). Therefore, Ge Hong (c. 284-364 or 343 AD) in his *Zi Yuan* (*Chinese Characters Dictionary*) clearly stated that "the *stūpa* is a Buddha-hall"[3]. The idea that to build a *stūpa* is to set up a temple can be found in numerous Chinese Buddhist texts[4].

---

[1] Su Bai, "*Dajin xijing wuzhoushan chongxiu dashikusi bei jiaozhu* [《大金西京武州山重修大石窟寺碑》校注, Annotation and Textual Research on a Copy of the '*Tablet of the Restoration of the Great Cave-temple Complex at the Wuzhou Hill near the Western Capital of the Jin Dynasty*']", in: *Zhongguo shikusi yanjiu* (*Studies of the Cave-temples of China*), Beijing: Cultural Relics Press, 1996:52-75, esp. 54, 65.

[2] In an archaeological excavation carried out in 2011 by the Shanxi Provincial Institute of Archaeology on the eastern part of the crest of the Wuzhou Hill, above Caves 5 and 6, a basement or foundation of a *stūpa* was unearthed, but none of the monks' cell came to light.

[3] The book *Zi Yuan* [字苑, *Chinese Characters Dictionary*] was lost long ago, but explanation of the *stūpa* was quoted in *Yiqiejing yinyi* [一切经音义, *Pronunciation and Meaning in the Buddhist Scriptures*] compiled by Xuanying [玄应] around the middle of the 7th century AD. Xuanying, *Yiqiejing yinyi* (*Pronunciation and Meaning in the Buddhist Scriptures*), emended by Sun Xingyan [孙星衍] et al, Shanghai: The Commercial Press, 1936: 264.

[4] Su Bai [宿白], "*Donghan Wei Jin Nanbeichao fosi buju chutan* [东汉魏晋南北朝佛寺布局初探, A Preliminary Study on the Layout of the Buddhist Monasteries from the Later Han down to the Southern and Northern Dynasties (1st to 6th century AD)]", in: *Wei Jin Nanbeichao Tang Song kaogu wengao jicong* [魏晋南北朝唐宋考古文稿辑丛, *Collected Papers on the Chinese Archaeology from the Wei down to the Song Dynasties* (3rd to 13th century AD)], Beijing: Cultural Relics Press, 2011: 230-247.

According to the *Weishu: Shilaozhi* (*History of the Wei Dynasties*: *Treatise on Buddhism and Taoism*) by Wei Shou (506-572 AD) in 554 AD, "in the first year of the Yuanshou period (2 BC) of Emperor Ai of the Han dynasty (206 BC -24 AD), a scholar named Qin Jingxian received oral instruction on the Buddhist scriptures from Yichun, envoy of the King of the Darouzhi (Indoscythe), but while China had heard of the scriptures, they were not yet part of their beliefs. Later, Emperor Ming (57-75 AD) of the Later Han dynasty (25-220 AD) dreamed one night of a golden man, sunlight issuing form the nape of his neck, flying in mid-air towards the palace courtyard. Thereupon the Emperor inquired from the assembled ministers. Fu Yi was the first to answer that it was the Buddha. The Emperor then dispatched Cai Yin and Qin Jing with a party on a mission to Hinduka to seek out or to copy the canon left behind by the Buddha. Cai Yin then returned East to Luoyang, capital of China at that time, with the monks Kāśyapa Mātaṅga and Zhu Falan. The existence in China of Buddhist monks and the kneeling ceremony dates from this time. Cai Yin also obtained a Buddhist scripture in forty-two chapters and a standing image of Śākyamuni. Emperor Ming commissioned artists to execute Buddhist images and install them on the Qingliang Platform atop the Xianjie Mausoleum. The scripture was sealed away in the stone chamber of the Lantai. Cai Yin placed the scripture on a white horse and returned to China. On account of how the scripture had travelled to Luoyang, the Baimasi (White Horse Monastery) was built west of the Yong Gate of the walled city of Luoyang ... After the White Horse Monastery had been built in the Luoyang capital, it was highly adorned with excellent and lovely paintings, which became the model for all corners of the Empire. The general rule that governed the construction of *gongta* (*grihya-chaitya*[1]/*caityagṛha*)[2] at that time was still based on the old

[1] M. C. Joshi, "Buddhist Rock-cut Architecture: A Survey", in: *Proceedings of the International Seminar on Cave Art of India and China,* Theme I: Historical Perspective, New Delhi: Indira Gandhi National Centre for the Arts, November 25, 1991: 1-28, esp. 7-8.

[2] The Chinese word *gongta*［宫塔］, which is composed of two characters, should be probably a derivative of the Sanskrit word *grihya-chaitya/caityagṛhā* or a similar Prākṛta word. 宫/*gong* was derived from *grihā* (house) or *grihya* that means belonging to a house, and 塔/*ta* was derived from *caitya/chaitya*. *confer*: 1) Monier Monier-Williams, *A Sanskrit-English Dictionary*, London: Oxford University Press, 1899: 361-363; 2) Unrai Ogiwara［荻原雲來］, *Bon-wa Daijiten*［漢訳対照梵和大辭典, *A Sanskrit-Chinese-Japanese Dictionary*］, Tōkyō: Kōdansha, 1974: 432b.

prototype of Hinduka, the *stūpas* are built with from one to three, five, seven or nine stories" [1].

Within the territory of ancient Hinduka [2], according to Édouard Chavannes, there were two regions that can be considered as sacred centers for Buddhism in a broad sense: the reaches of the Indus river and those of the Gaṅgā river. Buddhist monks and laymen from China in most cases first visited the Indus, which was closest to the Silk Road and then the Gaṅgā. Until the Tang dynasty (618-907 AD), the most direct route to central India via Nepal was not well known. Before the Tang times, among all the communication routes between ancient China and Hinduka, the most frequently taken was the "Jibin route ", because that was the only link from the Pamirs to Kāśmīra (present-day Kashmir) and Uḍḍiyāna (present-day Swāt). Some Buddhist monks and pilgrims like Song Yun and Huisheng never went to central India but stopped at Puruṣapura (present-day Peshawar) or Takṣaśila (present-day Taxila). That is why the region of Gandhāra is considered to have played a vital role in the early dissemination of Buddhism in China [3].

The meaning of the Chinese characters Jibin [4], a geographical term,

---

[1] 1) Wei Shou, *Weishu: Shilaozhi* (*History of the Wei Dynasties*: *Treatise on Buddhism and Taoism*), punctuated edition, Beijing: Zhonghua Book Company, 1974: 3025-3062, esp. 3025-26, 3029; 2) James R. Ware, "Wei Shou on Buddhism", in: *T'oung Pao* 30 (1930): 100-181, esp. 110-12, 122; 3) Leon Hurvitz, tr., *Treatise on Buddhism and Taoism* by Wei Shou, in: S. Mizuno and T. Nagahiro, *opere citato,* Vol. xvi supplement (1956): 23-103, esp. 28-29, 47.

[2] With regard to ancient Chinese names of Hinduka, see P. C. Bagchi "Ancient Chinese Names of India", in: *India and China: Interactions through Buddhism and Diplomacy; A Collection of Essays by Professor Prabodh Chandra Bagchi,* compiled by Bangwei Wang and Tansen Sen, Delhi: Anthem Press India, 2011: 3-11.

[3] Édouard Chavannes, "Voyage de Song Yun dans l'Udyana et le Gandhāra (518–22)", in: *Bulletin de l'Ecole française d'Extrême-Orient,* III (1903): 379–441.

[4] According to Xuanzang [玄奘, ca. 602-664 AD], Jiashimiluo [迦湿弥罗, Kāśmīra] was "formerly written Ki-pin (Jibin) by mistake", it other words, Jibin "was an old and incorrect name for the country". We are told also by Daoxuan [道宣, 595-667 AD] that "Jiashimiluo was called Jibin by Chinese, a popular name handed down from ancient times, but we do not know the origin of Jibin". Seishi Karashima [辛嶋静志] suggests that Jibin was probably a transliteration of the Prākrit term Kaśpīr and Kaśmīra was a corresponding Sanskrit homologue of the Prākrit Kaśpīr. According to Charles Willemen, however, Jibin "is not necessarily a phonetic rendering, but it may indicate the region of foreigners, guests [*bin,* 宾], who use *ji* [罽], a kind of cloth, very appreciated by the Han. (To be continued on the next page)

varies with different contexts in a discussion of the history of Central Asia. Although it generally covers the area of present-day Kashmir, it also comprised Uḍḍiyāna, Takṣaśilā, Gandhāra and Kāpiśa at least from the 4th to early 6th century AD[1]. Jibin region, for a period of time, "was northwestern India, of which Kāśmīrā was an important part, but not the only part"[2]. Jibin in ancient Chinese literature basically corresponds to the Greater Gandhāra[3]

Udyāna, the Gilgit area, may have been the original area, but it gradually developed to encompass the whole northwestern area, certainly in the 4th century". *confer:* 1) Xuanzang, *Datang xiyu ji*［大唐西域记, *Record of the Western Regions of the Great Tang Dynasty*］, emended and annotated by Ji Xianlin［季羡林］et al, Beijing: Zhonghua Book Company, 1985: 320; 2) Samuel Beal, *Si-Yu-Ki-Buddhist Records of the Western World; Chinese Accounts of India,* translated from the Chinese of Hiuen Tsiang, London: Trubner, 1884: 188, note 86; 3) Thomas Watters, *On Yuan Chwang's Travels in India AD 629-645,* London: Royal Asiatic Society, 2 vols., Vol. I, 1904; Vol. II, 1905; Vol. I: 259; 4) Daoxuan, *Xü gaoseng zhuan*［续高僧传, *Continued Biographies of Eminent Priests,* or *The Tang Dynasty Biographies of Eminent Priests,* or *A Continuation of the Memoirs of Eminent Monks*］, in: *Taishō*, Vol. 50: 449a; 5) P. C. Bagchi "Ki-pin and Kashmir", in: *India and China: Interactions through Buddhism and Diplomacy; A Collection of Essays by Professor Prabodh Chandra Bagchi,* compiled by Bangwei Wang and Tansen Sen, Delhi: Anthem Press India, 2011: 145-154; 6) Seishi Karashima, "*Hanyi fodian de yuyan yanjiu*［汉译佛典的语言研究, On the Linguistic Form of the Chinese Translated Versions of the *Tripiṭaka*］", in: *Fojiao hanyu yanjiu*［佛教汉语研究, *Studies of the Buddhist-Chinese*］, ed. Zhu Qingzhi［朱庆之］, Beijing: The Commercial Press, 2009: 33-74, esp. 56-57; 7) Charles Willemen, "Sarvāstivāda Developments in Northwestern India and in China", in: *The Indian International Journal of Buddhist Studies,* (New Series in continuation of the *Indian Journal of Buddhist Studies,* Vol. X, Varanasi: B. J. K. Institute of Buddhist and Asian Studies) No. 2 (2001): 163-169.

［1］1) S. Lèvi and É. Chavannes, "L'Itinéraire d'Ou-k'oung", in: *Journal Asiatique,* Octobre (1895): 371-84; 2) Edouard Chavannes, *Documents sur Les Tou-kiue (Turcs) Occidentaux: Recueillis et commentés,* St-Pétersbourg: Académie Impériale des Sciences de St-Pétersbourg, 1903: 130-132; 3) Kurakichi Shiratori［白鳥庫吉］",Keihinkouku［罽賓國考, On the Jibin Kingdom］", in: *Seiiki shi kenkyū*［西域史研究, *Collected Papers On the History of the Western Regions*］, Vol. 1, Tokyo: Iwanami Shoten, 1944: 377-462, esp. 460-462; 4) Cen Zongmian［岑仲勉］, *Hanshu Xiyuzhuan dili jiaoshi*［汉书西域传地理校释, *Collation and Annotation to the Monograph on the Western Regions in the History of the Western Han Dynasty*］, Beijing: Zhonghua Book Company, 1981: 150-164; 5) Chongfeng Li, "The Geography of Transmission: The 'Jibin' Route and Propagation of Buddhism in China", in: *Kizil on the Silk Road: Crossroads of Commerce & Meeting of Minds,* ed. Rajeshwari Ghose, Mumbai: Marg Publications, 2008: 24-31.

［2］1) Charles Willemen, *opere citato*: 167; 2) Chongfeng Li, *opere citato*: 25.

［3］Richard Salomon, *Ancient Buddhist Scrolls from Gandhāra: The British Library Kharoṣṭhī Fragments,* Seattle: University of Washington Press, 1999: 3.

or Gandhāran cultural area [1], two modern terms used recently in academic circles.

It is well-known that the Chinese have provided abundant data for the study of Central Asia civilization. According to the *Waiguo Shi* (*An Account of Foreign Countries*) [2] by the monk Zhi Sengzai, about 4th century AD, Jibin lies to the west of Śrāvastī; the King of Jibin and the people in the country all believed in the way and doctrine of Buddhism. In the winter, men and monks would drink a little fruit wine before noon, and they could not eat anything after noon time" [3]. This account seems to be the earliest extant Chinese record about Jibin.

From the 3rd to the 6th century AD, "Jibin abounds with saints and wise men" [4]. There were frequent exchanges between Jibin and China during this

---

[1] Charles Willemen believes that "the Gandhāran cultural area of Gandhāra and Bactria was known as *Jibin* 罽宾 in Chinese", or Gandhāran cultural area was non-Kāśmīra Jibin. 1) Charles Willemen, "Kumārajīva's 'Explanatory Discourse' about Abhidharmic Literature", in: *Kokusai Bukkyōgaku Daigaku-in Daigaku Kenkyū Kiyō* [国際仏教大学院大学研究紀要第 12 号 (平成 20 年), *Journal of the International College for Postgraduate Buddhist Studies*], Vol. XII (2008): 37-83 (156-110), esp. 39 (154), 69 (124); 2) Charles Willemen, *Outlining the Way to Reflect* [思维略要法] (T. XV 617), Mumbai: Somaiya Publications Pvt Ltd, 2012: 16.

[2] This book was lost after the 10th century AD, but some materials were quoted and preserved in some of the Chinese *leishu* [类书, a class of works combining to some extent the characteristics of encyclopedias and concordances, embracing the whole field of literature, methodically arranged according to subjects, and each heading giving abstracts from former works on the subject in question], such as *Taiping yulan* (*The Taiping Reign-Period Imperial Encyclopedia*). Xiang Da [向达], *Tangdai chang'an yu xiyu wenming* [唐代长安与西域文明, *The Tang Dynasty Chang'an and Civilization of the Central Asia*], Beijing: SDX Joint Publishing Company, 1957: 565-578, esp. 570-572.

[3] Ouyang Xun [欧阳询, 557-641 AD], *Yiwen leijun* [艺文类聚, *Encyclopedia of Art and Literature in Dynastic Histories*] in 624 AD, emended and annotated by Wang Shaoying [汪 绍 楹], Shanghai: Shanghai Chinese Classics Publishing House, 1965: 1294.

[4] Sengyou [僧佑, 445-518 AD], *Chu sanzang ji ji* [出三藏记集, *A Collection of Records concerning the Tripiṭaka* or *A Collection of Records of Translations of the Tripiṭaka*], emended and annotated by Su Jinren [苏晋仁] and Xiao Lianzi [萧錬子], Beijing: Zhonghua Book Company, 1995: 545; *confer*: *Taishō*, Vol. 55: 105a.

period[1]. Those who came from Jibin to recite or translate Buddhist scriptures and to propagate the doctrines in China, such as Buddhabhadra, Buddhajīva, Buddhayaśas , Dharmamitra, Dharmanandi, Dharmapriya, Dharmayaśas, Guṇavarman, Puṇyatāra , Saṃghabhadra, Saṃghadeva, Saṃgharakṣa and Vimalākṣa, were clearly recorded in the *Chu sanzang ji ji* (*A Collection of Records concerning the Tripiṭaka*) compiled by Sengyou, which is the oldest descriptive catalogue of the Chinese translations of the Buddhist canon in existence and contains prefaces and postscripts to the translations of the *Tripiṭaka* as well as biographies of some eminent priests or master monks[2]. On the other hand, those who went to Jibin from China during the 4th and 5th centuries AD, either in quest of Buddhist *sūtras* and images or simply on a pilgrimage, included Fayong, Zhimeng and Zhiyan, among many others[3]. Kumārajīva (344-413 AD), a great translator and eminent monk, is recorded as having traveled back and forth between Jibin and Kucha several times. Thus, a close relationship existed between Jibin and China as far as Buddhist cultural exchanges were

---

[1] According to *Zhongguo wenwubao* [中国文物报, *China Cultural Relics News,* October 26, 2005], a tomb dated to the Northern Zhou dynasty [北周, 557-581 AD] was discovered at Nankang [南康] village in northern Xi'an. In the light of an epitaph unearthed from the tomb, the deceased was Li Dan [李诞] of a Brahman race [婆罗门种], who came to China from Jibin during the Zhengguang period [正光, 520-525 AD] of the Northern Wei and died at the age of 59 at Wannianli [万年里] in 564 AD. He was buried in his home village and was conferred the posthumous honor of Hanzhou *cishi* [邯州刺史, Regional Inspector of Hanzhou] by the Northern Zhou. This is not only the first tomb that bears a name of a Brahman but also a tomb that records a foreigner who came from Jibin and lived in China. It further indicates that Jibin and China had a close contact besides the Buddhist relationship.

[2] Sengyou, *Chu sanzang ji ji* [*A Collection of Records concerning the Tripiṭaka* or *A Collection of Records of Translations of the Tripiṭaka*], emended and annotated by Su Jinren and Xiao Lianzi, Beijing: Zhonghua Book Company, 1995; *confer Taishō,* Vol. 55: 1-114.

According to Fei Zhangfang [费长房], *Chu sangzang ji ji* was compiled by Sengyou in the Jianwu period [建武, 494-497 AD] of the Southern Qi dynasty [南齐, 479-502 AD]. Fei Zhangfang, *Lidai sanbo ji* [历代三宝记, *Record of the Triratna through the Ages,* or *Record concerning the Triratna under Successive Dynasties*] in 597 AD, in: *Taishō,* Vol. 49: 125c.

[3] Fayong is said to have led a group of about 25 monks, Zhimeng led 15, and Zhiyan 4 monks from China to Jibin respectively. There are also other lists of monks in Chinese documents as well. So the number of Chinese monks was considerable.

concerned[1].

Jibin or Greater Gandhāra is rich in Buddhist sites and remains. Of the many Buddhist sites in Jibin none is better known than that of Takht-i-Bāhī and no place has been the object of so many excavations both illegal and systematic than these isolated ruins until the last few years.

The ruins at Takht-i-Bāhī are situated on the crest and northern slope of a detached spur rising abruptly from the plain about 13 kilometers north of Mardān in the North-West Frontier Province of Pakistan, i. e. in the center of the ancient territory of Gandhāra. The most important portion of the entire ruins, which extend altogether for close to one and a half kilometers east and west along the summit, is the monastic complex situated on a ridge to the north, somewhat lower than the crest of the hill itself, and toward the eastern end of the whole site (figs.5a, 5b, 5c). Since 1871 European scholars started focusing on these remains, when F. H. Wilcher superintended the excavation of the religious building which occupied the lower portion of the central spur. Although A. Cunningham made a detailed report of his reconnaissance on the ruins at Takht-i-Bāhī in 1875[2], further excavations on the site were carried out first in January 1907 by D. B. Spooner and then by H. Hargreaves in 1911. Both of them described their discoveries at some length and drew detailed plans of the entire monastic complex within the enclosing walls (figs.6a, 6b, 6c)[3].

On the basis of the above archaeological reports as well as some Buddhist texts in Chinese, the overall remains of the whole monastic complex at Takht-

---

[1] 1) Chongfeng Li, *opere citato* (The Geography of Transmission...): 24-31; 2) Chongfeng Li, "Jibin and China as seen from Chinese Documents", in: *Archaeology of Buddhism in Asia*, ed. B. Mani, New Delhi: Archaeological Survery of India (in press).

[2] A. Cunningham, *Archaeological Survey of India: Report for the Year 1872-73* (1875)/ Volume V: 23-36, Pl. VI-X.

[3] 1) D. B. Spooner, "Excavations at Takht-i-Bāhī", in: *Archaeological Survey of India: Annual Report 1907-08* (1911): 132-48, Pls. XL-L; 2) H. Hargreaves, "Excavations at Takht-i-Bāhī", in: *Archaeological Survey of India: Annual Report 1910-11* (1914): 33-39, Plates XVII-XXII.

i-Bāhī comprise a *stūpa*, a *vihāra*[1], a central court and an *uposathāgāra* or *prāsāda*, besides some other related structures such as low level chambers, a square court and a passage. The outer walls are generally very lofty, being built on the steep slopes of the spur. Thus, some of them present a wall from 18.29 meters to 24.38 meters high on the outside, but not higher than 6.1 meters inside. The main entrance to the monastic enclosure appears to have been on the south. From the entrance gate to the western end of the central court, one would have turned to the right and east to enter the court itself, which, as can be seen by the plans and illustrations, is a mass of small votive *stūpas* surrounded on three sides by lofty chapels, and bisected from south to north by a paved passage running between small *stūpas* and miniature shrines and connecting the *stūpa* court and the *vihāra* court, both of which lie at higher levels than the central court itself. The latter, the *vihāra* court proper, was approached by a short flight of five steps, the former by a loftier one of fifteen.

Ascending these 15 steps (the first flight) to the south, one enters the *stūpa* court and finds oneself in front of a square platform originally approached by a few steps now quite ruined. This is obviously the basement of the *stūpa* itself, but the continued and irresponsible activity of treasure hunters has resulted in its complete destruction. The *stūpa* stands in the midst of an oblong court 17.22 meters by 13.87 meters. The base of the *stūpa* is a square with sides measuring 6.25 meters, receding in three stages to 4.72 meters and with a total height of 2.6 meters from the ground. The top of the base, which served as a processional path around the drum, was approached by a flight of steps, located in the central projection of the north side, facing the entrance to the court. Around this courtyard on the three sides were a number of chapels, originally five on a side, each 2.44 meters square externally, with the side towards the court open. It is obvious from the structure of these buildings that when first planned they were separated

[1] According to *Da piluzhena chengfojing shu* [大毗卢遮那成佛经疏, *Annotations on the Mahā-vairocanābhisaṃbodhi-vikurvitādhiṣṭhāna-vaipulya-sūtrendra-vāja-nāma-dharmaparyāya* or *Annotation on Mahā-vairocanā-sūtra*], which is Yixing [一行, 683-727 AD]'s record of Śubhākarasiṃha [善无畏, 637-735 AD]'s lectures on the very *sūtra,* the Chinese charcters *sengfang* [僧坊] is a paraphrase of Sanskrit word *vihāra,* meaning a dwelling place. *confer Taishō,* Vol. 39: 615c.

one from the other by a considerable space, 0.86 meter broad, originally open. At a later date, when the court became crowded with images, these openings were filled with a segment of wall used for miniature shrines similar to niches. In this way the court was completely closed on the three sides (fig.7a). The only superstructure extant in the whole site is found in the *stūpa* court, with the exception of the vaulted passage underground to the west of the central court; but even here only two of the chapels retain their original roofing, while a third has the lower of its two domes and collar partly preserved. The ceilings of these chapels are spanned by corbels, while the roofs are domical, externally flattened at the top. Above each of them is a narrow collar surmounted either by a second smaller dome or by a vault, externally wagon-shaped and apsidal on plan with a trefoil opening on the façade and a pinnacle in the form of a mushroom above (fig.7b).

The central court, which occupies a hollow between the *stūpa* court and the *vihāra* court, is 35.36 meters long from east to west and 15.24 meters wide from south to north. The north, east and south flanks of this court have a number of narrow but high chapels, 29 altogether, some standing to a height of 7.62 to 9.14 meters. Each of these chapels is a separate and distinct building, entirely open towards the court. None of the roofs now remain, but there can be little doubt that these chapels were originally covered with domes like those in the *stūpa* court. All the chapels or most of them, judging from numerous fragments found in the ruins, must once have held a colossal statue of the Buddha in stucco. Because the central court is crowded with miniature or votive *stūpas,* it was called by some scholar "a court of many *stūpas*" . The precise use of this court has not been ascertained, but it is particularly rich in its display of sculptures made both of stone and stucco. Apart from shapeless fragments and those too badly damaged to recognize, fragments of stone sculpture unearthed here from 1907 to 1908 number 472 specimens and thus comprises the Peshawar Museum Nos. 679 to 1151 inclusive, besides the stucco fragments. Most of the sculptures discovered at Takht-i-Bāhī, however, were found in the central court. Of different artistic worth, they generally represent the Buddha, sometimes in larger compositions depicting his life-scene (fig.8).

A second flight, directly opposite to the first, against the northern wall of the central court, leads to the *vihāra* court, which is at a lower level than the *stūpa* court; it is called by most scholars the monastic quadrangle or monastery[1].This *vihāra,* a compact self-sufficient unit, is the largest block of building in the whole monastic complex. The quadrangle, 18.9 meters square inside, has 15 dwelling cells with high walls, each 3.05 meters in depth, arranged on three sides; the one at the north-west corner is somewhat longer than the others, but of the same depth. In the south-east quarter of the square courtyard there is a reservoir for water which was probably filled by drainage from the roofs of the cells. Toward the middle of the wall on the eastern side there is a door leading into a room measuring 6.1 meters square used as a kitchen. To the north of it there were two doors, one leading to a cell and the other to the upstairs; to the east there are also two doors, both leading outside, where two projecting buttresses look as if intended for the latrine of the establishment; and to the south there is a single door leading into a big room 9.75 meters by 9.14 meters, a refectory. The roofs of all the cells and rooms, which were originally covered with overlapping domes, have fallen apart long ago.

Immediately to the west of the *vihāra* court is another larger quadrangle on the north side of the site, which is a 15.24 meters square structure enclosed by walls, as high as 9.14 meters, with a single entrance opened in the south side. In terms of its function, F. H. Wilcher inferred it may have been used as a place of cremation, A. Cunningham believed "this was the place set apart for general meetings of the Fraternity" , i. e. the meeting court[2], and D. B.

---

[1] According to *Datang xiyu qiufa gaoseng zhuan* [大唐西域求法高僧传, *Biographies of Eminent Priests of the Great Tang Dynasty Who Sought the Law in the Western Regions*] by Yijing [义净, 635-713 AD], *piheluo* [毗诃罗, vihāra] means a dwelling place, that was called *si* [寺, monastery] but incorrectly translated" . When A. Cunningham wrote reports on his reconnaissance of the Buddhist sites, he sometime preferred to use *vihāra* rather than monastery. 1) Yijing, *Datang xiyu qiufa gaoseng zhuan* (*Biographies of Eminent Priests of the Great Tang Dynasty Who Sought the Law in the Western Regions*), emended and annotated by Wang Bangwei [王邦维], Beijing: Zhonghua Book Company, 1988: 115; *confer Taishō*, Vol. 51: 6a; 2) A. Cunningham, *Archaeological Survey of India: Report of a Tour in the Punjab in 1878-79* (1883)/ Volume IX: 12.

[2] A. Cunningham, *Archaeological Survey of India: Report for the Year 1872-73* (1875)/ Volume V: 23-36, esp. 32, Plate VII.

Spooner conjectured that "M. Foucher has shown to have been originally the Hall of Conference"[1]. From the Buddhist texts in Chinese, however, it may be considered as an *uposathāgāra*. The outer walls on the north and west of this enclosure rise from the hillside and are extant even today. Although this square structure has some small holes in the walls for oil-lamps, there are no traces of any other openings in the walls, nor of any seats or smaller buildings on the ground. It should be a place set apart for general meetings of the monks, an *uposathāgāra*[2]. The single opening and the high walls would secure privacy, and it is hard to imagine any other function for which they could have been intended.

To the south of the *uposathāgāra,* there are ten so-called "underground" chambers, which could be called "low-level" chambers, because their being underground was apparently accidental and they are not truly subterranean. These chambers which were constructed later than the wall of the west part of the central court are built against, but not bonded with, that wall. Their roofs consisting of corbelled arches, 4.27 meters high and covered with a thick layer of earth, are level with the said central court (fig.9a). A. Cunningham conjectured that these chambers were the store-rooms or granaries of the whole monastic complex.

And, to the south of these ten "low-level" chambers are another court and a long vaulted passage descending into the valley below. Here there are six pairs of colossal Buddhas' feet in stucco, placed against the southern wall of this court; the place was thus called "Court of the Colossi"; beneath the court is the vaulted passage (fig.9b).

The entire Buddhist remains at Takht-i-Bāhī[3] are really a typical model or prototype of the free-standing monastic complex of Gandhāra, in which, both the *stūpa* court and the *vihāra* court are the most important components.

---

[1] D. B. Spooner, *opere citato*: 132-148, esp. 134, Pl. I.

[2] Daoxuan [道宣], *Sifenlü shanfan buque xingshi chao* [四分律删繁补阙行事钞, *The Essentials of "The Fourfold Rules of Discipline"*], Fascicle 1, *Taishō,* Vol. 40: 35b.

[3] The above description of the ruined site at Takht-i-Bāhī is based on the reports made separately by A. Cunningham, D. B. Spooner and H. Hargreaves. 1) A. Cunningham, *Archaeological Survey of India: Report for the Year 1872-73* (1875)/ Volume V: 23-36, esp. 26-33; 2) D. B. Spooner, *opere citato*: 132-148; 3) H. Hargreaves, *opere citato*: 33-39.

Located in the center of the ancient territory of Uḍḍiyāna, the principal nucleus of the Buddhist sacred area of Saidu Sharīf I, Swāt, comprises "the *Stūpa* Terrace and the Monastery Terrace"[1], which indicate the *stūpa* court and *vihāra* court respectively (fig.10a). The *vihāra* court, which stands at a higher level to the east of the *stūpa* court and presents a stratigraphy and succession of floors pointing definitely to being in synchrony with those of the *stūpa* court, was founded together with the *stūpa* court as part of a unified scheme and connected with each other by a stairway[2]. According to Domenico Faccenna, who was in charge of the archaeological excavation on the Buddhist sacred area of Saidu Sharīf I, "the earliest construction stage of the sacred buildings probably dates to the 1st century AD", "Saidu Sharif I displays a certain decline extending through the 4th century" and ends "in the 5th century" (fig.10b-c)[3].

This type of layout, however, not only was very prevalent in Gandhāra proper and Uḍḍiyāna, but also in Takṣaśila, as the monastic complex at Jauliāñ, Taxila. In other words, a similar arrangement of a free-standing monastery was popular in Jibin/the Greater Gandhāra from the second century AD onwards. According to John Marshall, the monuments at Jauliāñ (fig.11) "comprise a monastery of moderate dimensions, and by its side two *stūpa* courts on different levels—the upper to the south, the lower to the north—with a third and smaller court adjoining them on the west. The Main *Stūpa* stands in the upper court, with a number of smaller *stūpas* closely arrayed on its four sides and with lines of chapels for cult images ranged against the four walls of the court and facing, as usual, towards the *stūpa*. Other *stūpas* and chapels similarly disposed stand in the lower and smaller court. The monastery, which is designed on the same lines as the one at Mohṛā Morādu,

[1] Pierfrancesco Callieri, *Saidu Sharif I* (*Swat, Pakistan*), 1 *The Buddhist Sacred Area; The Monastery*, Rome: IsMEO, 1989: 3-141, esp. 4; Figs. 2-3.

[2] Domenico Faccenna, *Saidu Sharif I* (*Swat, Pakistan*), 2 *The Buddhist Sacred Area; The Stūpa Terrace*, Text, Rome: IsMEO, 1995: 143-163, esp. 145, Figs. 22-23.

[3] 1) Francesco Noci et al, *Saidu Sharif I* (*Swat, Pakistan*), 3 *The Graveyard*, Rome: IsIAO, 1997: 107-111, esp. 111; 2) Domenico Faccenna, *opere citato*: 143-163, esp. 157-159.

contains an open quadrangle surrounded by cells, besides an ordination hall (assembly hall), refectory and other chambers. "[1] Here, the monastery is in fact a *vihāra* and the two *stūpa* courts recorded by John Marshall are two components of a large *stūpa* court. A big *stūpa* stands in the middle of the southern part of the large *stūpa* court, with smaller votive *stūpas* and niches arranged around it, and the large *stūpa* court is surrounded by the lofty chapels. The *vihāra* court here, which is similar to those at both Takht-i-Bāhī and Saidu Sharīf I in ground plan, has two storeys and is provided with *uposathāgāra* or *prāsāda,* kitchen and refectory, besides the stone pavement, stairs, niches, water reservoir and cells.

Such a design of the monastic complex completely coincided with the notes that the Chinese pilgrims took of the *saṃghārāma* or monastery of Greater Gandhāra while they made their pilgrimage to some Buddhist centers there. According to records by Song Yun and Huisheng, who visited this region early in 520 AD, "to the north of the [capital] city [of Uḍḍiyāna] is the Tuoluo Monastery, which has the largest number of the Buddhist relics. The *futu* (*stūpa*) is high and large, and the *sengfang* (*vihāra*) is crowded off to the side. It has six thousand (or sixty) golden statues arranged around"[2]. This indicates clearly that the *stūpa* was the center of a *saṃghārāma,* the *vihāra* was absolutely necessary or indispensable to a *saṃghārāma,* and the image-niches were a place set apart for making an obeisance and doing monastic

[1] 1) John Marshall, *Excavations at Taxila: The Stūpas and Monastery at Jauliāñ; Memoir No. 7 of the Archaeological Survey of India*, Calcutta: Archaeological Survey of India, 1921: 3-19, esp. 3; 2) John Marshall, *Taxila: An illustrated account of archaeological excavations carried out at Taxila under the orders of the Government of India between the years 1913 and 1934,* London: Cambridge University Press, 1951, Volume I: 368-387.

[2] 1) Yang Xuanzhi [杨衒之], *Luoyang qielan ji* [洛阳伽蓝记, *A Record of Buddhist Saṃghārāmas in Luoyang*] in 547 AD, emended and annotated by Zhou Zumo [周祖谟], Beijing: Zhonghua Book Company, 1963: 203; 2) Yi-t'ung Wang [王伊同], tr., *A Record of Buddhist Monasteries in Lo-yang* by Yang Hsüan-chih, Princeton: Princeton University Press, 1984: 231.

Both Giuseppe Tucci and Domenico Faccenna "wish to identify the Sacred Precinct of BI (Butkara I, Swāt) with the T'o-lo sanctuary (the monastery of T'a-lo)". 1) Giuseppe Tucci, "Preliminary Report on an Archaeological Survey in Swāt", in: *East and West,* IX/4 (1958): 279-348, esp. 280, 288; 2) Domenico Faccenna, *Butkara I* (*Swāt, Pakistan*) *1956-1962*, Part 1, Text, Rome: IsMEO, 1980: 171-172.

confession and repentance (*vandanā* and *pāpa-deśanā*). "Once a *bhikṣu* lives at an *araṇya* alone for 15 days, he should sprinkle water and sweep the courtyards of *ta* (*stūpa*), *si* (*vihāra*), *busachu* (*uposathāgāra*) and *zhongting* (*prāsādâṅgana* or central court), then lay and spread seats (*niṣidana*) one after another" [1]. Thus, the *stūpa*, *vihāra,* central court as well as *uposathāgāra* or *prāsāda* are a basic set or components of a large *saṃghārāma* of Hinduka.

On the basis of the *Fayuan zhulin* (*Forest of Gems in the Garden of the Law*) by Daoshi (？ -668 AD), "when a Buddhist monastery begins to be designed, *foyuan* (the Buddha's court/a court of the Buddha image) and *sengyuan* (*vihāra* court) have to be built separately, each has its own courtyard. If it is a large monastery, a separate *fota* (*stūpa*) should be added" [2]. In the light of *Foshuo zhude futian jing* (*Sūtra on the Field of Blessedness of all Virtues*), "the first of the seven fields of blessedness is to construct a *fotu* (*stūpa*), *sengfang* (*vihāra*) and *tangge* (*prāsāda*)" [3]. *Pusa benxing jing* (*Sūtra on Bodhisattva's Own Deeds*) emphasizes the resultant benefits of alms-giving to a hundred *Pratyeka-buddhas* is less than that of building a *ta* (*stūpa*) and a *sengfangjingshe* (*vihāra*)" [4]. We are also told by Kikkāya or Kinkara and Tanyao in the Chinese version of *Za baozang jing* (*Kṣudrakapiṭaka/Storehouse of Various Treasures Sūtra* or *The Scriptural Text: Storehouse of Sundry Valuables*) as follows: "While the Buddha stayed in Rājagṛha, Bimbisāra constructed a *futu* (*stūpa*) and a *sengfang* (*vihāra*) for him. Later, a householder or elder built a *jiangtang* (*prāsāda*) at Tathāgata's *caṅkramaṇa* [5], with its four gates open. The householder was reborn in the heaven after his death... the Buddha said 'the householder was among men who built a *prāsāda* for the Buddha. Because of such a good causal deed, he was reborn in heaven'" [6]. "A householder of Hinduka who lived in the south of Gṛdhrakūṭa

---

[1] Puṇyatāra［弗若多罗］and Kumārajīva［鸠摩罗什］tr., *Shisong lü*［十诵律，*The Ten Divisions of Monastic Rules/Sarvstivāda-vinaya*］, Fascicle 56, in: *Taishō,* Vol. 23: 411a.

[2] *Taishō,* Vol. 53: 751c.

[3] *Taishō,* Vol. 16: 777b.

[4] *Taishō,* Vol. 3: 114c.

[5] A Tathāgata's *caṅkramaṇa* was a place that Tathāgat used to walk about when meditating to prevent sleepiness.

[6] *Taishō,* Vol. 4: 475c.

requested to build a *futu* (*stūpa*) and a *sengfang zhuchu* (*vihāra*) for the Tathāgata after he saw the *stūpa* and *vihāra* constructed by Bimbisāra. Then the householder reincarnated in the heaven after his death... the Buddha said 'the reason why the householder was reborn in the heaven is because of such a good causal deed'"[1].

In accordance with *vinaya* rules, such as *Mohesengqi lü* (*Mahāsaṃghikavinaya*) and *Sifelü shanfan buque xingshi chao* (*Essentials of the Fourfold Rules of Discipline*)[2], the *stūpa* court and the *vihāra* court have been held in the greatest esteem. Besides self-cultivation (*caryā*), worship and confession (*vandanā* and *pāpa-deśanā*), *bhikṣus* "rise at dawn and should sweep the *tayuan* (*stūpa* court) and the *sengfangyuan* (*vihāra* court)"[3]; *bhikṣus* "rise at dawn and sweep *tayuan* (*stūpa* court) and *sengyuan* (*vihāra* court)"[4]. "One should give the *ta* (*stūpa*) and *sengyuan* (*vihāra* court) a thorough cleaning when the *poṣadha* takes place"[5]. "If one finds something untidy and dirty in the *tayuan* (*stūpa* court) and *sengyuan* (*vihāra* court), they should be swept clean. "[6] During the morning of the *poṣadha, bhikṣus* are requested to whisk or wipe off the *tamiao* (*stūpa*), sprinkle water and sweep the floor of the *siyuan* (*vihāra* court)[7]. "If it is the date of the *poṣadha,* the *ta* (*stūpa*) and the *sengyuan* (*vihāra* court) should be given a thorough cleaning."[8]

Therefore, the traditional idea that "to worship a *stūpa* is to worship the Buddha" and the belief of benefits deriving from building *stūpa* and *vihāra* as

---

[1] *Taishō,* Vol. 4: 475c.

[2] *Sifelü shanfan buque xingshi chao* (*Essentials of the Fourfold Rules of Discipline*) is a commentary on *Sifen lü* [四分律, *Fourfold Rules of Discipline/Dharmaguptaka-vinaya*]. It was compiled in 630 AD by Daoxuan, who was the founder of the Nanshan branch of the Precepts school in China. *confer Taishō,* No. 1804, Vol. 40: 1-156.

[3] Buddhabhadra [佛陀跋陀罗] and Faxian [法显] tr., *Mohesengqi lü* (*Mahāsaṃghika-vinaya*), Fascicle 25; see *Taishō,* Vol. 22: 429b.

[4] Buddhabhadra and Faxian tr., *ibidem,* fascicle 25; *Taishō,* Vol. 22: 433a.

[5] Buddhabhadra and Faxian tr., *ibidem,* fascicle 27; *Taishō,* Vol. 22: 450b.

[6] Buddhabhadra and Faxian tr., *Ibidem*, fascicle 34; *Taishō,* Vol. 22: 504c.

[7] Daoxuan, *Sifelü shanfan buque xingshi chao* (*Essentials of the Fourfold Rules of Discipline*), Fascicle 1; *Taishō,* Vol. 40: 23c.

[8] Daoxuan, *opere citato*: 35a.

well as *uposathāgāra* or *prāsāda,* accompanied by strict discipline rules, caused Buddhist believers to have the greatest esteem for those buildings—*stūpa*, *vihāra* and *uposathāgāra* or *prāsāda*. In other words, the Chinese translation of Buddhist texts underlines the high position the *stūpa* court and the *vihāra* court of Hinduka saṃghārāmas held in the mind of Buddhists.

In addition to the above design of the *saṃghārāma* of the Greater Gandhāra, there are two more Buddhist monastery sites deserving attention. One is the structural remains of mound B at Jaṇḍiāl, Taxila, the other is the ruins of Pippala in the same area.

The mound B at Jaṇḍiāl, which was called "*stūpa* and monastery at Babar-Khäna" by A. Cunningham and was numbered 40 in his map of the ruins of Taxila, was acknowledged to contain the remains of a *stūpa* set in a courtyard and surrounded by buildings (figs.12a-b)[1]. According to John Marshall, the *stūpa* in the centre is of two different time periods, having originally been built in Śaka-Parthian times, and rebuilt in the third or fourth century of our era. The most significant feature of the remains is "the unusual plan of the foundations on the north and west sides of the *stūpa*-court. In the Śaka-Parthian period to which this *stūpa* is referable, we should not, of course, expect to find a quadrangle enclosed by rows of symmetrical cells, such as are characteristic of later monasteries, nor can we in fact be sure that any of the surviving chambers were used for residential purpose. The small group Q, R, S, may have been so used, but the larger building T at the north-east corner was evidently an open court with a small chapel—possibly for an image—projecting into it from its northern side. And on the west side of the quadrangle, what appear at first sight to have been long narrow rooms (N, O, P), were in fact nothing more than the

[1] In 1863, this site was first excavated by A. Cunningham, who appears to have excavated as far as the later structure only. Description and plan (fig.12a) of the site by him have drawn the scholars' attention. "The central *stūpa*, about 45 feet (13.72 meters) in diameter, was surrounded by open cloisters 8 feet (2.44 meters) wide, forming a square of 90 feet (27.43 meters), behind which were the cells of the monks, each 9 $\frac{1}{2}$ feet (2.9 meters) broad and 14 $\frac{1}{2}$ feet (4.42 meters) long. 1) A. Cunningham, *Archaeological Survey of India: Four Reports made during the years 1862-63-64-65* (1872)/ Volume I: 111-135, esp. 120-21, 132, Pl. LVII; 2) A. Cunningham, *Archaeological Survey of India: Report for the Year 1872-73* (1875)/ Volume V: 74-75, Pl. XX.

foundations of a raised platform" [1].

The remains at Pippala, Taxila, are also of two different time periods. "To the east is the courtyard of a monastery (*vihāra*) dating from late Pathian or early Kushān times and comprising an open quadrangle in the centre with ranges of cells on its four sides. In the middle of the courtyard is the basement of a square *stūpa* facing north. " [2] (fig.13)

Because the *stūpa* and the *vihāra* were such important components in the plan of the *saṃghārāma* of Hinduka, such a monastic complex was also translated or commonly called *tasi* (*stūpa*-cum-*vihāra*/*stūpa* and *vihāra*) in Chinese [3]. On the basis of *Za baozang jing* (*Kṣudrakapiṭaka*/*Storehouse of Various Treasures Sūtra*), a *gṛhapati* (elder or householder) from Śrāvastī used to build *futu* (*stūpa*) and *sengfang* (*vihāra*). Later, the elder was born again in Trayastriṁśās after he died of illness. The *futu* (*stūpa*) and *sengfang* (*vihāra*) built by him, which were generally called *tasi* (*stūpa*-cum-*vihāra*) for short, were repaired or renovated by his wife who always thought of her husband and made offerings to Buddhists. The elder's wife was also reborn in the same heaven after she lived her full life span.

[1] John Marshall, who believes that the description and plan of the site published by A. Cunningham are fanciful and misleading, records the site as follows: The earlier structure "is a little less than 33 ft. (10.06 meters) square, with a projecting staircase on its southern face, and a relic chamber measuring 11 × 14 ft. (3.35 × 4.27 meters) in the center" . Leading from the entrance of the *vihāra* to the steps on the south side is a narrow causeway made of the stone. "When this *stūpa* and the buildings connected with it had fallen to decay, another *stūpa* and a second series of buildings were erected on their ruins. This later *stūpa* has a circular plinth, 35 ft. (10.67 meters) in diameter." (fig.12b) John Marshall, *Taxila: An illustrated account of archaeological excavations carried out at Taxila under the orders of the Government of India between the years 1913 and 1934,* London: Cambridge University Press, 1951, Volume I: 355-56; Volume III: Pls. 1, 91, 92a.

[2] This early monastery "must have fallen to ruin before the fourth to fifth century of our era; for at that time a second monastery was erected over the western side of it, completely hiding beneath its foundations all that remained of the old cells and veranda on this side. At the same time, also, the rest of the early monastery was converted into a *stūpa* court by dismantling and leveling with the ground everything except the *stūpa* in the open quadrangle and the back wall of the cells, which was now to serve as an enclosure wall for the new courtyard" . John Marshall, *opere citato,* Volume I: 365-67, esp. 365; Volume III, Pls. 98a, 99a-b, 100a.

[3] Huiyuan [惠苑], *Xinyi dafangguangfo huayanjing yinyi* [新译大方广佛花严经音义, *Pronunciation and Meaning for Buddhist Terms in the Buddhāvataṁsaka-mahāvaipulya-sūtra*/*Pronunciation and Meaning for Buddhist Terms in the Flower Garland Sūtra* (*Avataṃsaka-sūtra*)], Fascicle 2; in: *Taishō,* Vol. 54: 453c.

The reason why they were both reborn in the Trayastriṁśās is because of their merits and virtues[1]. According to Song Yun and Huisheng, "thence they traveled westward for five days before reaching the place where the Tathāgata [agreed to] be beheaded in compliance with someone's request. There too was a *tasi* (*stūpa*-cum-*vihāra* or a stūpa and a monastery) that housed more than twenty monks... Traveling westward for another day, they reached the place where the Tathāgata tore out his eyes to benefit others. There was also a *tasi* (*stūpa*-cum-*vihāra*)... Thereafter they traveled westward for seven days, and, after having crossed a large river, they reached the place where the Tathāgata, as King Śibi, saved the life of a dove. A *tasi* (*stūpa*-cum-*vihāra*) was built to commemorate this event"[2].

3. Origin of the Saṃghārāma in Pincheng

According to Fei Zhangfang, Tanyao, who held the position of national director of the Buddhist clergy of the Northern Wei, invited *bhikṣus* and monks of Hinduka to translate Buddhist scriptures at the Great Cave-temple Complex of Wuzhou in the third year of the Heping period of the Northern Wei (462 AD)[3]. This seems to prove that the construction of the cave-temples based on the original design, of which Tanyao was in charge, had been finished before that year[4]. In other words, if the cave-temples designed by Tanyao were not completely carved out, some rock-cut caves and timber structures such as the building where the *bhikṣus* of Hinduka translated scriptures had been put into use before 462 AD. The ruined temple unearthed at the western part of the summit of the Yungang cave-temples, above the five caves designed by Tanyao (Cave Nos. 16-20), should be the free-standing temple consisting of several cells on the crest of the Wuzhou Hill recorded in the *Jin Tablet*. This might be also the place where

[1] *Taishō*, Vol. 4: 473b-c.

[2] 1) Yang Xuanzhi, *opere citato*: 212-213, 220-221; 2) Yi-t'ung Wang, *opere citato*: 237, 238-243.

[3] Fei Zhangfang, *opere citato*: 85a-b.

[4] Tang Yongtong, *Han wei liang jin nanbeichao fojiao shi* [汉魏两晋南北朝佛教史, *A History of Buddhism from the Han down to the Southern and Northern Dynasties* (1st to 6th century AD)], Beijing: Zhonghua Book Company, 1982: 359.

the *bhikṣus* of Hinduka translated the Buddhist scriptures at the Wuzhou Cave-temple Complex. The construction of this free-standing temple may have been started simultaneously with that of the five caves by Tanyao and finished before the third year of the Heping period of the Northern Wei, in 462 AD as previously mentioned. When the free-standing temple atop the crest of the Wuzhou Hill was originally designed, it should have followed "the general rule that construction of the monastery and *stūpa* (in China) was still based on the old form or prototype of Hinduka" and combined the *stūpa* court and the *vihāra* court into one on the basis of the layout of the Buddhist monastery in Hinduka or the Greater Gandhara[1], or it may have directly accepted the design of the early *stūpa*-cum-*vihāra* type at Pippala[2], Taxila, with the *stūpa* in the center, the surrounding monks' cells and the cloister in front of the cells[3]. This free-standing temple at the crest of the

[1] Kikkāya/ Kinkara, who edited and translated *Fu fazang yinyuan zhuan* [付法藏因缘传, *A History of the Buddha's Successors*] into Chinese at Tanyao's request, might have come from the Greater Gandhāra. In 472, together with Tanyao, Kikkāya translated *Za baozang jing* [*Kṣudrakapiṭaka/ Storehouse of Various Treasures Sūtra* or *The Scriptural Text: Storehouse of Sundry Valuables*] and retranslated *Fu fazang yinyuan zhuan* [*A History of the Buddha's Successors*]. Many stories and plots in *Za baozang jing* [*Kṣudrakapiṭaka/Storehouse of Various Treasures Sūtra*], which probably belongs to the Dharmagupta school, occurred or were set in Greater Gandhāra. Therefore, it may not be accidental that the plan of the ruined temple atop the Yungang caves resembles that of the Buddhist monastery of Greater Gandhāra. Charles Willemen, "A Chinese Kṣudrakapiṭaka (T. IV. 203)", in: *Asiatische Studien Études Asiatiques* XLVI. 1. 1992: 507-515.

[2] According to *Fanwangjing pusa jieben shu* [梵网经菩萨戒本疏, *Annotation on the Latter Part of the Brahma-jāla-sūtra/Sūtra of Brahmā's Net*] by Fazang [法藏, 643-712 AD], however, "to construct a Buddha hall and a *stūpa* in the courtyard of the *vihāra* and to take water from a well in the courtyard of the *stūpa* were both serious fault. *Taishō,* Vol. 40: 615a.

[3] A brick-built *stūpa*-cum-*vihāra* on the right bank of River Waghora, Ajāṇṭa, was discovered in 2000, which is very similar to the ground plan of the free-standing *stūpa*-cum-*vihāra* at Pippala, Taxila. It "consists of row of cells on three sides (south, west and north) with perhaps a common entrance towards the River Waghora on the eastern side. The southern wing consists of a row of five cells, the northern wing consists of three cells, while the western wing has a single centrally located cell with a front passage. There are two more 1.3 m wide passages all along the entire length of the northern and southern wings connecting the central cell. The entrance of the cells open into these passages. Opposite to the central cell at distance of 2.20 m east, a rectangular brick platform meant for a stupa was located. This forms the centre of the monastery". On the basis of the polished wares and a gold coin of Byzantime king Theodosiu (datable to 402-450 AD) unearthed, the site can be dated to the fourth and fifth centuries A.D. There might be some relation between the brick-built *stūpa*-cum-*vihāra* at Ajāṇṭa and the free-standing *stūpa*-cum-*vihāra* at the crest of Wuzhou Hill, Datong. *confer: Indian Archaeology 2000-01: A Review:* 92-97.

Wuzhou Hill, however, was a very early attempt to sinicize the *saṃghārāma* of Hinduka. The Yongning Monastery built later at Luoyang, evolved from such a design, was a completely sinicized Buddhist *saṃghārāma* in China[1].

(The paper was presented to the Conference on the Occasion of the 50th Anniversary of the Department of Archaeology, Peshawar University and published in *Ancient Pakistan*, Vol. XXIII: 13-54)

---

[1] Yongning Monastery [永宁寺] was constructed in the first year of the Xiping period (516 AD) of the Northern Wei, by decree of Empress Dowager Ling, whose surname was Hu [灵太后胡氏]. It was located one *li* (0.5 km) south of the Changhe Gate [阊阖门] on the west side of the Imperial Drive [御道], facing the palace grounds... Within the precincts of the monastery was a nine-storied wooden *stūpa* [浮图]. Rising nine hundred Chinese feet (251 meters) above the ground, it formed the base for a mast that extended for another one hundred Chinese feet (27. 9 meters); thus together they soared one thousand Chinese feet (279 meters) above the ground, and could be seen as far away from the capital as one hundred *li* (50 km)... North of the *stūpa* was the Buddha hall [佛殿], which was shaped like the Palace of the Great Ultimate [太极殿]. In the hall was a golden statue of the Buddha eighteen Chinese feet (5 meters) high, along with ten medium-sized images—three of sewn pearls, five of woven golden threads, and two of jade. The superb artistry was matchless, unparalleled in its day... The monastery had over one thousand cloisters for the monks [僧房楼观], both single cloisters and multilevel ones, decorated with carved beams and painted walls... The walls of the monastery were all covered with short rafters beneath the titles in the same style as our contemporary palace walls. There were gates in each of the four directions. The tower on the South Gate rose two hundred Chinese feet (55. 8 meters) above the ground, had three stories, each with an archway, and was shaped like the present-day Duanmen Gate [端门] of the palace grounds. 1) Yang Xuanzhi, *opere citato*: 17-24; 2) Yi-t'ung Wang, *opere citato*: 13-17.

The Yongning Monastery took the wooden *stūpa*, square in plan, as the centre of the monastery. The main gate, the *stūpa* and the Buddha hall were constructed from south to north, forming a central axis, with additional architectures or buildings such as the cloisters for the monks arranged by side in bilateral symmetry.

The Institute of Archaeology, Chinese Academy of Social Sciences [中国社会科学院考古研究所], *Beiwei Luoyang Yongningsi* [北魏洛阳永宁寺：1979-1994年考古发掘报告, *The Yongning Monastery in the Northern Wei Luoyang*: *An illustrated account of archaeological excavations carried out between the years 1979 and 1994*], Beijing: The Encyclopedia of China Publishing House, 1996: 6-8, Figure 4.

Kumārajīva and Early Cave-temples of China: the Case of *Dhyāna-sūtras*

Kumārajīva [鸠摩罗什, 344-413 AD or 350-409 AD][1] was a great scholar of the Buddhist *Tripiṭaka* [三藏] and an eminent translator of the Buddhist scriptures. His teaching and translations exerted a far-reaching influence on Buddhism as well as Buddhist art in China. Therefore, Kumārajīva occupies a pivotal position in the history of Sino-Indian cultural relations.

1. Kumārajīva's Translations of the *Sūtras*

According to *Weishu: Shilaozhi* [魏书·释老志, *History of the Wei Dynasties: Treatise on Buddhism and Taoism*] by Wei Shou [魏 收], at that time there was in the Western Regions a foreign *śramaṇa* by the name of Kumārajīva who was eager of spreading the Dharma (Buddhism). The eminent Chinese monk Dao'an [道安, 312-385 AD][2] was much greatly interested to have discussions with Kumārajīva and often urged Fu Jian [符坚], founder of the Former Qin state [前秦, 351-394 AD], to send for him. Kumārajīva, in his turn, having heard of Dao'an's noble reputation,

---

[1] Lü Cheng [吕澂], *Zhongguo foxue yuanliu luejiang* [中国佛学源流略讲, *A Survey of the Chinese Buddhism*], Beijing: Zhonghua Book Company, 1979: 87.

[2] Dao'an was also a great scholar of the Buddhist *Tripiṭaka* and an eminent translator of Buddhist scriptures in the 4th century AD in northern China. Tang Yongtong [汤用彤], *Han wei liang jin nanbeichao fojiao shi* [汉魏两晋南北朝佛教史, *A History of Buddhism from the Han down to the Southern and Northern Dynasties* (1st to 6th *century* AD), Shanghai: The Commercial Press, 1938; 2nd ed., Beijing: Zhonghua Book Company, 1982: 133-163.

called him the Saint of the East. At times he paid him his respects by bowing to him from afar. Some twenty years after Dao'an's death, Kumārajīva arrived in Chang'an [长安, present-day Xi'an]. He regretted not finding Dao'an and was deeply sorrowed by his loss. The ideas in the texts corrected by Dao'an and the versions translated by Kumārajīva are in complete harmony and entirely free from disagreement. Through Kumārajīva's work, the content of the Dharma was made widely known throughout central China [中原][1].

When Kumārajīva arrived in Chang'an in 401 AD at the invitation of Yao Xing [姚兴], ruler of the Later Qin state [后秦, 384-417 AD], he was given the position of National Preceptor [国师, *purohita*][2]. At the Caotang Monastery [草堂寺] in Chang'an, eight hundred students gathered together to interpret or retranslate scriptures under his guidance. The eloquent and great thinker Kumārajīva knew both Chinese and the vernacular languages of the Western Regions. At that time *śramaṇas* such as Daorong [道彤], Senglue [僧略], Daoheng [道恒], Daobiao [道檦], Sengzhao [僧肇], Tanying [昙影] and others, along with Kumārajīva, helped one another to elucidate what was very obscure. They altered and fixed the composition of ten odd works consisting of long, profound *sūtras* and *śāstras,* so that the text might be clear and intelligible. Down to this day these works are taken as models by all *śramaṇas* in their studies[3]. According to *Jinshu: Yaoxing zaiji* [晋书·姚兴载记, *History of the Jin Dynasties*: *Biography of Yaoxing*] by Fang Xuanling [房玄龄], about five thousand *śramaṇas* and monks from far away areas

---

[1] Wei Shou, *Weishu* [魏书, *History of the Wei Dynasties*], punctuated edition, Beijing: Zhonghua Book Company, 1974: 3025-3062, esp. 3029-30. confer: 1) James R. Ware, "Wei Shou on Buddhism", in: *T'oung Pao*, 30 (1930): 100-181, esp. 125-126; 2) Leon Hurvitz, "Treatise on Buddhism and Taoism by Wei Shou", in: *Yun-kang; The Buddhist Cave-temples of the Fifth Century AD. in North China; detailed report of the archaeological survey carried out by the mission of the Tōhōbunka Kenkyūsho 1938-45* by S. Mizuno and T. Nagahiro, Vol. XVI, Supplement and Index, Kyoto: Jimbunkagaku Kenkyūshō, Kyoto University, 1956: 23-103, esp. 50.

[2] Sengyou [僧佑], *Chu sanzang ji ji* [出三藏记集, *A Collection of Records concerning the Tripiṭaka or A Collection of Records of Translations of the Tripiṭaka*), emended and annotated by Su Jinren [苏晋仁] and Xiao Lianzi [萧錬子], Beijing: Zhonghua Book Company, 1995: 533; *confer Taishō,* No. 2145, Vol. 55: 100-102, esp. 101b.

[3] Wei Shou, *opere citato*: 3031; *confer*: 1) James R. Ware, *opere citato*: 130-131; 2) Leon Hurvitz, *opere citato*: 54.

gathered at the capital (Chang'an), a *stūpa* was built at Yongguili [永 贵 里] and a *prajñā* platform [般若台] was set up in the palace [中宫]. The *śramaṇas* who practiced *dhyāna* numbered in the thousands, and all counties and prefectures were influenced by Kumārajīva's teaching and translations with the result that nearly ninety per cent of the people in the state converted to Buddhism[1].

During this period, regions and territories occupied by the Han nation lacked *sūtra* and *vinaya* texts in the vernacular language; they were, thus, inaccessible to the masses. Kumārajīva, consequently, was immersed in the translation of Buddhist scriptures. On the basis of a conversation between Kumārajīva and Vimalākṣa [卑摩罗叉], most of the new scriptures on the Buddhist *sūtra* [经, the Buddha's doctrinal teachings], *vinaya* [律, rules of the monastic discipline] and *śāstras* or *Abhidharma* [论, commentaries on *sūtras* and *vinaya*] were reinterpreted or translated into Chinese by Kumārajīva, and more than three thousands students of the Dharma studied with him[2]. According to *Chu sanzang ji ji* (*A Collection of Records concerning the Tripiṭaka*) by Sengyou, Kumārajīva continuously produced or translated 35 Buddhist texts into Chinese in 294 fascicles. Among them were *Emituo jing* [阿弥陀经, *Sukhāvatīvyūha, Amitabha-sūtra*], *Fahua jing* [法华经, *Saddharma-puṇḍarīka-sūtra, Lotus Sūtra*], *Weimojie jing* [维摩诘经, *Vimalakīrti-nirdeśa-sūtra*], *Shizhu jing* [十住经, *Daśabhūmikā sūtra, Sūtra on the Ten Stages*], *Yijiao jing* [遗教经, *The Buddha's Legacy Teachings Sūtra*], *Mile xiasheng jing* [弥勒下生经, *Maitreyavyākaraṇa, Advent of Maitreya Sūtra*], *Foshuo mile chengfo jing* [佛说弥勒成佛经, *Sūtra of Maitreya becoming a Buddha*], *Shisong lü* [十诵律, *Sarvāstivādavinaya, Ten Divisions of Monastic Rules*], *Dapin bore* [大品般若, *Mahāprajñāpāramita-sūtra, Larger Wisdom Sūtra*], *Xiaopin bore* [小品般若, *Smaller Wisdom Sūtra*], *Bailun* [百论, *Treatise in One Hundred Verses*], *Zhonglun* [中论, *Mādhyamika-śāstra, Treatise on the Middle Way*], *Shi'ermen lun* [十二门论, *Treatise on the Twelve Gates*], *Dazhidu lun* [大智度论, *Mahāprajñāpāramitā-śāstra, Treatise on the Great Perfection of Wisdom*] and *Chengshi lun* [成实论, *Satyasiddhi-śāstra*,

---

[1] Fang Xuanling [房玄龄] et al, *Jinshu* [晋书, *History of the Jin Dynasties*], punctuated edition, Beijing: Zhonghua Book Company, 1974: 2975-3006, esp. 2985.

[2] Sengyou, *opere citato*: 535; *confer Taishō,* Vol. 55: 102a.

Treatise on the Establishment of Truth]. In addition, Kumārajīva translated and compiled some *sūtras* on *dhyāna* such as *Chanfa yaojie* [禅法要解, *Interpretation of the Dhyāna-discipline* or *Essential Explanation of the Way to Meditate*], *Chanjing* [禅经, *Dhyāna-sūtra or Dhyāna-meditation-sūtra*]/*Zuochan sanmei jing* [坐禅三昧经, *Dhyāna-samādhi-sūtra, Sūtra on the Concentration of Sitting Meditation*]/ *Guanzhong chanjing* [关中禅经, *Dhyāna-sūtra translated in the Central Shaanxi Plain*] and *Chanfa yao* [禅法要, *Essentials of the Dhyāna-discipline*]/*Chanmi yaofa jing* [禅密要法经, *Secret Essentials of the Dhyāna-discipline* or *Sūtra about the Secret Essence of Dhyāna*][1].

Undoubtedly, it is clear that Emperor Xiaowen [孝文帝, 471-499 AD] of the Northern Wei Dynasty was honoring Kumārajīva as a Saint who had attained Mahāyāna enlightenment of the bodhisattva stage and who had been active in converting the people. According to the *Weishu: Shilaozhi* (*History of the Wei Dynasties: Treatise on Buddhism and Taoism*), in the fifth month of the twenty-first year (497 AD) of Emperor Xiaowen, the following imperial order was issued: "Whereas the Master of the Law (*Dharmācārya*) Kumārajīva may be called a man who has quitted the world like a divinity and who has resolutely entered upon the Four Practices; and whereas the monastery which he constantly inhabited still has surplus land; and whereas we respect and take pleasure in the traces of his practices and deeply regret the master's demise; permission is granted to erect in memory of him a three-storied *stūpa* on the site of the old building which he inhabited"[2].

According to *Lüxiang gantong zhuan* [律相感通传, *Responses to Dreamlike Dialogues with Devas*] by Daoxuan [道宣], Kumārajīva thoroughly understood Mahāyāna enlightenment, fully comprehended the Buddha's preaching and freely translated the scriptures on the *sūtra*, *vinaya* and *śāstra*. Kumārajīva's translations have brought honor to his ancestors and prosperity to his descendants, an achievement which most others aspire to but cannot attain. Because his versions are faithful to the originals of the *Tripiṭaka,* they have been chanted and studied by Buddhist followers since they were translated into Chinese and were not

---

[1] Sengyou, *opere citato*: 49-51, 534; *confer Taishō,* Vol. 55: 10c-11a, 101b.

[2] Wei Shou, *opere citato*: 3040. confer: 1) James R. Ware, *opere citato*: 156; 2) Leon Hurvitz, *opere citato*: 82-83.

replaced by others at least until the early 7th century AD[1].

With respect to the various versions of the Buddhist *Tripiṭaka* in Chinese, only those translated by Kumārajīva continued to be popular throughout the centuries all over China, a trend which exists even up to modern times. Kumārijīva's translations and interpretations were prized by later generations for their excellence and clarity and were without parallel, in terms of technique and correction; they ushered in a new epoch in the history of the translation of the Buddhist *Tripiṭaka* and greatly impacted the development of Buddhism in China[2].

Dhyāna or meditation is a practice that focuses the mind on one point in order to purify the spirit, thereby eradicating illusions and perceiving the truth. *Dhyāna* was widely practiced in Hinduka (present-day the South Asian Subcontinent) before Śākyamuni was born, and was incorporated into Buddhism later, which developed its own forms and approaches. "When the Chinese were first brought face to face with Indian Buddhism with its rich and elaborate imagery, concepts, and modes of thinking, they were fascinated at first and finally overwhelmed and conquered. After a few centuries, however, the practical nature of the Chinese began asserting itself; it began to search for certain features within Buddhism which it could understand and practice, and in this search it soon picked on the *dhyāna* exercise as the essence of Buddhist discipline"[3].

In fact, ways of practicing meditation and stages of attainment began to be transmitted side by side after Buddhism spread into China, but there was not a regular method or pattern of meditation-practice until the late 4th century AD. The monk Sengrui［僧叡］, who was one of the disciples of monk Dao'an and later became an assistant of Kumārajīva, was filled with emotion and stated that "the heart cannot be laid at any place, because the way of *dhyāna* discipline has not been introduced yet"[4], or, in

［1］Daoxuan, *Lüxiang gantong zhuan* (*Responses to Dreamlike Dialogues with Devas*), in: *Taishō,* No. 1898, Vol. 45: 874-882, esp. 877a.

［2］Lü Cheng, *opere citato*: 86-99.

［3］Kenneth Ch'en, *Buddhism in China: A Historical Survey*, Princeton: Princeton University Press, 1973: 350.

［4］Huijiao［慧皎］, *Gaoseng zhuan*［高僧传, *Biographies of Eminent Priests or The Liang Dynasty Biographies of Eminent Priests or Biographies of Eminent Priests or Biographies of Eminent Monks or Memoirs of Eminent Monks*］, emended and annotated by Tang Yongtong［汤用彤］, Beijing: Zhonghua Book Company, 1992: 244; *confer Taishō,* No. 2059, Vol. 50: 364a.

other words, the heart of *dhyana*-discipline had not been understood at that time. Sengrui was taught and given instruction in *dhyāna*-discipline by Kumārajīva, only six days after Kumārajīva had arrived in Chang'an. On the basis of *Guanzhong chu chanjing xu* [关中出禅经序, *Preface to the Dhyāna-sūtra translated in the Central Shaanxi Plain*] by Sengrui, "*dhyāna* is the ABC to the *mārga* (way of Buddhism) and a ferry crossing to the *Nirvāṇa* (enlightenment)" [1]. In addition, the contemporary Buddhist scriptures in the region of the Yangtze at the time, according to the *Chu sanzang ji ji* (*A Collection of Records concerning the Tripiṭaka*) by Sengyou, were mostly incomplete; the *dhyāna* method was unheard of, and the available collection of monastic rules (*vinaya-piṭaka*) was also fragmentary. Huiyuan [慧远], a great master of Chinese Buddhism in southern China, was saddened by the incompleteness of the Buddhist doctrine and ordered his disciples Fajing [法净] and others to go far distance in search of Buddhist scriptures [2]. These records indicate that not only *dhyāna* scriptures were lacking or incomplete in northern China before the 4th century AD, but *sūtra* texts were also less translated during the initial stage of dissemination of Buddhism in southern China. *Dhyāna* was unknown to the public and *vinaya* texts were incomplete or with parts missing even in the same region during the same period [3]. After Kumārajīva came to Chang'an, key *dhyāna sūtras*, besides various scriptures on the *sūtra*, *vinaya* and *śāstra*, were reinterpreted or translated into Chinese by him along with his brilliant disciples. As a result, Huiyuan "expresses his joy at the translations made by Kumārajīva in this field" [4] and said that Kumārajīva had opened up a realm of *dhyāna*-discipline [5].

With regards to Kumārajīva's translations, *Chanjing* (*Dhyāna-sūtra*), namely, *Zuochan sanmei jing* (*Dhyāna-samādhi-sūtra*, *Sūtra on the Concentration of*

---

[1] Sengrui, "*Guanzhong chu chanjing xu* (Preface to *Dhyāna-sūtra translated in the Central Shaanxi Plain*)", in: *Sengyou, opere citato*: 342-343; *confer Taishō*, Vol. 55: 65a.

[2] Sengyou, *opere citato*: 568; *confer Taishō*, Vol. 55: 110a.

[3] Sengyou, *ibidem*.

[4] Erik Zürcher, *The Buddhist Conquest of China: The Spread and Adaptation of Buddhism in Early Medieval China*, Leiden: E. J. Brill, 1972: 223.

[5] Huiyuan, "*Lushan chu xiuxing fangbian chanjing xu* [庐山出修行方便禅经序, Preface to *Dhyāna-sūtra of Buddhasena/Dharmatrāta Dhyāna-sūtra translated at Mt. Lu* or *General Introduction to Dhyāna Scriptures produced on Mt. Lu as Means to Religious Cultivation*]", in: Sengyou, *opere citato*: 343-345; *confer Taishō*, Vol. 55: 66a.

Sitting Meditation) or *Guanzhong chanjing* (*Dhyāna-sūtra translated in the Central Shaanxi Plain*) in two fascicles[1], which explains the method of *dhyāna* practice in detail, was compiled and produced on the basis of seven *sūtras* on *dhyāna* discipline in 402 AD. This work was simultaneously the outcome of both interpreting and editing *sūtras* on *dhyāna*[2]. Later, *Chanfa yaojie* (*Interpretation of the Dhyāna-discipline* or *Essential Explanation of the Way to Meditate*) in two fascicles[3] was compiled according to *Chishi jing*［持世经, *Upholder of the Age Sūtra*］in the same year.[4] This work is similar to the general practice of Hīnayāna Buddhism. Since he was not satisfied with what he had translated or compiled before, Kumārajīva checked up his previous versions carefully and re-edited what he had previously done; he also worked on some other *sūtras* about *dhyāna*-discipline. As a result, *Chanfa yao* (*Essentials of the Dhyāna-discipline*), viz. *Chanmi yaofa jing* (*Secret Essentials of the Dhyāna-discipline* or *Sūtra about the Secret Essence of Dhyāna*) in three fascicle[5] finally came out in 407 AD[6]. It considers contemplation of filthiness［不净观, *aśubhā-smṛti*］[7] as the dominant factor and elaborates on the *dhyāna* discipline belonging to Hīnayāna Buddhism. In addition, Kumārajīva used to translate *Guanfo sanmei jing*［观佛三昧经, *Buddha-dhyāna-samādhī-sūtra*］into Chinese, but it was unfortunately lost[8]; *Siwei*

---

[1] *Taishō,* No. 614, Vol. 15: 269-286.

[2] Sengrui, *opere citato*: 342-343; *confer Taishō*, Vol. 55: 65a-b.

[3] *Taishō,* No. 616, Vol. 15: 286-297.

[4] Sengrui, *opere citato*: 342; *confer Taishō*, Vol. 55: 65b.

[5] *Taishō,* No. 613, Vol. 15: 242-269.

[6] Sengrui, *opere citato*: 342; *confer Taishō*, Vol. 55: 65b.

[7] The contemplation of filthiness (*aśubhā-smṛti*) is also called meditation on the vileness of the body or meditation on the impurity of the body. The practice of meditation or contemplation on the inherent impurity of the human body is to overcome craving and greed, that is, it is aimed at stemming desire and quieting the mind.

[8] 1) Fei Zhangfang［费长房］, *Lidai sanbo ji*［历代三宝记, *Record of the Triratna through the Ages* or *Record concerning the Triratna under Successive Dynasties*］, in: *Taishō,* No. 2034, Vol. 49: 78c; 2) Daoxuan, *Datang neidian lu*［大唐内典录, *The Great Tang Dynasty Catalogue of Buddhist Scriptures* or *A Catalogue of the Buddhist Canon compiled under the Tang Dynasty*］, in: *Taishō,* No. 2149, Vol. 55: 253b; 3) Zhisheng［智昇］, *Kaiyuan shijiao lu*［开元释教录, *The Kaiyuan Era Catalogue of the Buddhist Canon* or *A Catalogue of the Buddhist Sacred Books of the Kaiyuan Period* or *A Catalogue of the Buddhist Canon compiled in the Kaiyuan Period*］, in: *Taishō,* No. 2154, Vol. 55: 513b.

lueyao fa［思维略要法, *An Outline of Meditation* or *Outlining the Way to Reflect*］, which records ten kinds of contemplation and wholely belongs to Māhayāna Buddhism, seems to have also been translated by Kumārajīva[1].These versions of the *dhyāna sūtras* fully testify that Kumārajīva taught and gave instruction in *dhyāna* discipline immediately after he came to Chang'an. In conclusion, he carefully reinterpreted and edited the *dhyāna* scriptures[2].

As a matter of fact, Kumārajīva's mother had a strong interest in *dhyāna* and devoted herself to practicing the *dhyāna*-meditation. According to *Gaoseng zhuan* (*Biographies of Eminent Priests*) by Huijiao, when she traveled out of the city, she saw a cemetery with bare bones between the tombs scattered around randomly. She was deeply moved by the thought of suffering and its origin and she vowed to become a nun. She said that if her hair were not cut to become a nun, then she would not drink nor eat. After going hungry for six days and nights, her energy and strength were exhausted and it was doubtful that she would live until the morning. Her husband became frightened, and allowed her to become a nun under the circumstances. However, without shaving her hair, she would not eat. Thereupon, by an imperial order, her hair was cut. After that, she began to drink and eat. Then the next morning she received the precepts and happily did her meditation practice as before[3]. On his way back from Jibin［罽

---

［1］As for *Siwei lueyao fa* (*An Outline of Meditation* or *Outlining the Way to Reflect*), Sengyou put it under the translations of An Shigao［安世高］, but Fei Zhangfang, Daoxuan and Zhisheng listed this text as Kumārajīva's translation. However, Lü Cheng argues that its translator was mislabeled as Kumārajīva by Zhisheng and Charles Willemen infers that this Chinese text was probably established in the early 5th century in Jiankang by Chinese monks using popular ideas of the time. If a Hinduka *dhyāna* master was involved in the compilation, it may have been someone like Dharmamitra, ca. 430-440 AD.

1) Sengyou, *opere citato*: 25; *confer Taishō*, Vol. 55: 6a-b; 2) Fei Zhangfang, *ibidem*, *Taishō*, Vol. 49: 78c; 3) Daoxuan, *ibidem*, *Taishō*, Vol. 55: 253b; 4) Zhisheng, *ibidem*, *Taishō*, Vol. 55: 513b, 668b, 721b; 5) Lü Cheng, *Xinbian hanwen dazangjing mulu*［新编汉文大藏经目录, *A New Catalogue of the Chinese Versions of the Buddhist Tripiṭāka*］, Ji'nan: Qilu Publishing House, 1980: 90; 6) Charles Willemen, *Outlining the Way to Reflect*［思维略要法］(T. XV 617), Mumbai: Somaiya Publications Pvt Ltd, 2012: 15-17.

［2］Lü Cheng, *opere citato* (*Zhongguo foxue yuanliu*...): 75-76.

［3］Huijiao, *opere citato*: 45-46; *confer Taishō*, Vol. 50: 330a.

宾, Greater Gandhāra or Gandhāran cultural area[1], Kumārajīva also stayed in Ush-Turfan [温宿] for a while. The king of the Kucha kingdom personally went to Ush-Turfan and welcomed Kumārajīva to return to his native country to preach widely on the various *sūtras*, since the whole world admired his school of thought as nothing could compare with it. At that time, the princess of Kucha had already become a Buddhist nun whose secular name was Ajieyemodi [阿竭耶末帝, Akāyamatī][2]. She was widely learned in many *sūtras* and she was especially proficient in *dhyāna* discipline[3].

On the basis of what he had learned from Greater Gandhāra as well as the Western Regions, Kumārajīva, whose thinking and ideology had very likely been influenced by his mother's *dhyāna* discipline, not only translated and edited *dhyāna sūtras*, but also fostered five thousand disciples and directed most of them to practice *dhyāna* at Chang'an. For instance, according to *Weishu: Shilaozhi* (*History of the Wei Dynasties: Treatise on Buddhism and Taoism*), when Shizu [世祖, i. e., Emperor Taiwu/ 太武帝, 424-452 AD] of the Northern Wei Dynasty defeated Helianchang [赫连昌] in 426 AD, he captured a master monk by the name of Huishi [惠始] who, hearing that Kumārajīva had translated some new *sūtras*, went to Chang'an to interview him. Directing his attention to the learning of *sūtra*, he sat in meditation north of the White Canal [白渠]. During the day he entered the city to listen to the expositions, but at night he returned to his abode to sit quietly... When Tongwan [统万] had been conquered, Huishi went to the capital (Pingcheng/ 平城, present Datong). He gave much instruction and guidance, but his contemporaries could not

---

[1] 1) Richard Salomon, *Ancient Buddhist Scrolls from Gandhāra: The British Library Kharoṣṭhī Fragments*, Seattle: University of Washington Press, 1999: 3; 2) Charles Willemen, "Kumārajīva's 'Explanatory Discourse' about Abhidharmic Literature", in: *Kokusai Bukkyōgaku Daigaku-in Daigaku Kenkyū Kiyō* [国際仏教大学院大学研究紀要第 12 号 (平成 20 年), *Journal of the International College for Postgraduate Buddhist Studies*], Vol. XII (2008): 37-83 (156-110), esp. 39 (154), 69 (124); 3) Charles Willemen, *opere citato* (*Outlining the Way to Reflect*...): 16; 4) Chongfeng Li. "Jibin and China as seen from Chinese Documents", in: *Archaeology of Buddhism in Asia*, ed. B. Mani. New Delhi: Archaeological Survey of India (in press).

[2] Here, Akāyamatī should be the mother of Kumārajīva. Tang Yongtong, *opere citato*: 201.

[3] Huijiao, *opere citato*: 48; *confer Taishō*, Vol. 50: 330c-331a.

fathom his manner. Shizu of the Northern Wei valued him greatly and often paid him homage. Huishi who practiced *dhyāna*-meditation from the time, up to his death, is said that for fifty odd years he never laid down to sleep even once.[1].

After the *dhyāna-sūtras* were translated into Chinese by Kumārajīva, the practice of *dhyāna* became progressively regular in northern China and the procedure of practicing *dhyāna*-meditation was also standardized in this vast region. Therefore, Kumārajīva, who not only produced *dhyāna sūtras*, but also gave instruction in *dhyāna* practice, did all he could in regard to this discipline. He is, thus, regarded as the great master of the *dhyāna*-discipline in northern China[2].

Besides Kumārajīva, some other Buddhist masters also translated *sūtras* on *dhyāna*-discipline into Chinese, such as *Damoduoluo chanjing*［达摩多罗禅经，*Dharmatrāta dhyāna-sūtra* or *Yogācārabhūmi*］, i. e., *Lushan chanjing*［庐山禅经，*Dhyāna-sūtra translated at Mt. Lu*］[3] and *Foshuo guanfo sanmeihai jing*［佛说观佛三昧海经，*Buddha-dhyāna-samādhisāgara-sūtra*, *Sutra on the Sea of Mystic Ecstasy Attained by Visualizing the Buddha* or *Ocean of Meditation on the Buddha Sūtra*］[4] by Buddhabhadra［佛驮跋陀罗，359-429 AD］, among others. Buddhabhadra arrived in Chang'an around 410 AD and at first assisted Kumārajīva

---

［1］Wei Shou, *opere citato*: 3032-33. confer: 1) James R. Ware, *opere citato*: 135-136; 2) Leon Hurvitz, *opere citato*: 63.

［2］1) Tang Yongtong, *opere citato*: 210, 213, 218-219; 2) Liu Huida［刘慧达］, "*Beiwei shiku yu chan*［北魏石窟与禅，*Dhyāna* and the Cave-temples of the Northern Wei Dynasty］", in: *Zhongguo shikusi yanjiu*［中国石窟寺研究，*Studies of the Cave-temples of China*］by Su Bai［宿白］, Appendix I, Beijing: Cultural Relics Press, 1996: 332.

［3］*Taishō*, No. 618, Vol. 15: 300-325. Hui-yuan wrote a preface to this *sūtra*, namely, Huiyuan, "*Lushan chu xiuxing fangbian chanjing xu*［Preface to *Dhyāna-sūtra of Buddhasena/Dharmatrāta Dhyāna-sūtra translated at Mt. Lu* or *General Introduction to Dhyāna Scriptures produced on Mt. Lu as Means to Religious Cultivation*］", in: Sengyou, *opere citato*: 343-345; *confer Taishō*, Vol. 55: 65-66.

［4］*Taishō*, No. 643, Vol. 15: 645-697. The text, generally called *Sea Sūtra*, belongs to a category of *Kuan Sūtras* on visualizing Amitayus. *Kuan* was a systematic system of building visual images through different steps, advancing from simple to complex. *Kuan Sūtra* refers to the images and statues as a first step towards visualizing the beauty of the divinity. The mental pictures were formed with the help of images that took the practitioner to ecstatic vision.

in the translation of the Buddhist scriptures. They often had discussions together and mutually explored some of the abstruse implications of canonical texts. Nevertheless, they breathed a different intellectual atmosphere later, as their scholastic lineages apparently derived from separate origins. The lectures on *dhyāna* by Buddhabhadra at Chang'an, however, seem to be very different from what was taught by Kumārajīva. Kumārajīva devoted himself to disseminating the teachings of *sūtras*, particularly the Mahāyāna doctrine of Nāgārjuna, and was favorably recognized by Yao Xing, ruler of the Later Qin state. Moreover, Kumārajīva and his disciples, more than three thousands in number, could freely go in and out of the palace and the court. Buddhabhadra, however, strictly adhered to the modes of teaching of the Sthaviravāde of the Śrāvakayāna, cultivating meditation and concentration, living a plain and simple life without any display or show. Owing to such divergences, gradually there arose discord between the disciples of the two great masters. In the 17th year of the Yixi [义熙] era (411 AD) of the Eastern Jin Dynasty, some disciples of Kumārajīva blamed Buddhabhadra as being guilty of telling a lie—thus breaking a fundamental commandment—and relying upon the support of the masses. This compelled Buddhabhadra to leave Chang'an, and he went southward to Mt. Lu where he was welcomed by Huiyuan, who had heard of Buddhabhadra's fame. During his residence at Mt. Lu, Buddhabhadra, at the request of Huiyuan, lectured on the doctrine of meditation and translated a special work on *dhyāna, Yogacaryā-bhūmi-sūtra,* and thus gave him great help in his meditation and contemplation[1].

According to Lü Cheng's study, though Buddhabhadra's translations touched upon different aspects of Buddhism, his special attention was concentrated on the methods of meditative contemplation. Buddhabhadra had translated the works of both Dharmatrāta and Buddhasena on the methods of *dhyāna*. Of course, Kumārajīva also taught methods of contemplation, but he recommended only some essentials

[1] 1) Sengyou, *opere citato*: 541-543; *confer Taishō*, Vol. 55: 103b-104a; 2) Huijiao, *opere citato*: 69-73; *confer Taishō*, Vol. 50: 334b-335c; 3) Lü Cheng, "Buddhabhadra" , in: *Encyclopaedia of Buddhism*, ed. G. P. Malalasekera, Colombo: The Government of Ceylon, Vol. III, 1971: 382-384; 4) Tang Yongtong, *opere citato*: 218-219.

of *dhyāna* of the old masters of the Sthaviravāde of the Śrāvakayāna without giving them an orderly and systematic formulation. Buddhabhadra's methods, however, were those handed down from master to disciples for generations and therefore kept their purity intact[1].

Chanfa yao (*Essentials of the Dhyāna-discipline*)/the *Chanmi yaofa jing* (*Secret Essentials of the Dhyāna-discipline* or *Sūtra about the Secret Essence of Dhyāna*), *Zuochan sanmei jing* (*Dhyāna-samādhi-sūtra*, *Sūtra on the Concentration of Sitting Meditation*)/ *Guanzhong chanjing* (*Dhyāna-sūtra translated in the Central Shaanxi Plain*), *Chanfa yaojie* (*Interpretation of the Dhyāna-discipline* or *Essential Explanation of the Way to Meditate*) and *Damoduoluo Chanjing* (*Dharmatrāta dhyāna-sūtra* or *Yogācārabhūmi*)/ *Lushan chanjing* (*Dhyāna-sūtra translated at Mt. Lu*) are all *sūtras* on mental *dharmas*, which explained the established *dhyāna* practice to the followers; they were held up as models by the devotees who intended to practice *dhyāna*[2]. The lost *Guanfo sanmei jing* (*Buddha-dhyāna-samādhī-sūtra*) translated by Kumārajīva and the extant *Foshuo guanfo sanmeihai jing* (*Buddha-dhyāna-samādhisāgara-sūtra*, *The Sutra on the Sea of Mystic Ecstasy Attained by Visualizing the Buddha* or *Ocean of Meditation on the Buddha Sūtra*) translated by Buddhabhadra, as the titles indicate, are mainly devoted to the contemplation of the Buddha (*buddhānusmṛti-samādhi*), precisely the kind of mental concentration which was much in vogue among the followers of Huiyuan. Thus, it can be inferred that the pursuit of *dhyāna*-discipline was a matter of philosophical discussion in the 5th century AD. In the early 5th century, in other words, Kumārajīva in the North, and Buddhabhadra as well as Huiyuan in the South, disseminated *dhyāna* discipline and enabled the Hinduka *dhyāna* to become progressively popular in China[3].

---

[1] 1) Lü Cheng, *opere citato*: 382-384; 2) Chongfeng Li, "Jibin and China as seen from Chinese Documents", in: *Archaeology of Buddhism in Asia*, ed. B. Mani, New Delhi: Archaeological Survey of India (in press).

[2] Tang Yongtong, *opere citato*: 552.

[3] Hu Shih [胡适], "*Chanxue gushi kao* [禅学古史考, On the History of the *Dhyāna*-discipline]", in: *Hushi xueshu wenji: Zhongguo foxueshi* [胡适学术文集：中国佛学史, *Collected Works of Hu Shih: A History of Chinese Buddhism*], Beijing: Zhonghua Book Company, 1997: 38-54, esp. 42.

2. Dhyāna-meditation

The aim of *dhyāna*-meditation is to free oneself from worldly worries and to become a Buddha, in other words, this is a meditative practice for the Buddhists who were eager to attain enlightenment. An idea place for *dhyāna* practice should be both monastery and *araṇya* (forest hermitages), as it is often the case. According to *dhyāna sūtras*, the practice of *dhyāna*-meditation needs to take place in extremely quiet surroundings. A place suitable for meditation must be extremely peaceful, such as a forestland, places between tombs, under trees, and *araṇya*. Therefore, it tends to be found in mountains, forest, marshes, or near streams, *dhyāna* practice should be carried out in places far from cities and towns, and in locations where people rarely go[1].

Originally, caves in different areas were used by monks as places of meditation where they could discipline themselves in order to rid their hearts of any vestiges of worldly thoughts, such as Buddha allowing *bhikṣus* to walk around [经行, *caṅkramana*] and to dwell in *chanku* [禅窟, meditation-cave][2]; Mahākyāsyapa used to sit in meditation in a cave named Pippala [宾钵罗窟] near Gṛdhra-kūṭa [耆阇崛山, Vulture mountain][3]. According to *Faxian zhuan* [法显传, *Travels of Faxian*], when Faxian arrived at the Vulture-mountain, three *li* from

[1] 1) Kumārajīva, *Zuochan sanmei jing* (*Dhyāna-samādhi-sūtra, Sūtra on the Concentration of Sitting Meditation*)/ *Guanzhong chanjing* (*Dhyāna-sūtra translated in the Central Shaanxi Plain*), in: *Taishō,* No. 614, Vol. 15: 269b-270c; 2) Kumārajīva, *Chanfa yao* (*Essentials of the Dhyāna-discipline*)/ *Chanmi yaofa jing* (*Secret Essentials of the Dhyāna-discipline or Sūtra about the Secret Essence of Dhyāna*), in: *Taishō,* No. 613, Vol. 15: 252a.

[2] Kumārajīva, *Miaofa lianhua jing* [妙法莲花经, *Saddharma-puṇḍarīka-sūtra or Lotus Sūtra of the Wonderful Law*], in: *Taishō,* No. 262, Vol. 9: 1-62, esp. 45c.

[3] 1) Kinkara and Tanyao, *Fu fazang yinyuan zhuan* [付法藏因缘传, *A History of the Buddha's Successors*], in: *Taishō,* No. 2058, Vol. 50: 298c; 2) Faxian, *opere citato*: 114; 3) H. A. Giles, *The Travels of Fa-hsien (399-414 AD)*, or *Record of the Buddhistic Kingdoms by Faxian*, Cambridge: Cambridge University Press, 1923: 52; 4) Xuanzang, *Datang xiyu ji* [大唐西域记, *Record of the Western Regions of the Great Tang Dynasty*], emended and annotated by Ji Xianlin [季羡林] et al, Beijing: Zhonghua Book Company, 1985: 730; 5) Samuel Beal, *Si-Yu-Ki—Buddhist Records of the Western World; Chinese Accounts of India, translated from the Chinese of Hiuen Tsiang*, London: Trubner, 1884: 374-375, footnote 53.

the summit he found a cave in the rock, facing south, where Buddha used to sit in meditation. Thirty paces to the northwest there is another such cave, in which Ānanda used to sit in meditation when Māra-pāpmen or Pāpīyas [魔波旬] changed himself into a vulture and stood before the cave in order to frighten Ānanda. Nevertheless, the Buddha by his divine power pierced the rock and stretched out his hand to stroke Ānanda's shoulder, so that his fear was allayed. The tracks of the bird and the hole for Buddha's hand are both still to be seen; hence the name Vulture-cave Mountain. In front of the cave is the place where the four Buddhas sat down, and also the caves where each one of the *arhats* sat in meditation, several hundred in all[1].

At that time these caves were natural ones and many Buddhist monks went to the forest and lived in natural caves to meditate. Usually, forests and caves were associated with meditation as there were no people living there and there was less disturbance.

There were certainly rock shelters used by ascetics of many creeds in the times before Aśoka, but no ruler or king ever thought of furnishing them with permanent settlements chiselled out of solid rock. It was Aśoka, king of the Maurya Empire, who initiated cutting living rocks into architectural forms. As proof of his tolerance towards all the religious sects, he had caves built in the Barābār hills in Gayā and presented them to the Ājīvikas [邪命外道] in 257 BC; one of his successors donated three caves at Nāgārjuni hills to the same Ājīvikas[2]. Sometime in the post-Aśoka period, the activity of hewing out an abode into the living rock spread to the Deccan under the patronage of the Buddhists of the Theravāda school. Some irregularly open or single monastic cells at Bhāja, Kāṇhēri and other sites may be regarded as the earliest examples of rock-cut architecture on the Western Deccan. With the liberal donations by the public and preserving efforts made by the Buddhist

[1] Faxian, *opere citato*: 113. *confer*: 1) H. A. Giles, *opere citato*: 50; 2) Xuanzang, *opere citato*: 727-728; 3) Samuel Beal, *opere citato*: 373.

[2] Harry Falk, *Aśokan Sites and Artefacts: A source-book with bibliography*, Mainz am Rhein: Verlag Philipp von Zabern, 2006: 255-279.

monks, more and more cave-temple complexes came into existence in Hinduka[1].

This kind of custom spread to China along with the transmission of Buddhism, and *dhyāna* was the only activity practiced by Buddhist monks, besides the *Annuttara-pūjā* or highest worship[2], in northern China from the late 4th to the early 7th century AD[3]. Construction of the Buddhist rock-cut temples in China as well as arrangement of the Buddhist images inside seem to be closely related to the *dhyāna*-discipline.

On the basis of *Weishu: Shilaozhi* (*History of the Wei Dynasties: Treatise on Buddhism and Taoism*), when Gaozu [高祖, i. e. Emperor Xiaowen] ascended the throne in 471 AD, Xianzu [显祖, i.e. Emperor Xianwen/献文帝 465-471 AD] went to live in the Chongguang Palace [崇光宫] in the Northern Park [北苑], where was said to always read books on the Mystery. Xianzhu ordered construction of a Deer-park Monastery and Temple [鹿野佛图, Mṛgadāva *Stūpa*] on the western mountain within the park, about 10 *li* to the right of Chongguang Palace, with meditation-cells hewn in to the rock, and monks who practiced *dhyāna* dwelt therein[4]. Therefore, Gao Yun [高允] who was a famous scholar of the Northern Wei Dynasty said: "To carve *or hewn* out a celestial cave in the rock is to supply a place for a monk sitting in meditation"[5]. The remains of a rock-cut temple (fig.1) found in 1987 in a mountain valley near Xiaoshisi village [小石寺村] at Datong, moreover, tallies with the record in *Weishu* and is considered to be a component part of the ruined Deer-

---

[1] Chongfeng Li [李崇峰], *Zhongyin fojiao shikusi bijiao yanjiu: Yi tamiaoku wei zhongxin* [中印佛教石窟寺比较研究：以塔庙窟为中心, *Chētiyagharas in Indian and Chinese Buddhist Cave-temples: A Comparative Study*], Beijing: Peking University Press, 2003: 2-4.

[2] Chongfeng Li, "Gandhāra and Kucha: The Case of an Iconological Relationship", in: *Historical, Cultural and Economic Linkages between India and Xinjiang Region of China: New Challenges and Opportunities*, ed. K. Warikoo (in the press).

[3] Tang Yongtong, *opere citato*: 570-572.

[4] Wei Shou, *opere citato*: 3038. confer: 1) James R. Ware, *opere citato*: 149-150; 2) Leon Hurvitz, *opere citato*: 75.

[5] Gao Yun [高允], "*Luyuan fu* [鹿苑赋, Rhapsody on the Deer-park]", in: *Guang hongmingji* [广弘明集, *Further Anthology of the Propagation of Light*] by Daoxuan, *confer Taishō*, Vol. 52: 339b.

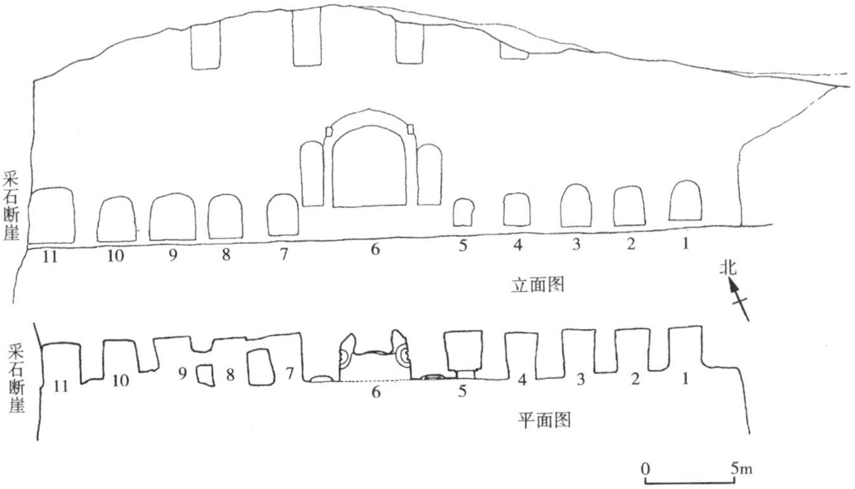

fig.1 Remains of the rock-cut temple at Deer-park, Datong

park Monastery and Temple[1].

Buddhism was formally disseminated into China proper in the middle of the Yongping era［永平，58-75 AD］of Emperor Ming［明帝］of the later Han Dynasty［后汉，25-220 AD］, which had a strong influence on Chinese culture and ideology from the 3rd century onwards[2]. The Buddhist monasteries、temples and images, however, most likely made their debut somewhat later. The cave-temples were but a special kind of temple or monastery. Therefore it is reasonable to suppose that they appeared in China only after some time, evolving from the more common types of temple building and image making.

The cave-temple complex at Mogaoku［莫高窟，fig.2］, Dunhuang, according to a stone tablet named *Dazhou lijun mogaoku fokan bei*［大周李君莫高窟佛龛碑，*A Tablet Commemorating a Buddhist Cave built by an Individual named Li at Mogao in the Great Zhou Period*］and dated to 698 AD, was started

［1］1) Li Zhiguo［李治国］and Liu Jianjun［刘建军］, "*Beiwei pingcheng luyeyuan shiku diaocha ji*［北魏平城鹿野苑石窟调查记，A Survey of Rock-cut Caves at the Deer-park Monastery and Temple of the Northern Wei Dynasty at Pingcheng］", in: *Zhongguo shiku: Yungang shiku* (*The Cave-temples of China: Yungang Caves*) I, Beijing: Cultural Relics Press, 1991: 212-215; 2) Liu Jianjun, "*Luyeyuan shiku diaocha baogao*［鹿野苑石窟调查报告，A Report on Rock-cut Caves at the Deer-park Monastery and Temple at Datong］", in: *Shikusi yanjiu*［石窟寺研究，*Studies of the Cave-temples*］, Vol. I, Beijing: Cultural Relics Press, 2010: 1-9.

［2］Tang Yongtong, *opere citato*: 1-21.

in 366 AD. by a hermit monk named Lezun [乐僔] and continued by another hermit monk named Faliang [法良], to be developed later by Prince Dongyang [东阳王] and Lord Jianping [建平公]. Both Lezun and Faliang were monks who practiced meditation[1]. There is reason to believe that each of these men came from central China, east of Dunhuang[2]. Hence it would appear that the history of the Mogaoku caves can only be understood as part of the history of central China.

fig.2 The cave temple complex at Mogaoku, Dunhuang

The cave-temple complex at Binglingsi [炳灵寺, fig.3] in Yongjing, which was also known as Mt. Tangshu [唐述山] or Mt. Jishi [积石山] in the historical records, became an integral part of the religious activities of the Western Qin state [西秦, 385-431 AD][3]. According to an inscription found at niche 6 (fig.4) in cave 169, construction of the cave-temples at Binglingsi was initiated around 420 AD[4].

---

[1] Liu Huida, *opere citato*: 331-348, esp. 332.

[2] Su Bai, *Zhongguo shikusi yanjiu* (*Studies of the Cave-temples of China*), Beijing: Cultural Relics Press, 1996: 262-269, 355-356, esp. 265, 355.

[3] 1) Li Daoyuan [郦道元], *Shuijing zhu* [水经注, *Commentary on Waterways Classic*], sub-commentated by Yang Shoujing [杨守敬] and Xiong Huizhen [熊会贞], Nanjing: Jiangsu Chinese Classics Publishing House, 1989: 138-40; 2) Daoshi [道世], *Fayuan zhulin* [法苑珠林, *Forest of Gems in the Garden of the Law*] in 668 AD, emended and annotated by Zhou Shujia [周叔迦] and Su Jinren [苏晋仁], Beijing: Zhonghua Book Company, 2003：1247; *confer Taishō*, No. 2122, Vol. 53: 269-1030, esp. 595a-b.

[4] Cave 169 at Binglingsi is a large natural cave, the Buddha images made in clay sculpture and Buddhist motifs or subjects represented on the mural were added around 420 AD. According to the Buddhist tradition, monks usually went to the forest and lived in natural caves to meditate in the early period. In this way, Cave 169 probably used to be a place for monks to practice *dhyāna*-meditation and contemplation.

fig.3 The cave temple complex at Binglingsi, Yongjing

fig.4 Amitāyus-niche dated to 420 AD, Cave 169 at Binglingsi

Although we do not know who was the first to hew out a temple in the rock here, we do know that the *dhyāna*-discipline was very popular in Western Qin state and monk Tanwupi / Tanmopi [昙无毗, Dharmapriya?] who came from a foreign country taught *dhyāna*-discipline and led followers to practice meditation in the state[1]. Monk Tanmopi's portrait was even painted in the mural of cave 169 at Binglingsi (fig.5). Moreover, Xuanshao [玄绍], who was one of the disciples of monk Xuan'gao [玄高], devoted himself to *dhyāna*-discipline and went to Binglingsi to practice meditation later. Binglingsi was, for this reason, an important place where meditating monks gathered and learned *dhyāna* discipline during the period of the Western Qin state.

The cave-temple complex at Maijishan [麦积山, fig.6] in Tianshui, wherein many meditating monks such as Xuan'gao, Tanhong [昙弘] withdrawn from society, and lived in seclusion, accommodated more than one hundred hermit monks who practiced *dhyāna*. Xuan'gao, who was a great master of *dhyāna*-discipline in northwest China at that time, used to have three hundred disciples who

[1] Huijiao, *opere citato*: 410; *confer Taishō*, Vol. 50: 397-398, esp. 397a.

fig.6 The cave temple complex at Maijishan, Tianshui

fig.5 Portrait of Monk Tanmopi (Dharmapriya?), mural painting, Cave 169 at Binglingsi

dwelt in the rock-cut *dhyāna*-cells at Mt. Tang［堂山 / 常山?］in Linyang［林杨］[1]. Xuan'gao was later invited as a teacher of Prince Huang［太子晃］of the Northern Wei Dynasty after 439 AD[2]. Yu Xin［庾信］, who was a famous scholar in the Southern and Northern Dynasties period, called Maijishan the "Vulture-island［鹫岛］[3] where meditating monks dwelt as hermits"[4]. This indicates

［1］Huijiao, *opere citato*: 409-410; *confer Taishō*, Vol. 50: 397a-b.

［2］Tang Yongtong, *opere citato*: 353-357.

［3］The term Vulture-island originates probably from the Indian *Gṛdhra-kūta* (Vulture Peak) where, according to various *sūtras* and historical records, the Buddha, Mahākyāsyapa, Ānanda and lot of *bhikṣus* used to sit in meditation in the caves over there.

［4］Yu Xin, "*Qinzhou tianshuijun maijiya fokan ming bing xu*［秦州天水郡麦积崖佛龛铭并序, Preface and Epigraph to the Buddhist Niches at Maijiya, Tanshui District, Qinzhou Prefecture］", in: *Wenyuan yinghua*［文苑英华, *The Best Works in the Literary and Art Circles*］compiled by Li Fang［李昉］, Facsimile edition, Beijing: Zhonghua Book Company, 1966: 4149-4150, esp. 4149.

that Maijishan used to be another important place in which meditating monks gathered and practiced *dhyāna*-discipline.

The cave-temple complex at Yungang [云冈, fig.7] in Datong is believed to have been constructed on the initiative of Monk Tanyao [昙曜], who seems to have been one of Xuangao's disciples and was also famous for his *dhyāna*-discipline in northern China[1]. According to *Weishu: Shilaozhi* (*History of the Wei Dynasties: Treatise on Buddhism and Taoism*), in the first part of the reign period of Heping [和平, 460-466 AD] of Emperor Wencheng [文成帝, 452-465 AD]

fig.7 The cave temple complex at Yungang, Datong

[1] 1) Huijiao, *opere citao*: 413; *confer Taishō*, Vol. 50: 398b; 2) Daoxuan [道宣], *Xü gaoseng zhuan* [续高僧传, *Continued Biographies of Eminent Priests*], in: *Taishō*, No. 2060, Vol. 50: 427c-428a.

the *śramaṇa* Shixian［师贤］[1] died; monk Tanyao succeeded him and changed his title to *Shamentong*［沙门统, Chief of the Śramaṇas］. As a result, Buddhism became the official religion of the Northern Wei Dynasty in 452 AD, having being restored after the persecution, and Tanyao was ordered to come from Zhongshan［中山］to the Capital Pingcheng. When he met the Emperor on the road, who had come to welcome him, one of the horses (of the Emperor's chariot) advanced and took Tanyao's robe in his teeth. This event was deemed to be auspicious as it was believed that even the horse recognized a good man. The Emperor afterwards respected him as a teacher. Monk Tanyao humbly begged the Emperor to chisel out the rocky wall of the mountain of Wuzhou pass［武州塞］, west of the capital, to open up five caves and carve out an image of the Buddha in each one. The tallest image was seventy feet high, the next tallest sixty feet high, with superb carvings and decorations, a crowning glory to the world[2].

The rock-cut caves at Wuzhou hills［武州山, an old name of Yungang］and those at the Deer-park Monastery and Temple in Datong were opened up or hewn out simultaneously or successively, and both of them are located in the suburbs of Pingcheng. The rock-cut caves at the Deer-park Monastery and Temple were hewn out to create a space for meditating monks[3] and those at Wuzhou hills too may have been set up for the hermit monks who practiced *dhyāna*[4].

---

［1］Śramaṇa Shixian (Siṃhabhadra？, ？-460 AD), who was a relative of the King of Jibin and entered the Buddhist order at a young age, came East to Liangzhou［凉州］, a Buddhist center of then northern China. After Liangzhou was subdued by the Northern Wei Dynasty in 439 AD, Siṃhabhadra went on to its capital (Pingcheng). While Buddhism was forbidden by Emperor Taiwu of the Northern Wei in 444 AD, Siṃhabhadra, who disguised himself as a medical practitioner, reverted to the lay life but observed the doctrine without alteration. On the very day of the restoration of Buddhism by Emperor Wencheng of the Northern Wei Dynasty in 452 AD, Siṃhabhadra became a *śramaṇa* again. The Emperor personally performed the hair-cutting ceremony for Siṃhabhadra and his associates, altogether five men, and the *sramaṇa* Siṃhabhadra was appointed *Daorentong*［道人统, Chief of the Clerics, in Control of the Religious］, as before, by the Emperor in the same year.

Wei Shou, *opere citato*: 3036. confer: 1) James R. Ware, *opere citato*: 145; 2) Leon Hurvitz, *opere citato*: 71.

［2］Wei Shou, *opere citato*: 3037. confer: 1) James R. Ware, *opere citato*: 146-147; 2) Leon Hurvitz, *opere citato*: 72.

［3］Gao Yun, *opere citato*: 339b.

［4］Tang Yongtong, *opere citato*: 558.

When a Hinduka monk named Fotuochanshi [佛陀禅师, Buddha-*dhyāyin*？], who was a famous master of *dhyāna* as his name implies, arrived in the capital, Emperor Xiaowen requested the building of an appropriate grove and a rock-cut niche, which were suitable for this hermit monk and convenient for him to gather followers and to practice *dhyāna*-meditation[1]. Therefore, it is very clear that to hew out a cave in the rock is mostly to provide a place for monks to practice *dhyāna*-meditation[2].

The cave-temples carved out in the region around the Capital Ye [邺城, present-day Linzhang][3] in the second half of the 6th century AD, such as those at Xiaonanhai [小南海], Xiangquansi [香泉寺], Daliusheng [大留圣] and Xiangtangshan [响堂山], were also closely related to monks who practiced *dhyāna*[4].

After the fall of the Western Jin Dynasty [西晋, 266-316 AD] in 316 AD, a large number of northern literati migrated to southern China and brought the *Xuanxue* [玄学, metaphysics] school[5] to the South. It later flourished in southern China, especially in the area around Capital Jiankang [建康, present-day Nanjing]. The southern style of Buddhism began to taka its inspiration from *Xuanxue* and had a strong philosophical aspect to it, which emphasized discourse and theory. In this way, Buddhism in southern China came to be very different from that in northern China which emphasized *dhyāna* practice[6]. Therefore, Buddhists in northern China not only built free-standing monasteries or temples, but also carved out caves in which monks meditated.

---

[1] Daoxuan, *opere citato* 551, esp. 551a.

[2] Tang Yongtong, *opere citato*: 559.

[3] Capital Ye used to be successively capitals of the Wei [曹魏, 221-265 AD], Later Zhao [后赵, 319-352 AD], Former Yan [前燕, 333-370 AD], Eastern Wei [东魏, 534-550 AD] and Northern Qi [北齐, 550-557 AD] kingdoms or states.

[4] Li Yuqun [李裕群], *Beichao wanqi shikusi yanjiu* [北朝晚期石窟寺研究, *A Study on the Cave-temples of the Late Northern Dynasties Period*], Beijing: Cultural Relics Press, 2003: 234.

[5] *Xuanxue* was a mystical school in the realm of philosophy, which developed in the 3rd and 4th centuries AD, characterized by metaphysical speculations seeking to adapt Daoist theories to a Confucian milieu. Bai Shouyi [白寿彝], ed., *An Outline History of China*, Beijing: Foreign Languages Press, 1982: 177-178.

[6] Tang Yongtong, *opere citato*: 350-394.

In the south, however, Buddhists tended to emphasize monastery or temple ceremonies and to discourse on theory[1]. Should they meditate, it would be generally in a monastery or temple, not in a cave, that is, a devotee would sit in meditation in *Fatang* [法堂, the chief temple or main hall] of a monastery, cleansing his heart and mind[2]. In other words, in northern China *dhyāna* was following the Indian tradition of moving away from the secular world but in southern China *dhyāna* was influenced by *Xuanxue*, where religious life was closely associated with meditation and philosophical discussion. The Buddhist monks in southern China preferred a free-standing monastery or temple to a rock-cut cave.

A relation between a rock-cut cave and *dhyāna*-practice, however, can be also found in *Songshu* [宋 书, *History of the Song Dynasty*] by Shen Yue [沈约]. In fascicle 97, it records that meditation monks from northern China all gathered in the free-standing Douchang Monastery [斗场寺][3] after they moved to Jiankang. For this reason, the common saying that "Douchang Monastery is a cave for the meditation monks"[4] was born in the capital, which indicates that the "rock-cut cave" had a close relation with *dhyāna* and even the people who lived in southern China.

---

[1] Shenqing [神清], *Beishan lu* [北山录, *Buddhism recorded at the Northern Mountain*], in: *Taishō*, No. 2113, Vol. 52: 573-636, esp. 596c.

[2] Huiyuan, "*Nianfo sanmei shiji xu* [念佛三昧诗集序, Preface to *A Collection of Poems on Buddhānusmṛti-samādhi*]", in: *Guang hongmingji* (*Further Anthology of the Propagation of Light*) by Daoxuan; in: *Taishō*, Vol. 52: 351, esp. 351c.

[3] Douchang Monastery was named after Douchang Alley [斗场里]. It was called Daochang Monastery [道场寺] in the *Biographies of Eminent Priests* by Huijiao, who seems to think that meaning of "斗 (*dou*, fight)" was not suitable for a Buddhist monastery, so he changed it to "道 (*dao*, way)" whose tone sounds like "斗 (*dou*)". Douchang Monastery was a very important monastery in southern China during the Southern Dynasties period, where eminent monks such as Buddhabhadra and Huiyuan used to stay for a while.

Sun Wenchuan [孙文川] and Chen Zuolin [陈作霖], *Nanchao fosizhi* [南朝佛寺志, *Record of the Buddhist Monasteires of the Southern Dynasties*], in: *Jinling suozhi jiuzhong* [金陵琐志九种, *Nine Annals of the Local History of Jinling*], Nanjing: Nanjing Publishing House, 2008: 139-285, esp. 188-190.

[4] Shen Yue, *Songshu* (*History of the Song Dynasty*), punctuated edition, Beijing: Zhonghua Book Company, 1974: 2391-2392.

It is noteworthy that a number of hermit monks gathered to meditate at Mt. She [攝山, old name of Qixiashan 棲霞山] near Jiankang at the end of the 5th century AD, and it is only at this time that we begin to find cave-temples in this region. These rock-cut caves are the Buddhist cave-temple complex at Mt. Qixia near Nanjing (fig.8), which was designed by Fadu [法度], a hermit monk known for meditation, along with Ming Sengshao [明僧绍] and his son Ming Zhongzhang [明仲璋], both of whom were devout secular Buddhists[1].

fig.8 The cave temple complex at Qixia, Nanjing

In addition, Monk Senghou [僧侯, 395-484 AD], a native of Xiliangzhou [西凉州, present-day Zhangye], who devoted himself to reciting *Fahua* (*Lotus Sūtra*) and *Weimo* (*Vimalakīrti-nirdeśa*) as well as *Jinguangming* [金光明, *Suvarṇaprabhāsottama-sūtra*], came to Jiankang around 454 AD. Later, Senghou was invited by Xiao Huikai [萧惠开, 423-471 AD] to go to Sichuan for a while. When Senghou returned to the capital (Jiankang), he requested that a cave should

[1] Jiang Zong [江总], *Jinling sheshan qixiasi bei* [金陵摄山棲霞寺碑, *A Tablet on the Qixia Monastery at Mt. She, Jinling*]; *confer* Su Bai, *Zhongguo shikusi yanjiu* (*Studies of the Cave-temples of China*), Beijing: Cultural Relics Press, 1996: 176-199, esp. 177-178.

be carved in the rock at Hougang [后冈] for the practice of *dhyāna*-meditation[1].

3. Cave Temple Complexes

With respect to the study of the cave-temple, however, not only a comparison and analysis of its images should be made, but special attention should be paid to its contents. The contents of the cave-temple may be viewed from two aspects: on the one hand, it caters to the wishes of four kinds of the Buddhist followers (*catasraḥ parṣadaḥ*) and, on the other, it appeals to the tastes of secular people. Concerning monks' demands and secular tastes, there are some matters of common concern, but there are also some differences in their interests and views. The common interests of monks and secular people include making offerings and worshiping images as well as some of the worldly secular requirements, but the different interests lie in monks' demand for religious practice or activity. The only activity of monks who lived from the 4th to the early 7th century AD. in northern China, as it has been demonstrated, was to practice *dhyāna*.

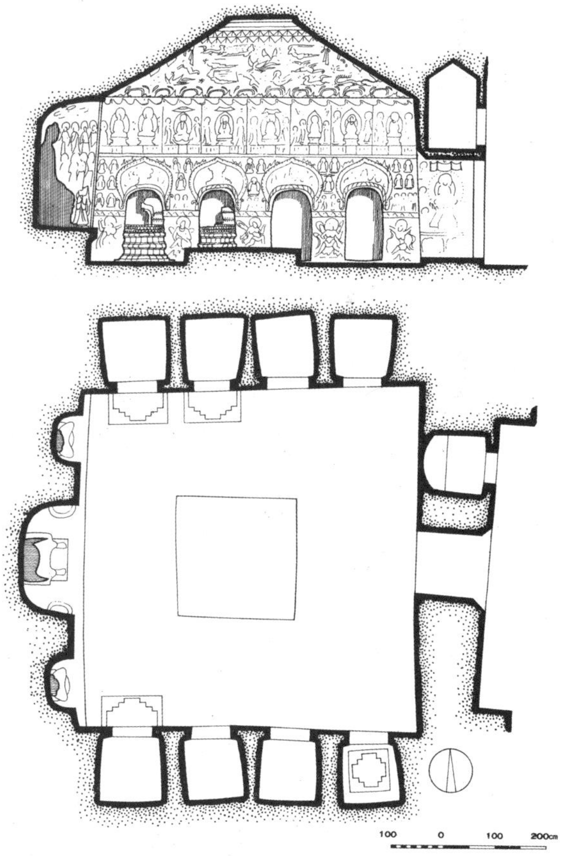

fig.9 *Lēṇa,* plan and longitudinal section of Cave 285 at Mogaoku, Dunhuang

On the basis of form and structure, many extant caves in China can be classified according to the nature or functions for which they were originally

[1] Huijiao, *opere citato*: 472; *confer Taishō*, Vol. 50: 408, esp. 408c.

designed. Therefore, any cave which was made expressly for meditation is called a meditation-cave. Some meditation-caves are single cells, while the others form part of a group (fig.9). There were also some caves designed as living quarters or habitation so that monks may actually live there, and these of course were larger than a normal meditation-cave. The latter is called *sengfangku* [僧房窟, habitable cave or dwelling cave], which is similar to the Mahārāshṭran *lēṇa*[1].

It is known from the *sūtras* that monks need to contemplate on the Buddha image during meditation. Therefore, prior to engaging in *dhyāna*-meditation they must first carry out ceremonies of worship before an image of the Buddha[2]. For this reason we find a Buddhist rock-cut temple in the vicinity of the meditation-caves. In the early period of cave-temples we generally find a *stūpa* in the center of a cave (fig.10), a feature in keeping with the fact that Buddhist *sūtras* often mention "going into a *stūpa* to view the image of the Buddha"[3].

This kind of cave is to be distinguished from the previously mentioned meditation-caves and habitable caves, and is known as *tamiaoku* [塔庙窟, *stūpa*-cave] or *zhongxinzhuku* [中心柱窟, central pillar cave], which is analogous to the Mahārāshṭran *chētiyaghara* both in form and nature[4]. Later there

---

[1] In this article, I sometimes use *lēṇa* as a convention for the characteristic cave structures of China which was used for dwelling. The term is known from Prākṛit or Prākṛta inscriptions from the Buddhist caves of the Western Ghats, and has been popularized since the time of colonial Indology. *confer* H. Lüders, "A List of Brāhmī Inscriptions from the Earliest Times to about A.D. 400 with the Exception of those of Aśōka", in: *Epigraphia Indica*, Volume X (1909-10), Appendix, Calcutta: Superintendent Government Printing, 1912: Nos. 998, 1000-1001, 1006-1007, etc.

[2] 1) Kumārajīva ? *Siwei lueyao fa* [*An Outline of Meditation* or *Outlining the Way to Reflect*], in: *Taishō,* No. 617, Vol. 15: 297-300, esp. 298a, 299a; 2) Kumārajīva, *Chanfa yao* (*Essentials of the Dhyāna-discipline*)/ *Chanmi yaofa jing* (*Secret Essentials of the Dhyāna-discipline* or *Sūtra about the Secret Essence of Dhyāna*), in: *Taishō,* No. 613, Vol. 15: 242-269, esp. 258b.

[3] Buddhabhadra, *Foshuo guanfo sanmeihai jing* [*Buddha-dhyāna-samādhisāgara-sūtra, The Sutra on the Sea of Mystic Ecstasy Attained by Visualizing the Buddha* or *Ocean of Meditation on the Buddha Sūtra*], in: *Taishō,* No. 643, Vol. 15: 645-697, esp. 655b, 688c-689a.

[4] In this article, I sometimes use *chētiyaghara* as a convention for the characteristic cave structures of China with a central *chētiya/stūpa* surrounded by an open circumambulatory passageway. The term is known from Prākṛit inscriptions from the Buddhist caves of the Western Ghats, and has been popularized since the time of colonial Indology. *confer* H. Lüders, *opere citato*: No. 1050, 1058, 1072, 1141, 1153, 1178, 1179, 1183, etc.

fig.10 *Stūpa*-cave, viz, *chētiyaghara,* Cave 2 at Yungang, Datong

appeared some caves especially designed for displaying Buddhist images and for contemplation of Buddha. This kind of cave is called *zunxiangku* [尊像窟, Buddha-image cave or Buddhist icon cave] or *fodianku* [佛殿窟, Buddha-hall cave] (fig.11). Sometimes a master monk would attract a number of disciples around one of these cave-temples. Naturally, the master monk had to lecture or held discussions on the *sūtras*, and for this purpose a *jiangtangku* [讲堂窟, lecture-hall or preaching hall cave] was constructed in some sites of the rock-cut cave-temples. Sometimes the lecture-hall cave has an image in it, in which case the cave could serve both as a Buddha-hall and as a lecture-hall.

In some places, where numerous caves were set up, we can really speak of a Buddhist cave-temple complex. Not all the caves we discuss necessarily merit the label of cave-temple complex, but for the sake of convenience we shall refer to all of them as cave-temples[1]. It is not the number that should matter but

[1] Su Bai, *Zhongguo fojiao shikusi yiji* [中国佛教石窟寺遗迹, *The Buddhist Cave-temples of China*], Beijing: Cultural Relics Press, 2010: 7.

fig.11　Buddha-hall-cave, Cave 272 at Mogaoku, Dunhuang

whether the basic requirement of a monastery were respected.

The remains of the cave-temples in Xinjiang are all to be found in the northern belt of the Tarim basin. Both Hīnayāna and Mahāyāna Buddhism were transmitted into Xinjiang through the Silk Roads. Along the northern route, east of Kashgar, Hīnayāna Buddhism was more popular, which emphasizes meditation even more than Mahāyāna, so to this extent, one can understand why many cave-temples were carved out. The earliest caves in Xinjiang (fig.12) are mostly single meditation caves and habitable caves with a long foyer. Before long we begin to find rectangular *stūpa*-

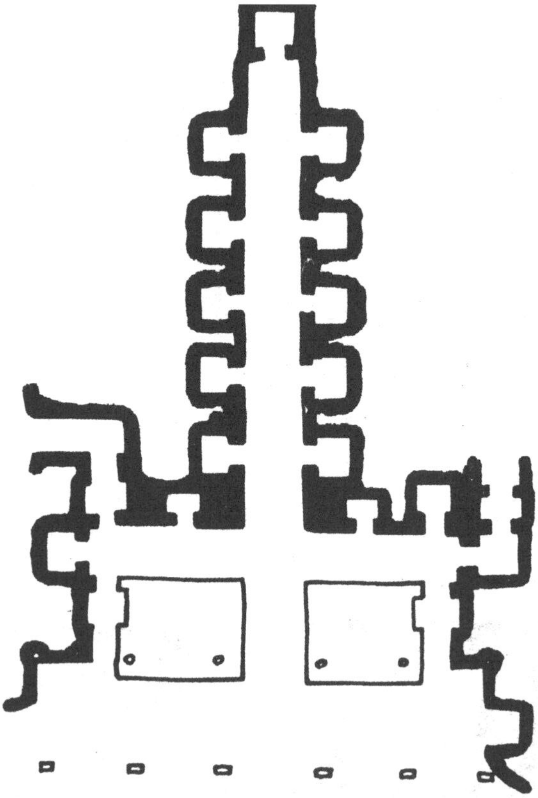

fig.12　*Lēṇa,* plan, Cave 5 at Subashi, Kucha

caves with a Kuchean style *stūpa* inside (fig.13), and later we also find lecture-hall caves. Prior to the fact that construction of lecture-hall caves became the fashion, there was also a period in which a complex consisting of several kinds of caves such as meditation-cave and *stūpa*-cave seem to have flourished. This kind of cave group gets more complicated over time. In the later period it developed to such a degree that the rock-cut caves were combined with surface-timbered constructions outside the caves. Therefore, it became a Buddhist temple with the cave itself serving as the main hall[1].

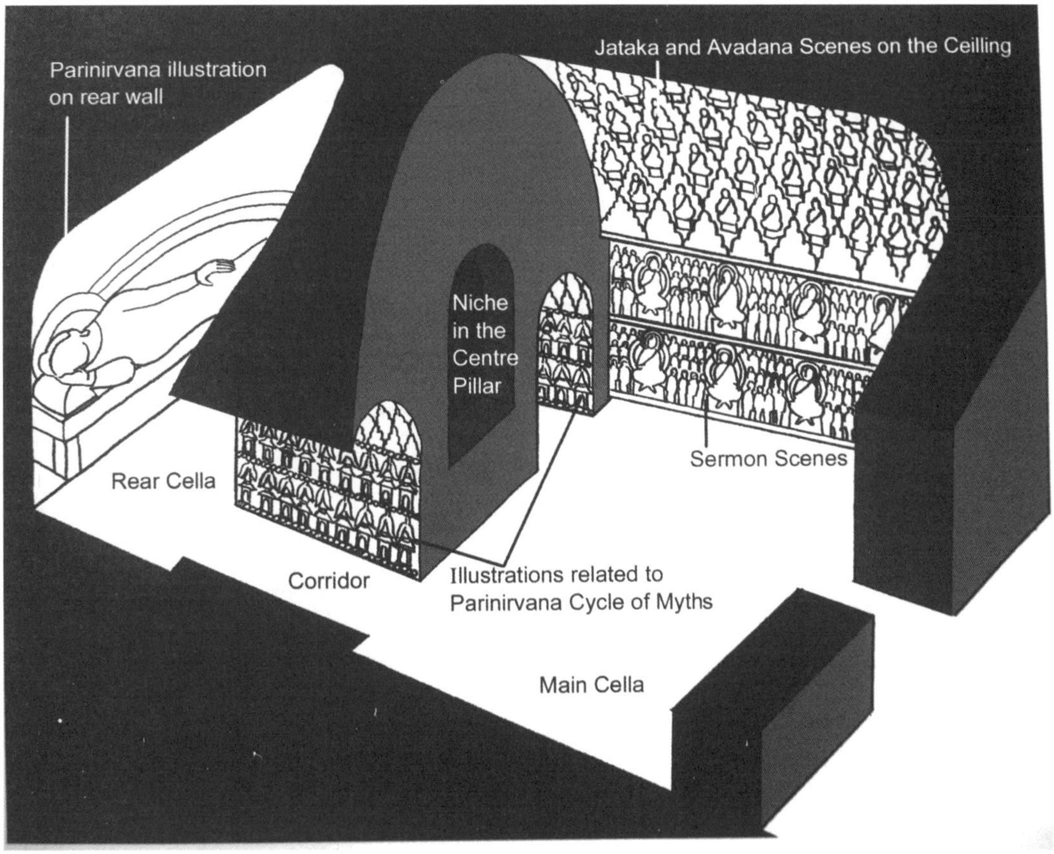

fig.13 Typical iconographic program of a *chētiyaghara* (central pillar cave) at Kizil

In addition, *Shier yinyuan jing* [十二因缘经, *Twelve Nidānas*] inscribed on votive stone *stūpas* found at Jiuquan and Turfan, the term *dhyāna*-cave [定

[1] Su Bai, *opere citato*: 11.

窟] appeared in the tablet commemorating a monastery set up by Juqu Anzhou [沮渠安周, 444-460 AD] of the Northern Liang state unearthed in Turfan, and representations of monks practicing *dhyāna*-meditation and contemplation in Cave 42 at Toyuk all seem to have a close relation with the *dhyāna sūtras* produced by Kumārajīva[1].

As one of the four prefectures in the Hexi Corridor [河西走廊][2], Liangzhou [凉州, present-day Wuwei] was both a political and Buddhist center of the corridor, especially during the period of the Northern Liang state. According to *Weishu: Shilaozhi* (*History of the Wei Dynasties: Treatise on Buddhism and Taoism*), Liangzhou had believed in Buddhism from the time of Zhang Gui [张轨, 313 AD, founder of 前凉 / Former Liang state] onward for generations. When Juqu Mengxun [沮渠蒙逊] ruled over Liangzhou, he also had a liking for Buddhism. At that time there was a *śramaṇa* by the name of Tanmochen [昙摩谶, Dharmarakṣa, 385-433 AD] who came to Liangzhou from central Hinduka in 412 AD. Dharmarakṣa, who was familiar with the *sūtras* and *śāstras* and translated at least ten *sūtras* including the *Daboniepan jing* [大般涅槃经, *Mahāparinirvāṇa sūtra*], was skilled in fortune-telling and predicting in detail events which took place in other states, which came to be true. Juqu Mengxun often consulted him on affairs of the state[3]. It is said that Juqu Mengxun sponsored the making of a sixteen-feet stone Buddha image for his mother[4] and he also had a cave-temple carved out in a mountain about one hundred *li* to the south of Liangzhou around 397 AD, that is, the cave-temple complex at Tiantishan [天梯山][5]. While the *dhyāna*

---

[1] Jia Yingyi [贾应逸], "*Jiumoluoshi yijing he beiliang shiqi de gaochang fojiao* [鸠摩罗什译经和北凉时期的高昌佛教, Kumārajīva's translated versions of the *sūtras* and the Turfan Buddhism in the Northern Liang state]", in: *Dunhuang Research*, No. 1 (1999): 146-158.

[2] Hexi or Gansu Corridor is located in northwestern Gansu, it is so called because it lies to the west of the Yellow River.

[3] Wei Shou, *opere citato*: 3032. confer: 1) James R. Ware, *opere citato*: 133-134; 2) Leon Hurvitz, *opere citato*: 57-61.

[4] Huijiao, *opere citato*: 78; *confer Taishō*, Vol. 50: 335-337, esp. 336b.

[5] Daoxuan, *Ji shenzhou sanbao gantong lu* [集神州三宝感通录, *Collection of the Strange and Extraordinary Deeds of the Buddhist Triratna in China*], in: *Taishō*, No. 2106, Vol. 52: 404-435, esp. 417c-418a.

master Dharmamitra [昙摩蜜多, 356-442 AD] stayed in Liangzhou before 424 AD, his disciples and followers were numerous and the practice of *dhyāna*-meditation was very earnestly pursued[1]. It is noteworthy that Buddhism of Liangzhou was famous not only for translation of the scriptures, but also for *dhyāna*-discipline. For instance, Juqu Jingsheng [沮渠京声], a young cousin on the paternal side of the Northern Liang ruler, was a monk who practiced *dhyāna*-meditation in Liangzhou[2]. Monks Xuan'gao, Xuanshao and Tanyao, who all practiced *dhyāna*-meditation and supported the activity of opening of rock-cut temples, did have a close relation with the *dhyāna*-discipline of Liangzhou. Therefore, any place with a rock-cut temple was created for hermit monks to practice *dhyāna*-meditation; any devotee who practiced *dhyāna*-meditation must have had ties with Liangzhou, because *dhyāna*-meditation needed instruction from others and couldn't be studied independently. A monk or a lay devotee, without the guidance or supervision of a *dhyāna*-master, was unable to learn the art of concentration, he would perform heterodox and false contemplation and would not be able to achieve proper *dhyāna*-meditation[3].

In 439 AD, the Northern Wei Dynasty conquered the Northern Liang state and occupied Liangzhou. Immediately they deported Juqu Maoqian [沮渠茂虔 or Juqu Mujian/沮渠牧犍, ruler of then Northern Liang, 433-439 AD] and his clans as well as all the elites and many commoners from Liangzhou to Pingcheng, about 100, 000 families in all[4]. According to *Weishu: Shilaozhi* (*History of the Wei Dynasties: Treatise on Buddhism and Taoism*), "Liangzhou was conquered and the people of the state moved to the capital. The *śramaṇas* and Buddhist paraphernalia as well as practices all came to East,

[1] Sengyou, *opere citato*: 546; *confer Taishō*, Vol. 55: 105, esp. 105a.

[2] Huijiao, *opere citato*: 78; *confer Taishō*, Vol. 50: 337a.

[3] Tang Yongtong, *opere citato*: 278-283.

[4] Cui Hong [崔鸿], *Shiliuguo chunqiu: Beiliang lu* [十六国春秋：北凉录, *Annals of the Sixteen States: the Northern Liang*], in: *Taiping yulan* [太平御览, *The Taiping Reign-Period Imperial Encyclopedia*] compiled by Li Fang [李昉] et al, facsimile edition, Beijing: Zhonghua Book Company, 1960: 603.

and *xiangjiao* [象 教 image-religion, viz. Buddhism][1] prospered more and more and increased far and wide" [2]. The focus of monastery or temple building activity had definitely shifted to the vicinity of the political center of gravity, i. e., Pingcheng. Not long after the Buddhist craftsmen were moved to Pingcheng, a number of eminent monks followed, some of them coming from Liangzhou during the emigration[3]. If we look at the individual Buddhist images remaining from before and after the restoration of Buddhism during the Northern Wei Dynasty in 452 AD, we can see that in subject matter, style and clothing, the images of Buddha all reflect the earlier traditions popular under the Northern Liang. These factors, taken together with records of forced immigrations to the Northern Wei capital, lead us to conclude that the early Buddha images of the Northern Wei Dynasty are closely related to those of the Northern Liang[4]. In short, the Buddhism of the Northern Wei Dynasty definitely followed that of the Northern Liang[5]. In addition, from 409 to 469 AD, for a period of about 60 years, the Northern Wei Dynasty made it a policy to gather the combined expertise of the

---

[1] As for term *xiangjiao* [象教 or 像教], some scholars believe it is the equivalent of the Sanskrit word *pratirūpakadharma* or *saddharma-pratirūpaka* [像法], the second period in the teaching of the Good Law. According to an explanatory note in the *Toutuosi beiwen* [头陀寺碑文, *Inscription on the Tablet of Dhūta Monastery*] in *Wen Xuan* [文选, *Anthology Through the Ages*] by Xiao Tong [萧统, 501-531 AD], however, we are told by Li Zhouhan [李周翰] that "*xiangjiao* means to use the image to teach people". Here, the Chinese word *xiangjiao* were composed of two characters, "*xiang* [像]" and "*jiao* [教]", the former signifies image and the latter religion, compounded together as image-religion, which indicates or implies Buddhism, because Buddhist followers all worship the image of Buddha. From the late Northern Wei Dynasty onwards, Buddhism was often called image-religion by the Chinese, the Buddha image became the most important means for the dissemination of Buddhism, and the idea that "to erect the image is to establish the religion" was deeply rooted in medieval China.

Li Shan [李善] et al, *Liuchen zhu wenxuan* [六臣注文选, *Annotations to Anthology Through the Ages*] compiled by Xiao Tong, in 718 AD, facsimile edition, Beijing: Zhonghua Book Company, 1987: 1089.

[2] Wei Shou, *opere citato*: 3032. confer: 1) James R. Ware, *opere citato*: 135; 2) Leon Hurvitz, *opere citato*: 61.

[3] For instance, Xuangao went to Pingcheng during this time and became a teacher of Prince Huang. He used to stay in a *dhyāna*-cave and carried forward *dhyāna*-practice in the capital. Huijiao, *opere citato*: 411-412; *confer Taishō,* Vol. 50: 397c-398a.

[4] Tang Yongtong, *opere citato*: 359.

[5] Tang Yongtong, *opere citato*: 557.

major talents in all trades and professions in northern China in the area of the capital. With the accumulation of talent and the restoration of Buddhism, the Northern Wei Dynasty, under the direction and guidance of Monk Tanyao who came from Liangzhou[1], had the means to construct the mammoth-scale cave-temples at Wuzhou hills, west of the Capital[2].

Because of such patronage by the Northern Wei imperial house and other ruling groups, Buddhist cave-temples were carved out in various sites in northern China, beginning with the latter half of the 5th century AD and continued to be patronized by the ruling families of the Sui [隋, 581-618 AD] and Tang [唐 618-907 AD] dynasties all the way to the mid 8th century in China[3].

Within this development, we only find three types of rock-cut cave in the cave-temple complex set up from the latter half of the 5th century to the early 6th century, namely meditation-caves, *stūpa*-caves and Buddha-hall-caves. As for the rock-cut caves hewn out in the early 6th century, the number of meditation-caves and the *stūpa*-caves are relatively small, while Buddha-hall-caves became predominant at this stage. The types of rock-cut cave opened up during the mid-late 6th century remain virtually the same, but at this time a *stūpa* was often carved out on the open face of the cliff above the entrance of the caves as in Xiangtangshan. If a devotee enters this kind of cave to worship the Buddha image, the point of this may well be to represent the idea expressed in *sūtras* that a devotee "enters a *stūpa* to view the Buddha image"[4]. This is a necessary requirement of monks carrying out meditation. From this, we may infer that up to this period the caves carved out in northern China still included the provision of a space for monks carrying out *dhyāna*[5].

---

[1] Tang Yongtong, *ibidem*.

[2] Su Bai, *Zhongguo shikusi yanjiu* (*Studies of the Cave-temples of China*), Beijing: Cultural Relics Press, 1996: 114-144.

[3] Su Bai, *Zhongguo fojiao shikusi yiji* (*The Buddhist Cave-temples of China*), Beijing: Cultural Relics Press, 2010: 16-18.

[4] Buddhabhadra, *opere citato* (*Foshuo guanfo sanmeihai jing...*): *Taishō*, Vol. 15: 645-697, esp. 656b, 665b, 681c, 688c-689b, 694c.

[5] Su Bai, *opere citato* (*Zhongguo shikusi yanjiu...*): 16-20.

In addition, some reliefs or murals depicting monks in *dhyāna*-meditation can also be found in a cave-temple complex such as those in Yungang Caves 7, 8, 12 and in Mogaoku Cave 285 (fig.14), which provide us the visual evidence that "to carve a celestial cave in the rock is to supply a place for a monk sitting in meditation"[1]. The cave-temple complexes constructed from the 4th to the 6th century AD in northern China, with respect to function and nature, were mostly to provide a place for monks practicing *dhyāna*-meditation and contemplation.

fig.14 A Monk in *dhyāna* meditation, Cave 285 at Mogaoku

4. Contemplation of the Buddha's Images

The method of meditation was earlier on found in the practice of "remembrance［念, *anusmṛti*］" of Buddha Amitābha as described in the *Bozhou sanmei jing*［般舟三昧经, *Pratyutpanna-buddha-sammukhāvaṣṭhita samādhi-sūtra, Sūtra of the Meditation to behold the Buddhas*］by Lokakṣema［支娄迦谶, 147 AD-?］in 179 AD[2]. The subject of this important *sūtra* is a form of mental concentration which enables a devotee to behold all Buddhas as if they were standing before his eyes[3]. The object of this meditation is to cause the spirit to liberate itself from the cycle of birth and death, pain and trouble, and to achieve a state of *Nirvāṇa*. The method of this meditation is to concentrate mentally on one

［1］Gao Yun, *opere citato*: 339, esp. 339b.

［2］Lokakṣema, *Bozhou sanmei jing* (*Pratyutpanna-buddha-sammukhāvaṣṭhita samādhi-sūtra, Sūtra of the Meditation to behold the Buddhas*), in: *Taishō*, No. 417, Vol. 13: 902-919.

［3］E. Zürcher, *opere citato*: 220.

particular object, thought, etc., thereby creating conditions favorable to acquiring the power of vision. In practice, a devotee could concentrate on anything at all, but the most important object of early Chinese Buddhism was to concentrate with his whole heart on the image of Buddha[1]. This is to say, a devotee was thought to be able to achieve a mental state in which he could not distinguish between himself and Buddha by concentrating his thoughts entirely upon the image of Buddha. The practitioner can eventually become a Buddha himself. A devotee must faithfully observe all the rules of religious life; then he must go to a secluded spot and there concentrate his mind upon the Buddha, for one day and one night, or for a whole week, continuously, until he is able to achieve his objective. Having achieved this concentration, Buddha will manifest himself before the devotee's eyes and preach the doctrine to the latter, like an image in a dream or a shape reflected in a mirror[2]. According to the *Yu yinshi liu yimin deng shu* [与隐士刘遗民等书, A Letter to Hermit Liu Yimin and others] by Huiyuan, when Liu Yimin had spent just half a year concentrating his thought and sitting in meditation, he saw in *samādhi* the Buddha. Whenever he met a Buddhist image on the way, the Buddha would manifest himself in the air, his halo illuminating heaven and earth all bathed in a golden color, and again he would see himself wearing a *kāṣāya* and bathing in the jewel pond of *Sukhāvatī*. When he had come out of *samādhi*, he asked the monks to recite the *sūtra*[3].

The content of a monk's meditation inside a cave, however, is mainly to practice remembrance of Buddha. According to *Siwei lueyaofa* (*An Outline of Meditation* or *Outlining the Way to Reflect*), "Buddha is the king of the Law. He can let one obtain all kinds of good qualities. That is why someone who practices meditation should first be mindful of Buddha"[4], to be precise, a devotee who desires to attain enlightenment should practice the remembrance of Buddhas in the ten directions (*daśa diśaḥ*) and Buddhas of the past, present and future

---

[1] Kumārajīva, *opere citato* (*Zuochan sanmei jing*...): 269-286, esp. 276a.

[2] E. Zürcher, *opere citato*: 221.

[3] Huiyuan, *opere citato* (*Yu yinshi liu yimin deng shu*...): 304, esp. 304b.

[4] Kumārajīva?, *opere citato* (*Siwei lueyao fa*...): 297-300, esp. 299a; *confer* Charles Willemen, *opere citato* (*Outlining the Way to Reflect*...): 31.

(*trayo-dhvanaḥ*) before entering *dhyāna*[1]. According to *Chanmi yaofa jing* (*Secret Essentials of the Dhyāna-discipline* or *Sūtra about the Secret Essence of Dhyāna*), Buddha told Nandhi［难提 / 禅难提］and Ānanda to teach, in the future, all human beings who had committed many sins in, to practice the remembrance of Buddha in order to put an end to their faults, vexations or retributions in this life for the sins of previous existence. A devotee who intends to practice the remembrance should first of all sit up straight, with his hands crossed, eyes closed and tongue touching the palate. Once he is calmed down by this posture, the devotee should be totally absorbed in remembrance, his attention completely concentrated. Before carrying on the remembrance, the devotee should sit in front of an image and practice the contemplation of Buddha. After Buddha's *Parinirvāṇa, bhikṣu*［比丘］, *bhikṣuṇī*［比丘尼］, *upāsaka*［优婆塞］and *upāsikā*［优婆夷］should be yearning to contemplate on Buddha, seek peace and quietness, and if they repent their faulty behavior, to confess their sins[2]. In the same text, Buddha told Ānanda that if a *bhikṣu* desires licentious possion he should be taught to contemplate Buddha; this contemplation will help him to move away from faults and sins. Then, he might be taught to practice the remembrance of Buddha with his whole heart or mind[3]. According to *Siwei lueyaofa* (*An Outline of the Meditation* or *Outlining the Way to Reflect*):

> Mindfulness of Buddha makes one's serious wrongs of immeasurable eons trifling, and one may reach concentration. If one is earnestly mindful of Buddha, Buddha is mindful of you too. Just as enemies and creditors do not dare to approach him who is held dear by the king, any remaining evil factor will not come to disturb the person who is mindful of Buddha. If one is mindful of Buddha, Buddha is always present. How must one be mindful? One's confidence must not go beyond ones' eyes. One should visualize a fine image to be like the real Buddha. First one should descend to the feet from the cranial knot and from the white tuft of hair between the eyebrows, and from

[1] Kumārajīva, *opere citato* (*Zuochan sanmei jing...*): 269-286, esp. 281a.

[2] Kumārajīva, *opere citato* (*Chanfa yao...*): 242-269, esp. 255a-256a.

[3] Kumārajīva, *opere citato*: 258b.

the feet one should again reach the cranial knot. When the characteristics are thus carefully grasped, one should turn to a tranquil place. Reflecting with eyes closed, one should be concentrated on the image, so that one does not think of anything else. If one thinks of another object, one should control one's thoughts and make them return. If one observes with one's mental eye, seeing as one wishes, this is the concentration attaining visualization of the image. One should perform this mindfulness: "I will not go to it, and the image will not come either, but what I have seen will dwell in my thoughts because of my mental concentration" .[1]

The process of contemplation entails observing the sitting Buddha first, then the standing Buddha and finally the Buddha in *Parinirvāṇa*[2]. The contemplation of Buddha's physical features and characteristics [相好, *lakṣaṇa* and *vyañjana*] as well as that of the seated Buddha, standing Buddha and the Buddha in *Parinirvāṇa* are called "*Guanfo sanmei* [观佛三昧, Buddha-*dhyāna-samādhī*, contemplation of Buddha]"[3]. After the contemplation of the image, the devotee should continue to examine *shengshen* [生身, the body of birth], such as his previous life and present life, and *fashen* [法身, the body of qualities or *dharma-kāya*], such as the *maṇi* [摩尼] pearl[4]. Then, the devotee has to contemplate the seven Buddhas[5], who would be witness to the devotee's practice of *dhyāna*-meditation[6].

By this time, the devotee, having seen all the Buddhas to whom he had

---

[1] Charles Willemen, *opere citato*: 31; *confer*: Kumārajīva?, *opere citato* (*Siwei lueyao fa*...): 297-300, esp. 299a.

[2] Kumārajīva, *opere citato* (*Chanfa yao*...): 242-269, esp. 255a-256a.

[3] Kumārajīva, *opere citato*: 255a-256c.

[4] 1) Kumārajīva, *opere citato*: 265b; 2) Kumārajīva?, *opere citato* (*Siwei lueyao fa*...): 297-300, esp. 299a-c.

[5] The term "Seven Buddhas" means seven Buddhas of the past, that is, Śākyamuni [释迦牟尼佛] and six Buddhas said to have preceded him. The six Buddhas are Vipaśyin [毗婆尸佛], Śikhin [尸弃佛], Viśvabhū [毗舍佛], Krakucchanda [拘留孙佛], Kanakamuni [迦那含牟尼佛] and Kāśyapa [迦叶佛]. Among them, the first three Buddhas appeared in the past Glorious *Kalpa*, while the other four Buddhas including Śākyamuni appeared in the present Wise *Kalpa*. *confer* Kumārajīva, *opere citato* (*Chanfa yao*...): 242-269, esp. 254a.

[6] 1) Kumārajīva, *ibidem*; 2) Buddhabhadra, *opere citato*: 645-697, esp. 693a.

contemplated, is aware that one Buddha is the equivalent of all Buddhas and all Buddhas are of one Buddha[1]. If the devotee returns to the cave and fails to meditate on the Buddha whom he had contemplated on, or what he meditated on differs from what he contemplated, then the devotee has to enter a *stūpa-gṛha/caityagṛha* to contemplate on the Buddha again[2]. If he succeeds, it means that the devotee has escaped from the bonds of various cravings or secular life and obtained the freedom from transmigration, from *karma*, from illusion and from sufferings. At this point the devotee needs to worship Maitreya, the future Buddha, because he will meet Maitreya during his *dhyāna*-meditation and contemplation[3]. The contemplation of Maitreya is based on the versions written by Kumārajīva, such as *Mile xiasheng jing* (*Maitreyavyākaraṇa, Advent of Maitreya Sūtra*)[4], *Foshuo mile chengfo jing* (*Sūtra of Maitreya becoming a Buddha*)[5] and *Chanmi yaofa jing* (*Secret Essentials of the Dhyāna-discipline* or *Sūtra about the Secret Essence of Dhyāna*)[6]. In terms of the content of contemplation, furthermore, *Fahua sanmei guan* [法华三昧观, *Saddharma-puṇḍarīka-samādhi, Samādhi of the Lotus of the Law*][7] is one of the most important contemplations[8] as it enables a devotee to worship Śākyamuni and Prabhūtaratna [释迦、多宝] together. They are recorded in detail in *Fahua jing* (*Saddharma-puṇḍarīka-sūtra, Lotus Sūtra*)[9] which was translated into Chinese by Kumārajīva in 406 AD. Kumārajīva's version was regarded as the best among the Chinese translations and was widely read and quoted[10]; and it

---

[1] Kumārajīva, *opere citato* (*Zuochan sanmei jing*...): 269-286, esp. 277a.

[2] Buddhabhadra, *opere citato*: 645-697, esp. 665b, 681c.

[3] Kumārajīva, *opere citato* (*Chanfa yao*...): 242-269, esp. 268a.

[4] Kumārajīva, *Mile xiasheng jing* (*Maitreyavyākaraṇa, Advent of Maitreya Sūtra*), in: *Taishō,* No. 454, Vol. 14: 423-425.

[5] Kumārajīva, *opere citato* (*Foshuo mile*...): 428-434.

[6] Kumārajīva, *opere citato* (*Chanfa yao*...): 242-269, esp. 254c, 268a

[7] Kumārajīva?, *opere citato* (*Siwei lueyao fa*...): 297-300, esp. 300b-c; *confer* Charles Willemen, *opere citato*: 45-47.

[8] Liu Huida, *opere citato*: 339.

[9] Kumārajīva, *opere citato* (*Miaofa lianhua jing*...): 1-62, esp. 32b-34b.

[10] Among various translated versions of the *Lotus Sūtra*, as Daoxuan pointed out, only the version produced by Kumārajīva was taken as the model and widely quoted by Buddhist followers. Daoxuan, "*Miaofa lianhuajing hongchuan xu* [妙法莲花经弘传序, Preface to Dissemination of the *Saddharma-puṇḍarīka-sūtra* or *Lotus Sūtra of the Wonderful Law*]", in: *Taishō*, Vol. 9: 1, esp. 1b.

exerted a great influence on Buddhism in medieval China[1].

In short, if we consider the content and meaning of the above described contemplation and meditation activity, it really identifies with or corresponds to that of the cave-temples carved in China from the 4th to the 6th century AD. A small cave was hewn out of living rock for meditation, a big Buddha-hall-cave was designed for contemplation, and a *stūpa*-cave was especially carved for a devotee who had to enter the cave again to practice contemplation and meditation, besides circumambulation of the *stūpa*.

This phenomenon is reflected most clearly in the cave-temple complex at Yungang, and becomes even more pronounced over time[2]. The huge Buddha images carved out in the cave-temples of the first period at Yungang present the notable marks or features and physical characteristics of the Buddha before our eyes, which are recorded in detail in the *dhyāna sūtras* translated by Kumārajīva. For instance, most of the thirty-two features [三十二相, *dvātriṃśan mahā-puruṣa-lakṣaṇāni*] and some of the eighty characteristics [八十种好, *aśīty-anuvyañjanāni*] of Buddha, which are recorded in details in the *Chanmi yaofa jing* (*Secret Essentials of the Dhyāna-discipline* or *Sūtra about the Secret Essence of Dhyāna*)[3] and regarded as necessary for image contemplation [观像法], are the most important part of the monks' *dhyāna*-contemplation[4]. The features and characteristics of Buddha recorded in the text are as follows: the *uṣṇīṣa*, a growth of flesh on the head like a topknot or cranial knot; hair on the head is dark purple, one hair grows from each pore and the total number of the hair is 84. 000, each graceful hair became a dextro-curl, stretching for 13 *chi* (about 318 cm) when it was uncurled; the round face like a full moon, having an impressive bearing and a commanding presence; the *ūrṇā*, a white tuft of hair between the eyebrows, curling to the right, like a white glass pearl; the nose like the beak of an eagle-king; the mouth and lips are red-colored, in them it appears the shape

---

[1] Su Bai, *opere citato* (*Zhongguo shikusi yanjiu...*): 39-51, esp. 50; 76-88, esp. 83.

[2] 1) Su Bai, *opere citato*: 76-88; 2) Su Bai, *Zhongguo fojiao shikusi yiji* (*The Buddhist Cave-temples of China*), Beijing: Cultural Relics Press, 2010: 34-35.

[3] Kumārajīva, *opere citato* (*Zuochan sanmei jing...*): 269-286, esp. 276a-c.

[4] Kumārajīva, *opere citato* (*Chanfa yao...*): 242-269, esp. 256a.

of the *bimba*; the even teeth number forty, close, white and regular; the neck like a glazed tube, showing a golden color; the *śrīvatsalakṣana* (卐) on the chest is very clear and obvious among other marks; arms look like the trunk or proboscis of an elephant-king, extremely flexible, soft and lovely; the pliant hands grow hair, with fingers uneven and golden colored; the finger was connected by pearl-net shaped membrane, just like the feet of a goose king; body seated steady like a golden hill, properly dignified and straight; the calf of a lower leg looks like the calf of an antelope or deer king, straight and round; the level feet stood or seated on the lotus, with a thousand-spoke-wheel-sign on the soles and toes; the base of the toes was connected by a pearl-net shaped membrane, like the feet of a wild goose, and so forth. In addition, Buddha has aureole and nimbus around his body, *nirmāṇa*-buddhas［化佛］, *bhikṣus* and bodhisattvas can be seen in the light radiating from the body. If a devotee contemplates the Buddha from the *uṣṇīṣa* (cranial protuberance) to feet, it is called favorable contemplation, if done in reverse order it is called inverse contemplation[1].

Such notable features and physical characteristics of Buddha were fully represented in the early cave-temples at Yungang (fig.15)[2]. If a devotee carries on the contemplation in such a way or sits in meditation, his heart will be perfectly clear[3]. Consequently, a devotee can eventually come to think that there is no distinction between Buddha and himself. In short, a kind of hallucination or mirage in which one beholds Buddha will appear in the end[4]. For Buddhist adepts or monks, an act of worshipping Buddha is the same as concentrating their mind on the image of Buddha. During meditation, if a devotee fails to see the real Buddha, then he must enter the caves again and again to view the image of Buddha and to meditate. However, if, after a long time a devotee still fails to see Buddha, then the devotee may begin to have doubts. When this happens he must seek the aid of Maitreya, who stays in our world to

［1］Kumārajīva, *opere citato*: 242-269, esp. 255b-c.

［2］Liu Huida, *opere citato*: 335-36.

［3］Kumārajīva, *ibidem*.

［4］A monk named Daojiong［道冏］used to have such a dreamland when he practiced *dhyāna*-meditation. Daoshi, *opere citato*: 1962; *confer Taishō,* No. 2122, Vol. 53: 785a.

fig.15 Main Buddha, cave 20 at Yungang

help him in his crisis of the faith[1]. But how can a devotee approach Maitreya? Simply by worshipping before the image of Maitreya and, the image of Maitreya will appear (fig.16)[2]. The most important Buddhist images of the first period at Yungang, moreover, are the Buddhas of the three existences [三佛][3], which were not only especially emphasized by monk Tanyao[4], but also recorded in the *dhyāna sūtras* translated by Kumārajīva[5]. These of course include Śākyamuni

[1] Kinkara and Tanyao, *opere citato* (*Fu fazang yinyuan zhuan*...): 297-322, esp. 320a.

[2] *Foshuo mile xiasheng chengfo jing* (*Sūtra of Maitreya becoming a Buddha*) was produced by Kumārajīva in 402 AD, who was requested to translate and to meet the need of the Buddhist followers in the Later Qin state. Su Bai, *opere citato* (*Zhongguo shikusi yanjiu*...): 176-199, esp. 190-191.

[3] The Buddhas of the three existences [三佛, or the Buddhas of the three epochs], which means the Buddha in past existence, the Buddha in present existence and the Buddha in future existence, are used to indicate all of time, from the eternal past, through the present, to the eternal future. In the Buddhist *sūtras*, expressions such as "the Buddhas of the three existences [三世佛]" and "the Buddhas of the three existences and ten directions [十方三世诸佛]" indicate all Buddhas throughout eternity and boundless space. The subject of "the Buddhas of the three existences" was in full vogue after the restoration of Buddhism in 452 AD in northern China, because Monk Tanyao, by translating the *Fu fazang yinyuan zhuan* (*A History of the Buddha's Successors*), demonstrated that Buddhism has an extremely long, long history.

[4] Tang Yongtong, *opere citato*: 357-360.

[5] 1) Kumārajīva, *opere citato* (*Chanfa yao*...): 242-269, esp. 267c; 2) Kumārajīva, *opere citato* (*Zuochan sanmei jing*...): 269-286, esp. 281a.

fig.16 Maitreya image, Cave 13 at Yungang

and Maitreya[1].

The subject matter of the second period at Yungang is more complex. Apart from Śākyamuni, scenes from the life of the Buddha, *jātaka* stories and *stūpas* which naturally represent Śākyamuni, we also find Śākyamuni and Prabhūtaratna in pairs (fig.17), the thousand Buddhas [千佛, Budhāsahasa] in large scale, the seven Buddhas as well as Samantabhadra [普贤] riding on an elephant, etc.[2]. In addition, the importance of Maitreya becomes more and more obvious. The

[1] Liu Huida, *opere citato*: 340-341.

[2] Liu Huida, *opere citato*: 339-342.

fig.17 Śākyamuni and Prabhūtaratna, Cave 6 at Yungang

variety of images to be found in these later cave-temples has expanded to include the rather extraordinary phenomenon of two Maitreyas together. This evidence points out that monks carrying on meditation at that time were seeking increasingly various images and ways of imagining the Buddha image, in order to free themselves from the cycle of rebirth. This may also reflect the boredom and vexation of monks resulting from constant meditation[1]. Since the *dhyāna sūtras* deal especially with the methods employed in meditation and the ways of contemplating the Buddha image, as a result only the objects that monks should contemplate on are pointed out. Details of specific stories such as the life of the Buddha and *jātaka* were not mentioned.

The cave-temples of the third period were carved out after the move of the capital from Pingcheng to Luoyang in 494 AD. The cave-temples at Yungang in this period clarify several important points worth noting in this context. For instance, medium and small sized caves became especially numerous. There are quite a number of caves that are so small as to "allow

[1] Su Bai, *opere citato* (*Zhongguo fojiao shikusi yiji...*): 34-35.

room for only one seated person"[1]. From this we can deduce that a great many of the caves opened up during this period were intended as cells for the meditation of individual monks. This kind of caves is exemplified by cave 38. Since the sidewalls of this cave are covered with images of monks meditating and since this cave also displays the story of Śākyamuni comforting Ānanda (fig.18)[2], such images speak eloquently of the nature and function of such a cave[3].

fig.18 Śākyamuni comforting Ānanda, Cave 38 at Yungang

(This paper was published in *Kumārajīva: Philosopher and Seer,* ed. Shashibala, New Delhi: Indira Gandhi National Centre for the Arts, 2015: 190-221.)

[1] Daoxuan, *opere citato* (*Xü gaoseng zhuan...*): 557, esp. 557c.

[2] 1) Faxian, *opere citato*: 113; 2) H. A. Giles, *opere citato*: 50; 3) Xuanzang, *opere citato*: 727-728; 4) Samuel Beal, *opere citato*: 373.

[3] 1) Su Bai, *opere citato* (*Zhongguo shikusi yanjiu...*): 76-88; 2) Su Bai, *opere citato* (*Zhongguo fojiao shikusi yiji...*) : 34-35.

关于鼓山石窟中的高欢柩穴

鼓山石窟（邯郸北响堂山石窟）北洞（现编为第3窟），开凿于鼓山西崖北端，坐东朝西，是鼓山现存最早的一座石窟。窟外立面高约18米，面阔20米；窟前门道两侧原雕立柱、上有仿木结构的瓦垄和窟檐，顶部雕出覆钵及刹幡，整个外观形如一座高大的覆钵塔（图1）。窟内平面方形、平顶，进深12米，面阔13米，高12.5米，中央雕出方形塔柱（佛塔），塔柱周围凿出礼拜道。塔柱正面及左右两侧面中部各开一大龛（图2），大龛上部为列龛，下部造神王小龛。其中，塔柱正壁大龛内雕造结跏坐佛（图3），右壁（北壁）大龛内半跏坐佛（图4），左壁（南壁）大龛内倚坐佛（图5）。窟内前壁门道两侧浮雕礼佛人物，周壁雕造16座精美的塔形龛，唯龛内原始造像已失（图6、7）。

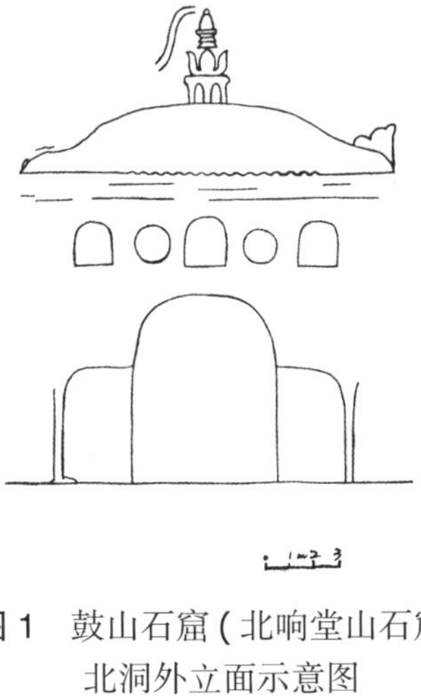

图1　鼓山石窟（北响堂山石窟）北洞外立面示意图

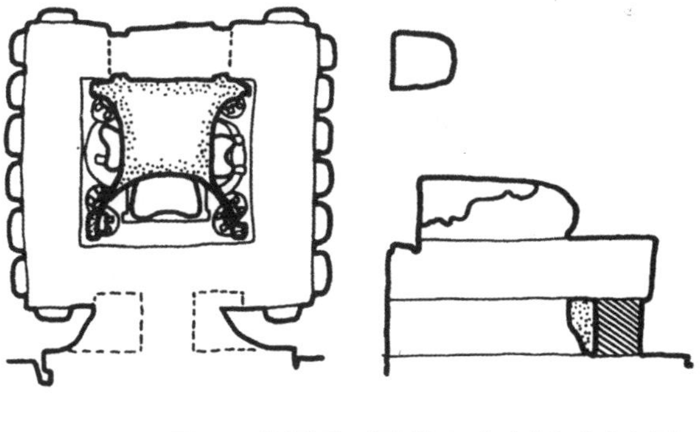

图2　北洞平面及纵向垂直剖面示意图

图 3　北洞中心塔柱正壁龛内佛像

图 4　北洞中心塔柱右侧（北）壁龛内佛像

图 5　北洞中心塔柱左侧（南）壁龛内佛像

图 6　北洞北侧壁塔形龛

从洞窟形制、题材布局、装饰纹样及宏大规模推断，北洞绝非一般人所能供养，处处显示出最高统治阶层的非凡气度，其开凿似与东魏权臣、北齐的实际创建者高欢有密切关系[1]。

图7　北洞侧壁塔形龛立面图

北洞中心塔柱南壁顶部西起第三龛（现编为3-33龛），龛内原有造像不存，现露出一小型龛室入口（图8）。2001年9月27日，笔者在现场考察时曾登临此室，并做了测绘和文字记录：龛室分门道和内室两部分（图9）。门道立面外侧作帐形、内侧呈圆拱状，面阔109厘米，进深105厘米，高168厘米。门道前端底部中央有一梯形石台，宽45厘米，高14厘米，其两侧各有一直径14厘米、深10厘米的圆孔。在门道后侧下部有两块55×63×25厘米的封门石，表面雕饰火焰、忍冬和莲花（图10）。封门石所在壁面及门道顶，有一匝深约1厘米的凹槽，原为安置封门之用。内室平面略呈梯形，顶边略弧，前端面阔128厘米，高171厘米，后端面阔118厘米，高163厘米，进深281厘米。小室壁面錾凿较平整，表面无雕饰。室内中央地面零乱摆放石块五块，分别编为A、B、C、D、E号，其中A石尺寸为61×54×22.5厘米，B石为61×57×23.5厘米，C石为48×24厘米，D石为40×22厘米，E石为33.5×23厘米。五块石块中，A、B两石表面雕饰火焰、忍冬和莲花，其纹样可与门道下部两块残石对接（图11），另三石亦可置放于A、B两

[1] 据文献记载，高欢是信奉佛教的。唐道世《法苑珠林》卷十三引《齐志》及《旌异》，表述《高王观世音经》的流行与之密切相关。唐法琳《辩正论》卷四《十代奉佛篇下》记载："魏齐献武王（高欢），思随冥运，智与神行；恩比春天，威同夏日。恒至心于万物，被大道于八方。修心克己，回向正法，造大悲寺，普济群生。"杨衒之《洛阳伽蓝记》卷五更记洛阳北邙山上有"齐献武王寺"。又，唐代道宣在编著《续高僧传》之前，曾"往相部寻鼓山"、游历石窟寺，并记述"自神武（高欢）迁邺之后，因山上下并建伽兰，或樵采陵夷，工匠穷凿"。参见：1) 道世《法苑珠林》，周叔迦、苏晋仁校注，北京：中华书局，2003年，第466-467页；2) 法琳《辩正论》，见《大正藏》第52卷，第515a页；3) 杨衒之《洛阳伽蓝记》，周祖谟校释，北京：中华书局，1963年，第228页；4) 道宣《续高僧传·圆通传》，见《大正藏》第50卷，第648c页；5) 丁明夷《巩县、天龙、响堂、安阳数处石窟寺》，见《中国美术全集》雕塑编13《巩县天龙山响堂山安阳石窟雕刻》，北京：文物出版社，1989年，第34页。

石之上，由此可以断定，五块石块系封堵龛室门道所用，即封门石。遗憾的是，另外三块残石不见，否则可拼接成完整的封门。封门石表面，处理成像龛正壁，且浮雕出头光和背光。其样式，与相邻左右两龛造像的头光、背光纹饰无异。至于底部石台及其两侧圆孔，原应置放造像。由此可见，该小室是当时特为藏纳某物所设计，隐蔽性极好。除封门石之外，小室内再无其他遗物。

图 8　北洞 3-33 龛室外立面

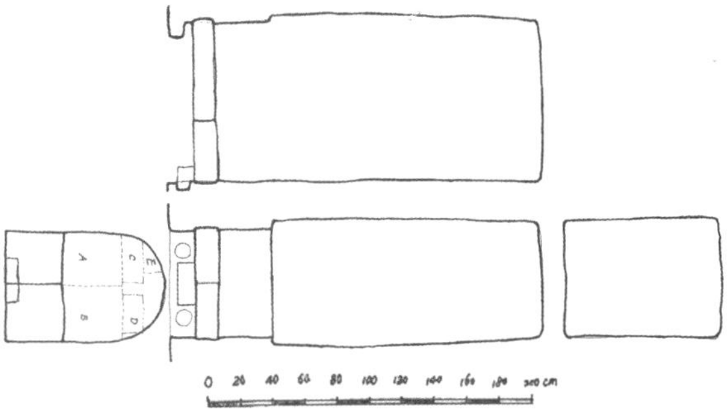

图 9　北洞 3-33 龛室平面、剖面及立面示意图

图 10　北洞 3-33 龛室入口封门石下部

图 11　北洞 3-33 龛室内残存石块 A、B

关于小龛室之原始用途,目前学界说法不一。有的学者认为它是东魏高欢的陵藏[1],也有的学者认为它有可能是一种天宫设置[2]。

北朝晚期,中原北方流行俗人死后瘗埋石窟的做法；而石窟作为陵墓的最早实例,可能是西魏乙弗后540年首葬麦积崖[3]。麦积崖第43窟为仿木石雕三间单檐四阿殿阁,正中开一龛,内造倚坐佛像；倚坐佛后为一低矮后室,平面作刀形(图12)。这种平面是当时墓葬流行的形制,因此有人推断它是乙弗后瘗窟[4]。我们认为这个推测是可信的。

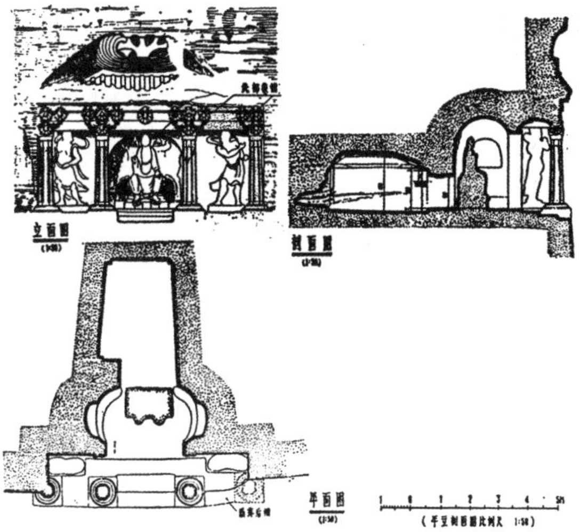

图12　麦积山第43窟外立面、平面及纵向垂直剖面图

据《资治通鉴》卷一百六十《梁纪》十六,“(梁武帝太清元年正月)丙午(547年2月13日),东魏渤海献武王欢卒……世子澄秘不发丧……(八月)甲申(9月19日),虚葬齐献武王于漳水之西；潜凿成安鼓山石窟佛寺之旁为穴,纳其柩而塞之,杀其群匠。及齐亡也,一匠之子知之,发石取金而逃”[5]。这段文字明确记载东魏权臣、北齐高祖高欢藏于鼓山石窟。文中的“献武王(高)欢卒”、“秘不发丧”、“(葬)于漳水

---

[1] 当地民间一直传说“高王藏在佛顶”的故事。参见：1)马丰《赴磁县武安县南北响堂寺及其附近工作报告》,见《国立北平研究院院务汇报》,1936年第7卷4期,第117页；2)宿白《三国——宋元考古》上(铅印本讲义),北京：北京大学历史系考古教研室,1974年,第19页；3)柴俊林《试论响堂石窟的初创年代》,刊《考古》,1996年第6期,第73-77页。

[2] 唐仲明《晋豫及其以东地区北朝晚期石窟寺研究——以响堂山石窟为中心》(博士学位论文),北京：北京大学,2004年,第21页注2、第67页注5。印度塔庙窟中不见佛塔顶部设置天宫,但塔基藏纳舍利却在塔庙窟中时有发现,如比德尔科拉第3窟和珀贾第12窟。

[3] 据《北史·后妃传》上:“文帝文皇后乙弗氏……逊居别宫,出家为尼……六年(540年)春……(帝)乃遣中常侍曹宠赍手敕令后自尽。后奉敕……召僧设供,令侍婢数十人出家,手为落发。事毕,乃入室,引被自覆而崩,年三十一。凿麦积崖为龛而葬,神柩将入,有二丛云先入龛中,倾之一灭一出,后号寂陵。”《北史》,点校本,北京：中华书局,1974年,第506-507页。

[4] 1957年4月下旬,洪毅然先生率西北师范学院艺术系学生在麦积山考察时发现了第43窟后室,后与麦积山文物保管所同行一道共同记录了该窟,并推定它可能是“寂陵”遗址。参见洪毅然《西魏文皇后乙弗氏“寂陵”遗址蠡测》,见《麦积山石窟资料汇编》初集,铅印本,天水：麦积山文物保管所、麦积山艺术研究会,1980年,第135-137页。

[5] 司马光《资治通鉴》,胡三省音注,标点本,北京：中华书局,1956年,第4948、4957页。

之西"[1]，疑抄自《北齐书·高祖纪》[2]，但"虚葬"之说和"潜凿"石窟之事，疑司马光另据其他相关文献精心写成。因此，鼓山石窟中应有一座藏纳高欢灵柩之穴，即高欢陵藏；而这座石窟从雕造时间、形制及规模等多方面考虑，应以北洞最为合适。

《资治通鉴》中的"佛寺"二字，即石窟寺，或许也可以理解为佛塔，因为建寺即立塔，是当时北朝习用的佛寺布局[3]；而"佛寺之旁"，应为石窟或佛塔之侧[4]。不过，《资治通鉴》所记墓穴位置似与上述北洞塔柱南壁顶部龛室略有出入[5]。经检《资治通鉴考异》和《资治通鉴目录》，发现：司马光"撮新书精要之语散于其间"[6]的《资治通鉴目录》[7]卷十六，明确记述"东魏孝静帝武定五年（547年），齐献武王欢卒，秘不发丧……澄还晋阳发丧，澄辞丞相，潜葬齐献武王于石佛顶。盗发之"[8]。《资治通鉴》与《资治通鉴目录》两者文字结合起来，正好符合鼓山石窟北洞现状，即潜葬墓穴位于北洞佛塔左侧（南壁）倚坐大佛顶部龛室[9]。现存龛室及封门石，更符合

[1] 在磁县西南部的漳河两岸，分布着134座北朝墓群。1979年发掘的茹茹公主墓，乃东魏高欢之子高湛之妻墓。该墓出土的墓志，记述茹茹公主"葬于滏水之阴，齐献武王茔内"。因而有人怀疑今磁县大冢村西的M1可能是高欢的义平陵（参见中国社会科学院考古研究所、河北省文物研究所编著《磁县湾漳北朝壁画墓》，北京：科学出版社，2003年，第198页）。若然，它是虚葬的高欢衣冠冢？

[2]《北齐书·高祖纪》作："（武定五年正月丙午，高欢）崩于晋阳，时年五十二，秘不发丧……八月甲申，葬于邺西北漳水之西。"《北齐书》，点校本，北京：中华书局，1972年，第24页。

[3] 宿白《东汉魏晋南北朝佛寺布局初探》，见《庆祝邓广铭教授九十华诞论文集》，石家庄：河北教育出版社，1997年，第36页。

[4] 据《大广益会玉篇》卷一《上部》，"旁：犹侧也"。中华书局1987年影印清张氏泽存堂本，第3页。

[5] 李裕群《北朝晚期石窟寺研究》，北京：文物出版社，2003年，第48页。

[6] 司马光《资治通鉴目录·序》，宋刊本，见《四部丛刊》初编缩印本，上海：商务印书馆，1936年，第1页。

[7]《资治通鉴》卷帙浩繁，司马光在修书的同时，做成《资治通鉴目录》三十卷，这是司马光《资治通鉴》的最后工作，"略举事目，年经国纬，以备检阅，别为目录"（晁公武语）。陈振孙曰："目录仿《史记》年表，年经国纬，用刘羲叟《长历》气朔，而撮新书精要散于其中。"遗憾的是，现通行本《资治通鉴》没有把目录印上。参见：1）晁公武《郡斋读书志》，孙猛校证，上海：上海古籍出版社，1990年，第209页；2）陈振孙《直斋书录解题》，徐小蛮、顾美华点校，上海：上海古籍出版社，1987年，第113页。

[8] 司马光《资治通鉴目录》，宋刊本，见《四部丛刊》初编缩印本，上海：商务印书馆，1936年，第259页。又，嘉靖《漳德府志》卷二引《通鉴》作"东魏大将军高澄虚葬齐献武王欢于漳水西，潜凿鼓山石窟佛顶之傍为穴"（参见嘉靖《漳德府志》，影印本，上海：中华书局上海编辑所，1964年）。

[9] 据《永乐大典》卷一万三千八百二十四《寺》引《元一统志》，"（智力寺）在磁州武安县。齐高欢薨于太原，默置（棺椁）于鼓山天宫之傍，即此滏阳乃虚陵也"（参见中华书局1986年影印本第5926页）。这条文献，明确记载默置之棺椁靠近天宫；而天宫应位于佛塔顶部，鼓山塔庙窟中只有3-33龛室与此记载相符。唯"此滏阳乃虚陵也"与之矛盾。

"纳其柩而塞之"。因此,该龛室为"潜葬"高欢之所、北洞为高欢瘗窟,似应无疑[1]。北齐亡后,一石匠之子曾"发石取金";而棺椁被窃,或在近代[2]。

最后要说的是,古代天竺一座大型佛塔的周围通常建造有许多形制各异的小塔,如斯瓦特地区的布特卡拉I (Butkara I)号遗址[3]。这些小塔[4],学界通称奉献塔或还愿塔(votive stūpa),是古代天竺四种佛塔之一[5]。北洞中心塔柱及北洞侧壁所开16座塔形龛[6],在总体布局上与斯瓦特地区的许多佛寺遗址类似,或许具有相同属性。据鼓山石窟南洞外《齐晋昌郡公唐邕刻经记》,"大齐之君,区有义□□思,家传天帝之尊,世祚轮王之贵"[7]。这里的"轮王",应为cakravartin(轮王、转轮王、转轮圣王),也可能泛指如来(佛)。北齐宠臣唐邕"善揣上意"[8],在发愿文中称颂皇帝有"世祚轮王之贵",尽管目的是取悦其主,但也说明"轮王"思想曾一度盛行;而"佛言:所有四种人应起塔,如来、圣弟子、辟支佛、转轮圣王"[9]。又,"释尊涅槃时,付嘱魔王造塔,令付帝释及四天王并大魔王:汝自守护。我涅槃后,正法灭尽已,将我钵

[1] 文献中亦有响堂山石窟为北齐文宣帝高洋陵藏之说。据《续高僧传·明芬传》,"仁寿下敕,令置塔于慈州之石窟寺,寺即齐文宣之所立也。大窟像背文宣陵藏中,诸雕刻骇动人鬼"(《大正藏》第50卷,第669c)。这里的慈州石窟寺,即响堂山石窟;响堂山石窟中之大窟乃北洞,而能作陵藏之用的唯有北洞,雕刻非凡、骇动人鬼的也仅此一洞。又,据《大广益会玉篇》卷第七"背:脊"(中华书局1987年影印泽存堂本第35页)也,"像背"即像脊;现存墓室正好位于像脊之上。因此,"大窟像背文宣陵藏"中的"文宣"二字,是否为"神武"之误?!

[2] 峰峰矿区文物保管所原工作人员柴俊林曾收集当地传说并走访有关人员,认为"高欢墓是'七七事变'(1937年)时才发现的",主谋是武安县苑城村人、时任日伪县长的李聘三,他们盗走墓内石棺一口、万年灯一盏(参见:柴俊林,上引书,第75页)。然而1935年10月16日,北平研究院史学研究会考古组马丰、龚元忠考察北响堂山石窟,并登"上北堂(北洞)方柱龛上高欢廓,廓离地高计11.70米,内什物全无,被盗一空"(参见:马丰,上引书,第117页)。故此传说疑与1922年11月日人常盘大定游访常乐寺时所见《(民国七年)募化启簿》有关:响堂石窟于"民国元年(1911年)冬月,遭权势恶劫,致使大小佛像无一不身手离异……"(常盤大定、關野貞《支那佛教史蹟》第三集評解,東京:佛教史蹟研究會,1926年,第92页)。

[3] D. Faccenna, *Butkara I* (*Swāt, Pakistan*) *1956-1962*, Part 3 (text), Rome: IsMEO, 1980: Pl. XIII.

[4] 依据法显记载,这种塔式建筑有些可能是罗汉塔或辟支佛塔,因为古代那竭国有"诸罗汉、辟支佛塔乃千数"。参见:法显《法显传》,章巽校注,上海:上海古籍出版社,1985年,第47页。

[5] 关于古代天竺的四种佛塔,参见李崇峰《中印佛教石窟寺比较研究:以塔庙窟为中心》,北京:北京大学出版社,2003年,第27页。

[6] 这十六座塔形龛内原雕的十六佛,结合南响堂第2窟周壁十六佛题名列龛,疑为法华题材。

[7] 参见水野清一、长广敏雄《河北磁县河南武安响堂山石窟》,京都:东方文化学院京都研究所,1937年,第143页。

[8]《北齐书·唐邕传》,点校本,北京:中华书局,1972年,第530页。

[9] 佛陀什/竺道生译《弥沙塞部和醯五分律》,见《大正藏》第22卷,第173a页。

塔安置戒坛南……又敕龙王：当造十六塔，为钵塔眷属"[1]。作为高欢陵藏，北洞周壁雕造十六座塔形龛，或许具有供奉和眷属双重属性，因为6世纪时天竺佛像一再直接东传、"生身供养者即是塔像"[2]思想广为流布、西胡化浪潮在邺城愈演愈烈[3]。北洞的雕造，可能就是在这种背景下完成的。

（本文内容于2006年5月2日和5日下午分别在美国宾夕法尼亚大学博物馆和芝加哥大学艺术史系做过演讲，演讲题为：On Gaohuan's Tomb Cave at Xiangtangshan.）

---

[1] 道世《法苑珠林》，第2825-2826页。

[2] 昙无谶等译《大方等大集经》，见《大正藏》第13卷，第214b页。

[3] Chongfeng Li, "Gandhāra, Mathurā and Buddhist Sculptures of Mediaeval China", in: *Glory of the Kushans: Recent Discoveries and Interpretations,* ed. Vidula Jayaswal, New Delhi: Aryan Books International, 2012: 378-391, esp. 384-388.

僧璨、定禅师与水浴寺石窟

河北邯郸水浴寺西窟前壁门道两侧，上部浮雕千佛四排，下部镌刻供养人五列；所有供养人皆面向窟门。其中，窟门东侧（左侧）上排第一身供养人，上衣“被服”双肩，大衣作“右袒式”披覆，双手曲肘前伸，左手作禅定印，右手托钵[1]，雕像前方阴刻“比丘僧璨[2]供养佛时”（图 1）。窟门西侧（右侧）雕刻内容与东侧对称，上排第一身供养人服饰同东侧，唯双手合十，雕像前方阴刻“昭玄大统定禅师供养佛”（图 2）。上述两僧，分居每侧供养人行列之首，地位显著。

经检有关文献，疑僧璨和定禅师分别为中土禅宗第三祖僧璨和北齐统领佛事的最高僧官——昭玄大统神定。

图 1 水浴寺西窟窟门东侧（左侧）上排第一身供养比丘僧璨

[1] 这种一手托钵、另一手大拇指与食指相勾作禅定印的供养高僧形象，在佛教石窟及单体造像中很少见。

[2] 铭刻中的“僧璨”应为僧璨，敦煌写卷《历代法宝记》也作“僧璨”。“璨”乃“璨”之俗字。参见潘重规编《龙龛手鉴新编》，北京：中华书局，1988 年，第 350 页。

一、三祖僧璨

图2 水浴寺西窟窟门西侧（右侧）上排第一身供养比丘神定禅师

关于僧璨，唐初高僧道宣在叙述楞伽宗师承时曾有简单记载，兹录如下："今叙师承，以为承嗣所学，历然有据。达磨禅师后，有惠可、惠育二人。育师受道心行，口未曾说；可禅师后，粲禅师、惠禅师、盛禅师、那老师、端禅师、长藏师、真法师、玉法师，已上并口说玄理，不出文记。"[1]道宣所言粲禅师，应为僧璨。

据唐神龙二年（706年）张说撰《荆州玉泉寺大通禅师碑》，中土禅宗祖师"自菩提达磨天竺东来，以法传慧可，慧可传僧璨，僧璨传道信，道信传弘忍。继名重迹，相承五光"[2]。张说碑文中的传法世系，大都有7世纪史料作证明。此碑出后，这个谱系遂成定论[3]。

[1] 道宣《续高僧传·法冲传》，《大正藏》第50卷，第666b页。

[2] 李昉等编《文苑英华》卷八百五十六《荆州玉泉寺大通禅师碑》，影印本，北京：中华书局，1966年，第4521页。

又，法国巴黎国家图书馆藏敦煌藏经洞出土的唐杜朏撰《传法宝记》(P2634)，沿用了这一谱系，即中土禅宗祖师及传承关系为：东魏嵩山少林寺释菩提达摩、北齐嵩山少林寺释惠可、随（隋）皖公山释僧璨、唐双峰山东山寺释道信、唐双峰山东山寺释弘忍、唐嵩山少林寺释法如、唐当阳玉泉寺释神秀。"唯东魏惠可以身命求之，大师（达摩）传之而去；惠可传僧璨，僧璨传道信，道信传弘忍，弘忍传法如，法如及乎大通。"参见黄永武主编《敦煌宝藏》第123册，台北：新文丰出版公司，1985年，第53页。

关于《传法宝记》的成书年代，周叔迦认为"不出开、天之际"，杨曾文定在开元四年至二十年(716-732年)之间，Philip B. Yampolsky和柳田圣山推测还要略早。参见：1) 周叔迦《释典丛录》，见《周叔迦佛学论著集》，北京：中华书局，1991年，第1105页；2) 杨曾文《唐五代禅宗史》，北京：中国社会科学出版社，1999年，第142页；3)Philip B. Yampolsky, *Platform Sūtra: The Text of the Tunhuang Manuscript*, New York: Columbia University Press, 1967: 5；4) 柳田聖山《初期の禪史》I《楞伽師資記、傳法寶記》，東京：築摩書房，1971年，第329-351页。

不过，1983年在洛阳龙门西北宝应寺遗址出土的《大唐东都菏泽寺殁故第七祖国师大德于龙门宝应寺龙岗腹建身塔铭并序》，由神会弟子慧空撰写于永泰元年（765年）。该塔铭所述禅宗五祖以下与《传法宝记》不同，此乃弘忍之后门下分为南北二宗之故："粤自佛法东流，传乎达摩，达摩传可，可传璨，璨传道信，信传弘忍，忍传惠能，能传神会，宗承七叶，永播千秋。"参见温玉成《记新出土的菏泽大师神会塔铭》，刊《世界宗教研究》，1984年第2期，第78-79页。

[3] 胡适《楞伽宗考》，刊《中央研究院历史语言研究所集刊》第五本第三分，后收入（北京）中华书局1997年出版的《胡适学术文集：中国佛学史》，第94-129页。

上述禅宗五代祖师，惟三祖僧璨在道宣《续高僧传》中无传[1]。由于僧璨的特殊地位，隋代薛道衡曾为之撰碑，惜早已亡佚；不过，唐天宝年间房琯撰《唐山谷寺璨大师碑》[2]、大历二年（767年）郭少聿撰《黄山三祖塔铭并序》[3]、大历七年（772年）独孤及撰《舒州山谷寺上方禅门第三祖僧璨大师塔铭》[4]及《舒州山谷寺觉寂塔隋故镜智禅师碑铭并序》[5]、咸通二年（861年）张彦远撰写的《三祖大师碑阴记》[6]，对僧璨均有详略不等的记载。

兹录《舒州山谷寺觉寂塔隋故镜智禅师碑铭》如下：

> 案前志，禅师号僧璨，不知何许人也，出于周隋间，传教于惠可大师[7]。抠衣于邺中，得道于司空山[8]。谓身相非真，故示以疮疾；法无我所，故居不择地。以众生病为病，故所至必说法度人。以一相不在内外，不在中间，故必言不以文字。其教大略：以寂照妙用摄，流注生灭，观四维上下，不见法，不见身，不见心。

---

[1] 参见陈垣《释氏疑年录》，北京：中华书局，1964年，第56页。

道宣虽不为僧璨立传，但《续高僧传·法冲传》则有"可禅师后粲禅师"记载。又，《续高僧传·辩义传》的记述，值得注意："（仁寿）四年（604年）春末，又奉敕于庐州独山梁净寺起塔。初与官人案行置地，行至此山。忽有大鹿，从山走下，来迎于义。腾踊往还，都无所畏。处既高敞，而恨水少，僧众汲难。本有一泉，乃是僧粲禅师烧香求水，因即奔注。至粲亡后，泉涸积年。及将拟置，一夜之间，枯泉还涌，道俗欣庆。"《大正藏》第50卷，第666b、510c页。

独山在安徽庐江县西北，皖公山之东北。这里的僧粲，可能是禅宗三祖僧璨禅师。参见：胡适《楞伽宗考》，上引书，第114页。

[2] 此碑现存的最早记录，是宋赵明诚的《金石录》："第一千三百七十八，《唐山谷寺璨大师碑》，房琯撰，徐浩八分书，元年建辰月"（参见赵明城《金石录》卷七，影印南宋刻本，北京：中华书局，1983年）。碑全文收入智炬于唐德宗（780-805年）时编撰的《双峰山曹侯溪宝林传》（简作《宝林传》）卷八。参见：1）上海影印宋版藏经会1935年《景印宋藏遗珍》上集第四函；2)（北京）中华书局1994年出版、中华大藏经编辑局编《中华大藏经：汉文部分》第73册，第665-675页。虽然胡适先生认为此碑是神会和尚托房琯作于天宝五、六载之间（746-747年），但它的确是一部重要的禅宗史料。参见胡适《跋〈宝林传〉残本七卷》，载（台北）胡适纪念馆影印《胡适手稿》第七集，后收入（北京）中华书局1997年出版的《胡适学术文集：中国佛学史》，第171-182页。

[3] 董诰等编《全唐文》卷四百四十，影印本，北京：中华书局，1983年，第4486页。

[4] 独孤及《毗陵集》卷九，《四部丛刊》本。

[5] 李昉等编《文苑英华》卷八百六十四，影印本，北京：中华书局，1966年，第4561-4562页。

[6] 姚铉纂《唐文粹》卷六十三，《四部丛刊》本。

[7] 据道宣《续高僧传·僧可传》，僧可（慧可）在洛滨"奋其奇辩，呈其心要……后以天平（534-537年）之初，北就新邺，盛开密苑"。《大正藏》第50卷，第552a页。

[8] 司空山在安徽太湖县北，潜山县西；太湖县治距东北潜山县治（唐代舒州）42公里。司空山唐代属舒州境，山极高峻，山半有洗马池，即古司空原。唐代大诗人李白曾避地于此，有诗曰："卜居司空原，北将天柱邻。"

乃至心离名字，身等空界，法同梦幻，亦无得无证，然后谓之解脱。禅师门率是道也。上膺付嘱，下拯昏疑；大云垂阴，国土皆化。谓南方教所未至，我是以有罗浮之行。其来不来也，其去不去也。既而以袈裟与法俱付悟者，道存形谢，遗骨此山，今二百岁矣。皇帝后五年，岁次庚戌（770 年），及剖符是州，登禅师遗居，周览陈迹，明证故事。其茶毗起塔之制，实天宝景戌（754 年）中别驾前河南少尹赵郡李公常经始之[1]；碑板之文，隋内史侍郎河东薛公道衡、唐相国刑部尚书赠太尉河南房公琯继论撰之。而遵弘道之典，易名之礼，则朝廷方今以多故而未遑也。长老比丘释湛然，诵经于灵塔之下，与涧松俱老，痛先师名氏未经邦国焉；与禅众寺大律师释澄俊，同寅叶恭，亟以为请。会是岁，嵩岳大比丘释惠融至自广陵，胜业寺大比丘释开悟至自庐江，俱纂我禅师后七叶之遗训。曰：相与叹塔之不用命，号之不崇，惧象法之本根坠于地也。愿申无边众生之弘誓，以摅罔极。扬州牧御史大夫张公延赏以状闻，于是七年（772 年）夏四月，上沛然降兴废继绝之诏，册谥禅师曰"镜智"，塔曰"觉寂"，以大德僧七人洒扫供养[2]。天书赐命，辉焕崖谷，众庶踊跃，谓大乘中兴。是日，大比丘众议立石于塔东南隅，纪正法兴废之所以然。及以谓初中国之有佛教，自汉孝明始也，历魏晋宋齐，施及梁武，言第一义谛者，不过布施持戒，天下惑于报应，而人未知禅，世与道交相丧。至菩提达摩大师，始示人以诸佛心要，人疑而未思。惠可大师传而持之，人思而未修。迨禅师三叶，其风浸广，真如法味，日渐月渍，万木之根茎枝叶，悉沐我雨。

[1] 智藏、智空等曾于唐广德三年至大历二年（765-767 年）在黄山东建造僧璨禅师灵塔，郭少聿《黄山三祖塔铭并序》记载颇详："原夫像教东倾，正宗西域；大塊连铸，造化无功；应现十方，渐流万品，惟正觉之玄妙也。传如来之正教，得佛法之宝印者，即我和尚三祖讳僧璨矣。澄神寂靖，散识归贞，耆艾相承。传云黄山东，是有窀穸元宫焉。殁故僧智藏，寻此圣山，经遘铭记，苔文半灭，微辩云和尚讳僧璨矣。遂瞻仰于青山之下，顶礼于荒坟之前。于大唐广德三年岁次乙巳（765 年），发心建启灵塔元宫之上，未圆备卒此。助成僧智空，睹此营修，果未圆满，师资相传，愿绪构兴。功德主霍待璧孙待敬等，各施净财，成兹胜业。各愿生生值善，四行果圆，难苦脱尘。又为大唐宝应玄圣文武皇帝陛下圣化无竭，大宝常存，福祚遐长，万品安乐，蠢动含灵，同沾斯福。于唐大历二年岁次丁未（767 年），庆赞已毕，传芳永代，称庆远年。若不刻石镌铭，无以示其来者。其词曰……"董诰等编《全唐文》卷四百四十《黄山三祖塔铭并序》，影印本，北京：中华书局，1983 年，第 4486 页。

[2] 独孤及《舒州山谷寺上方禅门第三祖璨大师塔铭》进一步记述到："右淮南节度观察史扬州大都督府长史兼御史大夫张延赏状，得舒州刺史独孤及状，得僧湛然等状，称：大师迁灭，将二百年，心法次第，天下宗仰。秀和尚、寂和尚传其遗言。先朝犹特建灵塔，月加塔册谥。大师为圣贤衣钵，为法门津梁。至今分骨之地，未沾易名之礼。伏恐尊道敬教，盛典犹阙。今因肃宗文明武德大圣大宣孝皇帝斋忌，伏乞准开元中追褒大照等禅师例，特加谥号，兼赐塔额。诸寺抽大德僧一七人，洒扫供养，冀以功德，追福圣灵。中书门下　牒淮南观察使　牒奉　敕宜赐谥号镜智禅师，其塔余依。牒至准敕故牒。大历七年四月二十二日（772 年 5 月 17 日）牒。"独孤及《毗陵集》卷九，《四部丛刊》本。

然后空王之密藏，二祖之微言，始璨然行于世间，浃于人心。当时闻道于禅师者，其浅者知有为法，无非妄想；深者见佛性于言下，如灯之照物，朝为凡夫，夕为圣贤，双峰大师道信其人也。其后信公以教传弘忍，忍公传惠能、神秀。能公退而老曹溪，其嗣无闻焉；秀公传普寂，公之门徒万，升堂者六十有三；得自在惠者一，曰弘正。正公之廊庑，龙象又倍，或化嵩洛，或之荆吴，自是心教之被于世也。与六籍侔盛焉，呜呼，微禅师吾其二乘矣，后代何述焉？庯讵知禅师之下生不为诸佛，故现比丘身以救浊劫乎，亦犹尧舜既往，周公制礼，仲尼既没，游夏弘之，使高堂后苍徐孟戴庆之流，可得而祖焉。夫以圣贤所振为木铎，其揆一也。诸公以为司马子长立夫子世家，谢临川撰惠远法师碑铭，今将令千载之后，知先师之全身，禅门之权舆，王命之追崇，在此山也。则扬其风，纪其时，宜在法流及当味禅师之道也。久故不让，其铭曰：

人之静也，性与生皆植；知诱于外，率为妄识；如浪斯鼓，与风动息；淫骇贪怒，为刃为贼；生死有涯，缘起无极；如来悯之，为辟度门；即妄了真，以证觉源；启迪心印，贻我后昆；间生禅师，俾以教尊；二十八劫，迭付微言（自摩诃迦叶以佛所付心法，递相传至师子比丘，凡二十五世；自达摩大师至禅师，凡三世，共二十八劫）。如禅师，膺期弘宣，世溷法灭，独以道全（后周武帝下令灭佛法，禅师随可大师隐遁司空山十有三年）；童蒙求我，我以意传；摄相归性，法身乃圆；性身本空，我无说焉。如如禅师，道既弃世，将三十纪，妙经乃届，皇明昭贲，亿兆膜拜。凡今后学，入佛境界，于取非取，谁缚谁解（初禅师谓信公曰："汝何求？"曰："求解脱。"曰："谁缚汝，谁解汝？"曰："不见缚者，不见解者。然则何求？"信公于是言不证解脱知见，遂顶礼请益。是日，禅师授以祖师所传袈裟）。万有千岁，此法无坏。[1]

唐开元年间净觉编撰的《楞伽师资记》，系依玄赜《楞伽人物志》而作，为禅宗重要史料[2]，惟于僧璨记述颇简且把其称作四祖："第四隋朝舒州思（司）空山粲禅

---

［1］李昉等编《文苑英华》卷八百六十四《舒州山谷寺觉寂塔隋故镜智禅师碑铭》，影印本，北京：中华书局，1966 年，第 4561-4562 页。

唐张彦远《三祖大师碑阴记》补述了此后情况："大历初，彦远曾祖魏国公留守东都，兼河南尹。洛阳当孽火之后，寺塔皆为丘墟，迎至嵩山，沙门澄沼修建大圣善寺。沼行为禅宗，德为帝师，化灭沼谥大譻，即东山第十祖也。洎镇于蜀，皆有崇饰。在淮南，奏三祖大师谥号与塔额，刺史独孤君为之碑，张从申书字。夫禀儒道以理身理人，奉释氏以修心修性。其揆一也。会昌天子灭佛法，塔与碑皆毁。像虽毁而法不能灭，是法也不在乎塔，不在乎碑。大中初，塔复置而碑未立。咸通二年（861 年）八月，遂与沙门重议刊建。舒州刺史河东张彦远书于碑之阴。"姚铉纂《唐文粹》卷六十三《三祖大师碑阴记》，《四部丛刊》本。

［2］参见：1）胡适《论禅宗史的纲领》，载亚东图书馆 1930 年出版《胡适文存三集》，后收入（北京）中华书局 1997 年出版的《胡适学术文集：中国佛学史》，第 34-38 页；2）胡适《〈楞伽师资记〉序》，刊《海潮音》第十三卷第四期，后收入《胡适学术文集：中国佛学史》，第 54-60 页；3）吕澂《中国佛学源流略讲》，北京：中华书局，1979 年，第 145 页。

师，承可禅师后。其粲禅师，罔知姓位，不测所生。按《续高僧传》曰：‘可后粲禅师’。隐思空山，萧然净坐，不出文记，密不传法。唯僧道信奉事粲十二年，写器传灯，一一成就。”[1]

敦煌遗书 P2125 号和 S516 号写卷，系唐大历（766-779 年）以后保唐寺派高僧所作《历代法宝记》的两个不同抄本，部分内容采自早期史料[2]。两抄本详细记述了禅宗六祖及其传承情况，唯文字略有出入。其中，关于僧璨事迹可补述如下：“隋朝第三祖璨禅师，不知何处人。初遇可大师……可大师知璨是非常人，便付法嘱及信袈裟与僧璨。可大师曰：汝善自保爱，吾有难，汝需避之。璨大师亦佯狂市肆，后隐舒州司空山[3]。遭周武帝灭佛法，隐皖公山[4]十余年[5]。此山北多是猛兽，常损居人。自璨大师至，并移出境。付法并袈裟与道信后，时有皖禅师、月禅师、定禅师、岩禅师来至璨大师所。云：‘达摩祖师付嘱后，此璨公真神璨也，定惠齐用，深不思议也。’璨大师遂共诸禅师往隐罗浮山[6]。三年后，至大会斋出，告众人曰：‘吾今欲食。’诸弟子奉饮食。大师食毕，告众人曰：‘诸人叹言，坐终为寄。唯吾生死自语由己。’一手攀会中树枝，掩然立化，亦不知年几。塔庙在皖山寺侧。弟子甚多，唯道信大师传衣得法承后。薛道衡撰碑文。”[7]

根据上述材料，我们获知：僧璨俗姓、籍贯不详，生卒年不确[8]，曾受业于禅宗

---

[1] 净觉《楞伽师资记》，见《大正藏》第 85 卷，第 1286b 页。这段文字，似净觉依据《续高僧传·道信传》写成。参见：1）胡适《跋〈宝林传〉残本七卷》，载姜义华主编《胡适学术文集：中国佛学史》，北京：中华书局，1997 年，第 177 页；2）吕澂《中国佛学源流略讲》，北京：中华书局，1979 年，第 145 页。

[2] 胡适《楞伽宗考》，上引书，第 121 页。

[3]《历代法宝记》关于惠可大师付法事，有如下记述：“（惠可大）师付嘱僧璨法已，入司空山隐。可大师后佯狂，于四衢城市说法。”参见黄永武主编《敦煌宝藏》第 115 册，台北：新文丰出版公司，1985 年，第 132 页。

[4] 皖公山，一名皖山，亦名潜山，在安徽潜山县西，绵亘深远，最高峰曰天柱。皖公山与司空山两山相连，这一带是僧璨故事的中心，似可无疑。

[5] 李昉等《文苑英华》卷八百六十四《舒州山谷寺觉寂塔隋故镜智禅师碑铭》双行小注作“十有三年”。参见（北京）中华书局 1966 年影印本，第 4562 页。

[6] 罗浮山，位于广东博罗县西北，以瑰奇灵秀著称，山中寺院道观颇多。相传晋代葛洪于此得仙术，谢灵运作《罗浮山赋》后为世所知，史载东晋沙门单道开为最早入罗浮山之佛教徒，其后僧人往来者渐多。

[7] 参见：1）黄永武主编《敦煌宝藏》第 4 册，台北：新文丰出版公司，1981 年，第 234 页；2）《敦煌宝藏》第 115 册，台北：新文丰出版公司，1985 年，第 132 页；3）《历代法宝记》，《大正藏》第 51 卷，第 181b-c 页。

[8] 智炬《宝林传》记僧璨卒于隋大业二年丙寅（606 年），道原《景德传灯录》卷三延续此说。不过，依据道宣《续高僧传·辩义传》记述，僧璨应卒于仁寿四年（604 年）之前。参见：1）胡适《楞伽宗考》，上引书，第 116-117 页；2）胡适《跋〈宝林传〉残本七卷》，上引书，第 179 页；3）印顺《中国禅宗史》，南昌：江西人民出版社，1999 年，第 38 页。

二祖惠可。惠可于东魏天平初年(534年)至邺都传法[1],僧璨"抠衣于邺中",投惠可门下。"可大师知璨是非常人,便付法嘱及信袈裟与僧璨"。惠可告诫僧璨：吾有难,汝需避之。璨大师故而佯狂市肆,后隐舒州司空山。周武帝灭佛(574年)并平齐(577年)之后,僧璨随可大师隐遁司空山或皖公山十有三年,"得道于司空山"。其间,定禅师等亦往僧璨居所[2]。开皇十二年(592年)道信来投[3],此后"道信奉事璨十二年(592-603年)[4],写器传灯"。传法与道信后,僧璨和定禅师等"往隐罗浮山。三年后,至大会斋出",归返皖公山,掩然立化,"葬在山谷寺后"[5]。

由于僧璨等只"口说玄理,不出文记"[6],因此关于他的记载极少[7]。道宣在叙述禅宗历史时,起初殊感材料缺乏；后来虽偶获新数据,也只能补入相关传记之

---

[1]《续高僧传·僧(慧)可传》,《大正藏》第50卷,第552a页。

[2] 据敦煌藏经洞出土、唐杜朏撰写的《传法宝记》,僧璨"后遭周武破法,流遁山谷,经十余年,至开皇初,与同学定禅师隐居皖公山"。参见杨曾文编校《敦煌新本六祖坛经》附编(一)《传法宝记》,北京：宗教文化出版社,2001年,第178页。

[3] 清宣统元年(1909年)十月印行的端方《匋斋藏石记》,卷十五收有"僧璨皖公山塔记"砖。砖面刻"大隋开皇十二年七月,僧璨大士隐化于舒之皖公山岫,结塔供养,道信为记"；左侧面刻"大隋开皇十二年作"。1982年4月,浙江省杭州市出土一块铭文砖,砖面及左侧面刻有完全相同的铭文。该砖现藏浙江省博物馆。参见陈浩《隋禅宗三祖僧璨塔铭砖》,见《文物》1985年第4期,第8页。

据端方按语,"此塔记作于四祖礼谒之年。曰'隐化'者,谓隐居山岫化导众生耳。结塔供养,谓供养诸佛……隐化'化'字若作怛化解,则以《五灯会元》证之年岁不合。《会元》三祖章次云：初以白衣谒二祖,既受度传法,隐于舒州之皖公山。属后周武帝破灭佛法,祖往来太湖县司空山,居无常处积十余载,时人无能知者。据此,则隐化二字当作隐居行化解无疑。是时隋革周命,苛禁甫除,宗风未畅,佛教尚寂,本不求显。曰隐化者,殆承三祖之微指欤？矧塔记云云,略无伤痛之意。曰结塔供养,决非藏骸之塔。可知无庸误解化字,而以年岁为疑也"(端方《匋斋藏石记》卷十五叶七,见《石刻史料新编》第一辑,第11册,台北：新文丰出版公司,1982年,第8121-8122页)。不过值得注意的是,577年北周武帝灭北齐及其佛教,道信生于580年,开皇十二年(592年)仅12岁,能否有此砖铭？

[4]《宝林传》卷八作"(道信)侍奉左右经八、九年于吉州受戒,却来侍奉璨大师"(参见上海影印宋版藏经会1935年《景印宋藏遗珍》上集第四函)；而《续高僧传·道信传》则作十年(参见《大正藏》第50卷,第606b页)。

[5] 敦煌藏经洞出土的《南阳和尚问答杂征义》,一作《神会语录》,也有类似记载："璨大师与宝月禅师及定公,同往罗浮山……璨大师至罗浮山,三年却归至岘山……葬在山谷寺后,寺内有碑铭形象,今见供养。"参见杨曾文编校《神会和尚禅话录》,北京：中华书局,1996年,第106页。

[6]《续高僧传·法冲传》,《大正藏》第50卷,第666b页。

[7] 2010年7月30-31日,北京大学东方文学研究中心举办"跨文化的佛教神话学研究"国际学术研讨会(Conference on Cross-Cultural Researches on Buddhist Mythology)。陈金华博士在会上宣读了"Fact and Fiction: The Creation of the 'Third Chan Patriarch' and his Legends"论文,对唐宋时期有关僧璨的史料作了详细梳理,可参看该会议《论文汇编》第170-195页。

中[1]，无法为僧璨单独立传。僧璨死后，隋内史侍郎河东薛道衡曾撰碑文；唐天宝五载（746年）河南少尹赵郡李常在山谷寺起塔，相国刑部尚书赠太尉河南房琯又撰碑文；广德三年至大历二年（765-767年），智藏、智空于黄山东敬造灵塔；大历五年（770年）独孤及任舒州刺史，比丘湛然和惠融等希望朝廷为僧璨敕谥号及塔额，于是独孤及与淮南节度史、扬州大都督府长史兼御史大夫张延赏奏明朝廷，朝廷降诏敕僧璨"镜智"，敕塔额"觉寂"。会昌毁佛后，张延赏之孙张彦远亦镌碑阴记之。

二、大统神定

同僧璨一样，定禅师在《续高僧传》中亦无传。不过该书卷二十一《道信传》对我们颇有启示。"释道信，姓司马，未详何人。初七岁时，经事一师，戒行不纯，信每陈谏，以不见从，密怀斋检，经于五载，而师不知。又有二僧，莫知何来，入舒州皖公山静修禅业。闻而往赴，便蒙授法，随逐依学，遂经十年。师往罗浮，不许相逐：'但于后住，必大弘益。'"[2]这里的二僧，道宣虽未明言，但据《历代法宝记》及有关史料，应是僧璨与定禅师[3]。

虽然前引《双峰山曹侯溪宝林传》是一部杂凑的禅门伪史[4]，但卷八所记惠可大师传承谱系颇为重要："可大师下除第三祖自有一支，而有七人。第一者皖山神定，第二者宝月禅师[5]，第三者花闲居士，第四者大士化公，第五者向居士，第六者弟子和公，第七者廖居士。第二宝月者有一弟子名曰智岩，后为牛头第二祖师是也。第三花居士有弟子名曰昙邃，雪人也。此昙邃出三弟子，第一者延陵惠简，第二者彭城惠差，第三者定林寺惠刚下自出四代；惠刚弟子六合大觉，大觉弟子高邮昙影，弟子泰山明练；明练弟子扬州静泰。此上七代并是可大师之苗裔矣。"[6]由此可见，神定

[1] 胡适《〈楞伽师资记〉序》，上引书，第56页。

[2]《大正藏》第50卷，第606b页。

[3] 1) 胡适《楞伽宗考》，上引书，第117页；2) 胡适《跋〈宝林传〉残本七卷》，上引书，第177页；3) 印顺，上引书，第37页；4) 忽滑谷快天《中国禅学思想史》，朱谦之译，上海：上海古籍出版社，2002年，第106页。

[4] 胡适《跋〈宝林传〉残本七卷》，上引书，第172页。汤用彤也认为唐代时晚出之禅宗史记，所述禅宗祖师生平不尽可信。参见汤用彤《汉魏两晋南北朝佛教史》，北京：中华书局，1983年，第561页。

[5]《续高僧传·智严传》记载智严于唐武德四年（621年）弃官入舒州皖公山，从宝月禅师出家。此宝月禅师疑为《历代法宝记》中的"月禅师"，与僧璨有关系。参见：胡适《楞伽宗考》，上引书，第116页。

[6] 上海影印宋版藏经会1935年《景印宋藏遗珍》上集第四函。

是二祖惠可门下地位仅次于僧璨之高徒。取材于《宝林传》的《景德传灯录》[1]，卷三列“中华五祖并旁出尊宿”。其中，第二十九祖慧（惠）可大师旁出六世共一十七人[2]，与《宝林传》所记略有出入，惟把“皖山神定”写作“岘山[3]神定禅师”。

此神定禅师，疑为水浴寺西窟前壁“昭玄大统定禅师”[4]及南响堂山第2窟中心柱右壁的“昭玄沙门统定禅师敬造六十佛”[5]之定禅师。据前引《历代法宝记》，定禅师曾与月禅师等至皖公山僧璨大师住所，后与僧璨等同往罗浮山。唐独孤及《毗陵集》卷九《舒州山谷寺觉寂塔隋故镜智禅师碑铭并序》后附录《山谷寺觉寂塔禅门第三祖镜智禅师塔碑阴文》，引薛道衡撰僧璨大师碑文[6]曰：“大师与同学定公南隐罗浮山，自后竟不知所终。”此定公，应是皖山或岘山神定禅师，简称定禅师。作为禅宗二祖惠可的两大弟子，僧璨与神定禅师一直关系融洽。

据《续高僧传 · 法上传》，北齐“天保（550-559年）之中，国置十统。有司闻奏，事须甄异。文宣乃手注状，云：‘上法师可为大统，余为通统。’”[7]法上“年阶四十，游化怀卫，为魏大将军高澄奏入在邺。微言一鼓，众侣云屯。但上戒山峻峙，慧海澄深。德可

---

[1] 1) 胡适《跋〈宝林传〉残本七卷》，上引书，第171-182页；2) 陈垣《中国佛教史籍概论》，北京：中华书局，1962年，第106页。

[2] 道原《景德传灯录》，参见《大正藏》第51卷，第216c-217a页。

[3] 此岘山疑为皖山之舛。退一步说，岘山可能也与僧璨有关。岘山位于湖北襄阳县境，著名的光福寺距此不远，传说僧璨曾在光福寺受具。至于僧璨受戒之年，《宝林传》卷八作“天平中后周第二祖己卯之岁”或“后周第二祖天平三年己卯之岁”（参见上海影印宋版藏经会1935年《景印宋藏遗珍》上集第四函）。北周无“天平”年号，“天平”乃东魏孝静帝元善见年号，天平二年为乙卯（535年），三年为丙辰。后周第二祖乃周明帝宇文毓，三年为己卯，即559年。景德元年（1004年）道原纂《景德传灯录》卷三把此纪年改作“北齐天平二年”，不过宋仁宗后期或更晚校刊的《景德传灯录》，则校注为“当作天保二年（551年），乃辛未岁也”（参见《大正藏》第51卷，第220c页）。

[4] “昭玄大统定禅师供养佛”题名，最初由北京大学历史系考古实习队1957年12月调查水浴寺石窟时发现，并推测此“定禅师”与南响堂山第2窟题铭中的“定禅师”为同一人。参见刘慧达《北魏石窟与禅》，刊《考古学报》，1978年3期，该文订补后以附录形式收入（北京）文物出版社1996年出版的宿白先生《中国石窟寺研究》，第331-348页。

[5] 此题记所在岩石，于20世纪40年代被炸掉后埋入第二窟前室券顶通道两侧，80年代中期被重新清理出来。何士骥与刘厚滋编《南北响堂寺及其附近石刻目录》及水野清一和长广敏雄编写的《响堂山石窟》皆作“统定禅师敬造六十佛”，无“昭玄沙门”四字；常盘大定、关野贞编著的《支那佛教史蹟》第三集《评解》第114页作“沙门统定禅（师）敬造六十佛”；而北京图书馆金石组编辑的《北京图书馆藏中国历代石刻拓片汇编》（郑州：中州古籍出版社，1989年，第八册第220页），则作“昭玄沙门统定禅师敬造六十佛”。

[6] 胡适认为：皖公山山谷寺建立所谓薛道衡《粲禅师碑》，大概是禅宗神秀门下普寂、义福等人势力最盛的时候，可能与《宝林传》卷八所附法琳《可禅师碑》一样，是同期编造出来的假史料。胡适《跋〈宝林传〉残本七卷》，上引书，第178-179页。

[7] 《大正藏》第50卷，第485c页。

轨人，威能肃物。故魏、齐二代，历为统师，昭玄一曹，纯掌僧录。令史员置五十许人，所部僧尼二百余万。而上纲领将四十年……末敕住相州定国寺。而容德显著，感供繁多；所得世利，造一山寺，本名合水，即邺之西山，今所谓修定寺是也。山之极顶造弥勒堂，众所庄严，备殚华丽，四事供养百五十僧。及齐破法湮（577 年），僧不及山寺。上私隐俗服，习业如常……卒于合水故房，春秋八十有六，即周大象二年七月十八日（580 年 8 月 13 日）也”[1]。据此，法上入邺应在 534 年左右，统领东魏北齐僧录将四十年后，被敕住相州定国寺，时在 574 年左右；而就任北齐昭玄大统，当在 554 年左右。

作为北齐“昭玄十统”[2]之一，定禅师曾于天统元年（565 年）[3]参与营造滏山石窟（南响堂山石窟），在第 2 窟敬造六十佛，署名“昭玄沙门统定禅师”。稍后不久，僧璨与神定禅师倡首在鼓山水浴寺开窟造像，并写真留名。此时的神定禅师已经接掌僧录，荣任北齐统领佛事的最高僧官——“昭玄大统”，时在天统五年（569 年）之前，或接替法上而任，因为僧璨于“是年自北齐来司空山，遂隐于舒州皖公山，今所谓山谷山寺也”[4]。换言之，僧璨与神定禅师在水浴寺开窟造像应在北齐天统五年之前[5]。

三、石窟与禅修

南北朝时期，“北土佛徒深怵于因果报应之威，汲汲于福田利益之举。塔寺遍地，造像成林”[6]，开窟不绝。当时修造石窟的目的，除了进行礼忏、供养、做功德、修福田以及个人的造像愿望之外，禅修应是僧人开窟造像的重要目的之一[7]。“夫坐禅者，宜山栖穴处，则凿窟以为禅居，亦意中事。”[8]禅修应先观像，而习禅所观的各种形象多雕塑在石窟之中，释迦（包括本生和佛传）、释迦多宝并坐、三世佛和十方诸

[1]《大正藏》第 50 卷，第 485b、c 页。

[2] 关于北齐昭玄寺僧官及数目，文献有歧异，目前学者多认为沙门统和都维那各有若干员，其中沙门统中有一人为大统。参见：1) 白文固《南北朝隋唐僧官制度探究》，刊《世界宗教研究》，1984 年第 1 期，第 53-59 页；2) 谢重光《中古佛教僧官制度和社会生活》，北京：商务印书馆，2009 年，第 74-81 页。

[3] 参见南响堂山第 2 窟前室后壁《滏山石窟之碑》。

[4] 觉岸编《释氏稽古略》卷二《高祖宣帝》，《大正藏》第 49 卷，第 804a 页。

[5] 据现存遗迹，水浴寺西窟后壁两侧龛像为后来补凿。其中，后壁左侧的“定光佛并三童子阿育王施土”是武平五年（574 年）由邑主张元妃捐资雕造的，故西窟开凿年代应早于该年。参见李裕群《中原北方地区北朝晚期的石窟寺》（博士学位论文），北京：北京大学，1993 年，第 12 页。

[6] 汤用彤，上引书，第 574 页。

[7] 刘慧达《北魏石窟与禅》，上引书，第 331 页。

[8] 汤用彤，上引书，第 558 页。

佛、无量寿、四方佛、七佛及弥勒等是禅观的主要内容。此外，在观像仪式之中也规定有礼佛供养，即入定之前和入定之后都要礼佛。由此可见，造像、观像、礼忏、供养和坐禅都是禅僧修持的课题，亦即北朝时期禅僧们大行开窟造像的重要原因[1]。

北魏晚期，中原北方义学兴盛，僧人俱修定法，且有所宗之经[2]。惠可、僧璨一系名楞伽禅，"依据则为《胜鬘》[3]、《楞伽》[4]也。《楞伽》于《胜鬘》，犹三《传》之于《春秋》。《胜鬘》，经也；《楞伽》，则经之传也"[5]。作为禅僧，僧璨和神定在信守"萧然净坐，不出文记"[6]之时，必定奉行楞伽经者处处着眼于破除妄想，显示真如法身，亦即涅槃。虽然他们亦顺应当时"禅智兼弘"的风气，纠正一般禅僧之失[7]，"定惠齐用，深不思议"[8]。不过，"坐禅行道，重在澄心"[9]。身为禅宗二祖惠可弟子，僧璨和神定应潜心禅修[10]，精进不懈，补偏救弊[11]。水浴寺窟群中央主窟，即西窟是一座典型的

---

[1] 刘慧达《北魏石窟与禅》，上引书，第 334-346 页。

[2] 汤用彤，上引书，第 561 页。

[3] 此《胜鬘经》全称《胜鬘狮子吼一乘大方便方广经》，一卷，刘宋求那跋陀罗于元嘉十三年(436年)出。该经反复说明如来藏乃出世正因。关于如来藏之说，《楞伽经》里也有专章阐述。由此可见《楞伽经》与《胜鬘经》之关系，以及教义上彼此互相阐发的共同之处。北齐晋昌郡公唐邕曾于天统四年至武平三年(568-572年)在鼓山石窟(北响堂山石窟)南洞刻写佛经四部，其中第二部就是《胜鬘经》，应为求那跋陀罗译本。此外，惠可同门"林法师在邺盛讲《胜鬘》并制文义。每讲人聚，乃选通三部经者得七百人，预在其席。及周灭法，与可同学同护经像"(《续高僧传·僧可传》，《大正藏》第 50 卷，第 552b 页)。这说明此经在北齐都城颇为流行。

[4] 此《楞伽经》全称《楞伽阿跋多罗宝经》，四卷，刘宋求那跋陀罗于元嘉二十年(443年)出。史载菩提达磨授与惠可的四卷《楞伽经》，就是此本。"我观汉地，惟有此经，仁者依行，自得度世。"道宣《续高僧传·僧可传》，《大正藏》第 50 卷，第 552b 页。

[5] 吕澂《禅学述原》，载《吕澂佛学论著选集》卷一(第 396-409 页)，济南：齐鲁书社，1991 年，第 396 页。

[6] 净觉《楞伽师资记》，《大正藏》第 85 卷，第 1286b 页。

[7] 汤用彤，上引书，第 561-570 页。

[8]《历代法宝记》，参见黄永武主编《敦煌宝藏》第 4 册，台北：新文丰出版公司，1981 年，第 234 页。

[9] 汤用彤，上引书，第 574 页。

[10] 据吕澂研究，禅宗之"禅"，原意止观，止观方法即禅法。大乘禅法的流行，远在东晋鸠摩罗什和佛陀跋陀罗时期。"他们译出《坐禅三昧经》、《达摩多罗禅经》等，介绍了各种方法，尤其重要的是'念佛法门'。由观念佛的相(三十二相)、好(八十随形好)、佛的功德(百四十不共法)，以至诸法实相，都从念佛法门引申而来，却没有更上一着。到了南朝刘宋求那跋陀罗翻译《楞伽经》，列举愚夫所行禅、观察义禅、攀缘如禅、如来禅四种名目，而以具备自觉圣智内容的如来禅为止观的最高层，契合于'如来藏心'的攀缘如禅作它的阶梯，这样直截指示佛家实践的究竟和源头，便启发了当时讲究禅法的人去另辟途径。"吕澂《中国佛学源流略讲》，北京：中华书局，1979 年，第 369 页。

虽然惠可、僧璨都用《楞伽经》来做实践的印证，但为避免与传统禅法冲突，必须顺应当地习俗，采纳一些早期止观思想和当时流行的禅观形式。参见：吕澂，上引书，第 144-145 页。

[11] 当时楞伽诸师多偏于细析经文，执着名相，而少能坐禅修心，精进不懈。参见：汤用彤，上引书，第 568 页。

塔庙窟，中心塔柱正面及左右侧面造三世佛，窟前壁上方雕出七佛，左右侧壁浮雕千佛（十方诸佛）并各开一坐佛龛。为“静修禅业”，僧璨与神定禅师开凿此窟[1]，除了供养、礼忏及做功德之外，很可能以该窟造像作为禅观对象，满足“入塔观像”之需[2]。通过观释迦像，坐禅会现见佛幻境；观三世佛，乃修习“菩萨念佛三昧”；而观七佛，是祈求七佛为他修禅作证并听七佛说法[3]。

（本文原刊《石窟寺研究》第二辑第165-175页，收入本书时仅改正若干印制错误。）

---

[1] 独孤及《毗陵集》卷九《舒州山谷寺觉寂塔隋故镜智禅师碑铭并序》后附录《山谷寺觉寂塔禅门第三祖镜智禅师塔碑阴文》。碑阴文撰者在征引薛道衡、房琯分撰僧璨大师碑文之时，亦对僧璨事迹有所考述。“有隋薛内使道衡及皇朝房尚书琯与今独孤使君及三子慧炬相烛也，文峰相摩也，嗣为之碑，森列净土，如经星五纬更为表里焉。然述者之词各因所见，言或踳驳，将贻惑与来世，吾所辩焉。薛碑曰：‘大师与同学定公南隐罗浮山，自后竟不知所终。其铭曰：留法服兮长在，入罗浮兮不复还。’据此，南游终不复此地也。房碑曰：‘大师告门人信公曰：有人借问，勿谓于我处得法。遂托疾山阿，向晦寓息。忽大呼城市曰：我于岘山设斋，汝等当施我食。于是邑民咸集，乃斋于杨树下立而终焉。’今以两碑参而言之，则薛内史制碑之后，大师从罗浮还，付嘱信公，然后涅槃于兹。房公以得于传记而述之，非徒然也。其余事业，则三碑载之详也，今则不书。其锡名之诏，与有地者之爵里、行教护塔者之名号，不可以莫之，传于后也，皆刻于独孤氏之碑阴。”（《四部丛刊》本）这里征引的房琯碑文与《宝林传》所录房碑文字略有出入。不过，薛道衡在这里明确指出僧璨与定公系同学，《续高僧传·道信传》亦记“有二僧，莫从何来，入舒州皖公山静修禅业”。水峪寺西窟前壁僧璨与神定禅师分列窟门两侧，是否也表现二者为同学密友呢？

[2] 刘慧达先生认为北朝时期开凿的中心柱窟，如云冈和响堂山石窟中的中心柱窟，中心柱多作塔形，有的在顶部还雕出覆钵。因此，当时僧人进入这类石窟中观像，也就等于“入塔观像”。刘慧达《北魏石窟与禅》，上引书，第345页。

[3] 参见：刘慧达，上引书，第337-345页。

敦煌莫高窟北朝晚期洞窟的分期与研究

一、绪　　论

公元557年，宇文泰嫡子宇文觉废魏自立，建立北周，这标志着中国历史上长达25年的宇文氏王朝从此开始。

北周的统治者，政治上仍袭西魏旧制，改组中央政府的组织形式，采用浓厚复古色彩的西周六官制度，充实关陇统治集团；军事上继续实行府兵制，扩大府兵来源，以"除其县籍"[1]、"无他赋役"[2]等政策，将招募对象扩充到所有均田户，从"初期的兵农分立制，走向和均田制结合起来的兵农合一制"[3]；经济上仍实施均田制，限制大土地所有者的发展，建德元年（572年）诛戮专权的宇文护之后，周武帝"始亲万机，克己励精，听览不怠"[4]，继续推行改革措施。其中最重要的是先后五次下诏释放奴婢和杂户，放免为民。同时，接受卫元嵩的建议，采取灭佛政策，打击僧侣地主阶级在经济上的势力，把"关、陇、梁、益、荆、襄地区几百年来僧侣地主的寺宇、土地、铜像、资产全部没收，充作以后伐齐的军事费用，近百万僧侣、僧祇户和佛图户，编为均田户，作为北周境内生产战线上的重要力量；把合龄的壮丁，编为军队，扩大了府兵队伍"[5]。这样，既增加了国家的财富，调整了民众的赋役负担，也在一定程度上缓和了国内的阶级矛盾。在国际交往和对外关系方面，北周统治者采用"定四表以武功，安三边以权道"的政策，"结姻于北狄"，娶突厥可汗的女儿阿史那氏为皇后，并与突

[1]《隋书·食货志》，点校本，北京：中华书局，1973年，第680页。
[2]《北史·李弼》等传后论，点校本，北京：中华书局，1974年，第2155页。
[3] 王仲荦《魏晋南北朝史》，上海人民出版社，1980年，第618页。
[4]《周书·武帝纪》，点校本，北京：中华书局，1971年，第107页。
[5] 王仲荦，上引书，第622页。

厥连兵伐齐，“通好于西戎”[1]，致使嚈哒、安息、高昌、吐谷浑、粟特、龟兹和焉耆等连年入贡不绝，南与陈朝和好，互相多次遣使聘问[2]。

由于宇文氏在政治、经济、军事和对外关系方面进行了一系列改革，使地狭民贫、人口九百多万[3]的北周王朝，国力迅速加强，社会基础进一步稳固，终于在公元577年消灭北齐，统一了中原北方。灭齐之后，周武帝“遂欲穷兵极武，平突厥，定江南，一二年间必使天下一统”[4]。可他不久病死（578年），统一中国之大业，由隋文帝杨坚完成。

北周时期的敦煌，作为西陲重镇和中西交通的咽喉，受到了宇文氏王朝的极大重视。当时的瓜州刺史，无论是韦瑱、段永、李贤，还是于义，大多为宇文氏的宠臣、关陇统治集团的骨干人物[5]。

基于宇文氏王朝当时实施的一系列改革措施，加之瓜州几任刺史的稳固统治以及敦煌大族的辅佐[6]，北周时的敦煌，呈现出繁荣安定的局面。

北周时期的佛教，尽管有周武帝建德三年（574年）的“法难”，但由于当时佛教有深厚的社会基础，加之北周几个皇帝大都佞佛[7]，就是武帝本人最初也厚供高僧[8]，敬“重佛法，下礼沙门”[9]，并多造功德，广度僧尼[10]。即使在禁“断佛、道二教”[11]之后，他还设立通道观，主张会通三教。其目的，“在于把佛教和道教完全与国家的政治组织结合起来”[12]，以利治国教民。整个宇文氏王朝，先后造寺“九百三十一所”[13]，由此可见，当时的佛教还是十分兴盛的。

在皇帝佞佛思想的影响下，当时王公大臣多笃信佛教。宇文周时的瓜州刺史，明确记载有两人信佛：一是大将军段永（详见本文附录一），另一位是建平公

[1]《周书·异域传》，点校本，北京：中华书局，1971年，第884页。

[2] 参见《陈书·宣帝纪》、《周书·武帝纪》。

[3]《通典》卷七《食货典·历代盛衰户口》，点校本，北京：中华书局，1988年，第147页。

[4]《周书·武帝纪》，点校本，北京：中华书局，1971年，第107-108页。

[5] 参见《周书·韦瑱传》、《北史·段永传》、《周书·李贤传》、《隋书·于义传》。

[6]《北史·令狐整传》，点校本，北京：中华书局，1974年，第2349-2354页。

[7] 参见法琳《辩正论》卷三《十代奉佛篇》、《周书·宣帝纪》、《周书·静帝纪》。

[8]《续高僧传·道判传》，见《大正藏》第50卷，第516c-517b页。

[9] 道宣《广弘明集》卷八《周灭佛法集道俗议事》，参见《大正藏》第52卷，第136a页。

[10]《辩正论》卷三《十代奉佛篇》上，参见《大正藏》第52卷，第508b页。

[11]《周书·武帝纪》，点校本，北京：中华书局，1971年，第84页。

[12][法]谢和耐《中国五至十世纪的寺院经济》，耿昇译，兰州：甘肃人民出版社，1987年，第361页。

[13]《辩正论》卷三《十代奉佛篇》上，上引书，第508b页。

于义[1]。段永曾修造“尔绵寺”[2],并于瓜州任上请高僧于宅院讲经说法,弘扬佛教[3]。显贵于义,曾在莫高窟“修一大窟”[4],是与莫高窟修窟造像有直接关系者。在统治阶级的大力提倡下,这一时期敦煌的佛事活动再次兴盛起来,莫高窟的开窟造像也有了较大的发展。“中原在北朝晚期兴起的新型的佛教艺术,又一次向西影响了敦煌莫高窟。”[5]

与国内其他同期佛教石窟寺一样,莫高窟北朝晚期的塑像和壁画,可以看作是隋代修窟造像活动的一个序曲。从这时起,造像风格已从强调线条的传统阶段,过渡到了追求、再现体型这样一个更趋成熟的造型风尚之时。对这一时期洞窟的分期研究,在探讨早期洞窟艺术演变和追溯隋代石窟艺术渊源上,具有十分重要的价值。同时,北朝晚期洞窟对研究整个敦煌,乃至全国的石窟艺术,也是一个不可缺少的重要环节。

基于这点,笔者对莫高窟隋代以前诸窟进行了全面考察,发现以第428窟为代表的十几座洞窟,造像面相方圆、头大、上身长、下身短、形体丰壮,与前期清瘦体态,如第285窟的佛和菩萨像,迥然有别;褒衣博带式的服饰也逐渐消失,取而代之的是多层次的下摆宽大的大衣。这种佛像,在中原,无论是响堂山、安阳,还是麦积山、须弥山,都属于齐、周时期的作品。因此我们有理由怀疑上述诸窟是北朝晚期,即北周时所造[6],最后初步确定塑像和壁画保存相对完好的15座洞窟,作为本文分期研究的对象。这批洞窟,除第461窟位于莫高窟北区之外,其余皆分布在南区中段第二、三层崖面上(图1),左右与前后代洞窟毗邻。

关于北朝晚期洞窟的划分和年代,前人做了不少工作,但多从艺术角度,限于个别洞窟的考证和年代推测[7]。真正从考古学角度,首次提出分期排年的,应是宿师季

---

[1] 有关于义事迹,宿师季庚先生考证甚详。参见:1)宿白《敦煌莫高窟早期洞窟杂考》,刊《大公报在港复刊三十周年纪念文集》上,香港:大公报社,1978年,第393-415页;2)宿白《东阳王与建平公》,载《向达先生纪念论文集》,乌鲁木齐:新疆人民出版社,1986年,第155-173页;3)宿白《东阳王与建平公(二稿)》,载《敦煌吐鲁番文献研究论集》第四辑,北京:北京大学出版社,1987年,第38-57页。

[2]《辩正论》卷四《十代奉佛篇》下,上引书,第518c页。

[3] 参见附录一。

[4] 1)宿白《敦煌莫高窟早期洞窟杂考》,上引书,第408-410页;2)宿白《东阳王与建平公(二稿)》,上引书,第49页。

[5] 宿白《敦煌莫高窟早期洞窟杂考》,上引书,第402页。

[6] 同上。

[7] 参见:1)张大千《漠高窟记》,台北:故宫博物院刊行,1985年;2)谢稚柳《敦煌艺术叙录》,上海:古典文学出版社,1957年;3)水野清一《敦煌石窟ノート》,載水野清一《中國の仏教美術》,東京:株式会社平凡社,1968年,第386-444頁。

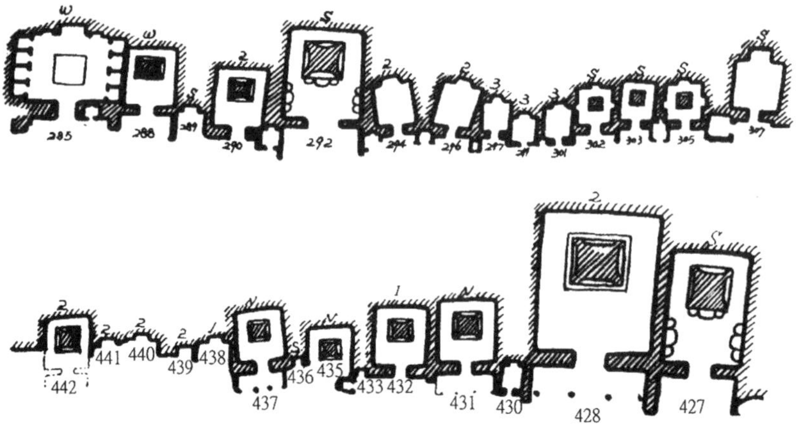

图 1　莫高窟北朝至隋代部分洞窟连续平面图

庚先生[1]。1978年，为了庆祝《大公报》在香港复刊30周年，季庚师应邀撰写了《敦煌莫高窟早期洞窟杂考》一文，确定第430、428、438-442、290、294、296、299、301等窟为北周窟[2]。尔后，樊锦诗、马世长、关友惠合作完成了《敦煌莫高窟北朝洞窟的分期》，对其中的15座北周洞窟做了系统的论证，并推测其年代“始于西魏大统十一年(545年)，下迄隋开皇四、五年(584、585年)之前”[3]。1985年，季庚师又对上述诸窟做了进一步分期排比[4]。

为了对上述诸窟做深入、细致的研究，本文以前人对莫高窟北周洞窟的断代和分期研究成果为起点，以纪年洞窟为标尺，用考古学方法，对北朝晚期十五座洞窟的年代和特征试作进一步探讨。至于研究中所依据的项目，由于各洞窟的保存状况不同，我们仅选择了窟龛形制、塑像、壁画布局、壁画中个体形象的类型及技法、主题故事画的构图等五部分，作为我们分期排队的内容。在此基础上，进而对整个北朝晚期洞窟做较全面的阐述。

二、北朝晚期洞窟的分期

依据洞窟建筑结构的特点，西魏末至隋初的15座洞窟，可以分作方形窟和中心

[1] 宿白《参观敦煌第285号窟札记》，见《文物参考资料》，1956年第2期，第19-21页。

[2] 宿白《敦煌莫高窟早期洞窟杂考》，上引书，第401-402页。

[3] 樊锦诗、马世长、关友惠《敦煌莫高窟北朝洞窟的分期》，见《中国石窟·敦煌莫高窟》一，北京：文物出版社，1981年，第185-197页。

[4] 宿白《东阳王与建平公(二稿)》，上引书，第55-56页注[22]。

塔柱窟两种主要类型。按照不同的窟型,我们分别对上述两类洞窟的形制、塑像和壁画等进行考古类型学分析,尔后分组排比,找出洞窟的先后发展序列,并在此基础上进行分期。

(一) 方形窟各部分类型分析

这种洞窟通常具有前后室,但前室大多坍塌毁坏,现仅存主室(后室)。主室平面方形,顶部大多凿成覆斗状,少数凿成前部人字披、后部平顶的形状。一般于正壁(西壁)开一大龛,内塑像,其他壁无龛。南北侧壁、东壁及窟顶均满绘壁画。下面,我们将方形窟分作五部分标型分式,进而排比分组。

1. 窟龛形制

在这部分中,我们选择了具有分期意义的平面、窟顶和龛式三项进行分析。

(1) 平面布局

依据洞窟的平面布局,可将方形窟分作二型。

A 型:平面方形,四壁无龛,仅在西壁影作尖楣圆拱龛(图 2)。1 个,第 461 窟。

B 型:平面方形,正壁开一龛,其他壁无龛(图 3、4)。10 个,第 294、296、297、299、301、430、438、439、440、441 窟。

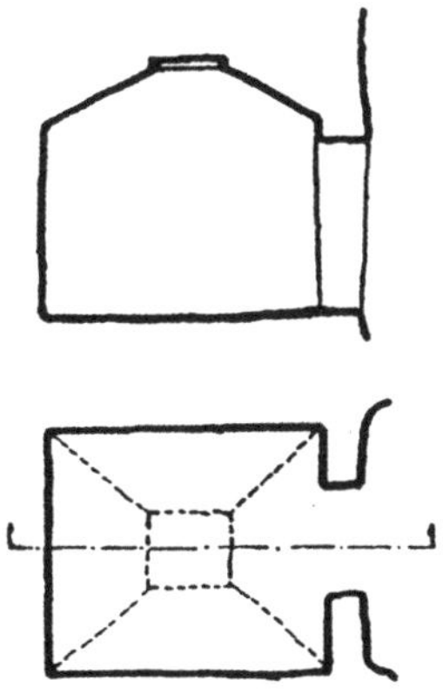

图 2　第 461 窟平面及纵向垂直剖面图

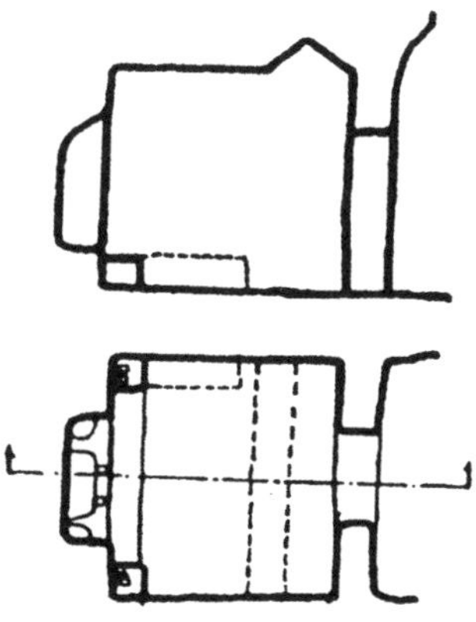

图 3　第 430 窟平面及纵向垂直剖面图

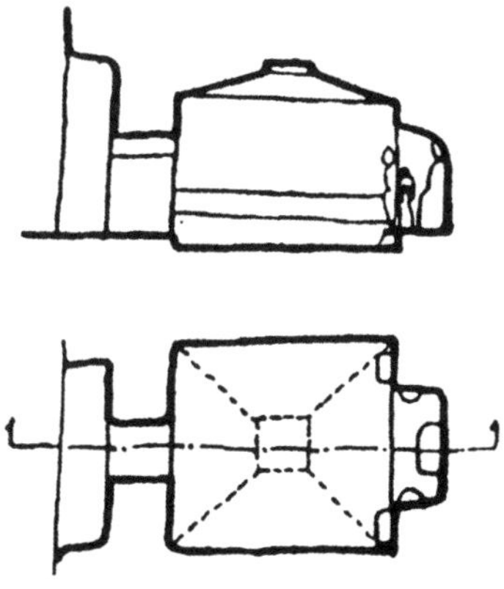

图 4　第 296 窟平面及纵向垂直剖面图

(2) 窟顶结构

按洞窟的顶部构造,可将方形窟分作二型。

A 型:覆斗顶。窟顶从四壁的顶部向上斜收,聚向中心,最后形成方形的藻井,形似覆斗,故名(参见图 2、4)。9 个,第 294、296、297、299、301、438、440、441、461 窟。

B 型：人字披顶。窟顶分前后两部分；后部凿成平顶，前部是一个与洞窟纵深正交的人字形窟顶，俗称人字披（详见塔柱窟的窟顶结构），故名（参见图 3）。2 个，第 430、439 窟。

(3) 佛龛样式

方形窟内佛龛，只有尖楣圆拱龛一种形制。按龛楣梁与龛柱的组合可分二式。

Ⅰ式：龛楣梁尾部饰忍冬，龛柱头束帛（图 5）。3 个，第 438、441、461[1]窟。

Ⅱ式：龛楣梁尾部饰龙首或忍冬，龛柱头饰覆莲（图 6、7）。7 个，第 294[2]、296、297[3]、299、301、430、439、440 窟。

图 5　第 461 窟龛梁尾部与龛柱头装饰

图 6　第 430 窟龛梁尾部与龛柱头装饰

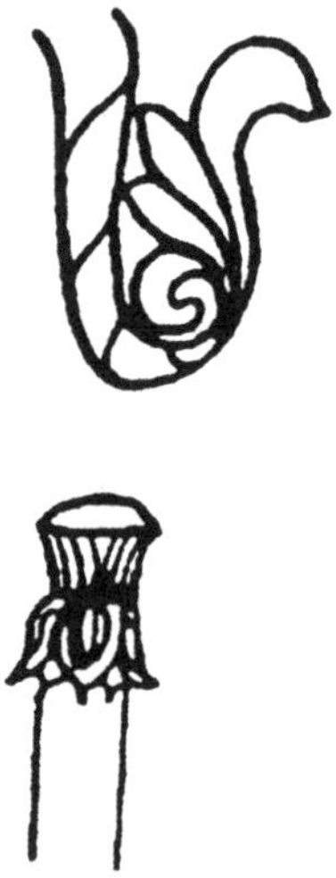

图 7　第 297 窟龛梁尾部与龛柱头装饰

2. 造像题材、组合及技法

在造像题材这部分中，我们选择了佛、菩萨和弟子像三项进行类型分析；而塑像技法，仅仅分析了塑像[4]衣褶的制作方法。至于其他方面的技法，由于能力所限，未能进行分析。

(1) 佛像

方形窟内的佛像[5]，皆善跏趺坐（倚坐），内着僧祇支，上衣覆搭双肩，有的于胸

[1] 第 461 窟虽未开龛，但西壁影作的圆拱形佛龛，龛梁尾部饰忍冬，龛柱头画成束帛式。

[2] 第 294 窟西壁佛龛，龛柱头为覆莲式，龛楣梁尾部饰物已残毁。从现存遗迹来看，应为龙首龛梁。

[3] 第 297 窟龛楣梁尾部饰忍冬，龛柱饰覆莲。暂入此式。

[4] 这里主要分析各窟龛内主尊塑像的衣褶制法，胁侍像衣褶的分期意义不明显。

[5] 第 461 窟西壁所绘佛龛中的二佛并坐，右侧佛大衣“通肩被服”，左侧佛内着僧祇支，上衣覆搭双肩且于胸前束带，大衣作“右袒式”披覆。参见：《中国石窟：敦煌莫高窟》一，图版 155。

前束带打结[1]；外着褒衣博带式大衣（图 8-11）。9 个，第 294、296、297、299、301、430、438、439、440 窟。

图 8　第 438 窟彩塑佛像

图 9　第 430 窟彩塑佛像

图 10　第 301 窟彩塑佛像

图 11　第 297 窟彩塑佛像

(2) 菩萨像

菩萨立姿，头戴花鬘冠，配耳饰和月牙形项饰。有的发髻插簪，有的饰宝缯、臂钏和手镯。从服饰上看，可分作二型。

A 型：裙披式，即袒上身，下着裙，披披巾；依披巾的不同披着方式下分三式。

Ai 式：披巾自双肩顺臂搭下后，于双肘处各自向内略为折转或重心垂至腹下，后末端上挂双肘外垂（图 12、13）。4 个，第 296[2]、299、430、438[3]窟。

Aii 式：披巾自双肩下搭后，于腹前相交打结（图 14）。2 个，第 296、430 窟。

Aiii 式：披巾自双肩下搭后，横于腹前两道（图 15）。1 个，第 297 窟。

B 型：上着僧祇支，下着长裙，披披巾（图 16）。1 个，第 439 窟。

---

[1] 关于佛法衣束带打结，目前学界多认为系僧祇支束带打结。经检索相关律典并考察云冈、龙门、麦积山和敦煌北朝时期洞窟中的佛像，我们发现这种束带应为上衣覆搭双肩后所系，是佛法衣 / 法服汉化的一种结果，疑受南朝汉化佛像影响所致。如云冈石窟第 5 窟西壁、第 6 窟塔柱南壁上层和第 6 窟东壁上层的立佛，龙门石窟宾阳中洞、普泰洞、魏字洞、皇甫公窟和路洞正壁的坐佛，特别是麦积山第 138 龛正壁、142 窟左壁、120 窟和 127 窟正壁的坐佛、第 135 窟立佛、第 20 窟正壁及左壁、第 55 龛和第 62 窟正壁的坐佛以及莫高窟第 285 窟正壁、第 432 窟塔柱正壁、第 438 窟和第 297 窟正壁的坐佛等，表现得极为清晰。参见：1)《中国石窟 · 云冈石窟》一，北京：文物出版社，1991 年，图版 31、91-92、115；2)《中国石窟 · 龙门石窟》一，北京：文物出版社，1991 年，图版 7、75、85-86、186、208；3)《中国石窟 · 麦积山石窟》，北京：文物出版社，1998 年，图版 102、109、126、151、173、210、218；4)《中国石窟 · 敦煌莫高窟》一，北京：文物出版社，1982 年，图版 114、149、156、183 等。

[2] 第 296 窟菩萨披巾自双肩搭下后，重心垂至腹下，后两末端分别上挂双肘外垂。

[3] 第 438 窟菩萨披巾自双肩顺臂搭下至肘内，下垂部分绘出。

(3) 弟子像

图 12　第 438 窟
彩塑菩萨像

图 13　第 430 窟
彩塑菩萨像

图 14　第 296 窟
彩塑菩萨像

图 15　第 297 窟
彩塑菩萨像

图 16　第 439 窟
彩塑菩萨像

图 17　第 430 窟
彩塑弟子像

图 18　第 297 窟
彩塑弟子像

依据第 461 窟西壁壁画中的弟子法服，可以分作两种类型。一种内着僧祇支，大衣作通肩式披覆；另一种内着僧祇支，上衣遮搭双肩，大衣作“右袒式”披覆。至于像设中的弟子立像，多内着僧祇支，束下衣（内衣），上衣遮搭双肩，大衣作“右袒式”披覆。脚下着鞋或长靿靴（图 17、18）[1]。6 个，第 294、296、297、299、430、439 窟。

(4) 造像组合

方形窟的造像组合，可分二型。

A 型：一铺三身像。龛内塑一佛，龛外两侧各一菩萨。1 个，第 438 窟。

B 型：一铺五身像。龛内塑一佛二弟子，龛外两侧各塑一菩萨。9 个，第 294、

[1] 参见：1)《中国石窟·敦煌莫高窟》一，北京：文物出版社，1982 年，图版 153、159、183；2)《中国石窟雕塑全集》第 1 卷《敦煌》，重庆：重庆出版社，2001 年，图版 41、42。

296、297、299、301、430、439、440[1]、441[2]窟。

(5) 佛衣褶襞

据断面形状,可将方形窟内佛像大衣衣褶的制作形式分作三型。

A 型：贴泥条式。在塑像大的体面上,贴上一条条凸起的泥条；泥条断面有半圆或三角形之别(图 19b)。1 个,第 438 窟。

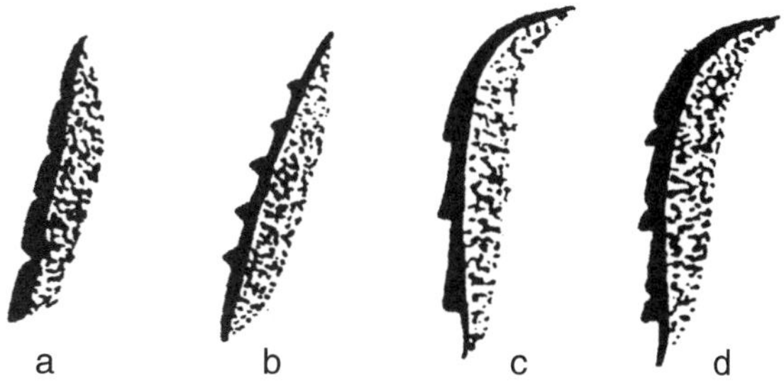

图 19　莫高窟彩塑佛像衣纹断面示意图

a. 第 432 窟；b. 第 438 窟；c. 第 430 窟；d. 第 290 窟

B 型：阴线式。其作法,是在塑像大的体面上用刀等挖或划出一道道沟槽；其断面为半圆或三角形,且有疏密、深浅、主辅等变化(参见图 19a)。2 个,第 439、440 窟。

C 型：阶梯式。佛像身上的衣褶自上而下或自下而上做成一折比一折高或低的形式；其断面层层错起,棱角分明,犹若阶梯,故名(图 19c)。6 个,第 294、296、297、299、301、430 窟。

3. 壁画布局

在这部分中,我们选择了如下五项进行分析。

(1) 正壁龛内

据龛内正壁和侧壁的壁画题材,可将正壁龛内壁画分作三型。

A 型：正壁绘火焰背光,两侧画花草。1 个,第 461 窟。

B 型：正壁绘火焰背光,侧壁画飞天、供养菩萨、弟子等。5 个,第 297、301、430、438、439 窟。

C 型：正壁绘火焰背光,侧壁上绘弟子、飞天和菩萨,下绘鹿头梵志(南侧)和婆薮仙(北侧)。3 个,第 294、296、299 窟。

(2) 正壁龛外

按壁画题材和内容,龛外两侧壁画可分四型。

A 型：两侧绘弟子和供养菩萨。1 个,第 461 窟。

---

[1] 第 440 窟龛内现存一佛二弟子。龛外两侧的菩萨已残毁,但菩萨像座仍在,故将其归入 B 型。

[2] 第 441 窟西龛内五身像皆毁。从现存像座遗迹来看,原塑一倚坐佛、二弟子、二菩萨。

B 型：龛外两侧上绘飞天和供养菩萨，下绘鹿头梵志和婆薮仙。1 个，第 438 窟。

C 型：龛外两侧上绘天宫伎乐或帝释天与帝释天妃，下画供养菩萨。3 个，第 294、296、439 窟。

D 型：龛外两侧壁上部画菩萨。4 个，第 297、299、301、430 窟。

(3) 南北侧壁

依题材内容及布局，南北两侧壁壁画可分作二型。

A 型：壁面大部分画千佛，按内容及经营位置下分三式。

Ai 式：壁面顶部绘帷幔，中画千佛，下绘三角形垂饰（图 20）。1 个，第 461 窟。

Aii 式：上绘天宫伎乐、三角形垂饰和帷幔等，中画千佛，下绘供养人（图 21）。2 个，第 430、439[1]窟。

Aiii 式：壁面大部画千佛，下绘供养人，再下为药叉（夜叉）或边饰（图 22）。3 个，第 297、299、438 窟。

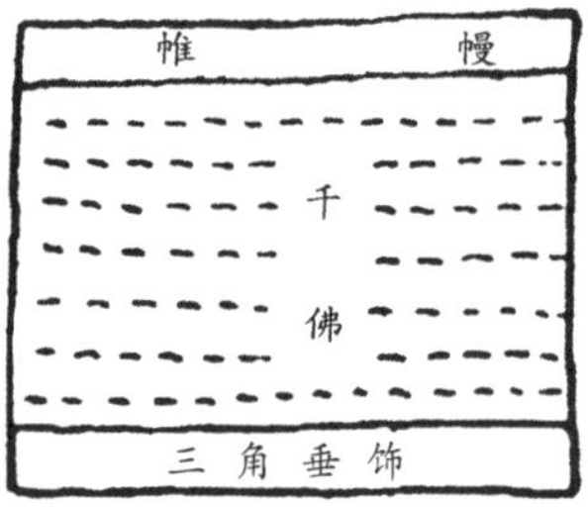

图 20　第 461 窟侧壁壁画题材布局示意图

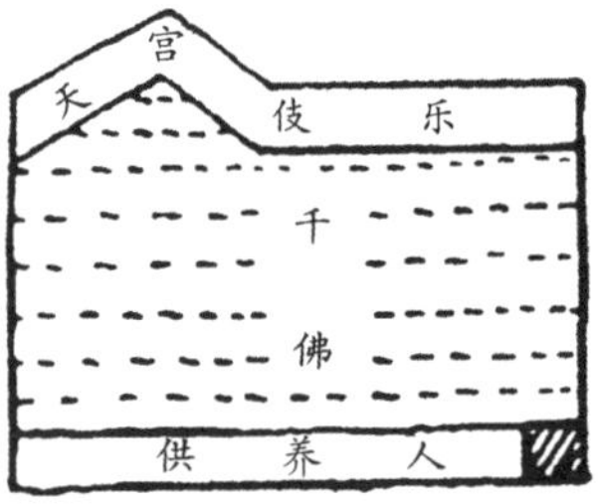

图 21　第 430 窟侧壁壁画题材布局示意图

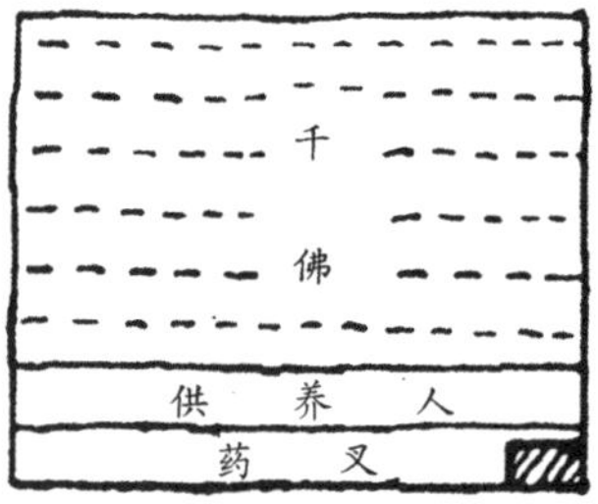

图 22　第 297 窟侧壁壁画题材布局示意图

B 型：壁面大部分绘千佛，中央画说法图或故事画，按经营位置下分二式。

Bi 式：壁面中央画说法图，左右及上部绘千佛，下画供养人等（图 23）。2 个，第 294、301 窟。

Bii 式：上画千佛，中绘故事画，下画药叉（图 24）。1 个，第 296 窟。

(4) 东壁壁画[2]

方形窟东壁壁画，按题材内容和布局可分作二型。

A 型：顶部绘天宫伎乐，门上方画一佛四菩萨说法图，门两侧及其余壁面绘千佛，下部画供养人（图 25）。1 个，第 430 窟[3]。

---

[1] 第 439 窟南壁（残）千佛下面有树残迹。是否原绘故事画，有待进一步研究。

[2] 现存第 438、439、440、441、461 窟东壁已塌毁。原画内容不清。

[3] 第 430 窟四壁底部供养人，大都被宋代（？）重绘的供养人覆盖，仅在北壁西侧露出一身原画供养人。

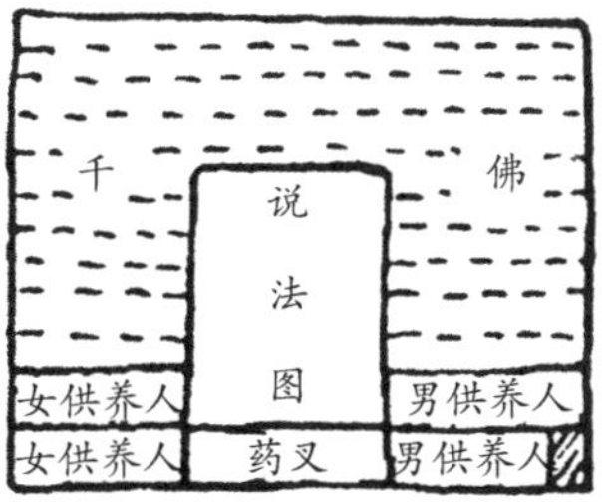

图 23　第 301 窟侧壁
壁画题材布局示意图

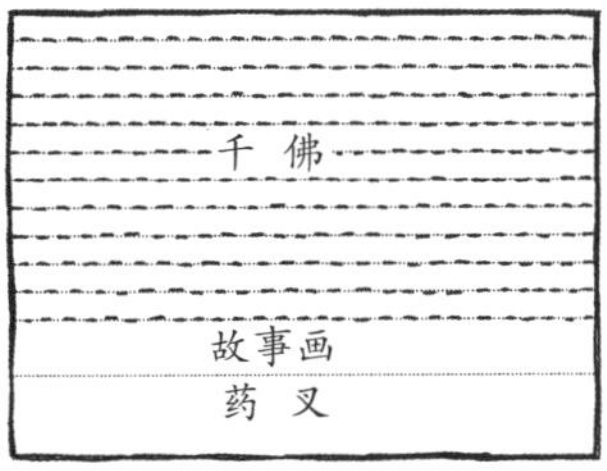

图 24　第 296 窟侧壁
壁画题材布局示意图

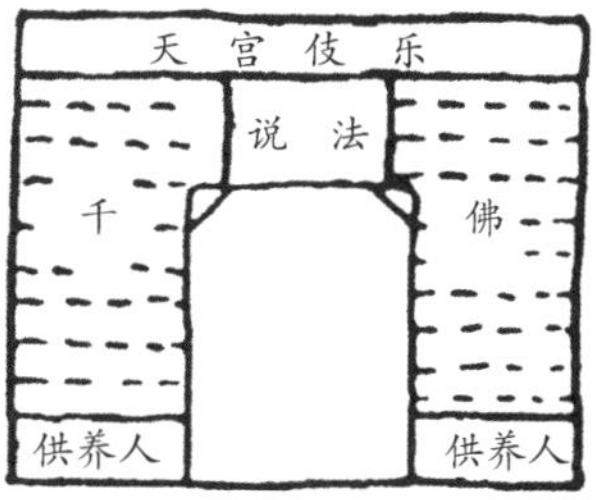

图 25　第 430 窟东壁
壁画题材布局示意图

B 型：门上方及门南北侧壁面画千佛，下画供养人、供养车马等，再下为药叉或供养人（图 26）。5 个，第 294、296、297、299、301 窟。

(5) 窟顶壁画[1]

依据题材内容与布局，窟顶壁画可分二型。

A 型：窟顶藻井画斗四井心，垂角、帷幔等铺于四坡，下画天宫伎乐、故事画等，按经营位置下分三式。

Ai 式：斗四莲花井心，垂角、帷幔铺于四坡，下画天宫伎乐（图 27）。1 个，第 461 窟。

Aii 式：斗四莲花井心，垂角、帷幔、忍冬和千佛等铺于四坡，下画故事画，再下为天宫伎乐及边饰（图 28）。5 个，第 294、296、299、301、438 窟。

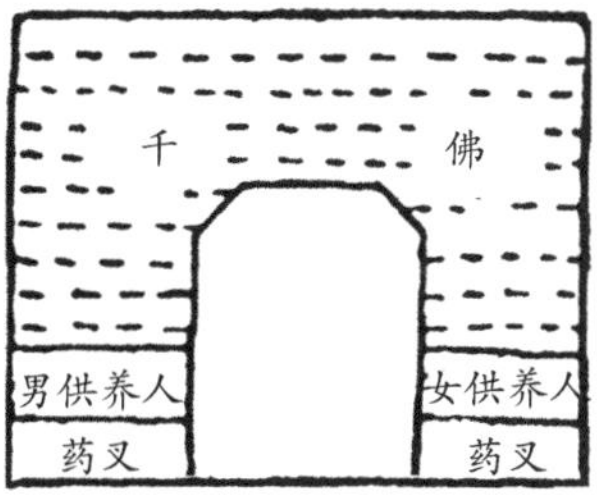

图 26　第 296 窟东壁
壁画题材布局示意图

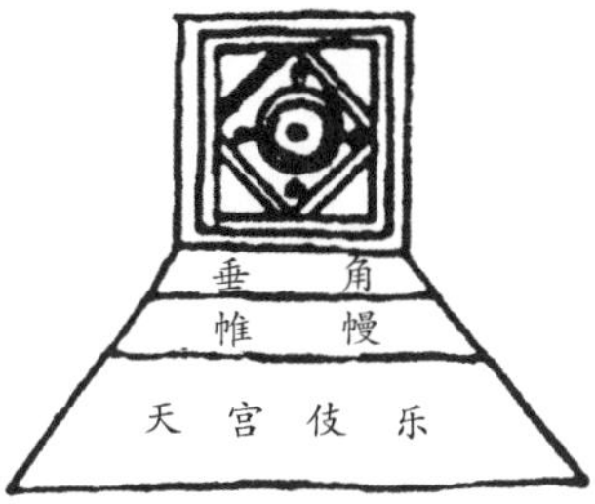

图 27　第 461 窟窟顶
壁画题材布局示意图

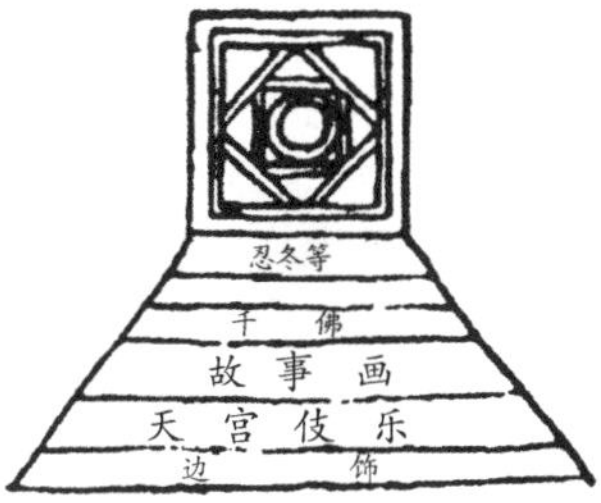

图 28　第 296 窟窟顶
壁画题材布局示意图

Aiii 式：斗四莲花井心，垂角、帷幔铺于四坡，下绘千佛三列，再下为天宫伎乐及边饰（图 29）。1 个，第 297 窟。

B 型：前部人字披画忍冬、莲花和摩尼宝珠等，后部平顶画斗四莲花、忍冬图案及飞天等（图 30）。1 个，第 430 窟。

[1] 第 439 窟窟顶壁画大多塌毁，原画布局及内容不清。

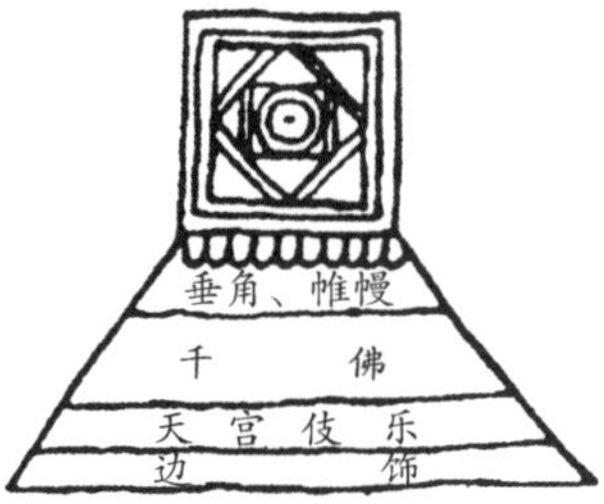

图 29　第 297 窟窟顶
壁画题材布局示意图

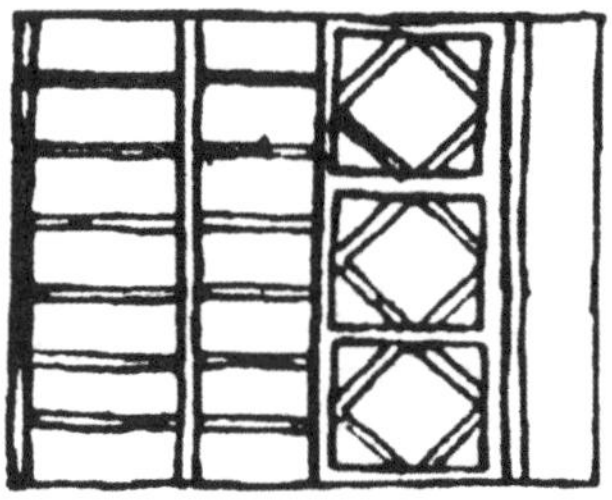
图 30　第 430 窟窟顶
壁画题材布局示意图

4. 壁画中个体形象及技法

这部分，我们选择了菩萨、千佛、天宫伎乐、飞天、供养人及菩萨面部晕染方式等六项进行考古类型学分析。

(1) 菩萨像

壁画中的菩萨，与塑像基本相同。菩萨头戴花鬘冠或三珠冠，有的配臂钏和手镯，还有的头饰宝缯。参照菩萨塑像的类型，壁画中的菩萨按服饰可分三型。

A 型：裙披式，依披巾的不同披着方式下分二式。

Ai 式：披巾自双肩下搭后于胸前交叉或顺臂自肘内垂下（图 31、32)。6 个，第 294、296、430、438、439、461[1]窟。

Aii 式：无。

Aiii 式：肩挂缨络两条，有的于胸前呈交叉状，有的一长一短垂于胸腹前。披巾自双肩搭下后，横于腹前两道（图 33)。2 个，第 297、301 窟。

图 31　第 461 窟
壁画菩萨像

图 32　第 296 窟
壁画菩萨像

图 33　第 301 窟
壁画菩萨像

图 34　第 439 窟
壁画菩萨像

[1] 第 461 窟菩萨的披巾自双肩下搭后于胸前交叉。

B 型：上着僧祇支，下着长裙，披披巾。1 个，第 299 窟。

C 型：大衣作通肩式披覆（图 34)。1 个，第 439 窟。

(2) 千佛

依据法服与颜色的组合，千佛可分二型。

A 型：千佛法服为通肩与褒衣博带式相间，土红地。千佛面呈灰色、黑褐色[1]，小字脸，手染三道。据法服颜色，基本四个一组（图 35)。1 个，第 438 窟。

B 型：千佛大衣皆作通肩式披覆，手作禅定印。千佛面呈灰色、黑褐色或黑色晕染，小字脸，大多耳染三点，手染三道（图 36)，据法服颜色下分二式。

Bi 式：千佛八个一组。1 个，第 461 窟。

Bii 式：千佛四个一组（图 37)。7 个，第 294、296、297、299、301、430、439 窟。

图 35　第 438 窟壁画千佛

图 36　第 294 窟壁画千佛细部

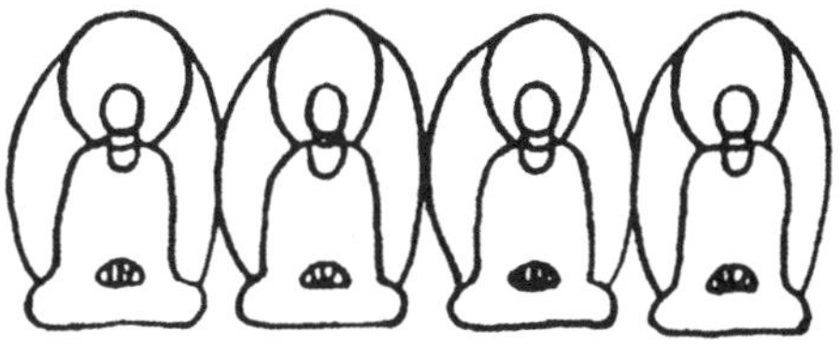

图 37　第 294 窟壁画千佛

(3) 天宫伎乐

按构图形式，天宫伎乐可分二型。

A 型：圆拱形与汉式屋形天宫相间画出，每阁内画一伎乐，居宫歌舞奏乐，天宫楼阁下方的凹凸状装饰，是承托楼阁的平台（图 38)。1 个，第 438 窟。

B 型：构图较 A 型简化。画面上不出现天宫楼阁，仅画出由方砖等构筑的象征性凹凸平台；伎乐天于平台上方凌空舞乐（图 39、40)。8 个，第 294、296、297、299、301、430、439、461 窟。

---

[1] 关于面部颜色及晕染等，皆指现在所呈颜色。壁画现在显示的颜色，有些系变色所致，如原来人物面部的肉红色，现变成了灰黑色，晕染色变成了粗壮的黑线；原来并不显著的白眉、白眼等，现在黑白分明。下文凡涉及颜色的描述，皆指现呈颜色。

图 38　第 438 窟天宫形制

图 39　第 461 窟天宫伎乐

图 40　第 301 窟天宫伎乐

(4) 飞天

方形窟内的飞天，从服饰上看可分作三型。

A 型：裙披式（俗称西域式），按服饰下分二式。

Ai 式：袒上身，下着裙。大多双足外露，披巾于头后扬成一大圆环（图 41、42、43）。5 个，第 294、296[1]、430、438、439 窟。

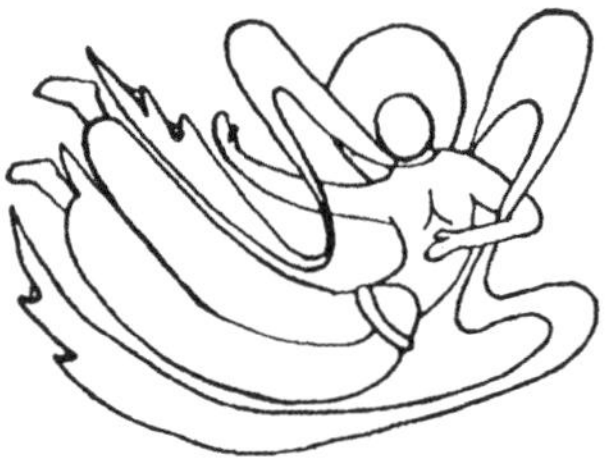

图 41　第 438 窟飞天

图 42　第 439 窟飞天

图 43　第 296 窟飞天

Aii 式：飞天头束大首髻，大多面染圆圈，戴项饰；袒上身，下着袖腿长裙，大多肩挂缨络（图 44）。3 个，第 297、299、301 窟。

B 型：头束鬟髻，两颊、额际和下巴均呈褐色；身着汉式对襟大袖长袍（俗称汉式或中原式），大多袖足；披巾于头后扬成一至三个环状（图 45）。5 个，第 294、296、430、439、461 窟。

C 型：上着僧祇支，下着袖腿大裙，双足微露；披巾于头后扬成一大圆环（图 46）。

[1] 第 296 窟有的飞天袒上身，下着袖腿大裙，裙腰外翻如短裙，披巾于头后扬成三个大环。

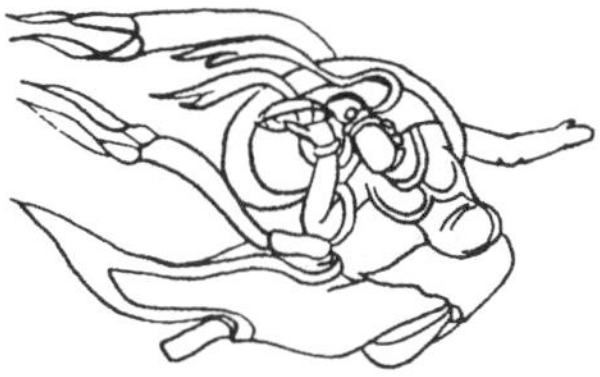

图 44　第 297 窟飞天

图 45　第 439 窟飞天

图 46　第 299 窟飞天

1 个,第 299 窟。

(5) 供养人像

供养人(包括僧人)的服饰,分男、女两部分分析。

甲、男供养人

按服装,方形窟内的男供养人或比丘可分四型。

A 型：着上衣和内衣,大衣作"右袒式"披覆(图 47)。6 个,第 294、296、297、299、301、438 窟。

B 型：内衣与上衣披覆方式不清,大衣摆似于胸前交系外翻。5 个,第 294、296、297、299、301、438 窟。

C 型：身着"绯衲小口袴褶",即上着圆领小袖褶,下着小口裤,腰束蹀躞带。有的于袴褶外穿对襟窄袖大衣(图 48、49)。6 个,第 294、296、297、299、301、430 窟。

D 型：着深衣袍,脚穿笏头履(图 50)。2 个,第 294、299 窟。

图 47　第 294 窟
男供养人

图 48　第 430 窟
男供养人

图 49　第 296 窟
男供养人

图 50　第 299 窟
男供养人

乙、女供养人

据服饰，方形窟内的女供养人可分二型。

A 型：内着白纱裙，外着对襟大袖襦。有的于裙襦外加搭披帛（图 51）；有的于裙襦外罩圆领长袖大衣（图 52）。5 个，第 294、296、297、299、301 窟。

B 型：上着窄袖衫，披披帛，下系曳地长裙。有的束蔽膝（图 53）。3 个，第 297、299、301 窟。

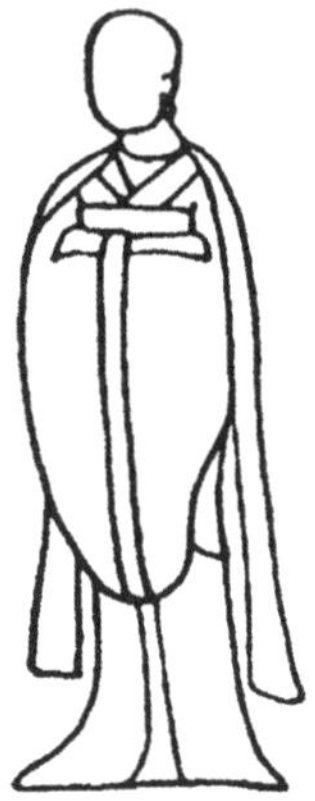

图 51　第 297 窟女供养人

图 52　第 301 窟女供养人

图 53　第 297 窟女供养人

(6) 面部晕染[1]

菩萨面部的晕染方式，可分为三型。

A 型：面颊染色块，通常为倒桃形。另染上眼睑及下巴等（图 54）。1 个，第 461 窟。

B 型：面部染法为西域式凹凸法，且在鼻梁等部位施白粉，以强调高光。依染法和点高光的部位下分二式。

Bi 式：面部染法为§或ᑕ形，同时在鼻梁和眼睛处涂白粉。2 个，第 438、439 窟。

Bii 式：面部染法为ᑕ形，通常用白粉点两眼、鼻梁、牙齿和下巴，个别的还有将两眉棱以白粉连在一起成为"五白式"[2]。3 个，第 294、296、430 窟。

C 型：两腮处染圆圈，并染眼睑和下巴，多用白粉点两眼和鼻梁（图 55）。3 个，第 297、299、301 窟。

---

[1] 绘画技法，主要分析了菩萨面部的晕染方式，因为这项具有分期意义，尤其是下述的"五白式"晕染，乃北周时期洞窟特有的一种表现形式。

[2] "五白式"晕染法之名，系段文杰拟定，指白鼻、白眼、白连眉、白齿和白下巴五个部分。这是北周洞窟特有的一种晕染方式，似"源于西域龟兹壁画"。参见段文杰《敦煌壁画の様式の特色と芸术的成果》，载日中国交正常化十周年记念《中国敦煌壁画展》图录，东京：每日新聞社，1982 年。后该文转载于同年出版的《敦煌研究》试刊第 2 期，第 1-16 页，题为《略论敦煌壁画的风格特点和艺术成就》。

图 54　第 461 窟菩萨面部晕染方式

图 55　第 301 窟菩萨面部晕染方式

5. 故事画[1]构图

方形窟内主题壁画(故事画)的构图形式,可分二型。

A 型:横卷式连续构图。2 个,第 296、461 窟。

B 型:"凹" 形连环画构图。5 个,第 294、296、299、301、438 窟。

(二)方形窟的分组

方形窟各部分的类型大体如上。其中上述五项保存基本完好的洞窟共九座。经过类型排比,这九座洞窟,可以归纳为两组(见表一)。

第一组:2 个,第 461、438 窟;

第二组:7 个,第 439、430、294、296、299、297、301 窟。

第一组洞窟的窟顶结构为 A 型,佛龛样式为Ⅰ式,菩萨像作 Ai 式,造像组合及佛衣褶襞皆为 A 型。正壁龛内外壁画为 A 或 B 型,千佛构图及天宫伎乐半数为 A 型。这些都是北魏和西魏时期洞窟[2]的特征,而为第二组洞窟所不见或少见。而第一组洞窟中 Bi 式千佛、B 型天宫伎乐及 B 型故事画构图等,又不见于西魏以前诸窟(以有西魏大统四、五年题记的第285窟为标尺)[3]。因此,第一组洞窟晚于西魏初,而早于第二组是显而易见的。

第二组洞窟的平面布局为 B 型,佛龛样式作Ⅱ式。菩萨像为 Ai、Aiii 式或 B 型,塑像中出现了弟子像,造像组合皆为 B 型。龛外两侧壁画为 C 或 D 型,千佛造型皆

[1] 这里所说的故事画,包括本生、因缘和佛传。

[2] 参见《中国石窟·敦煌莫高窟》一,北京:文物出版社,1981 年,图版 26、58、84。

[3] 参见:上引书,图版 95-96、154。

表一　方形窟各部分类型表

项目 / 型式 / 窟号	窟龛形制			造像题材、组合及技法					壁画布局					壁画中个体形象及技法							构图	分组
	平面布局	窟顶结构	佛龛样式	佛像	菩萨	弟子	造像组合	佛衣褶襞	正壁龛内	正壁龛外	南北侧壁	东壁	窟顶	菩萨	千佛	天宫伎乐	飞天	男供养人	女供养人	面部晕染	故事画	组别
461窟	A	A	I						A	A	Ai		Ai	Ai	Bi	B	B			A	A	第一组
438窟	B	A	I	√	Ai		A	A	B	B	Aiii		Aii	Ai	A	A	Ai	A/B		Bi	B	
439窟	B	B	II	√	B	√	B	B	B	C	Aii			Ai/C	Bii	B	Ai/B			Bi		第二组（甲）
430窟	B	B	II	√	Ai/Aii	√	B	C	B	D	Aii	A	B	Ai	Bii	B	Ai/B	C		Bii		
294窟	B	A	II	√		√	B	C	C	C	Bi	B	Aii	Ai	Bii	B	Ai/B	A/B/C/D	A	Bii	B	
296窟	B	A	II	√	Ai/Aii	√	B	C	C	C	Bii	B	Aii	Ai	Bii	B	Ai/B	A/B/C	A	Bii	A/B	
299窟	B	A	II	√	Ai	√	B	C	C	D	Aiii	B	Aii	B	Bii	B	Aii/C	A/B/C/D	A/B	C	B	第二组（乙）
297窟	B	A	II	√	Aiii	√	B	C	B	D	Aiii	B	Aiii	Aiii	Bii	B	Aii	A/B/C	A/B	C		
301窟	B	A	II	√			B	C	B	D	Bi	B	Aii	Aiii	Bii	B	Aii	A/B/C	A/B	C	B	
440窟	B	A	II	√			B	B														
441窟	B	A	I				B															

为 Bii 式,天宫伎乐皆作 B 型,菩萨面部晕染方式大多为 Bii 式或 C 型。这些大多是隋代初期流行的题材和特征[1],而为第一组洞窟所不见或少见。因此,第二组洞窟晚于第一组也是毫无疑问的。

第二组洞窟,经过我们排比分析,还可细分为甲、乙两小组。

甲组：4 个,第 439、430、294、296 窟。

乙组：3 个,第 299、297、301 窟。

甲组洞窟 B 型窟顶,B 型菩萨像,C 型龛外两侧壁画布局,壁画中 Ai 式和 C 型菩萨,Ai 式和 B 型飞天,Bii 式菩萨面部晕染方式等皆不见于乙组洞窟。

乙组洞窟的窟顶结构均为 A 型,塑像中出现了 Aiii 式菩萨像,龛外两侧壁画布局均为 D 型,壁画中出现了 Aiii 式和 B 型菩萨、B 型女供养人,菩萨面部晕染方式皆为 C 型。上述特征,均为甲组洞窟所不见或少见。

经过与莫高窟唐代以前的洞窟对比,我们看出：乙组洞窟的窟龛形制、塑像和壁画布局、个体形象及技法等,多与隋初洞窟的相关部分[2]接近；而甲组洞窟的上述特征,则与隋初洞窟有较大差异。因此可以说,乙组洞窟的时代,较甲组略晚。

这样,原来的两大组洞窟,可细分为下列三组：

第一组：2 个,第 461、438 窟。

第二组：4 个,第 439、430、294、296 窟。

第三组：3 个,第 299、297、301 窟。

因此,上述三组洞窟的顺序,可以看作是西魏末至隋初九座方形窟的相对早晚序列。其余两个内容不齐全的方形窟,依据其现存遗迹,可对照上述诸窟的相关部分,分别归入上述三组。

第 440 窟的残存部分,平面布局为 B 型,窟顶结构作 A 型,佛龛样式作Ⅱ式,造像组合及佛衣褶襞皆为 B 型。第 441 窟除佛龛为Ⅰ式外,平面布局、窟顶结构和造像组合均同第 440 窟。经过与上述三组洞窟进行比较,我们看出：第 440、441 两窟的残存部分,与第 439 窟的同类部分是十分接近的,故将其归入第 439 窟与第 430 窟之间,即归入上述第二组洞窟之中,这样,上述三组洞窟分别为：

第一组：第 461、438 窟,2 个。

第二组：第 439、440、441、430、294、296 窟,6 个。

第三组：第 299、297、301 窟,3 个。

---

[1] 参见《中国石窟·敦煌莫高窟》二,北京：文物出版社,1984 年,图版 13、15、17、18、19、22。

[2] 出处同上。

（三）中心塔柱窟各部分类型分析

中心塔柱窟（塔庙窟），是北朝时期中原北方石窟寺营造中普遍采用的一种形制，敦煌地区也是如此。莫高窟的中心塔柱窟通常具有前、后室。但前室大多残毁，仅存主室（后室）。主室平面为一纵长方形，从空间上看，这种洞窟主室可分作前、后两部分，前部约占纵深的1/3，有一个与洞窟纵深正交的人字形窟顶，俗称人字披顶。在人字披的前后披上，塑或画出椽子，椽间绘作望板，两披之间塑或绘出脊槫；后部凿出平顶，与人字披的后披相接。塔柱周围形成通道——礼拜道。中心塔柱分塔基与塔身两部分，其中塔身四面开龛塑像，塔基绘制壁画。塔柱周围的窟顶和洞窟四壁均绘壁画。

对中心塔柱窟，我们也同方形窟一样做考古类型学分析。中心塔柱窟的内容，也主要包括五个部分，即：1. 窟龛形制；2. 造像题材、组合及技法；3. 壁画布局；4. 壁画中个体形象及技法；5. 故事画构图形式。下面我们对照方形窟，分别对西魏末至隋初的四个中心塔柱窟标型分式。需要说明的是，如果塔柱窟的某项与方形窟的某项相同，则采用方形窟该项所标定的型与式，并将该型、式的文字叙述省略。否则，拟定新的型与式。

1. 窟龛形制

在这部分中，我们也同方形窟一样分三项记述。不过将方形窟的平面布局一项，改为塔柱形制，因为中心塔柱窟的平面布局分期意义不明显，只有窟内塔柱的立面结构才能反映演变过程。余两项同方形窟。

(1) 塔柱形制

按塔柱四面开龛的情况，可分作二型。

A型：塔柱正面（东向面，下同）开一较大圆拱龛；南、西、北三面各开上、下两层龛；上层龛为较浅的横长方形，下层龛形同正面龛（图56)。1个，第432窟。

B型：塔柱四面各开一大圆拱龛（图57)。3个，第290、428、442窟。

(2) 窟顶结构

对照方形窟，中心塔柱窟窟顶形制仅有一型。

A型：无。

B型：同方形窟B型（参见图56、57)。4个，第290、428、432、442窟。

(3) 佛龛样式

对照方形窟，中心塔柱窟的佛龛可分二型。

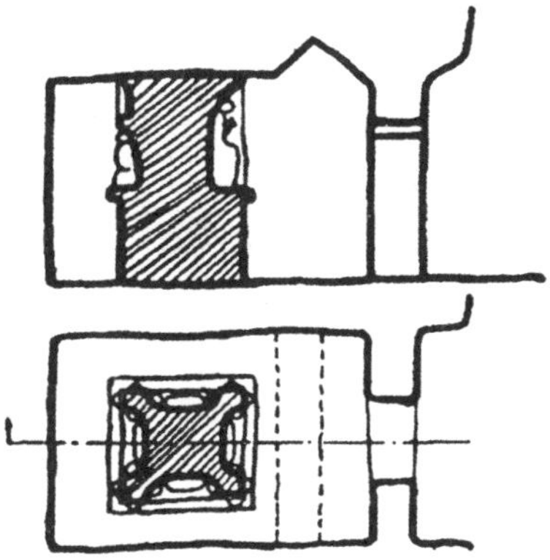

图 56　第 432 窟平面及纵向垂直剖面图

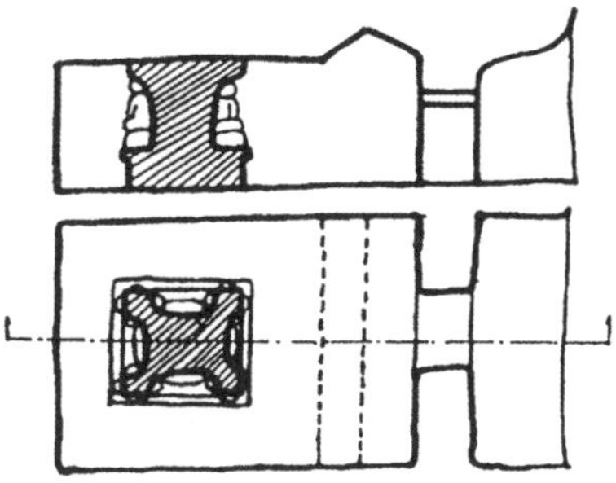

图 57　第 428 窟平面及纵向垂直剖面图

A 型 *[1]：浅长方形龛，无龛楣梁和龛柱。1 个，第 432 窟塔柱南 (S)、西 (W)、北 (N) 面上层龛。

B 型：圆拱形龛。与方形窟所有佛龛样式相同，按龛梁与龛柱头的组合下分二式。

Bi 式：同方形窟Ⅰ式 (图 58)。2 个，第 290 窟塔柱南、西、北面龛，第 432 窟塔柱南、西、北面下层龛。

Bii 式：同方形窟Ⅱ式 (图 59)。4 个，第 290、432 窟塔柱东 (E) 面龛，第 428、442 窟塔柱四面龛。

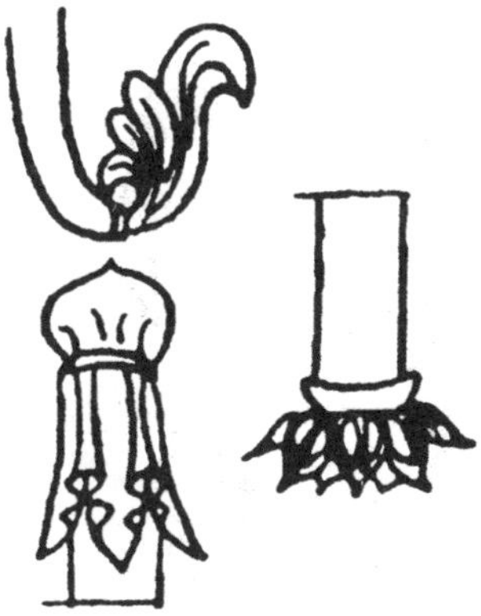

图 58　第 290 窟龛梁尾部与龛柱头装饰

图 59　第 428 窟龛梁尾部与龛柱头装饰

2. 造像题材、组合及技法

在这部分中，我们选择了佛像、菩萨像、弟子像、造像组合、龛两侧影塑和佛衣褶襞作法等六项进行考古类型学分析。

[1] 在类型分析中，如塔柱窟的某项较方形窟的同类项新出现一种型或式，以 * 号表示，下同。

(1) 佛像

对照方形窟，中心塔柱窟的佛像按坐势分作二型。

A 型：佛结跏趺坐，依大衣披覆方式下分三式。

Ai 式*：大衣作通肩式披覆，“以衣右角，宽搭左肩，垂之背后……衣便绕颈，双手下出”[1]（图 60）。1 个，第 432 窟塔柱南、北面上下龛，西面上层龛。

Aii 式*：大衣敷搭双肩后衣摆于腹前交系外翻掩手（图 61）。1 个，第 432 窟塔柱西面下层龛。

Aiii 式*：内着僧祇支，上衣覆搭双肩，有的束带打结，外着褒衣博带式大衣（图 62、63）。1 个，第 428 窟塔柱四面龛。

B 型：佛善跏趺坐，依大衣披覆方式下分二式。

Bi 式*：大衣作通肩式披覆（图 64）。1 个，第 290 窟塔柱北面龛。

Bii 式：同方形窟所有佛像，即内着僧祇支，上衣覆搭双肩，有的束带打结，外着褒衣博带式大衣（图 65）。3 个，第 290 窟塔柱东、南面龛，第 432 窟塔柱东面龛，第 442 窟塔柱四面龛。

(2) 菩萨像[2]

对照方形窟，中心塔柱窟的菩萨像大多为立姿，个别交脚坐，按服饰可分六型。

A 型：裙披式，同方形窟 A 型，即袒上身，下着裙，披披巾；依披巾的不同披着方式下分三式。

Ai 式：同方形窟 Ai 式。3 个，第 290 窟塔柱东面龛，第 428 窟塔柱东、南、西面龛，第 432 窟塔柱东面龛和南、西面下层龛。

图 60　第 432 窟彩塑佛像

图 61　第 432 窟彩塑佛像

图 62　第 428 窟彩塑佛像

[1] 义净《南海寄归内法传》卷二，见《大正藏》第 54 卷，第 215a-b 页。

[2] 第 442 窟中心塔柱各龛的菩萨像皆毁，原来服饰不清。

图 63　第 428 窟彩塑佛像

图 64　第 290 窟彩塑佛像

图 65　第 432 窟彩塑佛像

Aii 式：同方形窟 Aii 式。3 个，第 290 窟塔柱东、南、西面龛，第 428 窟塔柱东面龛，第 432 窟塔柱东面龛和南面下层龛。

Aiii 式：无。

Aiv 式*：披巾于胸前交叉或交叉穿璧（图 66-68）。2 个，第 290 窟塔柱南、西、北面龛，第 428 窟塔柱南、北面龛。

B 型：同方形窟 B 型（图 69）。1 个，第 290 窟塔柱西、北面龛。

图 66　第 428 窟彩塑菩萨像

图 67　第 290 窟彩塑菩萨像

图 68　第 428 窟彩塑菩萨像

图 69　第 290 窟彩塑菩萨像

C 型*：大衣作通肩式披覆（图 70）。1 个，第 432 窟塔柱南、西、北面上层龛。

D 型*：上身着僧祇支（斜披络腋），下着长裙（图 71）。1 个，第 432 窟塔柱南、西、北面上层龛。

E 型*：着汉式对襟大袖长袍，披巾自双肩搭下后于腹前交叉穿璧，脚穿笏头履（图 72）。1 个，第 432 窟塔柱北面下层龛。

F 型*：上着对襟小衫，束腰带，下着长裙。披巾自双肩搭下后重心垂至腹前，后两末端分别上挂双肘外垂（图 73）。1 个，第 290 窟塔柱西面龛。

图 70　第 432 窟彩塑菩萨像

图 71　第 432 窟彩塑菩萨像

图 72　第 432 窟彩塑菩萨像

图 73　第 290 窟彩塑菩萨像

(3) 弟子像

对照方形窟，中心塔柱窟的弟子立像按法服披覆方式可分二型。

A 型：同方形窟所有弟子像[1]（图 74）。3 个，第 290 窟塔柱东、南、北面龛，第 428 窟塔柱四面龛，第 442 窟塔柱南、西、北面龛。

B 型*：上衣、大衣皆作“右袒式”披覆，有的大衣右肩系带（图 75）。1 个，第 290 窟塔柱南面龛。

图 74　第 428 窟彩塑弟子像

图 75　第 290 窟彩塑弟子像

(4) 造像组合

对照方形窟，中心塔柱窟的造像组合可分二型。

[1] 塑像中的弟子内着僧祇支，束下衣，上衣遮搭双肩，大衣作“右袒式”披覆。参见：1)《中国石窟·敦煌莫高窟》一，北京：文物出版社，1982 年，图版 174；2)《中国石窟雕塑全集》第 1 卷《敦煌》，重庆：重庆出版社，2001 年，图版 34-36、40、46。第 442 窟塔柱西面龛弟子大衣边缘似交系外翻，暂入此式。

A 型：一铺三身像，同方形窟 A 型。1 个，第 432 窟塔柱东面龛和南、西、北面下层龛。

B 型：一铺五身像，按造像题材下分二式。

Bi 式*：龛内塑一佛四菩萨。1 个，第 290 窟塔柱西面龛[1]，第 432 窟塔柱南、西、北上层龛。

Bii 式：同方形窟 B 型。3 个，第 290 窟塔柱东、南、北面龛，第 428、442 窟塔柱四面龛。

(5) 龛外影塑

中心塔柱四面龛的龛外两侧，以影塑形式代替方形窟佛龛的两侧壁画；按题材可分作三型。

A 型：龛外两侧影塑供养菩萨和化生。1 个，第 432 窟塔柱东面龛和南、西、北面下层龛。

B 型：龛外两侧影塑千佛。2 个，第 290、442 窟。

C 型：龛外两侧影塑供养菩萨。1 个，第 428 窟。

(6) 主尊衣褶[2]

对照方形窟，中心塔柱窟主尊衣褶仅有二型。

A 型：无。

B 型：同方形窟 B 型。1 个，第 432 窟塔柱南、西、北面上下层龛。

C 型：同方形窟 C 型（图 19d）。4 个，第 290[3]、428、442 窟塔柱四面龛，第 432 窟塔柱东面龛。

3. 壁画布局[4]

在题材布局这部分中，我们选择了龛内壁画、南北侧壁壁画、西壁壁画、东壁壁画和窟顶壁画五项进行类型学分析。

(1) 龛内壁画

对照方形窟，中心塔柱窟各龛内壁画有三型。

A 型：无。

---

[1] 第 290 窟塔柱西面龛内塑一交脚菩萨和二胁侍菩萨，龛外两侧再各塑一菩萨。暂入此式。

[2] 中心塔柱窟塑像的衣褶亦以佛像为准；第 290 窟塔柱西面龛主尊虽为交脚菩萨，但衣褶分析亦视作佛像。

[3] 第 290 窟佛像衣褶在阶梯式边缘再刻阴线，应为阶梯、阴线混合式。

[4] 第 432 窟主室四壁及窟顶壁画，皆为后代绘画覆盖，原画内容不清。

B 型：同方形窟 B 型。4 个，第 290 窟塔柱南、西、北面龛，第 432 窟塔柱东面龛，第 428、442 窟塔柱四面龛。

C 型：同方形窟 C 型。1 个，第 290 窟塔柱东面龛。

D 型*：龛内正壁画火焰背光，侧壁绘化生(图 76)和供养菩萨。1 个，第 432 窟塔柱南、西、北面下层龛。

图 76　第 432 窟化生童子

(2) 侧壁壁画

对照方形窟，中心塔柱窟南北两侧壁壁画可分二型。

A 型：同方形窟 A 型。

Ai-Aiii 式：无。

Aiv 式*：前部上画天宫伎乐，人字披下画禅定佛一铺，中画千佛，下画供养人，再下为药叉；后部上画天宫伎乐，中画千佛，下画供养人，再下为药叉(图 77)。2 个，第 290、442 窟。

B 型：同方形窟 B 型。

Bi-Bii 式：无。

Biii 式*：前部人字披下画说法图，通壁上部影塑千佛，中画说法图等，下画供养人行列[1]，再下为三角垂饰(图 78)。1 个，第 428 窟。

(3) 西壁壁画

---

[1] 第 428 窟四壁下部供养人行列有重绘现象。现将笔者实地踏查所看到的一些迹象以及对迹象的看法，分析如下：1) 现存四壁下部供养人行列，只有南壁西段的二排供养人，是最先画于壁面的。因为南壁(中层)西端的说法图中，东侧菩萨莲座的底轮廓线，叠压在下部供养人的头上。依据这种层位关系，我们可以确定其下部供养人(两排)是先于说法图绘出的。不过，与供养人同时的底层壁画内容是什么，底层是否有壁画，现难以断定，因为表层的说法图已将其全部覆盖。2) 东壁、北壁、西壁和南壁东段的供养人行列，皆为三排，其形体较南壁西段的为小，服饰也与之不同。现在东、北、西和南壁东段供养人行列的许多部位，都露出了底层的两排供养人。其服饰、形体均与南壁西段的供养人相同。据现存遗迹，表层供养人行列，仅仅是在底层供养人行列的表面粉刷一层白粉后绘出，而且是后于说法图等壁画绘出的，因为表层供养人行列的上边线，叠压在上述壁画的底边轮廓线上。3) 由上述遗迹，我们推测：a. 表层的三排供养人行列与底层的两排供养人，在时间上相差不远，或许同时。因为按照惯例，如果是后代重绘的壁画，通常于原画表面涂敷一层较厚的泥皮，然后于覆盖原画的泥层表面作画。b. 至于为何在这么短的时间内绘画两次，大概有两种可能：其一，当时供养人的数量过多，画两排安排不下，而改作三排。其二，为了强调千佛、说法图和故事画等，即强调窟内的宗教气氛，而将处于从属地位的供养人的形体缩小。供养人形体缩小后，留下的空间只有改绘三排。这里也不排除，此窟是利用前代洞窟重绘的。不过，就塔柱四面开单层龛这点来看，似乎又排除了利用前代洞窟重绘或重塑的可能性。当然，上述推测，只是笔者的主观臆度。要想获得较准确的答案，有待进一步研究。

西壁壁画，按题材和布局可分作二型。

A 型：上绘天宫伎乐，中画千佛，下画供养人，再下为药叉（图 79）。2 个，第 290、442 窟。

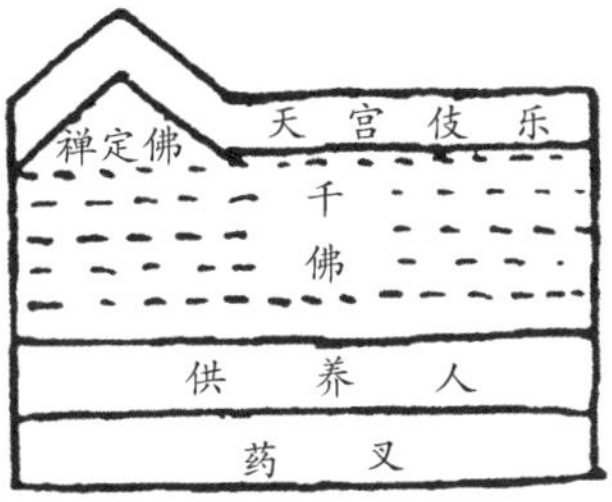

图 77　第 290 窟侧壁壁画题材布局示意图

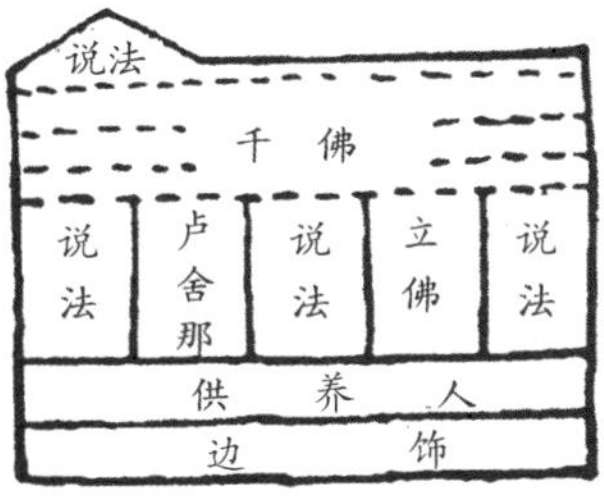

图 78　第 428 窟侧壁壁画题材布局示意图

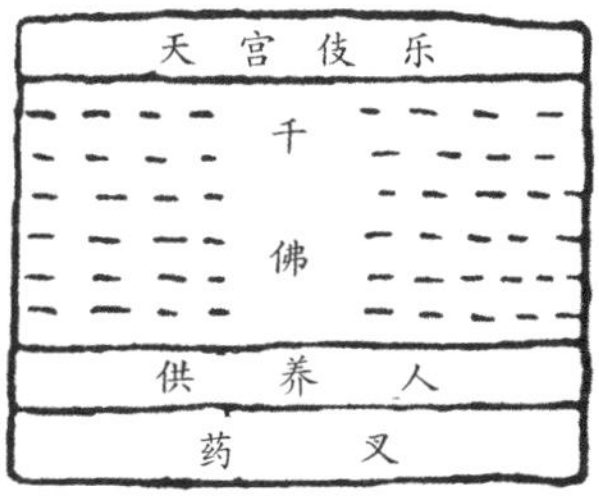

图 79　第 290 窟西壁壁画题材布局示意图

B 型：上部影塑千佛，中画说法图等，下画供养人，再下为三角形垂饰（图 80）。1 个，第 428 窟。

(4) 东壁（前壁）壁画[1]

对照方形窟，中心塔柱窟东壁壁画有二型。

A 型：无。

B 型：无。

C 型*：门上方及南北侧影塑千佛，千佛之下画故事画，再下绘供养人和三角形垂饰（图 81）。1 个，第 428 窟。

D 型*：上画天宫伎乐，中画千佛，下画供养人及供养车马，再下为药叉（图 82）。1 个，第 290 窟。

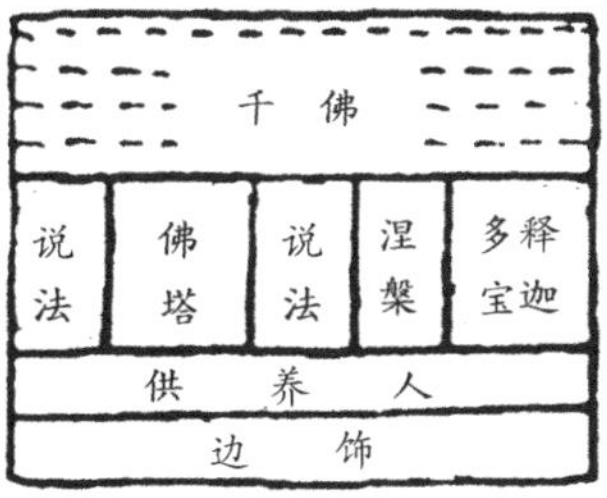

图 80　第 428 窟西壁壁画题材布局示意图

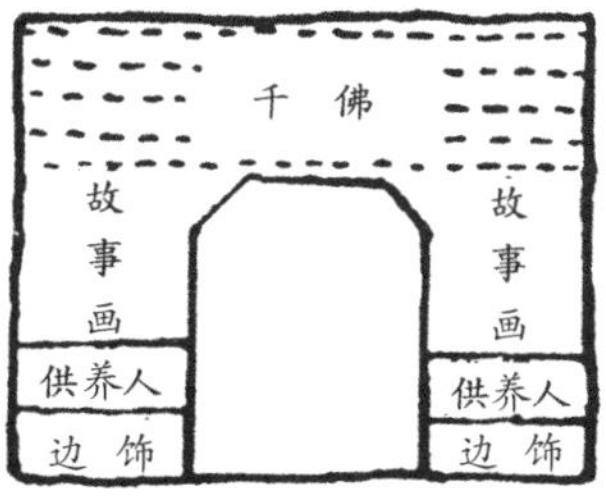

图 81　第 428 窟东壁壁画题材布局示意图

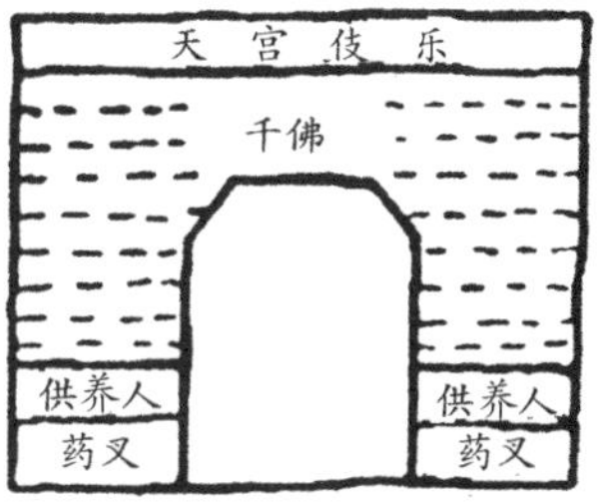

图 82　第 290 窟东壁壁画题材布局示意图

(5) 窟顶壁画

对照方形窟，中心塔柱窟窟顶壁画仅有一型。

A 型：无。

---

［1］第 442 窟前壁已塌毁，原画内容不清。

B 型：同方形窟 B 型。3 个，第 290、428、442 窟。

4. 壁画中个体形象及技法

(1) 菩萨像

对照方形窟，中心塔柱窟壁画中的菩萨像可分二型。

Ai 式：同方行窟 Ai 式。4 个，第 290、428、432、442 窟。

Aii-Aiii 式：无。

B 型：同方行窟 B 型，1 个，第 428 窟。

(2) 千佛

对照方形窟，中心塔柱窟的千佛壁画仅有一型。

A 型：无。

B 型：同方形窟 B 型。

Bi 式：无。

Bii 式：同方形窟 Bii 式。3 个，第 290、428[1]、442 窟。

Biii 式：无。

(3) 天宫伎乐

对照方形窟，中心塔柱窟的天宫伎乐壁画可分二型。

A 型：同方形窟 A 型。1 个，第 442 窟。

B 型：同方形窟 B 型。1 个，第 290 窟。

(4) 飞天

对照方形窟，中心塔柱窟壁画中的飞天有三型。

A 型：同方形窟 A 型。

Ai 式：同方形窟 Ai 式。4 个，第 290、428、432、442 窟。

Aii-Aiii 式：无。

B型：同方形窟B型。2个，第290、428窟。

C 型：无。

D型*：裸体飞天。飞天全身裸露，戴项饰，披披巾，肢体修长（图 83）。1 个，第 428 窟。

图 83　第 428 窟飞天

(5) 供养人像

甲、男供养人

对照方形窟，中心塔柱窟内的供养人或比

[1] 第 428 窟千佛虽为影塑，但性质与壁画同。暂入此式。

丘画像分四型。

A 型：同方形窟 A 型。1 个，第 428 窟。

B 型：同方形窟 B 型（图 84）。2 个，第 290、428 窟。

C 型：同方形窟 C 型。3 个，第 290、428、442 窟。

D 型：同方形窟 D 型。1 个，第 290 窟。

乙、女供养人

对照方形窟，中心塔柱窟内女供养人像可分二型。

A 型：同方形窟 A 型（图 85）。1 个，第 428 窟。

B 型：同方形窟 B 型（图 86）。1 个，第 442 窟。

图 84　第 428 窟男供养人

图 85　第 428 窟女供养人

图 86　第 442 窟女供养人

(6) 菩萨面部晕染

对照方形窟，中心柱窟中的菩萨面部晕染方式仅有一型。

A 型：无。

B 型：同方形窟 B 型。

Bi 式：同方形窟 Bi 式。2 个，第 432、442 窟。

Bii 式：同方形窟 Bii 式。2 个，第 290、428 窟。

5. 故事画构图

对照方形窟，中心塔柱窟中故事画的构图有二型。

A 型：无。

B 型：无。

C 型*：故事画构图作 S 或“已”形排列，形成情节完整的连环图画。2 个，第 290、428 窟。

D 型*：故事画作单幅构图。1 个，第 428 窟。

（四）中心塔柱窟的分组

中心塔柱窟五个部分的考古类型学分析大体如上。经过排比，这四座中心塔柱窟可以分作前后两组（见表二）。

第一组：第 432 窟。

第二组：第 442、428、290 窟。

第一组只有第 432 窟一座。该窟塔柱形制为 A 型，佛龛样式多为 A 型或 Bi 式。佛像多作 Ai 式。菩萨像多为 C、D 型，龛外两侧影塑为 A 型，造像组合为 A 型或 Bi 式，主尊衣褶处理多用 B 型。龛内壁画多为 D 型。这些都是北魏和西魏洞窟[1]所具有的特征，为第二组洞窟所不见或少见，因而，第 432 窟早于第二组洞窟。

第二组的三座中心柱窟，塔柱形制均为 B 型，龛式多用 Bii 式。佛像多为 Bii 式或 Aiii 式，造像中出现了弟子像，造像组合多为 Bii 式，主尊衣褶处理采用 C 型。龛内壁画多为 B 型。这些特征多不见第 432 窟，而为隋代洞窟[2]所普遍采用。因而，第二组洞窟晚于第 432 窟。

（五）北朝晚期洞窟的分期

由于中心塔柱窟数量甚少，自身无法代表这一时期洞窟的发展序列。经过实地考察，我们发现：塔柱窟的窟龛形制、造像题材、壁画布局以及壁画中几类个体形象等，皆与方形窟的相应部分大致相同或接近。因此，对照方形窟的相关部分，我们可将上述四座中心塔柱窟分别归入方形窟的三组序列之中。

第 432 窟的佛龛样式（Bi 式）、造像组合（A 型）、衣褶制法（B 型）、飞天造型（Ai 式）和菩萨的面部晕染方式（Bi 式），大多与第 461 窟和第 438 窟的同类接近或相同。因此，我们将第 432 窟归入方形窟的第一组之中。

第 442 窟在窟顶结构（B 型）、佛龛样式（Bii 式）、佛像造型（Bii 式）、弟子像（A 型）、造像组合（Bii 式）、龛内壁画（B 型）、窟顶壁画（B 型）、千佛造型（Bii 式）等方面，多与第 430 窟的相关部分一致或接近，而第 428 窟和第 290 窟，许多方面与第 442 窟相同。又，第 290 窟佛龛样式、菩萨造型、造像组合、龛内壁画、千佛及天宫伎乐的构图等与第 294 窟和第 296 窟的相同或大体接近。基于上述，可将第 442、428、290

---

［1］参见《中国石窟·敦煌莫高窟》一，北京：文物出版社，1981 年，图版 66、108。

［2］参见《中国石窟·敦煌莫高窟》二，北京：文物出版社，1984 年，图版 19。

表二　中心塔柱窟各部分类型表

<table>
<tr><th colspan="2" rowspan="2">项目 / 型式 / 窟号</th><th colspan="3">窟龛形制</th><th colspan="6">造像题材、组合及技法</th><th colspan="5">壁画布局</th><th colspan="7">壁画中个体形象及技法</th><th>构图</th><th>分组</th></tr>
<tr><th>塔柱形制</th><th>窟顶结构</th><th>佛龛样式</th><th>佛像</th><th>菩萨</th><th>弟子</th><th>造像组合</th><th>龛外影塑</th><th>主尊衣褶</th><th>龛内</th><th>南北侧壁</th><th>西壁</th><th>东壁</th><th>窟顶</th><th>菩萨</th><th>千佛</th><th>天宫伎乐</th><th>飞天</th><th>男供养人</th><th>女供养人</th><th>面部晕染</th><th>故事画</th><th>组别</th></tr>
<tr><td rowspan="7">432</td><td colspan="2">E</td><td rowspan="7">A</td><td rowspan="7">B</td><td>Bii</td><td>Bii</td><td>Ai/Aii</td><td></td><td>A</td><td>A</td><td>C</td><td>B</td><td rowspan="7"></td><td rowspan="7"></td><td rowspan="7"></td><td rowspan="7"></td><td rowspan="7">Ai</td><td rowspan="7"></td><td rowspan="7"></td><td rowspan="7">Ai</td><td rowspan="7"></td><td rowspan="7"></td><td rowspan="7">Bi</td><td rowspan="7"></td><td rowspan="7">第一组</td></tr>
<tr><td rowspan="2">S</td><td>上</td><td>A</td><td>Ai</td><td>C/D</td><td></td><td>Bi</td><td></td><td>B</td><td></td></tr>
<tr><td>下</td><td>Bi</td><td>Ai</td><td>Ai/Aii</td><td></td><td>A</td><td>A</td><td>B</td><td>D</td></tr>
<tr><td rowspan="2">W</td><td>上</td><td>A</td><td>Ai</td><td>C/D</td><td></td><td>Bi</td><td></td><td>B</td><td></td></tr>
<tr><td>下</td><td>Bi</td><td>Aii</td><td>Ai</td><td></td><td>A</td><td>A</td><td>B</td><td>D</td></tr>
<tr><td rowspan="2">N</td><td>上</td><td>A</td><td>Ai</td><td>C/D</td><td></td><td>Bi</td><td></td><td>B</td><td></td></tr>
<tr><td>下</td><td>Bi</td><td>Ai</td><td>E</td><td></td><td>A</td><td>A</td><td>B</td><td>D</td></tr>
<tr><td rowspan="4">442</td><td colspan="2">E</td><td rowspan="4">B</td><td rowspan="4">B</td><td>Bii</td><td>Bii</td><td rowspan="4"></td><td></td><td>Bii</td><td>B</td><td>C</td><td>B</td><td rowspan="4">Aiv</td><td rowspan="4">A</td><td rowspan="4"></td><td rowspan="4">B</td><td rowspan="4">Ai</td><td rowspan="4">Bii</td><td rowspan="4">A</td><td rowspan="4">Ai</td><td rowspan="4">C</td><td rowspan="4">B</td><td rowspan="4">Bi</td><td rowspan="4"></td><td rowspan="12">第二组</td></tr>
<tr><td colspan="2">S</td><td>Bii</td><td>Bii</td><td>A</td><td>Bii</td><td>B</td><td>C</td><td>B</td></tr>
<tr><td colspan="2">W</td><td>Bii</td><td>Bii</td><td>A</td><td>Bii</td><td>B</td><td>C</td><td>B</td></tr>
<tr><td colspan="2">N</td><td>Bii</td><td>Bii</td><td>A</td><td>Bii</td><td>B</td><td>C</td><td>B</td></tr>
<tr><td rowspan="4">428</td><td colspan="2">E</td><td rowspan="4">B</td><td rowspan="4">B</td><td>Bii</td><td>Aiii</td><td>Ai/Aii</td><td>B</td><td>Bii</td><td>C</td><td>C</td><td>B</td><td rowspan="4">Biii</td><td rowspan="4">B</td><td rowspan="4">C</td><td rowspan="4">B</td><td rowspan="4">Ai/B</td><td rowspan="4">Bii</td><td rowspan="4"></td><td rowspan="4">Ai/B/D</td><td rowspan="4">A/B/C</td><td rowspan="4">A</td><td rowspan="4">Bii</td><td rowspan="4">C/D</td></tr>
<tr><td colspan="2">S</td><td>Bii</td><td>Aiii</td><td>Ai/Aiv</td><td>B</td><td>Bii</td><td>C</td><td>C</td><td>B</td></tr>
<tr><td colspan="2">W</td><td>Bii</td><td>Aiii</td><td>Ai</td><td>B</td><td>Bii</td><td>C</td><td>C</td><td>B</td></tr>
<tr><td colspan="2">N</td><td>Bii</td><td>Aiii</td><td>Aiv</td><td>B</td><td>Bii</td><td>C</td><td>C</td><td>B</td></tr>
<tr><td rowspan="4">290</td><td colspan="2">E</td><td rowspan="4">B</td><td rowspan="4">B</td><td>Bii</td><td>Bii</td><td>Ai/Aii</td><td>A</td><td>Bii</td><td>B</td><td>C</td><td>B</td><td rowspan="4">Aiv</td><td rowspan="4">A</td><td rowspan="4">D</td><td rowspan="4">B</td><td rowspan="4">Ai</td><td rowspan="4">Bii</td><td rowspan="4">B</td><td rowspan="4">Ai/B</td><td rowspan="4">B/C/D</td><td rowspan="4"></td><td rowspan="4">Bii</td><td rowspan="4">C</td></tr>
<tr><td colspan="2">S</td><td>Bi</td><td>Bii</td><td>Aii/Aiv</td><td>A/B</td><td>Bii</td><td>B</td><td>C</td><td>B</td></tr>
<tr><td colspan="2">W</td><td>Bi</td><td></td><td>Aii/Aiv/B/F</td><td></td><td>Bi</td><td>B</td><td>C</td><td>B</td></tr>
<tr><td colspan="2">N</td><td>Bi</td><td>Bi</td><td>Aiv/B</td><td>A</td><td>Bii</td><td>B</td><td>C</td><td>B</td></tr>
</table>

窟插入第430窟与第294窟之间，即归入方形窟的第二组之中。

这样，西魏末至隋初的15座洞窟，按照它们的窟龛形制、造像题材及组合、壁画布局及个体形象造型的类型及其分组，可以并为以下三期。

第一期：第432、461、438窟，3座。

第二期：第439、440、441、430、442、428、290、294、296窟，9座。

第三期：第299、297、301窟，3座。

三、各期洞窟的主要特点、相互关系及其年代

经过考古类型学分析，我们发现，莫高窟北朝晚期各期洞窟在形制、造像和壁画三方面，相互间既有承袭关系，彼此又有许多不同。现在我们按三期洞窟的先后次第，分述一下各期洞窟的主要特点及相互关系。尔后，对于各期洞窟的相对年代试作初步推测。

（一）第一期洞窟

第一期的洞窟形制，既有为隋唐以后普遍沿用的方形覆斗顶窟[1]，又有在北魏乃至西魏时期盛行的中心塔柱窟[2]。方形窟有的于西壁开龛（B型），有的不开龛（A型），窟顶皆为覆斗形（A型）。中心塔柱窟的塔柱形制为A型，顶为人字披式（B型），佛龛多为圆拱形，忍冬龛梁、束帛龛柱头（Ⅰ式或Bi式），同时也出现了龙首龛梁、覆莲龛柱头这种新的组合形式（Bii式）；少数佛龛为浅长方形（A型）。佛面相方圆而稍长（图87），多为结跏趺坐，大衣作通肩式披覆（Ai式）；少数为善跏趺坐，着褒衣博带式大衣（Bii式）。菩萨面形多为长方桶状（图88），服饰有四种：裙披式（Ai-Aii式）、通肩式（C型），斜披络腋、下着裙（D型），汉式大袖长袍（E型）。造像组合多为一佛二菩萨（A型），少数为一佛四菩萨（Bi式），主尊大衣褶襞大多采用阴线式（B型），或贴泥条式（A型），新出现了阶梯式（C型）。壁画中佛、菩萨像的造型，与塑像基本相同，略有差异。壁画中的弟子，内着僧祇支，上衣覆搭双肩，有的于胸前束带作结下垂；大衣作“右袒式”披覆（图89）。主室的壁画布局，龛内正壁多绘火焰背光，侧壁画

[1] 这种洞窟最早出现在第272窟。不过其覆斗顶坡度平缓，且坡面略呈凹弧状。西魏第249窟，应该是莫高窟现存最早的典型覆斗顶窟。这种窟形，可能意在模仿传统的覆斗形“小帐”，隋唐以后普遍流行。以莫高窟隋代洞窟为例，在保存较好的80座洞窟中，覆斗顶窟就有50座，占总数的62.5%。

[2] 敦煌这种中心塔柱窟，应是在云冈和巩县中心柱窟（塔庙窟）基础上的进一步演化。属于西魏以前的21座洞窟，中心塔柱窟共12座，占总数的57%。

图 87　第 438 窟佛像头部

图 88　第 432 窟菩萨像头部

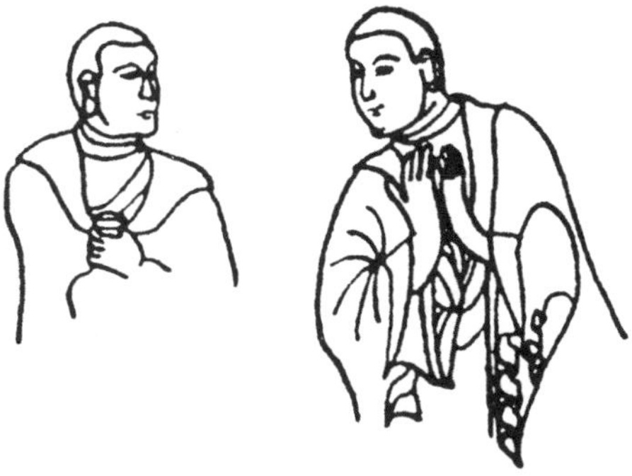

图 89　第 461 窟壁画弟子像

飞天、供养菩萨、弟子等（B 型）；有的侧壁绘化生和供养菩萨（D 型）。南北两侧壁壁画，有的上绘帷幔，中画千佛，下绘三角边饰（Ai 式）；有的壁面大部分画千佛，下画供养人，再下为药叉或边饰（Aiii 式）。方形窟的覆斗顶中央画斗四莲花井心，垂角帷幔铺于四坡，下画天宫伎乐（Ai 式）；有的于天宫伎乐之上加绘故事画（Aii 式）。千佛造型有两种：一为通肩与褒衣博带式法服相间画出，四个一组（A 型）；另一种法服均为通肩式，基本八个一组（Bi 式）。天宫伎乐构图也为两种：一种是圆拱形与汉式屋形天宫相间，伎乐天居宫舞乐（A 型）；另一种是新出现的，画面上不绘天宫楼阁，仅画出象征性的凹凸平台，伎乐天于上方凌空舞乐（B 型）。第一期的飞天，有的袒上身，下着裙，双足外露，披巾于头后扬成一大圆环（Ai 式）；有的头束鬟髻，着汉式对襟大袖长袍（B 型）。由于四壁底部保存不好，或者被后代壁画覆盖，第一期的供养人，仅见到大衣作“右袒式”披覆（A 型）和内着上衣、大衣衣摆于胸前交系外翻（B 型）两种形式。这一时期菩萨和某些飞天的面部染法，既有西魏出现的中原式面颊染色块的形式（A 型）[1]，又有西域式的凹凸晕染法（Bi 式），二者并存。主题故事画的构图，既有横卷式连续构图（A 型），又有“凹”形连环画构图形式（B 型），后者系在前者基础上演变而来。第一期的纹样，总的说来较为简单，计有单叶波状忍冬

[1] 参见《中国石窟・敦煌莫高窟》一，北京：文物出版社，1981 年，图版 113、126。

纹（图 90）、云气纹（图 91）、龙头忍冬卷草纹（图 92）、缠枝花草（图 93）和缠枝忍冬禽鸟图案（图 94）等。颜色的使用，这一时期还沿袭西魏时期的旧制，较多使用湛蓝色。

图 90　第 438 窟纹样

图 91　第 461 窟纹样

图 92　第 461 窟纹样

图 93　第 432 窟纹样

图 94　第 438 窟纹样

第一期洞窟的许多特点，如中心塔柱窟的 A 型塔柱形制、方形窟的 A 型平面布局，Ⅰ式或 Bi 式佛龛、Ai 式佛像，C、D、E 型菩萨像，A 型和 Bi 式造像组合，A 型佛衣褶襞，A 型龛外两侧影塑或 A、B 型龛外两侧壁画，A 型和 Bi 式千佛、A 型菩萨面部晕染法，释迦多宝并坐之题材以及大量使用湛蓝色等，皆不见于第二期，而大多接近西魏洞窟的特征。至于 B 型平面布局，Ⅱ式或 Bii 式佛龛，Bii 式佛像、Aii 式菩萨像、C 型主尊衣褶，B 型龛内壁画、Aiii 式侧壁壁画，Aii 式窟顶壁画，壁画中 Ai 式菩萨像造型、B 型天宫伎乐、B 型飞天、B 型故事画构图等，又为第二期洞窟继续沿用。

既然第一期洞窟的许多特征被第二期洞窟继续沿用，表明第一期洞窟与第二期洞窟之间有承袭关系；而第一期洞窟中不见于第二期洞窟的那些特征，与莫高窟西魏中期以前洞窟大多接近。因此，第一期洞窟晚于西魏中期、早于第二期是很明显的。结合敦煌当时的历史，我们认为敦煌莫高窟北朝晚期洞窟的上限，即第一期洞窟的上限，“始于西魏大统十一年”之说[1]是可信的。至于第一期洞窟的下限，如果考虑到西魏中期以后敦煌的历史，我们发现，西魏大统十二年（546 年）继邓彦之后，成庆任瓜州刺史，但不久就为张保所杀。同年，被授“河西大使、密令图彦”的申徽，以

[1] 樊锦诗、马世长、关友惠，上引书，第 197 页。

其“信洽西土”,刺史瓜州。“在州五稔(年),俭约率下,边人乐而安之。”[1]魏废帝元年(551年)至魏恭帝(554-556年)初,性情清静的王子直“行瓜州事……务以德政化民,西土悦附”[2]。京兆望族韦瑱,于魏恭帝三年(556年)“除瓜州诸军事、瓜州刺史,州通西域,蕃夷往来……瑱雅性清俭,兼有武略。蕃夷赠遗,一无所受。胡人畏威,不敢为寇。公私安静,夷夏怀之”[3]。通过研讨上述文献,我们认为:一方面,由于这几位“政绩”突出刺史的统治,这一时期的敦煌应该说是比较安定的;但从另一方面来看,他们不奉佛教(至少从笔者目前所见到的文献看是这样),因而不会给敦煌的佛教信仰带来多大的影响,也不会对当时的开窟造像活动产生多大的推动作用。这一时期洞窟数量少,题材和内容多沿袭旧制、很少新东西,大概与之不无关系。因此我们估计:第一期洞窟的下限,应在北周明帝宇文毓统治时期。这样,莫高窟北朝晚期第一期洞窟的年代,约在西魏大统十一年至北周明帝武成二年之间,即545-560年左右。

(二)第二期洞窟

第二期洞窟的建筑形制也有两种:一为方形窟,一为中心塔柱窟。不过这一期的两种窟形,均较第一期的两种形制有了一些变化。方形窟的某些窟顶,凿成了前人字披、后平顶的新型式(B型),这似乎是由中心塔柱窟的窟顶演变而来。中心塔柱窟较前期的明显变化是塔柱四面皆开单层龛(B型),佛龛皆为尖楣圆拱形,大多为龙首龛梁、覆莲龛柱头(Ⅱ式或Bii式);少数沿袭旧制,龛梁尾部饰忍冬,龛柱头束帛(Bi式)。

图95　第428窟佛像头部

第二期洞窟中的佛像,面形方圆丰满(图95)。从造型通体比例看,头大、上身长、下身短。佛大多善跏趺坐,内着僧祇支,上衣覆搭双肩,有的束带打结,外着褒衣博带式大衣(塔柱窟的Bii式和方形窟内的所有佛像);少数结跏趺坐,外着褒衣博带式大衣(Aiii式);个别佛像善跏趺坐,大衣作通肩式披覆(Bi式)。菩萨像面形与佛像相同(图96),服饰多为裙披式,富于变化,有Ai式、Aii式、Aiv式之分,出现了上着僧祇支,下穿长裙(B型)和上着

[1]《北史・申徽传》,点校本,北京:中华书局,1974年,第2390页。

[2]《周书・王子直传》,点校本,北京:中华书局,1971年,第701页。

[3]《周书・韦瑱传》,点校本,北京:中华书局,1971年,第694页。

对襟小衫、下穿长裙 (F 型) 两种新形式。第二期洞窟中新出现的弟子像，一开始便塑造出了二人年龄上的差异。阿难面相方圆丰满，年少聪俊，为一汉僧形象；迦叶则塑成胡貌，高鼻深目，大眼宽腮，瘦骨松肌，一副老态 (图 97)，个别的迦叶像，还塑造出西域式的连眉[1]。弟子大多内着僧衹支，束下衣，上衣遮搭双肩，大衣作“右袒式”披覆 (塔柱窟的 A 型和方形窟内的所有弟子像)；少数上衣、大衣皆作“右袒式”披覆，有的大衣于右肩束带 (B 型)。与一期洞窟相比，第二期洞窟的又一变化是造像的组合。这一期的彩塑，均为一铺五身，除第 290 窟中心塔柱西龛内为一交脚菩萨坐像、二胁侍菩萨立像和龛外两侧各塑一菩萨立像外，其余龛内造像皆为一佛二弟子，龛外两侧各一立菩萨 (B 型或 Bii 式)，即较一期洞窟增加了二弟子形象。而这种一铺五身像之组合，对我们来说是有绝对分期意义的。造像衣褶，主要采用阶梯式 (C 型)，个别为阴线式 (B 型)。

图 96　第 290 窟菩萨像头部

图 97　第 430 窟弟子像头部

图 98　第 428 窟壁画佛像

壁画中佛、弟子和菩萨像，基本上与塑像相同，略有差异。有的佛像内着僧衹支，大衣偏覆右肩，结跏趺坐于须弥座上 (图 98)。有的菩萨着通肩式大衣。

第二期洞窟的壁画布局：龛内正壁绘火焰背光，侧壁有的画飞天、供养菩萨、弟子等 (B 型)；有的侧壁上绘弟子、飞天和菩萨，下画鹿头梵志和婆薮仙 (C 型)。南、北两侧壁壁画，有的上绘天宫伎乐、三角边饰等，中画千佛，下绘供养人 (Aii 式)；有的壁面上部画千佛，中绘说法图或故事画等，下绘供养人或药叉 (Bi-Biii 式)；也有的上画天宫伎乐，前部人字披下画禅定佛一铺，中画千佛，下绘供养人等 (Aiv 式)。窟顶壁画，方形窟覆斗顶中央画斗四莲花井心，垂角、帷幔等铺于四坡，下画故事画，再

[1] 参见《中国石窟 · 敦煌莫高窟》一，北京：文物出版社，1981 年，图版 159。

下为天宫伎乐 (Aii 式)。中心塔柱窟于前部人字披画忍冬、莲花、摩尼宝珠等图案,个别的画故事画；后部画斗四莲花、忍冬和飞天等 (B 型)。

第二期洞窟中千佛的比重增大,除画在四壁之外,个别窟还画到了窟顶。千佛构图皆为 Bii 式。这一期的天宫伎乐,除第 442 窟仍袭北魏和西魏普遍采用的旧制 (A 型) 之外,其余各窟皆为 B 型。洞窟中的飞天,种类增多,形象丰富,姿态变化较大。除沿袭一期的 Ai 式和 B 型飞天外,新出现了裸体飞天 (D 型)。二期洞窟中的男供养人除沿袭第一期的 A、B 型外,新出现了 C、D 型两种形式。女供养人的服饰有两种：一种内着白纱裙,外着对襟大袖襦 (A 型),裙襦外,有的加搭披帛,有的罩圆领长袖大衣；另一种上着窄袖衫,下系曳地长裙,披帔帛 (B 型)。菩萨的面部,主要采用 Bii 式晕染法。

第二期洞窟中,故事画的数量较第一期明显增加,出现了许多新题材,如《须大拏太子本生》、《独脚仙人本生》、《梵志夫妇摘花坠死缘》、《微妙比丘尼缘品》等。此外,还出现了情节达 87 幅之多的长篇佛传及福田经变[1]。构图上,既有横卷式的连环画形式 (A 型),也有数条并列、情节呈 S 或"己" 形走向的连续经营 (C 型),还有因地制宜、充分利用壁面的"凹" 形构图 (B 型) 以及单幅构图 (D 型)。

这一期洞窟中的纹样,仍以忍冬纹为主,除第 428 窟较多地沿用旧式,如单叶波状忍冬纹 (参见图 103)、连锁忍冬纹 (图 99)、单叶藤蔓分枝忍冬纹 (图 100)、散点花叶纹 (图 101) 等之外,其他各窟多为前期不见或少见的双叶交茎套联忍冬纹 (图 102)、双叶分枝回卷忍冬纹 (图 104)、四出忍冬纹 (图 105)、禽鸟忍冬图案 (图 106)。

图 99　第 428 窟纹样

图 100　第 428 窟纹样

图 101　第 428 窟纹样

图 102　第 294 窟纹样

[1] 史苇湘《福田经变简论》,见《向达先生纪念论文集》,乌鲁木齐：新疆人民出版社,1986 年,第 300-312 页。

图 103　第 290 窟纹样

图 104　第 439 窟纹样

图 105　第 442 窟纹样

图 106　第 296 窟纹样

综上所述，莫高窟北朝晚期第二期洞窟，在窟龛形制、造像组合、造像特征、壁画布局以及塑绘技法等方面都发生了较大的变化，出现了许多新特征，有些还是第二期洞窟所特有的，如 Bii 式晕染法、D 型飞天等。为了推测第二期洞窟的年代，我们拟从两方面试作论证。

第二期洞窟中，也没有明确的开窟纪年。不过，有些洞窟的供养人题记，对我们推测其相对的开凿年代有较大帮助。

第 428 窟东壁门南表层供养人行列，上排北起第三身题作“晋昌郡沙门比丘庆仙供养”，同列第四身题名为“晋昌郡沙门比丘□志供养”[1]。

据宋人乐史《太平寰宇记》卷一百五十三《陇右道》“瓜州”条，“晋惠帝始分置晋昌郡……至凉武昭王遂以南人置会稽郡，以中州人置广夏郡。至后周初并之，复为晋昌郡。至武帝改晋昌为永兴郡。隋初罢郡，立瓜州。炀帝初废之，以其地并入敦煌。至唐武德五年 (622 年) 复立为瓜州……天宝元年 (742 年) 改为晋昌郡。乾元元年 (758 年) 复为瓜州”[2]。

由上我们知道，宋太平兴国时期 (976-984 年) 乐史撰《太平寰宇记》之前，敦煌地区设置晋昌郡共三次：一为西晋，一为北周，最晚一次为唐天宝元年。莫高窟第 428 窟，从窟龛形制、塑像、壁画以及塑绘技法等方面来看，既不会早至西晋，也不会

[1] 1) 史岩《敦煌石室画像题识》，石印本，成都：华西大学比较文化研究所、国立敦煌艺术研究所、华西大学博物馆，1947 年，第 73 页；2) 谢稚柳，上引书，第 279 页；3) 敦煌研究院编《敦煌莫高窟供养人题记》，北京：文物出版社，1986 年，第 160 页；4) Paul Pelliot, *Mission Paul Pelliot documents archéologiques XI; Grottes de Touen-houang: Carnet de Notes de Paul Pelliot, inscriptions et peintures murale, V*, eds. , N. Vandier-Nicolas et M. Maillard. Paris: Collège de France, 1986: Grotte 135.

[2] 乐史《太平寰宇记》，王文楚等点校，北京：中华书局，2007 年，第 2959 页。

晚到唐天宝时期。所以这条题记的时间,上限应在北周初(557年),下限为周武帝宣政元年(578年)病死之前。又,建德三年(574年)武帝“法难”曾波及到瓜州(详见附录二),故题记的书写时间应在建德三年之前,而开窟的时间也应在此之前。

据敦煌遗书S. 2935号《大比丘尼羯磨经一卷》尾题:“天和四年岁次己丑六月八日(569年7月7日)写竟,永晕(晖)寺尼智瓆受持供养,比丘庆仙抄讫。”[1]尾题中的庆仙,很可能是在第428窟题名的比丘庆仙[2]。假如这一推断成立,那么比丘庆仙于天和四年仍在从事佛事活动。不过尾题中为何没有题写晋昌郡,却是一个有待探讨的问题,是由于天和四年晋昌郡已改置,还是因受雇于人、不便题写地名?我们认为两种可能性都存在。不过,比丘庆仙的画像及题名出现在第428窟东壁,从另一方面证实第428窟开凿于北周初(557年)至武帝建德三年(574年)之间,即公元557-574年。

莫高窟第442窟北壁西侧供养人行列,现存第七身供养人(自东向西)题名为“弟……主簿鸣沙县丞张缌供养佛时”[3]。据法国伯希和1908年考察敦煌莫高窟时所做的笔记[4],还可将这条题记补充为“弟子□州主簿鸣沙县丞张缌供养佛时”。

据唐人李吉甫《元和郡县志》卷四十《陇右道》下“瓜州”条:“敦煌县,本汉旧县,属敦煌郡。周武帝改为鸣沙县,以界有鸣沙山,因以为名。隋大业二年(606年),复为敦煌。”[5]又《太平寰宇记》卷一百五十三《陇右道》“沙州”条:“后周保定三年(563年)改敦煌为鸣沙县,以县界鸣沙山为名。隋初复为敦煌县。”[6]

因此,我们认为:第442窟北壁供养人题名,应是保定三年改为鸣沙县后迄隋大业二年复为敦煌县之间所题。这样,第442窟的开凿时间不会早于北周保定三年(563年)[7]。

第二期洞窟之所以发生这样大的变化,出现这么多新题材、新内容、新布局、新构

---

[1] 商务印书馆编《敦煌遗书总目索引》,北京:商务印书馆,1962年,第169页。

[2] 贺世哲《敦煌莫高窟供养人题记校勘》,见《中国史研究》,第3期(1980年),第29页。

[3] 敦煌研究院编,上引书,第166页。

[4] Paul Pelliot, *opere citato:* Grotte 120s.

[5] 李吉甫《元和郡县图志》,贺次君点校,北京:中华书局,1983年,第1026页。

[6] 乐史,上引书,第2956页。

[7] 至于第442窟的下限,据同排第八身供养人题名“弟子武将军帅都督前敦煌郡主簿张𫘝”可作进一步推测。“帅都督”一职,据《周书·武帝纪》,天和五年(570年)夏四月,“省帅都督官”;建德二年(573年)春正月“庚戌,复置帅都督官”。结合第442窟中许多旧的因素,如天宫伎乐构图(A型)和飞天造型(Ai式)等,我们推测该窟的下限,不应在建德二年复置帅都督官以后,而应在天和五年省此官之前。这样,第442窟的年代大约可定在保定三年至天和五年之间,即563-570年左右。当然,在没有找到确切的年代资料以前,这只是我们的推测而已。

图以及新的塑绘技法等，应与当时的历史，尤其是佛教史有关。

北周受西魏禅，西魏相宇文泰，宇文泰子北周明帝宇文毓，泰兄子北周大冢宰宇文护，都是笃信佛教的。"当泰执西魏国柄，护总北周权重时，关西一地，佛法逾盛，译筵频开。"[1]北周武帝可能早年受其父兄的影响，"初本循例事佛，造功德"[2]。曾于"武成二年(560年)为文皇帝造锦释迦像，高一丈六尺，并菩萨圣僧、金刚狮子周回宝塔二百二十躯……造宁国、会昌、永宁等三寺……凡度僧尼一千八百人，所写经论一千七百余部"[3]。周武帝还"遵贤待德……敕公卿、近臣、妃后、外戚咸受十善，因奉三归"[4]，并"特所钦承，乃下敕'释昙崇'为周国三藏，年任陟岵寺主"[5]，后"祈请"倡禅于长安的释僧实，为周"国三藏"[6]。"建德中年"，授昙延为"国统"[7]。另外，建德元年(572年)以前，北周大权实际上掌握在大冢宰宇文护之手[8]，而宇文护是十分崇奉佛法的[9]。在皇帝的倡导下，王公大臣大多佞佛，据不完全统计，北周一代，共有30人之多[10]。由于他们的倡导与影响，佛教又得到了进一步发展，各地讲经说法，开窟造像活动十分盛行。

敦煌莫高窟北朝晚期第二期洞窟，开始出现了具有分期意义的新的造像组合形式——一佛二弟子二菩萨，同时出现了许多新特征。这使我们有理由推想：信奉佛教的大将军段永(详见附录一)，于北周武成二年至保定二年(560-562年)刺史瓜州；任职期间，曾请高僧于斋上讲经说法。西京盛族李贤继段永之后，自保定二年至四年(562-564年)接任瓜州刺史。李贤是北周著名显贵之一，史称李门"声彰内外，位高望重，光国荣家……冠冕之盛，当时莫比焉。自周迄隋，郁为西京盛族"[11]。他与宇文家族过从甚密，以致宇文泰曾将幼时的宇文邕和宇文宪寄养在李贤家达六年之久。刺史瓜州期间，虽"分竹敦煌，仍专万里之务"[12]；而周武帝亦"思贤旧恩"，值保定三

[1] 王仲荦《北周六典》，北京：中华书局，1979年，第213页。
[2] 汤用彤《汉魏两晋南北朝佛教史》，北京：中华书局，1983年，第389页。
[3]《辩正论》卷三《十代奉佛篇》上，《大正藏》第52卷，第508b页。
[4]《续高僧传·释僧玮传》，《大正藏》第50卷，第558b页。
[5]《续高僧传·释昙崇传》，上引书，第568b页。
[6]《续高僧传·释僧实传》，上引书，第558a页。
[7]《续高僧传·释昙延传》，上引书，第488b-c页。
[8]《周书·晋荡公护传》，点校本，北京：中华书局，1971年，第175页。
[9] 费长房《历代三宝记》，《大正藏》第49卷，第94-101页。
[10]《辩正论》卷四《十代奉佛篇》下，上引书，第517-518页。
[11]《周书·李贤传》，点校本，北京：中华书局，1971年，第424页。
[12]《大周柱国河西公墓铭》，见《文物》，1985年第11期，第19页。

年“七月戊辰(563年8月10日)行幸原州”之时,并“幸贤第……令中侍上士尉迟恺往瓜州,降玺书劳贤……”[1]虽然文献没有言明李贤信奉佛教,但既然宇文泰家族佞佛,公卿宠臣大多笃信佛法,想必他也会受到一定的影响,即使他不奉佛,至少在当时也不会反对佛教活动。至于在莫高窟“修一大窟”的建平公于义,自中原西刺瓜州,当在周武帝建德三年(574年)灭佛道之前的北周盛世,曾为莫高窟“弘其迹”[2]。

因此,第二期洞窟发生的较大变化和出现的许多新东西,与段永、李贤和于义等刺史瓜州不无关系,有些特征,应该是他们从东方带来的。广义地说,是受当时全国上下佞佛风气的影响产生的。

由于佛教的迅速发展,寺院占有肥沃的土地,僧尼又皆享受免除租、调和徭役的特权[3]。这样势必加重编户人口的赋役,长此下去阶级矛盾必定激化,关陇统治集团的政权一定会动摇。另外,北周武帝要完成消灭北齐、统一中原的大业,必须励精图治,富国强兵。于是,他便采取“求兵于僧众之间,取地于塔庙之下”[4]的政策,于建德三年五月“丙子(574年6月21日),初断佛、道二教,经像悉毁,罢沙门、道士,并令还民。并禁诸淫祀,礼典所不载者,尽除之”[5]。周武帝的这次灭佛,也曾波及到了瓜州,致使莫高窟的开窟造像活动受到了影响(详见附录二)。

基于上述两方面的分析,我们估计:莫高窟北朝晚期第二期洞窟的上限,应在明帝宇文毓统治后期,即段永刺史瓜州之后;下限不会晚于建德三年北周武帝灭佛之前,即公元560-574年之间。

(三)第三期洞窟

第三期洞窟,只有覆斗顶正壁一龛窟单一形制,佛龛样式为Ⅱ式。

佛像的面相及服饰基本同二期。从整体上看,这期佛像较第二期更趋头大,上身长,下肢短;菩萨像大多臂长,腿短,腹部渐圆突。菩萨的服饰,出现了披巾横于腹前两道的新型式(Aiii式),弟子像的造型同第二期。造像组合及衣褶,皆沿袭第二期旧制。

壁画中的佛、弟子和菩萨,与塑像基本相同,但略有差异。第301窟南壁说法图

---

[1]《周书·李贤传》,上引书,第417页。

[2] 1)宿白《敦煌莫高窟早期洞窟杂考》,上引书,第408-410页;2)宿白《东阳王与建平公》(二稿),上引书,第45-49页。

[3] 任继愈主编《中国佛教史》第三卷,北京:中国社会科学出版社,1988年,第64页。

[4] 道宣《广弘明集》卷二十四昙积《谏周祖沙汰僧表》,《大正藏》第52卷,第279b页。

[5]《周书·武帝纪》,点校本,北京:中华书局,1971年,第85页。

中的佛像(图107),肉髻低平,面相方正,外着褒衣博带式田相大衣,坐于束腰须弥座上。佛的坐姿较为特殊,与其说结跏趺坐,不如说交脚坐更为合适,这是不见于第一、二期洞窟的新型式。菩萨的服饰,新出现了Aiii式。

图107　第301窟壁画佛像

第三期洞窟的壁画布局,大多与第二期相近,唯窟顶壁画新出现了Aiii式。千佛和天宫伎乐构图皆为二期旧制,分别为Bii式和B型。这一期的飞天新出现了C型。壁画中菩萨的两腮,均染圆圈(C型)。供养人的服饰和装饰纹样,与第二期洞窟基本相同。

故事画的数量较第二期明显减少,种类单一,只有本生故事,构图皆作"凹"形(B型)。

另外,第297窟西壁龛沿下出现的舞乐供养图(图108),是莫高窟罕见的题材。此窟的龛梁下还出现了莫高窟唯一的浮塑羽人像(图109)[1]。

图108　第297窟乐舞壁画(欧阳琳临本)

图109　第297窟羽人塑像

综上所述,我们看出:第三期洞窟中的许多特征,如B型平面布局、A型窟顶、Ⅱ式佛龛、Aii式菩萨像、B型造像组合、C型佛衣褶襞、Bii式千佛、B型天宫伎乐和故事画构图以及各部分的壁画布局等,都是二期特征的延续,这表明二、三期洞窟是有承袭关系的。

至于第三期洞窟中的许多新特点,如Aiii式菩萨像、Aiii式窟顶壁画布局、壁画中Aiii式菩萨像、C型飞天、C型菩萨面部晕染方式等,又不见第一、二期洞窟,而多为隋初洞窟大量采用[2]。这表明,第三期洞窟是晚于第二期的。

---

[1] 羽人是"儒家从神仙家那里接过来的"。洞窟中出现这种题材(莫高窟第249窟壁画最早出现了这种题材),反映出佛教思想与中国传统儒家思想在当时逐渐融合。这或与周武帝会通三教有关。参见北京大学历史系考古教研室编《中国考古学之五:三国—宋元考古》上,铅印本讲义,北京大学,1974年,第56页。

[2] 参见《中国石窟·敦煌莫高窟》二,北京:文物出版社,1984年,图版7、8、10、12、18、19。

不过,隋初洞窟,尤其是有开皇四年题记的第302和305窟的许多特征,如佛内着僧祇支,上衣遮搭双肩,大衣作“右袒式”披覆且以钩纽系之(图110),菩萨披巾于腹前交叉打结后饰璧之作法(图111),洞窟三壁三龛之布局和平面呈凸形的佛龛形制(参见图1),胁侍菩萨像进入龛内之作法以及天宫伎乐中象征性平台上加木质栏杆等[1],又都不见于第三期以前诸窟,因此,第三期洞窟早于隋初诸窟,又是显而易见的。换言之,第三期洞窟在时间上介于第二期与隋初诸窟之间,应是毫无疑问的。

图110　第305窟佛像

图111　第302窟菩萨塑像

关于北朝晚期洞窟,即第三期洞窟“下迄隋初开皇四、五年(584、585年)之前”[2]的判断,我们认为是可信的。至于第三期洞窟的上限,如果考虑到周武帝建德三年法难对敦煌的影响,那么这期洞窟的开凿,就应在武帝病死,“重隆佛日,光后超前”[3]的北周宣帝宇文赟继位之后。周宣帝于大成元年正月十五日(579年2月26日),下诏:“弘建玄风,三宝尊重,特宜修敬……其旧沙门中德行清高者七人,在正武殿西安置行道。二月二十六日(4月7日),改元大象。又敕:‘佛法弘大,千古共崇……’至四月二十八日(6月7日),下诏曰:‘佛义幽深,神奇弘大,必广开化义,通其修行。崇奉之徒,依经自检。遵道之人,勿须剪发’。……令选旧沙门中懿德贞洁、学业冲博、名实灼然、声望可嘉者一百二十人,在陟岵寺为国行道”[4]。尔后,宣帝于大象元年(579年)“冬十月壬戌(579年11月8日)……初复佛像及天尊像。至是,(宣)帝与二像

[1] 参见《中国石窟·敦煌莫高窟》二,上引书,图版6、27。

[2] 樊锦诗、马世长、关友惠《敦煌莫高窟北朝洞窟的分期》,上引书,第197页。

[3]《辩正论》卷三《十代奉佛篇》上,上引书,第508b页。

[4]《广弘明集》卷十《周高祖巡邺除殄佛法有前僧任道林上表请开法事》,《大正藏》第52卷,第156c-157a页。

俱南面而坐，大陈杂戏，令京城市民纵观”[1]。大象二年六月“庚申(580年7月3日)，复行佛、道二教，旧沙门、道士精诚自守者，简令入道”[2]。自此，佛教正式恢复。

1975年，敦煌文物研究所保护组(敦煌研究院保护研究所前身)对莫高窟第220窟宋修甬道进行搬迁，于甬道南壁宋代壁画下发现五代后唐同光三年(925年)翟奉达所写《检家谱》一方。《检家谱》位于甬道南壁小龛外，其内容有翟氏追述其先辈在莫高窟开窟造像的历史，“大成元年己亥岁(579年)□□迁于三峗□□镌龛□□□圣容立像……”[3]

据《通志》卷二十五《氏族略》序，“自隋唐而上，官有薄状，家有谱系；官之选举必由于簿状，家之婚姻必由于谱系……凡百官族姓之有家状者则上之，官为考定详实，藏于秘阁，副在左户。若私书有滥，则纠之以官籍；官籍不及，则稽之以私书……人尚谱系之学，家藏谱系之书”[4]。由此可见，谱牒在封建地主阶级的政治生活和婚姻关系等方面起着十分重要的作用。故而第220窟这条记载是可信的。“大成”是北周宣帝的年号，只有一年(579年)。这从另一方面证实：北周大成年间，莫高窟就已经恢复开窟造像活动了。

基于上述分析，我们认为：莫高窟北朝晚期第三期洞窟的上限，应在北周大象元年(579年)“初复佛像及天尊像”之后，不会早于宣政元年(578年)六月武帝崩殂以前[5]。这样，第三期洞窟的年代，大约在公元578-584年。

---

[1]《周书·宣帝纪》，点校本，北京：中华书局，1971年，第121页。

[2]《周书·静帝纪》，点校本，北京：中华书局，1971年，第132页。

[3] 敦煌文物研究所《莫高窟第220窟新发现的复壁壁画》，见《文物》，1978年第12期，第43-44页。

[4] 郑樵《通志》，影印万有文库十通本，北京：中华书局，1987年，第439页。

[5] 据笔者目前所知，周武帝建德三年(574年)灭佛后，现存最早的有明确纪年的“法难”之后的佛教造像，是北周宣政元年(578年)所造的一尊交脚像，原藏南朝鲜汉城李氏王室博物馆。这尊像，双脚由从地涌出的怪兽承托，手作转法轮印。身形背光较大，其外缘饰化佛和火焰纹；背光两侧，雕出双狮面部。座下浮雕两排供养人。

这尊像的造型较特别，有待进一步研究。不过值得注意的是，在佛教尚未恢复的宣政元年，雕造这样一身佛像与建德六年平齐后武帝改元宣政、遂欲统一中原北方的志向不符。因此，这尊像的出现可能与下述原因有关。据《广弘明集》卷十引《周高祖巡邺除殄佛法有前僧任道林上表请开法事》，宣政元年六月丁酉夜，武帝崩于乘舆，宣帝“登祚在同州。至九月十三日，长宗伯岐公奏讫。帝允许之，曰：‘佛理弘大，道极幽微。兴施有则，法须研究。如此累奏，恐有稽违’。奏曰‘臣本申事，止为兴法。数启殷勤，惟愿早行。今圣上允可，议曹奏决。上下含和，定无异趣。一日颁行，天下称庆’”(《大正藏》第52卷，第156c页)。由于朝廷意在恢复佛教，这一消息，用今天的话说，会很快透露、传播出去。佛教当时在北方，乃至全国有深厚的社会基础。善男信女、高僧大德早就盼望这一天的到来，以求精神上的解脱。在这样的历史背景下，这尊像出现在北周宣政元年也就没有什么奇怪的了。参见 Osavld Siren, *Chinese Sculpture from the fifth to the fourteenth century*, London: E. Benn, 1925, Vol. Ⅰ: 74; Vol. Ⅲ, Plate 277a.

四、莫高窟北朝晚期洞窟演变所反映的若干历史问题

综观莫高窟北朝晚期洞窟的主要特点和各期之间的相互关系，我们发现：北朝晚期洞窟的演变，既有本地因素，又有外来影响，而形成北朝晚期洞窟特点的各要素及产生这种变化的原因是错综复杂的。下面我们拟从渊源和流变两方面试对这个问题作一初步探讨。

(一)

经过与莫高窟早期洞窟、国内外各地石窟群以及其他零散造像进行比较，我们认为莫高窟北朝晚期洞窟演变的本地及外来因素，主要体现在下述几个方面。

从洞窟形制上看，北朝晚期洞窟的两种主要窟形，均较前期有了变化。中心塔柱窟，除第432窟塔柱形制为A型外，其余三窟皆采纳B型，即塔柱四面开单层龛。这种B型塔柱，在云冈第6、11窟早已出现[1]，后来巩县第1、3窟和须弥山石窟中也被大量使用[2]。在敦煌，它始见于西魏第248窟；至北周，在仅有的四座中心塔柱窟中使用率为3/4。这种形制，在新疆和中亚各地石窟群中罕见[3]。方形窟大多承袭西魏第249窟旧制，采用覆斗顶结构。这种窟顶，与敦煌魏晋墓覆斗形墓室顶，"在建筑形制上，明显地有着渊源关系"[4]。方形窟这时新出现的B型窟顶，即前部人字披、后部平顶的形式，应该是从中心塔柱窟窟顶移植过来的，因为这种窟顶不见于国内外其他石窟群[5]，是敦煌石窟特有的一种建筑形制。概而言之，北朝晚期，方形窟已占

[1] 水野清一、長廣敏雄《雲岡石窟：西曆五世紀における中國北部佛教窟院の考古學的調查報告》，東方文化研究所調查，昭和十三年至昭和二十年，京都：京都大學人文科學研究所，第三卷(1955年)：第28-35页；第八卷・第九卷(1953年)：第26-29页。

[2] 1)河南省文化局文物工作队编《巩县石窟寺》，北京：文物出版社，1963年，实测图第1-2、9-18页；2)宁夏回族自治区文物管理委员会、中央美术学院美术史系编《须弥山石窟》，北京：文物出版社，1988年，图版9、44、48-51、69-70、74、76、93。

[3] 库车森木塞姆第26窟平面为长方形，中央偏后有一方形塔柱，塔基为叠涩束腰式，塔身四面开龛。"就柱身而言，与内地的中心柱极为相似；但甬道为券顶，则是龟兹石窟所习见的。克孜尔的第99窟，柱身的四面开龛，与森木塞姆第26窟近似。克孜尔石窟的中心柱窟与以上二例，同属一种窟形，即同属具有龟兹特点的中心柱窟"。马世长《克孜尔中心柱窟研究》(硕士学位论文)，北京：北京大学，1982年，第9-10页。

[4] 敦煌文物研究所考古组《敦煌晋墓》，见《考古》，1974年第3期，第198页。

[5] 拜城克孜尔第77窟后室窟顶凿成具前后坡的梯形顶，敦煌石窟的人字披窟顶与之是否有关系值得研究。

绝大多数；这种窟形，更适于僧、俗观佛和礼拜，而“中心塔柱窟，是为了‘入塔再观’之用”[1]。

北朝晚期洞窟中的佛像，大多善跏趺坐，着褒衣博带式大衣。菩萨像的服饰，仍以裙披式为主。这些特征，大多是莫高窟北魏晚期和西魏时期洞窟的遗风。始见于西魏第288窟中心塔柱上的影塑千佛，此时在塔柱四面大量采用；这种形式，在隋代中心塔柱窟中不见。

洞窟四壁壁画的布局，沿袭北魏、西魏旧制，基本上有两种：其一，上画天宫伎乐，中画千佛或故事画，下绘药叉等；其二，壁面大部分画千佛，下绘供养人或边饰等。两者之中以后者占多数。

故事画的构图，除沿用早期单幅（D型）和情节连续铺排的横卷形式（A型）之外，新出现S形或“己”形构图（C型），应是在A型的基础上发展而来的。至于“凹”形构图（B型），则是画工为充分利用石窟壁面所创造的。

在充分利用本土因素，继承当地优良传统的前提下，这时的画工或雕塑匠人，也乐于博采东西方艺术之长，补己之短，借以提高自己的画塑艺术水平。

莫高窟北朝晚期洞窟中的佛像，皆作低平肉髻，面相方圆，眉细长，鼻高直，嘴角稍上翘；菩萨的面相与佛基本相同，只是冠饰繁丽。从通体比例来看，无论佛或菩萨，皆头大，上身长，下身短，形象丰壮[2]。这种特征，在麦积山[3]、须弥山[4]等石窟及其他零散造像[5]中都已大量采纳，尤其是形体丰壮这点，应是南朝张僧繇“骨气奇伟”[6]画风，即变重神骨而为“得其肉”[7]的完美体现。菩萨像的Aiii式服饰，即披巾

[1] 宿白《敦煌七讲》，油印本，敦煌：敦煌文物研究所，1962年，第42页。

[2] 这一时期，壁画中佛与菩萨的通体比例比较合适，只有彩塑的造型比例发生了变化。这是一个值得研究的问题。

[3] 郑振铎主编《麦积山石窟》，北京：文化部社会文化事业管理局，1954年，图版52、61、70、144。

[4] 宁夏回族自治区文物管理委员会、中央美术学院美术史系编，上引书，图版9-13、44、56、78、84、86。

[5] 传世和出土的具有这种特征的造像很多，兹举三例：1. 现藏日本大阪市立美术馆的一通北周保定三年（563年）造像碑上的佛像；2. 甘肃省张家川回族自治县1973年出土的北周建德二年（573年）王令猥造像碑上的佛像；3. 陕西博物馆藏北周建德三年（574年）造像碑上的佛像。上述佛像的造型，皆为童颜，头大，上身长，下身短。参见：1) 大阪市立美術館編《六朝の美術》，日本：平凡社，1976年，図版257；2) 吴怡如《北周王令猥造像碑》，见《文物》，1988年第2期，图版八；3) 陕西博物馆藏《石刻选集》，北京：文物出版社，1957年，图版23-25。

[6] 张彦远《历代名画记》卷七引李嗣真语（《续画品录》）。明王世贞万历初年郧阳初刻《王氏画苑》本。

[7] 张彦远《历代名画记》卷七引张怀瓘语（《画断》）。明王世贞万历初年郧阳初刻《王氏画苑》本。

横于腹前两道之制，与麦积山北周第36、62、82等窟菩萨像和须弥山北周第45窟塔柱正壁右胁侍菩萨[1]的服饰作法极为相似。

从现存的佛教石窟寺来看，弟子像最早出现在甘肃省肃南县金塔寺东窟[2]，时间大约在北凉或北凉亡后[3]。后来，云冈第9窟前室北壁上层明窗西侧又出现了这种二弟子[4]。至于二弟子与菩萨一并列入佛的辅弼像，即一佛二弟子二菩萨之组合，现存最早的实例应是龙门莲花洞和宾阳中洞的五身像[5]。其后，巩县第1、3、4、5窟，也承袭了这种一铺五身之规制[6]。麦积山石窟现存最早的弟子像，位于北魏中期开凿的第155窟左壁。到了北魏晚期和西魏，第122、92、161等窟均出现了一佛二弟子二菩萨之组合[7]。麦积山的弟子像，多为一老一少，内着僧祇支，外着褒衣博带式大衣，足穿靴或履；尤其是西魏第87窟和第161窟的弟子像[8]，迦叶高鼻深目，完全是西域人的形象。这一点，与敦煌第439窟的弟子造型是极为相似的。到了北齐、北周，河北南响堂山第1、7窟和北响堂山南洞[9]，宁夏固原须弥山第46窟门上小龛和第48窟塔柱东面[10]，也都雕出弟子像，组合大多为一佛二弟子二菩萨。弟子像，似不见于敦煌以西各石窟群，因此，莫高窟北朝晚期洞窟中新出现的一佛二弟子二菩萨之组合，应是从东方传来的。

西魏中期以前，莫高窟天宫伎乐构图有两种。其一，天宫圆拱形，下画凹凸状条砖平台，台下绘托梁，如第251、288窟。其二，天宫为圆拱形与汉式屋形相间画出，下绘平台和托梁，如第257、249窟。上述两种天宫，每一阁内皆画一伎乐天居宫舞乐。到了北朝晚期，除个别洞窟（如第438、442窟）仍保留着旧有天宫形式外，大多数洞窟已不画天宫，仅绘出由方砖构筑的象征性平台，汉式装束的飞天于上方凌空舞乐。这种不画天宫之制，在现存国内外石窟中，以开凿于北凉时期的酒泉文殊山前山

---

[1] 参见：1) 郑振铎主编，上引书，图版70；2) 宁夏回族自治区文物管理委员会、中央美术学院美术史系编，上引书，图版44。

[2] 甘肃省文物考古研究所等编《河西石窟》，北京：文物出版社，1987年，图版29-30。

[3] 宿白《凉州石窟遗迹和"凉州模式"》，见《考古学报》，1986年第4期，第441页。

[4] 水野清一、長廣敏雄，上引书，第六卷（1951年）：图版13。

[5] 龙门文物保管所编《龙门石窟》，北京：文物出版社，1980年，图版55-58。

[6] 河南省文化局文物工作队编《巩县石窟寺》，北京：文物出版社，1963年。

[7] 李月伯等《麦积山石窟的主要窟龛内容总录》，见阎文儒主编《麦积山石窟》，兰州：甘肃人民出版社，1983年，第156-200页。

[8] 郑振铎主编，上引书，图版150。

[9] 水野清一、長廣敏雄《河北磁縣河南武安響堂山石窟》，京都：東方文化學院京都研究所，1937年，图版3A、34B、46A。

[10] 宁夏回族自治区文物管理委员会、中央美术学院美术史系编，上引书，图版88。

千佛洞窟顶的天宫伎乐为最早[1]。

北朝晚期洞窟绘画特有的一种技法——“五白式”晕染法，应该是受天竺或西域式画法的影响产生的[2]。克孜尔第38窟主室门道上部弥勒说法中的菩萨和第167窟右甬道外侧壁的礼佛供养菩萨头像[3]，都是标准的“五白式”画法。这种“五白式”画法，除炳灵寺第169窟出现过“四白式”孤例外[4]，似不见于天梯山、麦积山、金塔寺、文殊山和莫高窟早期洞窟。因此可以说，它是由西域传入敦煌的[5]。

另外，这一时期壁画中世俗人物和大多数飞天的两腮均染色块，多为圆形或倒桃形，晚期则演化成小圆圈。这种“染高不染低”[6]的中原画法，在西魏大统年间开凿的第285窟已见端倪，此时大量使用。东西方两种晕染法在莫高窟合璧使用，应是当时中西文化交流的产物。

北魏和西魏时期，莫高窟主题故事画（包括佛传、本生和因缘）均绘于主室的南北壁或东西壁显著位置[7]。到北周，故事画大多移至窟顶；入隋，则更以窟顶为主[8]。为何将故事画移至窟顶，确切地说，移至不太引人注意的次要部位？对此，过

[1] 甘肃省文物考古研究所等编，上引书，图版115、116、167-170。

[2] 从绘画技法来看，敦煌北朝洞窟中的壁画，主要采纳了西域式的凹凸法，即“天竺遗法”。许嵩《建康实录》记一乘寺“寺门遍画凹凸花，代称张僧繇手迹，其花乃天竺遗法，朱及青绿所成，远望眼晕如凹凸，就视则平，世咸异之，乃名凹凸寺”。这种天竺传来的“凹凸法”使人物和花卉等产生立体感。画家当时在佛、菩萨以及飞天的面部、裸露的肌肤以及服饰上大多以土红色分别浓淡逐层晕染，眉、眼、鼻、下巴等凸起部位点高光，强调色彩的鲜艳和人物形象的三维效果。据研究，印度阿旃陀石窟壁画的制作程序是：画家在制作好的粉底/地仗上，用土红色起稿和构图，之后修改并涂色，最后用墨色或深棕色定稿。若有必要，再渲染一点阴影。新疆龟兹石窟中的壁画，基本上因循此制。“凹凸法”的骨架仍然是线条，长于表现肌肉的立体感；当时中原绘画的设色，大都以单线平涂为主，色阶层次缺少浓淡、明暗的变化。参见：1) 许嵩《建康实录》，张忱石点校，北京：中华书局，1986年，第686页；2) B. B. Lal, “The (Ajaṇṭā)Murals: Their Composition and Technique”, in: *Ajanta Murals,* ed A. Ghosh, New Delhi: Archaeological Survey of India, 1967:53-55; 3) 黄苗子《克孜尔断想》，载黄苗子《艺林一枝：古美术文编》，北京：生活·读书·新知三联书店，2003年，第302-307页。

[3] 中国美术研究所、中国外文出版社编《新疆の壁畫》，2册，东京：株式会社美乃美，1981年，上册图版86-87，下册图版70。

[4] 甘肃省博物馆、炳灵寺石窟文物保管所《炳灵寺石窟》，北京：文物出版社，1982年，图版22。

[5] 1) 段文杰《敦煌壁画の様式の特色と芸术的成果》，载日中国交正常化十周年記念《中国敦煌壁画展》图录，东京：每日新聞社，1982年；2) 段文杰《略论敦煌壁画的风格特点和艺术成就》，见《敦煌研究》试刊第2期，第1-16页。

[6] 这一术语，系敦煌研究院美术研究所谢成水见告。谨此致谢。

[7] 参见樊锦诗、马世长《莫高窟北朝洞窟本生、因缘故事画补考》所附《莫高窟北朝洞窟本生、因缘故事画统计表》，见《敦煌研究》，1986年第1期，第36-38页。

[8] 高田修《佛教故事画与敦煌壁画》，见《中国石窟·敦煌莫高窟》二，北京：文物出版社，1984年，第203页。

去有的学者曾做过推论，认为这是由于“人们对本缘故事画的兴趣下降”[1]。假如此说成立，为什么北朝晚期故事画比重增大、出现那么多新题材？如果是人们的“兴趣下降”，那么削减故事画比重，似乎更合情理，或以旧的内容填充壁画，更为简便易行。因而，在没有找到充分的证据之前，这还是一个有待深入研究的问题。况且，为了迎合6世纪后半叶中原北方禅业盛行这一潮流，作为坐禅观相的重要一观——观佛生身像，主题故事画对僧俗都具有更大的吸引力。

不过有一点是可以肯定的，那就是把大幅故事画绘在窟顶，现存最早的实例是麦积山北魏第127窟。该窟窟顶为覆斗形，四坡绘舍身饲虎、睒子本生等故事画[2]。以睒子本生为例，其故事情节与莫高窟的睒子本生大体相同，整个画幅较莫高窟的为大，情节表现更为明显。另外，在赋色和构图方面，它也与莫高窟北朝晚期的睒子本生有许多相同之处。因此，莫高窟主题故事画移至窟顶，或许是受到麦积山的影响才出现的，有些故事画的题材，可能也与麦积山石窟壁画有某种渊源关系。

(二)

自汉武帝于公元前111年在敦煌设郡，公元2世纪初西域副校尉常驻敦煌以来，敦煌不仅是通向中原的门户、统辖西域的军政中心，而且成为中西陆路交通的重要枢纽，“华戎所交一都会也”[3]。

西魏、北周的统治者，为了“安三边”、“定四表”，在与南朝和睦的基础上，采取联姻北狄、通好西戎之政策，与葱岭东西各族人民加强了政治上的通使、经济上的互市、文化艺术方面的交流。这一时期，无论是柔然、高车、突厥，或者是其他地方，都与中原地区有着密切的往来[4]。高昌、鄯善、焉耆、龟兹、于阗、渴盘陀、疏勒等地也都经常派人到中原馈赠方物，对西魏、北周保持着特定的从属关系，而宇文氏也回赠了许多礼品，加强了彼此间的经济、文化交流[5]。随着当时西域与内地交往的日益加强，西域以西各国，也同中原建立了联系，嚈哒、粟特、波斯等先后遣使来访，赠送礼品[6]。

---

[1] 高田修《佛教故事画与敦煌壁画》，上引书，第208页。

[2] 董玉祥主编《中国美术全集：麦积山等石窟壁画》，北京：人民美术出版社，1987年，图版59、62-65。

[3] 晋司马彪《后汉书·地理志》萧梁刘昭注引《耆旧记》，见范晔《后汉书·郡国志》，点校本，北京：中华书局，1965年，第3521页。

[4] 参见《北史·蠕蠕传》、《北史·高车传》和《北史·突厥传》。

[5] 参见《周书·异域传》下和《北史·西域传》。

[6] 参见《周书·嚈哒传》、《周书·粟特传》和《周书·波斯传》。

政治关系的改善，导致葱岭东西各族商人纷纷到我国内地贸易。对此，统治者亦持鼓励和保护态度。如西魏末西域商人到河西地区经商，刺史韩褒为了济贫，曾实施"每西域商货至，又先尽贫者市之"的政策[1]。当时"河西诸郡，或用西域金银之钱，而官不禁"[2]。历史上"自葱岭以西，至于大秦[3]，百国千城，莫不欢附，商胡贩客，日奔塞下"[4]之情景，到北周时更是有增无减。莫高窟第296窟福田经变中的商旅图[5]，应是这一时期中西交通频繁的真实写照。该图中央画一桥，两支商队相遇于桥头。桥上为中原商贾，着袴褶、戴幞头[6]，骑在马上，赶着满载货物的毛驴；桥下商胡牵着骆驼等待过桥。这种情景，与《周书·异域传》所言"卉服毡裘，辐辏于属国；商胡贩客，填委于旗亭"[7]是一致的。而联想到第294窟北壁"清信商胡无（？）主（？）翟一卑迦"；"清信商胡都爝（？）心（？）世（？）居罗供养"；"清信子（？）商胡竹鲁（？）□□养□佛□"；"清信子（？）商胡女（？）夫翟舒（？）……"等题名[8]，我们进一步认识到：商旅的往来，贸易的发展，既促进了东西方的经济繁荣，又增进了彼此之间的文化交往。

北朝晚期，高僧西行求法、东来弘教者络绎不绝，译筵频开[9]。这对佛教艺术的发展应有某种直接的影响，因为开窟造像本身就是一种公德，它是弘扬佛教的重要

[1]《周书·韩褒传》，点校本，北京：中华书局，1971年，第661页。

[2]《隋书·食货志》，点校本，北京：中华书局，1973年，第691页。

[3] 1949年以后的国内考古发掘中，在河北赞皇县南邢郭村北齐武平六年(575年)李希宗妻崔氏墓中，出土了东罗马帝国金币三枚，其中的两枚，是查士丁一世(518-527年在位)和他的外甥查士丁尼(527-565年在位)舅甥共治时(527年4月1日至8月1日)所铸造的。崔氏入藏时间为576年，而东罗马527年铸造的两枚金币，下距埋入的年代不足50年。这说明，6世纪中、后叶，中国与东罗马两国的交往很频繁。参见：1) 石家庄地区革委会文化局文物发掘组《河北赞皇东魏李希宗墓》，见《考古》，1977年第6期，第382-390、372页；2) 夏鼐《赞皇李希宗墓出土的拜赞庭金币》，见《考古》，1977年第6期，第403-406页。

[4] 杨衒之《洛阳伽蓝记》，范祥雍校注，新1版，上海：上海古籍出版社，1978年，第161页。

[5]《中国石窟·敦煌莫高窟》一，北京：文物出版社，1981年，图版189。

[6] 画面上的幞头形态，与宋郭若虚《图画见闻志》"后周以三尺皁绢向后幞发，名折上巾，通谓之幞头，武帝时裁成四脚"和宋俞琰所言"幞头起于周武帝，以幅巾裹首，故曰幞头……周武所制不过如今之结巾，就垂两角"是完全吻合的。这是莫高窟壁画中最早出现的幞头。参见：1) 郭若虚《图画见闻志》卷一《论衣冠异制》，《四部丛刊续编》本（宋刻配元钞本）；2) 俞琰《席上腐谈》卷上。《宝颜堂秘笈》本。

[7]《周书·异域传》上，点校本，北京：中华书局，1971年，第884页。

[8] 1) 敦煌研究院编《敦煌莫高窟供养人题记》，北京：文物出版社，1986年，第123页；2) Paul Pelliot, *Mission Paul Pelliot documents archeologiques XI; Grottes de Touen-houang: Carnet de Notes de Paul Pelliot, inscriptions et peintures murale, V*, eds. , N. Vandier-Nicolas et M. Maillard. Paris: Librairie Adrien-Maisonneuve, 1986: Grotte 126.

[9] 参见冯承钧《历代求法翻经录》，上海：商务印书馆，1931年，第37-41页。另外，莫高窟第428窟东壁门南"凉州沙门比丘道玲供养"、"甘州沙门孙义供养"和第294窟"清信商胡竹……供养时"，也可证实此时东西方佛教上的交往频繁。

方式之一[1]。又据《隋书·音乐志》:“太祖(宇文泰)辅魏之时,高昌款附,乃得其伎……其后(武)帝娉皇后于北狄,得其所获康国、龟兹等乐。”[2]这从另一方面说明,北朝晚期中原与西域文化艺术的交往进一步加强了。

宇文周时期的敦煌,由于受到关陇统治集团骨干人物的扼守,社会局面比较安定。文献明确记载信佛的大将军段永和建平公于义,对这一地区的佛事活动起到了一定的推动作用。“上有好者,下必甚焉。”两位好佛的刺史都来自东方,因而莫高窟这时出现的许多新题材、新特征等,应该与之有关。换言之,这种新型的佛教艺术,是他们从东方带来的,或许赴任时也从中原带来了一批工匠。因为中原的僧俗来这里开窟造像,会很自然地把他们所熟悉的东方式样和东方当时的佛教思潮反映出来。又,作为中西交通的重要枢纽,它也必然是一重要的文化交汇处。既然商胡能在洞中留下题名,此时天竺或西域“五白式”晕染法传至敦煌,亦入情入理。这些都是中西政治、经济、文化交流的结果。

(三)

这一时期造像广额方颐、体态丰壮之特点率先出现在长安地区[3],进而流布中原北方,应是画史上“张家样”北传的一种反应。

据姚最《续画品录》,张僧繇“善图塔庙超越群工”[4],创立了佛教画之“张家样”[5]。其画风富于肌肉的肥胖感,形象丰腴,故唐人张怀瓘赞叹道“象人之妙,张得其肉”[6]。张氏画了大量佛事画,究其缘由,唐代张彦远认为:“(梁)武帝崇饰佛寺,多命僧繇画之”[7]。

“不依国主,则法事难立”[8],“必假时君,弘传声略”[9],是历代僧俗奉行的法度。

---

[1] 刘慧达《北魏石窟与禅》,见《考古学报》,1978年第3期,第347-348页。

[2]《隋书·音乐志》中,点校本,北京:中华书局,1973年,第342页。

[3] 这种样式的佛像,学界有“陕西派”之称,系日本学者松原三郎拟定,因这种面相童颜、头大、上身长、下身短之造像多发现于当时宇文氏统治的长安及附近地区,故名。松原三郎《改訂東洋美術全史》,東京:株式會社東京美術,1981年,第182页。不过,我们认为,这种造型特点,也同样见于北齐造像,北周造像只是更突出一点罢了。

[4] 姚最《续画品录》。明王世贞万历初年郧阳初刻《王氏画苑》本。

[5] 张彦远《历代名画记》卷二,叶二。明王世贞万历初年郧阳初刻《王氏画苑》本。

[6] 张彦远《历代名画记》卷七,叶七引张怀瓘《画断》。明王世贞万历初年郧阳初刻《王氏画苑》本。

[7] 张彦远《历代名画记》卷七,叶五。明王世贞万历初年郧阳初刻《王氏画苑》本。

[8] 僧佑《出三藏记集》卷十五《道安传》,《大正藏》第55卷,第108a页。

[9] 道宣《大唐内典录》序,《大正藏》第55卷,第219b页。

这一准则，我们认为同样适于佛教造像。由于受到帝王的推崇，作为佛事画之张家样，可以想象当时笼罩着整个南方地区，是南朝佛教艺术的标准样式。成都万佛寺遗址出土的梁普通四年（523 年）、大通元年（527 年）、中大通五年（533 年）、大同三年（537 年）、中大同三年（548 年）等梁武帝纪年铭的石刻造像[1]，都具有丰腴健壮的特点。

南北朝时期，尽管政治上出现了两个对立的朝廷，但南北交往从未间断。"以张僧繇为代表的南朝新风，大约在梁武帝中期，其影响已及于北魏新都洛阳。当时，中原人士似又掀起一次南方热。"[2]到西魏末、北周初，南北交往逐渐频繁，萧梁宇文周之间"通和"，并多次相互遣使聘问[3]。至周世平定巴蜀（553年）、兼并江陵（554年）之后，文人僧侣北上者渐多，南方文化艺术等大量传入中原北方。

萧梁著名宫体诗人庾信，先前曾出使西魏；灭梁后，因其文学成就，被强留长安，"特蒙恩礼"[4]。诗人王褒，值江陵破后，亦随驱归关中十万余口百姓之列，"俱至长安"，以文学才识受到宇文氏的优待[5]。江陵破后，流寓北朝的诗人，还有颜之推[6]。庾信等人入关后，对南北文风的融合，起到了重要的作用[7]。

"逮太祖平梁荆后，益州大德五十余人，各怀经部送像至京（长安）。"[8]当时北入长安者，还有著名高僧释亡名[9]。他们的北上，对佛教"南北疏通"[10]和南北佛教文化艺术的交流，产生了较大的影响。

破江陵之时，于谨等人在"虏其男女十余万人，收其府库珍宝"之后[11]，亦"于煨烬之中收其书画四千余轴，归于长安"[12]。

当时北上的十余万人，其中不乏画塑人才，只是目前限于资料我们无法确定而

---

[1] 刘志远、刘廷壁《成都万佛寺石刻艺术》，北京：中国古典艺术出版社，1958 年，图版 1、2、4、6、8、10。

[2] 宿白《北朝造型艺术中人物形象的变化》，见哲敬堂珍藏选辑《中国古佛雕》，新竹：觉风佛教艺术文化基金会，1989 年，第 220 页。

[3] 参见《梁书·武帝纪》和《周书·文帝纪》。

[4]《周书·庾信传》，点校本，北京：中华书局，1971 年，第 734 页。

[5]《周书·王褒传》，点校本，北京：中华书局，1971 年，第 731 页。

[6]《北齐书·颜之推传》，点校本，北京：中华书局，1972 年，第 617 页。

[7] 王仲荦《魏晋南北朝史》，上海：上海人民出版社，1980 年，第 976 页。

[8]《续高僧传·释僧实传》，《大正藏》第 50 卷，第 558a 页。

[9]《续高僧传·释亡名传》，上引书，第 481b-482b 页。

[10]《续高僧传·释僧实传》，上引书，第 558a 页。

[11]《周书·于谨传》，点校本，北京：中华书局，1971 年，第 248 页。

[12] 张彦远，上引书，第 6 页。关于此事，参见《北齐书·颜之推传》和《隋书·牛弘传》。

已。不过,既然文人和高僧北上,僧侣携持经像入关,于谨等人运载书画北归,那么,以张僧繇为代表的南朝画风——张家样,大约在魏末周初时,也随北上大军一道直接传至长安,并与北方佛教艺术有机结合,产生出一种新型的佛教艺术式样,俗称“陕西派”。尔后,作为宇文氏佛教造像之模式,它径相流布、广被四方,麦积、须弥、水帘等地窟龛及其他零散造像,就是这种模式的完整再现。这种式样,也被东来的刺史带到了西陲重镇敦煌,莫高窟北朝晚期洞窟中广额丰颐、身体矮壮之佛像新样,与张氏“骨气奇伟”、“面短而艳”[1]之画风是一脉相承的。

北朝晚期洞窟中,千佛比重有所增加,释迦多宝并坐和弥勒题材延续使用,佛光中无量“化佛”数量递加[2],四方佛[3]和卧佛开始出现,故事画的题材、数量和构图等也较前期有很大发展。这些都反映出禅僧观像内容有增无已;出现这种情况,大概与周“国三藏”僧实倡禅长安、各地僧人争相效法有关[4]。同时,这也符合“从十六国到隋,石窟的性质主要是为了坐禅观相”[5]。

最后要说的是,北朝晚期洞窟中的本生故事,大多以“忠君孝亲”为主题,如睒子本生和须阇提太子本生。尤其是北周时期出现的睒子本生,在北周1/4洞窟中一再出现,反映出以孝道为主要内容的本生故事,在当时极受人们推重,应与自宇文泰以来“崇尚儒术”[6]复古制有关。周武帝亦奉儒学为正统,曾集群臣、百僚、沙门及道士等“亲讲《礼记》”[7]。灭佛之后还设立通道观,主张会通三教。认为“六经儒教之弘政术,礼义忠孝于世有宜”[8]。北周统治者的这种“忠孝”思想,与上述壁画“忠君孝亲”之主题是有某种联系的。壁画之内容,应是当时社会思潮的一种真实写照。其余本生和因缘故事画,主题大多为“忍辱牺牲”(舍身饲虎)和“乐善好施”(须达拏太子本生),宣传佛教固有的“因果报应”思想。这也是莫高窟北朝晚期主题壁画的一大特点。第296窟的微妙比丘尼,采用比丘尼现身说法的形式,迎合当时关西佞

[1] 米芾《画史》。明万历庚寅金陵“王氏淮南书院重刻”《王氏画苑》本。

[2] 参见:1)佛驮跋陀罗《佛说观佛三昧海经》卷四《观相品》,《大正藏》第15卷,第663-668页;2)鸠摩罗什《禅密要法经》,《大正藏》第15卷,第253a-254b页。

[3] 莫高窟中心柱窟塔柱四面单龛内所造佛像,如第428窟塔柱四面龛内佛像,有人认为可能依据《金光明经》雕造,内容为四方佛。塔柱四面开单层龛之目的,或许为了突出四方佛“护持是经”。参见阎文儒《中国石窟艺术总论》,天津:天津古籍出版社,1987年,第83-84页。

[4] 汤用彤,上引书,第570-572页。

[5] 宿白《敦煌七讲》,油印本,敦煌:敦煌文物研究所,1962年,第43页。

[6]《周书·文帝纪》,点校本,北京:中华书局,1971年,第37页。

[7]《周书·武帝纪》,点校本,北京:中华书局,1971年,第72、75页。

[8]《广弘明集》卷十惠远《周祖平齐召僧叙废立抗拒事》,《大正藏》第52卷,第153b页。

佛之风，借以“转相教诫”[1]，安抚民众，为统治阶级服务。

（四）

北朝晚期出现的这种新型的佛教艺术，对隋代洞窟的修建产生了较大的影响。覆斗顶方形窟与前部人字披后部平顶方形窟，皆成为隋代洞窟的主要窟形。造像头大、肩宽、上身长、下身短、形体丰壮之“陕西派”作风，一直延续使用到隋末才消失。一佛二弟子二菩萨之组合、Aiii式菩萨像以及主尊大衣的阶梯式衣褶，皆被隋代洞窟采用。隋代的本生和因缘故事画，绝大多数绘在窟顶；面部“染高不染低”之中原画法，在隋窟延续使用且有所演进。总之，莫高窟北朝晚期洞窟，在直接承袭北魏、西魏石窟艺术的基础上，汲取了中原和西域文化艺术中的有益成分，创造出许多新特征并担负起承前启后之重任，为莫高窟隋代石窟艺术的繁盛奠定了坚实的基础。

五、结　　语

上述四节，已从窟龛形制、造像、壁画、塑绘技法及构图等方面，对莫高窟北朝晚期洞窟的分期及有关问题作了初步探讨。其要旨，可以概括为以下三点：

1. 在段永、于义等刺史佞佛思想的影响下，莫高窟北朝晚期开凿了一大批洞窟。这批洞窟，大多占据莫高窟崖面较好的位置——南区中段二、三层，左右与前后代洞窟毗邻，在年代上呈交错状态，洞窟的分期与分区有关。

2. 运用考古类型学的方法，对莫高窟两个类型洞窟的窟龛形制、造像题材及组合、壁画布局、壁画中个体形象的造型及技法、主题故事画构图等进行了分析。在此基础上进行类型排比、分组，进而将莫高窟北朝晚期开凿的十五座洞窟分作三期，并推测了各期洞窟的相对年代。

第一期：第432、461、438窟，3个，开凿年代约在西魏大统十一年至北周明帝武成二年之间，即公元545-560年左右。

第二期：第439、440、441、430、442、428、290、294、296窟，9个。它们是莫高窟具有时代特征的较典型的北周洞窟，雕造年代相当于北周明帝武成二年至武帝建德三年，即公元560-574年左右。

第三期：第299、297、301窟，3个，时代约在北周宣政元年至隋开皇四年之间，即公元578-584年左右。

［1］《贤愚经》卷三《微妙比丘尼品》，《大正藏》第4卷，第368c页。

3. 经过与莫高窟早期洞窟、国内外相关石窟群以及其他零散造像进行比较，我们认为：莫高窟北朝晚期洞窟的演变，既有本地因素，又有外来成分。这种新型的佛教艺术，对隋代洞窟的修建产生了较大的影响，如头大、上身长、下身短、形体丰壮之"陕西派"作风，一直延续到隋末。总之，莫高窟北朝晚期洞窟包前孕后，是连接北魏、西魏古典艺术和隋代唐初成熟佛教艺术的一条纽带。

附　录

一、由敦煌遗书 S. 2732 号卷子尾题想到的

敦煌遗书 S. 2732 号卷子，名《维摩经义记》卷第四，为英人斯坦因掠去，现收藏于伦敦不列颠博物馆。限于种种原因，这份卷子过去没有得到足够的重视。由于工作需要，笔者于 1988 年和 1989 年初检索了藏经洞出土的全部汉文纪年卷子，发现 S. 2732 号卷子对我们研讨敦煌北周时期的佛教史具有一定的参考价值，同时也补正了历代佛经目录编纂中的一个失误。

S. 2732 号卷子尾题共四行，不包括卷子名称。现根据缩微胶卷（图 112）和翟理斯所编《不列颠博物馆藏敦煌汉文写本解题目录》[1]，将 S. 2732 号卷子尾题抄录如下：

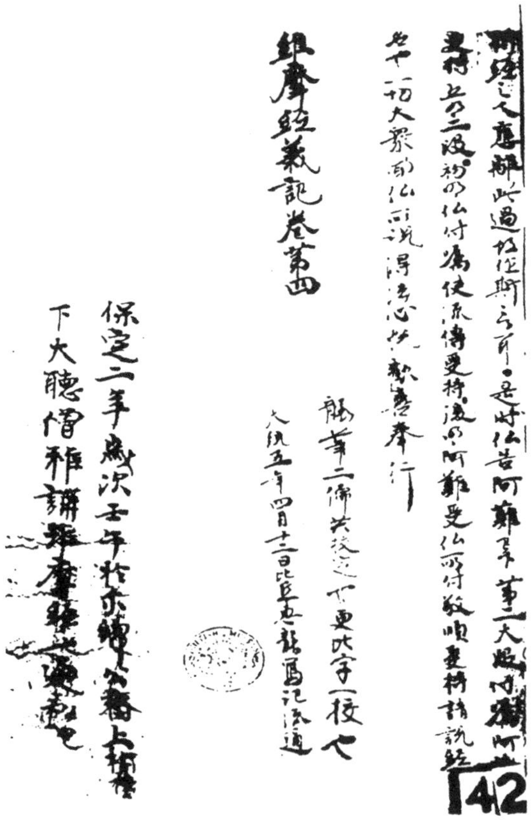
維摩經義記卷第四

图 112　敦煌写本 S. 2732 号尾题

[1] Lionel Giles, *Descriptive Catalogue of the Chinese Manuscripts from Tunhuang in the British Museum*, London: The Trustees of the British Museum, 1957: 167.

维摩经义记卷第四

龙华二儒共校定也更比字一校也

大统五年四月十二日(539 年 5 月 15 日)比丘慧龙写记流通

保定二年岁次壬午(562 年)于尔绵公斋上榆树

下大聴(德?　)僧稚讲维摩经一遍私记

由上述尾题,我们想到三点。

首先,尾题中的“尔绵公”,据我们考证,应是北周时期刺史瓜州的大将军尔绵永。尔绵永即段永,尔绵为赐姓[1]。据庾信《周柱国大将军大都督同州刺史尔绵永神道碑》[2],“公讳永,字永宾,东燕辽东石城县零泉里人也,本姓段”,后于西魏大统年间被“赐姓尔绵氏”[3]。“国家以玉门西拒,久劳亭障;阳关北牧,多事风尘。武成二年,有诏进公都督瓜州诸军事、瓜州刺史。是以名驰梓岭,声震榆关,无雷畏威,负霜怀惠。保定二年[4]还朝,授工部大夫,寻迁军司马……(四年)授使持节、大将军、都督,治左八军,总管军事……(天和)五年六月十六日(570 年 8 月 3 日)薨于贺葛城,春秋六十有八。将军死绥,三十行哭,都护丧还,缘边追祭……皇帝临丧,百寮赴弔……赠使持节、柱国大将军、同华宜敷册五州诸军事、同州刺史。谥曰基公。”[5]“(段)永历任内外,所在颇有声称,轻财好士,朝野以此重焉。”[6]由上,我们看出,段永是宇文周关陇统治集团的骨干人物,是统领北周二十四军之一的大将军[7]。

---

[1] 朱希祖《西魏赐姓源流考》,见胡适、蔡元培、王云五编《张菊生先生七十生日纪念论文集》,上海:商务印书馆,1937 年,第 563-564 页。

[2]《周柱国大将军大都督同州刺史尔绵永神道碑》,载《文苑英华》卷九百零五《碑》六十三《神道》二十四。北京:中华书局 1966 年影印本,第 4763-4765 页。

该碑文最早收入《庾信集》中。《庾信集》二十卷,《隋书·经籍志》作二十一卷,《旧唐书·经籍志》和《新唐书·艺文志》皆作二十卷。自元代以后,《庾信集》实际上已经散失。明清书目关于二十卷的记载,大抵沿袭旧说。我们今天尚能看到的《庾信集》早期刊本,是在宋刊诗集本的基础上,经明人抄录《艺文类聚》、《初学记》、《文苑英华》等编成的。明刊诗文合编本主要有两种:屠龙合刻评点本《庾子山集》(十六卷),张燮辑《庾开府集》(十六卷)。二书均成于明天启元年(1621 年)以前,而宋李昉和宋白奉敕编辑的《文苑英华》成书于雍熙三年(986 年),较上述二书早六百多年。因而,《文苑英华》所载该碑文,应是目前最早的版本,故选之。

[3]《北史·段永传》,点校本,北京:中华书局,1974 年,第 2348 页。

[4] 上海涵芬楼影印明屠龙合刻评点本《庾子山集》卷十四《周柱国大将军大都督同州刺史尔绵永神道碑》作三年,见《四部丛刊》初编集部,上海:商务印书馆,1922 年。

[5]《文苑英华》,上引书,第 4764 页。

[6]《北史·段永传》,上引书,第 2348 页。

[7] 谷霁光《府兵制度考释》,上海:上海人民出版社,1962 年,第 63-64 页。

据文献记载，段永是信奉佛教的，曾修造过“尔绵寺”[1]。刺史瓜州后，仍保持自身的宗教信仰，笃信佛法，任职期间，曾请高僧于斋上讲经，弘扬佛教。由 S. 2732 号卷子尾题，我们可以想见，在其佞佛思想影响下，敦煌地区当时讲经说法，传抄佛经颇盛。作为一州刺史，段永既然能够邀请高僧于府邸讲经，就也有可能顺应当时“赖经闻佛，借像表真”[2]之风气，在莫高窟修龛造像。借助于他的影响与势力，加之佛教本身深厚的社会基础，敦煌当时的开窟造像活动曾盛极一时。可以说，瓜州刺史段永，与莫高窟北周洞窟的开凿，有某种直接的关系，并对当时的开窟造像活动有较大的推动作用。北周洞窟中出现的许多新特征，可能就是他与其他几位刺史从中原带来的。只是目前限于种种条件，我们尚未找到直接、可靠的证据。

其次，《维摩经义记》这部经疏，在梁僧佑《出三藏记集》、隋费长房《历代三宝记》、唐智昇《开元释教录》、元庆吉祥《至元法宝勘同目录》[3]及明末蕅益智旭所撰《阅藏知津》[4]等目录中皆未著录。日本学者编辑的《大正新修大藏经著译目录》[5]和中国学者吕澂编撰《新编汉文大藏经目录》[6]，均将隋慧远撰《维摩义记》（八卷）误作《维摩经义记》。据笔者勘查，慧远撰《维摩义记》和 S. 2732 号卷子所写《维摩经义记》是两部不同的此土撰述，皆为“手记”性质，属注疏范畴之内“义疏”之列，其特征为“明经大义，不逐句释文”[7]。

敦煌本《维摩经义记》，现存有三个卷子：一为 S. 3878 号，尾题“《维摩经义记》卷第一，空藏禅师撰”[8]；一为北京图书馆藏辰 32 号卷子，尾题“《维摩经义记》卷第三，释琼许□□，大统三年正月十九日（537 年 2 月 19 日）写讫”[9]；另一卷，即是 S. 2732 号。至于上述三个卷子是否同为空藏禅师所撰，现难以断定。不过从现存三个卷子的内容来看，北图藏辰 32 号卷子和 S. 2732 号卷子，可能为同一人所撰的不同抄本，注疏所用经文底本，为姚秦鸠摩罗什译三卷本《维摩诘所说经》。辰 32 号卷子，为《维摩经义记》卷三，内容从《问疾品》至《观众生品》；S. 2732 号卷子，为《维摩经义记》卷四，内容为《佛道品》至《嘱累品》。这两个卷子从内容到顺序均可对接，

[1]《辩正论》卷四《十代奉佛篇》下，《大正藏》第 52 卷，第 518c 页。
[2]《续高僧传 · 释慧远传》，《大正藏》第 50 卷，第 490b 页。
[3] 庆吉祥《至元法宝勘同目录》，见《昭和法寳總目録》第二卷，第 179-238 页。
[4] 智旭《阅藏知津》，见《昭和法寳總目録》第三卷，第 1007-1252 页。
[5]《大正新修大藏经著译目录》，见《昭和法寳總目録》第一卷，第 658 页。
[6] 吕澂《新编汉文大藏经目录》，济南：齐鲁书社，1980 年，第 124 页。
[7] 汤用彤《汉魏两晋南北朝佛教史》，北京：中华书局，1983 年，第 395-400 页。
[8] Lionel Giles, *opere citato*: 67.
[9] 陈垣《敦煌劫余录》第二册，南京：国立中央研究院历史语言研究所，1931 年，第 89 页。

其抄写年代应相差不远。S. 3878 号卷子,为《维摩经义记》卷第一,与上述两卷没有衔接关系,加之现存只有一小残卷,品名不清,字体与上述二卷有异,因而要判定它与上述两卷《维摩经义记》是否有关,即是否为同一人所撰的不同抄本,还有待进一步研究。不过,《维摩义记》与《维摩经义记》是《维摩诘所说经》两种不同的注疏本,则是毫无疑问的。经过仔细比较,我们发现,不但两个注疏本的名称不同,而且文字内容相差也较大。总的说来,隋慧远所撰《维摩义记》,较敦煌本《维摩经义记》要详。

由上,我们认为敦煌本《维摩经义记》,可补各代佛经目录及大藏之不足。

最后要说的是,S. 2732 号《维摩经义记》于大统五年 (539 年) 四月十二日由比丘惠龙写记后,一直在民间广为流通。保定二年,当时该卷持有者于尔绵公斋上听僧稚讲《维摩经》之后,又私记此事于该卷卷末。S. 2732 号卷子尾题关于这两件事的记载,卷面上也有一段间隔,而且书法风格也不相同。有大统五年年号的书法与正文,即所抄经疏字体一样,笔力遒劲;而保定二年这条题记,书法要略次于"大统五年"那条。这从另一方面说明,敦煌当时的讲经说法、传抄佛经是颇为兴盛的。

综上所述,我们认为,敦煌遗书 S. 2732 号卷子,对我们研究北周时期敦煌的佛教史等,具有不可忽视的重要价值。

二、从藏经洞出土写经看北周武帝灭佛对敦煌的影响

据前引《周书·武帝纪》,北周建德三年 (574 年) 五月"丙子,初断佛、道二教。经像悉毁,罢沙门、道士,并令还民"。关于这次武帝废佛,隋代费长房记载颇详:"武帝邕世,建德敦牂,迄于作噩,毁破前代关山西东数百年来官私所造一切佛塔,扫地悉尽;融刮圣容,焚烧经典。八州寺庙,出四十千,尽赐王公,充为第宅;三方释子,减三百万,皆复军民,还归编户。"[1]

上述记载,就是中国封建社会曾发生的"三武一宗"灭佛事件之一 ——北周武帝的"法难"。关于这次灭佛的起因乃至经过,许多学者都做过详细的论述[2],此不赘言。本文所要阐述的,是这次灭佛对敦煌的影响。

有关北周武帝灭佛,敦煌是否受到影响,目前国内外学者主要有以下几种看法。

1. 宿师季庚先生认为:"北周武帝建德三年 (574 年) 毁佛、道二教,这应该影响

[1] 费长房《历代三宝记》,《大正藏》,第 49 卷,第 94b 页。

[2] 1) 余嘉锡《卫元嵩事迹考》,见《余嘉锡论学杂著》上册,北京:中华书局,1963 年,第 235-265 页;2) 汤用彤,上引书,第 389-394 页。

到敦煌”[1]；

2. 史苇湘认为：“宇文邕灭佛也曾波及瓜州……但是这并不影响莫高窟的镌龛造像”[2]；

3. 美国李铸晋认为：“以敦煌而论，武帝之破坏，想不受波及”[3]。

依据笔者目前掌握的有限资料，我们认为第一种观点较为妥当。现从三个方面试做初步探讨。

（一）经检索目前国内外刊布的敦煌藏经洞所出全部汉文卷子，我们发现，北周写经有明确纪年的共 19 件。现抄录如下：

1. 中村不折藏《妙法莲华经》，武成元年十二月二十日（560 年 2 月 2 日）[4]；

2. 中村不折藏《诸经抄》一卷，武成二年元月八日（560 年 2 月 19 日）沙门慧觉写记[5]；

3. 中村不折藏《梵网经 · 心地品》卷第十下，武成二年岁在辰年三月二十三（560 年 5 月 3 日）比丘僧欢释敬写供养[6]；

4. 清野谦次藏《杂宝藏经》卷第五，武成二年（560 年）写[7]；

5. S. 2664《律戒本疏》，保定元年岁次辛巳三月丁未朔八日（561 年 4 月 8 日）“玄觉抄记”[8]；

6. S. 2082《大般涅槃经》卷第十八，保定元年九月十七日（561 年 10 月 11 日）佛弟子张砛生为家内大小，一切众生，敬写流通[9]；

7. S. 2732《维摩经义记》卷第四，保定二年岁次壬午（562 年）于尔绵公斋上榆树下大聴（德？）僧稚讲维摩经一遍，私记[10]；

8. S. 1717《大般涅槃经》卷第一，宝（保）定四年六月戊子朔廿五壬子（564 年 7 月 19 日）比丘道济敬写[11]；

---

[1] 宿白《参观敦煌第 285 号窟札记》，见《文物参考资料》，1956 年第 2 期，第 21 页。

[2] 史苇湘《关于敦煌莫高窟内容总录》，见敦煌文物研究所编《敦煌莫高窟内容总录》，北京：文物出版社，1982 年，第 179 页。

[3] 李铸晋《敦煌隋代叙事画的几个问题》（摘要），见《敦煌研究》，1988 年第 2 期，第 96 页。

[4]《燉煌本古逸經論章疏並古寫經目録》，见《昭和法寶總目録》，第一卷，第 1064b 页。

[5]《燉煌本古逸經論章疏並古寫經目録》，上引书，第 1062c 页。

[6]《燉煌本古逸經論章疏並古寫經目録》，上引书，第 1064b 页。

[7]《燉煌本古逸經論章疏並古寫經目録》，上引书，第 1067b 页。

[8] Lionel Giles, *Descriptive Catalogue of the Chinese Manuscripts from Tunhuang in the British Museum*, London: The Trustees of the British Museum, 1957: 177.

[9] Lionel Giles, *opere citato*: 47.

[10] Lionel Giles, *opere citato*: 167.

[11] Lionel Giles, *opere citato*: 42.

9. S. 1945《大般涅槃经》卷第十一,周保定五年乙酉(565年)朔比丘洪珍写[1];

10. P. 2104《十地义疏》卷第三,保定五年岁次乙酉(565年)比丘智辩写[2];

11. 北图藏《大般涅槃经》卷第九,天和元年岁在辰巳(应为丙戌)十二月七日(567年1月2日)[3];

12. 北图藏《大般涅槃经》卷第十四,天和二年岁次丁亥五月卅日(567年6月22日)比丘僧济写[4];

13. S. 0616《金光明经》卷第四,天和三年岁次戊子五月廿一日(568年7月1日)[5];

14. S. 2935《大比丘尼羯磨经》一卷,天和四年岁次己丑六月八日(569年7月7日)写竟[6];

15. 中村不折藏《建章初首故称》第一,天和五年四月五日(570年4月25日)沙弥昙奣敬写[7];

16. 中村不折藏《十方千五佛名经》,建德元年九月十五日(572年10月7日)写竟[8];

17. Дх 1604/2199《大般涅槃经·功德品》第三,建德二年岁次癸巳正月十五日(573年3月4日)清信弟子大都督吐知勤明发心……[9]

18. 上海博物馆藏《大般涅槃经》卷第九,建德二年岁次癸巳正月十五日(573年3月4日)清信弟子大都督吐知勤明敬写[10];

19. 守屋孝藏藏《大集经》卷第十,大定元年岁次辛丑正月壬子朔十五日丙寅

[1] Lionel Giles, *opere citato*: 45.

[2] Jacques Gemet, *Catalogue des Manuscrits Chinois de Touen-Houang* (*Fonds Pelliot Chinois*), Vol. I, Paris, 1970: 68.

[3] 北京图书馆善本组编《敦煌劫余录续编》,石印本,北京:北京图书馆,1981年,第45页。

[4] 北京图书馆善本组编,上引书,第47页。

[5] Lionel Giles, *opere citato*: 61.

[6] Lionel Giles, *opere citato*: 165.

[7]《燉煌本古逸經論章疏並古寫經目録》,上引书,第1062c页。

[8]《燉煌本古逸經論章疏並古寫經目録》,上引书,第1062c页。

[9] Под редакцией Л. Н. Меньшикова, ОПИСАНИЕ КИТАЙСКИХ РУКОПИСЕЙ ДУНЬХУАНСКОГО ФОНДА ИНСТИТУТА НАРОДОВ АЗИИ, выпiуск II, ИЗДАТЕЛЬСТВО ВОСТОЧНОЙ ЛИТЕРАТУРЫ, Москва, 1967: 203.

[10] 上海博物馆、香港中文大学文物馆《敦煌吐鲁番文物》(敦煌吐鲁番文物展展品图录),香港:香港中文大学,1987年,第17页,图版三三。

(581 年 2 月 4 日) 清信女张阿珍敬写[1]。

上列 19 件经卷中，年代最早的是北周明帝宇文毓武成元年 (560 年) 的写经，最晚的则是静帝宇文衍大定元年 (581 年) 清信女张阿真敬写的《大集经》。因此可以说，自周初迄周末，整个宇文周王朝都有传抄佛经的活动。不过这里需要注意的是，上述 19 件经卷，在年代序列上有三处缺环。

第一处是第 7 与第 8 号之间，即公元 562-564 年间；

第二处是第 15 与第 16 号之间，即公元 570-572 年间；

第三处是第 18 与第 19 号之间，即公元 573-581 年间。

由于藏经洞写经出土后，曾一度被人掠夺、窃取而散失，因而在年代上出现像第一、二处时间较短的缺环，可谓正常情况。但第三处时间上的空缺，即公元 573-581 年这七年间没有任何纪年写经，应该引起我们注意。据笔者目前所知，敦煌藏经洞出土的西魏至隋代纪年卷子，在年代序列上最大的缺环就是这次[2]。联想到武帝建德三年 (574 年) 灭佛、静帝大象二年 (580 年) 复行佛、道二教这一段历史，那么这第三处缺环即建德二年至大定元年 (573-581 年) 之间没有任何纪年卷子的出土，就不是偶然的现象了。它应是这段历史的真实反映，是武帝灭佛的必然结果。因此，北周武帝的灭佛的确波及到了当时的瓜州。既然书写、传抄佛经暂停，那么势必导致开窟造像活动也受到了影响，莫高窟在此灭佛期间没有镌龛造像应是毫无疑问的。

(二) 据唐道宣《集神州三宝感通录》卷上记载，“瓜州城东古基者，乃周朝阿育王寺也。废教已后，隋虽兴法，更不置寺……沙州城内废大乘寺塔者，周朝古寺”[3]。上述文献证实，武帝当时废佛确实波及到了瓜、沙二州，这与前述费长房所言 “毁破前代关山西东数百年来官私所造一切佛塔，扫地悉尽” 相符。同时，这也从另一方面证明，敦煌当时的开窟造像可能同传抄佛经活动一样不得不暂时终止了。

(三) 至于莫高窟的塑像和壁画是否在这次废佛运动中受到破坏，乃至毁掉？因为迄今在现存洞窟中找不到确切的例证和任何较可靠的迹象，故很难对此下一结论。下面笔者试图通过有关文献，谈谈对这个问题的粗浅认识。

北周灭佛，主要是武帝采纳卫元嵩的建议，出于经济和政治上的考虑才进行的[4]。为了强国富民、消灭北齐、统一中原，他必须 “求兵于僧众之间，取地于塔庙之

[1] 北周大定元年正月朔日为壬午，推十五日为丙申。参见陈祚龙《敦煌古钞内典尾记汇校初编》，见陈祚龙《敦煌文物随笔》，台北：商务印书馆，1979 年，第 153-174 页。

[2] 参见薄小莹《敦煌遗书汉文卷编年》，铅印本，北京大学，1988 年。

[3] 道宣《集神州三宝感通录》，《大正藏》第 52 卷，第 407c 页。

[4] 1) 余嘉锡《卫元嵩事迹考》，上引书，第 235-265 页；2) 汤用彤，上引书，第 389-394 页。

下”[1]，“融刮圣容”，以充国家赀财。基于这个目的，武帝虽废佛教，未诛沙门，而是强迫他们还编为民，同时设立通道观，提倡会通三教，以利治国教民。“自废（佛）已来，民役稍希，租调年增，兵师日盛；东平齐国，西定妖戎，国安民乐。”[2]这可谓北周后期社会状况的一大概括。

另外，从《出三藏记集》、《历代三宝记》、《大唐内典录》和《开元释教录》等佛经目录，我们知道北周以前各朝代僧俗所著译之经、律、论，大多“未尝因武帝废佛而遂以焚毁不传也”[3]。敦煌藏经洞出土的北周以前各代纪年经卷，也从另一方面证实了这点。

至于《历代三宝记》所说“融刮圣容”，似主要针对佛像而言。笼统所说的佛像，应包括佛、菩萨、弟子、天王等。就其制作的材料而言，佛像有金铜、木石、泥瓷、纸绢等之分。金铜像，顾名思义是以金或铜铸造的；木石和泥塑像表面，信徒为了增强佛像的庄严，即为了表现佛的三十二相之一也有贴金箔或涂金粉之习惯。熔铜像以铸钱，毁土石像以刮金，对此文献上不乏记载：“周建德元年（572年）[4]，濮阳郡有石像，郡官令载向府，将刮取金。”[5]至于熔铜像以铸钱，则有“焚烧圣典，灵像铸钱”[6]为证。

鉴于上述武帝毁佛之本意，那些土、木、石像，“毁之固得，留之亦不以为深责，传世佛经，烧之固得，不烧亦未尝以为大罪也”[7]，加之“宗教信仰，最为坚实”[8]。灭法期间，高僧、信徒护持经像之事，在文献中屡见不鲜。如高僧释静端于武帝灭佛时，“竭力藏举诸经像等百有余所，终始护持，冀后法开，用为乘绪”[9]；“周建德六年（577年），国灭三宝，（慧）瑱抱持经像，隐于深山”[10]；大德法林“及周灭法，与（僧）可同学共护经像”[11]。

---

[1] 道宣《广弘明集》卷二十四昙积《谏周祖沙汰僧表》，《大正藏》第52卷，第279b页。

[2]《广弘明集》卷十《周高祖巡邺除殄佛法有前僧任道林上表请开法事》，《大正藏》第52卷，第154c页。

[3] 王仲荦《北周六典》，北京：中华书局，1979年，第232页。

[4] 百衲本《隋书·五行志》（元大德刊本）和中华书局点校本《隋书·五行志》皆作元年。联系下文“时（武）帝既灭齐”，疑建德元年乃六年之误，因武帝灭齐在建德六年（577年）。又，建德三年灭佛，毁像之事不会发生在灭佛前的建德元年。

[5]《隋书·五行志》，点校本，北京：中华书局，1973年，第643页。

[6]《续高僧传·法上传》，《大正藏》第50卷，第581a页。

[7] 王仲荦，上引书，第232页。

[8] 梁思成《中国雕塑史》，见《梁思成文集》三，北京：中国建筑工业出版社，1985年，第336页。

[9]《续高僧传·释静端传》，《大正藏》第50卷，第576c页。

[10]《续高僧传·释慧瑱传》，上引书，第649c页。

[11]《续高僧传·僧可传附法林师传》，上引书，第552b页。

基于上述原因，北周以前许多土、木、金、石像得以保存下来[1]，仅陕西耀县博物馆一处，就保存了13通北周造像碑[2]。至于佛教石窟保存至今的更多，如须弥山石窟保存北周洞窟16座[3]，麦积山石窟保存北周洞窟多达42座[4]，甘肃武山水帘洞也保存北周窟龛30多个[5]。既然在当时国都长安的北大门耀县及其附近能保留这么多造像碑，在当时关陇之要地原州和秦州有这么多窟龛完好地保存下来，除考虑佛教当时有深厚的社会基础和高僧信徒的尽力护持之外，想与武帝"融刮圣容"的作法不无关系[6]。既然他废佛目的之一是熔金铜以充国家赀财，那么对于莫高窟的泥塑和壁画来说，与"融刮圣容"的策略不符。因而我们推测，敦煌莫高窟在北周武帝法难期间基本没有遭到毁坏，现存石窟的状况及外观也从另一方面证实了这一推论。

综上所述，北周武帝建德三年的灭佛的确波及到了敦煌，并终止了传抄佛经和莫高窟的开窟造像活动，但此前的莫高窟塑像和壁画并未因此遭到破坏。

人们总是在实践中不断开拓认识客观真理的道路。本文立足于洞窟现存遗迹特征的分析，并以这种特征为标尺，研究其前后发展的逻辑规律，探讨在特定的历史条件下，北朝晚期洞窟的渊源与流变，最后论述了两个与分期研究有关的问题。不过，由于这一时期洞窟本身成分复杂，因而上述意见还是初步的。不妥之处，敬请方家指正。

（本文原为我1989年在敦煌莫高窟写就的硕士学位论文，后刊甘肃人民出版社2000年出版的《敦煌研究文集：敦煌石窟考古篇》第29-111页，2003年收入台湾佛光山出版的《法藏文库：中国佛教学术论典》84册第152-266页。此次重刊前，调整了考古类型学分析中的部分形式及注释体例，增补了5个注释，并改正了诸多印制错误。）

---

[1] 参见：1) Osavld Siren, *Chinese Sculpture from the fifth to the fourteenth century*, London: E. Benn, 1925, Vol. Ⅰ: 61, 71-75, Vol. Ⅲ: Plates 231, 265A-277B, 280A, 280C；2) 梁思成，上引书，第336-340页。

[2] 耀县药王山造像碑，有很多是从附近迁到这里来的。参见耀生《耀县石刻文字略志》，见《考古》，1965年第3期，第135页。

[3] 宁夏回族自治区文物管理委员会、中央美术学院美术史系编《须弥山石窟》，北京：文物出版社，1988年，第27-55页。

[4] 阎文儒主编《中国石窟艺术丛书：麦积山石窟》，兰州：甘肃人民出版社，1983年，第95页。

[5] 董玉祥、臧志军《甘肃武山水帘洞石窟群》，见《文物》，1985年第5期，第7-16页。

[6] 据笔者实地考察，上述几处石窟群没有贴金箔现象。莫高窟北周以前洞窟中的彩塑和壁画，除个别洞窟（254窟）外，大多也未贴金箔或涂金粉。